ENCYCLOPEDIA OF
WORLD CRICKET

ENCYCLOPEDIA OF WORLD CRICKET

Roy Morgan

Published in Great Britain by
SportsBooks Limited
PO Box 422
Cheltenham
GL50 2YN
Tel: 01242 256755
Fax: 01242 254694
www.sportsbooks.ltd.uk

Cover designed by Alan Hunns.

A catalogue record for this book is available from the British Library.
ISBN 9781899807 51 2

Printed by Cromwell Press

CONTENTS

INTRODUCTION

CRICKET HISTORY, as a subject, has changed over the last twenty or so years. It is no longer simply a description of key events and key dates. Inspired by the pioneer work of C.L.R. James it now encompasses an understanding of the economic, social and political context in which cricket is played. Thanks to writers like Hilary Beckles, Boria Majumdar, Greg Ryan and Derek Birley, detailed histories of this kind are now available on the development of the game in the West Indies, India, New Zealand and England. More recently, the historical approach has been supplemented by the work of Andrew Hignell who has promoted the idea of a geography of cricket.

This book starts from the fact that cricket is now played in some 150 countries. By integrating history and geography, a holistic view is presented of the way the game has spread across the globe from its origins in south-east England and how it has developed in the different countries in relation to their socio-economic and political backgrounds. In the process, the presentation has necessarily become somewhat encyclopedic; hence the choice of title.

The first chapter shows how the spread of cricket followed typical geographical patterns of diffusion in relation to lines of transport. Once the game was reasonably well-established in England, it was taken by British migrants, military and civilian, to many countries overseas both within and outside the Commonwealth. More recently, immigration from the Indian sub-continent has reinvigorated the game in some countries and taken it to others. The second chapter, which forms the bulk of the book, provides profiles of the game in every country where it is or has been played. Both men's and women's cricket are covered. For the test-playing countries, changes in the geography of touring itineraries and in the distribution of the first-class game are examined. For the more important countries a statistical section covers the playing record, famous victories and short profiles of key players. No attempt is made to produce the best side of all-time but rather to choose cricketers, men and women, who have made major contributions to the game at different times in the country's history. The country profiles reflect cricket's geography and not a definitive list of countries. Thus, England, Scotland, Wales, Isle of Man, Jersey and Guernsey are considered separate countries whilst Ireland (Republic and Northern Ireland) is treated as a single unit. Similarly, the various countries of the Caribbean are combined as the West Indies.

The third chapter covers international cricket competitions, excluding the World Cups, which are reasonably well-established and for which some form of cup or trophy is awarded. The men's and women's World Cups are described in chapter four alongside the various qualifying contests involving associate and affiliate countries. The final chapter discusses some of key issues which have emerged from the previous chapters and which affect the future of cricket as a world-wide game. Statistics are complete to 30 April 2007. However, for some of the associate and affiliate countries the difficulty of obtaining scorecards for many matches means that the statistical records represent the best information available; there is a chance that a few better performances have been missed.

The writing of this book was inspired by a forty-year interest in cricket in associate and affiliate countries. If it can go some way to stimulating a wider recognition of the game in these countries thereby promoting cricket as a truly international sport, it will have succeeded in its aim. I am grateful to my wife, Gillian, and my two sons, Richard and Gerald, for not only allowing me time to indulge my interest but actually encouraging it. I am also thankful to Randall Northam of SportsBooks Limited for believing in my vision and helping to bring the book to fruition.

Abbreviations

The following abbreviations occur regularly throughout the book. Other abbreviations occur locally, particularly but not exclusively in Chapter 2, where their definitions are provided in context.

ACC   Asian Cricket Council
ECB   England and Wales Cricket Board
ICC   Imperial Cricket Council (1912-1969);
          International Cricket Conference (1969-1989)
          International Cricket Council (since 1989).
IWCC   International Women's Cricket Council
MCC   Marylebone Cricket Club
TCCB   Test and County Cricket Board
WSC   World Series Cricket

Internet Sites

General

www.cricketarchive.co.uk
www.cricinfo.com
www.cricketfundas.com
www.cricketworld.com
www.worldcricketcentre.co.uk

Asian Cricket Council
www.asiancricket.org

European Cricket Council
www.cricketeurope.net

International Cricket Council
www.icc-cricket.com

Countries

Argentina
www.cricketargentina.com

Australia
www.cricket.com.au

Austria
www.austrian-cricket.info

Bangladesh
www.banglacricket.com

Belgium
www.cricket-belgium.com

Bermuda
www.bermudacricketboard.com

Bhutan
www.bhutancricket.org

Canada
www.canadiancricket.org

Chile
www.cricketchile.cl

Croatia
www.croatiacricket.4t.com

Cyprus
www.cypruscricket.com

Czech Republic
www.cricket.cz

Denmark
www.cricket.dk

England
www.ecb.co.uk

Estonia
www.cricket.ee

Finland
www.cricketfinland.com

France
www.cricketeurope.net/FRANCE
www.ffbsc.org

Germany
www.cricket.de

Gibraltar
www.cricketeurope.net/GIBRALTAR

Greece
www.cricketeurope.net/GREECE

Guernsey
www.cricketeurope.net/GUERNSEY
www.guernseycricket.com

Hong Kong
www.cricket.com.hk

Ireland
www.cricketeurope4.net/IRELAND

Isle of Man
www.cricketeurope.net/ISLEOFMAN

Israel
www.israel.cricket.org

Italy
www.crickitalia.org

Japan
www.cricket.or.jp

Jersey
www.cricketeurope.net/JERSEY

www.jerseyislandcricket.co.uk

Kenya
www.cricket.co.ke

Kuwait
www.cricketkuwait.com

Luxembourg
www.cricket.lu

Malaysia
www.malaysiacricket.com

Maldives
www.maldivescricket.com.mv

Namibia
www.cricketnamibia.com

Nepal
www.cricket.com.np

Netherlands
www.kncb.nl

New Zealand
www.nzcricket.co.nz

Norfolk Island
www.nlk.nf/cricket

Norway
www.cricketeurope.net/NORWAY
www.norwaycricket.no

Pakistan
www.pcboard.com.pk

Poland
www.cricket.pl

Portugal
www.cricketeurope.net/PORTUGAL

Saudi Arabia
www.saudicricket.com

Scotland
www.cricketeurope4.net/SCOTLAND

Singapore
www.cricket.org.sg

Slovakia
www.kriket.sk

Slovenia
www.ljcricket.com

South Africa
www.cricket.co.za

Spain
www.cricketeurope.net/SPAIN

Sri Lanka
www.srilankacricket.lk

Sweden
www.cricketforbundet.com

Switzerland
www.swisscricket.ch

Tanzania
www.tanzaniacricket.com

United Arab Emirates
www.emiratescricket.com

United States of America
www.usaca.org
www.haverford.edu/library/cricket

Vanuatu
www.vanuatucricket.com

Wales
www.cbw.org.uk
www.wales.play-cricket.com
www.welshcricket.org

West Indies
www.windiescricket.com

Zimbabwe
www.zimcricket.org

CHAPTER 1

THE GROWTH OF CRICKET

IN 1900 the only countries playing test cricket were England, Australia and South Africa. First-class cricket was played in New Zealand, the Indian sub-continent, parts of the West Indies and Philadelphia and the game had also been recorded in some forty other countries. Today ten countries have test-match status, cricket is firmly established in an additional 32 countries and the game is played in a recognisable form in a further 85 countries. In total, 73 countries entered the 2007 World Cup although only sixteen reached the final stages in the West Indies. This is a remarkable growth for a game which is generally regarded as a minority sport of English invention, largely restricted to countries of the British Commonwealth. How did this growth come about? And how, prior to 1900, did the game spread across the World from a small area of south-east England?

PATTERNS OF GROWTH

CRICKET HISTORIANS dispute how and when cricket began but it is generally accepted that an early form of the game was well-established by the early 1600s in The Weald of south-east England, near where the county boundaries of Kent, Surrey and Sussex meet. It was essentially a rural game played between villages. From its place of origin, the game spread outwards following the typical patterns of spatial diffusion proposed by the geographer, Torsten Hägerstrand, whereby ideas spread outwards from a central point either radially, passing from one locality to its neighbour, or linearly, along roads, railways or rivers. The initial spread of cricket followed a radial pattern through contacts between people in adjacent villages. Considering that, in the seventeenth century, the majority of people did not

travel outside their village and those that did could not get very far in a day because transport was either on foot, horseback or by stagecoach along bumpy, unsurfaced and often muddy roads, the game spread remarkably quickly. Within seventy years, it was common throughout the three south-eastern counties and had reached the outskirts of London at Richmond and Eltham. It was probably spread by farmers and traders, moving from market to market.

By the 1700s members of the aristocracy had developed a keen interest in the game. From their country estates, they became patrons of cricket and used their wealth to organise personal teams for matches against sides raised by rivals. The teams comprised people from all classes, the ability to play cricket being far more important than social background. The nobility provided transport, food and accommodation which meant that the distances travelled could be much greater. In the 1720s, matches were arranged between teams of the Second Duke of Richmond at Slindon, Sussex, Sir William Gage of Firle, near Eastbourne and Edwin Stead of Maidstone, Kent. The nobility split their time between the countryside and London and, thereby, brought cricket to the capital where, by the mid eighteenth century, it had become firmly established as an urban game. For the next half-century, the diffusion of cricket emanated from two centres, continuing its outward spread, village to village, from its rural focus in The Weald and moving out from London in a new pattern, along the lines of transport as first, better roads, and later, railways were developed. In one location, these two routes of diffusion converged, namely Hambledon in Hampshire. The game here was a logical westward extension from its presence in west Sussex

1

but it was strongly supported by the nobility who took advantage of increasingly speedy transport to and from London. The dual nature of the game's diffusion laid the foundation in England for the separation of cricket as an idyllic rural activity, mostly seen in the counties of the south and east, and cricket as an urban game as it spread from London to the industrial towns of the midlands and the north. By the end of the eighteenth century, the game had reached all the counties of England except Cornwall, Cumberland and Westmorland. Although, as far as is known, cricket began as a man's game, by the middle of the eighteenth century, a small number of women in rural south-east England and in London saw no reason why they should not play too. In terms of diffusion theory, however, women fall into the category of early to late adopters rather than innovators. The social status of women at the time of cricket's expansion meant that they travelled less and did not pioneer the transport routes along which the game spread.

The take-up of cricket by the aristocracy and members of the upper class, such as wealthy industrialists, was vital to the transfer of the game overseas. Through these people, cricket was adopted in the public schools, the leading universities and the armed forces and the alumni of these institutions were key to the establishment and maintenance of British interest in other countries. With the exception of the spread of the game into Wales and Scotland, which occurred overland, the diffusion of cricket beyond England followed the major sea routes. In most cases, cricket was taken overseas first by the military since, only when peace was established, could trade and settlement follow. Quite often trade followed the setting-up of the local garrison remarkably quickly, sometimes in less than a decade, so that the military, traders and settlers all functioned simultaneously in promoting the game. Since British interests depended on the garrison and on trade, in virtually all countries of the British Commonwealth cricket began as an urban game focused on the main port of entry. From there it moved inland with British influence along the main transport routes, be they rivers, roads or railways. In Australia and South Africa it might be argued that the game followed a pattern of spread from multiple centres but this would ignore the fact that at the time cricket was becoming established, these countries did not exist. Melbourne acted as the

dispersion point for Victoria, and Sydney for New South Wales. Similarly, Cape Town was the centre for the Cape of Good Hope and Durban for Natal. Multiple-centre diffusion, however, is appropriate for New Zealand where Auckland, Wellington and Canterbury acted as separate centres, and India where cricket developed separately in Kolkata and Mumbai. Once established, the way cricket evolved depended very much on how it was taken up by the local population which, in turn, depended on how the British and the local people chose to interact.

Exclusive Existence

The British community generally chose to follow a separate, exclusive existence, limiting contact with the existing population to what was necessary to develop and maintain trade. The British established their own clubs which became the focal points for both social and sporting activity. Often there were distinctions within the British community relating to social class and occupation. The civilians and the military established their own clubs which would challenge each other perhaps two or three times a year. The ways in which cricket diffused from the British to the local population largely reflected the relative numbers of the two groups. The simplest pattern is associated with Australia and New Zealand where the British soon outnumbered the local population and became the dominant ethnic group. They brought the game to the country and, through their descendants, it became self-generating until it effectively developed as an indigenous sport. As communities became larger and more settled, schools were founded and the teachers imported from Britain ensured that cricket held a strong place in the curriculum. A typical pattern of diffusion was established starting with the schools, going on to the formation of cricket clubs and leading, eventually, to the setting-up of inter-town and inter-provincial competitions.

Although the above pattern of British society was replicated in other Commonwealth countries, the British did not always form the dominant population. Attitudes towards the spread of cricket outside the British community were frequently equivocal. On the one hand, the British wished to remain exclusive which resulted in the local population viewing cricket as an activity of the colonial power. Sometimes this led to movements to discourage locals from taking up the game. In Ireland during the 1880s to early 1900s the Gaelic Athletic Association promoted hurling and gaelic football and any person who took part in cricket was immediately banned by the GAA from all sport; although not always implemented, the rules supporting this ban were not rescinded until 1970. In many African countries, the association of cricket with the British led to a failure of their governments to support the game following independence in the 1960s and 1970s.

In contrast to this exclusivity, which served as a social barrier to diffusion, was the need to educate and train at least the elite of the local population to become administrators. Locals thus learnt cricket in the schools that were established for this purpose. In this way, the game developed its roots in the Caribbean, amongst the Coloured and Xhosa peoples of South Africa, in India, Pakistan and Sri Lanka, and in Fiji. Schools like the Royal College and St Thomas's College in Colombo; Harrison College, The Lodge and Combermere in Barbados; and Lovedale College in the Eastern Cape, South Africa, were all important in the take-up of cricket by the local population. Another route by which cricket was introduced to local people was through individual administrators and missionaries who set out to teach the game along with other attributes of the British way-of-life.

Whilst cricket and social life generally remained organised along racial lines, matches between British and local sides became increasingly common and were often encouraged by the British administrators. The British supported an annual two-day cricket carnival for local teams in Bermuda as early as 1872. Matches between the Europeans and the Parsis began in Mumbai in 1877. Through these contacts, cricket was increasingly seen by local communities as a way of increasing their social status. For people from the lower and middle classes, cricket became a route up the 'social ladder', just as it did for able sportsmen of working-class origins in England. As the game became more firmly established, wealthy patrons emerged from the local communities to organise and support the game. The rulers in the princely states of India developed a keen interest in promoting cricket and several employed English professionals as coaches.

Much in the same way as the British aristocracy had done in southern England, the maharajas assembled their own teams, vying with each other to obtain the most accomplished players.

A Strange Recreational Pastime

The simplest way that cricket spread into the local community was where locals observed what must have seemed a strange recreational pastime and decided to copy it. It has been suggested that this was how cricket first became established amongst the Parsis in Bombay and may well be how cricket started amongst the Greek community in Corfu in the 1830s. A more recent example is the take-up of the game by Afghans whilst living in refugee camps in Pakistan. In extreme cases, the game is not only taken-up but is modified to produce a local variant which sometimes becomes more popular than the original game. This is what occurred in many countries of the South Pacific where, today, teams of fifteen to twenty per side engage in 'cricket traditionnel'. The South Pacific is also one of the few areas outside of England where cricket developed as a rural rather than an urban game. But this probably reflects the settlement pattern at the time of contact with the British rather than any characteristic inherent in the game of cricket. There were simply lots of villages and scarcely any towns.

The importance of individuals in encouraging the diffusion of cricket is best seen where they came to Britain for education and work, learnt the game and then introduced it back home on their return. The Hansen family, educated in England, were among the pioneers of the game in Denmark in the 1860s and the Rana family introduced cricket to Nepal on their return from education in India and England in the 1920s. Usually such contacts were not the sole method of diffusion but tended to reinforce other influences. Thus, British railway engineers took the game to Denmark at the same time as the Hansens were endeavouring to promote it and it was Dutch aristocratic families with strong English connections who were instrumental in founding the major cricket clubs in the 1870s to 1890s. The extent to which cricket extended from the preserve of the British into an accepted recreational activity of the local people largely determined how well it survived. Its position could also be strengthened by further cycles of diffusion. In the early twentieth century migrants from the Indian sub-continent were imported into East Africa to help in the construction of the railways and into Malaysia, Fiji, Trinidad and Guyana as indentured plantation labour. In all cases, these were quickly followed by Indian traders and shopkeepers and, soon after, by the establishment of cricket clubs.

Expansion and Contraction

Throughout most of the late nineteenth and the first seventy years of the twentieth century, the fate of cricket depended on how firmly the game was established among the local population. With a strong foundation, cricket survived and grew but where this was not the case, its existence relied solely on the British presence. Where political and economic changes caused the British to withdraw from all or part of a country, the game contracted accordingly and, as happened in Montevideo, Uruguay, and Shanghai, China, ultimately died out. In East Africa cricket underwent periods of expansion and contraction. The game spread from Zanzibar throughout much of Kenya, Uganda and Tanzania as the railway network extended inland and the British set up administrative centres in the small towns and farms in the highlands. In Kenya cricket spread from Mombasa inland to Nairobi and thence into the highlands and the rift valley to places like Kisumu, Nyeri, Nakuru and Eldoret, reaching its maximum extent by the 1960s. With independence, many British left East Africa and the game contracted to larger cities, a contraction which was reinforced when political conditions also encouraged many of the Asian community to leave.

Although cricket became a major sport among the descendants of the British in Australia, New Zealand and South Africa, the presence of a dominant population of British descent did not everywhere guarantee that the game would survive and develop. Much depended on how the first and second generation descendants viewed the sport and their country's relationship with Britain. In Australia particularly, the desire to demonstrate the country's equality with the 'mother country' in political, economic, social and cultural development was expressed in part through sport. It became important to show that

Australia could produce a cricket team which was capable of beating the best of England. This attitude contrasted with that of the British descendants in Canada and the United States. By the late 1860s, cricket was arguably the most popular sport in British Canada and by the First World War it had spread to the main towns throughout the whole country, from Vancouver on the Pacific Coast to the cities of the Atlantic Provinces. Its weakness, however, was that it relied on players educated in the main public schools such as Upper Canada College and Trinity College School. By the 1920s and 1930s, the majority of the population had come to see cricket as an elite game associated with a British past. It was more important for Canadians to express their differences to Britain rather than the similarities. Thus cricket went into decline. It survived as a minority sport and was later reinforced by immigrants from the Caribbean. In the United States the chances of cricket becoming a major sport suffered during the Civil War between 1861 and 1865. Thereafter it survived as a minority sport played by an elite group of the leisured class and, in this form, reached very high standards in Philadelphia. By the 1910s, however, more difficult economic conditions made it harder for the leisured class to retain their way-of-life. It became more important to earn a living and fewer people took up the game. The decline of cricket was even more marked than in Canada both in terms of speed and spread. Its survival today is highly dependent on migrants from the Caribbean and the Indian sub-continent.

The different attitudes towards cricket also had a major effect on the evolution of the women's game. Only where cricket became a stable part of sporting culture did women start to take the sport seriously. Cricket was then taught in the leading girl's schools and women organised clubs, either separately from the men's or as women's sections. The small number of players and lack of finance restricted women's cricket to the major urban centres and were probably more important constraints than the often unsupportive views of male cricketers towards their female counterparts. Where there were enough women wanting to play, any adverse attitudes were generally ignored but where the number of players was tiny, getting started was much harder. The view that cricket was a male preserve hindered women's cricket in South Africa, the West Indies and on the Indian sub-continent until very recently. Nevertheless, the situation in these countries is better than in those where men's cricket was never established beyond a minority sport or where it has been in decline. With the exception of The Netherlands, where women's cricket began in the 1930s, the women's game is either a development of the last few decades or has yet to start.

In the 1960s cricket was a major sport in England, Australia, South Africa, New Zealand, India, Pakistan and the West Indies and an important game in Ceylon, Scotland, Ireland and Wales. It was also played regularly in Bermuda, Malaysia, Singapore, Hong Kong and Fiji. Outside of the Commonwealth, it was a minority sport in The Netherlands, Denmark and on the Greek island of Corfu. In most other countries where the game had penetrated it was in decline. The change from cricket as a minority sport in world-wide terms to a global game has taken place over the last thirty years invigorated by a fresh cycle of diffusion brought about largely by immigrants from India, Pakistan, Sri Lanka and Bangladesh. Virtually everywhere these people have settled, they have organised cricket clubs. In promoting the game world-wide they have eclipsed the role of migrants from the West Indies whose influence was largely restricted to the USA, Canada and Britain. Almost every European country now has a a national cricket team. Although the standard of these national sides varies from close to English minor counties to probably no better than weekend club side second eleven, this does not detract from cricket now being a truly world-wide phenomenon.

AUTHORITIES

FROM THE time that cricket spread from The Weald to London and matches became more frequent, there was a need for some authority to oversee and unify the rules. Until that time local variations in practice existed. In 1727 the Duke of Richmond and Alan Brodrick met prior to the match between their respective sides to draw up *Articles of Agreement* as to how the game should be played and as a code for the umpires to follow. Members of the English aristocracy continued to assume responsibility for the way cricket was played and in 1744 met at The Star and Garter in Pall Mall, London, to agree rules in advance of the match between Kent and All-England. These became known as the 1744 Code. As the committee from The Star and Garter evolved into The White Conduit Cricket Club and, in 1788, into the Marylebone Cricket Club, so the latter took on responsibility for the rules of the game by default.

The MCC's main interest, however, was in organising matches for their members and, although they were increasingly consulted as a responsible body on matters relating to disputes and interpretation of the laws, they shied away from any involvement in administering the game. From the mid eighteenth century, cricket matches in England were organised by private individuals starting with the likes of the Duke of Richmond and Lord John Sackville and progressing through people such as Richard Nyren at Hambledon to the activities of William Clarke who ran the All-England Eleven in the midnineteenth century. Cricket tours overseas, beginning with George Parr's side which visited Canada and the United States in 1859, were also privately organised until the early 1900s. English county matches were arranged by the various County Cricket Clubs from the 1860s on. Not surprisingly, this *laisse-faire* approach led to numerous disputes over the status of matches and the selection of the English side for international matches. In 1887/88 two privately-financed teams, both representing England, toured Australia simultaneously, a situation which also reflected a similar lack of an overall administrative authority in Australia; one side had been invited by the Melbourne Cricket Club, the other by the New South Wales Cricket Association. Team selection for English international matches in England was made by the County authority on whose ground the match was played, leading to comments about bias in favour or against certain players. Gradually the separate organising groups regarded the MCC as an independent arbiter in settling disputes. In 1898, a Board of Control was established to regulate home internationals. Although instigated by the counties, the board looked to the MCC to ensure its independence and gravitas. Thus the MCC was slowly brought into the position of responsibility for administering cricket in England, a position it held until 1969 when the Test and County Cricket Board was established. The responsibility became extended to overseas tours in 1903/04 when the MCC stepped in to select a side to tour Australia after A.C. MacLaren had declined the invitation received from the Australian authorities.

England was relatively late on the scene in having a recognised body to administer cricket. In the United States, a Cricketers' Association was set up in 1878 to select the teams to represent Philadelphia against the touring Australians. It had a short life and by 1895 was defunct, leading to the founding of the Associated Cricket Clubs of Philadelphia to run the game locally at club and international level. The Nederlandsche Cricket Bond was founded in 1883, the South African Cricket Association, a body to administer cricket among the white community, in 1890, and the Canadian Cricket Association in 1892.

The Australasian Cricket Council was also formed in 1892 to cover Australia and New Zealand but it was never effective and was dissolved in 1900. New Zealand formed its own association in 1894 and the current Australian Cricket Board was founded in 1905. Thus by the 1900s the pattern was set for countries to establish their own national associations to organise the game. Most took a long time to do so. Ceylon founded its association in 1922. India and the West Indies only developed theirs in 1927 when it became necessary as a prerequisite for membership of the Imperial Cricket Council. In most other countries, national bodies were only formed between 1950 and 2000.

Narrow Focus

By the early 1900s with cricket tours between England, Australia and South Africa becoming regular occurrences, the question of a world authority to coordinate international activities arose. The first proposal came in November 1907 from Abe Bailey, then President of the South African Cricket Association, but with an agenda attached, namely his idea of promoting a triangular contest in 1909 between the three countries to establish their relative strengths. Although the Australians rejected the proposal, probably because they had already agreed to tour England in that year and did not want competition from South Africa affecting public interest and, therefore, likely profit. But Abe Bailey was not a person who was easily deterred and he continued to push his proposal. On 15 June 1909, representatives of

the MCC, the ABC and SACA met at Lord's for further discussions, the outcome of which was an agreement to hold the triangular tournament in England in 1912, and to establish an international body known as the Imperial Cricket Council. With its very narrow focus on the triangular tournament, the ICC's remit became quickly limited to test match cricket between countries of the Commonwealth. Its role as an organiser of international cricket was also hampered by its infrequent meetings. After its foundation, it did not meet again until 1921 and thereafter not until 1926. The lack of vision of its founders meant that the ICC ignored cricket in Canada and the USA, even though English and Australian teams had toured there regularly before the First World War. It also took no account of New Zealand, India, the West Indies, Argentina or Fiji where the game either was or had been played at first-class level. Perhaps international support at this stage could have prevented the decline of cricket in North America.

The 1926 meeting was attended by representatives from New Zealand, the West Indies and India and these countries were accorded test match status. At a second meeting in late summer of that year, the ICC adopted a resolution proposed by Lord Harris that its membership should comprise the governing bodies of those countries within the British Empire which send cricket teams to England or which are visited by teams from England. The ICC thereby confirmed its remit as being limited to cricket at test-match level within the Commonwealth. It now started to meet annually and gradually increased its responsibilities to deciding the timetables for future tours, the qualification requirements for cricketers to represent their country, and the nature and preparation of cricket pitches. These arrangements continued largely unaltered until the mid 1950s, the only major change being the admission of Pakistan as a separate country with test match status in 1952.

The 1950s saw the ICC face a major political crisis. In 1955, the South African Cricket Board of Control (SACBOC) which represented non-white cricket applied for membership. The ICC was forced to reject the application, partly because it could not sanction two bodies representing one country and partly because SACA would never have agreed to SACBOC's admission anyway. The debate, however, led to disagreements between essentially the 'white' members of the ICC and the representatives of India, Pakistan and the West Indies on how to deal with the racially-based organisation of cricket in South Africa and the exclusion of the majority of South Africa's cricketers from ever representing their country. The issue became inextricably linked to the international movement favouring a boycott of South African sporting connexions. Perhaps fortunately for the ICC, the South African government resolved the situation by leaving the British Commonwealth which meant that SACA's membership of the ICC automatically lapsed. South Africa were eventually readmitted in 1991. The crisis brought into question the extent to which the ICC could or, indeed, should intervene in the internal affairs of the representative national bodies. The ICC still finds it difficult to accept that cricket and politics cannot always be separated and therefore, when political difficulties arise, seems to prefer a policy of ignoring them in the hope that they might go away. The lack of leadership at this level invariably passes decision-making to the respective national associations and national governments which cannot always be in the best interests of cricket. Most recently, the ICC has shown that it has no way of dealing with the problems besetting cricket in Zimbabwe arising from government interference in the way the national association operates, the contractual conditions offered to players and team selection. No action has been taken to protect the future of cricket in the country.

This inability to provide a political lead contrasts strongly with the work of the ICC in promoting cricket as a world-wide game. Moves in this direction began in 1964 when, acting on a proposal from Pakistan, the ICC changed its name to the International Cricket Conference, formed a new category of membership, known as associate, and accepted the USA, Ceylon and Fiji as members. Since then additional countries have been admitted regularly as associate members for which the requirement is that cricket is firmly established and organised within the country. A further category of membership was created in 1984, at affiliate level, open to countries where cricket is played in accordance with the laws of the game. The ICC started organising international tournaments at one-day level with the

World Cup in 1975. The ICC Trophy for associate countries was started in 1979. Numerous international tournaments are now organised at various levels throughout the world, a move which has undoubtedly helped to promote cricket in many countries. In 2005, many of these one-day international competitions were incorporated into the structure of a World Cricket League with various divisions, promotion and relegation. In 2005 the International Women's Cricket Council, which had been the equivalent body responsible for organising women's cricket world-wide, merged with the ICC. The ICC now needs to show that it can promote the women's game globally with the same enthusiasm it has adopted with men's cricket.

Increasing Risk

The ICC has taken on numerous other responsibilities, aided by a further change in name and constitution in 1989 when it became the International Cricket Council with the right to impose decisions on its members. The ICC now oversees the conduct of international matches through the appointment of umpires and match referees and the imposition of regulations which supplement the official laws of cricket, the latter still being the responsibility of the MCC. Regulations cover hours of play, use of floodlights, definitions of fair and unfair bowling actions and the classification of international matches, i.e. what constitutes an official test match and an official one-day game. Since a number of these regulations impinge directly on the laws and the way they are interpreted, there is an increasing risk that the distinction between the two will become blurred and that the ICC may usurp the role of the MCC as the custodian of the laws.

Among the very successful ICC initiatives has been the establishment of an international panel of umpires supported by appropriate training programmes. This has improved the overall standard of umpiring at the highest level, reduced on-field animosity between players and umpires, and made the public more generally aware of the difficulty of many of the on-the-spot decisions umpires are asked to make. Similar panels exist for umpires at associate and affiliate level. The ICC has also taken action, some would argue belatedly, on match-fixing with the setting-up of an anti-corruption panel to investigate possible irregularities. Players can be banned for periods of time ranging from one match to life for bringing the game into disrepute either by unacceptable behaviour on the field or by becoming involved in fixing the outcome of matches.

In order to fulfil its vision of cricket as a global sport, the ICC requires increasing amounts of money to carry out its programmes which range from the organisation of test cricket and the World Cup to the promotion of the game in new countries such as Mali and Burkina Faso. As a result, the ICC has become increasingly dependant on sponsorship to supplement the subscription income of its members. Sponsorship, however, is controversial because the largest sums of money are available only from exclusive arrangements. With its new powers the ICC is able to impose its sponsorship agreements on its members regardless of arrangements already made by the national associations or individual players. Under the agreement between the ICC and the Global Cricket Corporation covering the ICC World Cups for 2003 and 2007 and the ICC Champions Trophy tournaments during that period, each national board was required to field their strongest available team and no conflicting sponsorship or advertising was permitted either during the competitions or for a period of 30 days both before and after. Although these restrictions are not dissimilar to those accepted for the Olympic Games and the football World Cup, they were imposed by the ICC with little prior discussion. The greatest difficulties arose in India and the West Indies where individual player sponsorship is more common. Yet, rather than address the issue at source, the ICC left it to the national bodies and the players to sort out the implications.

Like most international sports bodies, the ICC arouses both support and anger. There is clearly a need for a body to adminster and oversee cricket internationally and the ICC plays that role. In terms of its mission to promote cricket as a global sport, protect the spirit of the game and optimise commercial opportunities for the benefit of the game, it has been generally successful and has shown leadership. That leadership now needs to be extented to issues external to cricket but which have a major influence on its development.

MATCH DEFINITIONS

INTERNATIONAL CRICKET matches are recognised today as falling into one of the following classes: test matches, first-class matches, official one-day internationals, List A matches and miscellaneous.

Whether an international fixture can be called a 'test match' is now determined by the ICC. A test match is currently defined as a two-innings game of not more than five days' duration played by two sides of eleven players selected by the national associations of full member countries of the ICC and qualified to represent their countries as nationals or by place of birth. The ICC has decided which matches should be classed as tests since its formation in 1909. Matches played before that date and recognised today as tests have had their status confirmed through history. The term 'test match' appears to have been used for the first time during the 1861/62 tour to Australia of H.H. Stephenson's English team. It was applied to matches where sides from the separate colonies of Victoria and New South Wales 'tested' their strength against the tourists. However, in these early matches, the English team played against teams of twenty-two. It was not until 1877 that Australia challenged England on equal terms. The match played on 15-19 March in Melbourne between Australia and J. Lillywhite's side is now universally regarded as 'The First Test Match'. Which other international matches between Australia and England were considered tests was disputed until 1894 when Clarence Moody published a list in his *Australian Cricket and Cricketers* which became accepted as official. Most of the matches now regarded as test matches do not fit the ICC definition given above. Many were not between the strongest possible teams that the countries could have fielded. Up until the First World War the English sides which went to Australia were weaker than those which met Australia at home simply because many of the best amateur cricketers could not afford to make the journey. Teams which visited South Africa, the West Indies and India were often 'second best' because the opportunity was taken to rest the top players and provide experience for promising new players, knowing that the opposition was limited in ability. The policy of sending virtually reserve sides to India continued into the 1950s. The enormous variability in standard between the countries was reflected in the two-tier nature of the matches according to duration. Whilst games against Australia and South Africa were scheduled for five days, those against India and New Zealand were only allocated three days, again until the 1950s. These differences in standard need to be remembered when discussing whether Bangladesh and Zimbabwe are truly worthy of test-match status.

During the 1950s it was not uncommon for India or New Zealand to be beaten by England within two or three days. During the 1920s and 1930s, six-day tests were played in Australia. Provision was also made for the last match in a test series to be played to a finish if the series was drawn to that point. This led to a nine-day match between England and the West Indies at Kingston in April 1930 and to a ten-day game between England and South Africa at Durban in March 1939; both matches were abandoned because the English team had to catch the boat to return home.

Political Reasons

It is clear that historically there has been considerable variation in what constitutes a test match. The only consistent feature is that it describes a match between sides officially representing full member countries of the ICC. This definition was broken in 1970 when a series of matches was played between England and the Rest of the World to replace the scheduled fixtures against South Africa after their tour of England was cancelled for political reasons. The games were described as test matches at the time by the English press and *Wisden's Cricketers' Almanack* and were recognised as such by the players. In 1972 the ICC retrospectively withdrew their test status, a decision which effectively established a principle that test matches could only be between national sides. In 2005, the ICC ignored both their rules and precedents when they organised a match between Australia and an ICC World XI. They classified the game as an official test match even though it was not between national sides and it was scheduled to last six days instead of five. Many cricket statisticians criticised the decision. Yet, it has to be accepted that the definition of a test match has always been flexible in terms of duration and

the quality of the players and that the ICC is the ruling authority in this regard. There is also an analogy within the first class game. In England, first-class matches have traditionally involved those county sides designated as first class, the MCC and Oxford and Cambridge Universities. Yet matches played between the Champion County and The Rest or an England XI and The Rest have always been considered first class without question. Apart from the level of the game it is difficult to see how Australia versus a World XI and the Champion County versus The Rest differ in principle.

First-class matches are now classified as two-innings games of three or more days' duration between teams recognised as first class by the national associations of the full member countries. Some matches which have traditionally been viewed as first class retain that status for statistical purposes even though they were twelve-a-side or of unlimited duration and played to a finish. The ICC has also decided that it has the power to rule on the status of matches outside the jurisdiction of the full member countries. Three-day matches between first-class teams and Kenya are classified as first class as are the games between associate member countries in the ICC Intercontinental Cup. These rulings have been questioned by some statisticians as extending the concept of first class to teams of too low a standard but such a view ignores the enormous variability in standard of the teams rated first class by the full member countries today or those considered first class in the past. Such critics tend to compare the national sides of say Canada or Namibia with the top English counties or Australian state sides whereas the comparison would be better made with the teams at the bottom of the English county championship in the 1920s and 1930s or present-day first-class provincial sides in Bangladesh or Zimbabwe.

The main problem for cricket statisticians is the retrospective classification of early matches prior to any rulings on status by national bodies. Some statisticians favour starting first-class cricket in 1864, the year when over-arm bowling was officially sanctioned which raises the question of whether 'first-class' should be judged by the standards of today or by the relative standards of the time. If these are taken to include the rules of the day, there is no logical reason why the leading matches played with round-arm or even underarm bowling should not be recognised as first class. A further problem is that the earlier the date chosen, the fewer are the available scorecards. Also, in the earlier records it was not the custom to assign dismissals by catches or stumpings to the bowler; only the name of the fielder or wicket-keeper was recorded. Bowling records were not kept so there is little or no information on the number of overs bowled or the runs conceded. The Association of Cricket Statisticians and Historians has produced its own lists of all matches world-wide considered first class since 1801. These have been generally accepted for statistical purposes. Some cricket historians would like to see the record extended back to 1772, the year from which scorecard records become available in reasonable numbers. A few propose that the record should be taken back to 1660, the time when cricket teams of 'county' representation first appear in England.

The classification of official one-day international matches is more straightforward. The conditions are specified by the ICC and cover matches played under one-day rules in the World Cup and the ICC Champions Trophy, the Asia Cup and matches between the teams of full member countries. Matches between full member countries and associate or affiliate countries can also be classified as official whenever those countries have been assigned an official one-day international status. Kenya and Bangladesh were granted that status in 1997 with Bangladesh's becoming permanent on their promotion to full membership in 2000. Bermuda, Canada, Ireland, The Netherlands and Scotland were granted it for the period from January 2006 to 2009. As with the definition of test matches above, the ICC can also designate one-day matches involving World or Continental (e.g. Asia, Africa) elevens as official.

A number of one-day matches are played between teams of first-class status, mainly in one-day domestic competitions within the full member countries. The Association of Cricket Statisticians and Historians maintains a list of such matches which it considers the first-class equivalent of the one-day game. It is known as List A and has now been accepted by the ICC.

The above categories of matches leave a large number of international matches played by associate and affiliate countries as unclassified or miscellaneous. If proper records and statistics are to be produced for these, there needs to be a list of recognised matches. Some national associations, notably Scotland, Ireland, The Netherlands and Denmark, have their own lists covering matches for which international caps have been awarded. Unfortunately, these are not all true international matches against other countries. They include matches against English first-class counties, many of two-day duration. If a list was produced which was restricted to matches between countries, the problem would arise as to whether the teams were truly 'national' teams. For official ICC-recognised competitions, the players chosen must satisfy certain requirements related to birth, citizenship or residence. However, these regulations have changed over time. Prior to the 1980s, regulations depended on the individual national associations or the organisers of the matches.

The fixtures between Malaysia and Singapore for the Saudara Cup which started in 1970 have been for national citizens only whereas the All-Malaya sides in the 1920s and 1930s were a mixture of civilians and military from Britain and Australia and local players. Deciding on the criteria for an official list of international fixtures would be far from a straightforward exercise but a necessary one if a proper statistical record is to be produced. It is also clear that collecting the necessary information would not be easy since the national associations adopt very different policies concerning archiving of records. In Scotland and Ireland, the national bodies have complete scorecards of all their matches and have placed these on the internet. Other authorities, however, seem unable to locate the scorecards of international matches played only two years ago.

GEOGRAPHICAL REQUIREMENTS

THEORETICALLY THE requirements for playing cricket are relatively simple. All that is needed is a flat piece of ground on which a pitch can be prepared and which is large enough to encompass a boundary line and room for spectators, sufficient daylight hours to enable a reasonable length of playing time, and a climate which provides enough rain for grass to grow but not so much rain as to prevent play. In practice, the provision of appropriate conditions is not so simple.

Up until 1774, little in the way of pitch preparation took place. The only objective was to keep the grass as short as possible which was usually achieved by allowing sheep to graze on it for a period of time prior to a match being played. The team which won the toss had the choice of where to pitch the wicket which gave an advantage to that side's bowlers who could choose an area which sloped either from end to end or across the wicket as appropriate. The changes to the laws in 1774 reduced the bias towards the home team's bowlers by allowing the visiting team to select a pitch within 30 yards of a point designated by the home side. From 1811, the choice of pitch was transferred to the umpires, a power which they retained in theory until 1947 when the laws were revised. The need to prepare a wicket rather than rely on the natural surface with all its irregularities became more important as bowling actions changed (Table 1.1).

Once the ball was allowed to pitch, irregularity in bounce became a concern particularly where it could cause injury to a batsman. Pitches therefore had to become flatter and 'true' in bounce. Developing a suitable playing surface is a science requiring a thorough understanding of soil properties, particularly texture and moisture, grass growth and management, the response or bounce of cricket balls in relation to different levels of soil compaction, and how all these factors are affected by both weather and climate. To be a successful cricket pitch curator or groundsman or woman requires great skill. The groundsman is effectively the key person on whom the future of world cricket, at all levels, depends. The safety of the players is directly related to the 'trueness' of the pitch. The more skilled the player in terms of the ability to bounce or spin the ball, the more dangerous to batsmen they will be on a rough surface. Thus test-match and first-class grounds have to be prepared to a higher level than club or school pitches. The consequences of getting it wrong can be very dramatic. In January 1998 the test match between the West Indies and England at

Table 1.1 Changes in bowling practice

Until 1750s	Underarm rolling	Ball brought in an action from under the armpit and propelled forwards by rolling along the ground. Bowlers relied on speed and lumps and hollows in the pitch.
1750s to 1828	Underarm pitching	Ball propelled in an action from below the armpit but allowed to pitch and bounce. Enabled the bowler to impart twist or spin. The natural action, developed successfully by Noah Mann of Hambledon, caused the ball to spin from leg to off to a right-handed batsman. William Lamborn, who played for various England elevens, developed the ball which turned the other way. David Harris (Hambledon) was the best exponent of fast under arm bowling.
1828-1864	Round-arm	Ball bowled with the arm stretched out horizontally from the shoulder. First used in 1780 and gradually accepted as the norm. Method allowed a longer swing of the arm with the possibility of increased speed and variation in bounce and flight. Ball also delivered with the palm of the hand facing downwards instead of upwards as with underarm bowling. Although legalised in 1828, round-arm and underarm continued in parallel as accepted methods of delivery for many years. Leading exponents of round-arm were Edward Willsher, a fastish left-arm spin bowler from Kent, Alfred Mynn, also from Kent, and the Nottinghamshire player, Alfred Shaw, who could spin the ball both ways.
1864 to present	Over-arm	Bowlers gradually allowed the level of their arm to rise from the horizontal to obtain greater control over direction. Delivery with a vertical arm was legalised in 1864 after which overarm, round-arm and underarm bowling were all accepted for many years. Underarm survived longer than round-arm with exponents of underarm 'lobs' continuing up to the First World War. Since over-arm bowling became the standard method of delivery, the main controversy has been whether a delivery is 'correct' or 'thrown', i.e. the arm starts bent at the elbow and is then straightened at the point of delivery. In 2005, the ICC agreed that a delivery was legal provided that the arm did not deviate from the vertical by more than 15°.

Sabina Park, Kingston, Jamaica, had to be abandoned after 61 balls when the umpires declared the pitch too dangerous. The pitch had been relaid but would not roll flat and the soil failed to bind together.

The preparation of a pitch which is true and consistent in bounce is achieved by compacting it with a smooth wheeled roller. Rolling, however, reduces the spaces between the soil particles through which water can drain and which hold the air which is essential for grass growth. Although the grass is largely removed from the surface of the playing area prior to the start of a match, its presence below ground is important because the root network helps bind the soil together and encourages uniform drying. At various times during the year, both in and out of the cricket season, the pitch is scarified by hand-forks or machine-powered tines to aerate the surface and provide vertical channels or slots to improve drainage. The pitch curator is therefore charged with producing both a compacted and aerated surface. It is also necessary to ensure that the surface remains smooth and that the soil binds together for the duration of a match and does not break up under the impact of ball and feet.

The ideal soil for a cricket pitch is a clay loam with a clay content of between 28 and 39 per cent for test and first-class matches although 24 to 30 per cent clay will produce a wicket suitable for club cricket. With the huge variability in soils throughout the world, ranging from heavy clays to sands, the groundsman has to add dressings to the surface, usually immediately after the cricket season has ended, in order to produce an artificial soil. It is necessary to ensure that the dressings are uniformly incorporated into the soil and that localised accumulations of matted grass and roots are removed. Local irregularities in densities of dressing and grass can lead to variations in bounce.

What is generally understood as the 'pace' of a pitch is determined by how much the ball bounces on impact. This can be measured by a simple test of determining how high a cricket ball bounces vertically when dropped from a standard height of 4.9 metres. At least 20 readings should be taken on the area of the pitch being examined. Ideally a hockey ball should be used since its weight of 156g is the same as that of a cricket ball but it is seamless and therefore does away with variations in the bounce depending on whether or not the ball has landed on its seam. Table 1.2 shows the relationship between 'bounce' and 'pace'.

The height of the bounce increases with the clay content of the soil and decreases with the water content. For most soils, maximum bounce seems to be achieved when the water content falls to below 10 per cent. Variations in water content as a result of the weather can give the greatest problems to groundsmen in pitch preparation. For a match lasting three or more days, a watering regime may be used to ensure that the pitch starts slightly below its maximum pace allowing the pace to increase with drying as the match proceeds. Spells of prolonged rain or drought can interfere with the preparation and prohibit this state from being achieved. Although the covering of wickets has reduced the variability in pace that can occur during a game, it cannot eliminate it completely because it is impossible to hold the water content of the soil beneath the covers constant or to control the rate at which it will alter over time.

Information on the pace of a pitch is only one indicator of how it will behave. It tells us nothing about the degree of turn or spin that can be achieved when the ball hits the pitch or the amount of swerve that can be obtained as the ball moves through the air. Turn or spin depends on the roughness of the surface. The greater the roughness, the more the ball grips the surface on impact and the more it will turn. So far, no standard test has been developed to assess this. Generally, turn will increase as a match progresses and the surface becomes rougher although the extent to which this is true will depend on how well the soil binds or whether it breaks up. Swerve has nothing to do with the qualities of the pitch and is entirely dependent on atmospheric conditions, the shine of the ball and the extent to which the players can

Table 1.2

The pace of a pitch in relation to the bounce of a ball when dropped vertically from 4.9 metres

Pace	Height of bounce (cm)
Very fast	> 75
Fast	64 - 75
Moderately fast	50 - 63
Easy paced	38 - 50
Slow	25 - 37
Dead	< 10

control shine to give a rough surface on one side of the seam and a smooth surface on the other.

Since it is the skill of the groundsman and the interaction of soil and grass that produces the ideal playing surface, it follows that there is considerable variation in the quality of pitches throughout the world and, indeed, within individual countries. The difficulties of preparing good grass wickets have meant that, in many countries, playing surfaces consist of matting laid on top of either soil or concrete. Where rainfall is inadequate for grass growth, there are particular difficulties in producing grass wickets although, if sufficient water is available for irrigation, the water regimes are often easier to control because the weather is more predictable. It is not surprising, therefore, that there is interest in the production of artificial wickets. In recent years where the ICC has been helping to promote the game in countries where it is not well-established, the assistance package has included flicx wickets. These comprise more than 6,000 interlocking plastic tiles, usually coloured green, which form a continuous surface with small hexagonal holes. When laid on a suitably-prepared underlying surface, the wicket produces consistent bounce and provides some assistance to spin. Such artificial surfaces are suitable for nets, practice pitches and games at school and club level but have not been approved for first-class or international matches. For these, the concept of a portable 'drop-in' grass wicket has been explored. Such a wicket can be produced off-site under controlled conditions as a single slab, 25m long, 3m wide and 200mm deep, and then slotted in position as and when required. On grounds which are also used for football or rugby, it can be removed again and replaced with a suitable surface for those sports. Portable wickets have been used for matches in Australia and New Zealand but have proved rather easy-paced. The MCC is currently experimenting with them at Lord's, though not in the main arena, but with mixed success. Obtaining the controlled weather conditions for preparation seems to be more of a challenge than in the southern hemisphere though why this should be so is not clear. British weather is not substantially different from that of Wellington or Dunedin in New Zealand where they have also been installed.

Climate and Weather Requirements

Cricket can be seriously affected by the weather. Wet conditions result in poor footing for the players, a wet ball and a soft pitch. Adverse weather can also affect the number of people attending cricket matches and the enjoyment they receive. In most situations, play simply stops when it rains. Other weather events can also prevent play. On the 2 June 1975 snow stopped the match between Derbyshire and Lancashire at Buxton, Derbyshire. A sandstorm prevented play on the 17 April 1938 between All-Egypt and H.M. Martineau's XI at Gezira. Thick fog at Faisalabad between 17 and 21 December 1998 caused the abandonment of the test match between Pakistan and Zimbabwe without a ball being bowled. The Pakistan Cricket Board was criticised for scheduling the game in Faisalabad in December when fog is quite a common occurrence. The Asian Under 17 tournament in Kuala Lumpur, Malaysia, had to be abandoned in August 2005 after atmospheric pollution from forest fires in Indonesia seriously reduced visibility and the smog created a health hazard.

In the 1999 issue of *Wisden Cricketers' Almanack*, Philip Eden proposed a Summer Index (I) as a way of analysing the suitability of the weather for cricket in England each year during the period between 1 May and 31 August. The index takes account of temperature, rainfall, the frequency of dry days and the hours of sunshine. With some modifications to allow for the availability of data, it is possible to apply the index on an annual basis to world climates. The modification is not to the formula but merely to the data used. The Modified Wisden Index (*MWI*) is calculated from:

$$MWI = 20(T-12) + [(S-400)/3] + 2D + [250-(R/3)]$$

where T is the mean annual temperature (°C), S is the average number of sunshine hours over the year, D is the average number of dry days and R is the mean annual rainfall (mm). Whilst, for England, the original summer index gave values between 0, the worst conditions, and 1000, the best possible conditions for cricket, the modified index, applied to annual data gives a greater range of values. Values range from 113 in Freetown, Sierra Leone, to 2200 in Muscat, Oman, and Riyadh,

Table 1.3 Values of the Modified Wisden Index for selected towns where test matches are played

Town	Country	MWI value
Conditions too dry		
Karachi	Pakistan	2026
Lahore	Pakistan	1876
Peshawar	Pakistan	1859
Conditions highly suitable		
New Delhi	India	1767
Bulawayo	Zimbabwe	1710
Cape Town	South Africa	1639
Chennai (formerly Madras)	India	1570
Kingston	West Indies	1565
Johannesburg	South Africa	1561
Adelaide	Australia	1542
Harare	Zimbabwe	1534
Bridgetown	West Indies	1427
Perth	Australia	1424
Brisbane	Australia	1308
Durban	South Africa	1303
Mumbai (formerly Bombay)	India	1295
Kolkata (formerly Calcutta)	India	1272
Conditions moderately suitable		
Sydney	Australia	1070
Port of Spain	West Indies	1069
Melbourne	Australia	1039
Christchurch	New Zealand	1021
Colombo	Sri Lanka	903
Auckland	New Zealand	825
London	England	822
Dhaka	Bangladesh	800
Wellington	New Zealand	779
Georgetown	West Indies	743

Saudi Arabia. Whilst the higher values indicate the more favourable conditions with respect to the number of dry playing days, they also indicate desert climates, where the lack of rainfall inhibits the preparation of grass wickets. The ideal conditions are defined by a Modified Wisden Index between 1200 and 1800, as found in many of the main centres in Australia, South Africa and India (Table 1.3). Less favourable conditions occur in England, New Zealand, Sri Lanka, Bangladesh and in Georgetown, Guyana. The most difficult conditions are found in Pakistan where the climate is too dry. In all these countries, however, climatic conditions are suitable for the preparation of grass wickets. Table 1.4 summarizes the conditions for selected associate and affiliate countries. Cricket can be played virtually anywhere but greater investment and enthusiasm are required to establish the game under very dry or very wet conditions.

Table 1.4 Values of the Modified Wisden Index for selected associate and affiliate countries

Town	Country	MWI value
Conditions too dry		
Muscat	Oman	2200
Riyadh	Saudi Arabia	2200
Sharjah	United Arab Emirates	2170
Windhoek	Namibia	1984
Haifa	Israel	1875
Los Angeles	USA	1830
Conditions highly suitable		
Kabul	Afghanistan	1618
Gibraltar	Gibraltar	1530
Port Moresby	Papua New Guinea	1491
Buenos Aires	Argentina	1270
Conditions moderately suitable		
Nairobi	Kenya	1179
Hamilton	Bermuda	1123
New York	USA	1111
Kampala	Uganda	1000
Lagos	Nigeria	952
Kathmandu	Nepal	947
Toronto	Canada	921
Hong Kong	Hong Kong	793
Vancouver	Canada	786
Dublin	Ireland	779
Copenhagen	Denmark	768
Kuala Lumpur	Malaysia	729
Singapore	Singapore	674
Apia	Samoa	667
Amsterdam	Netherlands	650
Edinburgh	Scotland	635
Conditions too wet		
Douglas	Isle of Man	551
Belfast	Ireland	509
Suva	Fiji	290
Freetown	Sierra Leone	113

CHAPTER 2
COUNTRY PROFILES

PROFILES ARE PRESENTED of the history and current status of cricket in every country in which it is or has been played. For the more important countries, a playing record is provided along with statistical information on the highest and lowest team scores and the best individual batting and bowling performances; best wicket-keeping achievements are listed where the number of victims in an innings is four or more. The records are given first for test matches or for international games of two innings. Performances in one-day internationals follow where they are superior. Short profiles are provided for some of the most important players in a country's history. The statistical details for these cover the player's achievements for their country in test cricket, other international matches (defined as games of two innings played over two or more days), one-day internationals

(defined as international matches with List A status – see Chapter 1) and other limited overs internationals. Other leading players at different periods in a country's history are then listed.

The following abbreviations are used in the player profiles and lists of leading players:

b = born; d = died
rhb = right-hand bat; lhb = left-hand bat
for bowling, r = right-arm; l = left-arm; f = fast; m = medium; s = slow; ob = off-break; lb = leg break; g = googly; sla = slow left-arm; (r) = round-arm; (u) = underarm
wk = wicket keeper; occ wk = occasional wicket keeper
* = not out
+ followed by a number in the bowling statistics indicates wickets taken in matches for which the bowling analysis has not been published, e.g. 26+4 indicates 26 wickets included in the calculation of the bowling average and 4 wickets for which information on runs conceded is not available.

AFGHANISTAN

Affiliate Member of ICC: elected 2001

Although cricket is recorded as having been played in Kabul by British troops in 1839, the British left no lasting legacy of the game. In the mid 1990s, cricket became very popular amongst Afghans in the refugee camps in Pakistan and, on returning home, the refugees continued to organise regular cricket matches. The Afghanistan Cricket Federation was formed in 1995. Cricket academies have been started in Khost, Jalalabad and Kabul. A national squad was formed in 2001 and for three seasons competed in the second division of Pakistan's domestic competition, playing in the zone covering the Tribal Territories of the North West Frontier Province. In all, six matches were won, six lost and one drawn.

The first appearance in international competition was in the Asian Cricket Council Trophy in 2004. The team reached the quarter-final where they lost to Kuwait. This qualified them for the Plate Competition in which they finished runners-up to Nepal. By 2006, they had become one of Asia's emerging countries, finishing second in the Middle East Cup, losing by 3 wickets to Bahrain in the final, and coming third in the Asian Cricket Council Trophy. They met and defeated a strong MCC side by 179 runs in Mumbai, India, and made their first tour of England, playing club sides and county second elevens and winning seven out of their eight matches.

Leading players: *Present day:* Muhammad Nabi (rhb. rob); Hamid Hassan (rhb. rf).

Playing record
One-day matches

	Played	Won	Lost	No Res
Asian Cricket Council Trophy	12	7	5	0
Middle East Cup	5	2	1	2

Highest team score

ODI

| 270-8 | v Nepal, Kuala Lumpur | 2006 |

Lowest team score

ODI

| 100 | v Nepal, Kuala Lumpur | 2004 |

Highest individual score

ODI

| 101 | Nowroz Khan Mangal v Oman, Kuala Lumpur | 2004 |

Best bowling

ODI

| 5-14 | Ahmed Shah Hamadi v Nepal, Kuala Lumpur | 2004 |

ARGENTINA

Associate Member of the ICC: elected 1974

IN 1806, A British expedition to the River Plate, under the command of Alexander Gillespie, was captured in Buenos Aires and the soldiers played cricket as a pastime whilst being held as prisoners of war. Although this was the first time cricket was played on the South American continent, it is unlikely there is any connection between these internees and the subsequent development of the game in Argentina. Those who formed the Buenos Aires Cricket Club in 1831 are more likely to have been traders. It was not until the British began to settle in the country in the 1860s to build the railways and set up sugar estates and cattle ranches, however, that cricket was established in an organised way. In 1868, Buenos Aires initiated the series of matches against Montevideo in Uruguay which continued into the late 1930s. Out of 29 games played, Buenos Aires won 21 and lost only 6. By the 1870s, the game was surprisingly widespread with clubs not only in the capital city and its suburbs but even further away in the province of Entre Ríos and at Rosario, in Santa Fé. By 1890, with the expansion of the railway network, the game had reached San Miguel de Tucumán where it was supported by the large number of British staff attached to the North West Argentine Railway under the management of Robert Stuart. William Leach established a 1,200,000 hectare sugar estate in Jujuy Province which was served by the sugar refinery of Carlisle and Methuen in Salta. Leach, who played first-class cricket for Lancashire in 1885,

came from a large family of seven brothers, all of whom either visited or worked on the estate at different times and played domestic cricket in Argentina. The British established a club at Tucumán to organise occasional matches at weekends which was so successful that it attracted players from as far away as Córdoba, some 600km to the south. Indeed, the cricketers of the day seemed oblivious of the difficulties of travel in order to get together and organise a game. In 1893, a team crossed the Andes through the Uspallata Pass to play against Chile, travelling by mule and taking three and a half days to get there. Cricket was clearly in the hands of the intrepid as well as the reasonably well-to-do.

In 1891, William Leach and Robert Stuart, acting on behalf of the cricketers in northern Argentina decided to challenge Buenos Aires. It was from this that the annual fixture between the North and South of Argentina was born. In 1891, the Hurlingham Club was established and they employed William Lacey, an English professional, to serve as coach and groundsman. Once cricket was placed on the curriculum of the English schools in Buenos Aires, it became well established as a focal point of social interaction for the British community in the city. A feature of the game at this time was the large number of players who had experience of first-class cricket in England.

Cricket in the north of Argentina soon faced problems of sustainability associated with the fate of the railways. One consequence of the mergers of the various railway companies was the closure of the sports club in Tucumán. This was followed by the decision of the Central Argentine Railway to move its head offices from Rosario to Buenos Aires. With the concentration of the railways into fewer companies, fewer British people and more local staff were employed. As the number of British in the north-west declined, so did the number of cricketers, many of whom either returned to Britain or moved to Buenos Aires. Economically, cattle ranching on the pasture lands within a 500km radius of the capital city became the focus of investment and increasingly cricketers came from this area. As a way of bringing players from the rural areas together, the Camps Week was introduced in 1910 whereby, prior to the annual North–South fixture, teams from the North gathered in Buenos Aires and played each other as Southern and Western Camps, Northern

Camps and Entre Rios. From these trial matches, the team to play the South was selected. This system lasted until the early 1930s.

The period before the 1914-18 War became known as the 'Golden Age' of Argentine cricket. The forerunner of the Argentine Cricket Association was formed in 1911 and the standard of play was extremely high due to the very large number of cricketers from English public schools. Shortly after its formation the ACA felt confident enough to invite the MCC to tour. Thus Argentina's period as a first-class international side began with three 'tests' in 1912 of which one was won and the other two lost. The results showed that the country could hold its own against a team of eleven English first-class players. However, of the eighteen players who represented Argentina only four were locally born and only one had learnt his cricket in the country.

After the 1914-18 War, Argentina lost its appeal as a place for British investment and settlement and the country had to rely increasingly on players educated locally in English-speaking schools. Nevertheless, this enabled cricket to continue as a social activity and at a high level in what was known as the 'Silver Age'. Regular international matches were staged against Brazil and Chile and visits were received from the MCC in December 1926, Sir Julien Cahn's side in March 1930 and Sir Theodore Brinckman's team in December 1937. In addition, largely due to the efforts of E.W.S. Thomson, secretary and treasurer of the ACA who managed to spend most English summers organising cricket for Anglo-Argentine sides, a South American team drawn from players in Argentina, Brazil and Chile toured England in 1932. These achievements, together with the success of the national side, obscured the other changes that were taking place in the game. As economic activity became more and more concentrated in Buenos Aires, the number of players in the country declined.

After the 1939-45 War, with a further decrease in the number of British residents, most schools became bi-lingual. With a greater number of Argentinian pupils from Spanish backgrounds, the sporting emphasis changed to rugby. Many schools dropped cricket entirely and others reduced the amount of time devoted to it. With the game confined to the second and third generation descendants of the British

businessmen, educated in fee-paying schools, there was a real danger of it dying out. Cricket retrenched to just five clubs in Buenos Aires and standards fell rapidly. In visits from the MCC in January 1959 and December 1964-January 1965, the national side were outclassed. They also performed poorly in the ICC Trophy in 1979 and 1986, failing to win a match. The period from 1961 to 1990 is sometimes described as 'the struggle for survival'.

In the 1990s, the ACA began a programme of development concentrating on schools and clubs. The number of players has begun to increase and the standard of the national side has started to rise. Under the inspirational leadership of Guillermo Kirschbaum, Argentina won four out of its five matches in the ICC Trophy competition in 2001. The improvement did not last and, in the following year, Argentina lost all their games in the Americas Cup. The side suffered a major set-back in April 2003 when Kirschbaum died from a severe asthma attack. In contrast to its rather low status amongst the associate countries, Argentina easily remains the leading cricket nation in South America. The game is also being introduced to girls and in January 2001, a girls team toured New Zealand. A girls side from the Hutt Valley and Wellington area returned the visit in December 2002.

Famous Victory
January 15, 16, 17, 1927 – Palermo, Buenos Aires
Argentina 134 (J.C. White 5-65) & 63 (J.C. White 4-21, G.O. Allen 4-32)
MCC 89 (H. Dorning 7-38) & 79 (D.E. Ayling 6-32)
Argentina won by 29 runs

On winning the toss, 'Plum' Warner, the MCC captain, made an error in asking the home side to bat on a wicket which quickly crumbled. Argentina's first innings score looked too low but the visitors found Dorning unplayable. Argentina performed even worse in their second innings, leaving the MCC to score 109 runs for victory with all of the third day remaining. Although faring slightly better against Dorning, they found Dennet Ayling's off-breaks too difficult and Argentina won a low-scoring game fairly easily. The victory tied the series but with the MCC complaining about the quality of the pitch, a further 'test' was arranged at Belgrano which the visitors won by an innings and 12 runs.

Player Profiles

Ayling, Dennet Ernest. b Buenos Aires 8 June 1906. d Los Cocos, Córdoba, 18 December 1987. rhb. rob. The most successful bowler for South America on the 1932 tour of England, he took 33 wickets in six first-class matches (average 16.06) and scored 342 runs (average 42.75). In 26 international matches for Argentina and South America he scored 1,538 runs (average 35.76) and took 113 wickets (average 20.38).

Dorning, Herbert. b Argentina 1874. d Perranmar, Cornwall, 2 February 1955. lhb. lfm. Considered to be best cricketer ever to come from Argentina, he has been described as the 'W.G. Grace of Argentine cricket'. In a career which began in 1894 and ended in 1935, he played 22 international matches for Argentina, scoring 627 runs (average 20.90) and taking 91 wickets (average 16.98).

Other leading players: *1890-1914:* P.A. Foy (rhb. rfm). *1920-1939:* C.D. Ayling (rhb. lb); C.E. Ayling (rhb, rfm); C.H. Gibson (rhb. rfm). *1945-1960:* D. Cavanagh (rhb. rm). *1960-1980:* D. Drewery. *1980-2000:* D. Forrester (rhb. rmob); G.P. Kirschbaum (rhb. rfm). *Present day:* A. Ferguson (rhb. wk); M.J. Paterlini (rhb. rm).

Playing record

	Played	Won	Lost
First class International matches 3		6	4
Other internationals*	13	5	3

* matches against Brazil and Chile between 1919 and 1939

One-day matches

	Won	Lost	No Res
ICC Trophy	8	26	1
Americas Cup	1	16	1
American Championships Division 2	4	0	0

Highest team score
612-6 dec   v Chile, Buenos Aires   1929/30

Lowest team score
41   v New Zealand Ambassadors, Buenos Aires   1969/70

Highest individual score
234   D.E. Ayling   v Chile, Buenos Aires   1929/30

Best bowling
9-20   D. Cavanagh   v Combined Brazil-Chile-Peru, Buenos Aires 1956/57

Best wicket-keeping
| 5 (4c 1st) | C.W. Brook | v Brazil, Buenos Aires | 1927/28 |
| 5 (1c 4st) | A.G. Mulcahy | v Chile, Buenos Aires | 1929/30 |

ODI
| 5 (4c 1st) | A. Ferguson | v Bahamas, Buenos Aires | 2001/2002 |

ASCENSION

CRICKET BEGAN on Ascension Island in the 1960s when West Indian workers arrived to construct a relay station. They set up a local league which was kept going by South Africans, working for a cable company, and the Royal Air Force, who returned to the island during the Falklands War. The game has since been taken up by workers from St Helena employed on the island. At first, the game was played on the old army parade ground. Since the Church of St Mary the Virgin lies inside the boundary line, Saturday afternoon matches were often interrupted when weddings took place. A new slate roof was put on the church in 1993 and to avoid any damage to it, cricket was forced to move to a new ground at the RAF station. League games are now organised by the Ascension Island Cricket Association.

AUSTRALIA

Founder Member of the ICC in 1909

CRICKET WAS the first team sport taken to Australia by British settlers. It was being played in Sydney by 1804, some eighteen years after the decision of George II to set up a penal colony in New South Wales. On 8 January that year, the *Sydney Gazette and New South Wales Advertiser* reported on a match played by the officers and crew of HMS *Calcutta*. Clubs began to be formed by the settlers in Sydney in 1826. In the 1830s cricket was recorded in Tasmania, Western Australia, South Australia and Victoria with clubs being established only a few years after the first settlements. Despite the vast distances between the main towns, which meant that each state was effectively a separate colony, the pattern of cricket development in each was remarkably similar. The early matches were usually between the settlers and the military but, as more clubs were created, matches between local sides became more frequent. Publicans played a crucial role in the organisation of the games because the hostelries were the only places which could provide food and accommodation for the players and spectators.

Strongly Egalitarian

With settler numbers being small, anyone who could play was welcomed so that, from its very beginning in Australia, cricket was strongly egalitarian with players ranging from administrators to tradesmen, mechanics, furniture makers and labourers. The only exceptions were clubs established by 'gentlemen of the colonies' of which the most influential was the Melbourne Cricket Club, founded on 15 November 1838 with a membership subscription of one guinea, so as to attract only the 'right kind of people'. By the end of the 1840s, cricket was well established in many of the smaller up-country towns, such as Geelong in Victoria and Maitland and Newcastle in New South Wales, as well as in the main cities. Matches between country and town clubs occurred as did games between British- and local-born. The British influence on the game was to last until the end of the century. The side which represented Australia in the first test match in March 1877 contained only five locally-born cricketers. Between 1877 and 1900, five players represented both Australia and England. By the 1850s clubs were being formed in the suburban areas of the main cities and also by institutions such as the fire brigade, tradesmen's organisations and the civil service. Cricket also began to attract people of middle-class and professional standing who helped establish the game in schools and the newly-formed universities.

Given the geography of Australia, with great distances between the main settlements and the poor quality of the local road network which, during the rainy season varied from muddy to impassable with river crossings changing from fords to raging torrents, the speed at which cricket spread across the country was surprising. Transport between the main towns, the capital cities of the separate colonies, was generally by sea. The challenge to test the strength of the local game against that in the other colonies was too great, however, to be daunted by any difficulties of travel. The first inter-colonial match took place at Launceston in February 1851 when a team

from Victoria, chosen by the Melbourne CC played Tasmania, a side selected by the club in Launceston but including leading players from Hobart. Tasmania won by three wickets. In 1856, New South Wales met Victoria at Melbourne on a surface that was so rough that any batsman who reached doubles figures was considered a hero. New South Wales won by only 3 wickets after having been set a target of 15 runs.

Throughout the 1840s and 1850s, contact between Britain and its colonies in Australia remained strong and the Australian players adopted the changes to the way the game was played. Round-arm bowling was introduced in Australia in the 1842/43 season, fourteen years after it was legalised in Britain. In the case of over-arm bowling, Australia adopted it in 1862/63 whereas it was not legal in Britain until 1864. When the Australian tourists came to Britain in 1878, they were superior to the English team in its use. Contact with Britain was further enhanced as the organisers of the game in the individual colonies, not satisfied with the inter-colonial matches, aspired to test the local standard of play against that in England. The initiative was taken by the catering firm of Spiers and Pond in Melbourne who managed to sign up twelve English cricketers at £150 each plus first-class travelling expenses, to play in Australia in early 1862. The English played all matches against local sides of twenty-twos and were beaten by the combined team of Victoria and New South Wales. The tour was a great success financially, socially and in terms of the cricket played. The Melbourne CC then unilaterally took over the organising role and arranged for English teams to visit in 1863/64 and 1873/74. The latter tour attracted a lot of interest because the Melbourne Club agreed to find the substantial sum of £1,500 for a personal fee for W.G. Grace plus expenses for his wife and £170 for each of the eight professional players in the party. G.F. Grace and two other amateurs made up the party. Again the tour was a success financially and playing-wise. The professionals made extra money by taking out cricket equipment and selling it at inflated prices and by betting on the matches. Although fixtures were still played against the odds, the standard of Australian cricket was now much improved and, in Victoria, was almost as good as that of the English players, W.G. Grace excepted.

With the growth of inter-colonial matches and the number of tours, the organisation of cricket needed to become more professional and was gradually taken over by men who had the time and money to devote to the task. There was a widespread belief, with some anecdotal evidence to support it, that Australian cricket passed into the hands of Protestants and Masons where it remained until the 1960s. These people had a strongly Victorian view of how the game should be played and were keen to rid it of its association with gambling and boorish behaviour. At the same time, however, they had a pragmatic approach and helped institute several aspects of the game which have become distinctively Australian. Although the working class were not involved in the organisation, they were welcomed as players and no separation of amateurs and professionals ever developed; all were cricketers. Indeed, many in Australia were critical of the way W.G. Grace was able to command such a large fee for playing cricket and yet retain his position as an amateur. Other contributions included the acceptance of league competitions, the development of large grounds and the use of detailed scoreboards.

Australian Cricket Council Formed

The ability of any central body to control the game remained limited whilst the organisation of tours remained in private hands. In 1883/84 there were disagreements between the Melbourne CC and the Australian players over expenses for matches against J. Lillywhite's English tourists. In 1887/88 two English teams found themselves touring Australia and competing for matches at the same time, one organised by Melbourne CC and the other through the auspices of the New South Wales Cricket Association. Financially, the outcome was a disaster, the Melbourne CC lost £3,583 on the venture and A. Shaw, A. Shrewsbury and J. Lillywhite lost at least £2,400 on their rival tour. As a result, the representatives of the cricket associations of Victoria, New South Wales and South Australia met in Melbourne on 21 December 1887 to establish a protocol for the organisation of tours. On 21 March 1892, delegates from the same organisations formed the Australasian Cricket Council to regulate all international and inter-colonial matches. Although the ACC was dissolved in January 1900, it was replaced on 6 January 1905 by the Australian Board of Control in which the key administrators were Ernest

Bean of Victoria and Billy McElhone of New South Wales, neither of whom had any experience of cricket as players. This brought relationships with the players over payments and team selection to a head. At its simplest, the players had, on these privately-arranged tours, acquired the power to select their manager and to influence the financial arrangements. The Board were determined to take control of the players' finances, holding the view that they should not draw professional fees whilst retaining an amateur status. Against the wishes of the players, the Board appointed Peter McAlister as deputy captain and treasurer for the 1909 tour of England whereas the players had chosen Frank Laver as manager, a position which included responsibility for the tour's finances. Neither apparently kept any financial records of the tour and were unable to answer the Board's later request to see the account books. The Board backed McAlister and embarked on a smear campaign against both Laver and the tour captain, Monty Noble whose reputation for high standards of conduct and sportsmanship was known throughout Australia.

Concerns were also expressed at this time about the behaviour of some of the Australian teams overseas and the inability of the manager and captain to discipline the players. There was a widely-held view in England that, with the exception of the 1899 side under Joe Darling, a strict Presbyterian who detested both drinking and smoking, the Australians were not only mercenary in their outlook but were also ill-mannered and drunk most of the time. The team which went to England in 1912 returned with the reputation of being the worst-behaved ever, setting records for alcohol consumption and brawling. To some extent, the Board was responsible for this situation. Six key players, Warwick Armstrong, Hanson Carter, Albert Cotter, Clem Hill, Vernon Ransford and Victor Trumper, refused to tour since they were not allowed to select the team manager. Instead of seeking a compromise with them, the Board was intransigent and therefore chose a side which was weak in playing ability and led by Syd Gregory, a batsman with a distinguished test record but by then 42 years of age and who was too kind-hearted to control his players. The side was managed by George Crouch who had no idea how to deal with the situation. The team was socially ostracised before the end of the tour in England and its behaviour worsened during its visit to the eastern United States on the way home. Matthews, Carkeek and Smith were later disciplined by the Board and never selected for Australia again. The Board then assumed the power to decide whether or not a person was 'fit and proper' to represent Australia in international cricket regardless of his playing ability. Although the Board has been rightly criticised for its high-handed way of dealing with the players, the attitudes of many of the players did not help their cause. At any rate, the Board now had total control with player resentment festering on-and-off beneath the surface until it emerged again in the 1970s.

Rapid Decline

Other attitudes of the Board of Control in the early 1900s left their mark on Australian cricket for many years. Whether or not there was any direct government control is not clear, but the Board clearly operated in line with the 'White Australia' policy. When arrangements were made for a side from Fiji to tour Australia in 1907/08, the Board at first rejected the tour because it would breach that policy. However, the captain and manager of the Fijian side was Lieutenant Eric Marsden, formerly in the Army in Victoria, and he used his military connections to get the decision overturned and the tour went ahead. Indeed, any mention of the original decision was removed from the Board's minutes of the meeting. Then there is the question of the very rapid decline of the game amongst the Aborigine community. In the mid-nineteenth century, the aborigines in western Victoria were enthusiastic about cricket and received coaching from William Hayman and Tom Wills, a third-generation Australian who, as a pupil at Rugby School in England had been coached by John Lillywhite. On 26 December 1866, the aborigines met Melbourne CC at Melbourne on equal terms but lost by eight wickets. Nevertheless, they continued to organise fixtures in Victoria and also in Sydney and then embarked on a tour of England in 1868 where they won fourteen out of the 47 matches played. The Australians seemed worried that the aborigines had become not far short of first-class standard in a game which belonged to the 'white' population. Although their best player, Johnny Mullagh, was appointed a professional at the Melbourne Club, the rest were lost to the game after the Victoria Government placed an embargo on the movement of the aboriginal population outside the state. After this, discrimination by race and class made it almost impossible, until recently, for aborigines to participate in cricket. Although a few have represented their states in the first-class game, none has represented Australia.

The Board's attitude towards Fiji was to a large extent replicated in its dealings with countries other than England and South Africa. Although the West Indies sent a side to Australia in 1930/31, the social arrangements had to conform to the White Australia policy and the Department of Home Affairs only reluctantly agreed to the eleven black players participating. The Board had to give a written undertaking that they would leave the country again. The Board only agreed to a privately arranged tour of Malaya in 1927 because the politically inexperienced chairman, Harry Gregory, accepted the proposal without the knowledge of the other Board members. The Board insisted on choosing the players to take part in a tour of Canada and the United States, organised privately by Arthur Mailey in 1932 and only grudgingly agreed to allow its players to take part in a privately arranged tour of India in 1935/36. In short, the Australian Board took no interest in encouraging the game in other countries. The attitude towards New Zealand was especially negative. Although New Zealand cricket has almost as long a history as Australia's, only one international was played between the two countries, a test match in 1945/46, before the 1970s. Fiji did not visit again until 1960 and it was not until the late 1990s that teams from Papua New Guinea and Tonga appeared in Australia. There is no doubt that Australia could have made a much greater contribution to the development of cricket in southeast Asia and the Pacific.

The late 1880s saw the beginnings of organised women's cricket in Australia. Women started playing recreationally with their brothers and fathers and then gradually began to arrange informal games amongst themselves. A few clubs were formed and the sport was introduced in a few girls schools. The first recorded match was played in April 1874 at Bendigo, Victoria, and the scorecard survives of a match between two scratch sides, the Fernleas and the Siroccos, played at Sydney on 8 March 1886. This contains the names of Nellie, Lily and Alice Gregory, the daughters of E.J. Gregory, who represented Australia in the first test match in 1877, and the sisters of Syd Gregory. By 1900, women's matches had been played in all the States. The first inter-colonial match occurred on 17 March 1906 when Tasmania were beaten by six wickets by Victoria at Collingwood. Further inter-colonials took place between these two States and between Victoria and New South Wales over the following five years but after 1910, the women's game suffered a rapid decline. Chauvinistic attitudes increasingly prevailed about women playing cricket and these discouraged girls from taking up the game.

Social Structure

The social structure of Australian cricket of a paternalistic Board of Control but an egalitarian make-up of the playing community lasted until the 1970s. The one occasion when the conservative attitude of the Board was arguably valuable, however, was in responding to the 'bodyline' controversy in the 1932/33 season. Australia had become the dominant world side in the early 1930s. They won the series in England in 1930 by two matches to one with one test drawn, due largely to the batting of Don Bradman and the spin bowling of Clarrie Grimmett. For their tour of Australia in 1932/33, England attempted to restrain the Australian batsmen, especially Bradman, by fast short-pitched balls aimed at the body. After injuries to Woodfull and Oldfield, the Australian Board sent a cable to the MCC in London to protest about the tactics being used by the English captain, Douglas Jardine. The Board's view was that England had elevated the objective of winning above that of sportsmanship and the cable referred to the bowling as 'unsportsmanlike'. The use of this word was sufficient to rile the MCC and cables were exchanged between the MCC and the Board in which the MCC invited the Australians to cancel the rest of the tour if they felt so inclined. The issue was taken up at Government level with the Secretary of State for the British Dominions becoming involved. Diplomatic relationships between Britain and Australia were at a low point at this time. Economically, Australia was seriously affected by the Great Depression and had asked the British Government to postpone payments of interest on a large war loan. The Australian Government then

introduced high protectionist tariffs on imported goods. Eventually a compromise was reached with an agreement giving Australian foodstuffs preferential treatment in Britain and British manufacturing exports preference in Australia. No compromise was forthcoming on the cricket field, however, and the Australian Board was forced to withdraw the accusation of unsportsmanlike behaviour. No apology was ever made by the MCC who never admitted any responsibility. The Australian Board went on to outlaw bodyline bowling in domestic cricket. The MCC did not follow suit but the tactic was never used again in international cricket and was eventually dealt with by leaving the umpires to interpret regulations on whether the bowling of short-pitched balls constitutes dangerous and unfair bowling. There can be no doubt, however, that the stance of the Australian Board prevented serious injuries occurring in the sport.

The next major controversy to confront Australian cricket was when payment to players re-emerged as an issue in the 1970s. The players compared their position with that of other sportsmen who were able to enter sponsorship contracts with companies and were receiving full-time contracts from their national sporting bodies. The team manager of the 1975 side which competed in the World Cup competition in England pointed out to the Board that whilst the Board had made a profit, the individual players had made a loss. The Board had no idea how to respond. By 1976, individual players were being approached by businessmen with sponsorship deals which required the Board's approval. The situation came to a head when Kerry Packer, owner of the Channel Nine television station offered the Board A$500,000 a season for five years for exclusive rights to broadcast test and inter-State matches. The Board rejected the offer because they had already renewed their long-standing arrangement with the Australian Broadcasting Commission in a deal worth A$207,000 over three years. Packer immediately set up a company called World Series Cricket and recruited twenty-eight Australian, eighteen West Indian and twenty-two other players for a series of matches between WSC Australia and the Rest of the World, during the 1977/78 season, in competition with the Board's international and domestic programme. It was some two years before the Board agreed to talk to Channel Nine to find a compromise by which time an attempt by the ICC and the Test and County Cricket Board in England to ban the WSC players had failed in the British High Court. The Court ruled that any ban constituted an unreasonable restraint of trade. In the meantime, World Series Cricket had introduced day-night limited overs matches, white cricket balls, coloured clothing and improved television technology. Most importantly, Packer's activities led to remuneration schemes for players comparable to those in other sports through individual and team sponsorship by companies and to contracts between players and the Board.

Australia has always been a dominantly urban society and hardly any attempt has been made to take the first-class game outside the main cities. Some 59 per cent of the population live in Sydney, Melbourne, Brisbane Perth and Adelaide. In 1880/81, first-class matches were held only at Melbourne (three games), Sydney (two games) and Adelaide (one). In 1910/11, Melbourne and Sydney each staged six matches, twice as many as any of the other towns, with Brisbane (three games), Launceston (one) and Hobart (one) forming the other venues. The situation changed only slightly from then to the 1960s, with a small increase in the total number of matches played and the addition of Perth (one game in 1960/61) to the list of centres. In 2003/04, five centres staged six matches each and one centre staged seven; St Kilda, Victoria, and Newcastle, New South Wales, hosted two games and one game respectively. Although good class grade cricket is played in the smaller country towns, the only opportunity their inhabitants had of seeing the top class players was when touring sides visited places like Geelong, Armidale, Newcastle and Toowoomba and played so-called Country XIs. In contrast, Packer took his World Series Cricket to Kalgoorlie, Bunbury, Cairns, Townsville, Wagga Wagga, Maitland, Newcastle, Armidale, Bendigo, Devonport and many other towns, as well as to New Zealand and the West Indies. This initiative has not been followed by the ABC or the State Cricket Associations. Geographically, Australian first-class cricket remains heavily centralised. In 2004/05, however, test cricket was taken to Darwin and Cairns, giving the chance for the inhabitants to see the best

Australian cricketers take on Bangladesh and Sri Lanka.

During the English tour of Australia in 1891/92, the manager, Lord Sheffield, was impressed by the standard of play of the Australians but believed it could be strengthened further by putting inter-colonial matches on a more organised footing. He therefore donated funds for a trophy to be awarded for an inter-state competition of first-class matches. It is possible that Lord Sheffield was using cricket as one way of promoting the British Government policy of the time which was to further inter-colonial activity and encourage the colonies to federate. Thus, in 1892/93, the Sheffield Shield was inaugurated. It remained the trophy for the inter-state competition until 1999/2000, when company sponsorship was obtained from National Foods Limited who donated the Pura Cup, based on the brand name of their milk products (Table 2.1). Compared with the English County Championship, the number of first-class games played each year is very small, with just three teams involved initially and only six today.

Major Adventure

Until the advent of regular passenger air transport, a cricket tour of Australia was always a major adventure. For a start, it took a long time to get there. The first English tourists in 1861/62 took over two months to reach Melbourne and the players found life on board ship very tedious. Having reached Australia, travel between the main centres was also by sea, so often a week elapsed between matches. The situation improved with the construction of the railways but this enabled itineraries to be developed like that followed by the English side in 1894/95. They travelled from Adelaide to Melbourne, Sydney and Brisbane, only to do the journey in reverse and then repeat the circuit.

Table 2.1. Teams involved in Australia's first-class domestic competitions: the Sheffield Shield (1892/93-1998/99) and the Pura Cup (1999/2000-2006/07)

Team	Date of first appearance	Number of times winners
New South Wales	1892/93	44
Queensland	1926/27	6
South Australia	1892/93	13
Tasmania	1977/78	1
Victoria	1892/93	26
Western Australia	1947/48	15

The English tour of 1950/51 was typical of those followed by most countries in Australia between 1920 and 1980, beginning in Perth and travelling via Adelaide, Melbourne and Sydney to Brisbane. Some shuttling between Sydney and Melbourne then followed, finishing with a visit to Tasmania and a final test match in Melbourne. Throughout the tour visits to smaller towns were included to play State Country sides. Newcastle, Armidale, Toowoomba, Geelong and Broken Hill were the more common locations. Gradually, with faster travel, the number of non-playing days decreased and the distances travelled per non-playing day increased (Table 2.2). The availability of air travel, the development of one-day internationals and back-to-back test matches has now produced horrendous itineraries like that of England in 2002/03 in which virtually all the days when cricket was not being played were spent travelling from one venue to another. Between 1 and 25 January 2003, the team played cricket on fifteen days and there were only two rest days. The number of kilometres travelled per rest day was 3,495. Admittedly virtually all of this was by air but from 20 January, when the team played in Melbourne, the venues were Sydney and then back Melbourne. The logic of playing two consecutive matches in Melbourne before moving to Sydney seemed to have escaped the organisers! The effect of continuous cricket – air travel – cricket – air travel and no rest on a player's health seems not to have been considered.

Australia played its first international match at Melbourne against England in March 1877 winning by 45 runs. Since then the pattern of Australia's record has been remarkably simple. Up to 1908, it was patchy, with successful seasons like those of 1897/98 and 1901/02 being interspersed with periods with very few victories. From 1908 until 1992, the overall picture is one of success. Although Australian cricket writers like Jack Pollard and Chris Harte refer to certain periods as 'cricket in the doldrums' and 'the end of a winning streak', in reality these periods were short-lived, lasting at most about five years. Always, Australia produced some outstanding new players, able to lift the fortunes of national side again. Since 1992 the record has been remarkable with Australia winning most of the games they played. Between 1999 and 2001, they were victorious in sixteen consecutive test matches. The summer of 2005, however, saw them lose the series to England. Although they recovered in 2006/07 by regaining The Ashes and winning the World Cup, there is concern as to whether they can find new players of the same quality to replace an ageing side.

Since the 1920s, the fortunes of the Australian women's side have closely followed that of the men's team. When the men were successful, it encouraged women to take up the game. After reorganising from scratch at the end of the 1914-18 War, women's cricket developed rapidly and in the 1930s entered its golden decade. The increasing strength of the game at state level encouraged the Australian Women's Cricket Council to invite England to tour in 1934/35. The success of this, particularly financially, led to Australia touring England in 1937 during which they achieved their first international victory. The story after the 1939-45 War, however, was one of initial enthusiasm followed by gradual decline. Australia beat England in three test series in the late 1940s and early 1950s. No further international matches were played until 1958 by which time lack of funding and very small crowds meant that public interest in the women's game was very low. Only a small corps of players and administrators prevented it from dying out. Their initiatives in schools and junior clubs led to the re-emergence of the game in the 1970s. An increase in the number of tours both overseas and in Australia and the inauguration of the Women's World Cup in 1973 further encouraged the game, enabling the Australian administrators to obtain a greater level of sponsorship than that achieved in

Table 2.2. Playing days, rest days and distances travelled on tours of Australia by England

Date	Playing days	Rest days	Ratio of cricket days to rest days	Kilometres travelled per rest day
1894/95	76	56	1.36	177
1950/51	82	35	2.34	308
2002/03	51	25	2.04	1119

Notes: Rest days are days when no cricket is played and no travel takes place. The ratio of kilometres travelled per rest day is an underestimate because kilometres are based on straight-line distances between the venues and not the actual distance travelled.

any other country. By investing money in better coaching and superior training, Australia have dominated women's world cricket since 1980. They have won 80 per cent of their one-day international matches and have been World Cup Champions five times out of the eight competitions played. The Australian captain of the 1990s, Belinda Clark, was one of *Wisden Australia*'s five cricketers of the year in 1999.

In both the men's and women's game Australia have achieved a dominance which no other country has been able to match. Throughout the 1990s and early 2000s, they have been clearly the world champions in both test matches and one-day internationals. During this time they have played aggressive, highly competitive and attractive cricket.

Famous Victories

August 28, 29, 1902 – The Oval, London
Australia 63 (R.G. Barlow 5-19, E. Peate 4-31) and 122 (H. Massie 55, E. Peate 4-40)
England 101 (F.R. Spofforth 7-46) and 77 (F.R. Spofforth 7-44)
Australia won by 7 runs

This was the match which led to the creation of The Ashes. Australia were dismissed in 2¼ hours on a wet pitch following two days of rain. England struggled in reply after Fred Spofforth bowled W.G. Grace for four and they lost six wickets before gaining first-innings lead. In their second innings, Australia owed all to Hugh Massie who decided to attack the bowling, scoring his 55 in only 45 minutes; otherwise only Alex Bannerman (13) and Billy Murdoch (29) reached double figures. England started well in the pursuit of 85 runs to win, the fifty coming up for the loss of only two wickets. Once W.G. Grace was caught at mid-off from the bowling of Henry Boyle, the batting struggled. The Hon. Alfred Lyttleton and Alfred Lucas played out twelve successive maiden overs but England then lost wickets regularly to Spofforth who bowled consistently on a good length with frequent variations in pace. Although runs continued to be scored, some of Spofforth's deliveries were unplayable and, amid great tension, England fell seven runs short. It is said that one spectator died of heart failure in the closing stages and another chewed right through his umbrella handle. After the match the *Sporting Times* published an obituary of

English cricket ending with the words: 'the body will be cremated and the ashes taken to Australia'.

August 18, 20, 21, 22, 1934 – The Oval, London
Australia 701 (W.H. Ponsford 266, D.G. Bradman 244, W.E. Bowes 4-164, G.O.B. Allen 4-170) and 327 (D.G. Bradman 77, S.J. McCabe 70, W.E. Bowes 5-55, E.W. Clark 5-98)
England 321 (M. Leyland 110, C.F. Walters 64) and 145 (C.V. Grimmett 5-64)
Australia won by 562 runs

The match was a prime example of Australia's dominance with the bat in the 1930s. Bill Ponsford and Don Bradman put on 451 runs for the second wicket. Bradman batted for 316 minutes and hit one six and 32 fours; Ponsford was in for 460 minutes and hit one five and 27 fours but he was dropped six times before being out hit wicket with the score on 574 for four. Australia batted until 4.55 p.m. on the second day whereupon Cyril Walters and Herbert Sutcliffe (38 runs) made an opening stand of 104 runs. Wickets then fell regularly to Clarrie Grimmett (3-103), Hans Ebeling (3-74) and Bill O'Reilly (2-93) with Maurice Leyland and Leslie Ames (33) the only batsmen to offer resistance before Ames was forced to retire with severe lumbago and took no further part in the match. Bill Woodfull did not enforce the follow-on. Frank Woolley, then aged 47, kept wicket in Ames's absence and let 37 byes. England were set a target of 708 runs but were unable to deal with the bowling of Grimmett.

October 11, 12, 2002 – Sharjah Cricket Association Stadium
Pakistan 59 (S.K. Warne 4-11) and 53 (S.K. Warne 4-13)
Australia 310 (M.L. Hayden 119, Saqlain Mushtaq 4-83)
Australia won by an innings and 198 runs

Pakistan won the toss and decided to bat on one of the world's slowest and flattest pitches. Their innings lasted just one ball short of 32 overs, the batsmen being completely bemused by Shane Warne's bowling which included his new 'slider'; three of his wickets were obtained by balls which kept low but did not turn and then trapped the batsman leg before. In temperatures approaching 50° C, Pakistan's pace attack was neutralised.

Matthew Hayden, dropped twice, batted for seven hours and received support from Justin Langer (37), Ricky Ponting (44) and Damien Martyn (34). Warne then dominated proceedings, Pakistan lasting less than 25 overs this time.

Women's match

June 12, 14, 15, 1937 – County Ground, Wantage Road, Northampton
Australia 300 (K.M. Smith 88, H.D. Pritchard 87) and 102
England 204 (M.E. Maclagan 89, P. Antonio 6-51) and 167 (E.A. Snowball 72, K.M. Smith 4-50)
Australia won by 31 runs

Australia achieved their first victory over England in the fourth match between the two countries. Australia batted well on winning the toss with Hazel Pritchard playing a delicate innings full of cuts and glances and putting on 127 runs for the second wicket in partnership with Margaret Peden (34 runs). Kath Smith then punished the English bowling, displaying her fierce hooking ability. Myrtle Maclagan held the English innings together whilst her colleagues succumbed to the guile of Peggy Antonio's leg breaks and googlies. Australia batted poorly in their second innings and it was expected that England would score the runs required for victory, especially when they reached 97 for the loss of only one wicket. They then collapsed to left-armer Smith and Antonio (3-40).

The tied matches

December 9,10, 12, 13, 14, 1960 – Woolloongabba, Brisbane
West Indies 453 (G.S. Sobers 132, F.M. Worrell 65, J. Solomon 65, F.C.M. Alexander 60, W.W. Hall 50, A.K. Davidson 5-135) and 284 (F.M. Worrell 65, R.B. Kanhai 54, A.K. Davidson 6-87)
Australia 505 (N.C. O'Neill 181, R.B. Simpson 92, C.C. McDonald 57, W.W. Hall 4-140) and 232 (A.K. Davidson 80, R. Benaud 52, W.W. Hall 5-63)
Match tied

The captains, Richie Benaud and Frank Worrell, agreed before the series started to play exciting cricket and then, in the first test, produced one of the best matches of all time. West Indies attacked the bowling from the start and amassed a very competitive total, despite excellent pace

bowling from Alan Davidson. Garfield Sobers scored his century in just over two hours. Australia responded in similar vein and achieved a first innings lead. West Indies then found batting difficult with Davidson again bowling well; only Frank Worrell came close to mastering him but a last wicket stand of 31 between Wes Hall and Alf Valentine left Australia to score 233 runs at a rate of 45 an hour. Hall bowled at a fiery pace and Australia slumped to 57 for the loss of five wickets and 92 for six before Davidson and Benaud added 134. Davidson was run out when Benaud called for a quick single. Wally Grout then scored a single leaving six runs to be scored from the last over with three wickets left. From the first ball Grout obtained a leg bye. Benaud was then caught at the wicket. Grout and Ian Meckiff managed four more runs before Grout was run out. Lindsay Kline came in with two runs needed from two balls. He hit the seventh ball of the over to square leg and Meckiff, backing up, called for a run only to be beaten by Joe Solomon's throw, a direct hit with only the width of the stumps to aim at. The match was tied with one ball left to play.

September 18, 19, 20, 21, 22, 1986 – M.A. Chidambaram Stadium, Chepauk, Madras
Australia 574-7 dec (D.M. Jones 210, D.C. Boon 122, A.R. Border 106, N.S. Yadav 4-142) and 170-5 dec
India 397 (Kapil Dev 119, R.J. Shastri 62, K. Srikkanth 53, M. Azharuddin 50, G.R.J. Matthews 5-103) and 347 (S.M. Gavaskar 90, M. Amarnath 51, R.J. Bright 5-94, G.R.J. Matthews 5-146)
Match tied

Australia completely outplayed India over the first three days and, at one time, there was the possibility of a victory by an innings. Australia batted positively into the third day with Dean Jones spending 8 hours 23 minutes at the crease, overcoming bouts of nausea and cramp in the hot humid conditions. India struggled against the spin of Greg Matthews and Ray Bright (2-88) and were saved from the follow-on by Kapil Dev's century reached off 109 balls. Australia declared their second innings at the start of the final day, setting India 348 to win in a minimum of 87 overs. India began by playing for a draw but a century partnership between Sunil Gavaskar and Mohinder Amarnath opened the door for a chase of 158 runs off 30 overs in the final session after tea. Once Gavaskar was out, Ravi Shastri (48 not out) took control and forced Australia more and more on to the defensive. With only 18 runs needed from the last 30 balls, Chetan Sharma and Kiran More were dismissed in one over from Bright. Shivlal Yadav was removed, leaving India to score four runs from eight balls. Shastri made three runs in the last over but Maninder Singh was leg-before to Matthews on the penultimate ball of the match.

Player Profiles

Bradman, Sir Donald George AC. b Cootamundra, New South Wales, 27 August 1908. d Kensington Park, Adelaide, South Australia, 25 February 2001. rhb. Known as 'the boy from Bowral' because he was brought up there after his parents moved from Cootamundra when he was two years of age, his batting achievements are without parallel in test and first class cricket; he scored a century in every third time he batted. He made over 300 in an innings six times, two of them in test matches against England. Although some critics considered his batting mechanical, his timing and footwork made his driving and cutting immaculate. He treated each ball on its merit but with his rapid judgement, power of concentration and self-confidence, he was able to dominate the bowling. In 52 test matches, he scored 6996 runs with 29 centuries (average 99.94). He captained Australia in five test series and did not lose any, winning four convincingly. On retirement from the game, he became the first Australian cricketer to be knighted and then gave many years of service as a selector and administrator. The internationally-acclaimed Bradman Museum was founded in his honour at Bowral. It is dedicated to both Bradman's career and the history of Australian cricket.

Chappell, Gregory Stephen MBE. b Unley, Adelaide, South Australia, 7 August 1948. rhb. rm. The most accomplished and technically-correct Australian batsman of his generation, he had an extensive repertoire of strokes which he played with elegance and composure. He was a useful swing bowler, able to pick up crucial wickets and break partnerships, and an outstanding close fielder. He shares the record, seven, for the most number of catches made in a test match. In 87 tests he scored 7110 runs (average 53.86), took 47 wickets (average 40.70) and made 122 catches. In 74 one-day internationals he made 2331 runs (average 40.18) and took 72 wickets (average 29.12).

Grimmett, Clarence Victor. b Caversham, Dunedin, New Zealand, 25 December 1891. d Kensington Park, Adelaide, South Australia, 2 May 1980. rhb. lbg. Despite not starting an international career until the age of 33, he became one of the world's greatest leg spin bowlers. Bowling mainly leg breaks interspersed with a somewhat innocuous googly, his main weapon was a fast top-spinner which surprised the batsman by dipping very late in its flight. He was exceptionally accurate and rarely bowled a loose ball. In 37 test matches he took 216 wickets (average 24.21), taking five or more wickets in an innings on 21 occasions. He also scored 557 runs (average 13.92).

Lillee, Dennis Keith MBE. b Subiaco, Perth, Western Australia, 18 July 1949. rhb. rf. The leading Australian bowler of his generation, he delighted the crowds with his belligerence and apparent hatred of all batsmen. Starting as a fast tearaway, he developed the art to include variations in pace, balls that swerved or cut either way, the yorker and the bouncer, to which he added the occasional verbal barrage. In 70 test matches he took 355 wickets (average 23.92) and scored 905 runs (average 13.71). In 63 one-day internationals he made 240 runs (average 9.23) and took 103 wickets (average 20.82).

Lindwall, Raymond Russell MBE. b Mascot, Sydney, New South Wales, 3 October 1921. d Greenslopes, Brisbane, Queensland, 22 June 1996. rhb. rf. Australia's leading bowler in the late 1940s and 1950s, he was admired for the smoothness of his run-up, delivery and follow-through from which he achieved real pace. In England, where the ball would swing more than in Australia, he added an effective inswinger to his normal outswing delivery. As a useful lower order batsman, he made two test centuries. In 61 test matches he took 228 wickets (average 23.03) and scored 1502 runs (average 21.15).

McGrath, Glenn Donald. b Dubbo, New South Wales, 9 February 1970. rhb. rfm. One of the most consistent bowlers of line and length, his ability to bowl at or just outside the off-stump creates just sufficient uncertainty in a batsman as to whether to play the ball or leave it alone. Coupled with a miserly approach which pins the batsman down and causes frustration, the result is often a nick and a catch to the wicket-keeper or the slips. The outstanding fast bowler of his generation, in 124 matches he has taken 563 wickets (average 21.64) and scored 641 runs (average 7.36). In 249 one-day internationals, he has taken 380 wickets (average 21.98) and scored 115 runs (average 3.96).

Matthews, Christina (née White). b Kew, Melbourne, Victoria, 26 December 1959. rhb. wk. The most successful wicket-keeper in Australian women's cricket, she holds the world record for the highest number of dismissals in a career and the most in a match, 8 caught and 1 stumped, achieved against India at Adelaide in 1990/91. As a child she wanted to play football but, eventually, chose cricket instead. In 20 test matches she obtained 46 catches and 12 stumpings as well as making 180 runs (average 10.58). In 47 one-day internationals she scored 141 runs (average 9.40) and made 35 catches and 14 stumpings.

Oldfield, William Albert Stanley MBE. b Alexandria, Sydney, New South Wales, 9 September 1894. d Killara, Sydney, New South Wales, 10 August 1976. rhb. wk. One of the greatest wicket-keepers of the 1920s and 1930s, he did his work with quiet efficiency. His appeals to the umpire were always polite and more like a request for information than a demand. He kept superbly standing back to fast bowling and rarely dropped a catch but he was a master of his craft when standing up to the spin attack of Grimmett and O'Reilly. Despite playing only half as many matches as modern players, he still holds the record for the most stumpings in test matches. He was also a useful middle-order batsman. In 54 test matches he obtained 78 catches and 52 stumpings; he made 1427 runs (average 22.65).

Ponting, Ricky Thomas. b Launceston, Tasmania, 19 December 1974. rhb. A sporting prodigy and considered one of the best teenage batsmen ever to emerge from the Australian cricket academy, he is the most consistent and one of today's most exciting batsmen. An attacking player, he has already scored four double centuries in test cricket and can adapt his style to succeed equally well in one-day and twenty20 matches. The current Australian captain, he inspires by his own performances of which some of the best have come as match-saving innings. He has the potential to become the leading run-scorer of all-time in international cricket. In 110 test matches he has scored 9,368 runs (average 59.29). In 279 one-day internationals he has made 10,280 runs (average 43.01).

Spofforth, Frederick Robert. b Balmain, Sydney, New South Wales, 9 September 1853. d Ditton Hill Lodge, Long Ditton, Surrey, 4 June 1926. rhb. rfm. Known as the 'demon', he was Australia's leading bowler in its early test-cricketing years. He was particularly successful in England. Relying originally on speed, he later developed a great variety in pace, becoming more accurate and using both off-breaks and fast yorkers to great effect. In 18 test matches he took 94 wickets (average 18.41) and scored 217 runs (average 9.43).

Warne, Shane Keith. b Ferntree Gully, Melbourne, Victoria, 13 September 1969. rhb. lbg. One of the outstanding bowlers of the 1990s and 2000s, he has taken more wickets than any other player in test cricket. Always willing to experiment, he developed a range of deliveries, leg spin, top spin, googly, flipper, slider and backspin, with which to bamboozle the batsman. In a colourful career, he was fined in 1995 by the Australian Board of Control for selling information to an Indian bookmaker and in 2003 he was sent home from the World Cup and banned for a year for taking drugs. In 145 test matches, he has scored 3154 runs (average 17.32) and taken 708 wickets (average 25.41). In 193 one-day internationals, he has made 1016 runs (average 13.02) and taken 291 wickets (average 25.82).

Wilson, Elizabeth Rebecca. b Melbourne, Victoria, 21 November 1921. rhb. rob. A talented athlete, she developed into the leading woman cricketer of her era, being an outstanding all-rounder. Against England at the St Kilda Oval, Melbourne, in February 1958, she took seven wickets for seven runs in 63 balls, including a hat-trick when helping to dismiss England for 35. She then scored 100 out of Australia's 202 for 9 wickets declared and took four wickets for nine runs when England held out for a draw (76-8). She was the first cricketer, male or female, to score 100 runs and take 10 wickets in a test match. In 11 matches, she scored 862 runs (average 57.46) and took 68 wickets (average 11.80).

Other leading players: *1835-1860:* T.W. Wills (rhb. rf(r)/rs(u)); G. Elliott (rhb. rf(r)). *1860-1890:* G. Giffen (rhb; rob/rm); W.L. Murdoch (rhb); J.M. Blackham (rhb. wk). *1890-1914:* W.W. Armstrong (rhb. rfm/lb); M.A. Noble (rhb. rob/rm); V.T. Trumper (rhb. rm); C.T.B. Turner (rhb. rmf). *1920-1939:* S.J. McCabe (rhb. rm); W.J. O'Reilly (lhb. lbg); W.H. Ponsford (rhb. rm); W.M. Woodfull (lhb). *1945-1960:* R. Benaud (rhb. lbg); A.T.W. Grout (rhb. wk); R.N. Harvey (lhb); K.R. Miller (rhb. rf). *1960-1980:* A.R. Border (lhb. sla); W.M. Lawry (lhb); R.B. Simpson (rhb. lbg); J.R. Thomson (rhb. rf). *1980-2000:* I.A. Healy (rhb. wk); M.E. Waugh (rhb. rob/rm); S.R. Waugh (rhb. rm). *Present day:* A.C. Gilchrist (lhb. wk); B. Lee (rhb. rf); M.E.K. Hussey (lhb).

Women: *1920-1939:* P. Antonio (rhb. lbg); A. Palmer (rhb. rob). *1945-1960:* U.L. Paisley (rhb. rob). *1980-2000:* D.A. Annetts (rhb); B.J. Haggett (rhb. rm); R. Thompson (rhb. rfm). *Present day:* B.J. Clark (rhb); K.L. Rolton (lhb; lm); C.L. Fitzpatrick (rhb. rf).

Playing record

Test Matches

	Won	Lost	Tied	Drawn
England	131	97	0	88
South Africa	44	15	0	18
West Indies	48	32	1	21
New Zealand	22	7	0	17
India	32	15	1	20
Pakistan	24	11	0	17
Sri Lanka	11	1	0	6
Zimbabwe	3	0	0	0
Bangladesh	4	0	0	0
Total	320	178	2	187

One-day matches

	Won	Tied	Lost	No Res
World Cup	51	1	17	0
Other ODI	355	7	210	18

Twenty20

3	0	2	0

Highest team score

758-8 dec	v West Indies, Kingston	1954/55

Lowest team score

36	v England, Birmingham	1902

Highest individual score

380	M.L. Hayden	v Zimbabwe, Perth	2003/04

Best bowling

9-121	A.A. Mailey	v England, Melbourne	1920/21

Best wicket-keeping

6 (6c)	A.T.W. Grout	v South Africa, Johannesburg	1957/58
6 (6c)	R.W. Marsh	v England, Brisbane	1982/83
6 (6c)	I.A. Healy	v England, Birmingham	1997

Women

Test Matches

	Won	Lost	Tied	Drawn
England	10	7	0	25
West Indies	0	0	0	2
New Zealand	4	1	0	8
India	4	0	0	5
Total	18	8	0	40

One-day matches

	Won	Tied	Lost	No Res
World Cup	54	6	1	3
Other ODI	104	28	0	2

Twenty20

1	0	1	0

Highest team score

569-6 dec	v England, Guildford	1998

Lowest team score

38	v England, Melbourne	1957/58

Highest individual score

209*	K.L. Rolton	v England, Leeds	2001

ODI

229*	B.J. Clark	v Denmark, Mumbai	1997/98

Best bowling

7-7	E.R. Wilson	v England, Melbourne	1957/58

Best wicket-keeping

5 (4c 1st)	C.Matthews	v India, Adelaide	1990/91
5 (5c)	C.Matthews	v India, Melbourne	1990/91

AUSTRIA

Affiliate Member of the ICC: elected 1992

RECREATIONAL CRICKET is recorded as having been played in the 1890s by gardeners on the Rothschild estate near Vienna but the next reference to the game in Austria is not until 1975 when Kerry Tattersall, an Australian teaching English, founded the Vienna Cricket Club. Other clubs soon followed and by 1990 it was possible to form a representative side to compete in the European Cricketer Cup in Guernsey, finishing seventh out of ten participants. Although some Austrians are enthusiastically involved in the game, the majority of players are of Indian, Pakistani or Sri Lankan descent. In 1996, a national cricket centre was opened at Seebarn, in the vine-growing area 20 kilometres north of Vienna, and a new pitch was established at Velden. Austria hosted the European Cricket Council Trophy in 2001 and finished second, thereby qualifying to play in Group B of the European Championships the following year. Unfortunately, they were outclassed and lost all five matches. Surprisingly, they played no international cricket between 2003 and 2006.

Leading player: *Present day:* A. Simpson-Parker (rhb. rob).

Playing record
One-day matches

	Won	Lost	No Res
ECC Trophy	8	4	0
European Championships	0	5	0

Highest team score
ODI

321-9	v Czech Republic, Vienna	2006

Lowest team score
ODI

76	v Germany, Belfast	2002

Austria were dismissed for 42 by Italy at Saintfield in 2002 in a warm-up match for the European Championships Division B.

Highest individual score
ODI

148	A. Simpson-Parker	v Greece, Oxford	1995

Best bowling
ODI

5-9	Babar Nadeem	v Czech Republic, Vienna	2006

AZERBAIJAN

A CRICKET club was established in Baku in 1995 by a group of Indian, Pakistani, Bangladeshi, Sri Lankan and British expatriates. Membership fluctuates depending on the length of time people working for foreign companies stay in the country but there is generally sufficient to organise a match between two teams every Sunday between June and November. Since 2002, the club has established a home at the International School. There is now a small number of Azeri players.

BAHAMAS

Affiliate Member of ICC: elected 1987

LITTLE IS known about the history of cricket in the Bahamas. Its geographical and political isolation from the nearest cricket centres in Bermuda and the West Indies prevented the game from becoming anything more than an informal recreational activity for settlers and administrators. Although Jamaica sent a touring side in 1964, it was not until the 1980s that the game became more organised. The national side toured England in 1994 and the MCC returned the visit in 1998 but the Bahamians provided little opposition and were easily defeated. The Bahamas Cricket Association then embarked on a structured programme of coaching and development and standards rapidly improved. They won the Americas Affiliates Trophy in 2001 and 2002, thereby qualifying on both occasions to play alongside associate countries in the Americas Cup. Not surprisingly, they struggled losing all their matches in 2004 but they gained a surprising victory over Argentina in Buenos Aires in 2002.

Leading players: *Present day:* D.G. Weakley (rhb. sla); N.H. Ekanayake (lhb. sla).

Playing record
One-day matches

	Won	Lost	No Res
Americas Affiliates Trophy	6	1	0
Americas Cup	1	8	1
American Championships Division 2	3	1	0

Highest team score
ODI

227-3	v Surinam, Howard (Panama)	2003/04

Lowest team score
ODI

69	v Cayman Islands, Buenos Aires	2001/02

Highest individual score
ODI

108	D.G. Weakley	v Surinam, Howard (Panama) 2003/04

Best bowling
ODI

6-51	G. Armstrong	v USA, Buenos Aires	2001/02

Best wicket-keeping

5 (1c 4st)	G.T. Taylor jnr	v Surinam, Buenos Aires 2005/06
5 (4c 1st)	G.T. Taylor jnr	v Panama, Buenos Aires 2005/06

BAHRAIN

Affiliate Member of ICC: elected 2001

FROM THE time the Awali Cricket Club was established in 1935 by expatriates working in the oil industry, Bahrain was the only country in the Persian Gulf where cricket was played regularly until the 1960s. The MCC toured in December 1994 to celebrate Awali's diamond jubilee but Bahrain did not make their international debut until 2004 when they competed in the Asian Cricket Council Trophy. The side is made up largely of expatriate workers from Pakistan with sufficient years of residence to meet the ICC regulations. Since 2000, there has been a development programme in schools and a national inter-school competition with a quota system to ensure that Bahraini children are encouraged to take part. There is a national league organised by the Bahrain Cricket Association as well as junior, inter-company and inter-hotel competitions. Bahrain nearly won the Middle East Cup in October 2004 when they tied with Oman in the final but, by the rules of the tournament, Oman won the trophy since they had beaten Bahrain by 12 runs in an earlier stage of the competition. Bahrain won the Cup in 2006.

Leading players: *Present day:* Abdul Waheed (wk); Qamar Saeed.

Playing record
One-day matches

	Won	Tied	Lost	No Res
Asian Cricket Council Trophy	4	5	0	0
Middle East Cup	5	2	1	1

Highest team score
ODI

401-5	v Iran, Ahmadi	2005/06

Lowest team score
ODI

172	v Afghanistan, Kuala Lumpur	2004

Highest individual score
ODI

154*	Asghar Bajwa	v Iran, Ahmadi	2005/06

Best bowling
ODI

4-44	Mirza Ashraf	v Oman, Ahmadi	2005/06

Best wicket-keeping
ODI

4 (2 ct 2st)	Abdul Waheed	v Nepal, Kuala Lumpur	2006

BANGLADESH

Associate Member of ICC: elected 1977
Full Member of ICC: elected 2000

In the area which is now Bangladesh, cricket made a very slow start. The social structure and attitudes of society followed those of Kolkata from where it was administered as the eastern part of Bengal. It was not until the 1860s and 1870s when the British constructed new roads and improved the water supplies and health facilities in Dhaka that economic conditions encouraged Europeans to settle. Cricket developed as a recreational activity of the British and was quickly copied by middle and upper class Bengalis. In 1876 a European XI met and defeated a Native XVIII. Cricket was further promoted by English teachers at Dhaka College, the forerunner of Dhaka University, and by the royal household at Mymensingh. From the 1920s until the partition of India and the formation of Pakistan, both economic and sporting activity went into decline. Dhaka suffered from the migration of many Europeans and wealthier members of the Hindu and Muslim communities to Kolkata. The area was additionally hampered by its remoteness and inaccessibility. The journey from Kolkata to Dhaka, some 360 kilometres, took thirteen hours and required a change from rail to river steamer. Despite its high density, most of the population lived in scattered villages and homesteads with limited contact with each other or the European administrators. Its isolation meant that it was never visited by touring sides from overseas and never became a venue for Ranji Trophy matches.

After the partition of the Indian sub-continent in 1947, large numbers of Muslims migrated from Bihar into what became East Pakistan. These included cricketers such as Subir Chakravorthy and Mohsin Kazi who had played for Bihar in the Ranji Trophy in the 1930s and their interest laid the foundation for the development of the game which was now administered by The Board of Control for Cricket in Pakistan. The Pakistani national side played two matches in Dhaka at the end of their 1952/53 tour of India, drawing one and winning the other by ten wickets. In 1954, East Pakistan entered the national Quaid-i-Azam Trophy and thereby began playing cricket at first-class level. Their record was poor, however, and they were clearly the weakest side in the competition. The game did not have widespread appeal, being confined to the richer and more educated members of the urban community. Interest at Dhaka University, where coaching and facilities were available, was strong, however, and in 1958, the university entered the Quaid-i-Azam in its own right. Pakistan's victory over England at The Oval in 1954 inspired schoolchildren to play cricket and in 1955, test cricket came to East Pakistan when Pakistan met India at the purpose-built Dhaka Stadium. With improvements in transport since 1947, Dhaka was regularly served by air, and roads and railways now linked the main centres. Thus both India and the MCC, when they toured Pakistan in 1956, were able to play at Chittagong as well as Dhaka. With Pakistan beating the MCC by an innings on the matting wicket in a game attended by 40,000 people, a further impetus was given to the sport, stimulating an interest throughout the country.

Although, by the 1960s, many more people were playing cricket, the standard of the East Pakistan sides in domestic Pakistani cricket remained low and the Pakistan Board of Control decided that their teams should be reinforced with cricketers from West Pakistan. This certainly improved results but after East Pakistan beat a combined side from Hyderabad, Khairpur and Quetta in the Quaid-i-Azam by five wickets, there was a protest from the losing team. They claimed that at least six of the players, Nasim-ul-Ghani, Naushad Ali, Mufasir-ul-Haq,

Masood-ul-Hasan, Muhammad Sadiq and Rahman Ali, belonged to either Karachi or the Pakistan Public Works Department and were therefore ineligible to represent East Pakistan. After this, the inclusion of cricketers from the West ceased. Some good local players did emerge, notably Niaz Ahmad, who became the first cricketer from the East to represent Pakistan at test level, and M.A. Latif, who played in an unofficial test for Pakistan against Ceylon. Both, however, were born in India and no cricketer born in the East ever represented Pakistan.

Cricket suffered a major setback during the first few years after Bangladesh gained its independence. Many facilities were damaged. By 1975, the Dhaka stadium was in disrepair, the buildings were shell-torn and the square had sunk by several centimetres. Attempts in 1972 and 1973 to revive the game foundered because of the lack of equipment and ground facilities. The Bangladesh Cricket Board was established in 1975 and the military government which took control in 1976 initiated a cricket restoration programme. The MCC toured in 1975/76, playing matches in Rajshahi, Chittagong, Dhaka and Jessore. The Bangladesh national side was able to include several players who, only a few years earlier, had made their first-class debuts in the Pakistani domestic game. These formed the nucleus of the team which played in the first ICC Trophy in 1979.

Widely Popular

The late 1970s were a critical time for cricket which was in strong competition with football for the status of the national game. Football had the advantage of requiring little in the way of equipment and being able to be played on almost any surface in both urban and rural areas. Exactly how cricket won the battle is not clear, especially after the standard of Bangladeshi cricket was cruelly exposed by the Sri Lankan tourists in January 1978 who won all three representative games by an innings. Nevertheless, crowds came to see the matches and when the MCC toured again in January 1979, playing in Jessore, Mymensingh, Rajshahi, Chittagong and Dhaka, it is estimated that some 200,000 people watched the thirteen days of play. Over the next decade or so, cricket became widely popular and in 1994, it was estimated by the ICC that some 93,000 people were involved in playing the game. Despite this, cricket remains an urban game largely focused on Dhaka where the university and the leading club sides are the main source of players. The top clubs, such as Abahani Krira Chakra, Mohammedan Sporting Club, Victoria Sporting Club and Biman Bangladesh Airlines, compete annually in a league competition with the matches attracting crowds of 30,000 to 40,000. The clubs obtain funds from government and industry which they use to attract the best players from all over the country as well as from overseas, particularly Pakistan and India. In addition there is a Corporate Cricket League comprising sides from leading local and multinational companies. In order to ensure that young people are attracted to the game, in 1982 the Bangladesh Cricket Board instituted a schools tournament which initially attracted 45 schools from Dhaka. By the mid 1990s, this was attracting entries from over 500 schools covering 21 different cities, thereby spreading the game to parts of the country where it was not previously played.

With large numbers of people playing cricket, it was not surprising that standards began to improve and the national side started having more success. Bangladesh easily won the South East Asian Cup in 1984, 1988 and 1992 and thereby qualified to play in the 1986, 1988 and 1990 Asia Cup competitions in which they were then easily beaten by India, Pakistan and Sri Lanka. The ICC Trophy allowed a comparison of standards against other associate countries. It was not until 1997 that they were able to win the competition, being losing semi-finalists in 1982 and 1990. The 1997 victory qualified them for the 1999 World Cup and led to the award of one-day international and first-class status by the ICC. By winning all their matches to take the Asian Cricket Council Trophy in 1996 and 1998, Bangladesh showed that they were the best team in Asia outside the three test-playing countries. A huge gap still remained, however, in comparison with the test sides who easily defeated Bangladesh in various one-day competitions. In their first-class matches on tour of New Zealand in 1997/98 they were also outclassed.

The 1999 World Cup in England provided an opportunity to show how far cricket in Bangladesh had progressed. In order to acclimatise to the playing conditions, the side had undertaken a tour of the British Isles in the previous summer, losing five out of the six one-day matches played (the other was abandoned) and also the three-day game against the MCC. They drew the two three-day fixtures against Scotland. In the World Cup they lost to New Zealand, West Indies and Australia but beat Scotland by 22 runs, thereby confirming their position as one of the leading associate countries. They then surprised everyone by beating Pakistan by the wide margin of 62 runs. Unfortunately, the honour of that victory was later somewhat tarnished by accusations that, having already qualified for the next stage of the competition, the Pakistani side was not really trying or that the result was fixed through Indian bookmakers. No evidence has been produced in support of either of these interpretations.

Full Membership

The 1999 World Cup performance, the development programme of the Bangladesh Cricket Board, the popularity of the game at club, company and school level and the large following for the game within the country were all factors which led to the Board seeking full membership of the ICC and, thereby, promotion to test-playing status. The ICC demanded that, before this could be achieved, the Board needed to develop a proper first-class structure for the game. As a result, the National League was started in 1999/2000, comprising six district teams (Table 2.3). The ICC awarded Bangladesh its test status in 2000. The league matches were not considered first-class in the inaugural season, the start of which was marked by a strike of the leading players who were opposed to the league since it competed with the club competition. Whilst the clubs were able to provide an income for the players, the district organisations had only limited funding and were not able to offer a viable alternative. The Board eventually intervened and provided the top eighteen players with central contracts. In its second year, the National League was granted first-class status and was extended to eight teams. Dhaka District was divided to form two teams: Dhaka Metropolis, which represented the city area, and Dhaka Division, representing the rest of District. Biman Bangladesh Airlines entered as an additional team. This arrangement lasted only one season, however, after which it was decided not to mix district and corporate teams in the same competition. So far the league has not attracted the same level of interest as the club competition partly because most of the players are from Dhaka. In order to make the competition more even, these have been shared amongst the sides. This means that neither the players nor the crowd identify with the district teams.

Despite the wide following for cricket, its battle with soccer as the national game of Bangladesh continues. Its greatest effect has been on the location of the national home for cricket. The National Stadium, renamed the Bangabandhu National Stadium, was always a multipurpose venue with the facilities being shared between cricket and football as well as being used for 'tamashas', a sub-continental word which covers anything from gala nights for film stars to popular music concerts and political meetings. In 1999 there was a proposal to use it solely for football and at the end of the 1998/99 season, five of the seven cricket pitches were dug up. However, the remaining pitches continued to be used for international cricket until 1 March 2005 when, despite protests from both players and spectators, cricket moved to a purpose-built sports complex, the Sher-e-Bangla Stadium, at Mirpur. In 2006, the Bangladesh Cricket Academy was established at the Shaheed Chandu Stadium, Bogra, which also became the centre for cricket development in the north of the country.

The gaining of test status was important for cricket in Bangladesh because it led to financial solvency through income from television rights. It has enabled the salaries of contracted players to be increased, indoor facilities to be established at the main centres and the employment of coaches from overseas. Unfortunately, by the time test status was obtained, the majority of the players who won the ICC Trophy in 1997 were reaching the end of their careers and the development programme had not been going long enough to provide a nucleus of new players. As a result, too many promising youngsters have been brought into the national side too early and have found the gap between cricket at the associate level and test level to be too great. The batting has lacked stability and the bowling has been short on both pace and consistency.

In addition to losing heavily in the test matches, the one-day side has struggled and fell to humiliating defeats in the 2003 World Cup to Kenya and Canada. A test victory was forthcoming at the 35th attempt but only against a weak side from Zimbabwe. The ICC has been strongly criticised for awarding test status to Bangladesh but, apart from the standard of play, everything was in place for promotion from associate status to be appropriate. Without promotion, it is doubtful if there was any way of raising standards because money would not have been forthcoming for development. It may take another five or six years before Bangladesh becomes a force to be reckoned with but the achievement of reaching the Super Eight stage of the 2007 World Cup is encouraging, as is the endeavour to establish the women's game. Despite the opposition of certain Islamic groups, the Bangladesh Cricket Board inaugurated a women's domestic tournament in 2007 with the intention of forming a national women's squad.

Table 2.3 Teams involved in The National League: the first class domestic competition in Bangladesh (1999/00–2006/07)

Team	Date of first appearance	Number of times winners
Barisal	1999/00	0
Chittagong	1999/00	1
Dhaka	1999/00	3
Khulna	1999/00	1
Rajshahi	1999/00	2
Sylhet	1999/00	0
Dhaka Metropolis	2000/01	0
Dhaka Division	2000/01	0
Biman Bangladesh Airlines	2000/01	1

Note: The National League was not first class in 1999/00. Dhaka Metropolis, Dhaka Division and Biman Bangladesh Airlines played only in 2000/01.

Famous Victories
April 12, 13, 1997 – Tenaga Nasional Sports Kompleks (Kelab Kilat), Kuala Lumpur
Kenya 241-7 (50 overs) (S.O. Tikolo 147)
Bangladesh 166-8 (25 overs)
Bangladesh won by 2 wickets (Duckworth-Lewis Method)

Play did not start in this final of the ICC Trophy until 1.45 p.m. on the first day because of rain. Bangladesh won the toss and asked Kenya to bat, a decision which seemed justified when the first three wickets went down for 58 runs. Steve Tikolo and Maurice Odumbe (43) then added

137 for the fourth wicket before Odumbe was stumped by Khaled Mashud off the bowling of Mohammad Rafique (3-40). Kenya completed their innings at the end of the first day. Rain delayed the match on the second (reserve) day until 3.30 p.m. by which time, under Duckworth-Lewis rules, the target had been reduced to 166 runs from 25 overs. With contributions from Mohammad Rafique (26 runs), Minhajul Abedin (26), Aminul Islam (37) and Akram Khan (22), Bangladesh both collected runs and lost wickets regularly. Eleven runs were still needed from the last over with two wickets remaining. Khaled Mashud hit the first ball from Martin Suji for a six. Although this eased the pressure, the tension continued to the last ball from which Bangladesh needed to score one run with Hasibul Hossain on strike. He swung at but missed the ball and set off immediately to complete a leg bye whilst the Kenyan fielders, in total confusion, missed the run out.

May 31, 1999 – County Ground, Wantage Road, Northampton
Bangladesh 223-9 (50 overs) (Saqlain Mushtaq 5-35)
Pakistan 161 (44.3 overs)
Bangladesh won by 62 runs
On being put into bat in this first round World Cup match, Shahriar Hossain (39) and Akram Khan (42) enabled Bangladesh to reach 69 for the loss of one wicket from 16 overs but once Saqlain Mushtaq entered the attack, wickets fell quite regularly. Aminul Islam, Naimur Rahman, Minhajul Abedin, Khaled Mahmud and Khaled Mashud all reached double figures but only Mahmud (27 runs) went beyond twenty. If it had not been for 28 wides, the Bangladesh total would not have been competitive. Nevertheless, the target of 224 runs should not have been a problem but, whether through complacency or just not trying, the Pakistani batting failed completely with five wickets being lost for 42 runs by the 13th over. Azhar Mahmood (29 runs) and Wasim Akram (29) attempted a rescue act to which the Bangladeshi bowlers contributed 21 wides but by then, the deficit was too great. Runs were too hard to come by off some steady economical bowling. Bangladeshi joy at their first victory over a test-playing country was temporarily stayed when the last Pakistani wicket to fall, the run out of Saqlain Mushtaq, was referred to the third umpire. Fortunately he was given out because, by then, the jubilant fans had invaded the pitch. Later there were rumours about match fixing and illegal betting but none of these was ever substantiated.

June 18, 2005 – Sophia Gardens, Cardiff
Australia 249-5 (50 overs) (D.R. Martyn 77, M.J. Clarke 54)
Bangladesh 250-5 (49.2 overs) (Mohammad Ashraful 100)
Bangladesh won by 5 wickets
The Bangladeshi bowlers did well to restrict Australia to 249 runs especially as Michael Clarke and Damien Martyn put on 108 for the fourth wicket and Michael Hussey and Simon Katich finished the innings with a stand of 63 runs in 6.3 overs. Although Tapash Baishya (3-69) picked up most wickets when the Australian batsmen went for their shots and miscued, it was the bowling of Mohammad Rafique (0-31) and Aftab Ahmed (0-48) in twenty overs in mid-innings which slowed the scoring rate. Bangladesh struggled in reply losing three wickets for 72 runs at which point Mohammad Ashraful and Habibul Bashar (47) started their partnership of 130 in 23 overs. Australia were clearly a bowler short as Habibul and Ashraful made light of Brad Hogg's and Clarke's left-arm spin. When Habibul was run out and Ashraful holed out to long-on after completing his century (from 100 balls with eleven fours), an Australian victory still seemed likely but Aftab Ahmed (21*) and Mohammad Rafique (9*) calmly added runs until seven were needed to win from the last over. Aftab hit Jason Gillespie for six off the first ball and then scampered the single from the next to complete a remarkable victory.

Player Profiles

Ashraful Haque, Syed. rhb. rob. Having played first-class cricket for East Pakistan and Dhaka University prior to the formation of Bangladesh, he was the leading all-rounder in the late 1970s and early 1980s. He played in the ICC Trophy in 1979 when he achieved his best bowling performance, taking seven wickets for 23 runs against Fiji. He later became a leading cricket administrator. In 10 international matches before Bangladesh gained test status, he scored 263 runs (average 15.47) and took 10 wickets (average 43.00). In 6 limited-over internationals he made 131 runs (average 21.83) and took 20 wickets (average 11.80).

Habibul Bashar Sumon, Qazi. b Nagakanda, Kushtia, 17 August 1972. rhb. A fast-scoring batsman, capable of taking the bowling apart when well set, he developed into his country's leading run scorer in its early days of test cricket. Renowned for his classic on- and square-drives, he was also an impulsive hooker which often led to his dismissal. In 42 test matches, he has scored 2838 runs (average 34.60). In 109 one-day internationals he has made 2125 runs (average 21.68).

Khaled Mashud Pilot. b Rajshahi 8 February 1976. rhb. wk. Considered by many as the best wicket-keeper of his generation in South Asia, he is also a free-striking batsman, yet able to curb his strokes when the situation demands. He has helped rescue several innings by dogged defence. In 41 test matches, he has scored 1361 runs (average 19.44) and made 75 catches and 8 stumpings. Prior to Bangladesh gaining test status, he played 10 internationals, scoring 406 runs (average 31.23) and made 17 catches and 5 stumpings. In 126 one-day internationals he has made 1818 runs (average 21.90) and made 103 catches and 35 stumpings. Prior to Bangladesh gaining official one-day status, he played 17 limited-overs internationals, scoring 145 runs (average 29.00) and making 26 catches and 15 stumpings.

Latif, Mohammad Abdul. b Kamthi, Maharashtra, India, 10 November 1938. rhb. lb. Although born in India, he moved to East Pakistan as a child where he learnt his cricket and became the leading all-rounder. He was selected for Pakistan against Ceylon in 1966/67 and was unlucky not to be chosen for official test matches. In 36 first-class matches he scored 1596 runs (average 28.00) and took 45 wickets (average 22.84).

Minhajul Abedin Nannu. b Chittagong 25 September 1965. rhb. rob. A batsman of correct technique and unflappable temperament, he was the leading player for Bangladesh from the mid 1980s to the early 1990s. He was very unlucky not to play test cricket being controversially discarded as too old and unfit. He continued to play first-class cricket for Chittagong and

in 2001/02 became the only person to score 1,000 runs in a Bangladesh season. In one international match, he scored 81 runs (average 81.00) and took 2 wickets (average 18.00). In 38 one-day internationals he made 868 runs (average 27.12) and took 16 wickets (average 39.37). Before Bangladesh gained official one-day status, he played 36 limited-overs internationals, scoring 888 runs (average 32.88) and taking 39 wickets (average 17.38).

Mohammad Rafique. b Dhaka 5 September 1970. lhb. sla. An accurate rhythmical bowler, able to turn the ball on helpful wickets but otherwise relying on line, length and changes in pace, he is the most successful bowler in Bangladesh test cricket. He is also a miserly bowler in one-day matches. He has often opened the batting in one-day matches, being promoted as a 'pinch hitter'. In 26 test matches he has scored 982 runs (average 21.82) and taken 87 wickets (average 36.59). In 121 one-day internationals he has made 1166 runs (average 13.55) and taken 116 wickets (average 38.84). Before Bangladesh obtained test-match status, he played three internationals, scored 9 runs (average 3.00) and took 10 wickets (average 23.60). Before Bangladesh gained official one-day status, he played 16 limited-overs internationals, scoring 87 runs (average 10.87) and taking 30 wickets (average 9.60).

Other leading players: *1960-1980:* N.K. Amirullah (rhb. rm); Ismail Gul (rhb. rmf); Shafiqul Haque (rhb. wk). *1980-2000:* Akram Khan (rhb. rm); Aminul Islam (rhb. rob); Nasir Ahmed (rhb. wk). *Present day:* Enamul Haque (lhb. sla); Mohammed Ashraful (rhb).

Playing record
Test Matches

	Won	Lost	Drawn
England	0	4	0
Australia	0	4	0
South Africa	0	4	0
West Indies	0	3	1
New Zealand	0	4	0
India	0	3	0
Pakistan	0	6	0
Sri Lanka	0	7	0
Zimbabwe	1	4	3
Total	1	39	4

Unofficial tests prior to test status

0	3	1

One-day matches

	Won	Lost	No Res
World Cup	5	14	1
Other ODI	31	106	1
ICC Trophy	26	14	3
Asian Cricket Council Trophy	12	0	0
South East Asia Cup	13	0	0

Highest team score

488	v Zimbabwe, Chittagong	2004/05

Lowest team score

86	v Sri Lanka, Colombo	2005/06

ODI

76	v Sri Lanka, Colombo	2002
76	v India, Dhaka	2003

Highest individual score

158*	Mohammad Ashraful	v India, Chittagong	2004/05

Best bowling

7-95	Enamul Haque Jnr	v Zimbabwe, Dhaka	2004/05

ODI

7-23	Ashraful Haque	v Fiji, Water Orton	1979

Best wicket-keeping

4 (4c)	Khaled Mashud	v Sri Lanka, Colombo	2002
4 (4c)	Khaled Mashud	v West Indies, Chittagong	2002/03
4 (2c 2st)	Khaled Mashud	v Zimbabwe, Harare	2003/04
4 (3c 1st)	Khaled Mashud	v India, Chittagong	2004/05
4 (4c)	Khaled Mashud	v Sri Lanka, Colombo	2005/06

ODI

5 (4c 1st)	Nasir Ahmed	v Kenya, Amsterdam	1990
5 (2c 3st)	Nasir Ahmed	v Fiji, Rotterdam	1990
5 (4c 1st)	Khaled Mashud	v Northern Ireland, Kuala Lumpur	1998
5 (3c 2st)	Khaled Mashud	v Kenya, Nairobi	2006

BELARUS

CRICKET WAS started in Belarus in 1990 by students from South Asia, particularly Nepal, Sri Lanka and Pakistan. Those students who stayed in the country to work in medical and technological services have kept the game going supported by staff attached to embassies and new students. With a 'floating population', the number of teams that can be supported varies but is commonly between four and six. The annual SINTEZ-MM Trophy has been running for twelve years and is now contested by teams from Minsk, Vitebsk and Gomel. Cricket is handicapped by the cool, wet climate and lack of grounds.

BELGIUM

Affiliate Member of ICC: elected 1991
Associate Member of ICC: elected 2005

THE FIRST record of cricket in Belgium dates to a letter written in 1748 by the Earl of Carlisle to his friend, George Selwyn, referring to a game at Spa, in the Ardennes, in what was then part of the Spanish Netherlands. Cricket was later played by officers of the British Army during the Napoleonic Wars. There are references to matches in Brussels in 1814 and to a match played on 12 June 1815 just before the Battle of Waterloo. However, none of these events presaged the immediate take-up of the game. Although a watercolour painting by Robert Streatfeild, about 1840, shows the game still being played at Spa, cricket did not develop permanence until the formation of Brussels Cricket Club in 1865. Another picture, this time anonymous and dated 1870, shows the Bourgmestre of Brussels opening the Brussels cricket ground, in the Bois de la Cambre, in 1866. Membership of the Brussels CC and also that of the Antwerp Club, formed in 1880, was restricted to British residents. No attempt seems to have been made to encourage Belgians to take up the game, although by the turn of the century memberships of other clubs were open to selected Belgians.

In 1905, Belgium met the Netherlands in the first of what became a regular series of internationals that lasted until 1937. A cricket tournament was organised as part of the 1910 Brussels World Fair. By this time a few Belgians were being selected for the national side, most notably Le Comte Jean d'Oultremont who was a most enthusiastic supporter of the game. He promoted and organised matches and, perhaps for this reason, he regularly captained the team, despite being a player of rather limited ability. A keen sports administrator, he later became President of the Belgian Football Association. Despite his efforts, cricket stagnated after the First World War. The game became restricted to the Brussels and Antwerp clubs who survived, despite a rather fluid membership of short-term British and, occasionally, Australian residents, by playing in the Dutch league and undertaking friendly matches against Standard Athletic Club in Paris and English club sides. It was the Brussels and Antwerp Cricket Clubs who revived the game after the Second World War, although following a change of rules in 1966, they were forced to withdraw from the Dutch League. In 1977, the heritage of the Brussels Cricket Club was recognised by royal decree, giving it the status of a Société Royale and the title of the Royal Brussels Cricket Club.

From the 1960s on, the population of Brussels became more international. Overseas countries set up offices through which they could perform ambassadorial links with the European Union and many multinational companies chose the city for their headquarters. The number of people interested in playing cricket increased. The late 1970s and early 1980s saw the formation of a cricket club in Mechelen and the Pakistan Cricket Club of Belgium, in Brussels. More clubs were formed in the late 1980s and in 1990 the Belgian Cricket Federation was founded. Belgium sent a scratch side to the European Cricketer Cup competition in Guernsey in 1990 and finished second. This provided a spur to develop a national team which has since taken part in various European competitions. Like the situation before the 1914-18 War, only a few of the players are Belgian born and the rest are expatriates. Instead of being British or Australian, however, the leading players are of Indian or Pakistani origin. A development programme is underway with an emphasis on youth. Most clubs have junior sections and the Brussels and Antwerp Clubs also have ladies sections. Although Belgium has yet to produce a women's international team, Brussels CC has started fixtures with the Luxembourg Maidens.

Leading players: *1890-1914:* G.R. Alpen; Comte J. D'Oultremont; L. Schots. *1980-2000:* Wasiq Ahmed. *Present day:* Shahid Mohammad.

Playing record
International matches
	Won	Lost	Drawn
Netherlands (1905-1937)	3	15	3

One-day matches
	Won	Lost	No Res
ECC Trophy	6	8	0
European Affiliates Tournaments	4	2	0

Highest team score
301-3 dec	v Netherlands, Mechelen	1994

Lowest team score
23	v Netherlands, Antwerp	1905

Highest individual score
122	Ayub Khan	v Luxembourg, Mechelen	1994

Best bowling
7-92	P. Wright	v Netherlands, The Hague	1912

BELIZE
Affiliate Member of ICC: elected 1997

ALTHOUGH CRICKET has a long history in Belize with the Belize Wanderers Cricket Club in existence by the 1880s, it has, until very recently, been a game of minority interest. British Honduras was ignored by the West Indies Board of Control and the game had to develop and survive entirely by the efforts of the local population and the British military stationed at Newtown Barracks. Some interest was generated by visits of teams from Jamaica in 1936, 1951, 1961 and 1962 and by the MCC in April 1960. The game is hampered by a conflict between two bodies, each of which claims to represent the sport nationally. The oldest is the Belize Cricket Association which is largely urban based and represents clubs with cricketers from many different countries. The organisation recognised by the ICC is the Belize National Cricket Association on which there is a strong representation of clubs from the rural areas. Until this situation is resolved, Belize will never be represented by its best possible team. The one which played in the 2004 Americas Affiliates Tournament, chosen by the BNCA was weakened by the feud between the two bodies. Belize won the inaugural Central American Championships in 2006 but then lost all their matches in Division 2 of the American Championships and were relegated to Division 3.

Leading player: *Present day:* C. Anthony.

Playing record
One-day matches
	Won	Lost	No Res
Americas Affiliates Tournament	2	2	0
American Championships Division 2	0	4	0

Highest team score
ODI
332-8	v Costa Rica, Belize City	2005/06

Lowest team score

ODI

95	v Panama, Buenos Aires	2005/06

Highest individual score

ODI

118	C. Young	v Surinam, Howard (Panama) 2003/04

Best bowling

ODI

5-13	C. Anthony	v Mexico, Belize City 2005/06

BERMUDA

Associate Member of ICC: elected 1966

CRICKET WAS brought to Bermuda by the British military based at the Garrison which was established in 1701 to protect Britain's interests in the western Atlantic. Although the first recorded cricket match was not until 30 August 1844, when the Garrison lost to another army team, progress from that date seems to have been rapid. By the following year, the Bermuda Cricket Club had been formed and the game was being played by British troops and the local civilian population, both white and black. The game was organised along racial lines with white sporting clubs, based on the military, administrators, agricultural exporters, merchants and bankers and local neighbourhood clubs which became centres for sport, entertainment and social interaction among the black population. At its height, in the 1890s, as many as 1,500 troops were stationed at the Garrison and the Garrison, together with Hamilton Cricket Club, became the focus of the white game. Black sporting clubs were especially strong in the east of the island where the population centred on extended families earning a living from local trades, running family stores, and part-time fishing and farming. The extended family heritage is seen throughout Bermudan cricket history with the same surnames appearing regularly in the national side over many years, with Edwards, James, Pitcher, Raynor, Simmons, Simons, Smith, Tucker and Trott being the most frequent. A distinction developed early between the game of the white aristocracy which was taken reasonably seriously and attempted, as far as possible, to emulate the cricket of late Victorian and Edwardian England, and the black game which had a more carnival atmosphere. The British gave encouragement to local cricket when, in 1872, Captain J. Moresby of the Royal Navy set aside an annual two-day cricket carnival for civilians at Somerset.

Contacts were made with clubs in Philadelphia which led to Philadelphia Zingari visiting Bermuda in 1891 and playing three matches against the Garrison. In 1905, Hamilton Cricket Club toured New York and Philadelphia. These contacts resulted in representative teams from Philadelphia coming to Bermuda in 1907, 1908, 1910, 1911 and 1912. Each tour comprised matches against The Garrison and Hamilton CC before culminating in a match between Philadelphia and All-Bermuda, a combined team from the Garrison and Hamilton CC. Since Philadelphia were of first-class status and since Bermuda won more matches than they lost, Bermudan cricket at the time must have been close to first-class standard. Admittedly the side were helped by their experience of playing on the difficult batting wicket at Hamilton which consisted of a mat over a concrete surface which gave rise to a very high bounce of the ball and explained the very low scores obtained by all teams. When Bermuda visited Philadelphia in 1911, however, they won three out of the five matches played despite being unfamiliar with grass wickets.

Bermuda was visited by the Australian teams of 1912 and 1913, as side trips to their matches in Canada and the United States. The 1912 team struggled against Gerald Conyers and Thomas Gilbert and were fortunate to win by 57 runs but the stronger 1913 side won easily by an innings and 112 runs. The 1913 side also played against a black Bermudan side winning by an innings and 114 runs. The similarity in results for the all-white and non-white teams suggests that there was little difference in standard and that the All-Bermuda team would have been stronger if black players had been included.

The annual carnival established in 1872 took on a new life in 1902 when it became the annual Cup Match between Somerset CC and St George's CC, two of the leading clubs of black players. The contest, held on public holidays on the Thursday and Friday closest to 1 August, commemorates the abolition of slavery in the British territories of the Caribbean in 1834. It attracts crowds of 10,000-15,000 in a carnival atmosphere with steel, brass and rock bands and masked mummers; the spectators wear a range of decorated T-shirts, blouses, trousers and dresses in what is locally termed the 'fashion show'. Much liquor and local speciality food are consumed and gambling is rife. The event has occurred every year since 1902 with no interruption for either the 1914-18 or 1939-45 Wars.

Controversial

After the First World War, there was little external interest in Bermudan cricket and there were no significant international contacts until the visit of Sir Julien Cahn's side in 1933. Cahn's team played five matches, the last against a representative Bermuda side which now included non-white players. It was not until the MCC played two matches in Bermuda in December 1953 as a warm-up to their tour of the West Indies that the country became recognised as a pleasant place to visit, relax, and play some cricket either prior to or after a West Indies tour. The MCC visited again in 1974 and Pakistan came in 1958 and 1993, New Zealand in 1965 and 1972, and Australia in 1978, 1991 and 1995. The two matches against the Pakistanis were controversial. In the first game on 27 and 28 April 1958, the Pakistanis inexplicably left the field at 3.15 p.m. on the second day when Bermuda had lost six of their second innings wickets and were still nine runs behind the Pakistani first innings total. The *Royal Gazette* suggested that this was in protest against the decisions of the local umpires whereas the Pakistani captain, A.H. Kardar, maintained that there was an agreement to end play at that time. In 1993, the Pakistanis played two matches with a squad reduced by injury and contractual arrangements and had to call on local reinforcements. In both games they included Kamran Khan, who had played first-class cricket in Pakistan for Punjab University and Lahore before migrating to and playing for the United States. Khan was in Bermuda with a touring side from Philadelphia. In the second game, injuries during the match forced them to seek the assistance of Nadeem Usmani, a waiter at the Southampton Princess Hotel, to field as substitute.

The period from the mid 1950s to mid 1970s saw a second flowering of Bermudan cricket with the level of activity and interest matching that before the First World War. Visits were made by E.W. Swanton's team in 1956, W.S. Surridge's team in 1961, Gloucestershire in 1962, Yorkshire in 1964 and the Hyderabad Blues in 1975. Bermudan teams toured England in 1961 and 1962 and Denmark and The Netherlands in 1969. An international series with the USA for the Sir Henry Tucker Trophy was started in 1970 but it was short-lived, lasting only three years. Bermuda performed so well against the New Zealanders in 1965, drawing the two-day match, that the New Zealand Cricket Board accorded first-class status to their match against Bermuda in 1972. This decision was somewhat premature, however, since Bermuda lost by an innings and 31 runs. The 1960s saw the official end of racial discrimination in Bermudan society, after which the white population gradually withdrew from cricket. With the Garrison closing in 1950 and the white population being increasingly restricted to expatriate managers of corporate businesses and hotels or wealthy residents, their age profile increased and there were fewer with an interest in playing the game. The national side changed from being a mixed team in the 1950s and 1960s to an entirely black side today. New clubs were established in the west of the island by the black urban population working in the hotel industry. These also included players of Asian origin.

The 1980s to mid 1990s represented a period of consolidation with the national side being reasonably settled in its make-up. The team reached the final of the ICC Trophy in 1982, losing to Zimbabwe, and made the semi-finals in 1986 and 1994. Thereafter, cricket entered a difficult time. There was a need to replace the older members of the side but insufficient numbers of high quality young players were coming through the youth system. Youngsters were more interested in American sports such as basketball than cricket. Two members of the national side failed drugs tests and were banned for several international matches after which several other players refused to be tested. Two further players were banned for verbal abuse of Cricket Board officials. Bermuda were therefore forced to field weakened sides during the five years (1996-2000) that they competed in the West Indies domestic one-day competition. They lost all their matches except one. In 2005, however, a team combining youth and experience, finished fourth in the ICC Trophy in Ireland, thereby qualifying for the

World Cup in 2007 in which they were outclassed. They won the American Championships in 2006. Bermuda were the first associate country to play international Twenty20 matches when they hosted the World Cricket Classic in April 2006. Bermuda also made their debut in women's international cricket in September that year, beating Canada in the American region qualifying tournament for the World Cup.

Famous Victory

July 14, 15, 1911 – Haverford PA
Bermuda 164 (A.D. Gaye 59) and 130 (J.B. King 5-43, H.G. Pearce 4-34)
Philadelphia 129 (J.B. King 62, G.C. Conyers 6-69) and 159 (G.C. Conyers 9-69)
All-Bermuda won by 7 runs

Bermuda were soon in trouble against the Philadelphian attack led by Bart King and only the innings of Lieut A.D. Gaye and rearguard contributions from W.B.T. Johnston (26) and D. Martin (21) enabled them to post even a moderate total. King then opened the batting and played soundly whilst his colleagues collapsed around him to the bowling of Gerald Conyers. Bermuda fared poorly in their second innings and set Philadelphia a moderate target of 165 runs. They started well with King (35) and John Evans (44) but then suffered a total collapse against Conyers who performed the hat-trick in their middle order and followed it with a second hat-trick to finish the match. He took the last six wickets to fall for two runs in successive overs to complete one of the most remarkable bowling feats of all time.

Player Profiles

Conyers, Gerald C. rhb. rs. The most consistent bowler for Bermuda before the First World War, he was equally successful on Bermuda's home wickets and on the grass wickets of Philadelphia. In his 9 wickets for 69 (15-138 in the match) against Philadelphia at Haverford in 1911, he obtained the last six wickets to fall by taking two hat-tricks. In six internationals against Philadelphia (1908-1912) and the Australians (1912) he scored 112 runs (average 12.44) and took 67 wickets (average 7.90) including five or more wickets in an innings on ten occasions and ten or more in the match on five occasions. He was a businessman and stamp collector.

Hunt, Alma Victor OBE. b Somerset, Bermuda, 1 October 1910. d Sandys, Bermuda, 5 March 1999. lhb. rfm. Considered by many to be the best cricketer ever to come from Bermuda, he played for G.C. Grant's XI in first-class trials for the West Indies tour of England in 1933 but was not chosen because of doubts about Bermuda's qualification as part of the West Indies. He also played first-class cricket for Scotland in 1938. On returning to Bermuda, he served as Secretary and later President (1966-1983) of the Bermuda Cricket Board of Control. He was influential in establishing the ICC Trophy for Associate Countries. He requested a piper to play a lament at his funeral to mark his connections with Scotland. In 2 matches for Bermuda he scored 27 runs (average 13.50) and took 4 wickets (average 8.00).

Other leading players: *1890-1914:* J.R. Conyers (rhb); T.S. Gilbert (rhb. rf). *1945-1960:* E. Woods (rhb. rf). *1960-1980:* C.A. Daulphin (rhb. rmf); C.L. Parfitt (lhb. lm/sla); W.H. Trott (rhb. lmf). *1980-2000:* C.M. Marshall (lhb. lm). *Present day:* D.M. Leverock (rhb. sla); D.A. Minors (lhb. wk); C.J. Smith (rhb).

Women: *Present day:* R. Richardson.

Playing record

International matches

	Won	Lost	Drawn
Intercontinental Cup	2	2	4
Other first class*	0	1	0
Other internationals+	7	2	4

* v New Zealand 1972
+ Matches against Philadelphia (1909-1923) and two-day matches against Canada, Denmark and The Netherlands

One-day matches

	Won	Lost	No Res
World Cup	0	3	0
Other ODI	5	14	0
West Indies domestic competitions	1	18	1
ICC Trophy	37	18	3
Americas Cup	7	6	1

Highest team score

620	v Netherlands, Pretoria	2006/7

Lowest team score

49	v Philadelphia, Hamilton	1906/07

ODI

48	v Windward Islands, Kensington Park		1999/00

Highest individual score

247*	D.L. Hemp	v Netherlands, Pretoria	2006/7

Best bowling

10-17	T.S.G. Gilbert	v Philadelphia, Hamilton	1906/07

Best wicket-keeping

4 (4c)	J. Edness	v Canada, Toronto	2004
4 (2c 2st)	D.A. Minors	v Cayman Islands, Toronto	2005

ODI

4 (4c)	D.A. Minors	v Fiji, Nairobi	1993/94
4 (4c)	J. Edness	v Bahamas, Hamilton	2004
4 (4c)	D.A. Minors	v USA, Waringstown	2005

Women

One-day matches

	Won	Lost	No Res
World Cup Qualifying American Region	2	1	0

Highest team score

ODI

201	v Canada, Victoria		2006

Lowest team score

ODI

127	v Canada, Victoria		2006

Highest individual score

ODI

86*	B. Marshall	v Canada, Toronto	2006

Best bowling

ODI

5-32	C. Fulbert	v Canada, Toronto	2006

BHUTAN

Affiliate Member of ICC: elected 2001

FOR MOST of its history Bhutan has been a 'closed' kingdom, contacts with the outside world being carefully controlled so as to protect the local culture and environment. Although from 1910 until 1947, Britain advised the king on foreign policy, the number of expatriate residents was small and there are no records of cricket being played. It was not until television was allowed in the kingdom in 1999 that the Bhutanese were introduced to cricket. A small group, led by Tshering Tashi, became addicted and decided it would be a suitable sport for young Bhutanese to learn. Developments were very rapid from this point with the Board of Control for Cricket in Bhutan being formed in 2000, affiliate membership of the ICC being obtained in 2001 and the country playing its first international matches in 2003. Bhutan achieved its first victory in its sixth match when they beat Iran by 86 runs in the 2004 Asian Cricket Council Trophy. The main constraint on the growth of the game is the lack of a ground on which domestic tournaments and home international matches can be staged. At present, the BCCB has been allocated a training ground at Changlimithang on land between the football stadium and the archery range. On numerous occasions, cricket practice has been interrupted by stray arrows but, so far, there have been no injuries. Every time domestic games are held, permission to use the ground has to be obtained from the local authorities and there is concern that the present level of support and enthusiasm may not be long lasting. The BCCB is making repeated requests to the government for space in either Paro or Thimpu.

Leading players: *Present day:* Damber Singh Gurung (rhb. rf); Lobzang Yonten (rhb. rmf).

Playing record

One-day matches

	Won	Lost	No Res
Asian Cricket Council Trophy	2	5	0
Emerging Nations Tournaments	1	7	1

Highest team score

ODI

277	v Brunei, Bangkok		2004/05

Lowest team score

ODI

36	v Nepal, Kuala Lumpur		2006

Highest individual score

ODI

67	Sanjog Chhetri	v Thailand, Bangkok	2004/05

Best bowling

ODI

5-14	Jigme Singye	v Myanmar, Kuala Lumpur	2006

BOTSWANA

Affiliate Member of ICC: elected 2001
Associate Member of ICC: elected 2005

CRICKET WAS introduced into Botswana after the construction of the railway line from Mafeking to Bulawayo. The first reference to the game is in 1879. From that time cricket was played recreationally at club level but no attempt was made to establish a national body or field a national side. Although a team called Bechuanaland played in the Kimberley Tournament in 1887 alongside Port Elizabeth, Natal and Kimberley, this was probably representing an area known as British Bechuanaland, now in the northern part of Griqualand West. Without any national organisation, cricket lost out to softball and football and gradually declined until it was restricted to a few clubs and selected private primary schools. It was not until the late 1990s that the situation changed when expatriates from South Africa, India, Pakistan and Sri Lanka began to revive the game. By 2001, it was being played in some thirty schools and in 2005 a decision was taken to introduce the game in state-run primary schools in Gaberone. At present, the number of players in the country is still rather few so that most leagues are based on six-aside but tournaments are held in Gaberone, Francistown, Jwaneng, Orapa and Selebi Phikwe. The national side has competed regularly in the tournaments organised by the African Cricket Association and has shown a steady improvement over the last decade. In 2006 Botswana finished second in Division 2 of the African Championships. There is a women's team based on students at the University of Botswana but it has not yet played an international fixture.

Leading players: *Present day:* J. Moses (rhb. rm); Aslam Chand (rhb. rm).

Playing record

One-day matches

	Won	Lost	No Res
African Cricket Association Cup	5	1	0
African Affiliates	4	1	0
African Six-Nations	2	3	0
African Championships Division 2	3	1	0

Highest team score

ODI

335-3	v The Gambia, Benoni	2003/04

Lowest team score

ODI

39	v South African Development XI, Lusaka	2002

Highest individual score

ODI

121*	J. Moses	v The Gambia, Benoni	2003/04

Best bowling

ODI

6-17	A. Chand	v Malawi, Benoni	2003/04

BRAZIL

Affiliate Member of ICC: elected 2002

CRICKET HAS a long history in Brazil with a club at Rio de Janeiro in existence by 1840. The game was taken up almost everywhere the British had a presence and by the 1900s it was played in Rio, São Paulo, Santos, Recife, Barretos and in the mining towns in Minas Gerais State. The present Rio CC was founded in 1872 and reformed in 1898. The São Paulo club was set up in 1888 and the Santos club in 1890. The players were largely farm or estate managers, company managers and other British businessmen, usually with a public school background. No attempt was made to encourage Brazilians to take up the game. Contacts between the various centres were limited by the great distances and the problems of transport before internal air services were established on a regular basis, so that matches between the leading clubs were rare. In the rural areas of São Paulo State fixtures were arranged between 'Camps', comprising coffee farmers and ranchers who came together in camps close to the ground before each match, and 'Frigorificos', made up of factory managers and other employees in the corned beef industry. The standard of cricket in Brazil was at its highest in the 1920s and 1930s. International matches were played regularly with Argentina. Although Brazil won only twice, Argentina were rated first-class at the time and Brazil were only just below that in standard.

After the Second World War, British business interest in Brazil declined. The game depended on the employees of British companies but since many of these were on temporary assignments, the number of players was always highly variable and there was little continuity. Matches continued with Argentina in the

1950s and 1960s but from then on the standard of cricket fell. By the late 1990s, the Brazilian team was barely a match for the Argentina A side. About this time, however, a revival began inspired by a small number of Indian expatriates in São Paulo and staff from the embassies of the Commonwealth countries in Brasilia. A third centre has been established at Curitiba, based on personnel from HSBC. Brazil competed in Division 3 of the American Championships in 2006.
Leading players: *1920-1939:* R.L. Latham (rhb); H.C. Morrisey; O.T. Cunningham. *Present day:* M.R. Featherstone (rhb).

Playing record
International matches

	Won	Lost	Drawn
Argentina (1921-1929)	2	7	3

One-day matches

	Won	Lost	Drawn
American Championships Division 3	0	3	0

Highest team score

534	v Argentina, Buenos Aires	1927/28

Lowest team score

55	v MCC, São Paulo	1964/65

Highest individual score

163	H.C. Morrisy	v Argentina, Buenos Aires 1927/28

Best bowling

7-45	C. Chatwin	v Argentina, Niteroí	1966/67

BRUNEI

Affiliate Member of ICC: elected 1992
UP UNTIL 2000 cricket was an almost entirely an expatriate game in Brunei with most of its players coming from staff attached to the oil industry. The game struggled to survive with only a few players, many on short-term contracts, and no permanent ground. Brunei participated regularly in the Borneo Championships against Sabah (formerly North Borneo) and Sarawak. A team also competed in the Asian Cricket Council Trophy in 1996. By 2003, there were only three teams in the domestic league and the game seemed about to disappear. However, in 2004, a new committee of Bruneians took control of the national body and in 2005, a national side, meeting the ICC residential requirements, competed in

an Emerging Nations Tournament in Bangkok but they lost all their matches. A similar record befell them in the 2006 Asian Cricket Council Trophy.

Playing record
One-day matches

	Won	Lost	No Res
Asian Cricket Council Trophy	1	6	1
Emerging Nations Tournament	0	3	0

Highest team score
ODI

230-9	v Japan, Kuala Lumpur	1996

Lowest team score
ODI

43	v Maldives, Bangkok	2004/05

Highest individual score
ODI

62	Bilal Javed	v Saudi Arabia, Kuala Lumpur 2006

Best bowling
ODI

3-7	Ahmed Maazuri	v Japan, Kuala Lumpur	1996

BULGARIA

CRICKET WAS unknown in Bulgaria until the early 2000s when Professor Nikolai Kolev of the National Sports Academy, who has championed the introduction of other minority sports such as rugby and baseball, decided to promote cricket. Within two years, there were four clubs, two of which, the National Sports Academy in Sofiya and a team from Varna on the Black Sea coast, are entirely Bulgarian. The Bulgarian CC in Sofiya comprises Pakistanis and the fourth consists of Indian medical students. In 2004, a national side took part in a European tournament for countries below the affiliate level. Although they were outclassed and, in three out of the five matches, their bowlers contributed 158 wides, it is hoped that the experience will lead to an improvement in standards.

Playing record
One-day matches

	Won	Lost	No Res
European Representative Championships	0	5	0

Highest team score

ODI

151	v Luxembourg, Ljubljana	2004

Lowest team score

ODI

38	v Croatia, Ljubljana	2004

Highest individual score

ODI

49	T. Buisseret	v Luxembourg, Ljubljana	2004

Best bowling

ODI

4-21	P. Gill	v Croatia, Ljubljana	2004

CAMBODIA

THE PHNOM PENH Cricket Club was formed in 1999 by the Indian expatriate community. Matches are played at the North Bridge International School. As yet, no international matches have been played but the club has attempted to develop fixtures with Hanoi.

CAMEROON

THE CAMEROON Cricket Federation was launched in October 2005. Its immediate aims are to identify possible venues for cricket grounds, train local coaches and promote the game. The inspiration behind the CCF comes from workers from various Commonwealth countries engaged on projects in the country.

CANADA

Associate Member of ICC: elected 1968

EXACTLY WHEN cricket was first played in Canada is not known. It is generally accepted that the game was introduced by the British military. British garrisons were established in the main towns along the St Lawrence River after the battle of the Plains of Abraham, near Quebec City, in 1759. Although the first recorded match was not until 1834, at Hamilton between Guelph and Toronto, the game was certainly established before then. Toronto Cricket Club was founded in 1827 by George Barber, an English schoolmaster who came to Canada in 1825 and was one of the few civilians to encourage the game. He promoted the game as meeting the high ideals of Victorian sportsmanship, at a time when the reputation of cricket in Canada was somewhat mixed because of its association with gambling.

By the 1840s, cricket was well-established in Toronto, Montreal and other towns along the St Lawrence and the shoreline of Lake Ontario, where it was played by the garrisons, the civilian population, mostly British settlers, and in the leading schools, particularly Upper Canada College in Toronto and Trinity College School at Port Hope. The garrisons and the civilians formed their own clubs. Fixtures were largely between the clubs within each individual town. Matches between clubs from different towns were rare because of the cost and slowness of transport. Railways were new and expensive and no meals were served, the trains stopping infrequently at wayside inns. Most transport was by water. Despite this, Guelph and Toronto played occasional matches and links developed, initially by a hoax, between Toronto CC and St. George's CC in New York. In 1840 a person under the name of Mr Phillpots, supposedly a respected member of Toronto CC went to New York and arranged with the St George's Club to play two matches, home and away with the first in Toronto, the travel expenses to be paid in each case by the host side. When St George's arrived in Toronto they found that no one in the town knew anything about either the arrangement or Mr Phillpots. Toronto hastily assembled a side, cancelling a fixture with Guelph to do so, and lost by ten wickets. Nevertheless the contact had been made which eventually led to the first international match between Canada and the USA in 1844. Although the title was somewhat pretentious since, at that time, Canada generally meant Toronto and the USA meant residents of New York, the match was always intended to include the best players on both sides of the border and cricketers from other centres, notably Montreal and Philadelphia, were selected.

In the middle 1800s Canada can be considered one of the pioneers of international cricket. In addition to taking part in the first international fixture, the first match outside the British Isles by any side against an English touring team was played in Montreal when twenty-two of Lower Canada met George Parr's XI on 24 and 26 September 1859. The visit of Parr's side to Canada was brought about by the efforts of William Pickering who, after appearances for Eton, Cambridge University and the Gentlemen, emigrated to Canada in 1852 to become manager of Canada Life Assurance in Montreal. He started correspondence with his contacts in England in 1856 and, working with Robert Waller in New York, obtained sponsorship of £1,300 which was sufficient to secure the tour. This tour and those made subsequently in 1868 by E. Willsher's team and 1872 by R.A. Fitzgerald's side were important in introducing to Canadian cricket the changes that were taking place in the game in England such as round-arm and later over-arm bowling.

International matches against the USA continued until 1860 when they were interrupted by the American Civil War. A further match was played in 1865 after which the series ceased until 1879. Up to 1865, although it was termed the 'international match', the atmosphere was rather informal and more like English country-house cricket. There were no residential qualifications for selection and one player, D. Winckworth, appeared for both sides. Visiting players from England were sometimes included and both sides fielded professional players who were attached to the various clubs as coaches. The Canadian side was generally composed of British residents and members of the military. The military were very supportive of the international fixture and in 1855, when many of the troops stationed in Canada were moved to Crimea, no match was played.

The visits from Willsher's and Fitzgerald's teams generated a lot of interest. Captain Nesbit Wallace, one of the movers in obtaining sponsorship for Fitzgerald's team with W.G. Grace as its captain, proposed a tournament between America, Canada, England and an All-Comers side, to be held in 1874 in Halifax, where he was stationed with the 60th Royal Rifles. Efforts to produce a representative American side failed and the invitation was accorded to Philadelphia instead. England were represented by a side selected from the officers of the military stationed in Canada. Philadelphia won the trophy, known as the Halifax Cup and retained it the following year when the tournament was staged in Philadelphia.

From 1878 to 1914, Canadian cricket benefited from the increasing strength of the game in Philadelphia since all the touring sides which played there also visited Canada. Thus Canada played host to the Australians (1878, 1893, 1912 and 1913); privately-organised teams led by R. Daft (1879), E.J. Sanders (1885, 1886), Lord M.B. Hawke (1891, 1894), F. Mitchell (1895), K.S. Ranjitsinhji (1899) and B.J. Bosanquet (1901); the MCC (1905, 1907); and the Gentlemen of Ireland (1879, 1888, 1892 and 1909). In thirteen matches where Canada, as opposed to provincial or district teams, played the tourists, nine were lost, six by an innings, and the rest were drawn. The Canadians also had the worst of the matches against the USA, winning only eight times compared to America's nineteen out of the thirty games played between 1879 and 1912.

Poorly Organised

In 1880, a group of Canadian cricketers arranged a tour of England under the captaincy of a certain Thomas Jordan. The venture was poorly organised with fixtures being arranged as the tour progressed. It attracted little interest and the side struggled to meet costs. In none of the matches played were the expenses covered by the gate receipts. The captain turned out to be operating under a pseudonym, his real name being Thomas Dale. At the end of the first day of the fifth match against Leicestershire, he was arrested as he left the field and charged with being a deserter from the Royal Horse Guards regiment in 1873 when it was stationed in Canada. The charge was proven and he was sentenced to thirty-five days in prison. However, he escaped custody in Knightsbridge, was then caught and sentenced to a further eleven months. It emerged that after his desertion, he had remained in Canada, changed his name and fathered six children in two marriages. It has been suggested that it was his second wife who betrayed him. On returning to Canada after completing his stay in prison, he divorced her, and then moved to the United States where he became a professional cricketer. After the loss of their captain, the tourists sent for the Reverend T.D. Phillips to take over the leadership but by the time he arrived, the tour was close to collapse financially and it was abandoned in mid-July. It was not until 1887 that a second tour of England was attempted. This time it was well organised by George Lindsay who found sponsorship, to which Lord Landsdowne, the Governor-General was a major contributor, appointed the captain, Dr E.R.Ogden, and selected the team, all of whom were Canadian-born. They won five of the eighteen matches played.

By the time the matches with the USA were resumed in 1879, the influence of the military had declined and Canadian-born players were outnumbering those born in Britain. The game was now being played in almost every town in Ontario and was well-established in Nova Scotia and New Brunswick. As Canada began to be settled to the west, so the game moved westwards too. The North West Cricket Club was founded in Winnipeg in 1864 and the Victoria Cricket Club on Vancouver Island in 1876. Other clubs quickly followed in the Prairie Provinces, Alberta and British Columbia. In 1892, the Canadian Cricket Association was formed to control the game nationally, although, until 1949, its officials came mainly from Ontario and Quebec. The spread of the game over the whole country was recognised in 1913 when the Australian tourists undertook a full tour beginning in Victoria, British Columbia, on 28 May and ending there on 27 September, after having completed 53 matches across Canada, the USA and Bermuda.

Despite the widespread nature of the game, cricket was regarded by many Canadians as an elite English activity, popular in a limited number of urban centres, where it was maintained by players emanating from the top public schools. The game was therefore strongest in Ontario, where the appropriate social conditions existed but weaker in the Prairie and Atlantic Provinces. According to cricket historian, Roland Bowen, the game was hampered because many Canadian-born were unwilling to participate in what was seen as an Anglo-Saxon pursuit and was neglected by English expatriates in a conscious effort to become Canadian. Cricket did not develop therefore as fast as it might have done and began to lose out to ice hockey and baseball.

In the 1920s and 1930s, interest in cricket waned. Matches against the USA had ceased and touring sides were no longer visiting North America on a regular basis. The game survived in the public schools and elite clubs, particularly in Ontario and, to a lesser extent, British Columbia. Toronto and Vancouver became the focus with well-appointed grounds at Armour Heights

and Brockton Point respectively. Norman Seagram of Toronto, a philanthropist and enthusiastic supporter of Canadian cricket organised the 1922 tour of England as a way of reviving interest after the First World War. Despite containing some of the best players of the time, the side did not win any of their eleven matches and were outclassed by the MCC at Lord's. Seagram was also instrumental in the invitation extended by the Canadian Cricket Association to the Free Foresters for a short tour of eight matches in September 1923. The Hon R.C. Matthews, a former Minister for National Revenue in the Canadian government, organised, at his own expense, the 1936 tour of England. This was the first representative side to include players from the Western Provinces. Although they played mainly club sides and schools, they defeated an MCC team, all of whom had first-class experience. In 1937, a Canadian eleven chosen by R.C. Matthews again beat the MCC during their tour of Canada, indicating, perhaps, that standards were beginning to rise again. Interest was also shown in the late 1930s in encouraging women's cricket. Under the auspices of the Overseas Educational League, a team from Harrogate Ladies College, Roedean and Newcastle School visited Canada on a demonstration tour in 1939 but the visit was curtailed when the Second World War was declared.

Very Positive

After the 1939-45 War, the CCA was very positive in reviving the game as quickly as possible. An Inter-Provincial Tournament was inaugurated in 1947 and the M.C.C. were invited to tour which they did in August and September 1951. Canadian cricket was also reinforced by the arrival of immigrants both from Britain and the Caribbean. The strength of Canadian cricket at this time was recognised when the MCC retrospectively awarded first-class status to the second of their two matches against Canada on the 1951 tour. The Canadian side which toured England in 1954 played four first-class matches, including one against Pakistan, who were making their first tour of England. The award of first-class status was somewhat premature since they lost by an innings to Pakistan and were outplayed in two of the other matches, the third being marred by rain.

Following this flurry of international activity, the Canadian game stagnated. Further tours to Canada did not take place until the late 1950s when visits from Pakistan (1958) and the MCC (1959) showed that standards remained low. In 1963 the international series with the USA was resumed with Canada winning sensationally by an innings and 164 runs. With financial support from both the federal and provincial governments, investments were made in coaching and umpiring, youth cricket and new grounds with grass wickets. From 100 senior clubs across the country in 1965, the number increased to 247 in 1985 and 350 in 1992. Despite this expansion in numbers, it still remained difficult to interest Canadians in the game and the growth was largely due to immigrants and their descendants. In the early 1990s, some 35 per cent of all immigrants to Canada came from Commonwealth countries, especially the Caribbean and the Indian sub-continent. Some of these had first-class cricket experience and, once they had met the ICC's residential requirements, they made up the bulk of the national side. The side that played in the 1979 ICC Trophy and World Cup contained only one Canadian.

Since the 1970s, Canada's playing record has been one of extremes. In the first ICC Trophy in 1979, Canada finished runners-up, losing to a strong Sri Lankan side in the final by 60 runs. This was sufficient to qualify them for the 1979 World Cup in which they were completely outclassed by England, Pakistan and Australia. England dismissed them for 45 runs, made excruciatingly in 40 overs and 3 balls. Performances in subsequent ICC Trophy competitions were rather mixed although, by finishing seventh in 1997 they qualified for the Commonwealth Games in Kuala Lumpur in 1998. Here they lost heavily to Australia, Antigua and Barbuda, and India.

Torrential Rain

The late 1990s saw Canada emerge as a venue for international cricket when it hosted the contest between India and Pakistan for the Sahara Cup at the Toronto Cricket, Skating and Curling Club in September 1996. The start of the tournament was delayed by two days because of torrential rain so that three of the five matches had to take place on weekdays with very small attendances. Only one match attracted as many as 5,000 people, mostly expatriate Indians, Pakistanis and West Indians. However, substantial money came to the CCA through television rights. The series was repeated in 1997 and 1998 after which Sahara withdrew their support. This was taken up for one year in 1999 by DMC since when no support has been forthcoming and the series has ceased. The loss of income has created severe financial problems because in 1996 the federal government drastically reduced funding for cricket, along with all other non-Olympic sports.

In 2001, Canada hosted the ICC Trophy and, by beating Scotland in a third place play-off, qualified for the 2003 World Cup. In their second attempt at this level, they gained a surprise victory over Bangladesh but, as expected, lost all their other matches. Their low point was their score of 36 against Sri Lanka where no one reached double figures and the innings lasted only 18 overs and four balls. Sri Lanka reached the victory target in just 28 balls. Offsetting this debacle was the performance of Jim Davison in scoring the fastest hundred of the tournament in 67 balls against the West Indies. Since 2000, Canada has become established as the leading cricket nation of the American continent behind the West Indies. However, their performances continue to be varied, depending on the availability of two players, both born in British Columbia but who have played their cricket overseas: Ian Billcliff in New Zealand and Jim Davison in Australia. In 2005, with Davison in the team, they finished third in the ICC Trophy in Ireland and became the first associate country to qualify for the World Cup three times. July 2005 should have seen the first international appearance of the Canadian women's team. They were due to play in the domestic West Indies competition in Jamaica but the tournament was postponed because of the threat of a hurricane. Unfortunately, they were unable to take part in the rescheduled competition in St Vincent the following month. Their international debut finally came in 2006 when they lost to Bermuda in the American region qualifying competition for the World Cup.

As Canada strives for recognition as a top class one-day international side, the CCA needs to solve two immediate problems. The first is the continued shortage of money. The second is the fight between Canada and South Australia for the services of Jim Davison. Meanwhile, there is considerable underlying strength in the number of people playing cricket, the interest of immigrants from the Caribbean, India and Pakistan and their descendants, and the fact that the country now has ten grass wickets.

Famous Victory

February 11, 2003
Kingsmead, Durban
Canada 180 (49.1 overs)
Bangladesh 120 (28 overs) (A.Codrington 5-27)
Canada won by 60 runs

IN THEIR first game of their second appearance in the World Cup, Canada surprised both themselves and the whole cricketing world by defeating a test-playing country. On choosing to bat after winning the toss in this day/night match, they were given a sound start by a patient Ishwar Maraj (24), a hard-hitting David Chumney (28) and Ian Billcliff (42), reaching 70 for the loss of only two wickets. On trying to increase the tempo, however, wickets fell regularly and only a last wicket stand of 21 runs between Austin Codrington and Davis Joseph allowed even a moderate total to be reached. In reality, it was more than enough. Bangladesh reached 106 for four wickets by the 21st over but their batsmen then panicked in an unnecessary attempt to raise the run rate. Codrington's medium pacers under the floodlights seemed to mesmerise the batsmen and the last six wickets fell for fourteen runs in 44 balls.

Player Profiles

Davison, John Michael. b Campbell River, Vancouver Island, British Columbia, 9 May 1970. rhb. rob. The leading Canadian player of the early 2000s, he came to prominence in the 2003 World Cup when he hit a century against the West Indies off only 67 balls. Although born in Canada, he moved to Australia and started his first-class cricket career with Victoria but could not gain a regular place in the team. He moved to South Australia in 2002/03. In 1999 he was offered a position as a club player and coach in Canada and, when available, quickly became a member and, later, captain of the national team. In 4 international matches for Canada he has scored 375 runs (average 53.57) and taken 27 wickets (average 14.92). In 41 one-day internationals he has made 1112 runs (average 27.80) and taken 54 wickets (25.59); in 32 limited-overs internationals he has scored 577 runs (average 23.08) and taken 42+3 wickets (average 18.11).

Laing, John Melville. b London, Ontario, 3 March 1874. d Toronto 1 November 1947. lhb. lf. Selected for Canada when only 19 years of age, he was a bowler with very high action, making use of his 1.93 m height. His best ball was a yorker on the leg side. In 13 matches for Canada he scored 236 runs (average 11.23) and took 77 wickets (average 11.87) including five or more in an innings on seven occasions and ten or more in a match three times. He was a barrister by profession.

Other leading players: *1835-1860:* J. Bradbury. *1860-1890:* A. Gillespie (rhb. rm(r)); E.R. Ogden (lhb. rm(r)). *1890-1914:* D.W. Willcocks (rhb. wk). *1920-1940:* L.C. Bell (lhb); W.E.N. Bell. *1945-1960:* B. Christen (lhb. lfm); W.A. Percival (rhb. wk); K.B. Trestrail (rhb. lb). *1960-1980:* J.C.B. Vaughan (rhb. rmf). *1980-2000:* I.F. Kirmani (rhb. rob); P. Prashad (rhb). *Present day:* I.S. Billcliff (rhb); Umar Bhatti (lhb. lm).

Women: *Present day:* A. Mogan (lhb. rob); C. Abbott (rhb. rob).

Playing record

International matches

	Won	Lost	Drawn
Intercontinental Cup	4	4	2
Other first class*	0	2	2
International Series+	23	32	10
Other matches†	1	3	4

* v MCC in 1951 and matches played on 1954 tour of England
+ Matches against the USA between 1844 and 1995
† Two-day matches against Ireland, Scotland, Denmark and Bermuda

One-day matches

	Won	Lost	No Res
World Cup	1	11	0
Other ODI	7	14	0
West Indies domestic competitions	3	21	4
ICC Trophy	32	18	5
Americas Cup	14	3	0
ICC Six-Nations Challenge	1	9	0

Highest team score

588	v Bermuda, King City	2006

Lowest team score

28	v USA, New York	1846

Highest individual score

176	R. Nascimento	v USA, Toronto	1963

Best bowling

9-6	J. Bradbury	v USA, Toronto	1854

Best wicket-keeping

4 (4c)	W.A. Percival	v Essex, Clacton	1954

ODI

5 (5st)	S. Griffith	v Antigua, St John's	1976

Women

One-day matches

	Won	Lost	No Res
World Cup qualifying American region	1	2	0

Highest team score

ODI

203-5	v Bermuda, Victoria	2006

Lowest team score

ODI

124	v Bermuda, Victoria	2006

Highest individual score

ODI

58	K. Coulter	v Bermuda, Victoria	2006

Best bowling

ODI

4-13	C. Abbott	v Bermuda, Victoria	2006

CAYMAN ISLANDS

Affiliate Member of ICC: elected 1997
Associate Member of ICC: elected 2002

IT IS not known when cricket was first played in the Cayman Islands. They were settled by the British in the eighteenth century and it is likely the game was played as a recreational activity from that time. Their distant location, some 285 kilometres north-west of Jamaica, meant that they were remote from the development of the game in the Caribbean and the islands have never been part of the West Indies cricket scene. Until the mid 1960s, cricket was played on mud or marl pitches. Matches were arranged against visiting ships from the Royal Navy and there were regular fixtures between the districts of West Bay, a dominantly Caymanian side, and George Town, a team of Jamaican expatriates, mainly teachers and lawyers, with a small number of Caymanians. In 1965 a concrete pitch was laid at West Bay but the cricketers had to compete for its use with footballers. In 1973, the government developed the West Bay site entirely for football, and a new cricket ground, the Smith Road Oval, was established in George Town using clay imported from Jamaica. The site was alongside the airport and within the main flightpath so the pitch had to be repositioned on an artificial surface where it did not interfere with flying activities. Renamed the Jimmy Powell Oval, after a former President of the Cayman Islands Cricket Association who worked extremely hard to develop cricket in the country and was awarded the MBE in 2000 for his achievements, it is now the focal point of the country's cricket with a new pavilion and improved facilities.

From the 1970s cricket underwent an expansion brought about by an increased number of immigrants from Barbados, Jamaica, Guyana and Britain, working in the tourist and financial industries. In the 1990s, the government started to support the game, allowing the Cayman Islands Cricket Association to introduce cricket into primary and secondary schools and promote a development programme at district and national levels. By 2000, although 95 per cent of the cricketers playing in the Cayman Islands Senior League were still expatriates, 98 per cent of those in the youth programme were Caymanian. In 1997 a women's cricket organisation was founded. The men's national side made their first appearance in the Americas Cup in 2000 when they beat Argentina. Two years later, in the same competition, they won three out of their five matches. Among the leading players are the Wight brothers, Christopher, David, Michael and Philip. For a country to have four brothers in the national side at the same time is rare but when two of them, Christopher and David, are twins, it must constitute some sort of record. In 2005, the twins retired from international cricket. When the Caymans were invited by the ICC to replace the USA in the ICC Intercontinental Cup, for the first time they fielded sides without any of the Wight family.

Famous Victory
August 22, 2006
Maple Leaf Cricket Club, King City

Canada 187 (43.3 overs) (G.R. Codrington 73*, T. Taylor 4-19, Ronald Ebanks 4-43)
Cayman Islands 194-2 (42.2 overs) (S.C. Gordon 70*, P. Best 67*)

Cayman Islands won by 8 wickets

THE CAYMANS recorded their best ever performance to win this Americas Cup match against apparently stronger opposition with ease. Troy Taylor and Ronald Ebanks destroyed the Canadian batting as they lost four wickets for 32 and eight wickets for 94. George Codrington hit nine fours and one six in an innings of 103 balls to help Canada to a defendable total which would have been much less if the Cayman bowlers had not contributed 32 wides. The Canadian bowlers never posed any problem and with Steven Gordon and Pearson Best in an unbeaten third wicket stand of 137 runs, the Caymans secured a straightforward, if unexpected, victory.

Leading player: *Present day:* P. Best (rhb).

Playing record

International matches

	Won	Lost	Drawn
Intercontinental Cup	0	2	0

One-day matches

	Won	Lost	No Res
West Indies domestic competition	0	4	0
ICC Trophy Qualifying	3	2	0
Americas Cup	6	7	1
Americas Affiliates Trophy	3	0	0

Highest team score
ODI
265-7	v Argentina, King City		2006

Lowest team score
ODI
62	v Canada, Toronto		2000

Highest individual score
ODI
116*	P. Best	v Argentina, King City	2006

Best bowling
ODI
5-12	D. Wight	v Bermuda, Buenos Aires	2001/02

Best wicket-keeping
ODI
4 (4c)	C. Wight	v USA, King City	200

CHILE

Affiliate Member of ICC: elected 2002

THE FIRST record of cricket in Chile was in *Memoirs of General Miller*, published in 1829 which refers to a match in Valparaíso in December 1818 between the officers and men from HMS *Andromache* and those from HMS *Blossom*. Valparaíso Cricket Club was formed in 1860 by British residents and its first recorded match was in 1863. In 1870 they met a team from Santiago. Cricket expanded rapidly across the country in the 1880s and 1890s reaching most places where there was a British community, including Iquique, Antofagasta, Concepción and Punta Arenas. It was especially strong in the north where the British invested heavily in the nitrate industry. Many of the individual nitrate plants in the desert raised their own sides and a team from the port of Iquique regularly played a combined team from the Tarapaca Pampa.

Chilean cricket was at its peak in the 1920s when it was played by the British in a country club atmosphere in Valparaíso, Santiago and Concepción. The game was strongest in Valparaíso where it was established in the English-style public schools of St Peter's and The Grange. It was rumoured that when young British staff came out to join British companies they were appointed to offices in Valparaíso if they could play cricket and, if not, they were sent to Santiago! International matches with Argentina were arranged on a regular basis in the 1920s. The MCC visited the country in 1927 after their tour of Argentina and beat the Chilean side by seven wickets.

In 1928 the market for sodium nitrate collapsed, British investment declined and many British firms withdrew from the country. With a shortage of money, international matches against Argentina ceased. By the time they were resumed in 1938, the standard of Chilean cricket had fallen. As the size of the British community dwindled, the game declined, retreating to Santiago and Valparaíso. Matches against Argentina ceased in the late 1960s when Chile found it difficult to raise a competitive side and by 1994, the game was reduced to some thirty enthusiasts attached to the Prince of Wales Club in Santiago.

The late 1990s witnessed a revival. A group British and Australian expatriates started a league based on four clubs within Santiago and in 2001 the Asociación

Chilena de Cricket was formed with the aim of restarting the game in Valparaíso. By 2002, there were some 100 players, including three women, and by 2004 there were over 200 senior players, including 50 Chilean nationals. In 1995, Chile reappeared in the South American Championships but lost most of their games. By 1999 they had improved and finished third and in 2000 and 2002 they were runners-up to the Argentina A team. In 2004, they hosted the tournament, using grounds in Santiago and Valparaíso, and were fourth. In 2006 they entered Division 3 of the American Championships.

Leading players: *1920-1940:* K.V. Everard; A.L.S. Jackson (rhb. wk); J.A.S. Jackson (rhb. lb). *Present day:* P. Hollis; S Shalders

Playing record

International matches

	Won	Lost	Drawn
Argentina (1921-1938)	3	7	0

One-day matches

	Won	Lost	No Res
American Championships Division 3	1	2	0

Highest team score

387-8 dec	v Argentina, Santiago	1955/56

Lowest team score

58	v Peru, Santiago	1957/58

Highest individual score

164	B. Neary	v Argentina, Santiago	1955/56

ODI

223*	P. Hollis	v Andean Masters, Buenos Aires	2002/03

Best bowling

6-103	L.G. Wayland	v Argentina, Viña del Mar	1920/21

ODI

7-32	J. Anglin	v Argentina A, Buenos Aires	2002/03

Best wicket-keeping

ODI

4 (3c 1st)	G. Hooper	v Brazil, Lima	1998/99

CHINA

Affiliate Member of ICC: elected 2004

SHANGHAI BECAME a Treaty Port in 1842, meaning that foreign residents were allowed to trade, free of Chinese jurisdiction. British merchants occupied a major role and they probably introduced cricket around that time. Shanghai Cricket Club was formed about 1851 but there are no records of matches extant until 22 April 1858 when a team from Shanghai beat a team of officers from HMS *Highflyer* by an innings and 87 runs. The culture of trade within the British community supported contacts with other ports in China and Japan and trade was closely followed by the establishment of sporting links. In 1866, a team travelled to Hong Kong and played what turned out to be the inaugural match in an Interport series which continued until 1948. Out of the 38 matches played, Shanghai won sixteen against Hong Kong's twenty. The whole venture for the visiting side required a sea voyage of 2,560 kilometres and at least two weeks' absence from business. The effects of the long sea journey were often apparent with the visiting team usually being given only two or three days to acclimatise and get used to being on land again after the motion of the boat. Hong Kong were victorious in 77 per cent of the matches played in Hong Kong and Shanghai won 60 per cent of those played in Shanghai. In 1893, Interport fixtures were started with Kobe and Yokohama in Japan and with Hangzhou, the next port along the Chinese coast, but these were more intermittent. Home matches were played on a ground established in 1861 within the racecourse on the corner of present-day Nanjing Lu and Jiangxi Lu. It survived until 1949 when it was turned into the People's Park. The ground had a true, if slow, grass wicket and many of the cricketers who played there commented on the excellent light conditions.

Although most of the cricket clubs in Shanghai, including Shanghai CC, were run by British expatriates, a Parsi club was formed in 1890, the first club of Indian expatriates anywhere in the world. Occasional matches were also played against a Chinese team made up of players who learned the game by being on the groundstaff of the major clubs. Up until the Second World War, the British community in Shanghai was relatively stable and many cricketers represented Shanghai for periods of ten years or more.

The Interport match against Hong Kong in 1936 was the last before the Second World War, the Japanese expansion into central China and along the Chinese coastline between 1937 and 1939 preventing further contests. An attempt was made to revive the series and matches were played in 1947, in Hong Kong, and 1948, in Shanghai but by this time political unrest in China and business uncertainty were causing a rapid decline in the size of the British community and very quickly there were too few players to raise a team. All cricket in China then ceased for some thirty years.

In the early 1980s, a small group of British and Australian expatriates founded the Beijing CC. Activity was restricted to a few friendly matches, however, until 1994 when an international six-a-side competition was held. This event has continued annually, attracting teams from Japan, Hong Kong, Korea and Thailand. In 1994, the Shanghai Cricket Club was reformed through the initiative of the Indian Consul General and the head of the British Chamber of Commerce. The Shanghai International Sixes competition was started in 2003. The Hong Kong Ladies came to Shanghai in 2004 to play two games. Hong Kong won the first but Shanghai Pearls won an exciting second game by 2 runs. The China Cricket Association was formed in 2004 with the support of the Chinese government which has ordered schools in Beijing, Shanghai and Guangzhou to introduce the game. A site in Beijing has been earmarked for an international cricket venue. The experience of current coaching courses in Shanghai is that Chinese women are more enthusiastic about the game than Chinese men who seem to prefer football and basketball.

Player Profile

Barrett, Edward Ivo Medhurst. Captain. b Churt, Frensham, Surrey, 22 June 1879. d Boscombe, Hampshire, 10 July 1950 (following an accident). rhb. One of the finest and hardest hitters of his day, he combined a sound defence with well-timed forcing strokes all round the wicket. He served in 2nd Lancashire Fusiliers in the South African War and was wounded. He then joined the police where he served in Malaya before migrating to Shanghai where he eventually became Commissioner of Police. He played first-class cricket for Hampshire and The Army and represented both the Straits Settlements and the Federated Malay States. In 14 matches for Shanghai, he scored 857 runs (average 35.71). He was also a Rugby Union international for England (1903).

Other leading players: *1890-1914:* A.G.H. Carruthers; W.H. Moule; V.H. Lanning. *1920-1940:* D.W. Leach; W.E. O'Hara (lhb. lm); T.W.R. Wilson (rhb. lb).

Playing record
International matches

	Won	Lost	Drawn
Interport matches (1866-1948)*	21	23	3

* matches by Shanghai against Hong Kong, Straits Settlements and All-Malaya

Highest team score

479	v Hong Kong, Shanghai	1936

Lowest team score

35	v Hong Kong, Shanghai	1948

Highest individual score

165	I.E.M. Barrett	v Hong Kong, Shanghai	1921

Best bowling

8-10	V.H. Lanning	v Hong Kong, Shanghai	1906

CHRISTMAS ISLAND

CRICKET IS played on Christmas Island, an Australian possession in the Indian Ocean, by workers, mainly from Australia and New Zealand, employed in the phosphate industry. Matches are organised by the Christmas Island Cricket and Sporting Club, formed in 1959. The ground lies on high plateau, within the precincts of the airport.

COLOMBIA

THE BOGOTÁ Cricket Club was founded in 1964. Membership fluctuates depending on the number of expatriates working in Colombia. Activity was greatest in the 1970s when the game also spread to Cali where employees from the Royal Bank of Canada, Lloyd's Bank and the British Consulate formed a team. Matches between Bogotá and Cali took place every six months on a home and away basis. Since then the Royal Bank of Canada has been sold and the British Consulate in Cali closed and many of the British businessmen in Bogotá have returned home. There was a revival of activity between 1985 and 1993 when British Petroleum were heavily involved in the Colombian oil industry but today BP retains only a small staff. Most of Bogotá's cricketers are either British or Canadian embassy staff or teachers at the Anglo-Colombian School. Matches are played on felt matting over a concrete pitch which does not take spin. Also, at the altitude of 2,600 metres the ball does not move in the air. The wicket is theoretically a batsman's paradise but run scoring is quite hard since running between the wickets at that altitude is an effort and the outfield is heavily grassed, so few balls make it to the boundary.

COOK ISLANDS

Affiliate Member of ICC: elected 2000

ALTHOUGH CRICKET has formed a part of village-based sport in the Cook Islands for at least fifty years and probably much longer, the game had stagnated by the late 1990s and was largely confined to the main island of Rarotonga. Most of the players were in their forties and fifties and it was difficult to attract youngsters to the game against the competition of rugby union, football and tennis. A new executive of the Cook Islands Cricket Association then put in place a structure for youth development and entered into an arrangement with Northern Districts of New Zealand to provide assistance with administration and coaching. The country took part in the Pacifica Championships in Auckland, New Zealand, in 2001, with a squad of six cricketers from the Cook Islands and seven islanders based in New Zealand. The side, under the captaincy of 52-year-old Lionel Browne, won three out of their five matches. In 2001, cricket restarted on the island of Aitutaki with six senior village teams, two under 19 boys teams and two women's teams. This increased the number of players from which the national side could be chosen. Although still winning only three out of five matches, it was a much stronger team which participated in the 2002 Pacifica Championships. Deunu Eliaba performed one of the most outstanding feats in international one-day cricket when, aged twenty, he took nine wickets for sixteen runs in eight overs against New Caledonia. Seven of his victims were bowled and he finished the innings with a hat-trick. In the East Asia Pacific Cup in 2005, the Cook Islands dismissed Samoa, a side reduced to nine players

after two of the team were declared ineligible under ICC qualification rules, for 19 runs and then reached 21 for the loss of one wicket in 3.3 overs, completing one of the fast victories recorded in one-day international cricket. The match was all over in 13.2 overs.

Leading players: *Present day:* C.M. Brown (rhb. rf); D. Eliaba (rhb. rfm); N.J. Kairua (alias R. Bates) (rhb. rfm).

Playing record
One-day matches

	Won	Lost	No Res
Pacific Championships	6	4	0
South Pacific Games	4	2	0
East Asia Pacific Cup	4	2	0
East Asia Pacific Trophy	1	3	0

Highest team score
ODI

357-7	v New Caledonia, Apia	2002

Lowest team score
ODI

27	v Papua New Guinea, Suva	2003

Highest individual score
ODI

101	Isaiah Isaiah	v New Caledonia, Suva	2003

Best bowling
ODI

9-16	Deunu Eliaba	v New Caledonia, Apia	2002

Best wicket-keeping
ODI

5 (5c)	N.J. Kairua	v Tonga, Port Vila	2005
5 (5c)	I. Tangimetua	v Japan, Port Vila	2005

COSTA RICA

Affiliate Member of ICC: elected 2002

JAMAICAN WORKERS who came to build the railways introduced cricket into Costa Rica in the late 1880s. The Jamaican descendants stayed to work in the banana and cocoa plantations and by the 1930s there were 45 teams along the Caribbean coast, centred on Limón, playing in three leagues. The game declined in the 1950s as the Jamaican youth turned to football and the popularity of cricket depended on the size of the British community. In the 1970s the Cavaliers Cricket Club in San José was founded by English expatriates and in 1986 the San José Cricket Club was revived. Since the mid 1990s there has been increased interest in the game. In 2002, the country played its first internationals, losing two one-day matches at home to Panama in April and winning one and losing one away to Nicaragua in December. In the 2006 Central American Championships they were easily defeated by both Belize and Mexico.

CROATIA

Affiliate Member of ICC: elected 2001

The first game of cricket to be played in Croatia was in 1815 on the island of Vis where William Hoste, the then governor, introduced the sport after Great Britain defeated Napoleon and gained a presence on the Dalmatian coast. The game died out once the British left and it was not revived until the late 1990s when an enthusiastic group of Croatians returning from Australia, where they had learnt the game, started a club in Zagreb. Initially they played friendly matches against Ljubljana Cricket Club in Slovenia. From this base, two players, Ivan Bilić and Robert Dumančić, laid the foundations of the Croatia Cricket Board. International fixtures commenced in 2000 when Croatia competed in a festival in Vienna. Unlike most European teams at affiliate level, the Croatian side comprises mainly indigenous players but bringing them together for a tournament is costly because many live in Australia, New Zealand or England.

Leading players: *Present day:* C. Pivac; J. Vujnović; P. Vujnović.

Playing record
One-day matches

	Won	Lost	No Res
ECC Trophy	2	9	0
European Representative Championships	4	0	0
European Affiliates Championship	2	3	1

Highest team score
ODI

261-0	v Sweden, Vienna		2001

Lowest team score
ODI

75	v Slovenia, Zagreb		2002

Highest individual score
ODI

126*	P. Vujnovic´	v Sweden, Vienna	2001

Best bowling
ODI

6-24	V. Zanko	v Sweden, Vienna	2001

Best wicket-keeping
ODI

4 (2c 2st)	A. Govorko	v Finland, Valburga	2004

CUBA

Affiliate Member of ICC: elected 2002

CRICKET WAS brought to Cuba by immigrants from the English-speaking Caribbean imported to work in the sugar industry in the early 1900s. It remained reasonably strong in the sugar-growing eastern part of the country, reaching its peak in the 1950s. The game died out after the 1959 revolution when Fidel Castro came to power and private sports clubs were abolished. In 1997 the Anglo-West Indian Cultural Association decided to restart the game among Cubans of West Indian descent. The game is recognised by the Cuban Sports Ministry as a recreational activity and not as a sport. This provides for access to sports facilities but not to equipment or travel costs.

CURAÇAO

THERE IS a small group of cricketers on the island of Curaçao associated with staff, mainly Dutch, British and West Indian expatriates, employed in the oil industry. They play mainly friendly matches between themselves but occasional games are played against visiting naval ships.

CYPRUS

Affiliate Member of ICC: elected 1999

CRICKET HAS been played by the British services in Cyprus for many years but only in the 1990s was an effort made to spread the game to other British residents and to the Cypriot population. There are now ten clubs on the island with six playing regularly in a national league. Fixtures are also arranged with visiting English club teams. Cyprus competed internationally for the first time in the 2006 European Championships Division 4.

Playing record

One-day matches

	Won	Lost	No Res
European Championships Division 4	2	1	1

Highest team score

ODI

195-6	v Luxembourg, Antwerp	2006

Lowest team score

ODI

60	v Finland, Brussels	2006

Highest individual score

ODI

72*	N.J. Pelawattna v Luxembourg, Antwerp	2006

Best bowling

ODI

3-16	L.P.A.S. Arthanayake v Finland, Brussels	2006

CZECH REPUBLIC

Affiliate Member of ICC: elected 2000

PRAGUE CRICKET Club was founded by British expatriates in 1997. Friendly matches are played against club sides from other European countries and, since 2002, a second Czech club from Olomouc. International matches are played between the Czech Republic, Slovenia and Slovakia. The Czechs won the tri-nations tournament for citizens only against Poland and Slovakia, staged at the Prague CC ground at Vypich in 2004. The Prague and Czech sides are unusual in that they often include one or two of the best women players. The most notable is Magda Pokludová, a left-handed bat and left-arm medium-paced bowler, who, whilst on a student exchange at the University of Bath, played for the Somerset women's team. At present, there are insufficient women players for form a separate Czech women's side.

DENMARK

Associate Member of ICC: elected 1966

IT IS not known when cricket was introduced to Denmark but it seems likely that by the time records of matches first appeared in 1865, the game had already been in existence for several years. The 1860s saw two separate movements influence the development of cricket. First, the game was played by workers of the Danish Railway network which was being constructed under the supervision of British engineers. In 1865, the railwaymen started a cricket club in Odense, on the island of Fünen, although it is not known how many Danes were members. Railway engineers were also playing the game in Zealand and Jutland. The first recorded cricket match in Denmark took place in the same year at Randers though it is not certain whether this was between teams of railway engineers or, as suggested by the Danish cricket historian, Douglas Steptoe, between the Aalborg and Randers Cricket Clubs.

Meanwhile, in Copenhagen the game was being introduced by a small group of the aristocracy, centred on the Hansen family, who had learned the game in England. The brothers, Professor Edmund Grut-Hansen, Harald Hansen and Gustav Hansen, together with their brother-in-law, Professor Peter Plum, a physician-in-ordinary to the Russian Empress Dagmar, and Captain of the Engineers, V. Hoskjær, were key members of the Copenhagen Ball Games Club, which is known to have existed as early as 1861. They encouraged club members to take up the game. They were also influential in persuading a physics teacher, Napoleon Eugen Ibsen, to introduce the game at the Sorø Academy.

Of the two routes by which the game developed, more is known of the aristocratic one. Cricket was introduced at a second public school, Herlufsholm, and the game was played enthusiastically by the Ball Games Club under the captaincy of Lieutenant-Colonel H. Hilarius-Kalkau. Unfortunately, when he was posted by the military to Helsingør, interest declined and the game in Copenhagen nearly died out. Cricket was rescued, however, by the efforts of two old boys of the Sorø Academy, V.C. Petersen and Ludvig Sylow. In 1879, they formed the Københavns Kricket Klub which in 1882 amalgamated with the Kjøbenhavns Boldklub, later to become one of the leading clubs in Denmark. In 1887 the KB side tested their strength in three matches against the officers and men from the Prince of Wales's Royal Yacht *Osborne* which was on a visit to Copenhagen. KB won the first game by 8 wickets, drew the second and lost the third by 13 runs. These matches were important because it was the first time that over-arm bowling was seen in Denmark.

By 1880, cricket was also well-established at several centres in Jutland. In 1889, Albert Ginge, who set up his export business in Danish bacon at Hjørring, founded the Hjørring Cricket Club which has been a leading centre of the game in Jutland ever since. Young cricketers from Fredericia founded the Fredericia Amateur Cricket Club when they went to study at Copenhagen University. Club membership was quickly opened to all students at the University and, in 1889, to students from the Polytechnic Institute as well, thereby forming the Akademisk Boldklub, which became a rival to KB for the position of the leading club in Copenhagen. The same year also saw the establishment of the Dansk Boldspil Union (Danish Ball Games Union) to organise football and cricket clubs for the whole country.

Until the 1890s most cricket in Denmark took place on rough grass wickets or on gravel, usually on public commons, military parade grounds or other public and waste ground. Once over-arm bowling became the norm, these surfaces proved extremely dangerous and clubs started to develop their own private grounds where games could be played on matting. The game thus became focused on clubs and a few elite schools. Although it was established in virtually all the main towns, it was a minority sport of the well-educated and the wealthy. In this condition, the game started to stagnate and little further progress was made before the First World War.

Promising Results

After 1918 steps were taken to improve the standard of play. Coaching manuals were imported and, through the offices of R.P. Keigwin, a master at Clifton College in England and an expert on Danish history and poetry, arrangements were made for the MCC to tour in 1922. A further tour was made in 1925 when the MCC visited Jutland and Copenhagen. The

following year saw the first tour to England. Costs and time meant that the team was not fully representative of Danish cricket. It was the first time that the players had experienced grass wickets. Although only one match out of seven was won, with three games drawn, the results were promising. The Incogniti side visited Denmark in 1927 and 1929. The latter received a shock at Hjørring when they were dismissed for only 27 runs but they managed to salvage a draw. Following this tour, Baron H. Rosenkrantz, who was one of the 1926 tourists to England and a patron of cricket in the English style, organised the finance for H.P. Chaplin of Sussex to come and coach in Jutland. In 1929, a group of enthusiasts in Copenhagen formed the Copenhagen Cricket Ring with the aim of organising tours to Denmark by English teams. The Gentlemen of Worcestershire came in 1930 and in 1932 Sir Julien Cahn brought a side. This saw the selection of the first ever All-Denmark side for an international match. Two games were played, both won by Cahn's XI. No further international matches were played until 1939 when the Danes managed a draw with the MCC at Aalborg.

Cricket was revived rapidly after the Second World War thanks to the presence of British military units stationed in Denmark and just across the border in Germany. Cambridge University visited in 1947 and the MCC in 1950 and 1952. These tours showed that whilst the Danish bowling was of a reasonable standard, their batting lagged behind. The Copenhagen Cricket Ring, which had become the Danish Cricket Ring in 1935, raised the issue with the Dansk Boldspil Union, asking them to take action and provide proper coaching facilities. The Committee of the DBU, however, was dominated by people who were only interested in football and who were happy to see cricket decline to a point when it could be removed from their responsibility. Against this background, Kurt Nielsen, the chairman of the Copenhagen Ball Games Union, and Henry Petersen, almost a lone voice for cricket within the DBU, established the Dansk Cricket Forbund (Danish Cricket Union) in 1953 as the governing body. In the same year, Denmark embarked on their second tour of England, winning three out of the eight matches played against club sides. Oxford University visited Denmark in 1954 and in 1955 the international series of matches against The Netherlands was started. It was not until 1973, however, that they beat The Netherlands when, winning by 10 wickets, they gained their first victory in international cricket. The matches against The Netherlands continued until 1980 after which the two-day international fixtures gave way to one-day contests.

The 1970s was a very successful decade for Danish cricket. In addition to matches against The Netherlands, a regular series was started with Ireland. The first tours outside of Europe were undertaken with visits to Canada and East Africa. In 1979, Denmark reached the semi-finals of the ICC Trophy where they lost to a strong Sri Lankan side. The 1970s also saw the emergence of women's cricket. Surprisingly, there was considerable prejudice on the part of the Danish cricket authorities to the women's game but, by the end of the decade, an annual championship for women's clubs had been inaugurated.

Financial constraints prevented the successes of the 1970s from being built upon. Denmark was unable to afford the expenses of participating in the 1982 ICC Trophy. They returned in 1986, again to finish as semi-finalists, losing the play-off for third position to The Netherlands. Overall the 1980s and 1990s were a time of consolidation rather than development for what still remained a minority sport with limited spectator appeal and played by a small group of enthusiastic amateurs. The best players were either bowlers or all-rounders which meant that, whilst the Danish side could often bowl the opposition out, they did not have the batting to score defendable totals. This weakness in batting remains to this day.

Italy Dismissed for 29

The year 1989 was one of the most successful in Danish cricket history. For the first time they beat the Dutch in The Netherlands, winning the one-day fixture by 33 runs. They also dismissed Italy for 29 runs to win a 40-overs match by 409 runs. The end of the summer saw the first visit to Denmark by an international test team when Australia played two one-day matches after their tour of England. The visit attracted over 4,000 people to the games. The Australian batting struggled against the Danish attack led by Øle Mortensen but

the batsmen could make little impression against the Australian bowlers. The only player to impress was Aftab Ahmed who made a not out 77 in the second game. Aftab was representative of a major change that was taking place in Danish cricket, namely the emergence of a large number of Pakistani players. By the early 1990s, three all-Pakistani sides had been formed in Copenhagen, namely Norrebrø, Ishøj and Albertslund. By the mid 1990s, the KB junior side was also almost entirely Pakistani. It was from this stable that Amjad Khan emerged as the prospective replacement for Øle Mortensen as Denmark's strike bowler. However, he chose to follow a successful first-class career with Kent and, in 2006, became a British citizen .

The 1980s and 1990s saw the rise and fall of women's cricket in Denmark. The Danes were admitted to the International Women's Cricket Council in 1983 and participated in a quadrangular tournament in Utrecht the same year. By 1989, they were a match in Europe for the Dutch and Irish sides, gaining their first international victory over the Dutch when they hosted the European Women's Championships at Nykøbing Mors. Although they were outclassed in the 1993 and 1997 World Cup competitions by England, Australia and New Zealand, they beat Pakistan and gained further victories over The Netherlands. Unfortunately, lack of finance prevented investment in coaching at women's junior level and after what was a promising young side in the early 1990s gradually retired from international cricket in the early 2000s, there were no new players coming forward. When Denmark again hosted the European Championships in 1999, they made their last international appearance to date in women's international cricket.

The last decade has seen Denmark establish itself as the fifth best cricketing country in Europe but the new generation of players will need to be of a higher standard if the country is to compete effectively with Scotland, The Netherlands and Ireland. The most important event of the early 2000s was the opening of the new cricket centre at Svanholm Parken, Brøndby, with a turf wicket, the first in Denmark. Perhaps this can become the venue for some two-day cricket as well as more one-day international fixtures. Perhaps too, a real effort can be made to re-establish women's cricket which seems to have stopped completely.

Famous Victory

July 21, 22 and 23, 1972
Bagsvaerd, Copenhagen
Netherlands 78 (C. Morild 4-25) and 180 (R.F.
Schoonheim 53, H. Mortensen 7-)
Denmark 251 (H. Sørensen 92*, H. Mortensen 50,
R.A.H. van Weelde 5-33) and 8-0
Denmark won by 10 wickets

DENMARK GAINED their first international victory surprisingly easily after the Dutch batsmen struggled in their first innings on the matting wicket against Henrik Mortensen (3-25) and Carsten Morild. Mortensen's wickets were all catches to wicket-keeper H. Fausbøll. Only four players reached double figures. Although opening bowler R.A.H. van Weelde got some assistance from the pitch, Hardy Sørensen batted throughout the innings and with the help of Mortensen, O. Isaksson (27) and Karl Buus (26 runs), Denmark achieved a reasonable total. The Dutch never mastered Mortensen and Morild (3 wickets) in their second innings but contributions from wicket-keeper René Schoonheim and P.J. Trijzelaar (46) were sufficient to cause Denmark to bat a second time. They achieved the target of eight runs without loss. Unfortunately, the bowling analyses of the Dutch second innings has never been published.

Player Profiles

Buchwald, Charles. b 1880. d 1951. rhb. rs. He scored the first century recorded in Denmark whilst still at school and went on to became the country's best batsman until he retired in 1929, by which time he had scored 9,758 runs in 235 innings for an average of 49.79. Against English sides he scored 1,112 runs in 35 innings. Captaining the Gentlemen of Denmark on their tour of England in 1926 he made 326 runs in 8 innings, batting on grass for the first time. He was a powerful driver of the ball and employed the 'draw' stroke long after it had gone out of favour. He also represented Denmark at football and played right-back for the side that lost 2-0 to England in the 1908 Olympic Games final. He was a Civil Servant by profession, becoming the Permanent Under-Secretary of State at the Ministry of Public Works. He was awarded the Knight of the Order of Dannebrog and Commander of the Norwegian Order of St.Olav.

Mortensen, Øle Henrik. b Vejle 29 January 1958. rhb. rfm. The first Dane to play first-class cricket in England, he became a hostile bowler of world class. Many considered he could have played test cricket if he had chosen to qualify for England. In four international matches for Denmark, he scored 78 runs (average 11.14) and took 13 wickets (average 20.92). In 28 limited-overs internationals he made 335 runs (average 22.33) and took 68 wickets (average 10.26).

Other leading players: *1945-1960:* Svend Morild (lhb. lm). *1960-1980:* Carsten Morild (rhb. rm/rob); H. Mortensen (rhb. rm), H. Sørensen. *1980-2000:* Aftab Ahmed (rhb. rm); S. Henriksen (lhb. rfm); S. Vestergaard (rhb. rf). *Present day:* T.M. Hansen (rhb. lfm); F.A. Klokker (lhb. wk); R.J.A. Malcolm-Hansen (rhb. rob).

Women: *1980-2000:* J. Jønsson.

Playing record

International matches

	Won	Lost	Drawn
The Netherlands	1	5	5
Other matches*	1	6	8

* Two-day matches against Bermuda, Canada, East Africa, Kenya, Namibia, Scotland and Sri Lanka.

One-day matches

	Won	Lost	No Res
English domestic competition	0	5	0
ICC Trophy	26	20	2
European Championships	7	20	0
Emerging Nations Tournament	2	3	0

Highest team score

369-8 dec	v Namibia, Windhoek		1997/98

ODI

438	v Italy, Ringsted		1989

Lowest team score

27	v Sir Julien Cahn's XI, Copenhagen		1932

Highest individual score

197	C.R. Pedersen	v Namibia, Windhoek	1997/98

Best bowling

8-84	H. Mortensen	v W. Isaac's XI, Aalborg	1996

Best wicket-keeping

ODI

6 (6c)	M. Saddique	v Israel, Nairobi	1993/94

Women

One-day matches

	Won	Lost	No Res
World Cup	2	11	0
European Championships	3	13	0
Other one-day internationals	1	3	0

Highest team score

ODI

185-8	v Ireland, Kirby Muxloe	1990

Lowest team score

ODI

46	v England, Haarlem	1991

Highest individual score

ODI

53	J. Jønsson	v Ireland, Dublin	1995

Best bowling

ODI

4-6	M. Gregersen	v Netherlands, Nykøbing Mors 1999

Best wicket-keeping

ODI

4 (3c 1st)	M. Frost	v Ireland, Oxford	1993

EAST AFRICA

Associate Member of ICC: elected 1966
Membership transferred to East and Central Africa 1989
THE EAST African Cricket Association was formed in 1951 to organise international matches between Kenya, Uganda and Tanganyika. Responsibilities soon extended to promoting games between teams comprising the best cricketers from these three countries and other international sides. At one time it was anticipated that East Africa might have become a cricket entity analogous to the West Indies. This possibility was thwarted, however, by politics. In the 1950s and 1960s, the best cricketers in East Africa were either European or Asian. When independence came to Kenya in 1963, many Europeans returned to Britain and the Asians to India and Pakistan. Following independence in 1964, the best of the Indian players in Tanzania (formed from the combined territories of Tanganyika and Zanzibar) either returned to the sub-continent or migrated to Zambia. A similar loss of cricketers occurred in Uganda and became even more serious with the large-scale deportation of the Asian community during the regime of Idi Amin. Fortunately, by the 1970s, the African community in Uganda had taken to the game more strongly than elsewhere in East Africa, otherwise it might well have died out. Sam Walusimbi, from Uganda, became the first African to gain representative honours at East African level. Zambia joined the EACA in 1970 and their participation strengthened the European contingent for a few years but, with the decline in the Zambian economy, they too departed for Britain. January 1970 also saw the cancellation of a proposed MCC tour when the governments of Kenya and Uganda refused to allow the visit in protest at the proposed tour of England by South Africa in the summer of that year. Against this background cricket was seen by the governments as associated with a 'white' colonial heritage supported by a minority but economically influential Asian population. It was not an activity which the new African governments could be seen to support.

Although in the 1950s and 1960s the standard of East African cricket was considered high with six matches between 1963 and 1975 being rated first class, the representative side never won a match. The 1950s saw tours from strong sides from the Indian sub-continent, beginning with the Pakistan Cricket Writers team in 1956, captained by A.H. Kardar and including Hanif Muhammad, Imtiaz Ahmad, Alimuddin and Zulfiqar Ahmad. The Sunder Cricket Club which came from India in 1957 was captained by Mushtaq Ali and included Nari Contractor, Vinoo Mankad and Pankaj Roy. The Gujarat side which toured in 1960 again included Contractor alongside Polly Umrigar, Farouk Engineer, M.L. Jaisimha and R.G. Nadkarni. Given the strength of these teams, it was not surprising that East Africa were defeated. In 1958 East Africa also played hosts to the non-white South African side.

Despite the political and economic problems facing the game in the early 1970s, East Africa undertook their first tour of England in 1972 with a team containing a mixture of experienced and young players. The sixteen strong party included no Europeans and only two Africans. They played 21 fixtures but, surprisingly for so recent a tour, few of the scorecards survive. When a second non-test-playing country was needed at short notice for the 1975 World Cup, East Africa filled the position but they were outclassed. After the World Cup they lost to Sri Lanka by

115 runs in a match classified as first class and then lost to Denmark in Aalborg by three wickets. Save for one-day cricket, only three more international fixtures by East Africa took place. They drew with Denmark at Nairobi in 1976, finishing 100 runs behind in their second innings with only one wicket to fall. The fixture against the Minor Counties at Nairobi in January 1978 was abandoned without a ball being bowled, and they were beaten by the MCC in Lusaka in October 1981.

By the time East Africa participated in the 1979 ICC Trophy, Malawi had become a member of the EACA but the inclusion of an extra country did not raise the standard of the team. In fact, only one player from Malawi was considered good enough for selection. The standard of the East African side declined further in 1981 when Kenya left the EACA and gained membership of the ICC in its own right. In 1989, Uganda followed Kenya and established its own cricket administration. The EACA was then reconstituted as the East and Central African Cricket Conference with its headquarters in Lusaka, Zambia.

Leading players: *1960-1980:* Jawahir Shah (rhb); Ramanbhai Patel; Salaudin Khan

Playing record
International matches

	Won	Lost	Drawn
First class	0	5	1
Other matches	0	9	8

One-day matches

	Won	Lost	No Res
World Cup	0	3	0
ICC Trophy	5	8	4

Highest team score

471	v Commonwealth, Nairobi	1961/62

Lowest team score

81	v Denmark, Aalborg	1975

Highest individual score

131	G.P. Jarman	v Commonwealth, Nairobi	1961/62

Best bowling

7-40	L. Fernandes	v Cambridge University, Cambridge 1972

EAST AND CENTRAL AFRICA

Associate Member of ICC: replaced East Africa in 1989 Membership ceased in 2001 when the individual countries established their own cricket associations

THE EAST and Central African Cricket Conference was established in 1989 to take over the responsibility for cricket in Zambia, Tanzania and Malawi from the East African Cricket Association. The sport remained an interest of the Asian minority in all three countries and, with limited support from the individual governments, most money was spent on ensuring participation in the ICC Trophy competitions. The poor overall competition record reflected the low standard of the game which was struggling to survive. Nevertheless, sufficient activity remained to enable each country to continue playing international cricket after the Conference was disbanded in 2001 and the countries established their own cricket associations.

Playing record
One-day matches

	Won	Lost	No Res
ICC Trophy	5	18	2

Highest team score
ODI

266-8	v Singapore, Nairobi	1993/94

Lowest team score
ODI

26	Netherlands, Kuala Lumpur	1996/97

Highest individual score
ODI

141	I.A. Brohi	v Singapore, Nairobi	1993/94

Best bowling
ODI

4-15	A. Ebrahim	v Israel, Toronto	2001

Best wicket-keeping
ODI

4 (4c)	M.S. Jetha	v Israel, Toronto	2001

EGYPT

NO ONE has established when cricket was first played in Egypt but the Alexandria Cricket Club was founded by the British in 1851. The game remained a recreational activity for a small group of residents until 1875 when the British presence in Egypt was considerably enlarged following the opening of the Suez Canal. Clubs were established by the military, British personnel in the Egyptian civil service and British merchants. Matches were arranged at Port Said against the officers and men of visiting ships of both the Royal Navy and the merchant marine. On 2 October 1884, a combined Army and Navy XXII met and managed to draw with James Lillywhite's team who called in at Port Suez on their voyage to Australia for their 1884/85 tour. Within the confines of the military and the expatriate community, cricket became the focus of sporting and social activity and standards rose sufficiently for the MCC to arrange a tour to Egypt in March 1909. With a team close to first-class standard, they played three matches against All-Egypt winning two and losing one.

Further tours to Egypt were made by I Zingari in 1914 and the Free Foresters in 1927. By the late 1920s, Egyptian cricket was reinforced by a strong RAF presence and the game was established at Victoria College in Alexandria, an elite public school in the English style. The leading cricket centres were the Gezira Sporting Club, which had a matting wicket and grass outfield, and Alexandria CC where there was a grass wicket. The overall standard of the All-Egypt side was probably close to one of the weaker first-class English county sides. In 1929, H.M. Martineau, a patron of cricket who organised his own sides in a country-house style, began his series of annual tours to Egypt. These took place each April and continued until 1939. Since local arrangements were in the hands of the military, it was not surprising that the All-Egypt sides were dominated by military players. This created problems, however, because the military personnel were consistently changing and, as a result, the quality of the Egyptian team fluctuated. In the mid 1930s, letters appeared in the local English press complaining that cricketers from the more permanent civilian residents were being ignored. Overall, the regular turnover of both military and civilian personnel meant that there was little continuity in the side.

The only Egyptian to play cricket for All-Egypt was the spin bowler, Abdou Hassanein. In addition to being the leading player of the Egyptian Cricket Club, founded in 1935, he was employed professionally as the ground bowler at Gezira, so his ability was well known to the selectors. His first appearance against Martineau's side was sensational as he took nine wickets in their second innings to secure victory for Egypt by 74 runs. The other Egyptian player of note was Z. Taher who scored 72 not out in a total of 122 for the Egyptian Club in a one-innings match against Martineau's XI in 1935. Despite this effort, the Egyptians lost by 19 runs.

The annual visits of Martineau's sides were stopped by the 1939-45 War. Nevertheless, much cricket was played in Egypt during the War as a recreational activity for the troops. The service games left no lasting impact on Egyptian cricket, however, and as the military withdrew and the British civilian population declined in the immediate post-war period, cricket virtually ceased. An attempt was made to revive the Egyptian CC and an Egyptian team toured England in 1951, losing to the MCC at Lord's in a one innings game by four wickets. Hasan Aly impressed by taking four for 72. However, this club was the preserve of upper class Egyptians who had a pro-British outlook and generally supported the Egyptian aristocracy and monarchy. The club did not survive the abolition of the monarchy in 1953. The new government took no interest in the game. Victoria College stopped teaching cricket and the various cricket grounds were either built upon or taken over by sporting clubs and used for other activities.

The late 1990s witnessed a small resurgence of cricket among the expatriate Indian, Pakistani, Sri Lankan and British communities. The main hindrance is the lack of a ground. Matches take place on the staff football ground of the Mena House Oberoi which is too small and the pitch, though grass, is somewhat uneven.

Player Profiles

Abdou Hassanein. The only native Egyptian to be chosen for All-Egypt, he was the leading player of the Egyptian Cricket Club and the professional ground bowler at the Gezira Sports Club. In his two matches for Egypt he scored 39 runs (average 19.50) and took 17 wickets (average 17.47) with a best performance of 9 wickets for 60 (13-76 in the match).

Cole, Eric Stuart. Major-General CB CBE. b Imtarfa, Malta, 10 February 1906. d Wandsworth, London, 19 December 1992. rhb. rm. Stationed in Egypt for much of the inter-war period, he became the most successful player for All-Egypt. With his highly-effective outswingers, he took five wickets in an innings on five occasions and was the only Egyptian player to take over forty wickets. In ten matches for Egypt, he scored 382 runs (average 20.11) and took 42 wickets (average 22.65). He had a distinguished career in Royal Corps of Signals and later became Director of Telecommunications in the War Office. He was the Army's light-weight boxing champion.

Other leading players: *1890-1914:* Rev J. Burrough (rhb. rm); Lt Col R.H. Crake DSO DL (wk); Dr J.A. MacLaren (rhb. rm). *1920-1940:* E.P.S. Booker; P.C. Organ; Lt G.A. Thomas. *1945-1960:* Hasan Aly.

Playing record

	Won	Lost	Drawn
International matches	8	16	5

Highest team score
507	v H.M. Martineau's XI, Gezira	1935

Lowest team score
50	v H.M. Martineau's XI, Alexandria	1939

Highest individual score
177	M.E. O'Brian	v H.M. Martineau's XI, Alexandria 1932

Best bowling
9-60	Abdou Hassanein	v H.M. Martineau's XI, Gezira 1937

Best wicket-keeping
4 (3c1st)	R. Barcilo	v H.M. Martineau's XI, Alexandria 1933
4 (0c4st)	G.L. Cruickshanks	v H.M. Martineau's XI. Gezira 1935

ENGLAND

Founder Member of the ICC in 1909

IN A form in which it might be recognised today, cricket was established by the early 1600s in the counties of Surrey, Sussex and Kent. The first definitive mention of cricket relates to a court case in Guildford, Surrey, in 1597 over the ownership of a plot of land. During his evidence, the coroner, John Derrick, who was aged 59 at the time, mentioned that he and some school friends had played cricket on the land in question some fifty years earlier, which would mean that the game was known about by 1550. Earlier references to various games in which a ball is hit with a stick have been proposed as relating to cricket but no direct link to them has ever been proven. Whilst south-east England is generally regarded as the birthplace of cricket, its origins are still the subject of debate. Some authorities believe it was started by shepherds and farm workers, possibly as early as 1300. The evidence to support this theory is largely circumstantial and is based on the similarity between the early bat and a shepherd's crook and the possibility that the wicket is derived from the wicket-gate used by shepherds to control their flocks. An alternative theory is that the game was developed by iron workers in the sixteenth and seventeenth century, at a time when The Weald was England's main iron-producing region. Support for this comes from the close association between the villages where cricket was known to have been played and the sites of forges and foundries. What is clear is that in the early 1600s cricket was essentially a village sport played by the working population.

By the middle of the seventeenth century there is evidence that the nobility and landed gentry were taking an interest in the game, organising inter-village matches and betting on their outcome. Through their sons, cricket was introduced into public schools, like Eton, Winchester, Harrow and Westminster, and then into Oxford and Cambridge Universities. By the late 1600s and early 1700s, the game was being played by upper-class boys and undergraduates and it was largely through them that cricket came to London. Cricket changed from a village pastime to a game of organised matches which, following the end of press censorship in 1696, started to be reported in newspapers. The Sussex cricket historian, Timothy McCann, has unearthed reference to a 'great match' in June 1697, reported in the *Foreign Post*, between two teams of eleven played for 'fifty guineas apiece'. On 30 March 1700, *The Post Boy* announced a series of cricket matches to be played over Easter on Clapham Common between 'ten gentlemen' per side for prizes of £10 and £20. It is not clear at this time whether references to a 'great' match refer to the quality of the players or to the size of the bet. Later, however, the description comes to be associated with matches between teams of the best players that can be assembled.

In the early 1700s, cricket became recognised by certain members of the nobility as a way of demonstrating their influence and wealth. Taking on the role of patrons, they financed their own sides and organised matches, usually for sizeable prize money. In addition they must have covered the transport and accommodation costs of their teams since most of the players would not have been able to afford them. These early patrons of the game included the Second Duke of Richmond who, from his country seat at Goodwood, Sussex, established one of the best teams in England at Slindon. His rival was Sir William Gage of Firle, near Eastbourne. Edwin Stead of Maidstone arranged for teams of Kentish cricketers to play the sides of the Duke of Richmond and William Gage at Dartford Heath. Alan Brodrick of Peper Harow, near Guildford, raised teams from Surrey for two matches against the Duke of Richmond's teams in 1727. As these matches became more common there was a need to have an agreed set of rules. Prior to the 1727 encounters, the Duke of Richmond and Brodrick drew up *Articles of Agreement* to act as a code for the umpires to use when settling disputes.

Since the nobility divided their time between their country estates and their houses in London, it is not surprising that they were involved in organising many matches in the capital city. By 1730 the Artillery Ground, near Chiswell Street in Finsbury, was established as the leading venue. The ground was run by George Smith, the lessee of the Pied Horse public house. The association of cricket and a local hostelry which could provide food and drink for the spectators was thus assured. In London the patrons were joined by Frederick Louis, the Prince of Wales, who arrived in England from Hannover in December 1728. He was passionate about women and gambling and soon found that cricket provided an ideal opportunity for the latter. He became President of the London Club. Along with the Dukes of Richmond and Cumberland and other nobility, he was present at the Artillery Ground on 18 June 1744 for the 'greatest cricket match ever known' between a side from Kent, raised by Lord John Sackville, and All-England, led by Richard

Newland, a leading player from the Duke of Richmond's Slindon team. The match was played to a set of laws drawn up by the London Club in advance and known as the 1744 Code. As well as being one of the first games for which a scorecard survives, the match was important for being the first at which an admission charge was made and at which crowd control became an issue. Gambling and unruly crowds became a feature of the game by the latter part of the eighteenth century. Large crowds were necessary to cover the costs of organising the matches, particularly where teams were brought from Sussex and Kent to London. In Georgian England, in addition to the aristocracy, cricket attracted many people at the lower end of the social scale, including vagabonds, pickpockets and other petty criminals. The atmosphere at the big London games was clearly very different from the village environment of the south-eastern counties.

New Patrons

The middle of the eighteenth century saw new patrons emerge in the southeast, including the Fourth Earl of Tankerville at Mount Felix, Walton-on-Thames, the Third Duke of Dorset at Sevenoaks, Kent, and Sir Horatio Mann who promoted the game at grounds close to Canterbury, Maidstone, Margate and at Sissinghurst. The Reverend Charles Powlett who became the curate at Itchen Abbas, Hampshire, provided patronage for the emerging Hambledon club. It started as a social club based on the Bat and Ball Inn where its members could meet for dinner, drinking and organising cricket matches. From these beginnings it became the focus of Hampshire's cricket between 1772 and 1796. At its peak the members effectively paid for Richard Nyren, the nephew of Richard Newland, to be the landlord of the Bat and Ball, arrange fixtures and captain the team. The club's bowling was noted for its innovation. Edward Stevens, known as 'Lumpy Stevens' was one of the first bowlers to pitch the ball and therefore attempt to bowl a length as opposed to the earlier method of rolling the ball along the ground. David Harris developed the technique of making the ball break either to the leg or to the off after pitching. Tom Walker, although not a regular bowler, was the first to raise his arm level with his shoulder when delivering the ball and therefore pioneered round-arm bowling, although it was pronounced illegal at the time. Although much has been written about Hambledon, it was only one of several important clubs in England in the eighteenth century.

The other major club to be founded at this time was the Marylebone Cricket Club. Based on continuity of activity and membership between the White Conduit Club of 1785-1787 and, before that, the club run from the Star and Garter in Pall Mall, the MCC's history has been traced back by cricket historian Peter Wynne-Thomas to 1744. The leading patrons of the club were the Ninth Earl of Winchilsea and the Hon. Charles Lennox, later to become the Fourth Duke of Richmond; both were also members of the Hambledon Club. In 1786, the Earl of Winchilsea and Lennox supported Thomas Lord, a cricketer and general factotum of the White Conduit Club, to enclose and layout a private ground for the club's use. He leased a tavern and land near New Road, Marylebone. In 1809 he laid out a new ground further to the northwest, selling the original ground for building. This second ground, however, lay along the line of the Regents Canal and so Lord had to establish a third ground at St John's Wood, where the Lord's ground remains to this day. The aristocracy who ran the MCC revised the laws of the game in 1774 and again in 1788. Although intended for use in MCC's own fixtures, they were gradually adopted by other clubs as printed editions obtained a wide circulation. The main role of the MCC, however, was the promotion of the game by travelling more widely than other clubs and arranging matches in the midlands and north of England. The MCC also accepted the professional support of players. Surprisingly, it was one of the aristocracy who benefited from this. Through the English law of primogeniture, the Reverend Lord Frederick Beauclerk, the fourth son of the Duke of St Albans, was left without the necessary income to support his life as a gentlemen of leisure. His skill as a slow bowler was recognised at Cambridge University where he was spotted by Winchilsea and taken into the MCC. On his own estimate, he was able to earn some £600 per year from playing the game and from betting on his team's and his own achievements.

Over time, the costs of organising and running teams became increasingly prohibitive and a new form of sponsorship emerged through syndicates. These supported a new type of professional who could earn a moderate living from the game without being in service to an individual member of the nobility. The amount of money provided must have been substantial because the majority of the players for Hambledon were imported from other villages as professionals and supported in this way. There is no doubt that this type of patronage was important for the development of the game. It allowed the best cricketers in the country to be assembled in a small number of prestigious teams, the rivalry between which enabled the standard of play to rise. When, in 1777, James Aylward, playing for Hampshire, made a score of 167, he was immediately poached by Sir Horatio Mann and moved to Kent. Patronage also led to the emergence of county teams since this was a way in which an individual member of the landed gentry could extend his sphere of influence beyond that of the estate. The first advertised county game took place at Dartford in 1709 between Kent and Surrey. As seen above, the 1744 match at the Artillery Ground was between Kent and an All-England side, the latter being the best team of cricketers that could be assembled who were not already in the Kent team. For much of the eighteenth century, it was difficult to distinguish between the teams of the most famous village sides and those representing the county. The sides of Hambledon and Hampshire were virtually the same.

Women Participate

Between the 1740s and 1770s women began to participate in cricket, albeit in small numbers. In Surrey and Sussex, several matches were organised between villages and in 1747 a women's game was staged on the Artillery Ground in London. Generally, women's matches paralleled the men's in being boisterous affairs, well attended and with much betting on both the outcome and the performances of individuals.

The late 1700s and early 1800s saw a considerable decline in both men's and women's cricket, particularly in the number of matches. From 1792, England was at war with France for 23 years. The cost of government taxation to support the war effort and the reduction in trade sent the country into economic decline. The costs of living increased, agricultural wages were depressed and the rural population migrated to the towns to work long hours in the new factories of the industrial revolution for low wages. Many cricket clubs could not afford the transport to away matches nor the prices of the food and wine for their players. Fewer people had the money for admission charges to the big games and, without income from the gate, club finances could only be maintained by increasing membership subscriptions. As a result, membership declined and many clubs folded, among them Hambledon in 1795. By the time economic conditions improved in the 1820s, several changes had taken place in the cricketing environment. With the increasing industrialisation, the importance of the landed gentry was challenged by an emerging middle and upper class based around the new factories in the towns. As these entrepreneurs organised factory clubs for their workers, cricket became an increasingly urban game. In many instances, the club sides consisted solely of artisans using a local inn as their headquarters. Betting on the matches led to increasing numbers of undesirables amongst the cricket crowds, increasing the problems of crowd control. Betting had reached the stage where players were fixing matches and obtaining financial benefit therefrom. In some instances both teams were offered money to lose the game.

By the end of the 1820s, a new generation educated through the public school and university system gradually took over the administration of the game from the aristocracy. The new administrators set out to clean up the game by removing gambling and promoting cricket as a cultural activity based on a code of good behaviour. The ethos of the game changed from one played for enjoyment to an activity undertaken for spiritual and mental benefit. Cricket became more scientific with the legalisation of round-arm bowling in 1835, the development of sprung bats and the use of pads and gloves. In 1845, Nicholas Wanostracht, who played cricket under the alias of Felix, had his book, *Felix on the bat*, published, dealing with the techniques of batting. The first match between the universities of Oxford and Cambridge took place in 1827 with further matches in 1829 and 1836, since when it has been an annual fixture, interrupted only by the two World Wars. The series between the Gentlemen and the Players began with two matches in 1806 and then became an annual fixture from

1819 until 1962, the year before the distinction between amateur and professional cricketers was abolished. County clubs began to be formed by the nobility and leading industrialists although most only lasted a few years. In 1825 Sussex met Kent and over the next twenty years, matches occurred irregularly involving teams from these counties, Surrey and Nottinghamshire.

Old Boys Clubs

So few county matches were played in the first part of the nineteenth century that it was difficult for a professional to earn a living from the game. The amateurs from the public schools, universities and the military played much of their cricket in their own social group. They formed old boys clubs, travelling sides like I Zingari, and continued the tradition of country house cricket from the previous century. The MCC remained a small club in terms of membership and made no attempt to take leadership of the game. Indeed, they were very conservative in outlook and, in 1827, voted against the use of round-arm bowling; they finally agreed to its used in 1835. The members organised a very short season so that they could retreat to the grouse moors in mid summer. The few professional staff they employed as ground bowlers were thus without employment for much of the year. Much cricket in England at this time, however, took place outside of the county, major club and country house circuit. In the south-east virtually every village had its team and, as transport became easier and cheaper with the development of the railways, could travel further afield and play more matches. Teams were characteristically made up of teachers, priests, local businessmen and labourers. In the north, cricket focused around town clubs and factories. Even though they were sponsored by publicans, industrialists and landlords, the majority of the players were working class. As economic conditions improved and government legislation reduced working hours, more people were able to participate in the game and more fixtures could be arranged. By the 1840s, cricket was starting to attract the interest of the general populace. The introduction of the penny post in 1840 allowed match scores and reports to be sent to the newspapers cheaply and rapidly and matches began to be reported regularly in the press.

It was against this background of greater national interest in cricket and limited opportunities for the leading professionals of the day to earn a decent wage that William Clarke formed his All-England Eleven. Originally a bricklayer, he was a cricketer of some skill and a businessman of some vision. At the age of forty, he married the widow of the landlord of *The Trent Bridge Inn* and laid out a cricket ground nearby, thereby creating what became the Trent Bridge ground in Nottingham. He believed that club sides around the country would welcome the chance to play against the leading cricketers of the day and that such matches would attract large crowds. Between 1847 and 1878, the AEE played 47 matches described as either first class or important, winning 20 and losing 14, twelve matches were drawn and one tied. Many of the matches were played against local sides of eighteens or twenty-twos, all of whom were generally allowed to field which made run-scoring difficult. The AEE bowlers, however, were generally far too good for the local players so that innings totals of between 100 and 150 could usually be successfully defended.

The AEE proved an extremely successful venture both for Clarke and for generating interest in cricket not only all over England but in Wales, Scotland and Ireland as well. Over time, however, some of Clarke's players grew tired of his autocratic nature and began to question whether they were receiving a fair proportion of the income earned. Not surprisingly, financial bickering led to breakaway movements. John Wisden, the Sussex cricketer, set up a rival United All England Eleven in 1853 which lasted until 1869. An additional factor contributing to the rivalry was a difference in attitude between the professionals of the north and the south. The AEE was centred on Nottingham and recruited many of its players from Yorkshire. The UAEE was focused on Surrey, Sussex and Kent, the counties where cricket had first developed. Although public interest in cricket continued to grow, it was not sufficient to support two itinerant professional elevens and in 1869, the UAEE collapsed. Attempts at a revival in 1870, by establishing the United South of England Eleven and the United North of England Eleven lasted only a few years.

From the 1860s the AEE had to contend with a much greater interest by the public in county matches. Yorkshire, Middlesex, Lancashire and Cambridgeshire were now playing other counties alongside Kent, Surrey, Sussex and Nottinghamshire. The national press began to raise the question of which county warranted the title of 'champion'. By 1870, the press were publishing ranking tables, even though all the counties did not play each other and each played a different number of games. Different publications used their own criteria for ranking and therefore produced different outcomes. The cricket historian, Roland Bowen, has produced a list of the champion counties in these early days, as generally accepted by contemporary sources (Table 2.4). In 1873, a meeting of representatives of Surrey, Sussex, Middlesex, Kent, Gloucestershire, Nottinghamshire and Yorkshire agreed some rules on the qualifications of players to represent their counties. The MCC were asked to rule where disputes arose. Some authorities have considered the present county championship to date from this year and in 1973 the British Post Office issued commemorative stamps for its centenary. However, most cricket historians today recognise the County Championship as beginning in 1890 when the counties agreed on a points system and

Table 2.4 County champions between 1864 and 1889 as recognised by contemporary sources according to Rowland Bowen. In 1878, the outcome was undecided.

County	Number of times outright winners	Number of times championship shared	Comments
Cambridgeshire	0	0	Ceased to be first class in 1869
Derbyshire	0	0	First class between 1871 and 1887
Gloucestershire	3	1	First class from 1870
Hampshire	0	0	First class 1865-67, 1870, 1874-78
Kent	0	0	
Lancashire	1	3	First class from 1867
Middlesex	1	0	
Nottinghamshire	10	5	
Somerset	0	0	First class in 1882 only
Surrey	3	1	
Sussex	0	0	
Yorkshire	2	1	

a recognised list of fixtures. Table 2.5 summarizes the results to date.

The growth of the county championship established a social structure of cricket in the late nineteenth century which was to last until the 1960s. The organisation of each county side was undertaken by amateurs, usually from a public school and university background. Each team comprised a mixture of amateurs and professionals but was captained by an amateur. Although not exclusively so, the amateurs tended to be batsmen and the professionals the bowlers. Since many of the amateurs were either at university or were school teachers, they would displace all but the best professional batsmen from July, once the university and school terms had ended, to September. Whilst the amateurs and professionals would mix on the field, they maintained their separate status off it. Whereas the professionals who played with Clarke and Wisden were akin to skilled artisans who entered into contracts on their own terms, the professionals with the counties were no different to labourers or to the hired hands employed by the landed gentry in the Georgian period. They travelled to away matches separately from the amateurs, stayed in different hotels, changed in different dressing rooms and frequently came on to the field through different gates. Nevertheless, for many working class, cricket offered a better and more lucrative way of life than labouring in factories or mines but it

was hard work. By the 1930s, professional batsmen were playing fifty or even sixty innings each season and the bowlers were delivering between 1,500 and 2,000 overs. Cricket was not, however, a secure career. Many professionals were paid by the match and received no wages when ill or injured. Alternative employment had to be found for the winter months; several played soccer professionally. The professionals had to meet their own expenses for travel and subsistence from what they were paid, so there was little money spare to invest for the future. Many professionals became destitute when their playing careers came to an end.

The wealthier counties were able to offer slightly better conditions to their professionals, a few of whom were retained over winter to carry out maintenance work on the ground. The best could supplement their wages from collections made during matches to reward particularly outstanding performance. With a successful county, a good player could earn about £100 a year in the 1870s and £250 by 1900. These figures compared to wages of £80 to £100 as a labourer or a factory worker. Players who offered loyal service over many years were awarded a benefit match whereby the player received any profit from the gate after the expenses of the fixture had been met. If the match was well attended, the weather good and it lasted all three days, a player could expect to receive up to about £800 prior to the First World War and between £1,000 and £3,700 in the 1920s and 1930s. However, if rain prevented play or the match finished in one day, the amount received could be very small and some players even made a loss on their benefit.

At the end of the nineteenth century, a new type of cricket organisation emerged in the urban centres of the midlands and the north. This was league cricket where, unlike the club cricket of the south which was essentially run by enthusiastic amateurs, the clubs hired professionals, charged admission fees and set out to make a profit. The most successful were the Lancashire League, founded in 1890, and the Central Lancashire League, founded in 1893. Similar leagues were started in Durham, Staffordshire, Warwickshire, Worcestershire

Table 2.5 County champions between 1890 and 2006

County	Date of first appearance	Number of times outright winners	Number of times championship shared
Derbyshire	1895	1	0
Durham	1992	0	0
Essex	1895	6	0
Glamorgan	1921	3	0
Gloucestershire	1890	0	0
Hampshire	1895	2	0
Kent	1890	6	1
Lancashire	1890	7	1
Leicestershire	1895	3	0
Middlesex	1890	10	2
Northamptonshire	1905	0	0
Nottinghamshire	1890	5	0
Somerset	1891	0	0
Surrey	1890	18	1
Sussex	1890	2	0
Warwickshire	1890	6	0
Worcestershire	1899	5	0
Yorkshire	1890	30	1

and Yorkshire. The returns to a professional were not as high as from a county side. A professional in the Lancashire League might have made £80 per season in the 1890s, supplemented by bonuses for wins and ground collections. League cricket served to enhance the differences in outlook between the north and south. The amateurs who ran and played for club sides in London and the Home Counties looked askance at the idea of cricket clubs being organised for profit and attracting large partisan crowds in an atmosphere closer to that of a soccer game. Yet, many amateurs saw nothing hypocritical in accepting that they could not afford to play county cricket on a regular basis without receiving some form of remuneration. To retain their amateur status, they could not be paid a wage, instead they received stipends, honoraria and match expenses. In some cases, they obtained more money from cricket than the professional players. The cricketer who attracted most attention for the amount of money received was Dr W.G. Grace. He was given about £50 per game as expenses by Gloucestershire; his two testimonials in 1879 and 1895 yielded some £10,400. It has been estimated that between 1870 and 1910 he made around £120,000 from playing cricket.

First Overseas Tour

One way in which cricketers could obtain an income during the off-season was by undertaking tours overseas. The first overseas tour occurred in September and October 1859 when twelve professional players, under the leadership of George Parr, visited Canada and the USA. It is estimated that, after covering expenses, each player earned about £90. Further professional tours followed to Australia in 1861/62 and 1863/64, though this team included one amateur in Dr E.M. Grace, and to Canada and the USA in 1868. It was not until 1872 that an all amateur side went overseas when R.A. Fitzgerald, then Secretary of the MCC took a team to Canada and the USA. The organisation of overseas tours remained in the hands of individuals until 1903/04. The lack of a central administrative body led to two separate parties going to Australia in 1887/88 (see Country Profile for Australia). The lack of a central authority also meant that touring sides to England had to arrange

their own itineraries. For international matches involving a representative England eleven, team selection was the responsibility of the county club on whose ground the matches were played. Not surprisingly, this led to accusations of favouritism. In 1898, the counties established a Board of Control to regulate home international matches. The Board nominated a selection panel whose remit was to choose the English team. Gradually, the counties looked more and more towards the MCC as an overarching body of control. As noted earlier, the MCC was recognised as an authority on the laws of the game. Further revisions were made in 1788, in 1835 when round-arm bowling was legalised and in 1864 when over-arm bowling was permitted. Now the MCC was being asked to take on a wider administrative role. When A.C. MacLaren declined the invitation from Australia to select a side to tour in 1903/04 because S.F. Barnes and W.H. Lockwood refused to play under him, the MCC intervened and sent a side under the captaincy of P.F. Warner. From that tour, all major overseas tours were organised by the MCC until 1977/78, when, in order to secure government money to encourage people to take up sport, the MCC relinquished control of the game, returning to its original status as a private club. Two new bodies were established: the Test and County Cricket Board responsible for the first class county and international game, and the National Cricket Association to organise the minor counties and support the game in clubs and schools. These bodies were not to last because the separation of functions made it difficult for the various levels of the game to link together. In 1997, the bodies were merged into the England and Wales Cricket Board with a remit to cover all cricket, men's and women's, both professional and recreational.

In contrast to the continuous growth of men's cricket throughout the nineteenth century, Victorian attitudes towards femininity almost killed the women's game. Women were discouraged from taking an active part in any sport and, if they did, were frequently subject to ridicule. It was not until the late 1880s that women's cricket underwent a revival. In 1887, a group of women from the aristocracy formed the White Heather Club. Based on the country houses of the Brassey and Neville families, it expanded from eight to fifty members within four years. In 1890, a semi-professional women's team was formed under the title of the 'Original English Lady Cricketers'. They played exhibition matches in the English midlands between their 'blue' and 'red' teams. Since playing sport professionally was considered improper for a woman, they played under assumed names. An estimated 15,000 watched their match at Liverpool and the other games also attracted sizeable crowds. Surprisingly the club was disbanded after only one season. One reason suggested for this is that the male manager absconded with all the money. Despite continued opposition from many male cricket administrators and players, the Edwardian era saw the formation of several women's cricket clubs, particularly in the north of England and the London area. The game was introduced into the leading girls public schools. Notwithstanding these developments, women's cricket lagged behind the men's game. The necessary organisation for county and international cricket was not yet in place.

Major Changes

The 1960s saw major changes to the structure of English men's cricket. The game was suffering from a severe financial crisis. Attendances at county championship matches had been in decline throughout the 1950s, as was county membership through subscription. Few amateurs could afford to play county cricket full-time and county finances were insufficient to pay professionals a competitive wage compared with industry or what sportsmen could obtain through football. Amateur status was abolished in 1963 which meant that all could be paid openly for playing cricket, thereby removing the distinction between wages and expenses. With the introduction of a national school curriculum and continuous testing and examination of pupil performance at virtually all ages, there was less time for summer sport. The 1980s and 1990s saw the public schools reduce the size of their fixture list and the game ceased in many state schools as their playing fields were sold for building land. Contrary to these trends, a public school background followed by a spell at either Oxford or Cambridge University was no longer a route for recruiting county and test cricketers. The majority of first-class cricketers were now from state school backgrounds, having received

coaching and encouragement through the English Schools Cricket Association. The standards of cricket at Oxford and Cambridge were in decline and other universities, particularly Durham and Loughborough, were an alternative source of players. There was a general belief that the overall standard of the county game was also falling. With the intention of rectifying this, from 1968 the county teams were allowed to field a limited number of overseas players without them having to fulfil a residential qualifying period. This change had the effect of levelling the standards between the counties, making the competition more open. Whilst there was concern that the presence of overseas cricketers would inhibit the opportunities for local players, the overall effect has been positive. The best overseas players became very loyal to their counties, encouraged local talent, assisted with coaching and helped promote the game in local clubs and schools. European Union legislation on the free movement of labour enabled cricketers from Denmark and The Netherlands to participate in the county game. It also brought about a further increase in the number of overseas players since those who can claim citizenship of a European Union country through their ancestry do not count towards a county's quota of registered overseas players. County one-day knockout and league competitions were introduced and, most recently, floodlight evening games of twenty overs per side, known as Twenty20. These have attracted larger audiences than the three or four day county games. In 2000 the county championship was split into two divisions with promotion and relegation between them.

Another change since the 1960s is the distribution of venues for international and first-class cricket. Test matches have always been held in the major towns with London, by virtue of having two grounds, Lord's and The Oval, staging more than most. In 2003, this pattern was broken when test cricket was played at a new, purpose-built, ground at Chester-le-Street. In 1890, 29 per cent of the relatively few first-class matches that were played took place in London. The remaining matches were distributed reasonably evenly among the other grounds around the country. By 1910, London was even more dominant, with the other matches falling into two groups: a small number of centres staging between seven and eleven matches a season and a larger number of centres staging one or two matches. This situation continued through the Inter-War period and into the 1960s by which time the number of centres holding one or two first class games had increased, making first class cricket accessible to a large proportion of the population. Although, in 1960, 47 first-class matches were staged in London, 29 towns hosted one first-class game and another 20 towns hosted two matches. Unfortunately, declining attendances meant that organising a few matches at lots of grounds was not economic and by 2000, considerable retrenchment had taken place; the number of towns staging one match was reduced to 18. Also, the dominance of London had decreased with only 18 matches taking place in the capital.

With first class cricket becoming concentrated in fewer centres coupled with the trend towards shorter tours, touring itineries in England have became more leisurely (Table 2.6). Compared to tours in other countries, the small area of England means that, for most matches, it is possible to travel from one venue to another in the evening after a match finishes and be ready to start a new game the following day. Only where the distance exceeds 250 kilometres is a separate day required for travelling. The 1899 tour by Australia is typical of those at the end of the nineteenth century when touring sides had to play as many matches as possible in order to cover their costs. Not only was the tour very long, lasting from 8 May to 6 September but the cricket was virtually continuous with eight playing days for every one rest day. Also there was very little logic to the itinerary which was controlled by the order in which matches could be arranged. In the last month of the tour the team visited the following towns in the order of Canterbury, London, Cheltenham, London, Taunton, Liverpool, Scarborough and Hastings. The 1948 tour, typical of those between 1920 and 1990 was less hectic. The tour was longer, from 28 April to 18 September but no cricket was played on Sundays and rest days were more frequent. There were even more rest days in the shorter tour by Australia in 2001. Half of the matches played were one-day internationals with one day's rest between each one; there were as many as two to four days without cricket between each of the

three-day county games or five-day test matches. With the increasing tendency to use these days for training and practice rather than sightseeing, however, the tour was probably not as leisurely as it appears on paper. It is also noticeable that the itineries are better organised so that the distance between consecutive venues is reduced.

The increasing emancipation of women in the 1920s combined with a larger number of women being taught cricket at school and wanting to carry on playing, prompted a small group of enthusiasts to establish the Women's Cricket Association to organise and promote women's cricket at a national level. The WCA was founded on 4 October 1929. By the early 1930s, a regular programme of fixtures was in place between five regional associations, North, Midlands, East South and West. In the late 1970s, however, women's cricket entered a difficult period, with lack of sponsorship, a low level of public interest and dwindling membership of club teams. Cricket was no longer so common in girls schools, where it suffered competition from athletics and swimming, and was not even offered as a subject in sports qualifications from physical education colleges. In 1977, Jack Hayward, a philanthropist and major sponsor of women's cricket, withdrew his support when, for reasons that have never been entirely clear, the WCA took away the captaincy of the national side from Rachael Heyhoe-Flint. From then on until 1997, when the English Cricket Board took over responsibility for women's cricket from the WCA, sponsorship for home internationals and overseas tours had to be sought season-by-season, with very little money available for the game in the counties, clubs and schools. It remains to be seen whether the ECB's involvement will be positive with women's cricket being encouraged to grow or whether the women's game will be given no higher status than the minor counties and the club game.

Table 2.6 Playing days, rest days and distances travelled on tours of England by Australia				
Date	Playing days	Rest days	Ratio of cricket days to rest days	kilometres travelled per rest day
1889	104	13	8.00	427
1948	109	31	3.52	185
2001	54	33	1.64	114

Notes: Rest days are days when no cricket is played and no travel takes place. The ratio of kilometres travelled per rest day is an underestimate because kilometres are based on straight-line distances between the venues and not the actual distance travelled.

Men's recreational cricket also underwent a major change in the mid 1960s with the establishment of league cricket in the southern counties. Brought about for financial reasons as the only way to receive government money through the Sports Council, this has encouraged local industrial sponsorship and undoubtedly helped the survival of many clubs. Clubs are now able to employ a professional, usually an overseas player with first-class experience but not quite good enough to gain a contract with a county side, or one from an associate country seeking experience of the English game. In 1969 a nationwide knock-out tournament was introduced for club sides, followed in 1972 by a separate competition for village teams. In many counties a league structure with divisions, promotion and relegation operates, creating pressure on club sides to succeed. As they try to recruit the best players, the traditional ethos of the club as a social centre for cricketers of varying skills to organise friendly matches is disappearing. The side which won the National Club Championship in 2004 included four cricketers with first-class experience. The team which won the Village Cup were also the champions of the South Wales Cricket League and included a county second eleven player and an England Under 19 player. The rules for the village competition were changed for 2005 to exclude any side from the strongest leagues and any side which includes a player contracted to a first-class county. Responding to the effects of population migration from the towns to rural areas, the upper limit of 3,000 inhabitants for villages taking part in the competition was raised to 4,000. Club cricket, particularly in the towns, has provided a home for many players of Caribbean and Asian extraction.

French Revolution

International cricket almost got underway under Georgian patronage when, in July 1789, the Duke of Dorset, whilst the British ambassador in France, arranged for a side led by William Yalden of Chertsey to play a team of English cricketers in Paris. The chosen side set off but when they reached Dover they met the Duke of Dorset in retreat from the French Revolution and the venture had to be abandoned. The start of England's international cricket therefore had to wait until James Lillywhite's side

on tour of Australia met a 'combined eleven' in Melbourne on 15-19 March 1878. The first home international took place in 1880 presaging an outstanding period for English cricket, often described as 'The Golden Age' which lasted until 1914. England took sometime to recover from the effects of the First World War and it was not until the late 1920s that they were again able to field a side capable of beating Australia. Since then England's record has been very inconsistent with short periods of success, usually lasting about four to five years, interspersed by periods of disappointment. In the late 1920s, mid 1950s and mid 1970s England were arguably the best side in the world. The early 2000s have seen England emerge as one of the strongest countries at test cricket and one of the weakest in the one-day, limited-overs, game.

Women's international cricket began in 1934 when the WCA accepted an invitation to send a team to Australia under the captaincy of Betty Archdale. England won the series by two matches to nil with one drawn. The first home tests were against Australia in 1937, the series being shared with one win each and the third test drawn. The high cost of touring and the shortage of money, however, prevented further international cricket before the Second World War. The period between the late 1940s and 1970 saw the English women involved in international cricket about every three years. Lack of finance prevented more frequent matches especially as, once selected, the players had to cover most of their own travelling and subsistence expenses which, for a tour of Australia and New Zealand could be quite substantial. Also, those women who worked had to arrange leave of absence which was not always granted and, if it was, was usually without pay. England were the most successful country in women's test cricket from the 1950s through to the 1970s and were able to take this record into the one-day game by winning the inaugural world cup in 1973. Since then, as other countries have raised their standards, England have experienced a very lean period. Whilst they still managed to draw most of the test matches played, the side proved ill-equipped for the one-day game, losing heavily to Australia and New Zealand. The exception was the 1993 World Cup when England emerged the winners, beating New Zealand in a televised final at Lord's. This apart, it was not until 2002 that results started to improve under the captaincy of Clare Connor.

Notwithstanding the loss of the Ashes in 2006 and an uninspired performance in the 2007 World Cup, the early 2000s have witnessed a period of successful international cricket by both the men's and women's teams. Yet, as noted above, this has coincided with a contraction in the number of centres where first-class cricket is played. International cricket has become separated from the county game by the establishment of a national squad with a management structure that controls when a player can and cannot play for his county. How long county sides will be prepared to invest in player development if they are then to lose the services of their best players may well be a key question for the future. Increasingly, the game has come to depend on sponsorship from industry and income from the sale of broadcasting rights, particularly television rights worldwide. By the mid 1990s, broadcasting, sponsorship and a share of the receipts from test matches accounted for over 80 per cent of the income of the first-class county cricket clubs, compared with less than 30 per cent in the 1960s. In 2004, the ECB agreed a deal with Sky Sports which, from 2006, has meant the removal of live test cricket from terrestrial television. Since only a minority of the population subscribe to the Sky satellite sports channels, there is concern that the game may decline through want of exposure. However, the televising of cricket is not profitable for the terrestrial companies and none can match the sums which Sky is prepared to offer. How the ECB responds to these challenges, all of which broadly mean less exposure of cricket to the general public, may well determine whether the current success rate of the men's and women's teams can be sustained.

Famous Victories
July 26, 27, 28, 30 and 31, 1956 – Old Trafford, Manchester
England 459 (Rev D.S. Sheppard 113,
P.E. Richardson 104, M.C. Cowdrey 80,
I.W. Johnson 4-151)
Australia 84 (J.C. Laker 9-37) and 205
(C.C. McDonald 89, J.C. Laker 10-53)
England won by an innings and 170 runs
ENGLAND WERE fortunate to win the toss on a pitch that gave no assistance to pace bowling and which started to break up around tea time on the first day. After Peter

Richardson and Colin Cowdrey put on 174 runs for the first wicket, David Sheppard and Peter May added 93 for the fourth wicket. Sheppard's chanceless century, containing one six and fifteen fours was remarkable since he had given up regular cricket after taking Holy Orders and had played only four first-class innings that season before the match. The Australian spinners obtained surprisingly little bite from the wicket and Godfrey Evans made a typical swashbuckling 47 runs in a seventh wicket partnership of 62 in only twenty-nine minutes. The Australian wicket-keeper, Len Maddocks, held three catches and made one stumping in the England innings. Australia made 48 before losing their first wicket but thereafter found Jim Laker unplayable, their last seven wickets falling for 22 runs in thirty-five minutes. Following on, Australia lost Colin McDonald who retired hurt with a knee injury after scoring eleven. Neil Harvey then went first ball, thereby failing to score in either innings. Australia finished the second day with 51 runs scored for the loss of one wicket. Overnight rain continued for much of the third day when only three-quarters of an hours play was possible, during which time Australia add six runs and lost one wicket. Conditions on the fourth day were worse.

Rain restricted play to two sessions of forty-five and fifteen minutes. A strong wind made cricket extremely difficult and heavy lignum bails had to be used since the normal bails were continually blown off the stumps. Play began only ten minutes late on the last day on a slow and seemingly easy-paced pitch but just before lunch the sun appeared and, as the wicket dried it increasingly took spin. McDonald and Ian Craig (38) held out for over four hours and it looked as though Australia would save the match but, in a devastating spell, Laker removed Craig, Ken Mackay, Keith Miller and Ron Archer in nine overs whilst conceding only three runs. When McDonald's vigil finally ended after five hours and thirty-seven minutes at the crease, the question was how many wickets Laker would obtain. With his bowling partner, Tony Lock, regularly beating the bat at the other end, a haul of all-ten seemed unlikely but Lock was without luck and Laker went on to complete the most remarkable bowling feat of all time. England's victory was helped by the superb close-in fielding of Alan Oakman who held five catches in the match.

June 16, 17, 18, 20 and 21, 1981 – Headingley, Leeds
Australia 401-9 dec (J. Dyson 102, K.J. Hughes 89, G.N. Yallop 58, I.T. Botham 6-95) and 111 (R.G.D. Willis 8-43)
England 174 (I.T. Botham 50, D.K. Lillee 4-49) and 356 (I.T. Botham 149*, G.R. Dilley 56, T.M. Alderman 6-135)
England won by 18 runs

England began the match without much expectation. Australia were one up in the series and the selectors had relieved Ian Botham of the captaincy and recalled Mike Brearley. On winning the toss, Australia batted methodically but without inspiration. Aided by dropped catches, they amassed a sizeable total before Botham took five wickets for 35 runs in a spell after tea on the second day; Australia then declared just before the close. England had no answer to the pace attack of Dennis Lillee, Terry Alderman (3-59) and Geoff Lawson (3-32). Only Botham, with an aggressive half century, contributed much and extras, at 34, were the second highest score. The follow-on was no better, Alderman finding the conditions ideal for swing bowling. After losing seven wickets for 135, an innings defeat for England looked certain, despite the effort of Geoffrey Boycott (46 runs) who batted for three and a half hours. Botham then hit an astonishing, unbeaten, 149 runs, adding 117 in 80 minutes with Graham Dilley, and a further 67 with Chris Old. Set a target of 130 runs to win, Australia looked on course at 56 for the loss of only one wicket but then, Bob Willis, with the wind behind him, bowled like a man possessed and Australia lost their last nine wickets for 55 runs. There was a slight hiccup whilst Ray Bright (19) and Lillee (17) added 35 for the ninth wicket but Willis eventually dismissed them both. England's fielding was outstanding in Australia's second innings. Wicket-keeper Bob Taylor held seven catches in the match.

August 4, 5, and 6, 2005 – Edgbaston, Birmingham
England 407 (M.E. Trescothick 90, K.P. Pietersen 71, A. Flintoff 68, S. K. Warne 4-116) and 182 (A. Flintoff 73, S.K. Warne 6-46, B. Lee 4-82)
Australia 308 (J.L. Langer 82, R.T. Ponting 61) and 279 (A. Flintoff 4-79)
England won by 2 runs

After losing the first test of the series at Lord's by 239 runs, England came back strongly having been, surprisingly, asked to bat when Australia won the toss. Australia were handicapped by an injury to Glen McGrath who turned an ankle when treading on a cricket ball in pre-match practice. Marcus Trescothick and Andrew Strauss put on 132 runs for the first wicket and Kevin Pietersen and Andrew Flintoff added 103 for the fifth wicket. The tail then frustrated Australia as Ashley Giles (23), Matthew Hoggard (16), Steve Harmison (17) and Simon Jones (19*) made useful contributions. Only Shane Warne troubled the English batsmen. In reply, Australia promised much with Justin Langer, Ricky Ponting, Damien Martyn (20) and Michael Clarke (40) all making starts but then failing to go on to make a large score. As Andrew Flintoff (3-52) and Simon Jones (2-69) removed the tail, Gilchrist, who seemed unable to farm the bowling, was left stranded on 49 not out. England quickly lost Strauss to a superb delivery from Warne which pitched in the rough well outside off-stump only to break back outside his bat and pad and hit the middle and leg stumps. Brett Lee's aggressive fast bowling and Shane Warne's subtleties would have bowled out England cheaply but for the resistance of Flintoff who, batting number seven, was the last to be dismissed after he and Simon Jones had added 51 for the tenth wicket. Australia reached 47 without loss in pursuit of 282 but then lost wickets regularly to reach seven down for 136. Clarke (30 runs) then added 38 in partnership with Warne before falling to Harmison. Warne and Lee put on a further 45 as Australia edged closer and closer to the target. Captain Michael Vaughan rotated his bowlers and continuously changed his field placings but without effect until, Warne, going for a big hit off Flintoff, lost his balance and trod on his wicket, having made 42. Still Australia would not be defeated and Lee and Michael Kasprowicz then amassed 59 for the last wicket before Harmison surprised Kasprowicz with an outstanding slower ball to be caught behind by Geraint Jones for 20. Brett Lee was left disappointed and frustrated on 43 runs not out, as England achieved the closest result by a runs margin in England–Australia test history. The victory was the turning point of the series which England went on to win by two matches to one and therefore secure The Ashes for the first time since 1987/88.

Women's match

August 24, 25, 26 and 27, 2005 – New Road, Worcester

Australia 131 (K.H. Brunt 5-47) and 232 (S. Nitschke 88, K.A. Blackwell 72, K.H. Brunt 4-64)

England 289 (K.H. Brunt 52, E. Liddell 4-57) and 75-4

England won by 6 wickets

Asked to bat in conditions helpful to seam bowling, an experienced Australian side struggled against Katherine Brunt, Jenny Gunn (17-10-17-1) and Isa Guha (13-3-32-1). Even when captain, Clare Connor, tried her slow spin to give the fast bowlers a rest, she kept Australia tied down, bowling eight overs for only nine runs and getting the valuable wicket of Cathryn Fitzpatrick. England responded strongly to Australia's small total with useful contributions from Gunn (38), Connor (37) and Clare Taylor (43) but it took a last wicket stand of 85 runs between Brunt (52) and Guha (31 not out) to really frustrate the Australia bowlers. England then reduced Australia to seven runs for the loss of three wickets before a partnership of 112 runs for the seventh wicket by Kate Blackwell and Shelley Nitschke retrieved Australia's position. Nitschke and Emma Liddell (24) then added 53 for the tenth wicket. Again Brunt and Gunn (2-35) took the most wickets but Connor's remarkable analysis of 26-20-25-1 ensured that Australia struggled to gain an advantage. Nevertheless, they gave England a fright when Liddell, left-arm fast medium, dismissed Laura Newton and Gunn with only one run on the board; Connor and Charlotte Edwards quickly followed to make it 39-4. Arran Brindle (24*) and Lydia Greenway (10*) then batted sensibly to ensure there were no further alarms. The victory meant that England won a series against Australia for the first time since 1963 and reclaimed the women's Ashes.

Player Profiles

Bakewell, Enid (née Turton). b Newstead Village, Nottinghamshire, 16 December 1940. rhb. sla. Having learned cricket with and been considered better than the boys at grammar school in Nottingham, she made her debut for Nottinghamshire when aged fourteen. In 1959 she graduated from Dartford College of Physical Education. She began her career as a watchful and solid opening bat but later developed a range of strokes and ability to use her feet. With her left-arm bowling, she drifted the ball across the wicket with the breeze and then straightened it sharply off the pitch. On her first overseas tour to Australia and New Zealand in 1968/69, she did the double of scoring 1,031 runs and taking 118 wickets in all matches. In 12 test matches she scored 1078 runs (average 59.88) and took 50 wickets (average 16.62) with a best performance of seven for 61. In 23 one-day internationals she made 500 runs (average 35.71) and took 25 wickets (average 21.12).

Barnes, Sydney Francis. b Smethwick, Staffordshire, 19 April 1873. d Chadsmoor, Staffordshire, 26 December 1967. rhb. rm/rmf. His ability to seam, swing, cut and spin the ball according to the conditions, an action which made it difficult for the batsman to 'read' each delivery, and a command of length and direction, made him one of the greatest bowlers of all time. His reputation as a difficult person to manage and his brooding, aloof character meant that he was not selected as often as his talents warranted. In 27 test matches he scored 242 runs (average 8.06) and took 189 wickets (average 16.43). Between 1927 and 1930 he also played for Wales.

Brearley, John Michael, OBE. b Harrow, Middlesex, 28 April 1942. rhb. wk. Following a success as a cricketer at school and Cambridge University, he was chosen for the MCC Under 25 tour of Pakistan in 1966/67 where he scored 312 not out against the North Zone. Although he was unable to reproduce this form in test cricket, his sensitive handling of individuals, his command of tactics and his analytical mind made him an ideal captain. Under his leadership, England won 58 per cent of their matches, an achievement which no other English player who has captained in 30 or more matches can match. In 39 test matches, he scored 1,442 runs (average 22.88). In 25 one-day internationals he scored 510 runs (average 24.28).

Grace, Dr William Gilbert. b Downend, Bristol, 18 July 1848. d Mottingham, Kent, 23 October 1915. rhb. rm(r). The outstanding cricketer of his generation from 1870 to the early 1900s, he was the first player in first-class cricket to score a triple century, score over 2,000 runs in a season, perform the double of 1,000 runs and 100 wickets in a season, achieve 2,000 runs and 100 wickets in a season, score 1,000 runs between the start of the season and the end of May, and make over 100 centuries. Between 1868 and 1874, his batting average exceeded 50 in every season when most other batsmen had averages in the thirties. By the time international test cricket began, he was past his prime although he underwent a resurgence of form in 1895 when, aged 47, he achieved his thousand runs in May, made his hundredth hundred and again scored over 2,000 runs and averaged over 50 in the season. He first played for England in 1880 and became the first English player to score a century in test cricket, 152 at The Oval. His 170 at The Oval in 1886 was the highest test score made by an Englishman to that date. In 22 tests, he captained England 13 times, scored 1,098 runs (average 32.29) and took 9 wickets (average 26.22). These achievements make Grace, arguably, the greatest all-rounder in English cricket history. He was certainly the best known sports personality in late Victorian England and it was said that, alongside W.E. Gladstone, he was the best known of all Englishmen.

Hammond, Walter Reginald. b Buckland, Dover, Kent, 19 June 1903. d Kloof, Durban, South Africa, 1 July 1965. rhb. rmf. The dominant batsman in first-class cricket in the 1930s, he headed the batting averages for eight consecutive seasons (1933-1939 and 1946). Only Don Bradman with 37 has exceeded his 36 double centuries. A very correct player, noble and statuesque in style, he was renowned for his driving through cover and mid-off. When he reached 1,000 runs by the end of May in 1927, he was only the second person, following W.G. Grace, to achieve the feat. Originally a professional cricketer, he changed his status to amateur in 1938 and then captained England. In 85 test matches he scored 7,249 runs (average 58.45) and took 83 wickets (average 37.80). He also held 110 catches, being the best slip fielder of his day.

Hobbs, Sir John Berry. b Cambridge, 16 December 1882. d Hove, Sussex, 21 December 1963. rhb. The greatest English batsman of his generation, he was known as 'the master'. He had such good technique and quick reaction that he could succeed even on the most difficult wickets that others found unplayable. He scored a record 197 hundreds in his career, ninety-eight of which were made after the age of forty. Seventeen times he scored more than 2,000 runs in an English season, also a record. He was the first batsman to score over 5,000 runs in test cricket. In 61 test matches, he made 5,410 runs (average 56.94). He was a 'model' professional, extremely modest, with a deep understanding of the game. He was knighted for his services to cricket in 1953.

Hutton, Sir Leonard. b Fulneck, Pudsey, Yorkshire, 23 June 1916. d Norbiton, Kingston-upon-Thames, Surrey, 6 September 1990. rhb. He was the first professional to captain England. In his second season in international cricket in 1938, he scored 473 runs (average 118.25) against Australia, including 364 out of England's 903 for seven wickets declared at The Oval, at that time the highest individual test score ever made. He lost six years of his cricket career during the 1939-45 War after which he developed a reputation as a rather dour batsman, largely because he often had to carry a side whose batting was unreliable. His natural style, however, was attacking with a wide range of strokes. In 79 test matches, he scored 6,971 runs (average 56.67). He was knighted for services to cricket in 1956.

Laker, James Charles. b Frizinghall, Bradford, Yorkshire, 9 February 1922. d Putney, London, 23 April 1986. rhb. rob. Arguably the best off-break bowler England has produced, he had a high arm action, great accuracy, used flight well and obtained sharp spin off the pitch. He had an excellent first-class record with Surrey when they were county champions for seven consecutive years from 1952 but, surprisingly, could not hold a regular place in the England team. He took 166 wickets in the 1950 season, including eight for two runs in a test trial. In 1956, he twice routed the Australians, taking ten wickets in an innings for Surrey and then ten in an innings (19 for 90 in the match) for England at Manchester. In 46 test matches, he scored 676 runs (average 14.08) and took 193 wickets (average 21.24). After retiring from playing, he became a television commentator.

Maclagan, Myrtle Ethel, MBE. b Ambala, Uttar Pradesh, India, 2 April 1911. d Farnham, Surrey, 11

March 1993. rhb. rob. The leading English woman cricketer throughout the 1930s and 1940s, she became nationally known on the pioneering tour of Australia when, in the first test, she scored 72 and took seven wickets for ten runs. In the second test, she scored the first century (119) in women's international cricket. She served as an officer in the ATS during the Second World War and rejoined the Women's Royal Army Corps in 1951 as an Inspector of Physical Training. In 14 test matches she scored 1,007 runs (average 41.95) and took 60 wickets (average 15.58).

Taylor, Robert William, MBE. b Stoke-on-Trent, Staffordshire, 17 July 1941. rhb. wk. He was the understudy in the English team to Alan Knott for much of his career. Modest, undemonstrative, he took wicket-keeping to the highest level of perfection but suffered from the well-known selectors' belief that a wicket-keeper who could score hundreds was of more value than one who was well-nigh infallible behind the stumps. Arguably the greatest English wicket-keeper of all time, he made more dismissals in his career than any other 'keeper. Against India at Mumbai in 1979/80, he made seven dismissals in an innings and ten in the match. He was a capable lower order batsman. In 57 test matches he scored 1156 runs (average 16.28), took 167 catches and made 7 stumpings.

Trueman, Frederick Sewards, OBE. b Stainton, Yorkshire, 6 February 1931. d Leeds, Yorkshire, 1 July 2006. rhb. rf. He made his mark internationally in his first season for England in 1952 when he took 29 wickets in the series against India. An aggressive bowler with a high arm action, he enjoyed demoralising the opposition. He commanded line and length and used the bouncer, yorker and outswing as his weapons. With increasing television coverage of cricket in the 1950s, he became a national sports icon. Outspoken in his early playing days, he carried this trait into later life, combining it with a good memory and a natural sense of humour to become a respected radio commentator and after-dinner speaker. In 67 test matches, he scored 981 runs (average 13.81) and took 307 wickets (average 21.57) and was the first bowler to achieve 300 test wickets.

Other leading players: *1700-1750:* T. Waymark; S. Dingate. *1750-1800:* J. Aylward (lhb); W. Beldham (rhb; rm(u)); D. Harris (lhb); lf(u)); E. Stevens (Lumpy) (rhb. rm(u)). *1800-1835:* Rev Lord F. Beauclerk (rhb. rs(u)); W. Lambert (rhb. rs(u)); F.W. Lillywhite (rhb. rsm(r)); W. Ward (rhb). *1835-1860:* N. Felix (lhb. ls(u)); A. Mynn (rhb. rf(r)); F. Pilch (rhb. rs(r)); E.G. Wenman (rhb. wk). *1860-1890:* W. Caffyn (rhb. rm(r)); G. Parr (rhb); A. Shaw (rhb. rm/rs); E. Willsher (lhb. lf(r)). *1890-1914:* C Blythe (rhb, sla); C.B. Fry (rhb. rfm); G.A. Lohmann (rhb. rmf); A.C. MacLaren (rhb). *1920-1940:* H. Larwood (rhb. rf); W. Rhodes (rhb. sla); H. Sutcliffe (rhb); H. Verity (rhb. sla). *1945-1960:* K.F. Barrington (rhb. lb); A.V. Bedser (rhb. rmf); D.C.S. Compton (rhb. sla); P.B.H. May (rhb); J.B. Statham (lhb. rfm). *1960-1980:* G. Boycott (rhb); M.C. Cowdrey (rhb); A.P.E. Knott (rhb. wk); R.G.D. Willis (rhb. rf); D.L. Underwood (rhb. sla/lm). *1980-2000:* I.T. Botham (rhb. rfm); G.A. Gooch (rhb. rm); D.L. Gower (lhb); A.J. Stewart (rhb. wk). *Present day:* A. Flintoff (rhb. rfm); S.J. Harmison (rhb. rf); K.P. Pietersen (rhb; rob); M.S. Panesar (lhb. sla); M.E. Trescothick (lhb).
Women: *1920-1940:* E.A. Snowball (rhb). *1945-1960:* M.B. Duggan (rhb. sla/lmf); M.E. Hide (rhb. rm). *1960-1980:* R. Heyhoe-Flint (rhb). *1980-2000:* J.A. Brittin (rhb. rob); C.A. Hodges (rhb. rob); L. Nye (rhb. wk). *Present day:* C.M. Edwards (rhb. lb); J. Smit (rhb. wk); S.C. Taylor (rhb)

Playing record

Test Matches

	Won	Lost	Tied	Drawn
Australia	97	131	0	88
South Africa	54	26	0	50
West Indies	38	52	0	44
New Zealand	41	7	0	40
India	34	17	0	43
Pakistan	19	12	0	36
Sri Lanka	8	5	0	5
Zimbabwe	3	0	0	3
Bangladesh	4	0	0	0
Total	298	250	0	309

One-day matches

	Won	Lost	Tied	No Res
World Cup	36	22	0	1
Other ODI	190	200	4	14

Twenty20

1	3	0	0

Highest team score

903-7 dec	v Australia, The Oval	1938

Lowest team score

45	v Australia, Sydney	1886/87

Highest individual score

364	L. Hutton	v Australia, The Oval	1938

Best bowling

10-53	J.C. Laker	v Australia, Manchester	1956

Best wicket-keeping

7 (7c)	R.W. Taylor	v India, Mumbai	1979/80

Women

Test Matches

	Won	Lost	Tied	Drawn
Australia	7	10	0	25
South Africa	2	0	0	4
West Indies	2	0	0	1
New Zealand	6	0	0	17
India	1	1	0	10
Total	18	11	0	57

One-day matches

	Won	Lost	Tied	No Res
World Cup	37	19	2	2
European Championships	20	1	0	0
Other ODI	47	68	0	3

Twenty20

0	3	0	0

Highest team score

503-5 dec	v New Zealand, Christchurch	1934/35

Lowest team score

35	v Australia, Melbourne	1957/58

Highest individual score

189	E.A. Snowball	v New Zealand, Christchurch	1934/35

Best bowling

7-6	M.B. Duggan	v Australia, Melbourne	1957/58

Best wicket-keeping

8 (6c 2st)	L. Nye	v New Zealand, New Plymouth	1991/92

ESTONIA

THE ESTONIAN Cricket Association was formed in 1998. The national side comprises players from Britain, India and Finland as well as some Estonians. Fixtures are held against club sides in Helsinki, Riga and Stockholm. Four international matches were played against Finland in 2000, Estonia losing all of them easily. During the winter, six-a-side tournaments are held on the ice at Jeti Hall, on the site of the former Soviet missile factory, and on Lake Harku, attracting club sides from many European countries.

ETHIOPIA

CRICKET WAS once played regularly at the General Wingate School in Addis Ababa by the British and Indian teachers but when they left the country under the rule of General Mengistu, the game almost died out. However, matches are now played between the British and Indian embassies on a pitch of rolled earth at the Indian Embassy. Local rules are used because the ground is very small, allowing batting from only one end. The small size and high turnover of the expatriate community make it difficult to organise a larger programme of matches.

FALKLAND ISLANDS

AFTER THE First World War cricket was played in the Falkland Islands by the staff of the Wireless Telegraph Station. Matches were held against the local inhabitants and teams from visiting ships. When the Station closed in the 1920s, interest in cricket declined and the game virtually died out until the 1950s when it was revived by a small group of enthusiastic British officials. Regular matches were organised between four teams but these ceased when the Argentine invasion in 1982 destroyed the pitch and pavilion. The facilities were repaired and since 1998 an annual fixture has been held at the Mount Pleasant Oval between the Governor's XI and the British Forces. A national team played two matches in Chile in February 2004 against a Santiago Festival side but lost both heavily. The Falkland Islands were invited to compete in the South American Championships in December 2004 but the invitation was withdrawn to avoid any incident with Argentina which does not recognise the British sovereignty over the islands.

FIJI

Associate Member of ICC: elected 1965

ALTHOUGH INFORMAL games of cricket may have been played earlier by the passengers and crews of ships calling into Fiji on the Sydney to San Francisco route, organised cricket in Fiji started on 2 January 1874 when seventeen European gentlemen met at the then capital, Levuka, and formed a cricket club. On 21 February that year they played against the officers and crew of HMS *Pearl* on a very bumpy pitch at Vagadaci and beat them by an innings and 24 runs. Two further matches were played which Levuka lost. The enthusiasm of the European administrators and settlers for the game led rapidly to further matches against the crews of visiting ships and to inter-island fixtures. Cricket was, however, purely a recreational activity for European gentlemen and no attempt was made to introduce the game to the Fijians.

The situation changed under the Governorship of Sir George des Voeux between 1878 and 1886. Des Voeux was a keen cricketer and he appointed, as his private secretaries, Sir Jocelyn Amherst, another enthusiastic cricketer, and Sir Edward Wallington, who had gained a blue for Oxford University in 1877. These appointees started to coach Fijians who quickly developed an aptitude for the game, demonstrating considerable skill in fast-scoring batting and fast bowling. European administrative officers, particularly Sir Basil Thomson and Adolph Joske, spread the game to the distant islands where the Fijian chiefs were particularly supportive and keen to participate. As a result, cricket developed among the Fijian population as a village game with virtually every small settlement having an area of land where it could be played. In contrast, among the more urban European population of traders and businessmen, enthusiasm for cricket began to wane. By the 1880s, tennis had become the sport for recreation and, without maintenance, the ground and pavilion of Suva CC, at Albert Park, were allowed to decay.

The year 1890 marked the arrival in Fiji of J.S. Udal as Attorney General. John Udal had played for the MCC and was invited by W.G. Grace to go with his team to Australia in 1873 but he declined in order to complete his studies as a barrister. Once in Fiji, he immediately set about reorganising the game. He repaired the facilities at Albert Park and invited the Australians, under J.M. Blackham, to play there in March 1893 on their journey to England. Unfortunately, there was an outbreak of measles on board their ship which was quarantined and the passengers forbidden to land. Undeterred, Udal planned something more ambitious and set about arranging for a Fijian representative side to tour New Zealand. With the assistance of W.L. Allardyce, the Native Commissioner, he overcame local European resistance to the inclusion of Fijians in the side. The Europeans argued that to visit New Zealand would be an unsettling and corrupting influence on the young Fijian chiefs. The touring side, under Udal's captaincy, consisted of eight Europeans and six Fijians. Allardyce was prevented from going because he had to take charge of relief operations following a hurricane two weeks before the team's departure. Six of the eight matches played are rated as first-class.

Extremely Important

Following the departure of Udal in 1899 to take up the post of Chief Justice in Antigua, Fijian cricket went through a period of consolidation. The Australians finally visited in 1905 with M.A. Noble's side, on their way to England, beating eighteen of Fiji by 121 runs. Cricket continued to be extremely important to native Fijians and, in particular, to the chiefs on the small island of Bau, off the east coast of the main island of Viti Levu from which it is separated by an 800-metre long causeway. Only 8 hectares in size, 1.6 kilometres in circumference and no more than 320 metres wide in any direction, and with an adult male population of sixty, Bau was the focal point of native Fijian cricket in the early 1900s. Four of the touring party to New Zealand came from Bau and the island started to challenge the European clubs in Suva and Levuka. Under the leadership of Ratu Penaia Kadavulevu, enthusiasm developed for a tour of Australia. With the assistance of Lieutenant E.J. Mardsen, captain of the Victoria Army cricket team, resistance from the Australian Board of Control was overcome (see Country Profile for Australia). After Marsden provided assurances that all the Fijians would return home, the Melbourne Cricket Club agreed to underwrite the Victorian section of the tour and the other states then gave their support.

The tour took place between 11 December 1907 and 30 March 1908, the party comprising fifteen Fijians, including Kadavulevu as captain, and one European, Marsden. The team won five matches, drew sixteen and lost five. The venture did not lead to any long-term supremacy of Bau within Fijian cricket. As Kadavulevu got older and his administrative duties as Head of the Council of Chiefs and Inspector of Native Labourers increased, the island played fewer matches. Also, the next generation of Bauans showed less interest in the game.

The Australian touring parties returning from England in 1912 and on their way to Canada and the USA in 1913 stopped in Fiji but played only Suva CC, winning both matches easily. In the first game, Suva was represented by an entirely European team and in the second game, Ratu Pope Cakobau was the only Fijian. After the First World War, European and Fijian cricket became segregated, a situation which was unknown in Udal's and Marsden's time. The Europeans were increasingly concerned about standards and the need to find new talent. However, since there were only four European sides in Suva and they only played each other, there was no opportunity to improve. As a spur to young Europeans to take up the game, enthusiasts from Suva and Levuka financed a visit by a New Zealand side in 1924. Consisting mainly of players from Auckland, the New Zealanders played seven matches, winning five, including the two representative games against Fiji. The Fijian side was selected by Suva CC and was therefore entirely European. The only time the New Zealanders met native Fijians was when they drew a one-day fixture with Bau Island, a team which included six of the players who had toured Australia fifteen years earlier. Matches were also arranged against the Australians, on their way to tour Canada in 1932, and the MCC, returning home from Australia in 1933, but both were abandoned because of rain. The Fijian side selected to play the MCC would have included three native Fijians. In 1936, a New Zealand Universities team, calling themselves the Maorilanders, visited Fiji and played four matches. Fiji won the representative match by five wickets.

Whilst the standard of cricket amongst the European population continued to decline through the late 1920s and 1930s, the native Fijian game was hampered by a combination of poor, inconsistent wickets, and the great distances between the islands. The segregation of the game meant that whilst both Europeans and Fijians played at Albert Park, Suva CC had the use of the best wickets and the Fijians were relegated to the more dangerous pitches on the outskirts of the ground. Under these conditions it was difficult for the Fijian game to improve. Surprisingly, the Indian population of Fiji were not yet involved in cricket even though they made up a higher proportion of the population than either the Europeans or Fijians. Imported as labourers for the sugar cane estates, they were generally poor and not sporting-minded. It was not until their sons moved to the towns in the late 1930s and 1940s that the Indians started to feature in the game.

The history of Fijian cricket underwent a rapid change in 1938 with the arrival of Philip Snow as an Administrator. A former captain of Leicestershire Second Eleven, he was elected Secretary of Suva CC and immediately set about opening its membership to all communities. With the onset of multiracial cricket, standards rose, aided by the stationing of New Zealand Forces in Fiji in the 1940s, among them several cricketers with first-class experience.

Multiracial Basis

The Fijian Cricket Association was formed in 1946 to promote the game on a multiracial basis. One of their first ventures was to organise a tour of New Zealand in 1948. Snow led a side of eleven Fijians and six Europeans against all of the first-class provinces. Seventeen matches were played of which six were won, including the game against Wellington and the second fixture with Auckland, which was made possible by a delay to the flying boat on which the team returned to Fiji. Based on the high standards set by this team, another tour was arranged for 1954 with the matches against provincial sides being granted first-class status in advance. The equivalent games on the 1948 tour were granted first-class status retrospectively in 1987. Captained by Patrick Raddock, the 1954 team was less successful even though the best New Zealand players were on tour in South Africa. They won only one of the four matches against the major provinces.

Three of the Fijians from the 1948 and 1954 tours went on to hold high office. In 1970, Kamisese Mara became

Prime Minister of Fiji with Etuate Cakobau, the Deputy Prime Minister. When Jaoji Cakobau was appointed Governor-General in 1973, the top three administrative positions in the country were held by first-class cricketers, making Fiji unique in both cricket and world political history.

Further tours to New Zealand took place in 1961/62, 1967/68 and 1977/78 but these consisted of matches against only the minor associations. The standard of Fijian cricket, having reached its peak in 1948, was in decline. Fiji toured New South Wales in 1959/60, playing sixteen matches, mostly against local district sides. Ten of these games were won, including a one-day fixture against a New South Wales team. Such a one-off success could not, however, offset the fact that cricket in Fiji was losing popularity to rugby union, especially seven-a-side, and rugby league. Fewer people were playing the game and there were fewer grounds on which to play as Fiji's increasing population caused many village 'greens' to disappear under housing. Despite the country's attraction as a tourist destination, external interest in Fijian cricket was also less. Although visits were received from the West Indies in 1956, Pakistan in 1977 and India in 1981, no major cricketing country has played in Fiji since England in 1984. Fiji's international cricket has thus become confined to the ICC Trophy and competitions involving the South Pacific islands. All domestic and international cricket is now restricted to one-day limited overs matches. Since the mid 1990s, the Fiji Cricket Association has implemented coaching and development work, assisted by the New South Wales Cricket Association. By winning the East Asia Pacific Cup in 2006, Fiji qualified for Division 3 of the World Cricket League.

Famous Victory

February 27, 28 and March 1, 1948 – Basin Reserve, Wellington
Wellington 124 (Viliame Mataika 6-34) and 193 (A. McLean 73, R. Phillips 67, D.S. Wilson 54)
Fiji 171 (J.K. Cakobau 67*) and 250-9 (I.L. Bula 88)
Fiji won by 1 wicket

Viliame Mataika was virtually unplayable in Wellington's first innings bringing the ball sharply off the pitch into the batsman and making the occasional ball move the other way. Fiji also found run-making difficult but a fighting innings by Jaoji Cakobau helped them secure a

first-innings lead. Wellington played more confidently in their second innings with Ronald Phillips, Trevor Barber (34), David Wilson and Alan McLean all making useful contributions. Fiji fielded brilliantly, with Aisea Turuva bringing off a superb left-handed catch, a centimetre from the ground, to dismiss Robert Vance. Cakobau kept wicket during the innings following an injury to Patrick Raddock and made a spectacular one-handed catch above his head to dismiss McLean. Raddock then opened the batting but was dismissed quickly, after which Harry Apted (32) and Cakobau (38) gave support to Ilikena Bula who hit thirteen fours. In contrast, Fiji's captain, Philip Snow batted defiantly for one and a half hours for his seven runs. Turuva then hit the bowling hard, and then, out of the seventh wicket, a run was added. When Viliame joined Maurice Fenn for the last wicket, nineteen runs were still needed but, with the aid of an all-run five and many scrambled singles, and despite the confusion of Viliame batting with a runner because of an injury, the target was reached and the crowd of some 10,000 stood and applauded the whole Fijian team. Frank Mooney kept wicket superbly for Wellington, taking four catches and making two stumpings in the match.

Player Profiles

Bula, Ilikena Lasarusa. b Tobou 15 November 1921. rhb. A most attractive and flamboyant batsman, he based his stroke-making on forward play with exceptionally quick footwork and a propensity for hitting sixes using a strong pull drive. He was a Civil Servant by profession. In 16 matches for Fiji, he scored 1,045 runs (average 33.71).

Tuivanuavou, Ratu Wilikonisoni. rhb. rf. He was the leading strike bowler on Fiji's first tour to New Zealand in 1895. In six matches for Fiji, he scored 38 runs (average 4.75) and took 37 wickets (average 10.56).

Other leading players: *1890-1914:* Ratu P.E.S. Cakobau (rhb); J.C. Collins (rhb); J.S. Udal (rhb). *1920-1940:* Ratu E.T.T. Cakobau (rhb. rmob); V.S. Mataika (rhb. rmf); A. Turaga (lhb. lf). *1940-1960:* Ratu J.K. Cakobau (rhb. rm); M.J. Fenn (rhb. lb); P.T. Raddock (rhb. wk). *1960-1980:* N.M. Uluiviti (rhb. rm/rmob); F.L.C. Valentine (rhb. rmf). *Present day:*

N.D. Maxwell (rhb. rfm); J. Mateyawa (rhb. rmf); A. Tawatatau (rhb. lmf).

Playing record

	Won	Lost	Drawn
First-class matches*	5	8	2

One-day matches

	Won	Lost	No Res
ICC Trophy	13	27	4
South Pacific Games**	6	4	0
Asian Cricket Council Trophy	4	2	0
Pacifica Championships	5	4	0
East Asia Pacific Challenge	4	0	0
ICC Qualifying Competition	4	1	0
East Asia Pacific Cup	4	0	0

* matches against provincial sides on tours of New Zealand
** matches played in 1979 and 2003 competitions; detailed records of the 1987 and 1991 competitions have proved unobtainable

Highest team score

351-7	v Auckland, Auckland	1947/48

ODI

469-7	v Japan, Kuala Lumpur	1996

Lowest team score

50	v New Zealanders, Suva	1923/24

ODI

41	v Scotland, Toronto	2001

Highest individual score

128*	J.C. Collins	v Hawke's Bay, Napier	1894/95

ODI

150	J. Bulabalavu	v Japan, Kuala Lumpur	1996

Best bowling

8-62	P. Muspratt	v Pakistan, Lautoka	1976/77

Best wicket-keeping

5 (5c)	I.V. Tambualevu	v Otago, Dunedin	1967/68

FINLAND

Affiliate Member of ICC: elected 2000

CRICKET WAS played as a demonstration sport during the 1952 Olympic Games in Helsinki. Staff from the British Embassy combined with some British residents to make up a side which played against a team of British sailors on the sports field adjacent to the Olympic Stadium. The demonstration did not encourage the take-up of the sport, however, and the game was not played in Finland again until the 1960s when some matches were organised by the Palmerstons Society in Tapiola, a Helsinki suburb. This also proved a one-off venture. In 1974, some British and Australians formed the Helsinki Cricket Club. Efforts were made to spread the game more widely and in the 1990s two new clubs were formed in the Helsinki region and one in Turku. The Finnish Cricket Association (Suomen Krikettiliitto ry) was established in 1999 and this now organises a national league and a development programme in clubs and schools. A ladies team also exists, run by the club known as Stadin Krikkettikerho. About one-third of the cricketers in the country are Finnish citizens, the remainder being mainly long-term residents of British and Asian origin. International cricket started in 2000 when four matches, two at home and two away, were played against Estonia. All were won easily. Since then Finland has competed in various European tournaments with rather moderate results. Finland were the European Division 4 Champions in 2006.

Leading players: *Present day:* A.K. Bhatia; M.P. Moilanen.

Playing record

One-day matches

	Won	Lost	No Res
ECC Trophy	4	6	0
European Representative Championships	4	1	0
European Affiliates Championship	1	5	0
European Championships Division 4	2	1	0

Twenty20

	1	0	0

Highest team score

ODI

333-9	v Estonia, Helsinki	2000

Lowest team score

ODI

45	v Malta, Vienna	2001

Highest individual score

ODI

137*	M.P. Moilanen	v Bulgaria, Ljubljana	2004

Best bowling

ODI

5-10	S. Viola	v Cyprus, Brussels	2006

FRANCE

Affiliate Member of ICC: elected 1987
Associate Member of ICC: elected 1998

IN 1998 celebrations were held at Liettres, near Calais, to commemorate the 500th anniversary of what is claimed to be the first written record of cricket. The Archives Nationales include a petition from 1478 which states that 'Gunner Estievenet Le Grant left the castle in Liettres... and arrived at a spot where people were playing with a ball near a stake at *criquet*'. Although no direct relationship between *criquet* and cricket has been proven, in honour of the occasion, a plaque was unveiled, a street was renamed Allée du Criquet and a match was played between France and the Nord Pas 90 club which, suitably, the French won by 52 runs.

The first definitive mention of cricket in France was by Horace Walpole in 1766. He recorded seeing a match between some English and French aristocrats at Neuilly-sur-Seine, near Paris. The game must have been reasonably well-established in north-east France in the late eighteenth century otherwise the Duke of Dorset, whilst he was the British Ambassador in France, would not have attempted to arrange for a team of English cricketers from Paris to meet a side captained by William Yalden of Chertsey in July 1789. In the event, the French Revolution prevent the fixture from taking place (see Country Profile for England).

How quickly cricket restarted after the Revolution is not known. The next records relate to the game being played in Dieppe, Calais, Boulogne and St Omer in the 1820s and 1830s by lace-makers from Nottingham. However, when they returned to England in the 1840s, cricket in the region ceased. The game seems to have established a more permanent presence in Paris where an English cricket club is believed to have existed in 1829 and English residents there were certainly playing cricket in the 1840s. The first documented match, in 1864, was between Paris CC and the Warwickshire Knickerbockers, played in the Bois de Boulogne. In August that year, a team of English residents from Paris travelled to Bad Homburg and beat an English side from Prussia by an innings and 41 runs (see Country Profile for Germany). In 1892, a group of British businessmen founded the Standard Athletic Club and by the end of the century there were at least twelve clubs taking part in a regional championship, including the Sporting Athlétique Garrénois, an all-French side. By now, cricket had developed a sufficient following among the French upper class for it to be included in the Olympic Games when they were staged in Paris in 1900 (see Chapter 3).

French cricket continued to flourish in the early 1900s. International matches were started against Belgium in 1906 and were held annually until 1914. France competed in the triangular tournament held as part of the Brussels World Fair in 1910. The game revived fairly quickly after the First World War and in 1922 the Fédération Française de Cricket was formed. Although nominally a national body, it was naturally centred on Paris where most clubs existed. Throughout the 1920s and 1930s, cricket was played mostly at club level by expatriates with only the occasional international fixture against Belgium. This was an insufficient base from which to secure a long-term future. During the Second World War the majority of the clubs folded, never to revive. The ground at Bois de Meudon, where Standard Athletic had established a permanent home in 1922, was ploughed up and used for allotments. After the War, only the Standard Athletic club continued, reclaiming their ground in 1947 and playing matches against military teams from SHAPE and the Allied Forces Central Europe. A further blow to cricket occurred in 1966 when the French government decided to withdraw from NATO and their military personnel left the country.

Sudden Resurgence

JUST AS it looked as though cricket in France would die completely, there was a sudden resurgence of activity in the 1980s brought about by the arrival of Asian immigrants. Their enthusiasm encouraged British residents and new clubs were started not only in the Paris region and the north-east but also in the south and west. With cricket being played more widely, the Fédération Française de Cricket was reformed in 1987. In 1989 it merged with the Fédération Française de Baseball et Softball in order to secure state funding. A national side was selected to play the MCC at the Bois de Meudon in 1989 to celebrate the centenary of the match which the Duke of Dorset organised but never happened. France gained a surprise victory by seven wickets, though this was largely due to an innings of 73 not out by John Short, the Irish international. Essex played France in 1991 to mark the opening of a new ground at Château de Thoiry and Nottinghamshire came in 1993 to celebrate the establishment of the first grass wicket in France at Saumur. International matches were restarted with Belgium in 1991 and France has competed regularly in European tournaments and, in 2001, in the ICC Trophy. Although made up largely of British and Asian expatriates, the team includes the brothers Guy and Valentin Brumant from Guadeloupe, in the French West Indies, and Arun Ayyavooraju, born in Pondicherry in former French India.

Frustrated

In October 1997, France Cricket was founded as the new ruling body for the game but affiliated to the FFBS. Considerable effort has since been placed on development, particularly at junior level. In its encouragement of youth, France has been frustrated by the various rules of the ICC and the European Cricket Council. In 1999, Matthieu Royant played as a twelve-year-old for the French senior side against Denmark but was then barred from playing against Israel in the Quadrangular tournament in Gibraltar as being too young. France refused to change their team and Israel were awarded the game on a walkover. Also in 1999, a fifteen-year-old leg spin bowler, Cindy Paquin, was picked for the French squad for the European Colts Championships. The ECC would not allow her to play because of a possible risk of physical injury to female players in an otherwise male tournament.

When France refused to alter their squad, they were barred from the tournament. Cindy Paquin has since been allowed to represent France in the European Indoor and the European Under 21 Championships. Whether she will be able to play for the national side in an official ICC Tournament remains to be seen. Since another promising female, Laura Codrons, played for France in the European Under 13 tournament in 2002 there is an obvious need for France Cricket to establish a ladies international team. Whether this will be possible

is likely to depend on funding. At present the future development of cricket in France is uncertain because in 2004 the state subsidy to the game fell to its lowest level since it started in 1987.

Famous Victory
August 23, 1997 – Lyceum Alpinum, Zuoz
France 267 (49.5 overs) (G. Brumant 42, S. Palmer 35, S.M. Hewitt 31, Saeed 3-61)
Germany 266 (50 overs) (Shamasuddin Khan 45, A. Dar 45, Younis Khan 44, T. Rathore 32)
France won by 1 run

Batting first in this final of the European Nations Cup, France obtained a competitive total, aided by 67 extras which included 33 wides. On the penultimate ball of the innings, the French number eleven, David Bordes, was hit on the head by a bouncer from Saeed but struggled through to complete a leg bye before collapsing with a fractured skull. The importance of this run did not become clear until the last ball of the match when Germany, despite the assistance of 58 extras which included 26 wides and 22 no balls, fell one run short. Their number ten, B. Patzwald, going for the winning hit missed the ball and was stumped by Shabbir Hussain. Bordes spent two weeks in hospital but was able to resume indoor cricket before Christmas.

Player profile
Hewitt, Simon Mark. b Radcliffe, Lancashire, 30 July 1961. rhb. rm. Before settling in France, he played four first-class matches for Oxford University in 1984. Between France's revival in the late 1980s and when he retired after the ICC Trophy in 2001 to become the national coach, he played in every international fixture. In 4 international matches he scored 71 runs (average 14.20) and took 8 wickets (average 24.37). In 25 limited overs matches he made 526 runs (average 22.86) and took 28 wickets (average 22.78).

Other leading players: *1890-1914:* M. Kellerman. *Present day:* A.V. Ayyavooraju (rhb. rm); Shabbir Hussain (rhb).

Playing record
One-day matches

	Won	Lost	No Res
ICC Trophy	1	4	0

European Championships	10	12	1
Quadrangular Tournament	2	2	0

Highest team score

296	v Italy, Château Thoiry	1991

ODI

330-6	v Switzerland, Geneva	2000

Lowest team score

33	v Belgium, Paris	1911

Highest individual score

74	S.W. Shahzada	v Italy, Château Thoiry	1991
74	M. Hafiz	v MCC, Château Thoiry	1995
74	N. Jones	v MCC, Château Thoiry	1995

ODI

162	S.M. Hewitt	v Luxembourg, Walferdange	2000

Best bowling

7-27	M. Kellermann	v Belgium, Paris	1911

Best wicket-keeping

ODI

5 (4c 1st)	Shabbir Hussain	v Switzerland, Zuoz	1997

GAMBIA

Affiliate Member of the ICC: elected 2002

CRICKET WAS rather late arriving in The Gambia since it was the 1920s before the Europeans started establishing clubs and organising matches. Nevertheless, rapid progress was made and international matches began against Sierra Leone in 1927. The small European population and the distance from other West African countries where cricket was played limited the development of the game which remained a minority interest among Europeans and a small number of middle and upper class Africans. Following independence in 1963, the new government took little interest in the game. Many Europeans departed and, not surprisingly, standards fell. When the MCC visited during their tour of West Africa in 1975, they won a two-day game by an innings and 65 runs and the one-day limited overs match by 116 runs. The Gambia became part of the West African Cricket Conference in 1976 but the country was always the weakest of the four member states and few of their players were good enough to represent West Africa in the ICC Trophy. Participation in the West African Quadrangular Tournament which started in 1991 was sufficient to keep the game alive but by the late 1990s,

cricket was low in popularity and facilities were poor and few. Many pitches had been dug up and turned into soccer grounds. Domestic cricket was reduced to two teams. Nevertheless, The Gambia was able to host the West African tournament in 2000 and 2004. Finance and a major development programme will be needed if the game is to survive.

Leading player: *Present day:* P. Johnson (rhb. rm).

Playing record

One-day matches

	Won	Lost	No Res
ICC African Affiliates	0	4	0
African Championships Division 3	2	3	0

Highest team score

233	v Nigeria, Banjul	1903/04

Lowest team score

41	v MCC, Banjul	1975/76

Highest individual score

66*	M.A. Saar	v Nigeria, Banjul	1967

Best bowling

5-35	M. Kah	v Nigeria, Banjul	1967

ODI

5-25	P. Johnson	v Mozambique, Benoni	2003/04

Best wicket-keeping

ODI

5 (5c)	M. Kamara	v Mozambique, Benoni	2003/04

GERMANY

Affiliate Member of ICC: elected 1991
Associate Member of ICC: elected 1999

THE FIRST definitive mention of cricket in Germany is in 1858 when a group of British and American residents formed a club in Berlin. The sport was gradually taken up by British, American, Australian and Danish residents and by the 1880s it was an important minority recreational activity in the Berlin region. Berlin Cricket Club was established in 1883, followed by the other Berlin-based clubs of Frankfurt in 1885, Germania in 1888 and Victoria and Stern in 1889. By 1907, the Britannia and Preussen clubs had arisen and the seven teams were competing in the Berlin Cricket League. With more clubs being formed, the League had increased to fourteen teams by 1914. With the exception of the Berlin Club, all the teams were wings of football clubs and it was not unusual for the leading players to be participants of both sports. In 1913 the club officials came together and founded the Deutsche Cricket Bund as an overall body responsible for the game in Berlin, Nürnberg, Fürth, Düsseldorf, Mannheim and Hamburg. The body lasted only a few years, however, and had disappeared by the end of the First World War. The first international match, loosely termed Prussia versus France, took place on 10 August 1864 when a team of English cricketers from the Paris Cricket Club met an English side drawn from the Frankfurt Club and English residents in Homburg. The match was played in the grounds of the Kurhaus in Bad Homburg and the French won by an innings and 41 runs.

Cricket recovered quickly after 1918. The presence of the British Army of the Rhine added to the game by attracting touring clubs from England, The Netherlands and Denmark who then included several German clubs in their itineraries. Cricket was no longer the preserve of expatriates. It was taken up by German nationals. In August 1930 a team drawn from the clubs in Berlin and known as the United Berliners toured England. Captained by Guido Menzel and including his brother, Felix, the leading German players of the period, the team comprised twelve Germans and an Indian student from Bombay, W.R. Kirloskar. In the side were A. Schmidt, who was the goalkeeper in the German ice-hockey team for 27 years, and Pastor Harold Pölchau who became a member of the anti-Nazi Kreisau Group and was awarded the Medal of the Just by the Israeli government for his work during the Hitler regime. The strongest English side to visit Germany was the Gentlemen of Worcestershire who played two matches in Berlin in August 1937. Since they included five players with first-class cricket experience, it was not surprising that they won both matches easily. The tour only emphasized the rather low standard of play by the local cricketers.

The Second World War almost witnessed the demise of cricket in Germany. By 1945, most of the grounds had been destroyed, there was no equipment and most of the players had either left the country or become too old to take up the game again. With assistance from the British Army, the Berlin, Germania, Preussen and Victoria clubs restarted and, under the leadership of Kurt Rietz who had played for Berlin against Worcestershire, the Berlin League was revived. However, very few Germans were involved and the game was almost entirely confined to service personnel and British civilians. With the construction of the Berlin Wall in 1961, many expatriate players left Berlin and the number of clubs dropped first to two and then to one. However, during the 1960s, Indian and Pakistani students started the game in various German universities both in West Germany and Berlin. They encouraged their fellow German students to play and by the 1980s a small but thriving cricket-playing community had emerged. New clubs were formed comprising expatriates, German businessmen and university students. A new Deutscher Cricket Bund was formed in 1988 and international contests were started in 1989 with two matches away to Denmark in which Germany were easily defeated. Germany won the ECF Nations Cup when it was held at Worksop, England, in 1992 and were rewarded with a match against the MCC at Lord's. The German side did well, holding out for a draw. Germany won Division 2 of the European Championships in 2002.

Famous Victory
July 18, 1998 – Craeyenhout, The Hague
Germany 265-8 dec (50 overs) (M. Brodersen 104*, Shamasuddin Khan 40, Zaheer Ahmed 40, D.J. Johnson 3-32)
Gibraltar 165 (41.2 overs) (D.J. Johnson 50)
Germany won by 100 runs

Germany obtained their first victory over an associate country in this European Championships Division B fixture. They owed much to Marc Brodersen who became the first German born cricketer to score a century in international cricket. With the aid of Shamasuddin Khan, Abdul Salam Bhatti (23), A. Dar (26) and Zaheer Ahmed, they reached a defendable total despite the efforts of Daniel Johnson who took his three wickets for only 32 runs in nine overs. Johnson was again prominent in Gibraltar's reply but only Nigel Churaman (22) and David Robeson (20) gave any support. Hamid Bhatti (2-42) dismissed both openers with only 30 runs on the board, after which the wickets were shared between J. Kruger, Zaheer Ahmed and Tayyab Rathore (one each) and Gerrit Müller (two). Gibraltar contributed to their defeat with three of their batsmen being run out.

Player Profiles

Bhatti, Abdul Hamid. b Mianwala, Punjab, Pakistan, 20 September 1965. lhb. rfm. A regular member of the German team between 1993 and 2004, he bowled from wide of the crease, aiming on or just outside off-stump and making the ball swing away from the bat. He had a slinging action and owed his pace to his powerful shoulders. He was a free-scoring batsmen in the middle order. Few of his innings did not contain at least one hit for six. In 28 limited overs internationals he scored 410 runs (average 19.52) and took 37 wickets (average 20.24).

Menzel, Felix. rhb. rm. The leading German player of the 1930s, he could bowl for long periods of time, just short of a length on the leg stump, to a strongly-set leg-side field. On a United Berlin tour of England in 1930 he took 24 wickets at an average of 6.04 against club sides and was very successful against the visiting teams of the Gentlemen of Worcestershire, Somerset Wanderers and various Danish sides, sometimes as captain. He had an astute cricket brain and was rated as about Minor Counties standard. After the Second World War, he was instrumental in getting cricket restarted in Germany.

Other leading players: *1920-1940:* G. Menzel (rhb. rm). *1980-2000:* G. Müller (rhb); Abdul Salam Bhatti (rhb). *Present day:* M. Ayub Pasha (rhb. wk); Rana Javed Igbal.

Playing record

One-day matches

	Won	Lost	No Res
ICC Trophy	1	2	0
European Championships	16	8	0

Highest team score
ODI
467-1   v Switzerland, Zuoz   1997

Lowest team score
ODI
58   v Austria, Vienna   1991

Highest individual score
ODI
200*   Shamasuddin Khan   v Switzerland, Zuoz   1997

Best bowling
ODI
6-24   Farooq Ahmed   v Gibraltar, Bready   2002

Best wicket-keeping
ODI
5 (3c 2st)   Ayub Pasha   v Portugal, Belfast   2002
5 (2c 3st)   Ayub Pasha   v Guernsey, Glasgow   2006

GHANA

Affiliate Member of ICC: elected 2002

BRITISH MILITARY personnel and businessmen introduced cricket into Ghana in the late nineteenth century. By the 1880s the game was being played in Accra by the British as a recreational activity and was being taken up enthusiastically by some of the local African population. Regular contact by the British between Accra and Lagos in Nigeria led to international matches between the Gold Coast and Lagos starting in 1904. A leading role was played by Frederick Guggisberg, a military engineer, who was in the country carrying out surveying work. A keen all-round cricketer, he encouraged the game amongst both the Europeans and the Africans. In common with all recreational and sporting activity of the time, cricket was segregated, however, but with the Africans being as enthusiastic as the Europeans they started their own international matches with Nigeria in 1907.

In 1919, Guggisberg returned to the Gold Coast as Governor, a position he held until 1927. During his period of office, he promoted cricket in schools especially among the African population. By overseeing the development of transport links, particularly the railways, he also provided the opportunity for contacts between Europeans and educated Africans in towns outside of Accra. In this way cricket started in Kumasi, in the north. In 1939, the international match with Nigeria was staged in Kumasi, the first time it had been played in the Gold Coast outside of Accra. Also in that year, the Gold Coast played a three-day fixture there against Rhodesia. Working with Shenton Thomas, his counterpart in Nigeria, Guggisberg helped re-establish the international series with Nigeria after the First World War, beginning in 1925 for the European matches and

1926 for the Africans. Both series continued annually until 1939. The military and colonial services attracted many first-class amateur cricketers among the European players. Whilst Nigeria were the more successful team in the European matches, Gold Coast generally won the African contests.

After the Second World War, cricket revived quite quickly and the game continued to develop, particularly among the Africans. European international matches with Nigeria resumed in 1947 and the African matches started again in 1949. The Europeans relied strongly on cricketers who had represented the Gold Coast in the late 1930s. Younger players were largely from military personnel on short-term postings. In contrast, the African side became a blend of experience and youth. In 1956, segregated cricket ended and the subsequent contests with Nigeria involved mixed European and African sides. As the European population declined in numbers following independence in 1957, the Ghanaian team became increasingly an African one. With the decline in the Ghanaian economy in the late 1960s and through the 1970s, less money was available to support cricket and the government showed little interest in promoting the game. Cricket began to suffer from the increasing popularity of soccer. Although in 1973 Ghana became the first West African country to play outside of West Africa when they toured Kenya, Tanzania and Uganda, standards were falling and the game was in decline. Some interest was revived with the establishment of the West African Cricket Conference in 1975 which was followed by a visit of the MCC in 1976. Problems of organising cricket at a West African level, however, meant that the WACC was not been able to reverse the decline. Although Ghana has competed regularly in the annual West African Quadrangular Tournament, the playing base from which to select an international side has become quite small. By 2000, the major cricket league comprised only four teams. Whether the expatriate European and Asian population is large enough to bring about a revival of the game is in doubt. The future of cricket in Ghana remains uncertain.

Leading players: *1890-1914:* Brig-Gen Sir F.G. Guggisberg. *1920-1940:* L.S. Gruchy; C.D.A. Pullan; H. Vane-Percy (alias H.V. Baumgartner). *1945-1960:* J.B. Fleischer; J.J. Janney. *Present day:* F.K. Bakiyewem (rhb); P.K. Ananya (rhb. rfm).

Playing record
International matches

	Won	Lost	Drawn
Europeans v Nigeria*	8	12	7
Africans v Nigeria†	10	5	3
Combined European and African v Nigeria‡	3	4	2

* matches played between 1904 and 1955
† matches played between 1907 and 1955
‡ matches played between 1956 and 1964

One-day matches

	Won	Lost	No Res
ICC African Affiliates	3	2	0
African Championships Division 3	3	2	0

Highest team score

423-6 dec	Gold Coast v Lagos, Lagos		1925

Lowest team score

39	Gold Coast v Lagos, Accra		1905

ODI

18	Ghana v South African Country Districts, Benoni 2003/04		

Highest individual score

173	W.R. Gosling	Gold Coast v Lagos, Lagos1924/25	

Best bowling

7-28	J.B. Fleischer	Gold Coast (Africans) v Nigeria (Africans), Lagos	1948

ODI

7-25	P.K. Ananya	Ghana v Malawi, Benoni	2005/06

GIBRALTAR

Associate Member of the ICC: elected 1969

CRICKET WAS probably first played in Gibraltar by the British military in the late eighteenth century. Although the British presence dates to 1704, it is unlikely that cricket started earlier than 1783 when the four-year long Great Siege came to an end. The first record of cricket is not until 1822 when the *Gibraltar Chronicle and Commercial Intelligencer* reported that the next game by Gibraltar Cricket Club would take place on 6 July on the Neutral Ground, land which once included a racecourse but which was taken over by the airfield and associated Royal Air Force buildings during the Second World War. Both civilians and the military were clearly playing cricket by this time because, one week later, the Civilians challenged the Officers to a match. Shortly after, the military formed the Garrison Cricket Club and the civilians, the Calpe Cricket Club which in 1858 became the Gibraltar Cricket Club.

The first cricket match against an overseas team occurred literally by accident. In April 1890, W.L. Murdoch's Australian cricket team called into Gibraltar on their way to England for their summer tour but their liner, the *Liguria*, collided with two other ships whilst entering the harbour. Whilst repairs were being carried out, the Australians played a one-day match against The Garrison. Despite batting seventeen, the Garrison had no answer to the speed of C.T.B. Turner (9-15) and J.J. Ferris (5-10) and were dismissed for 25. Australia then made 150 for the loss of eight wickets by the close, Briscoe taking four wickets for 49 runs. Following this encounter, Gibraltan cricket remained isolated for twenty-seven years. Nevertheless, standards slowly improved and some of the local-born population began to play and join Gibraltar CC. Visits were made by The Cryptics CC in 1927, H.D.G. Leveson-Gower's side in 1932 and a team raised by G.O.B. Allen in 1935. All played matches against The Rock, as the combined civilian and military team was known. The late 1930s saw Gibraltar travel overseas to play matches in Portugal against British residents in Lisbon and Oporto. Before any return visits could be organised, the Second World War intervened and cricket in Gibraltar ceased.

After the War, Gibraltar CC moved to a new ground, the Victoria Stadium, next to the airfield. Matches between GCC and the Combined Services started, new civilian cricket clubs were formed and visits from British county and club sides became more regular. The need for an overall organising body for civilian cricket was recognised and, in 1960, the Gibraltar Cricket Association was formed. With the cut back in the size of the British military personnel stationed in Gibraltar, the future of cricket became more dependent on the local population. Unfortunately, cricket stopped being taught in schools in the 1960s. Gibraltar intended to take part in the inaugural ICC Trophy competition in 1969 but had to withdraw because the dates clashed with a hockey competition for which several players were required. The need to meet ICC's eligibility criteria weakened the teams which competed in the ICC Trophy throughout the 1980s and 1990s. However, the 1980s saw cricket re-introduced into secondary schools and a youth development programme was initiated. In 1992 Gibraltar played their first home international against

another associate country, losing a one-day 40 overs game to Israel by 3 wickets. In 1999 they hosted a Quadrangular Tournament involving Israel, Italy and France, losing in the final to Italy by 3 wickets. With the availability of television coverage of test cricket, there is now much greater awareness of the game and more encouragement for people to play. The standard has risen and Gibraltar no longer has difficulty fielding teams which meet the ICC regulations. In 2000, Gibraltar won the B Division of the European Championships and then retained the title in 2002. In 2004, they finished runners-up to Italy but in 2006 they were a disappointing fourth.

Leading players: *1920-1940:* J. Hayward Jnr; J. Balbuena. *1980-2000:* G.M. De'ath (rhb. sla). *Present day:* C.M. Rocca (rhb); R.J. Buzaglo (rhb. wk).

Playing record
One-day matches

	Won	Lost	No Res
ICC Trophy	6	26	5
European Championships	13	14	0
Quadrangular Tournament	2	2	0

Highest team score

353-8 dec	The Rock v H.D.G. Leveson-Gower's XI, Gibraltar	1932	

Lowest team score
ODI

44	v Kenya, Kuala Lumpur	1996/97	

Highest individual score

114	J.Balbuena	The Rock v H.D.G. Leveson-Gower's XI, Gibraltar	1932

Best bowling
ODI

5-14	N. Churaman	v Israel, Kuala Lumpur	1996/97

Best wicket-keeping
ODI

7 (6c 1st)	R.J. Buzaglo	v France, Waterloo	2004

GREECE

Affiliate Member of ICC: elected 1995

THE BRITISH garrison were probably playing cricket on Corfu shortly after they had taken over the island from the French in 1814 following the defeat of Napoleon at the Battle of Leipzig. In his *Memoirs with the 32nd Foot*, Major H.R. Lewin refers to cricket being played on the Esplanade, in Corfu Town, on 23 April 1823. The matches between the Garrison and the crews of passing British ships were undoubtedly watched by the local population. What exactly encouraged them to try the game for themselves will probably never be understood but by 1835 two local clubs were in existence, the Megaloi (Big) Team, consisting of members of the nobility and well-to-do, and the Microi (Small) Team, drawn from the rest of the population, though it is likely that this comprised artisans and other reasonably well-educated people rather than farmers and labourers. The birth of Greek cricket thus took place in the 1830s in Corfu, well before the local inhabitants of many better-known cricketing countries had been introduced to the game. The game first played on Corfu was therefore one where curved bats were still in use and most bowling was underarm. The local sides played each other and organised matches against The Garrison, the Royal Navy and teams made up of foreign residents. The matches against visiting teams were important since they gradually introduced to Corfiot cricket round-arm and, later, over-arm bowling.

By the time the British left when the island was handed over to Greece in 1864, cricket was well-established among the local population. Matches between the Megaloi and Microi continued and games were regularly organised against visiting ships of the Mediterranean Fleet. The Megaloi Team evolved into two clubs, the Gongakis Company and the Kamvisis Club. But by the 1890s, the number of active players in Corfu had decreased so that it was necessary to merge the clubs into one, the Gymnastikos, formed in 1893, and widen the membership. Matches were now confined to occasional games against ships of the Royal Navy. The ground at the Esplanade was allowed to deteriorate with the grass giving way to a surface of bare earth liberally sprinkled with stones. Sufficient interest was retained to organise an annual cricket festival.

After the First World War, cricket underwent a revival. In 1923, the Ergatikos (Artisans) Club was formed, taking over the mantle of The Microi. In 1930 it was renamed the Byron Club and membership was opened to the aristocracy. Since that time, there has been intense rivalry between Gymnastikos and Byron. Otherwise cricket between the two World Wars continued as

before with matches against the Mediterranean Fleet, usually during the cricket week, being the only external contacts.

The Second World War nearly saw the demise of Corfiot cricket as the island was occupied by the Italians and then the Germans. Although the cricket ground escaped damage, all equipment was destroyed and only a few players remained. Fortunately, among the British Military Mission which arrived in Corfu in 1946, were Major George Laing and Major Guy Thorneycroft, two keen army cricketers. They organised equipment and started coaching sessions. Matches between Gymnastikos and Byron resumed and fixtures against sides from The Royal Navy restarted. The cricket revival was short-lived, however, because with the worsening relations between Great Britain and Greece over Cyprus in the late 1950s visits of the Mediterranean Fleet were suspended.

Star-studded

Another rescue act was needed. It came through Major John Forte, the British Vice-Consul in Corfu, who set up an appeal through readers of the *Daily Telegraph* to save cricket on the island. The response produced about £400 worth of equipment and enough publicity to establish Corfu as a suitable touring venue for British clubs. Ron Roberts included it in his itinerary in 1962 for his world tour with a star-studded international side of test cricketers. By 1966 as many as seventeen different teams from Britain were visiting Corfu each season. The Anglo-Corfiot Cricket Association was founded in 1970 with the remit of encouraging cricket on the island. This was later reformed into the Corfu Cricket Technical Committee which became a member of the Greek Federation for Amateur Sport (SEGAS), thereby securing government funding from the Greek Ministry of Sport.

Greece took part in the European Cricketer Cup in Guernsey in 1990, winning two out of their five games, and then participated regularly in the European Nations Cup organised by the European Cricket Federation. In 1996, the Hellenic Cricket Federation was formed with responsibility for cricket throughout Greece. The national side was no longer all Greek but included a new generation of players of Asian origin, based in

Athens. By winning all their matches when they hosted the ECC Trophy in Corfu in 1999, Greece qualified for the B Division of the European Championships in Scotland in 2000 in which they were outclassed. In 2005, Greece finished second in the European Affiliates Championships in Belgium and qualified for Division 2 of the European Championships in 2006. They won all their first round matches before running into conflict with the ICC regarding the eligibility of non-resident players with Greek citizenship. The team had all their points deducted and returned home, accepting relegation to Division 3 rather than contest the relegation play-off match.

Leading players: *1890-1914:* P. Paramithiotis. *1920-1970:* P. Iselos (rhb. rs). *1975-1980:* P. Kontos, G. Scourtis; S. Goustis. *1980-2000:* Sadiq Mehmood; Sajjad Anjum; C. Vassilas (rhb. wk). *Present day:* A. Koutsoufis; A. Manousis; P. Maraziotis (rhb).

Playing record
One-day matches

	Won	Lost	No Res
European Championships Div 2	3*	6	1
ECC Trophy	12	4	0
European Affiliates	4	2	0

* Although Greece won three matches, they were all awarded to the opposition after Greece were penalised for fielding ineligible players.

Highest team score
ODI

377-5	v Luxembourg, Vienna	2003

Lowest team score
ODI

75	v Guernsey, Guernsey	1990

Highest individual score
ODI

150	Sadiq Mehmood	v Croatia, Vienna	2001

Best bowling
ODI

5-8	Mehmood Ahmed	v Belgium, Antwerp	2005

GUERNSEY

Affiliate Member of the ICC: elected 2005

FEW RECORDS exist of early cricket in Guernsey. In 1813, a combined team from Guernsey and Alderney were defeated by Jersey by an innings. By the time Elizabeth College began its regular series of fixtures with Victoria College, Jersey, in 1862, the game was certainly well-established, probably in part as a result of fixtures between the local population and the British Garrison. In 1867 the United All England Eleven visited the island. From the early 1900s, matches were regularly organised against touring sides from England, some of which like the Cryptics, Incogniti and the MCC were of reasonable strength. Cricket declined during the 1939-45 War when the island was under German occupation but a few local enthusiasts managed to organise some matches and, more importantly, protect the wicket on the King George V ground of Elizabeth College. The Guernsey Island Cricket Association was formed in 1927. In addition to organising the island's weekend and evening cricket leagues and helping touring sides with their visits, it runs a development programme involving some 1,200 children each year and arranges the island's international fixtures. Since 1957, there has been an annual two-day fixture against Jersey in which Guernsey has been victorious in 15 of the 48 matches played, with 12 of the matches drawn. Guernsey hosted and won the European Cricketers Cup in 1990. They competed in Division 2 of the European Championships in 2006, finishing fifth. Since 2000, Guernsey has had a ladies club. Known as the Sirens, it has a regular squad of fifteen players and competes in Division 2 of the island league. It also runs an Under 11 squad, known as the Sirenettes.

Cricket is played on two of the other islands of the Bailliwick of Guernsey. Alderney and Sark have regular fixtures against club sides from England. They also play each other twice a year, home and away.

Leading players: *Present day:* L. Savident (rhb. rm); A. Banerjee (rhb. rm).

Playing record
One-day matches

	Won	Lost	No Res
European Championships Div 4	4	1	0

Highest team score
ODI

308-5	v France, Glasgow	2006

Lowest team score
ODI

131	v Greece, Prestwick	2006

Highest individual score
ODI

136	L. Savident	v France, Glasgow	2006

Best bowling
ODI

5-23	P.J.A. Moody	v Israel, Lossiemouth	2006

Best wicket-keeping
ODI

4 (4c)	M. Oliver	v Israel, Lossiemouth	2006

HONG KONG

Associate Member of ICC: elected 1969

THE FIRST record of cricket in Hong Kong is in 1841, one year before the island was ceded to Great Britain by the Treaty of Nanking in 1842. In 1846 the British Garrison drained an area at Wiang La Chung, now known as Wong Nai Chung, in the Happy Valley to construct a cricket ground and a racecourse. As Hong Kong developed into a thriving port, civilian numbers increased and there was a demand for additional facilities beyond those used by the military. Even though, excluding service personnel, there were only 776 Europeans in 1853, and they were spread amongst the officials of the civil service, businessmen in the trading companies or Hongs, and the professional classes of teachers and lawyers, there was sufficient enthusiasm to organise cricket. In 1851 the Hong Kong Cricket Club was formed. The military reluctantly agreed to a government proposal to convert their parade ground on the seafront alongside Chater Road into an area for public recreation. The concept of public use, however, was restricted to three sections of Hong Kong's society, namely the civil service, tradespeople and the military. The area was turfed and used by the Hong Kong CC to which membership, though theoretically open, was restricted by virtue of prospective members having to be elected by a ballot of the existing membership.

The Hong Kong CC organised matches between its own members and against service teams. These eventually led to triangular tournaments between the club, the Army and the Navy. Although the numbers recruited were small, the establishment in 1861 of a career civil service for Hong Kong encouraged young men from public school and university backgrounds to the colony, some of whom had first-class or minor counties cricket experience. Through trading contacts with their counterparts in Shanghai, the businessmen who ran Hong Kong CC established relationships with Shanghai Cricket Club. These led to the series of matches known as the Interports. The first match was at Chater Road in 1866 when Hong Kong easily beat the Shanghai side by an innings and 264 runs. The following year saw the return fixture in Shanghai which Hong Kong lost by an innings and 36 runs. There is no doubt that the performance of the visiting side was strongly affected by the long sea voyage. Since the journey took 56 hours each way, the match required the players of the visiting team to be away from business or military duties for several weeks. As a result, the team was often not the best that could have been selected. Thirty-two years were to elapse before the third match was played in 1889. In 1890, the concept of the Interports was extended when a team from the Straits Settlements visited Hong Kong.

The hazards of sea journeys for these international fixtures were all too vividly demonstrated on 10 October 1892 when the SS *Bohkara*, carrying the Hong Kong team home from Shanghai sank near Sand Island in the Pescadores during a typhoon. Out of 148 passengers, 125 drowned. Only two members of the thirteen-man cricket team survived, Dr J.A. Lowson and Lt F.D. Markham. In memory of the cricketers who perished, a bronze plaque was erected in St John's Cathedral by members of the Shanghai Cricket Club. Following the tragedy, the Interport matches did not start again until 1897.

By the end of the nineteenth century, additional civilian cricket clubs had been formed and cricket introduced into the leading boys schools, particularly the Diocesan Boys' School, Queen's College, St Joseph's College and the Victoria English School. In 1912, the University of Hong Kong was founded and their cricket club was formed in November of that year. With the extension of Hong Kong into the New Territories, Kowloon Cricket Club was founded in 1904. A cricket league was started in the 1903/04 season. The quality of play rose and by the onset of the First World War must have been close to first-class county standard.

During the 1914-18 War, cricket was restricted to a small number of friendly matches but the game expanded very rapidly after 1919. International matches with Shanghai and Malaya restarted in 1920. A stable civilian population allowed the national side to be built around a core of good players, supplemented by the best of the military cricketers on short-term spells of duty. Although cricket during the 1920s and 1930s was largely segregated at club level by ethnic background, the national side was multiracial. A.A.A. Rumjahn, from Hong Kong University and the Indian Recreation Club was the first non-European to represent Hong Kong.

Cricket was seriously affected by the impending 1939-45 War as businessmen and service personnel left the colony to return to England. During their occupation, the Japanese took over many of the cricket grounds for stabling horses and mules. The club houses and their furniture were destroyed, anything wooden being broken up and used for firewood. Three of Hong Kong's international players, Tam Pearce, Ernest Fincher and Donald Anderson, lost their lives in the Battle for Hong Kong against the Japanese Imperial Forces in December 1941. Although two naval teams played a cricket match at Chater Road in September 1945, it took several years for most clubs to repair their facilities after the War and obtain new equipment. International matches resumed in November 1947 when Hong Kong met Shanghai at Chater Road. After the return match in Shanghai the following year, the Shanghai club folded. Interport fixtures were thereafter confined to matches against Malaya, eventually turning into separate series against Malaysia and Singapore. These continued until 1987 when a combination of enthusiasm for one-day matches and a much larger international programme by all three countries saw an end to two-innings Interports.

The 1950s and 1960s produced a succession of strong touring sides visiting the colony. Starting with Jack Chegwyn's team of Australian test players in 1952, they included Ron Robert's Commonwealth (1962), E.W. Swanton's team (1964), Worcestershire (1965), the MCC (1966), the Cricket Club of India (1967) and J. Lister's International Team (1968). Although, as expected, Hong Kong were generally beaten, they were by no means outclassed. The standard of play remained high, strengthened by cricketers posted to the Far East in the armed services. With a fluctuating population of civilian and military cricketers, however, the side had little permanence. The most prominent exceptions were all residents of Asian extraction. Their presence was indicative of the multiracial character of Hong Kong cricket at the time, a strength which was to ensure its continued development and survival through the 1970s and 1980s.

Expatriate-based

The 1970s can, at best, be considered a period of consolidation. Visits from overseas teams were less frequent. International matches were limited to the Interports against Malaysia and Singapore. Hong Kong's cricket was still strongly expatriate-based but the number of players from the military became fewer with the cut-back in the British armed forces. On the positive side, Hong Kong sent touring sides to Ceylon in 1971, Australia in 1973 and 1979, and England in 1976. The 1970s saw an increase in the number of expatriate cricketers from Australia and New Zealand. The reliance on expatriates, however, threatened Hong Kong's participation in the international arena. They were unable to take part in the inaugural ICC Trophy competition in 1979 because nearly half of the national team could not meet the ICC residential requirements. The Hong Kong Cricket Association responded by introducing development programmes in the schools and clubs to encourage the permanent resident population to take up cricket. As fast as these could take effect, however, the ICC continually made the qualification requirements more stringent.

A major contributory factor to the difficulty of choosing a national side which met the ICC requirements was the very limited participation of the Chinese population. Up until the 1990s, only one Chinese player was good enough to represent Hong Kong despite the fact that both Hong Kong CC and Kowloon CC employed Chinese as net bowlers. One of these was Benny Kwong Wo, a leg-spinner, who went on to play twelve matches for the national side. As part of the development programme, the HKCA formed the Dragons CC in the 1990s as the first-ever Chinese team in the colony.

The effort expended in promoting the game among the Chinese, however, was considered by some to be disproportionate and many felt that money could have been better spent on assisting other locally-born players. So far, Roy Lamsam is the only player to come from this initiative who has secured a regular place in the national side. One locally-born player of promise to emerge in the 1980s was Dermot Reeve. Born in Kowloon, he was selected for the national side at the age of seventeen. He was only nineteen when he played in the 1982 ICC Trophy competition. He then chose to settle in England, ending his international career for Hong Kong to follow a successful professional one with Sussex, Warwickshire and England.

The 1980s and 1990s saw an expansion in the amount of international cricket played by Hong Kong, all of it one-day limited overs. In addition to the ICC Trophy competitions, Asian competitions for associate countries began in 1984 and the annual contest with Malaysia, Singapore and Thailand for the Tuanku Ja'afar Cup started in 1991. Generally, Hong Kong proved the best side in Southeast Asia but were easily beaten by Bangladesh and the United Arab Emirates. The team remained reliant on members of the British, Australian and Indian communities. Hong Kong finished second in the Asian Cricket Council Trophy held in Sharjah in 2000 and qualified for the Asia Cup contest, originally scheduled for 2002. When it was eventually played in 2004, they were easily defeated by Bangladesh and Pakistan.

Hong Kong is the pioneer of international six-a-side cricket. An annual contest attracting teams from all the test-playing countries started in 1991. Since each innings is only five overs, the contests require a combination of skill and luck which is a great leveller as far as standards are concerned. Hong Kong have thus been able to spring occasional surprises and beat one of the test sides. The most spectacular of these was in 1991 when Mohammed Zubair performed the hat-trick, helping to dismiss South Africa for 20 runs and achieve a victory for Hong Kong by 20 runs.

The development programmes of the HKCA have become even more important since 1997 when Hong Kong's status changed from a British colony to a Special Administrative Region of China. There are now fewer British and Australian expatriates and this is reflected in the composition of the national side. Although captained by Tim Smart, an Australian, it is largely made up of Asian expatriates and locally-born players, again mostly from the Asian community. Results in the early 2000s were disappointing and suggested that Hong Kong was no longer the leading cricket nation in Southeast Asia nor the second best associate country in Asia. In 2006, however, they returned to form and finished second in the Asian Cricket Council Trophy.

One outcome of the HKCA development programme has been the development of women's cricket. Kowloon, Hong Kong and Lamma Island Cricket Clubs have ladies teams. In 2004, a national side visited China and played two games against the Shanghai Pearls, winning the first by 14 runs and narrowly losing the second by two runs. Seven of the thirteen strong touring party were from the Chinese community. The women made their international debut in 2006 but were heavily defeated by Pakistan in an Asian region qualifying competition for the 2009 World Cup.

Shortage of Space

An effect of Hong Kong's urban development and prosperity has been a shortage of space for cricket grounds. The problem came to prominence in 1969 when the government decided not to renew the lease to Hong Kong CC for the use of the Chater Road ground on its expiration in 1971. Instead it was agreed to hand the ground over to the Urban Council for development as an open space for public use, thereby applying the intent of the agreement in 1851 to all sectors of Hong Kong's society. In return the government offered the club a site at Wong Nai Chung Gap together with a small grant for turfing and developing a new ground. The Hong Kong CC moved to its new home in 1975. This did nothing, however, to increase the number of grounds available. By the early 1990s, the shortage was limiting the number of clubs which could be accommodated within the national cricket league. In 2000, the government responded by allocating a site for cricket at Po Kong Village, Diamond Hill, Kowloon. The facility, with space for two large grounds where matches can be played simultaneously, was opened in 2004.

The future of cricket in Hong Kong remains

uncertain. Much will depend on the success of the development programme. Developing locally-born talent is a prerequisite for participating in international cricket, particularly if the ICC strengthen further the player qualification rules by requiring that all players qualify by birth or citizenship. There is also uncertainty as to if or when the HKCA will be expected to merge with the China Cricket Association, producing a single body and a single international side for the whole country.

Famous Victory
February 15, 16 and 17, 1866 – Chater Road, Hong Kong
Shanghai 107 (D.H. Mackenzie 5-) and 59 (D.H. Mackenzie 7-)
Hong Kong 430 (R.D. Starkey 99, T. Clifford 71, F.A. Groom 7-)
Hong Kong won by an innings and 264 runs

Hong Kong gained a resounding victory in what turned out to be the inaugural fixture in a long series of matches between the two sides. The Shanghai players struggled to overcome the effects of the long sea voyage and made a very moderate total against the bowling of D.H. Mackenzie and A.M. Case (3 wickets). Only tail-end contributions from H. Dent (23) and H.R. Hearn (25) enabled them to pass the century mark. Hong Kong then lost E.H. Pollard and Mackenzie cheaply but most of the middle and lower order batsmen found runs easy, particularly against Shanghai's lob bowlers who were very inaccurate. In addition to R.D. Starkey and T. Clifford, D. Davidson (45), T. Mercer (45) and E. Wallace (43 not out) made useful contributions to which were added 41 wides. Shanghai fell meekly in their second innings with only D. Welsh (38) showing any resistance. The bowling figures for this match have not survived.

Player Profiles

Pearce, Thomas Ernest. d Hong Kong 1941 (killed in action, Battle of Hong Kong). Tam Pearce was the most highly regarded of Hong Kong's cricketers in the inter-war period. He first played for Hong Kong in 1903 and played his last international match in 1935. He was the first Hong Kong player to score 1,000 runs in international cricket. In 23 matches, he made 1,206 runs (average 32.59).

Sharma, Rahul. b New Delhi, India, 14 September 1960. rhb. rob. Having played first-class cricket for Delhi between 1985 and 1988, he migrated to Hong Kong as a management consultant and quickly established himself as an attractive and reliable batsman of quality. Once he had satisfied the ICC residential qualifications, he became an indispensable member of the national side. He has played more matches and scored more runs for Hong Kong than any other player. In 6 matches he has scored 329 runs (average 36.55) and taken 4 wickets (average 47.75). In 63 limited overs matches he has made 2,607 runs (average 55.46) and taken 56 wickets (average 18.19).

Other leading players: *1890-1914* J. Dunn (rhb); R.E.O. Bird (lhb. lm); E.J. Coxon. *1920-1940:* A.C.I. Bowker; A.R. Minu; E.B. Reed. *1945-1960:* B.C.N. Carnell. *1960-1980:* J.S. Shroff (rhb); R. Lalchandani (rhb. wk); P.C. Myatt (rhb. rm). *1980-2000:* S.J. Brew (rhb. rm); J.P. Fordham (rhb. wk); N.P. Stearns (rhb). *Present day:* T.T. Smart (rhb. wk); Afzaal Haider (rhb. rm); Khalid Hussain Butt (rhb, rfm).

Women: *Present day:* N.A. Pratt (rhb, lsm); N. Miles.

Playing record
International matches

	Won	Lost	Drawn
Interports (1866-1987)*	33	27	15
ICC Intercontinental Cup	0	1	1
ACC Fast Track Nations Tournament/Premier League	3	7	2

*matches against Shanghai, Straits Settlements, All-Malaya, Malaysia and Singapore

One-day matches

	Won	Lost	Tied	No Res
Asia Cup	0	2	0	0
ICC Trophy	16	23	0	3
Asian Cricket Council Trophy	18	10	1	0
South East Asian Cup	3	7	0	0
Tuanku Ja'afar Cup	33	8	0	6

Highest team score
455-9 dec	v Shanghai, Hong Kong	1909

Lowest team score
35	v Malaya, Singapore	1926

Highest individual score
218*	Khalid Hussain Butt	v United Arab Emirates, Sharjah 2006/07

95

Best bowling

| 8-50 | Afzaal Haider | Malaysia, Kuala Lumpur 2006/07 |

Best wicket-keeping

4 (4c)	S. Jex	v Shanghai, Shanghai	1928
4 (3c 1st)	R. Lalchandani	v MCC, Kowloon	1966
4 (3c 1st)	T.T. Smart	v United Arab Emirates, Hong Kong	2005

ODI

| 6 (4c 2st) | J.P. Fordham | v Thailand, Bangkok | 1992 |

Women

One-day matches

	Won	Lost	Tied	No Res
World Cup qualifying Asian region	0	3	0	0

Highest team score

ODI

| 116 | v Pakistan, Lahore | 2006 |

Lowest team score

ODI

| 49 | v Pakistan, Lahore | 2006 |

Highest individual score

ODI

| 52 | N.A. Pratt | v Pakistan, Lahore | 2006 |

Best bowling

ODI

| 2-62 | K. Gill | v Pakistan, Lahore | 2006 |

HUNGARY

HUNGARY'S ONLY cricket club was established in 1991. Known at various times as Budapest Cricket Club and Magyar Cricket Club, its current title is Magyar Testnelevesi Foiskola (Hungarian Sports University) Cricket Club. Comprising enthusiasts from India, Sri Lanka, Pakistan, New Zealand and five Hungarians, it has about 20 players. Matches are played against sides in Germany and Austria but the lack of a proper pitch makes it difficult to receive clubs from overseas.

ICELAND

IN 1999, Ragnar Kristinsson, after having seen cricket on television and attended a test match between England and Pakistan at Lord's, established, with fellow students from the University of Iceland, the Kylfan Cricket Club in Reykjavík. Shortly afterwards, a second club, Ungmennafélagið Glaumur, was founded by Kári Ólafsson in Stykkishólmer, which at latitude of 65°05' north, is probably the most northerly club in the world. In 2000, the two sides played each other for the Iceland Championships which Stykkishólmer won. In 2001, a combined side from Kylfan and Ungmennafélagið Glaumur defeated a third team, Tryggingamiðstöðin for the Championship. An artificial pitch, provided by the ICC, was installed at Stykkishólmer in 2003.

INDIA

Full Member of the ICC: elected 1926

THE FIRST recorded reference to cricket in India is 1721 when it was played by British sailors from a ship at anchor off the coast near Khambat (Cambay). As Britain established a presence on the Indian sub-continent through the trading activities of the East India Company and the military garrisons set up in support, cricket became an increasingly important activity, all part of replicating British society in an alien environment. Indeed, cricket became a symbol of the separate relationship between the colonisers and the locals. Although the East India Company had acquired trading bases in Chennai (Madras) (1639), Mumbai (Bombay) (1664) and Kolkata (Calcutta) (1696), it was Kolkata which became the administrative centre. The first cricket club in India was established there in 1792, a date which makes it the second oldest in the world after the MCC.

As soon as the British realised that they needed an English-educated Indian elite to underpin their presence in both the bureaucracy and the military, they set up schools and military training establishments for the local population. Although there was no formal policy to promote cricket or, indeed, any form of sport, many of the teachers were enthusiastic about the game and taught it as part of the education process. Thus, a small and select proportion of the Indian population were introduced to it. Within the army, sport became a way in which the British and Indians could mix, whilst allowing the two groups to retain their separateness. For all practical purposes, there was segregation. The British lived in separate quarters of the towns, had their own clubs and their own first-class carriages on the railways. The sporting clubs in Kolkata, Chennai and Mumbai provided English food and English entertainment; they were places to escape the noise, squalor and dirt of much of India. With their good trading links to Britain, they were able to import all the equipment needed for cricket whereas, in other towns, an often much smaller British population had to improvise with locally-obtained materials for the matting wickets and balls.

Although the Calcutta Cricket Club endeavoured to develop its reputation as the equivalent of the MCC in India, the limited interest shown in cricket by the local Bengali population at the time meant that Kolkata was soon eclipsed by Mumbai as a cricket centre. Here the game was taken up by the Parsis, an elite minority community who, in the interests of promoting their status and wealth, readily adopted British customs. They formed their own Oriental Club in 1848 and in 1877 challenged the Bombay Gymkhana, the leading European club, to a game. The result of this match remains unclear with historians of Indian cricket giving conflicting outcomes: although the Parsis led on first innings, Mihir Bose suggests that they went on to lose whereas Ramachandra Guha states that the match was drawn. The enthusiasm of the Parsis was enormous and they sent touring teams to England in 1886 and 1888. They were warmly received and, on the invitation of Queen Victoria, who had a special interest in Indian affairs, were invited to play against a side captained by Prince Victor, the Queen's grandson, in Windsor Great Park.

Fight for Space

The reception afforded to the Parsis in England contrasted with the equivocal attitudes of the Europeans in Mumbai. The Parsis had to fight for space on the *maidan*, the area of open space known to the Army as the Parade Ground but used by Europeans and Indians as a place of recreation. Whilst the Bombay Gymkhana had their own ground, the Parsis were in competition for space with the British Polo Club, and the cricket clubs formed by the Hindus, in 1877, and the Mohammedans in 1883. Eventually a compromise was reached and the Parsis were able to develop their own ground in an area known as the Kennedy Sea Face, just a few kilometres away from the Bombay Gymkhana. Benefiting from the experience of their tours of England, the standard of the Parsis improved and in 1889 they beat the Bombay Gymkhana by three runs, largely due to the skill of Dr M.E. Pavri, their leading all-rounder. As Parsi cricket became stronger, the British decided that, rather than risk the ignominy of defeat by an Indian side, the combined strength of the Bombay and Pune Gymkhanas should form the European team. In 1892, largely at the encouragement of Lord George Harris, two matches were played between the Parsis and what was to become known as the Bombay Presidency. Harris was a leading supporter of cricket during his period as Governor of Mumbai between 1890 and 1895. However, he viewed India in communal terms and, believing that Indian cricket was the stronger for its communal structure, he ensured that cricket organisation in Mumbai matched the colonial objectives of encouraging the communities to mix on the sports field whilst retaining their social separateness off the field. The Parsis provided a model for the other communities to follow. The Presidency match became an annual fixture which was subsequently awarded first-class status; it became a three-way contest in 1907 when the Hindus entered a team. The Mohammedans made it Quadrangular in 1911 and in 1937, a fifth team was added, termed The Rest, comprising Indian Christians, Anglo-Indians and Jews.

The contest continued until 1945/46 by which time communal cricket had become unacceptable both politically and socially. The communal arrangement of cricket was repeated in many other towns where the British were established, particularly Chennai, Karachi and Lucknow. A Presidency fixture was also organised in Chennai but this was not accorded first-class status. Between 1900 and 1930, the educated middle class in Bengal also took up the sport as a way of challenging British rule and in the 1920s clubs like the Bengal Gymkhana met and, sometimes, beat Calcutta Cricket Club on equal terms. For this short period Kolkata rivalled Mumbai as the centre of Indian cricket.

The structure of Indian society was complicated by the influence of caste and tribes. The opportunities to progress, particularly in Hindu society depended on what caste one belonged to. At the bottom of the caste hierarchy are those who work in leather. Such a person was Palwankar Baloo who moved from the Deccan Plateau to Pune when his father took a job in the Army. Baloo and his brother Shivram learnt to play cricket in Pune using equipment discarded by the army officers. Later he obtained a job as an assistant to the ground staff at the Pune Gymkhana where he bowled in the nets at practice. He soon developed into a high class left-arm bowler and controversy arose as to whether he should be selected to play in the Presidency match for the Hindus. Despite opposition from the Brahmin members of the Hindu Club, he was chosen and his bowling helped the Hindus beat the Europeans easily. Nevertheless, as a Dalit or member of the 'untouchable' caste, he was forced to eat his lunch off a separate plate at a separate table and had to take his tea interval outside the pavilion whilst his colleagues ate inside.

Britain never had a sufficient presence in India to conquer the whole country. They occupied and took military control over about two-thirds and allowed the local princes to rule over their kingdoms in the remainder provided they paid appropriate allegiance to the Crown. Some of the princes expressed their support by promoting cricket. The royal households of Dhar, Dungapur, Idar, Gwalior, Limbdi, Patiala, Porbandar, Rajputana and Wadhwan all gave support to the game in the 1880s and 1890s. In the early 1900s, some, such as the Maharaja of Cooch Behar hired European players, whereas the Maharaja of Natore, an ardent nationalist, assembled a side solely of Indian players, regardless of caste and class. Rajendra Singh, the Maharaja of Patiala, built up his own team by employing some of the best Indian cricketers and paying the costs of William Brockwell and J.T. Hearne to come out from England to act as coaches. However, it was his son, Bhupendra Singh, who established Patiala as a great cricket centre. He built his own cricket field, the Bardari Palace Oval and brought leading cricketers from England and Australia, including Wilfred Rhodes, George Hirst, Maurice Leyland, Harold Larwood, Frank Tarrant and Ernest Bromley to coach and play for his side. In 1911, he organised his own tour of England. Patiala's example was copied by others but their interest was often rather short-lived until, in the 1930s, the Maharajkumar of

Vizianagram took to the game. Although no more than a son of a prince and never likely to rule, he used a combination of tenacity and intrigue to promote his position. He established his own ground at Varanasi and when the proposed MCC tour of India in 1930-31 was cancelled, he organised his own team to take over some of the fixtures and tour India and Ceylon; in addition to recruiting some of best Indian players, he succeeded in obtaining the services of Jack Hobbs and Herbert Sutcliffe. The success of this venture gave Vizianagram a status only just below that of the Maharaja of Patiala in Indian cricket circles.

Increasingly Clear

With both the Indian Princes and the various European clubs in British India all involved in organising cricket, it was becoming increasingly clear that a Board of Control was required to select All-Indian teams and arrange tours. A meeting was organised in Delhi on 22 November 1927, chaired by the Maharaja of Patiala and with Anthony de Mello, a young Cambridge-educated Goan and keen all-round sportsman, as Secretary. Even though 60 per cent of the delegates were British, a proposal that Europeans who had been resident in India for four years or more could represent All-India was rejected. Thus, the situation of the West Indies, where the national side was led by a white man, regardless of his cricket ability, was not repeated. Nor was there, as in England, the culture of requiring an amateur rather than a professional to serve as captain. Instead, the conflict was between having a prince rather than a commoner as leader. Further meetings were held during which the main concern was to prevent the headquarters of the Board going to Kolkata. In order to avoid conflict between Kolkata and Mumbai, a compromise decision was reached to locate the Indian Cricket Board of Control in Delhi. R.E. Grant-Govan, an English businessman, became the first President and de Mello was appointed Secretary. Once established, the priority of the Board was to appoint an Indian captain.

One of the surprising features of Indian cricket history is that two of the best Indian cricketers never played for their home country. K.S. Ranjitsinhji, the Jam Saheb of Nawanagar, played his cricket for Cambridge University,

Sussex and England, and, although he took part in a few friendly games in India, he did little to encourage the game in his principality. He also advised his nephew, K.S. Duleepsinhji, not to play for India where, he said, there was no top class cricket to be found. As a result, the opportunity was there for the Maharaja of Patiala to become leader. However, politics delayed this because the new Viceroy, Lord Willingdon, decided to intervene in Indian cricket affairs by opposing Patiala. It is not clear how the bitter relationship between Willingdon and Patiala came about. The Maharaja of Patiala had recently been elected as Chancellor of the Chamber of Princes and the Indian princes were generally supportive of British rule which they saw as protection against the rising nationalism under the influence of Gandhi.

Also, Willingdon, who had previously played cricket in India when Governor of Mumbai in 1915, had attempted to break down the barriers between the communities by setting up clubs in Mumbai and Chennai with membership open to all. The most likely explanation is that Willingdon disliked Patiala's womanising life style and his attempt to recreate English country-house cricket in India. Willingdon therefore turned to the Maharaj Kumar of Vizianagram as a potential leader. Patiala regained the initiative, however, by sponsoring the trials for the Indian team to tour England in 1932. He also managed to obtain the services of Ranjitsinhji as chairman of the selection committee. When the touring party was announced, Patiala was named captain with Prince Gyanashyamsinhji of Limbdi, the Deputy Captain and Vizianagram as Deputy Vice-Captain. For political reasons both Patiala and Vizianagram withdrew and the Maharaja of Porbandar, brother-in-law of Limbdi and with no pretensions as a player, was made captain. Fortunately, Porbandar was a conscientious leader and amenable to advice; he gave way to the best all-round cricketer in the side, C.K. Nayudu, to lead India in the test match at Lord's.

The problem of captaincy did not go away. Whilst Nayudu retained the captaincy when the MCC toured India in 1933-34, Vizianagram was appointed for the tour of England in 1936. Nayudu's position as a colonel in the Indian Army was not considered sufficient status to represent the team at the various social functions on an overseas tour. Despite very limited ability, Vizianagram

played in all three tests. Clearly, if the policy of princely leadership was to continue there was an urgent need to find a Prince who had real cricketing ability. The call was answered when the Nawab of Pataudi, who had followed Ranjitsinhji and Duleepsinhji by playing for England, was persuaded to change allegiance. He led the side to England in 1946. After Indian independence in 1947, the policy was discarded and India's leading batsman, Vijay Merchant, was offered the captaincy of the team to visit Australia. Unfortunately, he and other leading players, Rusi Modi and Mushtaq Ali, withdrew either through injury or for personal reasons, and Lala Amarnath led the side. Since that time, however, the captaincy has generally gone to one of the leading cricketers.

National First-class Competition

In the early 1930s it became clear that Indian cricketers were not playing enough matches of a sufficiently high standard to develop a reservoir of class players from which to select a national side. The Board of Control decided to establish a national first-class competition. The rivalry between the Maharaja of Patiala and the Maharaj Kumar of Vizianagram resulted in both producing trophies to present to the winner. Vizianagram proposed that the competition should be for the Willingdon Trophy and, given the dislike of Lord Willingdon for Patiala, he expected his trophy to be accepted. However, when Lord Willingdon presented a trophy to Mumbai, the winners of the first competition in 1934/35, he awarded that offered by Patiala and agreed to the suggestion that the contest be known as the Ranji Trophy.

The reasons for this late change of heart remain a mystery. Fifteen teams participated in the initial competition, representing, with the exception of The Army, either British administrative units or the Princely States. All teams were chosen, at least theoretically, on merit and therefore embraced all communities, although it is likely that individual patronage influenced selection. The leading omission from the inaugural contest was Bengal where cricket was still dominated by the Calcutta club whose European members saw no need for such a contest. The club officials later changed their minds and Bengal entered in the following year.

The early years of the contest saw no regulations on who could play for which team and Digvijayasinhji, Ranji's successor as the Jam Saheb of Nawanagar, effectively purchased a team, importing players from Northern India, Western India and Mumbai, to win the trophy in 1936/37. The trophy quickly became a victim of rivalry between the regions as first, Maharashtra, and then, Mumbai, attempted to buy back their players. It was eventually dominated by Mumbai (Table 2.7) who won it every year between 1958/59 and 1972/73. The trophy was instrumental in spreading first-class cricket over the whole country. In 1935/36, first-class matches were played in sixteen towns. As expected, Delhi, Mumbai, Kolkata and Chennai staged most matches but eleven other towns each hosted a single match. With new entrants being regularly admitted to the competition, first-class cricket reached all but the most peripheral parts of the country, namely the mountainous states to the north and north-east, the ports of former French India and the more recently-formed rural states of Chhattisgarh and Uttaranchal. In 2000/01, Delhi staged more fixtures than any other town but this was because three teams play there, Delhi and District, the Railways and the Services. Although Mumbai staged six first-class matches, Baroda and Guwahati each held more first-class games than Kolkata or Chennai. Such a wide dispersal of first-class cricket contrasts with the greater centralisation of the first-class game in countries such as England.

The first cricket tour of India took place in 1889/90 when G.F. Vernon's side played eleven matches, mainly against European teams which they beat but losing to the Parsis in Mumbai by 4 wickets. Touring itineraries have

Table 2.7		Ranji Trophy Champions between 1934/35 and 2006/07
Team	Number of times trophy winners	Comments
Andhra	-	Entered1953; originally the northern part of Chennai
Assam	-	Entered 1940; originally part of the Cricket Association of Bengal and Assam
Baroda	5	Entered1937; before that part of Gujarat
Bengal	2	Entered 1935
Delhi	6	Entered 1934
Goa	-	Entered 1985
Gujarat	-	Entered 1934
Haryana	1	Entered 1985; before that was part of Southern Punjab
Himachal Pradesh	-	Entered 1985 following its formation as a political unit; previously part of Punjab
Hyderabad	2	Entered 1934; the team represents the city which is the political capital of Andhra Pradesh
Jammu and Kashmir	-	Entered 1959
Jharkhand	-	Entered 1936, formerly known a Bihar
Karnataka	6	Entered 1934; formerly known as Mysore
Kerala	-	Entered 1951; formerly known as Travancore—Cochin
Madhya Pradesh	-	Entered 1934 as Central Provinces and Berar
Maharashtra	2	Entered 1934; the team represents the state, excluding Mumbai
Mumbai	37	Entered 1934; formerly known as Bombay; the team represents the city of Mumbai which is in the state of Maharashtra
Orissa	-	Entered 1949; originally the southern part of Bihar
Punjab	1	Entered 1934 as Southern Punjab; Haryana seceded in 1970 following its formation as a political unit
Railways	1	Entered 1958; based in Delhi
Rajasthan	-	Entered 1935; formerly Rajputana
Saurashtra	2	Entered 1934 as part of Western India; also played as Kathiawar. Its Ranji Trophy titles were as Nawanagar, a separate principality which became part of Saurashtra in 1949, and Western India
Services	-	Entered in 1934 as The Army but did not reappear until 1949; based in Delhi
Tamil Nadu	2	Entered 1934; formerly known as Chennai
Tripura	-	Entered 1985
Uttar Pradesh	1	Entered 1934; formerly known as United Provinces
Vidarbha	4	Entered 1934 as Holkar; changed name to Madhya Bharat in 1951 and Vidharba in 1957 politically a part of Madhya Pradesh. All its Ranji Trophy titles were as Holkar

changed considerably over the years, reflecting changes in the structure of Indian cricket and improvements in transport. Generally, the ratio of days when cricket is played to days spent travelling has declined. More towns are visited but, ironically, there is less time spent in any of them and so less chance to gain a feel for the country outside the atmosphere of the cricket ground. The MCC tour of 1926/27 (Table 2.8) lasted just over four months with 34 matches in India, Ceylon and Myanmar and involved transport by bus, train and boat. Surprisingly, it was carried out by a team of only fourteen players which meant that there was little cover for injuries and illness. Apart from its length, the itinerary initially looks quite attractive and leisurely, visiting all the main cricketing centres of the day and with as many as 59 'rest days' against 73 days on which matches were played. Long periods were spent in Karachi, Lahore, Mumbai and Kolkata which meant that 25 of the 'rest' days were spent without the need to travel or change hotels. With cricket in India being organised along ethnic lines, the MCC, when in Mumbai, played respectively the Hindus, a combined Parsi-European XI and a combined Hindu-Mohammedan XI before finally meeting multiracial sides representing the Bombay Presidency and All-India. Official functions, in honour of the tourists, were organised in line with the ethnic structure of the game. Each community in each town entertained the tourists separately. Virtually every night there was a dinner or a dance given by either the Europeans, Hindus or Mohammedans followed, in some centres, by functions hosted by Parsis or Sikhs and then, invariably, by cricket the following day. Apart from the cricket and the long distances travelled between towns, the team was quickly exhausted by the hospitality.

Perhaps because the hosts for the tour were the all-white Calcutta CC, the itinerary, with one exception, was restricted to British India, namely that part of the sub-continent ruled directly by the United Kingdom. Even though cricket was played in the Native States, the only game scheduled in them was the last, a one-day match against Patiala, undoubtedly in recognition of the

support provided by the Maharaja. The focus of the tour on local centres of British cricket probably explained the visit to Yangon to play the Rangoon Cricket Club and an All-Burma side, the only first-class cricket matches ever to be played in Myanmar. After their arrival from England in Mumbai, the team immediately sailed to Karachi where the tour began. The itinerary then took them north to Rawalpindi, before coming south again to Mumbai through Lahore and Ajmer. This was followed by the long train journey to Kolkata and a sequence of boat journeys from Kolkata to Yangon, Yangon to Chennai, Chennai to Colombo and Colombo to Mumbai. A logical end to the tour would have been after the four matches in Ceylon but then the tourists would not have played in the Delhi area. Why the Delhi leg could not have been scheduled in November 1926, between the matches in Lahore and Ajmer, is not obvious since cricket is regularly played in Delhi in November. However, the by now extremely tired tourists had to return by sea from Colombo to Mumbai and then journey north for matches at Aligarh, Delhi and, finally, Patiala. The team then accepted an invitation to visit K.S. Ranjitsinhji in his state of Nawanagar before returning home. Despite its length, the tour was a great success with the players considered much more friendly that the average British person in India. One illustration of this was when the captain, Arthur Gilligan, apologised for the behaviour of the local European umpire who angrily kicked away the caps of a Hindu and a Moslem boy who ran on to the field in celebration when All-India surpassed the first innings score of the MCC. The statistics of the itinerary show that the tourists played cricket on 73 days and had 59 rest days giving a ratio of 1.66 between playing and rest days.

The itinerary followed by the MCC team in their

Table 2.8 Playing days, rest days and distances travelled on tours of the Indian sub-continent by the MCC and England

Date	Tour	Playing days	Rest days	Ratio of cricket days to rest days	Kilometres travelled per rest day
1926/27	India, Burma and Ceylon	73	59	1.66	314
1951/52	India, Pakistan and Ceylon	85	65	1.31	199
2001/02	India	29	23	1.26	379

Notes: Rest days are days when no cricket is played and no travel takes place. The ratio of kilometres travelled per rest day is an underestimate because kilometres are based on straight-line distances between the venues and not the actual distance travelled.

1951/52 tour is typical of that of most tours to the Indian sub-continent in the 1950s and 1960s. Compared to the 1926/27 tour, no visit was made to Myanmar, a longer period of time was spent in Pakistan and matches were played in central India at Indore, Kanpur, Nagpur, Hyderabad and Bengalooru (Bangalore) (Table 2.8). The team comprised sixteen players which was sufficient to allow for illness and injuries. Again travel was by bus, train and boat but the itinerary was more compact allowing the number of playing days to be increased to 85 and the number of 'rest days' to 65, giving a ratio of 1.31 between playing and rest days. More time was therefore spent playing cricket. With Indian cricket now organised as multiracial teams based on states, almost all the matches were against either the stronger individual state sides or combinations of states in the regional zones of West, North, East, Central and South. As a result, more centres were visited and there were no long stays in any one centre. The number of days in which the team could stay in the same hotel between matches was almost halved. The matches were of three days duration instead of two. Five test matches were played, each scheduled for five days, although only three lasted that long. Four were in the main centres of New Delhi, Mumbai, Kolkata and Chennai, and one in Kanpur. There was at least one match between each test and one instance of six matches, although two of these were against Pakistan which did not have test-match status at the time of the tour. The tourists travelled an average of 199 km for every 'rest day', a reduction of nearly 40 per cent in travel.

The 2001/02 tour was organised in two parts (Table 2.8). Seventeen players made up the side for the first part which began in Mumbai on 18 November and ended in Bengalooru on 23 December. The team played only six matches in six centres, the last three of which were test matches. The second part of the tour began on 19 January at Kolkata and ended on 3 February at Mumbai and comprised seven one-day internationals. The team for this leg consisted of sixteen players. Only nine players participated in both parts of the tour. The touring itinerary therefore ignored the local structure of Indian cricket. No chance was provided for players in the state or regional sides to test their skills against leading players from overseas. Apart from an initial warm-up in Mumbai which was not first-class, all the fixtures

involved national Indian teams. The need to play the most important matches in the main cricketing centres was no longer a critical issue. Instead, international matches were spread more widely across the country with the test matches being taken to Mohali, Ahmedabad and Bengalooru. Only one playing day was spent in each of Mumbai, Kolkata, Chennai and New Delhi. Ignoring the time between the two legs and considering only the time spent in India, the total tour was quite short, only 29 playing days. However, the ratio of playing days to rest days showed a further decline and travel was involved between every game. There were no consecutive matches in the same town. With such a compact itinerary, there was clearly far less time for official hospitality or for the players to experience much of the culture and life of India. Indeed, most views of India must have been from the air. With the use of air transport, the number of kilometres travelled per 'rest day' increased markedly and was even greater than that of the 1926/27 tour. Compared with earlier tours, the more recent tour would appear to be much harder work with more cricket and more travel compressed into a very short time period.

The organisation of early Indian cricket on a communal basis meant that, as a country, India played very few international matches. Only three games involving All-India had been played before the country obtained test-match status in 1932. The team which played against Lord Hawke's XI in 1892/93 comprised eight Europeans and three Parsis. There were seven Europeans in the team which played the MCC in 1926/27 at Kolkata, the side having been selected by Calcutta CC. Only the side which met the MCC at Mumbai could be considered representative of Indian cricket. Thus, when India first played test cricket, very few of its players had any experience of the game at that level. It was not surprising, therefore, that they were easily defeated by England. What is more surprising is that they were not totally outplayed.

Golden Age of Batting

From 1932 until 1951, Indian international cricket was dominated by its attempts to obtain its first victory. However, after its promising start against England in the 1930s, the standard of cricket deteriorated during the

1939-45 War, a period described by Mihir Bose as the 'golden age of batting' when huge team and individual scores were made on flat green wickets. The flaws in batting technique were first exposed during a visit of an Indian side to Ceylon in 1945 and then cruelly so when they were easily beaten by England, Australia and the West Indies in the late 1940s and early 1950s. Victory came at Chennai in February 1952 but against a second-string English side. When they met the full England team in England in the summer of the same year, they were completely outplayed. The afternoon of 7 June 1952 was the nadir. In their second innings of the test match at Leeds they found themselves on 0 for four after just fourteen balls. Thus, after having obtained their first victory, Indian cricket entered a period in which the occasional victory was interspersed between periods heavy defeats and boring draws. Generally, India were able to hold their own at home but were unable to compete overseas.

India's poor record became a matter of national concern and was raised frequently in the Lok Sabha, India's parliament. A special committee was set up to examine the administration of Indian sport generally, including the influence of factionalism. The 'golden period' of Indian cricket occurred between 1967 and 1980. England, Australia, West Indies and New Zealand were all beaten and, for the first, time India was a dominant side away from home. Between 1980 and 2000, India went through alternating periods of success and failure. The most exciting result was the tie, the second in test cricket, against Australia at Chennai (see Country Profile for Australia). By the late 1990s, the makings of a new team were apparent with the potential to be one of the best teams in the world. But they are still vulnerable to lapses away from home, one of the most memorable being their failure to reach the Super Eight stage of the 2007 World Cup.

Whilst cricket as a man's sport in India has more than 250 years of history, the women's game is a relatively recent phenomenon. Whereas the men's game was brought to India by the British, the women's game has emerged from within India as a response to the widespread enthusiasm for the sport. It is likely that women played informally with their fathers and brothers for many years but it was not until the late 1960s and early 1970s that some of the more enthusiastic and better players started to push their way into boy's teams at club level. Some clubs then started having nets for girls. Unlike the men's game where, at least for middle and upper class Indians, it is well established in schools, very few girls schools play cricket. Despite this, the constraints of limited funding and a shortage of training and playing facilities, rapid progress was made in the 1970s. The Women's Cricket Association of India was founded in 1973, an inter-state domestic tournament was started in the same year, an Australian Under-25 side toured India in 1975, and test matches were played against the West Indies in 1976/77. In 1978, India hosted the Women's World Cup. The national one-day tournament for the Rani Jhansi Trophy comprises twelve teams. Women's test matches are often played before large crowds on the main grounds in Delhi and Kolkata in contrast to the situation in England where the women are usually relegated to the smaller county grounds with hardly any spectators. India is now recognised as one of the top four women's international sides.

Match-fixing

What began in India as a polite Victorian game played before a respectful audience has become a game closer in spirit to that of Georgian England, with its large, excitable and sometimes volatile crowds and the amount of betting that takes place. There is a strong similarity between the accounts of match-fixing in Georgian England and the events in India of the 1980s and 1990s when Mukesh Gupta changed his life from a bank clerk to a notorious match-fixer and made a fortune betting on the results of the games. The extent of the activity and number of Indian test players involved will probably never be known but Ajay Sharma, Gupta's main contact, and Mohammed Azharuddin, who had a close relationship with Gupta between 1997 and 1999, were banned for life from any kind of involvement in cricket. Two other test players, Ajay Jadeja and Manoj Prabhakar received five-year suspensions which effectively ended their cricketing careers. Doubts were raised about the results of some 50 matches world-wide between 1979/80 and 1999/2000 of which 62 per cent involved

India. Although the outcome of many of these may not have been fixed, it is tempting to question whether the results of these and the somewhat erratic performance of the national side in the 1980s and 1990s were in any way linked. Perhaps the consoling part of this somewhat shameful episode in Indian cricket is that it was an Indian detective, Ishwar Singh Redhu, who forced the issue into the open.

Famous Victories

April 7, 8, 10, 11, 12, 1976 – Queen's Park Oval, Port of Spain
West Indies 359 (I.V.A. Richards 177, C.H. Lloyd 68, B.S. Chandrasekhar 6-120, B.S. Bedi 4-73) and 271-6 dec (A.I. Kallicharran 103*)
India 228 (M.A. Holding 6-56) and 406-4 (G.R. Viswanath 112, S.M. Gavaskar 102, M. Amarnath 85)
India won by 6 wickets

Despite some effective spin bowling by Baghwat Chandrasekhar, who took all five of the wickets which fell on the first day, and Bishen Bedi, West Indies built up a commanding position. India's batsmen struggled against the pace of Michael Holding. After being 131 runs behind on the first innings, the Indian bowling restricted the West Indian scoring rate. On the fourth day, Alvin Kallicharran batted with great care and the West Indies spent nearly three hours adding 139 runs before declaring. Starting the last day at 134 for the loss of Anshuman Gaekwad, Sunil Gavaskar and Mohinder Amarnath shared a partnership of 108 runs. After reaching his century, Gavaskar lost his touch and the scoring rate slumped with only 22 runs being made in the second hour of play. The three West Indian spin bowlers could make little inroads, despite the advantage of a worn, turning wicket, and Clive Lloyd, the West Indies captain, was forced to take the new ball with 29 overs remaining. Bernard Julien bowled very loosely and 37 runs were scored in eight overs. Gundappa Viswanath became inspired and hit the returning West Indian spinners all over the field. After he was run out, Brijesh Patel took command and the spin attack collapsed completely under pressure. India thus became the second side to score over 400 runs in the fourth innings to achieve victory.

June 25, 1983 – Lord's, London
India 183 (54.4 overs)
West Indies 140 (52 overs)
India won by 43 runs

India won a low-scoring game of considerable excitement to become the World one-day champions. On a superb sunny day, Clive Lloyd won the toss and put India into bat. With the ball showing movement off the seam, India struggled to score against Joel Garner and Andy Roberts. Kris Srikkanth (38) rode his luck in one of his typical innings, hitting Roberts for two fours and one six before succumbing to the first change bowler, Malcolm Marshall. Madan Lal, Syed Kirmani and Balwinder Singh Sandhu each made double figures, taking the score from 130-7 to 183 all out, a total which many considered too difficult to defend against the West Indies batting line-up. In the event, every West Indies batsman managed to perish before getting set and Vivian Richards, Desmond Haynes and Hilary (Larry) Gomes fell in nineteen balls whilst making only six runs. After Amarnath broke the partnership between Jeffrey Dujon and Marshall, he and Kapil Dev brought the innings to a close. India's surprising victory showed what three apparently innocuous medium-paced bowlers, Mohinder Amarnath (3-12), Madan Lal (3-31) and Roger Binny (1-23), can do in one-day cricket if they bowl to line and length. Mohinder Amarnath was named man-of-the-match.

March 11, 12, 13, 14, 15, 2001 – Eden Gardens, Kolkata
Australia 445 (S.R. Waugh 110, M.L. Hayden 97, J.L. Langer 58, Harbhajan Singh 7-123) and 212 (M.L. Hayden 67, Harbhajan Singh 6-73)
India 171 (V.V.S. Laxman 59, G.D. McGrath 4-18) and 657-7 dec (V.V.S. Laxman 281, R. Dravid 180)
India won by 171 runs

India achieved an astonishing victory after following on 274 runs behind on first innings. The partnership of 376 runs between V.V.S. Laxman and Rahul Dravid was a fifth-wicket record for India and the second highest for any wicket. They batted for the whole of the fourth day and showed that the Australian attack of Glen McGrath, Jason Gillespie, Michael Kasprowicz and Shane Warne could be tamed. Laxman's innings, lasting ten hours 31 minutes, gave him India's highest individual test score. When captain, Sourav Ganguly, declared, setting Australia 384 runs to win, a tame draw seemed the most likely outcome since the wicket, though providing turn, was not apparently difficult. However, the wiles of Harbhajan Singh proved too much. Despite their high score, the Australians had found him troublesome in their first innings in which Harbhajan's seven wickets included a hat-trick when he dismissed Ricky Ponting, Adam Gilchrist and Warne. Despite some resistance by Matthew Hayden and Steve Waugh, Australia lasted only 61 overs against Harbhajan, with Sachin Tendulkar, taking advantage of the batsmen's doubts, picking up the wickets of Hayden, Gilchrist and Warne with his leg spin. The match brought Australia's run of 16 consecutive victories in test cricket to an end.

Player Profiles

Baloo, Babaji Palwankar. b Mumbai 19 March 1876. d Mumbai 7 July 1955. lhb. sla. One of the most successful bowlers prior to India playing test cricket. He was the first dalit (untouchable) to be accepted in domestic first-class cricket. He was easily the leading bowler on the Indian tour of England in 1911, taking 75 first-class wickets at an average of 20.12 and over 100 wickets in all matches. In his first-class career, playing mainly for the Hindus, he scored 753 runs (average 13.69) and took 179 wickets at an average of 15.21, seventeen times taking five or more wickets in an innings.

Bedi, Bishan Singh. b Amritsar, 25 September 1946. rhb. sla. Instantly recognisable because of his selection of brightly coloured patkas, he was a regular member of the Indian side for some twelve years. He was a master of his art, having command of flight, pace and degrees of spin. He reserved his best performances for matches against Australia, taking 21 wickets against them in 1969/70, including 9-108 at Delhi, and 31 wickets in 1977/78. As captain, he controversially declared India's first innings closed against the West Indies at Kingston in April 1976 as a protest against what he considered to be consistently dangerous and intimidatory bowling. He followed this by ending India's second innings after five wickets had fallen for 97 runs, claiming that the remaining five batsmen were all injured. West Indies made the thirteen runs

required to win without loss. In 67 tests matches he took 266 wickets (average 28.71) and made 656 runs (average of 8.98). In 10 one-day internationals he scored 31 runs (average 6.20) and took 7 wickets (average 48.57).

Chandrasekhar, Bhagwat Subramanya. b Mysore 17 May 1945. rhb. rmlbg. During his career, he was India's most consistent match-winning bowler, using an armoury of leg breaks, googlies and top spinners, delivered at near medium-pace and interspersed with the completely unplayable ball. He was particularly successful in England, taking 57 wickets on the tour of 1967 and 50 wickets on the 1971 tour, including 6 wickets for 38 at The Oval allowing India to beat England in England for the first time. Although right-handed, he threw with his left arm because his bowling arm was withered by polio at the age of five. He was one of the worst batsmen ever to play test cricket, scoring 23 ducks in the 41 innings in which he was dismissed. In 58 tests, he took 242 wickets (average 29.74) and scored 167 runs (average of 4.07). He played only 1 one-day international, making 11 runs not out and taking 3 wickets (average 12.00).

Dravid, Rahul Sharad. b Indore 11 January 1973. rhb. rob. occ wk. The most consistent batsman in modern Indian test cricket, his undemonstrative but determined style make him the ideal player in a crisis. He can hold one end tight whilst his partners score the runs or, if no one else takes on the role, he can dominate the bowling, accumulate large scores and keep lesser batsmen away from the strike. He rises to the challenge in the most difficult of conditions and has become one of India's most consistent performers on overseas pitches. In 106 test matches for India he has scored 9,151 runs (average 57.91). In 309 one-day internationals he has made 10,004 runs (average 40.01).

Edulji, Diana Fram. b Mumbai 26 January 1956. rhb. sla. The most successful woman cricketer to emerge from India, she continued the tradition of high-class spin bowling established in the men's game. She stands third on the all-time women's list for the number of wickets obtained in test matches. In 20 tests, she has taken 63 wickets at an average of 25.77 and scored 404 runs at an average of 16.16. In 34 one-day internationals, she has taken 46 wickets with the remarkable average of 16.84 and made 211 runs with an average of 8.79. She received the Castrol Award in 2002 for Outstanding Contributions to Indian Women's Cricket.

Gavaskar, Sunil Manohar. b Mumbai 10 July 1949. rhb. His career set the record for the most appearances in test matches by an Indian, the most centuries and the first player to score 10,000 runs. Known as 'Little Master', his sound technique made him one of the best opening batsmen in the world. He carefully built each innings before taking on the bowling with a range of strokes, including drives and cuts. He played many long innings, a tribute to his powers of concentration. His 221 runs in over 8 hours at The Oval in 1979 which took his team to within eight runs of victory is considered one of the greatest innings of modern times. In 125 test matches he scored 10,122 runs (average 51.12). In 108 one-day internationals he made 3,092 runs (average 35.13).

Hazare, Vijay Samuel. b Sangli, Maharashtra, 11 March 1915. d Baroda 18 December 2004. rhb. rm. One of India's greatest batsman on difficult wickets, he played with a straight bat and intense concentration. In the very wet summer of 1952, he averaged 55.50 in the four tests against England and was the only player to deal effectively with hostile pace bowling. He made hundreds against all four of the countries against which he played test cricket. Although he was the captain when India achieved their first test victory and he went on to captain India fourteen times, he was too introvert to inspire his players, except by example. In 30 test matches, he scored 2,192 runs (average 47.65) and took 20 wickets (average 61.00).

Merchant, Vijaysingh Madhavji. b Mumbai 12 October 1911. d Mumbai 27 October 1987. rhb. rm. India's most accomplished batsman in the 1930s and 1940s, displaying almost perfect footwork, he built his innings carefully but, once set, showed an array of cuts, hooks and drives; he was especially severe on fast bowling. He was the outstanding batsman on tours of England in 1936 and 1946. In 10 test matches he made 859 runs (average 47.72). His real name was Vijaysingh Madhavji Thackersey but when,

as a young boy, he entered Bharda High School and was asked his name, he became confused and was unable to answer; the Headmaster then decided to call him Merchant.

Tendulkar, Sachin Ramesh. b Mumbai 24 April 1973. rhb. rm/lb/rob. A schoolboy sensation, at the age of 14 years he scored 326 not out for Sharadashram Vidyamandir (English) School against St Xavier's High School, sharing in an unbeaten partnership of 664 runs for the third wicket with Vinod Kambli, who made 349 not out. He scored a century on his first-class debut for Mumbai against Gujarat, when aged 15. He became the youngest person to make a test century in England when, aged 17 years and 112 days, he scored 119 at Old Trafford in 1990 to save his side from defeat. In 135 tests, he has scored 10,668 runs (average 54.70) and taken 38 wickets (average 50.68). In 384 one-day internationals he has made 14,847 runs (average 44.05) and taken 149 wickets (average 43.76).

Other leading players: *1890-1914:* Dr M.E. Pavri (rhb. rf); B.P. Shivram (rhb. rob). *1920-1940:* L.N. Amar Singh (rhb. rfm); Mohammad Nissar (rhb. rfm); S. Mushtaq Ali (rhb. sla); C.K. Nayudu (rhb. rsm). *1945-1960:* N. Amarnath (Lala) (rhb. rm); Ghulam Ahmed (rhb. rob); S.P. Gupte (rhb. lbg); M.H. Mankad (Vinoo) (rhb. sla); P.R. Umrigar (rhb. rob/rm). *1960-1980:* F.M. Engineer (rhb. wk); E.A.S. Prasanna (rhb. rob); S. Venkataraghavan (rhb. rob); G.R. Viswanath (rhb); A.L. Wadekar (lhb). *1980-2000:* M. Azharuddin (rhb); Kapil Dev (rhb. rfm); R.J. Shastri (rhb. sla); J. Srinath (rhb. rfm); D.B. Vengsarkar (rhb). *Present day:* S.C. Ganguly (lhb. rm); Harbhajan Singh (rhb. rob); A. Kumble (rhb. lbg); V. Sehwag (rhb); Zaheer Khan (rhb. lfm).

Women: *1980-2000:* S. Agarwal (rhb); F. Khalili (rhb. wk). *Present day:* N. David (rhb. sla); A. Jain (rhb. wk); M. Raj (rhb).

Playing record
Test matches

	Won	Lost	Tied	Drawn
England	17	34	0	43
Australia	15	32	1	20
South Africa	4	9	0	6
West Indies	11	30	0	41

New Zealand	14	9	0	21
Pakistan	8	12	0	36
Sri Lanka	10	3	0	13
Zimbabwe	7	2	0	2
Bangladesh	3	0	0	0
Total	89	131	1	182

Other Matches

All-India prior to test status	0	2	0	1
Unofficial test matches*	13	7	0	13

* Matches against J. Ryder's XI, Australian Services, Commonwealth, Ceylon and East Africa

One-day matches

	Won	Lost	Tied	No Res
World Cup	31	25	0	1
Other ODI	272	287	3	26

Twenty20

1	0	0	0

Highest team score

705-7 dec	v Australia, Sydney	2003/04

Lowest team score

42	India v England, Lord's	1974

Highest individual score

309	V. Sehwag	v Pakistan, Multan	2003/04

Best bowling

10-74	A. Kumble	v Pakistan, Delhi	1998/99

Best wicket-keeping

6 (5c 1st)	S.M.H. Kirmani	v New Zealand, Christchurch	1975/76

Women

Test matches

	Won	Lost	Tied	Drawn
England	1	1	0	10
Australia	0	4	0	5
South Africa	1	0	0	0
West Indies	1	1	0	4
New Zealand	0	0	0	6
Total	3	6	0	25

One-day matches

	Won	Lost	Tied	No Res
World Cup	21	20	1	3
Other ODIs	59	47	0	2

Twenty20

1	0	0	0

Highest team score

467	v England, Taunton	2002

Lowest team score

65	v West Indies, Jammu	1976/77

ODI

26	v New Zealand, St Saviours	2002

Highest individual score

214	M. Raj	v England, Taunton	2002

Best bowling

8-53	N. David	v England, Jamshedpur	1995/96

Best wicket-keeping

5 (1c 4st)	F. Khalili	v Australia, Perth	1976/77
5 (3c 2st)	A. Jain	v England, Shenley	1999

ODI

6 (1c 5st)	V. Kalpana	India v Denmark, Slough	1993

INDONESIA

Affiliate Member of ICC: elected 2001

CRICKET WAS played by British and Dutch expatriates in Indonesia from the late nineteenth century up to the Second World War but the numbers involved were small and it was never more than an occasional recreational activity. The game virtually died out after the country gained independence from the Dutch and most expatriates left. With the economic expansion in the 1990s, however, the numbers of British and Australian businessmen increased and the game was revived. Today, Indonesia has two main cricket centres, Jakarta and Bali. The Jakarta Cricket Association consists of ten clubs, comprising mainly expatriate players from Britain, Australia and Asia. The Bali Cricket Foundation consists of five clubs which include Udayana Cricket Club, an all-Indonesian side with its own cricket training centre at the Udayana Eco Lodge. In April 2000, these two organisations formed the Indonesian Cricket Federation. ICF's development programme is concentrating on introducing cricket into schools throughout the country. The number of players has increased from about 300 in 2000 to 11,000 in 2004. In April 2005, an all-girls team was formed in Bali, playing matches against local boys schools. The national side has played with limited success in various East Asia and Pacific competitions.

Leading player: *Present day:* J.A. Stevenson (rhb. rob).

Playing record

One-day matches

	Won	Lost	No Res
East Asia Pacific Challenge	1	3	0
East Asia Pacific Cup	1	5	3

Highest team score

ODI

281	v Tonga, Port Vila		2005

Lowest team score

ODI

119	v Japan, Port Vila		2005

Highest individual score

ODI

70	J.A. Stevenson	v Cook Islands, Port Vila	2005

Best bowling

ODI

5-42	A. Sundar	v Japan, Port Vila	2005

Highest team score

ODI

152-9	v Thailand, Kuala Lumpur		2006

Lowest team score

ODI

29	v Nepal, Kuala Lumpur		2004

Highest individual score

ODI

68	Nariman Bakhtyar	v Qatar, Kuala Lumpur	2006

Best bowling

ODI

5-55	Abdul Ghaffar	v Saudi Arabia, Doha	2005/06

IRAN

Affiliate Member of the ICC: elected 2003

CRICKET WAS introduced into Iran by the British who worked in the oil industry in the 1920s and 1930s. Annual matches took place between Abadan and Masjed Soleyman and occasional games occurred between Abadan and Baghdad Cricket Club in Iraq. The sport ceased when the Iranians took over the oil industry and most expatriates left the country. It was revived some twelve years ago by a small group of enthusiastic Iranians returning to their country after higher education overseas where they were introduced to the game. The leading player and coach was Hossain Ali Saliman who learnt the game at Karachi University. There are now four clubs in Tehran, supported by expatriates from India, Pakistan and Sri Lanka. In contrast, the clubs at Chah Bahar, Iranshahr, Zahedan and Mashhad are made up of almost entirely of Iranians. Iran has taken part in the Asian Cricket Council competitions and the Middle East Cup but with no success. Against Nepal in 2004 they were dismissed for 29 runs and the whole game was competed in 24.1 overs.

Leading player: *Present day:* Nariman Bakhtyar

Playing record
One-day matches

	Won	Lost	No Res
Asian Cricket Council Trophy	0	5	0
Middle East Cup	0	3	1

IRELAND

Associate Member of ICC: elected 1993

IN 1656, Oliver Cromwell issued an edict ordering his Commissioners to destroy all bats and balls in Dublin. For some years this was interpreted as indicating that cricket must have been very popular in Ireland at the time but the cricket historian, Peter Wynne-Thomas, considers it more likely that the Commissioners mistook hurling for cricket and that cricket did not arrive in Ireland until the end of the eighteenth century. The first recorded match in Ireland dates to 1792 when the Dublin Garrison, captained by Colonel Lennox, later to become the fourth Duke of Richmond, beat an All-Ireland side, captained by Rt Hon Major Hobart, Chief Secretary to the Lord Lieutenant of Ireland, by an innings and 94 runs. There was a wager of one thousand guineas on the result. This match illustrates the importance of the British military in taking the game to Ireland. In the early 1800s, cricket spread to the garrison towns of Kilkenny and Ballinasloe and from there to other towns. A rapid growth of the game occurred in the 1830s when many clubs were founded. It seems unlikely, however, that this expansion led to cricket becoming a common activity amongst the rural population of Ireland. Most of the clubs were run by the Irish aristocracy, many of whom were also landowners in England. With the construction of the railway network, beginning in Dublin in 1834 and Belfast in 1839, matches between clubs in the main towns became possible on a regular basis. The improvements in transport enabled Charles Lawrence, a Londoner who played for Middlesex and Surrey before becoming the professional at Phoenix Cricket Club in Dublin, to spread the game throughout Ireland by forming a touring side and organising matches on a commercial basis. At the time, there was only a limited interest from the public and Lawrence almost certainly made a loss on his venture. However, he was successful in promoting the game and was asked by the then Lord Lieutenant, the Seventh Earl of Carlisle, to construct a cricket ground on the estate of the Vice-Regal Lodge which, for a time, became the focus of the game in Ireland.

Important Feature

Ireland played its first international match in 1855 against the Gentlemen of England. Although Ireland won by 107 runs, the English side was not representative and contained several Irish players. The Gentlemen of England played two more matches, in 1856 and 1857. Visits were also made by the various professional touring elevens which were an important feature of English cricket at that time. The United All England Eleven played one match in 1856, the United South of England Eleven came in 1856 and 1859, and the All England Eleven played four matches between 1860 and 1869. Among the amateur clubs, the MCC first visited in 1858 and I Zingari in 1859. Ireland also played the MCC at Lord's in 1858, winning by 110 runs largely due to the bowling of Lawrence who took 8-32 and 4-25. Lawrence was lost to Irish cricket in 1861 when he emigrated to Australia where he played for New South Wales and took a keen interest in the development of cricket among the aborigines. By the mid 1860s, cricket was clearly flourishing as an elite game amongst the aristocracy and the well-educated Irish and the English communities. Dublin University formed a cricket club in 1842 and rapidly established itself as the nursery for future Irish players. One of the earliest clubs in Cork, the Constitution CC, was started by Englishmen on the staff of the *Cork Constitution*. The only part of the island where the game was slow to develop was Ulster where it was hampered by the influence of the Scottish Presbyterian church. Nevertheless, some of Ulster's leading clubs have early foundations: the Belfast Club

was formed in 1830, the Lisburn Club in 1836 and the Ulster Club in 1839.

In 1879, Ireland made its first tour outside of the British Isles. A group of amateurs under the captaincy of Nathaniel Hone and with a professional, Arnold Rylott, as an umpire, accepted an invitation and sponsorship from St George's CC, New York. The side visited New York, Philadelphia and Canada. That such a tour was possible is indicative of cricket being, at that time, a pastime of the wealthy who could afford the costs of trans-Atlantic travel and had little need to worry about loss of income from time away from work. Further visits followed in 1888 and 1892. The Hones were a leading cricketing family and between 1861 and 1894, Nathaniel, William, Leland, William junior, Jeffrey and Thomas all played for Ireland. Another indicator that the game in the nineteenth century was essentially a recreation of the elite is that there is no record of it having suffered from the potato famines which began in 1845 and led to the migration overseas of much of the rural population. In fact, it was the traditional Irish sports of hurling and Gaelic football that suffered. During the 1860s and 1870s, cricket began to spread from the towns into the countryside, particularly in the south and east of the country. Many clubs were founded, supported by the wealthy landlords but which relied on farmers and local artisans for players. For a short period, cricket was both an urban and a rural pastime. The village of Clonbur in Galway, for example, played 38 matches in one season.

In the 1880s, the stirrings of Irish nationalism led to the establishment of the Irish Land League. The resulting wars between tenant and landlord affected the rural areas particularly and cricket, along with other sports and recreation, virtually ceased. The landlords, suffering from falling crop and land prices and local agitators, were no longer able to support local clubs and many village and small town teams folded. The game became increasingly confined to Dublin and a few of the larger towns. The formation of the Gaelic Athletic Association dealt a further blow as they actively promoted the Irish games of hurling and Gaelic football. Any player who participated in cricket or any other sport declared a 'foreign' game was banned by the GAA from all sport. Surprisingly, this regulation prevailed until 1970. As a result, cricket came to be viewed as a game of the English and the Anglo-Irish and not suitable as a truly Irish activity.

Despite these set-backs, cricket survived as an urban game and in the 1880s made considerable growth in Dublin. In 1890 the Irish Cricket Union was formed to oversee the selection of the national side but its efforts were not entirely successful. A dispute in 1892 among the Dublin clubs about the selection procedure meant that the first team to go overseas under the auspices of the ICU and the third to visit North America was not properly representative. The 1880s saw the visits reciprocated as Philadelphia played in Ireland in 1884 and 1889 and Canada in 1887. These contacts with North America were extremely important because they provided the only opportunities for international cricket. During the troubles of the Land War, 1879-1882, and the Plan of Campaign, 1886-1892, the British were the subject of considerable harassment and many English sides did not consider it safe to visit Ireland.

Acceptable Sport

By the early 1900s, cricket was re-establishing itself as an acceptable sport for Irish participation particularly in Dublin and Cork. Dublin University became a stronghold of the game and its matches against the MCC and Leicestershire in 1895 are ranked first class. Contacts with English clubs were resumed. Matches against Scotland were played in 1888 and 1890 and South Africa paid visits in 1894 and 1901. In 1902, Ireland sent a touring party to England where they played London County, MCC, Oxford University and Cambridge University, the first Irish matches to be accorded first-class status. Since that time, the status of the Irish side has been controversial. The annual series of matches against Scotland has been considered first class but matches against the MCC, various English counties and the touring sides of the test playing countries have sometimes been rated first class and sometimes not. The classification of which games are first class seems to defy logic.

Women in Ireland started to play cricket in the late eighteenth century. In July 1884, a women's side led by Claudine Humphreys beat a men's team by one wicket in a game at Strabane. The first known all-women's match took place in Cork in the 1890s. Cricket was also introduced into the leading girls schools, notably Sion Hill, Holy Faith and Glasnevin and Glengara. An Irish schoolgirls side met an English schoolgirls team at Woodbrook in July 1908 but the result does not survive. Despite these promising beginnings, women's cricket took many more years to develop as a national sport.

In 1909, a men's side made a fourth tour of North America. The two games against Philadelphia which Ireland lost respectively by an innings and 168 runs and an innings and 66 runs, were considered first class. The Irish batsmen had no answer to the fast swing bowling of Bart King and the leg spin and googlies of Herbert Hordern. Although the Irish side was chosen by the ICU, it was not the strongest possible because some of the best players were unable to make the journey. As the game was no longer restricted to the wealthy and the aristocracy but was being played by businessmen and skilled professionals, it was more difficult to find players with the time and money to spend a month or more away on an overseas tour. Apart from short visits to England and Scotland, this was the last overseas tour made by Ireland until 1973. However, the aristocracy still had an involvement in the game. Country-house style cricket continued, particularly at Bray which, in 1907, hosted the fixture between Ireland and Yorkshire. Otherwise international matches were confined to Trinity College Park in Dublin and the occasional fixture in Belfast.

After a break for the First World War, the international series with Scotland restarted in 1920. Before other international contacts got underway, however, the Government of Ireland Act in July 1921 led to the partition of the island between Northern Ireland and the Irish Free State, later to become the Republic of Ireland in 1937. With the change in political status, the British administrators, civil servants and the military all left the south and with them went several good cricketers. Despite partition, a meeting was held in July 1923 between representatives of the Leinster Cricket Union, based in Dublin, and the Northern Cricket Union, based in Belfast to establish an administration for cricket. As a result, the Irish Cricket Union was reformed in 1923 which ensured that Irish cricket would continue as an all-Ireland activity. By the mid 1920s, Ireland was playing two or more international matches each season with the matches against Scotland, the MCC and some English counties rated as first class. For a short period in the 1920s, Dublin University's matches against the English counties were also ranked first class, a status which, judged by the results, considerably inflated their ability. Visits were received from the West Indies in 1923 and 1928, India in 1936 and Australia in 1938. Although Ireland and Scotland were reasonably well-matched, Ireland lost most of the other matches played. In contrast to Ireland's increasing status in the men's game, little progress was made in women's cricket. There are very few records of matches until the late 1930s by which time the Leinster Women's Cricket Union had been formed and six clubs in the Dublin area were participating in an evening league competition. Although women elsewhere in Ireland may have played the game, there appears to have been no other organised women's competition. The Second World War brought a temporary halt to both men's and women's cricket.

Minority Sport

International cricket resumed very quickly after 1945, the series against Scotland restarting in 1946. Soon after, county sides, the MCC and the test playing countries began to visit. Throughout the 1950s and 1960s cricket in Ireland retained its amateur outlook and recreational status and, as a result, remained a minority sport compared to football and rugby. Like many amateur sides when up against apparently stronger opponents, they could, however, spring the occasional surprise. In 1969, they sensationally dismissed the West Indies for 25 runs and won the match by nine wickets. This victory marked the start of one the most successful five year periods in Irish cricket under the captaincy of Dougie Goodwin. For the first time, Ireland were winning more matches than they were losing. This success was even more surprising because many of the leading players had retired and Ireland was rebuilding its national side. One factor which undoubtedly helped was the change that was taking place in the fixture list. As the standard of Irish cricket had declined relative to that of the English counties, only the annual fixture against Scotland retained first-class status. The fixture list was widened, with matches against The Netherlands,

Denmark and Wales. Partly this was necessity because at the height of the sectarian crisis in Ulster in 1972, English sides were again reluctant to play in Ireland but, fortunately, this lasted only a few seasons. These changes meant that Ireland was now meeting sides of similar cricketing standard instead of being outclassed by English county teams. The ICU became more outward-looking and, in 1973, renewed their contacts across the Atlantic by touring Canada and the United States. In 1977, the biennial tour of the national side to England was revived. Between 1977 and 1980, the national side went through a sixteen match period without defeat. This success encouraged the growth of cricket. There was a substantial increase in the number of boys joining cricket clubs, an overall rise in club membership and the formation of new clubs.

In contrast to this expansion of the men's game, women's cricket in Ireland was in severe decline. The Second World War and shortage of petrol in the years following caused many clubs to fold. In Leinster, only Trinity College, Contarf and the Railway Union clubs revived with Trinity being the most successful, aided by students from England. Typical of the attitudes of the period, the Trinity women's team was not allowed to play at College Park where the men played and had to use a ground at Dartry. Interest in women's cricket continued to dwindle and by the 1970s, all clubs in the Dublin area had folded. The game survived a few more years in Ulster but the sectarian troubles brought the game there to a close in 1972.

Irish cricket underwent a huge change in the 1980s as cricket moved more and more to the one-day limited overs format. Prior to 1981, when they were granted entry to the English one-day knock-out competition, Ireland had played only two matches under one-day regulations. By 1996, eighty per cent of their annual fixtures were one-day matches. Cricket also received much more exposure. England's test matches could now be seen on television not just in Northern Ireland but also in the Republic. Telefis Eireann began to broadcast Irish home matches. More money became available for cricket from industrial sponsorships and from the Test and County Cricket Board. Much of this was invested in youth cricket, the development of coaches and the improvement of umpiring.

The Irish side of the 1980s suffered from the reverse of the problem of earlier years. Whilst the batting was now reasonably strong, the bowling was no longer as penetrative. In 1986 and 1987, the whole attack went for over 40 runs per wicket, partly because during their tour of Zimbabwe in 1986 they came across Graeme Hick who hit them for 309 runs in only 394 minutes in a three-day international and for 155 not out in a one-day match. Once Ireland entered the ICC Trophy in 1994, the availability of players became an issue. Many of the players used up their annual leave to play in the competition which meant fielding a weaker side for the remaining matches of the season. Despite these problems, Ireland had some successes, winning the Triple Crown and the European Championships in 1996.

A greater public awareness of cricket led to a revival of the women's game. A one-off festival match organised for Trinity Week in Dublin in 1975 between Trinity College and the Phoenix Cricket Club aroused great interest and by the following year the Leinster Women's Cricket Union had not only been reformed but a league was underway involving seven clubs. Cricket was reintroduced into the leading girls schools in 1979 and inter-provincial matches involving Leinster, Ulster and Munster started in 1980. The Irish Women's Cricket Union was formed in 1982. The following year, Ireland took part in a quadrangular competition in The Netherlands. They beat Denmark and a Young Netherlands team but lost to The Netherlands. The Irish women played their first three-day match in 1987 against The Netherlands. Since then they have played only one other three-day game, against Pakistan in 2000. The rest of the matches have been one-days. They have taken part in all the World Cup contests and the European Championships. In 2001 they won the European competition. Although they have only once beaten England and never beaten Australia, New Zealand, India or South Africa, they have excellent records against The Netherlands, Denmark, Scotland and Pakistan. They had to qualify to participate in the 2005 World Cup in South Africa and did so by winning all their matches. In 2001, the Irish Women's Cricket Union amalgamated with the ICU, a move which it is hoped will increase the amount of coaching and sponsorship available and encourage more women to play. However, so far an increase in resources has not been forthcoming. Some of the women players feel that, with the greater success of the men's team, any new sources of funding will be invested in the men's game and the women will be sidelined.

Ireland hosted the ICC Trophy in 2005 and, although losing to Scotland in the final, qualified for the 2007 World Cup. Then, after victories over Scotland, The Netherlands and the United Arab Emirates they beat Kenya in the final of the ICC Intercontinental Cup to complete the most successful year in Irish cricket history. The composition of the successful team, however, poses problems. With the rising standards of Irish cricket over the last decade, the English first-class counties have shown interest in the best players. Edmund Joyce, who would probably have become Ireland's best-ever batsman, is a regular member of Middlesex but, after being selected by England for a one-day international, ironically against Ireland, he is no longer eligible for the national side. Eoin Morgan is also on the Middlesex staff and Niall O'Brien and Andrew White are with Northamptonshire. The problem posed for the Irish selectors is that whilst the English counties must release their players if they are chosen for England, there is no regulation that compels them to do so to represent Ireland. Thus, Ireland cannot always rely on fielding their best side. A further issue is that players like Trent Johnston and Jeremy Bray are from Australia, Andre Botha from South Africa and Naseer Shaukat from Pakistan; they qualify to play for Ireland by either residence or citizenship. With such players making up a high proportion of the national side, there is concern that there will be less incentive for the next generation of Irish-born players. The future of Irish cricket will depend on how the Irish Cricket Union resolves these issues. The public interest generated by the outstanding performance of the Irish side in the 2007 World Cup (see Chapter 4) should provide an excellent opportunity, however, from which to promote the game at school, club and international level.

Famous Victory
March 17, 2007. Sabina Park, Kingston.
Pakistan 132 (45.4 overs)
Ireland 133-7 (41.4 overs) (N.J. O'Brien 72)
Ireland won by 3 wickets
(Duckworth-Lewis method)

Ireland won the toss in this first-round World Cup match and invited Pakistan to bat. David Langford-Smith (10-1-31-1) and Boyd Rankin (9-1-32-3), supported by keen fielding, exploited the overcast conditions to reduce Pakistan to 56 for three through some superb swing bowling. Andre Botha strangled the middle order with a spell of 8-4-5-2, leaving Kyle McCallan (5.4-1-12-2) to mop up the tail with his off-spin. Ireland struggled in reply against hostile bowling by Mohammad Sami (3-29) but Niall O'Brien produced a mixture of flamboyant stroke-play and periods of sound defence in partnerships of 47 with William Porterfield (13) and 38 with Kevin O'Brien (16*) to keep Ireland ahead of the required run-rate. The innings was interrupted by a 35-minute break for rain after which a revised target was set of 128 runs from 47 overs, using the Duckworth-Lewis method. The loss of Niall O'Brien, Andrew White and McCallan in quick succession to leave Ireland on 133 for seven gave Pakistan a chance of victory but, in gloomy conditions, Ireland refused to panic. They played the bowling on its merits until Trent Johnston (9*) won the match in fine style by driving Azhar Mahmood over long-on for six. Ireland's greatest ever victory qualified them for the Super Eight stage whilst Pakistan went out of the World Cup.

Player Profiles

Boucher, James Chrysostom. b Phoenix Park, Dublin, 22 December 1910. d Fuengirola, Spain, 25 December 1995. rhb. rob. An outstanding cricketer in a career which lasted from 1929 to 1954, he was criticised for expending unnecessary energy in a long run-up which he used to deliver his off-spin at a medium pace. An attacking bowler, he usually bowled with three short legs and no extra cover, and never changed this for defence even when collared. For bowlers taking ten or more wickets, he headed the English first-class averages in 1931, 1937 and 1948. In 60 matches for Ireland, he scored 1,161 runs (average 13.19) and took 307 wickets (average 15.25). He was the first Irish player to take over 300 wickets in an international career. He was Secretary to the Irish Cricket Union from 1954 to 1973. By profession he was a clerk with the electricity board in Dublin.

Monteith, James Dermott. b Lisburn, County Antrim, 2 June 1943. rhb. sla. A regular choice for Ireland between 1965 and 1984, he also played first-class for Middlesex. His cricket career ended in 1984 when he was seriously injured by a hit-and-run car driver. In 72 international matches he scored 1,712 runs (average 20.62) and took 326 wickets (average 17.37), becoming the second Irish player to take 300 wickets and surpassing Boucher's total for the most wickets ever taken.

Other leading players: *1835-1860:* C. Lawrence; A. Samuels. *1860-1890:* Rev J. Byrne. *1890-1914:* L.H. Gwynn (rhb. rm); R.J.H. Lambert (rhb. rob);. *1920-1940:* E. Ingram (rhb. lb/rm); T.G.B. McVeagh (lhb); E.D.R. Shearer (rhb). *1945-1960:* S.F. Bergin (lhb); S.S.J. Huey (rhb. sla); J.S. Pollock (rhb). *1960-1980:* I.J. Anderson (rhb, rob), O.D. Colhoun (rhb. wk), A.J. O'Riordan (lhb. lfm). *1980-2000:* P.B. Jackson (rhb. wk); D.A. Lewis (rhb; rm); S.J.S. Warke (rhb). *Present day:* J.P. Bray (lhb); W.K. McCallan (rhb. rob); N.J. O'Brien (lhb, wk).

Women: *1920-1940:* I. Howard (lhb. sla). *1980-2000:* S. Bray (rhb. rf); M.P. Moore (rhb. sla); S.A. Owens (rhb. rf). *Present day:* B.M. McDonald (rhb. rmf); C. O'Neill (rhb. rob).

Playing record
International matches

	Won	Lost	Tied	Drawn	Ab
Scotland (first-class 1909-2000)	19	20	0	36	3
ICC Intercontinental Cup	6	1	0	3	0
Other first-class	7	24	0	17	0
Other internationals (*)	19	10	0	18	0

* Matches against Canada, Denmark, Netherlands, Philadelphia, USA, Wales.

One-day matches

	Won	Lost	Tied	No Res
World Cup	2	6	1	0
Other ODIs	2	5	0	1
English domestic competitions	10	47	0	3
ICC Trophy	16	11	0	1
European Championships	16	10	0	1
Triple Crown	10	16	1	0
Emerging Nations Tournament	2	2	0	1

Highest team score
513-5 dec	v United Arab Emirates, Abu Dhabi	2006/07

Lowest team score
24	v MCC, Dublin	1871

Highest individual score
209*	E.J.G. Morgan	v United Arab Emirates	2006/07

Best bowling
9-26	F. Fee	v Scotland, Dublin	1957

Best wicket-keeping

| 6 (6c) | P.B. Jackson | v Scotland, Glasgow | 1984 |

ODI

| 6 (6c) | N.J. O'Brien | v Italy, Glasgow | 2006 |

Women

Test matches

	Won	Lost	Tied	Drawn
Pakistan	1	0	0	0

One-day matches

	Won	Lost	Tied	No Res
World Cup	7	26	0	2
European Championships	13	11	0	0
Other ODIs	12	27	0	2

Highest team score

| 193-3 dec | v Pakistan, Dublin | 2000 |

ODI

| 309-2 | v Netherlands, Miskin Manor | 2005 |

Lowest team score

ODI

| 46 | v Australia, Dublin | 2001 |

Highest individual score

| 68* | C.M. Beggs | v Pakistan, Dublin | 2000 |

ODI

| 120 | K.N. Young | v Pakistan, Dublin | 2000 |

Best bowling

| 6-21 | I.M.H.C. Joyce | v Pakistan, Dublin | 2000 |

ISLE OF MAN

Affiliate Member of ICC: elected 2004

THE ISLE of Man Cricket Association was formed in 1930. Until 2004, it existed as an affiliate organisation of the Lancashire County Cricket Club. A small number of matches are played each year between a representative Island team and club sides from England, including the MCC. At present, there are twelve cricket clubs registered with the Association and six of these play in a weekend league. In 2005, the Isle of Man participated in the European Affiliates Tournament.

Leading player: *Present day:* C. Byrne.

Playing record

One-day matches

	Won	Lost	No Res
European Affiliates Championships	2	3	1

Highest team score

ODI

| 258-4 | v Spain, La Manga | 2006 |

Lowest team score

ODI

| 106 | v Greece, Mechelen | 2005 |

Highest individual score

ODI

| 85* | G. Morris | v Spain, La Manga | 2006 |

Best bowling

ODI

| 5-22 | A. Sewell | v Spain, La Manga | 2006 |

Best wicket-keeping

ODI

| 5 (2c 3st) | R. Webber | v Finland, Mechelen | 2005 |

ISRAEL

Associate Member of ICC: elected 1974

CRICKET WAS introduced into the area which is now Israel by the British during the period of military occupation between 1917 and 1922 which ended the rule of the Ottoman Empire. During the period of the British Mandate in Palestine which lasted from 1922 to 1948, the British and Australian military and members of the Mandatory Civil Service regularly played cricket as a recreational activity. Civilian cricket clubs were formed in Jerusalem and Haifa. With the establishment of Israel in 1948, the occupying forces and the expatriate civil service left and cricket depended for its survival on the enthusiasm of a small number of settlers, particularly from South Africa and India. The first recorded match in the new country took place in 1956 at Tel-Hashomer between Tel Aviv and Be'er Sheva. The Be'er Sheva side was captained by Ben Abrahams, an immigrant from Mumbai, who is generally regarded as the founder of Israeli cricket; he continued playing and then umpiring until his death in 1974, aged 71. Cricket generally struggled, however, because of the very small number of players and the lack of facilities. The combination of economic austerity and compulsory military service meant that few people could either afford or had the time to play sport.

The period 1961 to 1966 marked the nadir of Israeli cricket when the game almost died out. However, among the Jewish settlers from Commonwealth countries were a few cricket enthusiasts. Clubs were started where the immigrants settled, including Haifa, Be'er Sheva, Ashdod, where Indians were involved in the construction of the new port, and Galilee, particularly in the *kibbutzim* of Amiad and Beit Ha'emek. In 1966, a national league was started with ten clubs and, in 1968, there was sufficient enthusiasm to form the Israel Cricket Association. Despite the effects of the Arab-Israeli Wars in June 1967 and October 1973 which increased the length of military service and cut into leisure time still further, the new league prospered. Under the enthusiasm of its first President, Colonel Maxim Kahan, the Assistant Chief of Police for West Galilee, the ICA encouraged clubs from overseas to visit. In 1972 cricket was included for the first time in the Maccabi Games, a Jewish sports festival held in Israel every four years.

Israel participated in every ICC Trophy competition between 1979 and 2001 but with little success. They have done slightly better in the European Championships which have been held every four years since 1996. Since 2000 the ICA has embarked on a major youth development programme which now involves over 1,000 boys and girls. A national cricket academy was established in 2003 at the purpose-built cricket facility at the Hadar Yosef Sports Stadium in Tel Aviv. Although cricket does not yet rival soccer and basketball as the leading sports, the game is now played by children across all levels of society.

Leading players: *1980-2000:* S.B. Perlman. *Present day:* I. Massil (rhb. rmf).

Playing record
One-day matches

	Won	Lost	No Res
ICC Trophy	3	40	2
European Championships	7	20	1
Quadrangular Tournament	1	3	0

One of Israel's victories in the ICC Trophy was by a walkover when Sri Lanka refused to meet them in the 1979 competition; the victory in the Quadrangular tournament was also by a walkover when France refused to play after they were not allowed to include a twelve-year old in their side. One of the victories in the European Championships was a walkover when Greece decided not to play after being penalised earlier in the tournament for fielding ineligible players.

Highest team score
ODI

269-9	v Gibraltar, Rotterdam	1990

Lowest team score
ODI

38	v England NCA, Ringsted	1996

Highest individual score
ODI

117*	N. Ward	v Gibraltar, Gibraltar	1992

Best bowling
ODI

6-61	S. Shein	v Norway, Mechelen	2004

Best wicket-keeping
ODI

7 (7c)	P. Amit	v France, Uddingston	2000

ITALY

Affiliate Member of ICC: elected 1984
Associate Member of ICC: elected 1995

THE FIRST official record of cricket in Italy relates to a painting by Jacques Sablet, signed and dated 1792, depicting Thomas Hope, a merchant from Amsterdam, playing cricket when on the Grand Tour. Since, as was customary with landscape painting of the time, the artist has used some poetic licence in portraying the background landscape, it is impossible to locate the exact place where the game was played. The traditional interpretation is that it was in Rome. It is also uncertain whether the game was a one-off fixture among friends or is representative of cricket being a common recreational pastime amongst the expatriate British and Dutch community. The next record of cricket is in 1811 when a club was formed in Naples by Colonel Maceroni, the recently appointed *aide-de-camp* to the new Emperor, Joachim Murat, to provide some form of entertainment for the many expatriates, both military and civilian. Cricket was organised as a recreational activity at the Capodimonte Royal Gardens. In 1893, the Genoa Cricket and Football Club was founded by the English, an initiative which was followed by English residents elsewhere, resulting in the Milan Cricket and Football Club and the International Cricket and Football Club in Turin which, later, became Juventus. By the early 1900s, however, most of the English had departed these cities leaving the clubs to concentrate on football. Cricket was played by students at the English College in Rome and, shortly after the First World War, the rector laid out a wicket at the Portuguese monastery at Palazola on the shores of Lake Albano which he had acquired as the college's summer residence. Thus, by the 1920s, cricket had a tenuous existence in Italy among the expatriate community only to decline and then virtually disappear in the 1930s, except for a few, very informal matches at the Villa Pamphili in Rome.

The game did not revive until the 1960s when a concrete pitch was laid at the Villa Pamphili by Admiral Frank Pogson who had married Princess Orietta Doria Pamphili. In 1962, Mr Hugh Jones, an official at the British Embassy, presented a trophy for a cricket gala at the Villa. Six teams participated with the Australian Sports and Social Club being the first winners of what became known as the 'Rome Ashes'. The clubs then founded the Rome Sports Association, which covered soccer, rugby, hockey and softball in addition to cricket. The highlight of what became known as the 'golden era' of Roman cricket was in 1964 when the Australians played in Rome during a stop-over on their way to England. This period of Italy's cricket history ended in 1972 when the Rome City Council turned the Villa Pamphili into a public park.

Before cricket died out completely, some enthusiastic Italians founded the Associazione Italiana Cricket (Italian Cricket Association) in 1980. The first objective was to revive the game in Rome and then encourage Italian participation. By 1984, the clubs of Capannelle, Lazio and Roma had been formed in the capital. Under the leadership of Simone Gambino, who became president in 1986, the AIC promoted the game throughout the country. In 1984 the national side went on the first of several tours to England with a party of seventeen players which included nine Italians. In 1987, clubs taking part in the national championships had to field at least seven Italians, a figure which was later increased to nine. Gambino insisted that the national side should be all Italian, a policy which led to some embarrassing defeats. In 1989, Denmark made 438 runs in a one-day match against the Italian bowling and then dismissed Italy for 29 runs. In 1992, the policy was eased slightly with the requirement that all cricketers in the national side should be Italian passport holders.

Won All Their Games

Italy embarked on ambitious overseas tours, visiting Argentina in 1995 and South Africa and Namibia in 1996. They entered the 1996 European Championships and the 1997 ICC Trophy competition. Under the coaching of Doug Ferguson, standards improved and, in 1998, Italy won all their games in Division B of the European Championships and gained promotion to Division A. Much of their success was due to the arrival of Joe Scuderi, an Italian passport holder, who had learnt his cricket in Australia and had played first-class cricket for both South Australia and Lancashire. Although Italy found the opposition in Division A of the European Championships too strong and finished last in 2000 and 2002, they achieved unexpected victories over Denmark in 2000 and The Netherlands in 2002. On returning to Division B, they won all their matches in 2004 and went forward to the qualifying competition in Kuala Lumpur to decide which country had the twelfth and final place in the ICC Trophy competition in 2005. They finished a disappointing seventh out of the eight participants. To date, Italy's best players have been Italians returning from overseas, having learnt their cricket in England, South Africa or Australia, or Sri Lankans who came to Italy in 1992 under an agreement between the Cesena Cricket Club and the Board of Control for Cricket in Sri Lanka. The challenge will be to produce players of comparable standard who have been introduced to the game entirely in Italy. To this end, in 2003, the AIC embarked on a five-year plan to introduce cricket into some of the state schools.

The future may also see the emergence of an Italian women's team. A small group of women have been involved in cricket since the 1980s but mostly in an officiating capacity as umpires and scorers. In the early 1990s, many of the umpires in Italian domestic cricket were women. Today the Italian umpires are predominantly male but women have started to play. In 2002, an Italian Women's Championship was inaugurated. For women's cricket to grow, however, it must be expanded since it is currently confined to the town of Catania, in Sicily.

Famous Victory

July 20, 2002 – Comber
Italy 144 (45.5 overs) (J.C. Scuderi 64)
Netherlands 143-9 (50 overs) (N.A. Statham 50,
A.G. Corbellari 4-33)
Italy won by 1 run

The surprise result of the 2002 European Championships saw the Dutch inexplicably unable to surpass a very moderate Italian total. Italy owed their innings entirely to Joe Scuderi who made 44 per cent of their runs. The rest of the batting struggled against some very tight Dutch bowling. Roland Lefebvre (8.5-3-12-3) was outstanding and well supported by the spinners, Adeel Raja (10-1-26-3) and Tim de Leede (10-1-25-2). Perhaps the Dutch were initially complacent in reply. They lost three wickets for five runs and the fourth fell with the total at 16, Scuderi (1-27) and Andrea Corbellari doing the damage. Nick Statham and Luk van Troost instituted some repair with a partnership of 69 but after van Troost was dismissed, the Dutch fell away. At the start of the last over six runs were required with three wickets in hand. The Italians entrusted the task to Samantha Ketipe and with his first ball he had Statham caught behind by Kamal Kariyawasam. The new batsman, Edgar Schiferli, went for a big hit with the next ball only to be caught by Hemantha Jayasena. The hat-trick was averted and two runs scrambled from the next three deliveries, leaving four to make off the last ball. Quick fielding and a smart return to the wicket-keeper by Corbellari prevented the boundary and kept the runs down to two, giving Italy their best win to date.

Player profile

Scuderi, Joseph Charles. b Ingham, Queensland, 24 December 1968. rhb. rfm. A pupil of the Australian Cricket Academy in Adelaide, he went on to play first-class cricket for South Australia and Lancashire. Having played for Australia at Under 19 level, he was in the Australian squad of eighteen players for the 1992 World Cup. Fortunately for Italy, he was not chosen for the final fourteen and therefore remained eligible to play for the country of his parents. Since his debut for Italy in 1998, he has been their outstanding player. In 28 limited overs matches he

has scored 1,054 runs (average 47.90) and taken 24 wickets (average 18.58).

Other leading players: *1980-2000:* Akhlaq Qureshi (rhb. rm); K. Kariyawasam (rhb. wk); S.V. de Mel (rhb. sla). *Present day:* Alaud Din (rhb. rfm); A. Bonora (rhb. rm); H.S. Jayasena (lhb. lb).

Playing record

One-day matches

	Won	Lost	No Res
ICC Trophy	0	4	1
European Championships	12	11	0
ICC Qualifying Competition	1	4	0
Quadrangular Tournament	3	1	0

Highest team score

ODI

274-7	v Gibraltar, Gibraltar	1999

Lowest team score

ODI

29	v Denmark, Ringsted	1989

Highest individual score

ODI

123	J.C. Scuderi	v Gibraltar, Gibraltar	1999

Best bowling

ODI

5-17	E. Gallo	v Gibraltar, Antwerp	2004

Best wicket-keeping

ODI

7 (7c)	G. Passaretti	v France, Mechelen	2004

JAPAN

Affiliate Member of ICC: elected 1989
Associate Member of ICC: elected 2005

THE BRITISH Navy introduced cricket to Japan around the time of the Meiji Restoration. The Japanese government decided where foreign residents could live and so, inadvertently, they influenced where cricket was first played. The first cricket club in Japan was established by British traders in Yokohama in 1868. A similar club was soon founded in Kobe and trading contacts between the two cities led to a match between them in 1884. A second match was played in 1888 and thereafter a regular interport series was established which lasted until the

1930s. The small number of British residents meant that, despite the enthusiasm of the players, the standard was fairly low. Shanghai sent a team to play both clubs in 1893 and further occasional visits were made into the 1920s. Generally, Shanghai won the games easily. In the 1880s and 1890s, cricket was introduced as part of the sporting curriculum into the upper class high schools but it never interested the local children and was eventually dropped. As a result, cricket remained confined to the ports of Kobe and Yokohama and to the foreign population within them.

The period between 1931 and the outbreak of the Pacific War in 1941 is often referred to in Japan as the 'dark valley' because this was when the ideals of liberalism and individual freedom which had emerged in the 1920s were effectively stifled. The description is equally appropriate for the history of cricket in Japan for this was the period in which it died out as the number of foreigners resident in the country declined with the approach of the Second World War. The revival of the game was brought about by Professor Makato Yamada of Kobe City University of Foreign Studies. He began research into cricket and became so interested that he introduced the game to some Japanese students and, in April 1980, formed the first Japanese cricket club at the university. Other universities followed the lead and clubs were founded at Keio University in 1987, Senshu and Chuo Universities in 1989, Waseda in 1990, Doshisha in 1991, Tokyo University of Technology in 1992 and the Aoyama Gakuin University and the University of the Sacred Heart in 1994. Many of the universities established both men's and women's teams. A university competition for men's sides was started in 1990 and the women followed in 1993. The 1990s saw the foundation of clubs by graduates who wanted to continue playing after leaving university, beginning with the Fuji Far East Cricket Club in 1993. The other stimulus for cricket in the 1990s came from the increasing number of foreign residents. Compared to Japanese clubs which are largely confined to the Kanto area around Tokyo and Yokohama, foreign resident clubs are much more numerous and now exist in many cities throughout the country.

Japan's involvement in international cricket began in 1989 with an overseas tour to the Pacific Islands. They took part in the Asian Cricket Council Trophy

matches in 1996, 1998 and 2000 but without success. The national side was almost entirely Japanese. Japan then dropped out of the Asian cricket arena and became part of a new East Asia and Pacific region established by the ICC. By the time of their next appearance in international competition, some of the foreign players had been living in Japan long enough to meet the ICC residential requirements. The Japanese women made their first overseas tour in 1999, visiting Australia. When they participated in the World Cup Qualifying contest in The Netherlands in 2003 they were outclassed in all their matches. In 2006 they were defeated by Papua New Guinea in the East Asia-Pacific region qualifier for the 2009 World Cup. Cricket in Japan remains a sport of the university-educated elite and foreign residents, particularly from Britain and the Indian sub-continent. The challenge is whether, through the introduction of cricket into the elementary and junior high schools, the playing base can be extended more widely.

Leading players: *Present day:* T. Chino (rhb. wk); N.A. Miyaji (rhb. rm); Munir Ahmed (rhb. lb). **Women:** *Present day:* E. Kuribayashi (lhb. rob).

Playing record
One-day matches

	Won	Lost	No Res
Asian Cricket Council Trophy	0	10	1
East Asia Pacific Challenge	1	3	0
East Asia Pacific Cup	5	1	0
East Asia Pacific Trophy	1	3	0

Highest team score
ODI
| 315-9 | v Indonesia, Fujigawa | 2004 |

Lowest team score
ODI
| 18 | v Hong Kong, Kathmandu | 1998 |

Highest individual score
ODI
| 94 | M. Ferris | v Indonesia, Fujigawa | 2004 |

Best bowling
ODI
| 5-26 | N.A. Miyaji | v Indonesia, Port Vila | 2005 |

Best wicket-keeping
ODI
| 4 (4c) | T. Chino | v Indonesia, Port Vila | 2005 |

Women
One-day matches

	Won	Lost	No Res
World Cup qualifying	0	5	0
World Cup qualifying East Asia-Pacific Region	0	3	0

Highest team score
ODI
156-5	v Papua New Guinea, Port Moresby	2006

Lowest team score
ODI
28	v Pakistan, Amsterdam	2003

Highest individual score
ODI
67*	E. Kuribayashi	v Papua New Guinea, Port Moresby	2006

Best bowling
ODI
3-36	M. Takemori	v Papua New Guinea, Port Moresby	2006

JERSEY

Affiliate Member of ICC: elected 2005

OCCASIONAL CRICKET matches were played in Jersey in the 1860s by the British garrison stationed at Fort Regent. Cricket was also introduced at Victoria College, the local public school and in 1861 they played the first of what has become an annual fixture against Elizabeth College, their counterpart on Guernsey. In 1813, Jersey played their first international match, beating a combined Guernsey and Alderney side by an innings. Despite these beginnings, cricket took a long time to get organised on the island. It was not until 1870 that the first cricket club, Jersey United, was formed. In 1906, officers from the garrison formed the Jersey Leopards Club. The two clubs amalgamated in 1911 to form the Jersey Island Cricket Club. Since that time, apart from gaps for the 1914-18 and 1939-45 Wars, cricket has largely consisted of visits to the island by English club sides and short tours of England by Jersey Island CC. In the 1920s, the club employed a professional, Ernest Remnant of Hampshire, who was instrumental in the Island beating a strong MCC side by eight runs on their first visit to Jersey in 1924. Until the 1960s, all home matches were played at Victoria College which had the only grass wicket on the Island. Since then other clubs

with grass wickets have been formed at Florence Boot Fields, Grainville and Les Quennevais. In 1979, a new sports centre was opened at Grainville, St Saviour, which is now the home of Jersey's cricket. International matches against Guernsey started in 1957 and Jersey have been victorious in 21 of the 48 matches played. Jersey played in Division 2 of the European Championships in 2006, finishing second to Norway.

Leading player: *Present day:* M.R. Hague (rhb. rm).

Playing record
One-day matches

	Won	Lost	No Res
European Championships Division 2	2	2	1

Highest team score
ODI
267-2	v Italy, Grosseto	2007

Lowest team score
ODI
159	v France, Glasgow	2006

Highest individual score
ODI
100*	M.R. Hague	v Italy, Grosseto	2007

Best bowling
ODI
4-32	M.R. Hague	v France, Glasgow	2006

Best wicket-keeping
ODI
3 (3c)	R.D. Minty	v Germany, Glasgow	2006

KENYA

Associate Member of ICC: elected 1981

CRICKET WAS first played in Kenya in 1896 between British residents in Mombasa and the crew of HMS *Sparrow,* a British naval vessel which had called into port. By 1899, British settlers in Nairobi were playing the game as recreation. In both cities, scratch matches were organised on an *ad hoc* basis such as the East African Protectorate versus the Rest of the World, An England XI versus The Rest, and Recent Arrivals versus Old Stagers. In 1914, Kenya played its first international match under the title of the East African Protectorate when a representative European side travelled to Entebbe and defeated Uganda by five wickets. The captain was Shenton Thomas who later helped to promote cricket in the Gold Coast and Nigeria before becoming Governor General of the Straits Settlements. Thomas was also instrumental in initiating the fixture between the Officials and Settlers on 14 February 1910. The contest developed into an annual fixture which lasted until 1957 and became the highlight of the Kenyan cricket season for Europeans. During the 1920s and 1930s, many cricketers with first-class experience in England and South Africa took part in these games and the standard is regarded by many to have been close to first class.

Although it was the British who brought cricket to Kenya, it was taken up enthusiastically by the Indians who came to the country as traders and to work on the railways. The Indians were the first to organise their sporting activities through an official body. The Kenya Asian Sports Association was founded in 1912 and it became the country's authority for Asian cricket. The increasing need for a parallel European organisation was met in 1927 by the founding of the Kenya Kongonis Cricket Club with the aim of organising tours in East Africa, visits to England and generally advancing cricket in the country. The Kongonis adopted the MCC as their model and in 1932 were recognised as the governing body for cricket in Kenya. Although with separate European and Asian organisations, cricket developed along racial lines, contact between them was friendly. On 11 and 12 March 1933, the first of what became an annual series of matches was organised between the Europeans, selected by the Kongonis, and the Asians, selected by KASA. The Europeans were far too strong in the early matches but by the time the series ended in 1966, many Europeans had left the country following its independence and the standard of European cricket was in decline whereas that of Asian cricket had greatly improved. The Kongonis were successful in all their objectives except for arranging tours in Kenya. Several approaches were made to Sir Julien Cahn, Sir Theodore Brinckman, H.M. Martineau, the MCC, and Incogniti but they all failed through lack of finance. The South African Cricket Association considered a tour for 1940 but the Second World War prevented it from taking place.

Cricket restarted quickly after 1945 with both the Officials–Settlers and the Europeans–Asians matches resuming in 1946. Kenya played their first international match in 1951 when a combined European and Asian side beat Tanganyika in Nairobi by an innings and 27 runs. The following year they beat Uganda by 254 runs. The need to select the best side for these fixtures pointed up the need for a single authority to control the game and in 1953, the Kenya Kongonis and KASA agreed to form the Kenya Cricket Association, the first inter-racial sports organisation in the country. The KCA immediately promoted international cricket and, by 1954, a regular series of fixtures was established involving Kenya, Uganda and Tanganyika. Initially, the KCA had little control over touring sides. After the failures of the 1930s, there was suddenly a great interest in touring Kenya and the other East African countries but most of the ventures were privately arranged and sponsored. Air Vice-Marshall Sir Brian Baker brought a United Services team from Cairo in 1946. A strong European side, the Rhodesian Stragglers, came in 1951 followed in 1955 by another all-European team, the Natal Crickets. The Muslim Sports Association sponsored a visit from the Pakistan Cricket Writers in 1956, a side which included seven test players. The Sunder Cricket Club, sponsored by the Kathiawar Sports Club and including nine Indian test players, visited in 1957, and the MCC made their first tour in December 1957 and January 1958. The Kenya Asian Sports Association also sent a side to South Africa in 1957 where they played three 'test' matches against a representative South African Non-European side.

High Reputation

FROM 1958 until the mid 1970s, the KCA encouraged an almost continuous flow of visiting teams, all with players of first-class or test-match standard. These included the South African Non-European side (1958), Gujarat (1960), the Commonwealth (1962), the MCC (1963 and 1974), Pakistan International Airlines (1964), Worcestershire (1965), India (1967), Warwickshire (1967), the Cricket Club of India (1970) and Hyderabad Blues (1971). Against such strong opposition it was not surprising that Kenya did not win any matches. However, they managed to draw the majority of games and many of their players gained high reputations. Basharat Hassan was taken on by Nottinghamshire where he had a long and successful first-class career. Ramanbhai Patel was chosen by R.A. Roberts for his international side which undertook a world tour in 1972. Under the auspices of the East African Cricket Conference, the matches against the other East African countries became formalised in an annual tournament for the Sir Robert Menzies Trophy. The series lasted from 1966 to 1980 during which time Kenya won the competition nine times. When East Africa competed in the 1975 World Cup, Kenya provided seven of the fourteen players.

During this period, major changes took place in Kenyan cricket, reflecting the changing political environment following independence. As many of the European settlers and officials left the country, so the number of Europeans involved in cricket declined. By the end of the 1970s there were no longer sufficient players to keep the game alive in the various centres of the Rift Valley where it had been part of the way of life for European farmers and traders. Cricket became confined to Nairobi and Mombasa. The Kenyan national side changed from one of European and Asian in equal proportions to one dominated by Asians. When the Asian community were expelled from Uganda in the late 1970s, many Asians also left Kenya. At the same time, fewer of the next generation of Asians were keen to take up the sport and those that did seemed to be of a lower standard. Thus the quality of Kenyan cricket generally declined. When Kenya embarked on their first overseas tour in 1980/81 to Zimbabwe, they were outclassed in the two international matches played. The KCA recognised that cricket was still a game largely for the Asian community and those Europeans who had stayed and taken Kenyan citizenship and that the vast majority of the population of the country were effectively excluded. A major development programme was therefore undertaken to encourage African participation.

Throughout the 1980s, a small number of Africans in Nairobi became involved in cricket and the best gradually made their way into the national side until, by the 1990s, the Kenyan team comprised Asians and Africans in similar numbers. African cricket has been dominated by a few key families with the names of Tikolo, Odumbe and Suji being particularly important. In 1981, Kenya left the East African Cricket Conference and played in the 1982 and 1986 ICC Trophies with mixed success. Gradually, results improved and in 1990 Kenya reached the semi-finals of the ICC Trophy where they lost to The Netherlands. Kenya hosted the 1994 competition and reached the final, only to lose to the United Arab Emirates. This result, however, was sufficient to qualify them for the 1996 World Cup. A flurry of activity then ensued by way of preparation. The KCA organised a triangular tournament with the UAE and The Netherlands; Transvaal, Border and India A toured Kenya; Kenya toured South Africa; and The Netherlands then returned to Kenya for a series of four one-day matches. Results were rather mixed and it came as no surprise when Kenya lost their first three matches in the World Cup. Then came the surprise result which thrust Kenyan cricket into the world arena – they beat the West Indies by 73 runs.

Last Ball

The 1997 ICC Trophy again saw Kenya as runners-up, this time losing to Bangladesh on the last ball of the final. In July that year, Kenya were awarded international one-day status. Since that time, they have participated in various one-day competitions with the test-playing countries with limited success. An increasing number of three-day international matches have been played, mainly against the A sides of the test-playing countries. Tours have been made to India (2000), South Africa (2001) and Sri Lanka (2002). In the few years either side of 2000, Kenyan cricket seemed to be growing in strength. The climax was reached with the 2003 World Cup. Although staged mainly in South Africa, Kenya hosted two of the matches, beating Sri Lanka and obtaining a walkover against New Zealand who refused to play in Nairobi because of concerns about security. In addition, Kenya beat Canada, Bangladesh and Zimbabwe to reach the semi-final of the competition where they lost to India. The country's performances in the ICC Emerging Nations Tournament of 2000 and the Six Nations Challenge in 2004 showed that they were the best of the non-test countries. With cricket now the third most popular sport in the country, behind athletics and soccer, Kenya were making a bid for test match status. Their application to the ICC in 2001 was considered premature, however, raising concern that the team would be past its best before test-match status was granted, thereby repeating the experience of many of the other test-playing countries.

The early 2000s saw the emergence of a Kenyan women's side but with only a small number of players to choose from and limited availability of coaching and facilities, they have been unable to match the success of the men's team.

Superficial Gloss

There are concerns that the success of the men's team in the early 2000s may turn out to be a superficial gloss with no foundation. Despite some strong batting performances, Kenya failed to win a match as the guest overseas team in the Carib Beer Cup, the West Indies first-class competition, in early 2004, and they were surprisingly beaten by Ireland in the final of the 2005 ICC Intercontinental Cup. In the 2006 competition, they suffered defeats by The Netherlands and Canada. The international investigations into match fixing which began in India and involved South Africa in particular, also led to Kenya. In 2004, Maurice Odumbe was given a five-year ban from cricket for frequenting with a well-known Indian bookmaker, his activities having been exposed by his ex-wife. The investigations were extended to other members of the Kenyan side but, so far, no strong evidence of their involvement has been forthcoming. Soon after the 2002 World Cup, the Government Minister for Sport accused the KCA of financial mismanagement and dissolved the association. Although this action was overruled by the Kenyan High Court, it soon became clear that the KCA was insolvent. Even allowing for corruption being a part of Kenyan life at all levels of society, the financial status of the KCA has been a major factor in the failure to find a sponsor for Kenyan cricket. With insufficient funds to pay the expenses of the players contracted to the national side, many went on strike in 2004, forcing Kenya to field weakened sides in the final stages of the ICC Intercontinental Cup. They were embarrassingly outclassed by Scotland in the semi-final. The Kenyan government has since provided the KCA with sufficient money to pay the players about two-thirds of what they are owed. Lack of confidence in and uncertainty about the status of the KCA made it impossible to arrange for Kenya's participation in official one-day tournaments. As a result, the team played very few international matches between the 2003 World Cup and mid 2006.

The lack of a formal structure to Kenyan cricket is hindering its development. With no national tournament and no provincial organisation, the nursery for future cricketers is very small, being dependent upon a few elite schools, a small number of clubs in Nairobi and Mombasa, and the ill-financed Cricket Academy. As the players in the Kenyan national side become older, there is a need to replace them, but the evidence to date is that the new players are not of the same quality. The number of good African players coming through the system is very small and the support for women's cricket is very limited. The future of Kenyan cricket is extremely uncertain. The failure of the ICC to award the country test status whilst the national team was at its strongest may well turn out to be a disincentive to the future development of Kenyan cricket. In January 2006, the KCA was officially dissolved and replaced by a new body, Cricket Kenya. Time will determine whether this is a cosmetic change or whether it will overcome the problems of poor management.

Famous Victories
February 29, 1996 – Pune
Kenya 166 (49.3 overs)
West Indies 93 (35.2 overs)
Kenya won by 73 runs

Kenya were expected to lose this World Cup match easily and this looked the likely outcome when they were 81 with six wickets down, having been asked to bat on losing the toss. Only Steve Tikolo (29) had any answer to Courtney Walsh (3-46) but he became the first of Roger Harper's (3-15) victims. The last four batsmen added 85, largely due to defiant work by Hitesh Modi (28) and Tom Odoyo (24). Through them and Asif Karim (11), they lasted into the final over. Jimmy Adams made four catches and a stumping as the West Indies stand-in wicket-keeper. After reaching 18 without loss, the West Indies inexplicably fell apart. Richie Richardson was bowled by

Rajab Ali (3-17). Martin Suji bowled Sherwin Campbell three balls later and then Brian Lara was caught at the wicket by Tariq Iqbal off Rajab. Shivnarine Chanderpaul (19) and Harper (17) were the only batsmen to reach double figures as the middle order collapsed to the off-spin of Maurice Odumbe (3-15). Rajab Ali returned to claim the last wicket of Cameron Cuffy before the Kenyans ran a lap of honour of the stadium to the cheers of the local spectators. Maurice Odumbe took the player of the match award.

February 24, 2003 – Gymkhana Ground, Nairobi
Kenya 210-9 (50 overs) (K.O. Otieno 60, M. Muralitharan 4-28)
Sri Lanka 157 (46 overs) (C.O. Obuya 5 24)
Kenya won by 53 runs

Before their home crowd, Kenya played with great enthusiasm and with a belief that they could create an upset. In contrast, the Sri Lankans gave the impression that their hearts were elsewhere. Put into bat, Kenya lost Ravindu Shah in the first over. Kennedy Otieno then attacked the bowling violently. When he was dismissed, the third wicket to fall, he had made 80 per cent of his side's runs. Hitesh Modi (26), Maurice Odumbe (26) and Peter Ongondo (20) made useful contributions. The Kenyans were, not unexpectedly, bemused by Muralitharan (10-1-28-4) but the other bowling gave no trouble. Apart from Aravinda de Silva (41), Sri Lanka batted as though the required runs would come automatically without too much effort. In the process, they fell to some accurate leg-spin from Collins Obuya who was declared the player of the match.

Player Profiles

Jawahir Shah. b 1942. rhb. The leading batsman in Kenya throughout the period from 1964 to 1981, his wide range of attractive strokes made him a delight to watch. In 36 matches for Kenya and East Africa he made ten centuries. Many observers regarded him as of first-class standard.

Karim, Aasif Yusuf. b Mombasa 15 December 1963. rhb. sla. His international career lasted from 1980 to 2003. From being an attacking bowler unafraid to buy his wickets in two- or three-day matches, he developed into a miserly one-day exponent. He took part in three World Cup competitions and four ICC Trophy contests. He saved his most remarkable performance for his penultimate match, a World Cup game against Australia in 2003 (see Chapter 4). A good lawn tennis player, he was captain of the Kenyan Davis Cup side. In 6 international matches he scored 87 runs (average 12.42) and took 18 wickets (average 26.00). In 34 one-day internationals he made 228 runs (average 12.66) and took 27 wickets (average 41.25). In 37 other limited overs matches he scored 280 runs (average 12.72) and took 61 wickets (average 16.50).

Odumbe, Maurice Omondi. b Nairobi 15 June 1969. rhb. rob. The leading all-rounder in Kenyan cricket throughout the 1990s, he played in three World Cup matches and three ICC Trophy contests. His reputation was lowered, however, when found guilty of associating with bookmakers who were involved in match fixing and he was given a five-year ban. In 19 international matches he scored 985 runs (average 36.48) and took 41 wickets (average 20.90). In 102 one-day internationals he made 2,363 runs (average 26.85) and took 88 wickets (average 33.88). In 33 other limited overs matches he scored 1,390 runs (average 57.91) and took 23 wickets (average 30.04).

Ramanbhai Patel. The leading Kenyan batsman of the late 1950s and 1960s, he scored three centuries in the Asians versus Europeans series and one for East Africa against a strong Commonwealth side. He was selected by R.A. Roberts for his international team which undertook a world tour in 1962.

Tikolo, Stephen Ogonji. b Nairobi 25 June 1971. rhb. rm. Arguably the best player ever to represent Kenya and the best all-round African cricketer of all time. For one season, he was a professional with Border in South Africa. In 31 international matches he has scored 3,037 runs (average 66.02) and taken 68 wickets (average 42.76). In 92 one-day internationals he has made 2,564 runs (average 31.86) and taken 68 wickets (average 31.58). In 28 other limited overs matches he has made 1,173 runs (average 55.85) and taken 27 wickets (average 24.85).

Other leading players: *1920-1940:* A.H. Kneller (rhb. wk); E.P. Nowrojee; G.N. Shah; M.W. Walter;

F.O. Wilson. *1945-1960:* Shakoor Ahmed (rhb. wk); G.B. Jhalla (rhb. rfm); B.A.L. D'Cunha (rhb. lbg). *1960-1980:* A. Lakhani; Raghuvir Patel (wk); Zulfiqar Ali (rhb. rm). *1980-2000:* E.O. Odumbe (rhb. rm); R.D. Shah (rhb. rmf); M.A. Suji (rhb. rmf). *Present day:* H.S. Modi (lhb); T.M. Odoyo (rhb. rmf); K.O. Otieno (rhb. wk).

Women: *Present day:* C. Nekesa (rhb. rm); M. Hassan; F. Nazerali (rhb. rm).

Playing record
International matches

	Won	Lost	Tied	Drawn
First-class matches*	4	9	0	8
ICC Intercontinental Cup	2	2	0	6

* Excluding ICC Intercontinental Cup

One-day matches

	Won	Lost	Tied	No Res
World Cup	6	16	0	1
Other ODIs	21	49	0	1
ICC Trophy	24	12	0	2
Emerging Nations Tournament	5	0	0	1
Six Nations Challenge	4	1	0	1

Highest team score
564	v Leeward Islands, The Valley	2003/04

Lowest team score
49	v South Africa (SACBOC), Mombasa	1958

Highest individual score
247	R.D. Shah	v Pakistan A, Nairobi	2004

Best bowling
8-28	B.A.L. D'Cunha	v Tanganyika, Dar es Salaam	1957

Best wicket-keeping
6 (6 ct)	K.O. Otieno	v Pakistan A, Nairobi	2004

Women
One-day matches

	Won	Lost	Tied	No Res
African Championships	1	2	0	0
East African Championships	1	3	0	0
World Cup Qualifying – African region	0	3	0	0

Highest team score
ODI
129-6	v Tanzania, Kyambogo	2002

Lowest team score
ODI
55	v Tanzania, Dar es Salaam	2004

ODI
28	Y. Mashedi	v Uganda, Kyambogo	2002

28	M. Banja	v Namibia, Dar es Salaam	2004

Best bowling
4-10	C. Nekese	v Tanzania, Kyambogo	2002

KIRIBATI

CRICKET WAS introduced to Kiribati in 1892 by the British and has remained a recreational activity ever since though only two or three matches are now played each year. The best players are those who have spent time in New Zealand as part of their education. Tentau Iotamo showed promise as a batsman when at the Central Medical School, Suva, in the late 1930s but, on returning home, he died of malnutrition during the Japanese Occupation. Occasional matches are played against Tuvalu.

KOREA

Affiliate Member of ICC: elected 2001

CRICKET HAS been played in Seoul, South Korea, since the early 1990s. An annual competition is held, involving four or five teams, mostly made up of expatriates. Some fifteen per cent of the players, however, are Korean, many being students of Sung Kyun Kwan University where there is a cricket club. Korea participated in the 2002 East Asian Eights, held in Perth, Australia, with an entirely Korean side drawn largely from current and recently graduated university students.

KUWAIT

Affiliate Member of ICC: elected 1998
Associate Member of ICC: elected 2005

BRITISH AND other expatriates attached to the Kuwait Oil Company began playing cricket in Kuwait in 1947. The Magwa Cricket Club was formed in 1948. This later became the Kuwait Cricket Club. Once it had become established, cricket was taken up by Kuwaiti residents from the Indian sub-continent. Various local tournaments were organised from the 1950s to the 1990s but the number of participating clubs varied. With no central organisation, some players represented more than one club each season, tournaments were completed in some years but not in others and, with a strong dependence on the expatriate community, teams suffered from occasional non-availability of players. International matches were restricted to occasional visits of overseas teams such as the New Zealand Colts in 1964 and Air India in 1978. In order to place the game on a more organised footing, the Kuwait Cricket Association was formed in 1996. The Kuwaiti national side toured Pakistan in 1999, playing district and club sides, in preparation for their entry into the Asian Cricket Council Trophy in 2000. By early 2001, some of the players and the KCA were in dispute over team selection and development policy. A group of players under the Kuwaiti captain, Taher Bastaki, felt that the Association was biased towards the expatriate community and that insufficient encouragement was being given to Kuwaitis. A rival body, the Kuwait Cricket Board, was established with the aim of increasing the number of Kuwaitis in the national team. Although there has been some mediation, the issue of encouraging more Kuwaitis to play still remains. In 2004, Kuwait won the Gulf Cup, a competition for the affiliate countries along the Persian Gulf and finished third in the Asian Cricket Council Trophy. They then failed to win the Middle East Cup because, instead of fielding their strongest side, they chose to enter two separate teams, Kuwait Reds and Kuwait Blues, in order to give experience to more players. In the ICC Qualifying competition in 2005 to decide the final place for the ICC Trophy contest, Kuwait finished a disappointing sixth, beating only Italy and Zambia. Failure to reach the final of the 2006 Middle East Cup indicates that the standard reached in 2004 is not being maintained.

Leading players: *Present day:* Mohammad Nawaz; Saud Qamar.

Playing record

One-day matches

	Won	Lost	Tied	No Res
Asian Cricket Council Trophy	10	6	1	0
ICC Qualifying Competition	2	3	0	0
Middle East Cup*	3	7	0	0

* includes matches by Kuwait Blues and Kuwait Reds in 2004.

Highest team score

ODI

451	v Bhutan, Kuala Lumpur	2006

Lowest team score

ODI

95	v Nepal, Kuala Lumpur	2004/05

Highest individual score

ODI

122	Saud Qamar	v Bhutan, Kuala Lumpur	2006

Best bowling

ODI

4-9	Azmatullah	v Malaysia, Kuala Lumpur	2004

Best wicket keeping

ODI

5 (3c 2st)	J. Roshanta	v Bhutan, Kuala Lumpur	2006

LATVIA

CRICKET WAS first played in Latvia in 1998 by staff of the British Embassy in Riga. The Latvian Cricket Club was formed in 1999 by players from the Indian sub-continent and they competed that year in the Tallinn Cup, hosted by the Estonian Cricket Club. The Latvian Cricket Federation was founded in 2001 with the aim of promoting cricket and encouraging Latvian participation.

LESOTHO

Affiliate Member of ICC: elected 2001

ALTHOUGH CRICKET was first played in Maseru, the capital of Lesotho, in 1881, it never developed, until recently, beyond a recreational activity for a minority, mainly white, expatriate population. Links were established intermittently with the white cricket authorities in Orange Free State, South Africa, but these never led to the expansion of the game in Lesotho. Occasional matches were played against Swaziland. On independence, cricket became multiracial with Asian and European participation. In 1995 the Lesotho Cricket Association was formed to promote the game and encourage Basuthos to play. Lesotho competed in the annual African Zone VI tournaments between 1995 and 1998 but with limited success. The Lesotho Government's Sports Council encouraged the LCA to spend their limited resources on youth development programmes rather than financing the national senior side. Cricket is now played in at least seven schools and the number of clubs is slowly increasing. In 2005, Lesotho competed in the African Under 17 and Under 19 competitions. Although they lost most of their matches, both teams were entirely Basutho in composition. The senior side returned to international competition for the African Championships Division 2 and showed their inexperience not only by losing all their matches easily but also by bowling 176 wides in their first four games.

Leading players: *1980-2000:* A. Senewiratne. *Present day:* S. Abdullah.

Playing record

One-day matches

	Won	Lost	No Res
African Championships Division 3	0	5	0

Highest team score

ODI

195-8	v Kenya Development XI, Harare	1997

Lowest team score

ODI

66	v Ghana, Benoni	2006

Highest individual score

ODI

55	A. Senewiratne v Kenya Development XI, Harare	1997

Best bowling

ODI

3-43	L. Nts'ekhe v Gambia, Benoni	2006

LIBERIA

CRICKET HAS been played intermittently in Liberia by a small number of expatriates. At one time there was a Liberian Cricket Association which organised a cricket league for the clubs in Monrovia. Liberia was a member of the West African Cricket Conference but never participated in any of the West African tournaments. With the disbandment of the WACC and almost three decades of economic decline, government mismanagement and civil war, the game has died out and seems unlikely to revive in the foreseeable future.

LIBYA

CRICKET CLUBS exist in Tripoli and Benghazi. In 2001 the Libyan Cricket Association was formed. Although the game is largely expatriate, being strongest amongst the resident Pakistani population, several Libyans do play, having learnt the game when studying abroad.

LUXEMBOURG

Affiliate Member of ICC: elected 1998

CRICKET STARTED in Luxembourg soon after the United Kingdom and Ireland joined the European Community in 1973 and sent civil servants to Luxembourg City. In 1976 the Optimists Cricket Club was formed. The Mayor of Walferdange offered the club a small playing field for use as a ground in 1978. The Communities Cricket Club was started in 1984 and, together with the Optimists, they organised the Luxembourg side which took part in the European Cricket Cup in Guernsey in 1990 where they finished ninth out of ten participants. In the following year, the Optimists moved to a larger ground, again made available by the Mayor of Walferdange. International matches against Belgium and France began in the 1990s and, from 1991, the Optimists played in the Belgian cricket league, winning the competition in 1991, 1994 and 1995. The Luxembourg Cricket Federation was founded in 1994 and a Luxembourg league established. The league title is now contested by seven men's clubs and the Optimists Maidens. The latter was formed in 1993 to provide an opportunity for women expatriates to play. In addition to the league fixtures, the Maidens play club sides in Belgium and Germany and, in 2003, hosted three games against the MCC Ladies, all of which were drawn. For many years the expatriate make-up of the game meant that Luxembourg was unable to participate in ICC-recognised competitions because most of the players could not meet the residential qualifications and there were no Luxembourgeois players. As the expatriate community has become more stable, it is now possible to field an eligible side. Luxembourg therefore competed in the ECC Trophy in 2003, the European Representative Championships in 2004 and the European Championships Division 4 in 2006. The results, with only two victories, indicate that much work needs to be done to raise the standard of play. However, there are now over one hundred cricketers in the country and so much activity that there is an urgent need to find a second ground.

Leading players: *Present day:* M. Ramachandran; R.J. Paul.

Playing record
One-day matches

	Won	Lost	No Res
ECC Trophy	0	6	0
European Representative Championships	1	4	0
European Championships Division 4	1	2	1

Highest team score
ODI
257-8	v France, Walferdange	2000

Lowest team score
ODI
52	v Greece, Vienna	2003

Highest individual score
ODI
132	R.J. Paul	v France, Walferdange	2000

Best bowling
ODI
5-28	M. Ramachandran	v Slovenia, Valburga	2004

Best wicket keeping
ODI
3 (3st)	K. Glover	v Switzerland, Seebarn	2003
3 (3c)	G.P. Cope	v Finland, Brussels	2006

MALAWI

Affiliate Member of ICC: elected 2003

ALTHOUGH MALAWI is part of the British Commonwealth, cricket has always struggled to become more than a recreational activity for a small elite group of expatriates. In the late 1930s occasional matches were played between Nyasaland, as the country was then called, and teams from Salisbury (now Harare), Zimbabwe. Whilst the Salisbury side was all-white, Nyasaland was represented by a team drawn from the British and Asian communities. The small size of the expatriate population meant that the national side had to be either extremely weak or multiracial. Perhaps this was one reason why the game barely flourished whilst Malawi was part of the Federation of Rhodesia and Nyasaland. The cricket authorities in Salisbury seemed to concentrate most of their effort in supporting the 'white' game and a multiracial game in what was essentially a backwater area was ignored. Independence in 1964 resulted in the departure of many of the British, leaving the future of the game in the hands of the small Asian community. Given the weakness of the country's economy, little finance was available from the government to support a sport with minority interest.

Through the efforts of a small group of enthusiasts, cricket became more organised during the 1970s. A national cricket association was formed and in 1980 Malawi joined the East and Central African Cricket Conference. The immediate effect was that Malawi received visits from the MCC in 1981 and a Minor Counties side in 1982 during their tours of East Africa. Unfortunately, these remain the only two teams from the leading test-playing countries to have visited the country. Malawian cricket gained some recognition when their best batsman, Iqbal Lorgat, was chosen for the East African side in the ICC Trophy in 1982. During the 1980s and 1990s, Malawi took part intermittently in the East and Central African Championships and the African Zone VI tournaments with mixed success. In 1993 and 1994, they won the East and Central African competitions but at a time when the sides from Tanzania, Uganda and Zambia were rather weak. Today they are again the weakest of the central and east African countries. Efforts are being made to promote the game amongst the African community. By 2004, some 20 per cent of the national side were African.

Leading player: *1980-2000:* M.I.M. Lorgat.

Playing record
One-day matches

	Won	Lost	No Res
ICC African Affiliates Competition	2	3	0
African Championships Division 3	3	2	0

Highest team score
ODI
355-7	v Gambia, Benoni	2006

Lowest team score
ODI
20	v South African Country Districts, Benoni	2004

Highest individual score
ODI

84	M. Qureshi	v Gambia, Benoni	2006

Best bowling
ODI

5-26	F. Panjwani	v Gambia, Benoni	2004

MALAYSIA

Associate Member of the ICC: elected 1967

CRICKET WAS brought to Malaysia by British officials, business men, military personnel, planters and traders. By the 1880s, the game was reasonably well established as a recreational activity of the European administrators and settlers. The Selangor Club was founded in Kuala Lumpur in 1884 and the first cricket match was played on The Padang sometime between 1884 and 1886. Rivalry was quickly established with the Singapore Cricket Club (founded in 1852) with which there was much joint membership and exchange of players as various government officials frequently changed their location between Singapore and Kuala Lumpur. Clubs were also founded in Penang and Malacca, which with Singapore, made up the Straits Settlements, administered directly from 1867 by the United Kingdom government as a British colony.

The remainder of the Malay Peninsula was made up of the Malay States, ruled by their respective Sultans, but with the United Kingdom appointing a Resident with responsibility for law and order and economic development. The development of cricket was hindered by the difficulties of transport and the very small number of Europeans. Transport was by river craft or horse-carts and bicycles on unsurfaced tracks, frequently impassable after monsoon rains. In the early 1880s, there were only eighty-two European and Eurasian persons in the whole of Perak and the European population of Malacca numbered thirty-two. Despite these obstacles, the planters and officials were keen to get together for both social contact and team sport and many of the Residents had an enthusiasm for cricket. Largely as a result of the efforts of Sir Frank Swettenham, Resident between 1889 and 1895, and Sir Ernest Birch, Resident from 1904 to 1910, Perak became the leading centre for cricket, briefly rivalling Singapore.

Frank Swettenham captained a team from the so-called Native States which travelled to Singapore to give the visiting Ceylonese team a warm-up fixture before they embarked on matches against the Straits Settlements and Hong Kong in January 1891. Swettenham was sufficiently impressed by two of the Ceylonese players, fast-bowler, E.A. Christoffelsz, and batsman, Oliver Marks, that he offered them positions in the Malayan Civil Service. It was generally recognised that, under Swettenham, a person's chances of being employed in government service were enhanced if cricketing skills formed an important component of one's curriculum vitae. Thus, Norman Bewick, who went to Malaysia as a rubber planter on the Muar River Estate, Johor, and played for the Federated Malay States, was able to enhance his career, becoming Private Secretary to the Sultan of Pahang. Although perhaps less overtly under other Residents, there is no doubt that many of the leading cricketers in Malaysia between 1900 and 1940 were either administrators or worked for the various trading companies. By the 1910s, cricket had become established as a European game in Selangor, Penang, Perak, Negeri Sembilan and Malacca, with Kuala Lumpur, through the influence of the Selangor Club, reasserting itself over Perak as the leading cricket centre, probably because, as the leading commercial town, it had a larger European population. The clubs became the focus of sporting and social activity among the widely-scattered European communities. As a result, cricket developed as an urban activity, concentrated in the main towns on the western side of the Malay Peninsular. Club members, particularly in Kuala Lumpur, included many cricketers who had played some first-class cricket in England. Money was invested in producing good facilities for cricket often with grass wickets.

The rivalry between the Selangor Club and the Singapore Cricket Club was extended to a wider remit in 1905 with the first of a regular series of matches between the Federated Malay States and the Straits Settlements (often referred to as The Colony). The fixture was played annually through to 1940 when cricket ceased during the Japanese Occupation. With the large number of first-class cricketers involved, the standard was high and probably close to that of the English county game. Even though most of the players with first-class experience played for the Straits Settlements, it was the Federated Malay States which won more matches.

Although the top-class game in Malaya before 1940 was dominated by Europeans, the game at district level had been played by Indians and some Chinese and Malays outside the main towns since the 1880s. The Europeans undoubtedly encouraged the other communities to take up the game in order to obtain sufficient players for matches. As these groups later established their own social clubs, the game also spread to these communities in the towns although, without the same financial support and inputs, it took some time for the players to reach a standard comparable to the Europeans. Once they did, however, even though they were not granted entry to the European clubs, they were increasingly chosen to represent the Federated Malay States.

At the very highest level, the best of the players from the Federated Malay States and the Straits Settlements combined to form an All-Malaya side. The first international was played against All-Burma in Yangon in 1906, followed by two games in 1909 against M.A. Noble's team during a stop-over in Singapore on their return journey from England to Australia. After 1920, All-Malaya replaced the Straits Settlements in the regular series of Interport matches with Hong Kong; when the matches were played in Hong Kong, they also met Shanghai. In 1927, Malaya played two games against Bertie Oldfield's Australians, a side that contained ten players with first-class experience, including, in addition to Oldfield, Bill Woodfull, Charles Macartney, Thomas Andrews and Edgar Mayne. When Malaya won the first of the two 'test' matches by 39 runs, they achieved one of their greatest performances. Australia won the return match and also beat the Federated Malay States. The highest standard of cricket in Malaysia was probably reached in the period between 1925 and 1935. After this, although they obtained a creditable draw against Sir Julien Cahn's side in 1937, they were easily defeated by Ceylon in all three internationals in 1938. Cricket then ceased completely during the Japanese Occupation.

The revival of cricket after the 1939-45 War was hindered by the lack of grounds, which the Japanese had destroyed, and by the absence of expatriate players. Few of the expatriates who returned to Malaysia had experience of first-class cricket, the best being good club or Minor Counties in standard. Offsetting this, however, was the pre-war inheritance which had ensured that cricket was a game of all communities. By the 1950s, when international cricket was re-established with matches against Singapore and Hong Kong, Malaya was represented by multiracial sides. Indeed, sport became an important way of promoting good relations between the races whereas an individual's every-day life tended to revolve round ones own ethnic group.

During the late 1950s and 1960s, Malaysia was recognised as a pleasant place for touring sides to visit and matches were played against Ceylon (1957), the MCC (1961), a Commonwealth side (1962), E.W. Swanton's team (1964), Worcestershire (1965) and J. Lister's International side (1968). These matches ended in heavy defeats. A major initiative to encourage the game for Malaysian nationals took place in 1970 when the Saudara Cup series of matches for citizens only was started against Singapore (see Chapter 3). Malaysia has won more matches in the series than Singapore, including victories by an innings and 76 runs in 1971, ten wickets in 1983 (when Krishnan Saker took all ten wickets for 25 runs in Singapore's first innings) and 149 runs in 1999 (when, on the day before his 16th birthday, Arul Suppiah took six wickets for 48 runs, including a hat-trick in Singapore's second innings). He then forsook Malaysian cricket, taking up a sports scholarship at Millfield School before moving on to Exeter University. He now plays regularly for Somerset, becoming the second Malaysian national, after Lall Singh, to play first-class cricket.

Raise the Standard

A major effort was made in the mid 1990s to raise the standard of cricket and boost the facilities. Improvements were made to the major grounds in Kuala Lumpur including constructing a National Sports Complex at the Kilat Club. The Royal Selangor Club moved from The Padang in the centre of Kuala Lumpur to new premises in the Kiara Hills. New grounds were constructed on the outskirts of Kuala Lumpur, the Bayuemas Oval at Pandamaran and the Kinrara Oval at Puchong. The latter was used when Malaysia hosted the tri-nations series between Australia, India and the

West Indies in September 2006. Malaysia also hosted the Asian Cricket Council Trophy in 1966, 2004 and 2006, the ICC Trophy in 1997 and the Commonwealth Games in 1998, the only time that cricket has been included as a games sport. The Malaysian Cricket Association aims to encourage cricket as a national sport with a view to the country obtaining test status by about 2020. Unfortunately, to date, the playing record has not matched the ambition. A women's squad was formed in 2003, comprising mainly former hockey players and athletes from the armed forces. They won their first international against Singapore in 2006 by 58 runs.

Famous Victory

December 12, 13, 14, 1959 – Chater Road, Hong Kong
Hong Kong 132 (M.C. Schubert 5-35, Cheah Teow Keat 4-12) and 291 (I.L. Stanton 80, B.P. Dhabher 54)
Malaya 170 (B.C.N. Carnell 4-39) and 254-9 (S. Nagaiah 81*, A. Murugesu 51, B.C.N. Carnell 6-97)
Malaya won by 1 wicket

Hong Kong were well on course for an easy victory as a result of excellent batting by Ivor Stanton and Buji Dhabher and the all-round bowling performance of Buddy Carnell. Despite being ahead on the first innings, Malaya had succumbed to 38 for 5 in their second innings. There was a slight recovery to 163-9 but Malaya were still 91 runs behind with 90 minutes of play left when Stan Nagaiah joined Carl Schubert. Both these players had failed to score in the first innings. Nagaiah decided to enjoy himself and hit the ball around but after some 40 runs had been added, the batsmen decided there was still a chance of victory and began to play more sensibly. The Hong Kong captain, Guy Pritchard, tried changing his bowlers and altering his field placings but nothing worked. Close to time, Carnell bowled a full toss to Nagaiah who attempted to pull it to mid-wicket. George Rowe, fielding at silly mid-on took evasive action and dived to the ground, only to see Nagaiah's mis-hit lob gently over his head and the batsmen go through for the winning run.

Player Profiles

Lall Singh. b Kuala Lumpur 16 December 1909. d Kuala Lumpur 19 November 1985. rhb. rsm. Sponsored by a Kuala Lumpur businessman to move to India, he found employment with the Maharajah of Patialia, becoming Assistant District Commissioner. Following test trials, he was chosen for the Indian touring party to England in 1932 where he played one test match. On returning to Malaya, he became Head Groundsman and coach to the Royal Selangor Club. For Malaya and the Federated Malay States, he played 13 matches, scoring 722 runs (average 30.08) and taking 34 wickets (average 19.74).

Navaratnam, Suresh. b Kajang, Selangor, 7 October 1975. rhb. rm. The leading Malaysian cricketer of the 1990s and 2000s, he has scored more runs and taken more wickets in representative matches than any other Malaysian. In 25 matches he has made 918 runs (average 22.39) and taken 83 wickets (average 21.91). In 94 limited overs matches he has scored 2,444 runs (average 35.94) and taken 141 wickets (average 17.61).

Other leading players: *1890-1914:* P.H. Hennessy (rhb. rob); R.M. McKenzie (rhb. rm). *1920-1940:* R.L.L. Braddell (rhb. rm); A.J. Bostock-Hill (rhb. rm). *1945-1960: 1960-1980:* A.E. Delilkan (rhb. lbg); Gurucharan Singh (rhb. rob); Jagdev Singh (lhb. sla). 1980-2000: P. Banerji Nair (rhb. rob); R. Menon (rhb. rob); M.A. Muniandy (rhb. rfm). *Present day:* R. Madhavan (lhb. rm); D.S. Muthuraman (rhb. lb); S. Retinam (rhb. wk).

Playing record

International matches

	Won	Lost	Drawn
All-Malaya (1906-1961)	8	17	3
Federated Malay States v Straits Settlements (1905-1940)	20	8	8
Malaysia v Singapore (Saudara Cup)	12	7	18
Malaya/Malaysia (1957-1983)	2	12	11
ICC Intercontinental Cup	0	2	0
ACC Fast Track Tournament/Premier League	3	5	4

One-day matches

	Won	Lost	No Res
ICC Trophy	12	27	4
Asian Cricket Council Trophy	17	13	1
Wills Cup (Pakistan)	0	4	0
Commonwealth Games	0	3	0
Tuanku Ja'afar Trophy	18	17	9
Stan Nagaiah Trophy	19	14	3

Highest team score

408-9 dec   Federated Malay States v Straits Settlements, Penang 1937

Lowest team score

30	Federated Malay States v Straits Settlements, Penang	1907

Highest individual score

218	C.N. Reed	Federated Malay States v Straits Settlements, Penang	1933

Best bowling

10-25	K. Saker	v Singapore, Kuala Lumpur	1983

Best wicket-keeping

5 (5c)	S. Retinam	v Nepal, Kuala Lumpur	2003/04

ODI

5 (3c 2st)	S. Sakhadevan	v England A, Kuala Lumpur	2003/04

Women

ODI

Won	Lost	No Res
1	0	0

Highest team score

ODI

93-3	v Singapore, Johor Baharu	2006

ODI

93-3	v Singapore, Johor Baharu	2006

Highest individual score

ODI

36*	Emylia Eliani binti Mohammed Rahim	v Singapore, Johor Baharu	2006

ODI

3-5	Mahani binti Malyar	v Singapore, Johor Baharu	2006

MALDIVES

Affiliate Member of ICC: elected 2001

CRICKET WAS played in the Maldive Islands in the 1940s by personnel of the Royal Air Force but when the troops left in 1946, it almost died out. It was revived when Britain returned to the military airforce base at Gan, on Addu Atoll, in 1957. With military and civilian staff from the United Kingdom, West Indies, Australia, New Zealand, Pakistan and Sri Lanka, league and knock-out competitions were regularly held and a small number of Maldivians started to play even though, generally, the local population preferred soccer. Enough locals took to the game to enable it to survive the closure of the base in 1976. Over the last decade enormous advances have been made, albeit as a minority sport, with the Cricket Control Board of the Maldives undertaking a major development programme to promote the game in schools and bring in coaches from Sri Lanka. In 2000 and 2003 they sent the national team on tours of Sri Lanka to play against club and district teams. The Maldives made their first international appearance in 1996 when they competed in the Asian Cricket Council Trophy, winning one of their five matches, that against Thailand. Although their record in the ACCT has not improved, they are now one of the leading affiliate countries in Asia. They won the Asian Emerging Nations tournament in Bangkok in 2005 and 2006. Perhaps these victories will lead to greater government support. Most of the players are government employees but, surprisingly, this has been a handicap because the long working hours have made it difficult for the players to find time for coaching sessions and practice.

Famous Victory

February 4, 2005 – Polo Club Ground, Bangkok
Maldives 486-5 (50 overs) (Moosa Kaleem 217, Ahmed Afzal Faiz 71, Ismail Anil 60, Ahmed Hussain 51)
Brunei 43 (19.3 overs) (Ahmed Neesham 6-1)
Maldives won by 443 runs

Maldives batted first on winning the toss and proved far too strong for the inexperienced Brunei bowlers, scoring at 9.7 runs per over. Moosa Kaleem was outstanding but he was well supported by Ahmed Neesham in a stand of 244 runs for the second wicket and Ahmed Afzal in a stand of 94 for the third wicket. Brunei added to their problems by bowling 32 wides. In reply, Brunei lasted fewer than 20 overs. Only nine players batted because of injuries to Mansur Ahmed and B. Cheema; only S. Thapa (12) made double figures. Ahmed Neesham was almost unplayable and finished with the remarkable analysis of 5.3-5-1-6, allowing the Maldives to achieve one of the largest one-day victories of all time.

Leading players: *Present day:* Abdullah Shafeeu (rhb. wk); Moosa Kaleem (rhb. rob).

Playing record
One-day matches

	Won	Lost	No Res
Asian Cricket Council Trophy	4	16	2
Asian Emerging Nations Tournaments	6	4	0

Highest team score

ODI

468-5	v Brunei, Bangkok		2004/05

Lowest team score

ODI

34	v Nepal, Kathmandu		2002/03

Highest individual score

ODI

217	Moosa Kaleem	v Brunei, Bangkok	2004/05

Best bowling

ODI

6-1	Ahmed Neesham	v Brunei, Bangkok	2004/05

Best wicket-keeping

ODI

| 4 (4c) | Abdullah Shafeeu | v Malaysia, Singapore | 2002 |
| 4 (3c 1st) | Abdullah Shafeeu | v Singapore, Kuala Lumpur | 2006 |

MALI

Affiliate Member of ICC: elected 2005

THE MALI cricket association, FeMaCrik, was established in 2003. Cricket was introduced into ten schools in Bamako and is now being started in schools in other towns. An inter-school tournament was held in 2004.

MALTA

Affiliate Member of ICC: elected 1998

ALTHOUGH CRICKET was undoubtedly played in Malta as early as 1800 by the British garrison, it was not until 1887 that the first match was recorded when the game in which the Band Boys' Black Watch beat the Duke of Cornwall's Light Infantry by 24 runs was reported in the *Malta Daily Chronicle*. Many of the early matches were played on the Floriana Parade Ground, adjacent to the walled city of Valletta. The ground is no longer in use since it was converted into Independence Arena in 1964. One of the sightscreens still survives, however, an enormous block of sandstone, 9.1m long and 3m high, one of the most remarkable and permanent sightscreens in the world. In the 1880s, the area was open to the public with the result that cricket attracted a local following and stimulated the local Maltese to form the Colonials Club in 1903. This later became Floriana Cricket Club. Other Maltese clubs in the early 1900s included Dockyard Albion, Sliema and Kalkara. Cricket was also taught at St Edward's School. In 1891, Malta played its first international when a combined Fleet and Garrison XVIII met twelve players from Lord Sheffield's side on their way to Australia. The English team, which included W.G. Grace, made 200 for the loss of nine wickets, six of which were taken by Moon. The Maltese replied with 88 for 13. The match was played at the United Services Ground, Marsa, which, to this day, is the major ground in Malta. The garrison entertained the amateurs of the English party in the evening. It is not known how the professionals in the touring party, left to their own devices, amused themselves.

Up until the 1950s, cricket was an important recreational pastime. Representative elevens met teams from the Services as well as the crews of ships visiting the harbour. In the 1950s, however, economic difficulties caused many Maltese to emigrate and others to work longer hours in order to make a living. As a result, Maltese involvement in cricket ceased. The Floriana Club celebrated its 50th anniversary in 1953 but disbanded in 1962. Cricket became an elite game played largely by the military. In the 1980s some expatriates of Asian origin restarted civilian cricket. Occasional matches were played against visiting club sides from England, including the Free Foresters, Incogniti, the Cricketers Club of London, a team raised by Bertie Joel, and a British women's team which more than held its own against the local men's elevens. Nevertheless, the departure of the British services in 1979 again severely threatened the existence of the sport. It was saved by the return of Maltese emigrants in the late 1980s. The Malta Cricket Association was formed in 1989 and in 1990 Malta sent a side to Guernsey to compete in the European Cricketers Cup, where they finished eighth out of the eleven countries. Since then Malta has regularly participated in European affiliate competitions, reaching the semi-final of the ECC Trophy in 2001. The national side is dominantly Maltese. The number of players in the country, however, remains small and there is concern about finding new players of sufficient quality. Cricket is also restricted by the need to find an additional ground so as to relieve pressure on the Marsa Oval. More positively, Malta has now become an attractive place for overseas sides to

visit. In 2003, some 26 clubs came to Malta to play cricket.
Leading players: *Present day:* M. Caruana; J. Grima (wk); F. Spiteri.

Playing record

One-day matches

	Won	Lost	No Res
ECC Trophy	7	6	0
European Affiliates Championships	1	5	0

Highest team score

ODI

367-3	v Greece, Zuoz		1997

Lowest team score

ODI

66	v Austria, Vienna		2003

Highest individual score

ODI

157*	F. Spiteri	v Greece, Zuoz	1997

Best bowling

ODI

5-11	M. Caruana	v Greece, Antwerp	2005

Best wicket-keeping

ODI

4 (4c)	C. Naudi	v Finland, Vienna	2001

MAURITIUS

DESPITE CRICKET having been brought to Mauritius by the British garrison as early as 1838 and the Mauritius Cricket Club being founded in 1845, the game has never progressed beyond that of a recreational pursuit of the British and Indian communities. In the nineteenth century, the small number of British residents limited its development whilst the majority of the 200,000 Indians, brought in as immigrants to work on the sugar plantations, were too poor and worked too long hours to participate in sport. Although later generations of the Indian community have been keen on cricket, it has remained an elite sport, largely restricted to the middle class and more wealthy members of the Asian population, and well behind football and horse racing in popularity. Opportunities for international matches are minimal because of the distance of the country from the African mainland and, following the opening of the Suez Canal, its location away from the major sea routes across the Indian Ocean. No overseas cricket team visited Mauritius until 1972 when the Lusaka Nondescripts from Zambia played two one-day single innings matches against the national side. Mauritius lost both games. The leading club in the country is Maurindia which, since the mid 1990s, has played the Seychelles Cricket Club annually for the Air India Challenge Cup. At present there is little likelihood of cricket developing beyond its limited base because it is not taught in schools. Its future depends on the ability of the four main clubs to attract young players into the game.

Leading player: *1960-1980:* G.B. Naik.

MEXICO

Affiliate Member of the ICC: elected 2004

CRICKET HAS a long history in Mexico. The game was introduced by the English sometime in the nineteenth century. There are records of a cricket club in existence in Mexico City in 1838. A photograph taken in 1865 shows the Emperor Maximilian with a cricket team. The current Mexico City Cricket Club was founded in 1894. In the 1960s they moved to their present ground at Reforma which, at an altitude of 2,194 metres, boasts one of the highest grass wickets in the world. Although the game is no longer restricted to the English, it is still an expatriate activity with players from Britain, India, Australia, South Africa and the Caribbean. Since the 1970s, Mexico City CC has played sporadically, home and away, against teams in Belize and the USA. Mexico's first international appearance was in 2006 when they finished second to Belize in the Central American Championships.

MONACO

THE MONTE Carlo Cricket Club, with a membership of around 25 to 30 players, plays friendly matches against club sides from England, France, Italy, Switzerland and Spain. Since the stadium in which they played was demolished to build a supermarket, all their home games are played at Levens, in the mountains some

18 kilometres north of Nice. Although the Club has ambitions for cricket to be recognised officially by the Monegasque sports authorities, the lack of space for a ground, the lack of coaches and the fact that cricket is not played in schools all hinder its development.

MONGOLIA

THE MONGOLIAN Cricket Club was founded in Ulaanbaator in 1995 by a group of British and Indian expatriates. The Marylebone Cricket Club has granted the club the right to use the title, MCC, in any activities provided there is no conflict of interest or 'grandfather' rights. The club organises local matches between scratch sides such as India versus The Rest and the President's XI versus The Rest, which are played in the Naadam Stadium. Membership fluctuates and is open to any player who is resident in Mongolia for more than four weeks. The club includes one Mongolian who was educated at Eton College.

MOROCCO

Affiliate Member of the ICC: elected 1999
IN THE 1990s cricket was started in Morocco by members of the British and Pakistani communities in Rabat attached to their respective embassies. The practice sessions that they held in the American School attracted both expatriates and locals. Soon there were five cricket clubs in Rabat, including one, Stade Marocain, consisting solely of Moroccan players. In 2001, the Fédération Royale Marocaine de Cricket was founded and by 2003, additional clubs had been started in Tangier and Casablanca. The latter club also has a women's team. Support was obtained from Sheikh Abdur Rahman Bukhatir, the benefactor of cricket in the United Arab Emirates, who organised and financed the construction of a purpose-built stadium in Tangier with seating for 10,000 people. Completed in 2002 at a cost of US$ 4 million, the aim was to provide a ground that could be used internationally. In August 2002, Morocco hosted the Morocco Cup, a competition between Pakistan, South Africa and Sri Lanka. Although a repeat competition was planned for 2003, it was not held and no further matches

involving the test-playing countries have been played at the stadium. Morocco played its first international matches there in April 2003, losing all three of the series of one-day games against France. Morocco were due to compete in the African Affiliates Tournament in 2004 but withdrew at the last moment for financial reasons. They finished fifth in the African Championships Division 2 in 2006.

Leading players: *Present day:* Mohammed Ennaoui (lhb. lm); Tarek El Ghani (rhb. rm).

Playing record
One-day matches

	Won	Lost	No Res
African Championships Division 3	3	2	0

Highest team score
ODI

359-7	v Lesotho, Benoni	2006

Lowest team score
ODI

168	v Sierra Leone, Benoni	2006

Highest individual score
ODI

92	Kamal Moudden	v Lesotho, Benoni	2006

Best bowling
ODI

6-29	Amine Moussaoui	v Rwanda, Benoni	2006

MOZAMBIQUE

Affiliate Member of ICC: elected 2003
CRICKET WAS first played in Mozambique by South African expatriates in the 1950s. It remained a game played by a small minority until the country became independent from Portugal in 1975. As a result of intermittent civil war, economic decline and the departure of most of the expatriate community, cricket virtually ceased. By the 1980s, the game was almost non-existent. In the mid 1990s, members of the expatriate Indian community revived the game in Maputo where there are now twelve clubs engaged in friendly matches and short one-day tournaments. The Associação de Cricket de Mozambique was formed in 2003. The country played its first international matches in the African Affiliates Competition in 2004. By 2006

their standard of play had risen considerably and they won Division 3 of the African Championships and they then finished third out of five countries in the Division 2 competition.

Leading players: *Present day:* S.K.R. Shah (rhb. rfm); Z.G. Patel (rhb. rm); M.A.A. Koliya (rhb. rfm).

Playing record
One-day matches

	Won	Lost	No Res
ICC African Affiliates Competition	2	2	0
African Championships Division 3	5	0	0
African Championships Division 2	2	2	0

Highest team score
ODI

275-6	v Morocco, Benoni		2005/06

Lowest team score
ODI

29	v South African Country Districts, Benoni		2003/04

Highest individual score
ODI

126	S.K.R. Shah	v Morocco, Benoni	2005/06

Best bowling
ODI

5-35	M.A.A. Koliya	v Zambia, Dar es Salaam	2006

MYANMAR

Affiliate country of the ICC: elected 2006

FROM THE time British troops took command of Yangon in 1824, cricket was played in Burma by the military and, by the end of the nineteenth century, by British and Indian civilians. Although it was taught in those Burmese schools run along English public school lines and some all-Burmese cricket clubs were formed, cricket was never popular amongst the local population. The highest standards were reached by the British players, several of whom had first-class experience in England. The leading club was the Rangoon Gymkhana. International fixtures began in 1894 when Burma lost to Ceylon in Yangon by 5 wickets. Matches against Malaya started in 1906 when Burma beat them in Yangon by 3 wickets. Although Myanmar was administered as part of British India, the distance of Yangon from Kolkata and Chennai meant that

it was rarely included in the itinerary of touring sides to the sub-continent. The Oxford University Authentics played in Myanmar during their 1902/03 tour of India. The next visitors were the MCC in 1926/27 when, somewhat surprisingly but recognising the standard of the local European players, their two matches against Rangoon Gymkhana and All-Burma were awarded first-class status. The MCC drew with the Gymkhana and beat Burma by 10 wickets. Cricket ceased during the Japanese Occupation in the Second World War but revived afterwards following the country's independence. The Burmese Cricket Federation was established in 1947. The small size of the expatriate population in the 1950s restricted the game and, apart from the visit of the Pakistani side after their tour of India in 1952/53, no interest in Burmese cricket was shown by other countries. Effectively, the game was left to wither through neglect and lack of facilities. With the isolation of the country after it became a socialist republic under a military regime in 1962, cricket in Burma was, until recently, considered dead. However, a revival occurred in the early 2000s and Myanmar sent a side to the Asian Cricket Championships in 2006 which included a mixture of players of Indian and Burmese origin. They were outclassed being dismissed for 20 by Hong Kong and 10, in 10.1 overs, by Nepal who then won by 10 wickets in 0.2 balls to complete the fastest victory in one-day international cricket in terms of balls bowled.

Leading player: *1920-1940:* Sir H. Ashton (rhb).

Playing record
First-class matches

	Won	Lost	Drawn
All-Burma	0	1	0
Rangoon Gymkhana	0	0	1

One-day matches

Asian Cricket Council Trophy	0	4	0

Highest team score

482-9 dec	Burma v Ceylon, Yangon		1912/13

Lowest team score

10	Myanmar v Nepal, Kuala Lumpur		2006

Highest individual score

137	F.G. Drayson	Burma v Ceylon, Yangon	1912/13

Best bowling

7-44	E.D. Marshall	Burma v Ceylon, Yangon	1894/95

NAMIBIA

Associate Member of ICC: elected 1992

CRICKET WAS first played in Namibia in 1915 at the Okanjande concentration camp, south west of Otjiwarongo, between South African soldiers and local settlers shortly after the German regime in South West Africa surrendered to South African troops. By the 1920s at least three cricket clubs had been formed in Windhoek and one in Walvis Bay to provide social and recreational activity to the South African civil servants, administering the country as a mandated territory of the League of Nations, and the engineers and managers responsible for the development of the road and railway network. Although cricket was promoted by the South African government officials, the number of players remained small and the game never developed beyond friendly matches between club sides. By the 1950s, the game had spread northwards along the railway line with clubs being established at Otjiwarongo and at the mining town of Tsumeb. The first match played by a representative South West African side was at Windhoek in 1954 against Liesbeek Park, a club side from Cape Town. In 1958, a South West African team toured Port Elizabeth, in South Africa, again playing club sides.

South West Africa took advantage of the failure of the Rhodesian Country Districts to take part in the annual South African Country Cricket Association festival in 1962 and offered to fill the gap. From that date until 1989, South West Africa competed in this competition against Country District teams from the major South African provinces. Although the latter sides were mainly made up of farmers and other rural dwellers and the South West African side was largely urban, the teams were well matched. South West Africa played 130 matches in the competition, winning 31 of them; 48 games were lost, 50 drawn and there was one tie. The period from 1970 to 1973 was the most successful, Namibia winning nine of their twenty matches.

Somewhat surprisingly, considering the political uncertainties arising from the struggle for independence in the 1970s and 1980s, cricket underwent substantial development. The previous two decades had seen the game become increasingly restricted to Windhoek because of the limited and unreliable transport links to other towns. Now there was a major deployment of South African troops at military bases in Walvis Bay, Grootfontein, Oshakati, Rundu and Tsumeb. Cricket was essentially a sport of the whites but following the relaxation of the South African government's policy towards mixed-race team sports in 1973, a few black players began to appear. Mervyn Phillips became the first non-white player to represent South West Africa when he played in the 1978 Country Districts tournament. Further encouragement to multiracial cricket was given by the presence of troops from the United Nations Transitional Assistance Group (UNTAG) in the late 1980s.

Sever Connections

In June 1989, the South West African Cricket Union decided to sever its connections with South Africa. The Namibia Cricket Board was formed and straightaway, a tour of the national side to Botswana was organised. Following the country's independence, Gloucestershire and The Netherlands visited Namibia in 1990 and the MCC in 1991. Thus, from its formation, the NCB acted rapidly to obtain suitable opponents, invest in schools and youth cricket and receive recognition as an associate member of the ICC. The level of activity was remarkable considering that the Board was extremely short of money. The atmosphere in Namibian cricket at the time was like that of the pioneers of the game in other countries a century earlier. For the tour of Botswana in 1989, one of the players, Richard Nineham, who was a registered pilot, flew the team to Gaberone in a chartered aircraft. For a tour of Zimbabwe in 1990, the team travelled overland, using three minibuses and a light truck, returning home through numerous roadblocks in the Caprivi Strip, operated by the Security Forces. At one checkpoint, the team's cricket balls were nearly confiscated as 'possible hand grenades'. The NCB continued to be opportunistic. Having played a major role in the formation of the Zone VI Cricket Association for Africa, they hosted and won the inaugural tournament in 1991.

Namibia competed in the 1994 ICC Trophy in Kenya and, in a very successful, debut, won the Plate

Competition. This success brought about increased government support and the recognition of cricket as a major sport of the country, along with athletics, boxing, football and netball. In 1995, Namibia played their first three-day match against another country, drawing at home to Malaysia. Unfortunately, cautious defensive batting ruined the game with only one innings being completed by each side. The following year, Namibia received Italy, and were easy winners by an innings and 188 runs. More serious opposition was obtained when Namibia renewed ties with South Africa and entered the UCB Bowl, a competition comprising both three-day and one-day matches involving the B sides of Zimbabwe and the South African Provinces. In six consecutive years of the competition, Namibia won only five of the 32 three-day matches played and lost sixteen, and won eight of the one-day games, losing the other 24.

Rising Standard

Regular exposure to South African cricket coupled with a policy of employing overseas coaches led to a continued rise in the standard of Namibian cricket, even though the number of players remained small and, at least at the top level, the game remained a white person's preserve. The 2001 ICC Trophy saw Namibia win all their matches to reach the final where they lost to The Netherlands in a closely-fought encounter by two wickets. This performance was sufficient to qualify them for the final stages of the 2003 World Cup in South Africa. In their first experience of cricket at this level, they were easily defeated in all their matches. Their best performance was against England where A.J. Burger won the player-of-the match award for his 85 runs from 86 balls. Rudi van Vuuren became the first person to play in the final stages of two World Cup sports having previously played for Namibia in the Rugby Union competition.

In contrast to the men's game, women's cricket has been slow to develop. It was not until 2004 that a Namibian women's team made its first appearance in international cricket. They took part in the African Championships in Tanzania but were seriously outclassed in all their matches. This was not surprising considering the small number of players from which to choose and their lack of experience. The squad from which the selection was made was only 45 strong, comprising mainly players from the Windhoek area. It is hoped to promote women's cricket countrywide by playing friendly exhibition matches in the main towns but given the vast distances between the towns and the high transport costs, corporate sponsorship will be essential if this objective is to be realised. If the schools and youth coaching programmes of the NCB can be extended to girls, this would help the women's game to become better established.

Since the 2003 World Cup, the results of Namibia's men's team have been disappointingly mixed. In 2004 they were excluded from South African domestic competition when the United Cricket Board of South Africa decided to reduce the number of teams with the objective of raising the overall standard. This decision took away the route that the NCB had been using to raise standards. Namibia was forced instead to seek greater contact with Zimbabwe and Kenya. In October 2006, however, Namibia returned to the provincial South African domestic competitions with the matches in the three-day tournament being accorded first-class status. Namibian cricket faces the problem that, despite the efforts that have gone into promoting the game, the number of players from which to select the national side remains small. Whether Namibia can continue to improve its standard of cricket and eventually attain test status remains uncertain. In the long term there is the underlying problem that cricket remains essentially a white persons game and the whites represent only 6 per cent of the country's population. Attempts to encourage African participation have yet to be successful. No African has yet reached the standard required to play for the national side. Only two Africans have played at Under 19 level and the national schools teams, down to Under 11, are all white. Should the political environment in the country ever to move one where the make-up of national teams had to reflect better the ethnic distribution of the population, Namibian cricket could have a real problem of survival.

Famous Victories
July 13, 2001 – Toronto Cricket, Skating and Curling Club

Namibia 256-6 (50 overs) (D. Keulder 104)
Scotland 247 (48.4 overs) (C.J.O. Smith 88, R.A. Parsons 53, B.O. van Rooi 6-43)
Namibia won by 9 runs

By achieving their most important victory in their history in this ICC Trophy match, Namibia qualified for the final stages of the 2003 World Cup. Winning the toss and batting first, Riaan Walters (43) and Danie Keulder put on 57 runs for the first wicket. Once Walters was out, Jan-Berrie Burger (30) gave good support to Keulder whose 104 runs came from 137 balls and included nine fours and a six. From 171-2, Namibia lost wickets trying to raise the scoring rate but contributions from Gavin Murgatroyd (35) and Melt van Schoor (32*) ensured a competitive total. On a good batting wicket, the Scottish bowling lacked penetration and went for over five runs per over. Scotland replied strongly with Colin Smith and Drew Parsons adding 127 for the third wicket to reach 178 for only two wickets at the end of the 36th over. Burton van Rooi then produced a superb spell of bowling. Aided by three run-outs through brilliant fielding by Murgatroyd, Keulder and Lennie Louw, Scotland lost their nerve and their last eight wickets for 35 runs.

Player Profiles

Burger, Andries Johannes (Jan-Berrie). b Newcastle, Natal, South Africa, 25 August 1981. rhb. lb. Since making his debut for Namibia in 2001, he has become one of the most consistent batsmen in all the associate countries. In 16 matches he has scored 1,005 runs (average 33.50) and taken 24 wickets (34.79). In 36 one-day internationals he made 1,083 runs (average 30.08) and took 10 wickets (average 33.50). In 66 other limited overs matches he has scored 2,144 runs (average 35.14) and taken 26 wickets (average 28.34).

Murgatroyd, Bryan Gavin. b Walvis Baai 19 October 1969. rhb. rm. Namibia's leading cricketer throughout the 1990s, he was the Player of the Tournament at the ICC Trophy in 1994. In his only international match he scored 146 runs (average 146.00) and took 1 wicket (average 50.00). In 59 limited overs matches, he made 1,562 runs (average 35.14) and took 25 wickets (average 13.44).

Other leading players: *1960-1980:* P. Norgarb; R. Brown; F. Loock. *1980-2000:* D. Keulder (rhb. rob);

M. van Schoor (rhb. wk); I.J. Stevenson. *Present day:* G. Snyman (rhb. rfm); M.C. van Zyl (rhb. rmf); S.F. Burger (rhb. rmf).

Playing record
First-class matches

	Won	Lost	Drawn
South African domestic competition*	5	2	1
ICC Intercontinental Cup	2	3	2

South African Airways three-day competition (2006/07)

One-day matches

	Won	Lost	No Res
World Cup	0	6	0
Domestic competitions in South Africa and Zimbabwe*	8	5	3
ICC Trophy	18	12	0
Six Nations Challenge	5	5	0
African Six Nations Tournament	5	5	0

Standard Bank Cup (2002/03) and South African Airways (2006/07) competitions in South Africa and Fairweather Clothing Competition in Zimbabwe (2004/05)

Highest team score

510-4 dec	v Italy, Windhoek	1995/96

Lowest team score
ODI

45	v Australia, Potchefstroom	2002/04

Highest individual score

227	D. Keulder	v Italy, Windhoek	1995/96

Best bowling

8-34	M.C. van Zyl	v Ireland, Dublin	2006

Best wicket-keeping

5 (5c)	T. Taibu	v Griqualand West, Kimberley	2006/07
5 (5c)	T. Taibu	v Free State, Bloemfontein	2006/07

ODI

5 (5c)	M. van Schoor	v Kenya, Nairobi	1993/94
5 (5c)	M. Karg	v Gauteng, Krugersdorp	2002/03

Women
One-day matches

	Won	Lost	No Res
African Championships	0	3	0

Highest team score
ODI

106	v Kenya, Dar es Salaam	2004

Lowest team score
ODI

29	v Tanzania, Dar es Salaam	2004

Highest individual score

ODI

23*	R. Viljoen	v Kenya, Dar es Salaam	2004

Best bowling

3-34	R. Viljoen	v Uganda, Dar es Salaam	2004

NAURU

CRICKET WAS an important recreational activity of the Australian civil servants on the island and staff of the mining company exploiting the phosphates. Regular matches were played between Australian, Indian and Nauruan teams. Although about half of the cricketers on the island were Nauruan, the Australians and a small number of Sri Lankans undertook most of the organisational and coaching work. With the demise of the phosphate industry, the expatriate population has declined very rapidly in recent years and cricket is in danger of decline. A shortage of equipment poses a severe constraint on keeping the game alive.

NEPAL

Affiliate Member of ICC: elected 1988
Associate Member of ICC: elected 1996

MEMBERS OF the Rana ruling family brought cricket to Nepal in the 1920s when they returned from studies in England and India. Like the clothes, furniture, medical advances and electricity that they imported from western countries, cricket was kept for the benefit of the Ranas and a few chosen families of the royal court. They set up grounds in their palaces around the country where they could practice and play the game. In 1928, General Brah Shumsher Jung Bahadur Rana established a team at Babar Mandal in Kathmandu and General Nara Shumsher Jung Bahadur Rana became patron of a team at Lalitpur (also known as Patan). In the late 1930s, General Nara established a ground at Jawlakhel, a settlement in Lalitpur which is now the home of a Tibetan refugee camp. In 1935, General Madan founded his Sri Durbar Eleven and built a small stadium in his palace of Sri Durbar. Although the Ranas adopted many aspects of western life and culture, they effectively isolated the country from the rest of the world. They ensured that cricket, along with other aspects of their lifestyle, was not extended to the general population. There were no newspapers in Nepal and it was forbidden to import newspapers from overseas. Radios were not allowed in the country until 1946. A high proportion of the population was rural and, although slavery was abolished in the 1920s, the land tenure system kept the farmers and their families in almost permanent servitude to local landlords. With communications severely limited by the terrain and the absence of roads, the majority of the people were probably unaware that cricket even existed. In order to promote the game amongst the aristocracy, however, the Cricket Association of Nepal was set up in 1946.

In 1951, King Tribhuvan overthrew the Rana rule. Nepal became open to the outside world. Indian traders began to settle in Kathmandu and in the small towns of the lowlands. Although still a sport of wealthy, the number of people interested in playing cricket increased. In 1954, General Nara took a team from Kathmandu to India where they played matches in Patna and Kolkata. In 1961, the Cricket Association of Nepal was incorporated within the National Sports Council, a government body set up by Prince Basundhara Bir Bikram Shah. Despite its aim of promoting cricket, however, CAN effectively restricted activity to Kathmandu. Some critics considered that CAN was virtually moribund from its inception until the 1990s, it doing little more than organising tournaments for the main club sides in the capital. Certainly the late 1960s to the late 1980s were a time of consolidation of the cricket in the Kathmandu area. However, improvements in air and road communications allowed the game to spread to other towns throughout the country. Suddenly, in the 1990s, CAN instituted a major development programme. Regional and district tournaments were established and cricket was actively promoted in schools. All too quickly, the demand to play the game from senior to junior level created great pressure on the available facilities. The number of teams which could enter tournaments had to be restricted because of the lack of grounds. New grounds were therefore quickly established and existing ones upgraded. Those at Tribhuvan University and the Institute of Engineers in Kathmandu were improved, allowing Nepal to host the Asian Cricket Council Trophy in 1998. The facility at

Tribhuvan University has since been further enhanced to international standards.

Nepal first appeared on the international scene in the 1996 Asian Cricket Council Trophy and they have appeared in every ACC Trophy competition since. In the late 1990s, a national squad of mainly young players was formed and overseas coaches employed at senior and junior levels, a policy which produced rapid rises in standard. Within a decade, Nepal went from being one of the minor Asian cricketing countries to one of the leading non test-playing Asian countries. On the way they have been responsible for three of the more remarkable victories in one-day international cricket. In the final of the Emerging Nations tournament in 2003, they dismissed the Maldives for 34 runs in 22.4 overs and then made 38 without loss in 7.1 overs. In the ACC Trophy in 2004, Iran were dismissed for 29 in 23.4 overs. Nepal then reached 30 without loss in only 1.3 overs. In the 2006 competition they dismissed Myanmar for 10, a total that they surpassed in two balls, but could only finish fourth after losing the third place play-off to Afghanistan. In 2005 they beat both Malaysia and the United Arab Emirates in two-innings matches. If sufficient finance is available to support the work of CAN, Nepal could well gain test-match status within the next ten to twelve years. In February 2005, Nepal instituted an inter-schools cricket tournament for girls. If the pattern of development of men's cricket can be emulated, there may well be a Nepalese women's team in the international arena in the near future.

Famous Victory

May 7, 8, 9, 2005 – Tribhuvan University, Kathmandu

Nepal 287-7 dec (S. Vesawkar 89, S.P. Gauchan 68) and 125-6 dec

United Arab Emirates 164 (Arshad Ali 81*) and 76 (B.K. Das 5-27)

Nepal won by 172 runs

This ICC Intercontinental Cup match started after lunch on the first day, the delay being due to a wet outfield after overnight rain. Nepal lost two quick wickets before Kanishka Chaugai (47) added 65 with Shakti Gauchan. Gauchan and Sarad Vesawkar then anchored the innings with a partnership of 106. With Mehboob Alam contributing 34 runs, Nepal were able to declare early on

the second day. Apart from Arshad Ali, whose innings lasted 250 balls, the Emirates succumbed to Nepal's all-round bowling attack; Raju Basnyet took 3-27 whilst Binod Das, Alam, Raj Kumar Pradhan and Dhirendra Chand each took one wicket. The start of the third day was delayed by rain but with Chaugai (48) and Gauchan (26) batting sensibly, Nepal ensured that they would at least draw the match before declaring. The Emirates never attempted to secure a victory and concentrated on scoring the 75 runs required to ensure their progression to the semi-finals of the competition. Das bowled really well for his five-wicket haul and the Emirates were reduced to 69 for nine wickets. Zahid Shah then hit Gauchan for a six. One run later, Gauchan had Rizwan Latif leg before to achieve Nepal's victory against the top associate country in Asia.

Player Profiles

Alam, Mehboob. b Rajbiraj-3, Saptari, 31 August 1981. lhb. lm. Nepal's leading all-rounder since his debut in 2000, in 13 international matches he has scored 596 runs (average 25.91) and taken 25 wickets (average 20.12). In 34 limited overs matches he has made 567 runs (average 21.00) and taken 60 wickets (average 9.15).

Thakuri, Ganesh Bahadur Shahi. b Bardia, 28 May 1972. rhb. wk. One of Nepal's leading cricketers in the 1990s and arguably their best wicket-keeper to date, he played 14 limited overs matches, scoring 226 runs (average 22.60) and making 6 catches and 7 stumpings.

Other leading players: *1980-2000:* P.K. Agrawal (rhb. rob); D. Chaudhary (rhb. rm). *Present day:* R.K. Pradhan (rhb. lb); S.P. Gauchan (rhb. lb); B.K. Das (rhb. rm).

Playing record

International matches

	Won	Lost	Drawn
ICC Intercontinental Cup	2	0	2
ACC Fast Track Countries Tournament/Premier League	4	3	5

One-day matches

	Won	Lost	No Res
ICC Trophy	2	1	0
ICC Trophy Qualifying Competition	3	2	0
Asian Cricket Council Trophy	17	13	2
Emerging Nations Trophy	5	0	1

Highest team score

ODI

397-8	v Bhutan, Kathmandu	2003

Lowest team score

64	v United Arab Emirates, Kathmandu	2004

Highest individual score

108	M. Alam	v Malaysia, Kathmandu	2005

Best bowling

ODI

8-23	M. Alam	v Maldives, Kathmandu	2003

Best wicket-keeping

ODI

4 (3c 1st) G. Bahadur Sahi Thakuri	v UAE, Kathmandu	1998

NETHERLANDS

Associate Member of ICC: elected 1966

CRICKET WAS observed being played in The Netherlands in the 1780s by the English traveller, Samuel Pratt, during a visit to Scheveningen. Since Thomas Hope, a merchant from Amsterdam also noted that cricket was an important recreational activity of the Dutch community in Rome in the 1790s, it seems reasonable to infer that the game must have been established in The Netherlands by the late eighteenth century, at least among a small group of the population. It is likely that the game was introduced by English traders and by Dutch merchants who travelled to England. Take-up must have been limited, however, because the next reference to cricket in The Netherlands is not until 1845 when the game was recorded as being played by pupils at a boarding school at Noorthey, near Voorschoten between The Hague and Leiden. It is not known whether cricket was introduced at the school by teachers from England or by some of the pupils. In the following year, cricket was recorded at the University of Utrecht where it was played mainly by students from South Africa. The first cricket club in The Netherlands was formed at Noorthey in 1857.

The growth of cricket remained slow until the mid-1870s after which many clubs were formed in the space of a few years, mostly by people who had learnt the game at school and wanted to continue playing. Generally they were from aristocratic families with English connections through family or trade. The Anglicising influence was particularly important because it meant that cricket was imported along with its Victorian values of fair play, amateurism and exclusivity. The Utile Dulci club at Deventer was formed in 1875 by Mr Romiju, a former British Consul. This was followed in 1878 by the Haagsche Cricket Club and in 1881 by Rood en Wit in Haarlem. By 1888 there were, according to James Lillywhite, eighteen cricket clubs in The Netherlands with a côterie of some 300 players. Each club instituted some form of membership qualification to ensure that only people from the appropriate social class could join. Often prospective members had to be nominated by at least two existing members and then voted in at a membership meeting. Members could also be expelled for inappropriate behaviour. Some clubs were very exclusive and restricted membership to those educated at particular types of school, for example the gymnasium. The clubs played cricket to their own rules which did not always correspond to those of the MCC. In Deventer, for example, it was considered unfair to score runs by hitting the ball behind the wicket. In 1881, Uxbridge Cricket Club made the first visit to The Netherlands by an overseas side and beat a representative Dutch twenty-two by an innings and 45 runs. Since the Dutch players only knew the game by the practices of their own club, it was clear that some central coordination was required. In 1883, the Nederlandsche Cricket Bond was founded with a membership of eighteen clubs. In 1958, it was granted the royal title, Koninklijke, by Queen Juliana, and became the KNCB. When responsibility for English cricket was transferred from the MCC to the Test and County Cricket Board in 1977, the KNCB became the oldest of the surviving national cricket bodies.

At the time the NCB was formed, Dutch cricket standards were low. Most of the bowling was underarm and matches were played on any reasonably level piece of ground that could be found. Wickets were rarely prepared and therefore extremely rough and dangerous. In 1899, in order to raise standards, the NCB employed an English coach, Arthur Bentley, who came from Newton Abbott in Devonshire and had visited The Netherlands with the Newton Blues in 1886. Under his tuition, modern bowling methods were introduced and batting and fielding standards rose. Between 1890 and 1894, the highest batting average in the Dutch cricket season went from 12.45 to 43.44 with a corresponding rise in the best bowling average from 2.57 to 5.47. Throughout the 1880s and 1890s, regular visits were made by club sides from England, particularly from Kent, Yorkshire and the London area. These clubs provided models of dress, behaviour and style of play which the Dutch sides tried to emulate. The national team also played matches against Clingendaal, a side comprising resident or visiting Englishmen which lasted through the 1880s and 1890s.

The increasing maturity and confidence of Dutch cricket led the NCB in August 1891 to send a team, the Gentlemen of Holland, to play five matches against club sides in Yorkshire. The Netherlands thus became the first cricketing country outside of the British Empire to tour England. A second tour was made in 1894 to the London area and Kent. This included a two-day fixture at Lord's against the MCC which, with the Reverend P. Hattersley-Smith and K.S. Ranjitsinhji both making centuries, was much too strong, winning by an innings and 169 runs. By the time the third tour was made in 1901, Dutch cricket had improved considerably.

Serious Loss of Players

Ironically, just as the standard of the national side was reaching that of the best English club sides, cricket was having a problem of maintaining and recruiting players. Many of the young people who had joined clubs after leaving school found that their work did not allow sufficient time for sport. Those in the diplomatic service and in commerce found themselves posted to the Dutch East Indies and Surinam. Although some managed to continue playing cricket overseas and also grouped together to form a 'Koloniale' side when on leave in The Netherlands, there was a serious loss of players. Further, as the Dutch sided with the Boers during the wars in South Africa, fewer young people were attracted to a game so strongly associated with Britain. The exclusivity of the Dutch clubs hampered recruitment. When Rood en Wit set up a junior section to attract cricketers between the ages of twelve and sixteen, they were forced to abandon the venture by other clubs because of fears that it would lead to the admission of the lower classes. By the end of the

1890s, cricket had decreased in popularity, even among the elite, and was restricted to a very small 'leisured' class. Many of the top schools had ceased to teach the game.

Despite the problems underlying the future of the game, the NCB continued to grow the international programme. The MCC visited The Netherlands in 1902 and tours were made to England in 1901 and 1906. International matches against Belgium started in 1905. These continued, with an interruption for the First World War, until 1937. In 1910, The Netherlands joined France, Belgium and the MCC in a tournament associated with the Brussels Exhibition. At first the 1914-18 War saw the virtual demise of cricket in The Netherlands as many players were recruited into the armed forces. However, by 1915, thousands of British soldiers were stranded in the country. Some of the best British players joined Dutch clubs and in 1918 the officers from Scheveningen entered two teams in the Dutch League, playing under the title of 'Prisoners of War'.

When the British troops returned home at the end of the First World War, the NCB acted quickly to ensure that the best Dutch cricketers gained experience against good class amateur opposition from overseas. The MCC and Free Foresters became frequent visitors. Another outcome was the founding in 1921 of De Flamingo's, a touring club with membership by invitation. It attracted the best Dutch cricketers so that when it went on its frequent tours to England or played the MCC at home, its side was equivalent to the Dutch national eleven. De Flamingo's also undertook tours in The Netherlands and organised an annual youth tournament. As a result of these developments, cricket underwent a revival with many new clubs being formed and others restarted between 1924 and 1929. Although, cricket remained a sport of the elite, there was an increase in the number of people wanting to participate in a leisured pursuit upholding amateurism and sportsmanship. Women, too, wanted to be part of the scene. The first women's club was formed in Haarlem in 1930. By 1934, there were two more clubs in the country. Despite receiving no encouragement from male cricketers, the players and officials of these pioneer clubs formed the Nederlandse Dames Cricket Bond in 1934. No more than four or five clubs were affiliated to the NDCB in any year prior to 1939 but there was sufficient enthusiasm for a short season of inter-club fixtures to be organised. With the help of the Women's Cricket Association in England, standards improved and in 1937, the NDCB persuaded the Australian Women's side to visit The Netherlands after their tour of England. It was another seventeen years before the NCB managed to get the Australian men's team to do the same.

Golden Age of Dutch Cricket

Some Dutch cricket historians consider the 1930s to be the Golden Age of Dutch cricket but such a description probably reflects the attitudes of the players in upholding the 'spirit of cricket' as much as the standard of play. When the South Africans visited in 1935, the status of Dutch cricket was more realistically demonstrated with the tourists winning by an innings and 128 runs. Nevertheless, standards were higher than before the First World War and there were some players who were probably close to English first-class standard.

That cricket survived the German occupation of the country between May 1940 and May 1945 was remarkable and due entirely to the enthusiasm of the players. Many grounds were requisitioned, transport by private cars was banned and train travel became increasingly restrictive and often prohibited at weekends. When the headquarters of the main sports dealers in Rotterdam was bombed, there was a national shortage of equipment. Despite these obstacles, the NCB was able to organise as many as 300 matches a year, mostly between local clubs. At the end of the War, many matches were played between local sides and the British troops. In 1945, the first post-war international was played against an army side raised by B.H. Valentine which the Dutch won by 158 runs. A repeat match was played in 1946, again won by the Dutch. A 'Save Dutch Cricket' fund organised in England by Sir Pelham Warner led to a gift to the NCB of some 200 bats and 100 balls.

Although cricket remained a minority sport, the Dutch clubs increasingly opened their membership to the growing middle class who also formed their own clubs. The number of teams participating in the Dutch League grew from 58 in 1946 to 97 in 1958 and 135 in 1968. The matches against the Free Foresters and the MCC were resumed as were the tours made by De Flamingo's. In addition, beginning with the South Africans in 1951,

many of the test-playing nations visited The Netherlands either at the end or in the middle of their tours of England. Usually the tourists won easily but in 1964 the Dutch surprised the Australians, winning the match by three wickets.

In 1955, the first of what became known as the series of 'continental tests' was played against Denmark. These continued until 1981 after which they were replaced one-day internationals. The matches against Ireland which started in 1970 and Scotland, in 1979, suffered the same fate, as Dutch international cricket moved entirely to one-day games. This was partly to provide the necessary experience for The Netherlands to compete successfully in the ICC Trophy but it also allowed more matches to be played without substantially increasing the time required for the leading players to seek leave from their work. The 1980s also saw an increase in the number of foreign-born players in the national side, mostly qualifying by residence or by taking Dutch citizenship. Although these players helped to raise the standard of the national side, they also increased its average age and reduced the opportunities for younger cricketers.

The mid-1980s saw some of the leading Dutch players choose cricket as their profession with the English first-class counties. The first to do so was Paul-Jan Bakker, a bowler of fast-medium pace, who played regularly for Hampshire between 1986 and 1992. The most successful of the Dutch players on the English county circuit was Roland Lefebvre, a useful right-hand bat and a miserly medium-fast bowler, who played regularly for Somerset (1990-1992) and Glamorgan (1993-1995). Both Bakker and Lefebvre endeavoured to make themselves available for The Netherlands when required and, for several years, Lefebvre was the captain of the national team. In contrast, those who followed, notably Adrianus van Troost (Somerset) and Bas Zuiderent (Sussex), opted to play for their chosen counties rather than for their country whenever a conflict of interest arose. Surprisingly, whenever they played for The Netherlands, neither achieved much. Zuiderent consistently underperformed for his country until the ICC Trophy in 2005 when he scored three centuries to finish the leading batsman of the tournament.

The period from 1986 to 2001 was the most successful in Dutch cricket history. They reached the final of the ICC Trophy in 1986 and 1990 but lost both times to Zimbabwe. The KNCB increased the number of international matches played each year and embarked on tours to the United Arab Emirates (1990), Namibia (1990), New Zealand (1994), Kenya (1994, 1995), India (1995), South Africa (1997, 1998, 1999, 2001, 2004, 2006) and Canada (2000). At home, the Dutch recorded victories in one-day matches against the West Indians (1991), a strong England XI (1993) and the South Africans (1994). In 1995, The Netherlands entered the English domestic one-day knock-out competition. The best year was 1999 when they beat Cambridgeshire, the Lancashire Board XI and Durham, their first victory over a first-class county, before losing to Kent in the fourth round. The Netherlands finished third in the ICC Trophy in 1994 with Nolan Clarke the outstanding batsman of the tournament, scoring three centuries. They qualified for the 1996 World Cup but were outclassed and, rather disappointingly, played below their best in the only fixture they might have won against the United Arab Emirates. Dutch cricket made a major advance in facilities in 1996 with the establishment of grass wickets at Deventer and Amstelveen. This allowed The Netherlands to play one-day matches in the English domestic competition at home and enabled the KNCB to host one of the matches, South Africa versus Kenya, in the 1999 World Cup. The Dutch won the European Championships in 1996, 1998 and 2000 and then went on to win the ICC Trophy in Canada in 2001, beating Namibia in a memorable final to qualify for the final stages of the World Cup for the second time.

The 1980s and 1990s saw advances in women's cricket. Although the game revived after the Second World War, it took many years before it expanded its activity beyond that of the 1930s. Largely ignored by the men's game, the NDCB suffered from a lack of facilities, particularly grounds since nearly all suitable ones were used at weekends for matches in the men's Dutch League. Although the women's cricket league resumed in 1949, the NDCB were forced to abandon it in 1958. Instead, a centralised women's academy was established where promising players could receive coaching. A women's touring side, 't Wilgenhout, was formed which played occasional matches against men's teams and visiting women's teams from overseas. By the 1970s there were sufficient numbers of players for some of the leading clubs

to form women's sections. The women's league restarted in 1976. The first international match was played in 1984, a one-day game against New Zealand resulting in a loss by 67 runs. In 1987, The Netherlands lost to Ireland by an innings and 19 runs in the only two-innings fixture the Dutch women have ever played. Not surprisingly, given the limited playing strength and the lack of opportunities for match practice, the team has not been very successful with only occasional victories over Denmark, Japan, Pakistan and Scotland. Since the mid 1990s, the level of activity has increased. Overseas tours have been made to Sri Lanka (1997, 1999), England (2000, 2002), New Zealand (2000) and Pakistan (2001). Much more encouragement will be required from the men's cricketing authorities if the women's game is to progress. There is an urgent need to increase the number of women cricketers and provide them with more match experience.

Patchy

Since 2001, the record of the Dutch men's side has been patchy. In the 2003 World Cup, the side struggled to make runs and take wickets against test-class opposition though they did have the satisfaction of recording their first win at this stage of the competition, beating Namibia by 64 runs. Results in the ICC Trophy, the European Championships and the ICC Intercontinental Cup, show that the Dutch have fallen behind Ireland and Scotland in the European rankings. They were reduced to fifth place in the 2005 ICC Trophy but this was enough to qualify for the final stages of the 2007 World Cup, the first associate country to reach this level for a third time. Although more youngsters in The Netherlands are playing cricket than ever before and some are keen to postpone university studies or employment in order to further their cricket career, the continuous diet of one-day cricket in the domestic game is not raising the playing standard. If Dutch cricket is ever to gain official one-day or even test-match status, the domestic game must be put on a professional footing. For this to happen, however, the KNCB will need to seek greater corporate sponsorship from industry. The main constraint on achieving this is that cricket is still a minority sport in The Netherlands; it is not even in the top forty. That needs to change.

Famous Victories

July 15, 2001 – Toronto Cricket, Skating and Curling Club

Namibia 195-9 (50 overs) (B.G. Murgatroyd 50)
Netherlands 196-8 (50 overs) (J.J. Esmeijer 58*, K.J.J. van Noortwijk 50)
Netherlands won by 2 wickets

Winning the toss, Namibia struggled to master the Dutch attack in this final of the ICC Trophy. Although starts were made by Danie Keulder (24), Jan-Berrie Burger (38), Dion Kotze (28) and Melt van Schoor (25), only Gavin Murgatroyd reached a half century. The Namibian total looked sufficient, however, when the Dutch lost their first two wickets for twelve. Despite a stylish innings from Klaas-Jan van Noortwijk, The Netherlands were in a poor position at 106 for six. Jan-Jacob Esmeijer, dropped when he had made 15, and Lefebvre then added 52 before Lefebvre became Rudi van Vuuren's (3-35) third victim. Thirty-eight runs were still needed from the last four overs but Esmeijer farmed the bowling and reduced that to ten from the final over and three from the last ball. The Dutch held their nerve whilst the Namibians faltered. With the aid of a fumble by Riaan Walters at short fine leg, the Dutch got home to secure the Trophy, the most prestigious win in their cricket history.

Player Profiles

Lefebvre, Roland Philippe. b Rotterdam 7 February 1963. rhb. rm. The leading Dutch all-rounder in the 1990s and, arguably, the most successful cricketer ever to come from The Netherlands, he played first-class cricket for Somerset, Canterbury (NZ) and Glamorgan, and represented The Netherlands in five ICC Trophy competitions and in two World Cup contests. He was a highly-regarded captain with a good grasp of tactics. In his later career, he was renowned for extremely economical bowling in one-day competitions. In two international matches he scored 11 runs (average 3.66) and took 11 wickets (average 9.54). In 24 one day internationals he scored 227 runs (average 17.46) and took 30 wickets (average 23.53). In 71 other limited overs matches he made 1,127 runs (average 25.04) and took 102 wickets (average 14.58).

Posthuma, Carst Jan. b Haarlem 11 January 1868. d

Heemstede 21 December 1939. lhb. lf. The best-known of the Dutch cricketers before the First World War, he was the first to play first-class cricket which he did in 1903 when invited by W.G. Grace to represent London County. Nicknamed 'The Lion', he was universally recognised as the Grand Old Man of Dutch cricket. In 15 matches for his country, he scored 286 runs (average 12.43) and took 72 wickets (average 22.06), including five or more wickets in an innings seven times. He was a skilled rose grower and one of the leading world authorities on roses.

Other leading players: *1890-1914:* C. Feith (rhb); F.J.W. Rincker (rhb. rf); J.C. Schröder (rhb. wk). *1920-1940:* M. Jansen (lhb. lm); L.J. Sodderland (rhb. rm); A. Terwiel (lhb. lfm). *1945-1960:* W. van Weelde (rhb. rs); E.W.C. Vriens (rhb. rm); R. Colthoff (rhb. wk). *1960-1980:* P.J. Bakker (rhb. rmf); N.E. Clarke (rhb. lbg); A. Bakker (rhb). *1980-2000:* T.B.M. de Leede (rhb. rm); J. Smits (rhb. wk); S.W. Lubbers (rhb. rob). *Present day:* D.L. S. van Bunge (rhb. lb); R.N. ten Doeschate (rhb. rmf); A.N. Kervezee (rhb).

Women: *1980-2000:* I. Dulfer-Keizer (rhb. rm); P.J. te Beest (rhb); N. Payne (rhb. rm). *Present day:* S. Kottman (lhb. lm); C.A. Salomons (rhb. rob).

Playing record

International matches

	Won	Lost	Drawn
ICC Intercontinental Cup	1	2	4
Denmark	5	1	5
Other matches*	0	6	2

* Two-day matches against Bermuda, Ireland, Scotland and Sri Lanka.

One-day matches

	Won	Lost	No Res
World Cup	2	12	0
Other ODIs	6	8	1
ICC Champions Trophy	0	2	0
England domestic competitions	3	10	0
ICC Trophy	42	15	6
European Championships	18	8	1
Emerging Nations Tournament	3	1	1
Six Nations Challenge	4	6	0

Highest team score

474	v Kenya, Nairobi	2006/07

Lowest team score

41	v Ireland, The Hague	1970

Highest individual score

259*	R.N. ten Doeschate	v Canada, Pretoria	2006/07

Best bowling

7-18	Z. Cornelis	v Denmark, Schiedam	1960

ODI

7-9	Asim Khan	v East & Central Africa, Kuala Lumpur	1987

Best wicket-keeping

6 (5c 1st)	H. van Nispen	v Pakistanis,	1974
6 (5c 1st)	R.F. Schoonheim	v Scotland, Schiedam	1979

Women

International matches

Won	Lost	Drawn
0	1	0

One-day matches

	Won	Lost	No Res
World Cup	2	24	1
World Cup Qualifying	3	2	0
European Championships	7	15	0
Other ODIs	8	17	0

Highest team score

165	v Ireland, The Hague	1987

ODI

375-5	v Japan, Schiedam	2003

Lowest team score

54	v Ireland, The Hague	1987

ODI

29	v Australia, Perth	1988/89

Highest individual score

61	A. van Lier	v Ireland, The Hague	1987

ODI

142	P.J. te Beest	v Japan, Schiedam	2003

Best bowling

3-42	E. Veltman	v Ireland, The Hague	1987

ODI

5-20	C.F. Oudolf	v Sri Lanka, Kandy	1997/98

NEW CALEDONIA

CRICKET WAS introduced into New Caledonia by English missionaries in the nineteenth century. However, this being a French colony, there was no follow-up so, instead of developing the game according to MCC rules, the local inhabitants adapted it into what is termed 'cricket traditionnel'. In this version, the game is played by women on a pitch, 62 feet (18.89 m) long, with 27½ inch (69 cm) high stumps and no bails. The batswoman or 'joueuse' stands inside a 3¼-foot (1 m) square in front of the stumps and yields a baseball-like bat, 3 inches (7.62 cm) wide and between 36 and 39 inches (91.4 and 99.1 cm) long. The ball, made of sap, is either thrown or lobbed and generally bounces well off the pitch which is usually made of slag since grass surfaces are kept for football. The women wear knee-length dresses but no pads or gloves. Matches are fifteen-a-side and an over comprises only one ball. The umpires and scorers are always men. There are fourteen teams in the capital, Nouméa, and three in the neighbouring Loyalty Islands of Mare and Lifu. This version of the game is also played by men although, in this case, the umpires and scorers are also male. Altogether, there are some 4,000 active participants. The game is administered by the Fédération de Régionale de Cricket Nouvelle Caledonie.

The FRCNC also runs the standard version of cricket and, under their auspices, New Caledonia has taken part in various Pacific competitions but with little success. In their first appearance in the South Pacific Games in 1979, they conceded 362 runs to Fiji before being dismissed for 26. In the Pacifica Cricket Championships in 2001, Fiji scored 433 runs for the loss of five wickets in their 50 overs to which New Caledonia contributed 71 extras, including 27 byes and 27 wides; in reply, they made 73. They did even worse in the 2003 South Pacific Games, allowing Papua New Guinea to reach 502 for nine wickets off 50 overs with 59 extras, including 35 wides, before being bowled out in ten overs for 34 runs, thereby suffering one of the largest defeats in one-day cricket. Since 2000, New Caledonia have lost every international match they have played and have been dismissed for under 50 runs six times in fourteen matches.

Leading player: *Present day:* N. Passil (rhb. rm).

Playing record

One-day matches

	Won	Lost	No Res
Pacifica Championships	0	9	0
South Pacific Games*	0	5	0

* 2003 only. Full scores of the 1979, 1987 and 1991 matches have proved unobtainable.

Highest team score

ODI

169	v Vanuatu, Nouméa	1991

Lowest team score
ODI
25	v Tonga, Auckland	2001

Highest individual score
ODI
49*	M. Stafford	v Japan, Nouméa	1991

Best bowling
ODI
4-29	J.P. Lalengo	v Samoa, Suva	2003

NEW ZEALAND

Full Member of ICC: elected 1926

THE BRITISH established a foothold in the north of New Zealand in the 1790s to exploit seals, whales and timber. By 1810, the British presence had become sufficiently secure to attract missionaries intent on converting the indigenous Maori population. It is likely that some form of cricket was played soon after their arrival. The first record of cricket, however, is not until Henry Williams, the leader of the Anglican Church Missionary Society, organised a cricket match for children of the English settlers at Pihea in the Bay of Islands on 20 December 1832. Charles Darwin noted young Maoris playing cricket with the son of a missionary at Waimate on 21 December 1835. With the establishment of the New Zealand Company by E.G. Wakefield to promote the systematic colonisation of the country, more settlers began to arrive, many imbued with the ideal of recreating the society of rural England in the eighteenth century. Some thirteen months after settlers attached to the Company arrived in Wellington, *ad hoc* cricket matches were being played. Although the New Zealand Company probably accounted for only about four per cent of the immigrant population between 1830 and 1880, its promotion of Britishness pervaded the social structure of most of the growing settlements. Only Otago, under a strong Scottish influence, and Auckland were unaffected. Each centre had its own history of development because contact between the settlements was limited to irregular coastal shipping services. In 1859, it took up to two weeks to travel from Dunedin to Auckland. Gradually, communications improved with the onset of steam shipping instead of sail and the use of

telegraph services but road and rail links between towns remained rudimentary until the 1920s.

Cricket was probably played in Auckland in 1841 and by October 1842 matches were being arranged between the 'civilians' and the 'garrison'. In November 1842, a Wellington Cricket Club was formed by the elite members of colonial society and on 28 December played their first game when the club 'blues' beat the club 'reds' by two runs in a two-innings match. Also in December that year, the tradesmen in the city founded the Albion club. A cricket match was played at Nelson on 1 January 1842 by cadets of the New Zealand Company and, according to a report in the *Nelson Examiner* a Nelson Cricket Club may well have existed by November that year. In all three centres cricket suffered from a lack of people and shortage of money. The difficulty of bringing the rural land into cultivation and disputes over land ownership with the Maori resulted in many settlers becoming disillusioned and leaving. The garrisons kept cricket alive in Wellington and Auckland until the early 1850s after which enthusiasm for the game fluctuated with the size of the military presence. Every time troops departed to fight various Maori campaigns, the number of cricketers was seriously reduced. The majority of the settlers in Wellington and Auckland were either government servants or artisans with insufficient wealth to finance cricket clubs and establish grounds. Most of the clubs founded in the 1840s folded and many of those formed later had short lives. By the 1860s cricket had established only a tenuous hold in the North Island.

In the South Island, the Canterbury Association, founded in 1848 and embracing the ideals of the New Zealand Company, attracted a clientele of English public school and Oxbridge graduates who settled in the province in the 1850s to 1880s. These upper and middle class immigrants secured a ground at Hagley Park in 1851 and founded the Christchurch Cricket Club which became the Canterbury Cricket Club in 1860. Although two matches were played against a Working Men's XI, the fixture did not survive because the labourers and artisans had neither the time nor the money to organise clubs. In contrast, the members of the Christchurch club had the leisure and resources to make the long and arduous journeys to play teams from outlying settlements like Kaiapoi, Lincoln and Rangiora. By the 1860s, they were travelling further afield to Rakaia, Ashburton and Ellesmere to meet teams organised by the managers of pastoral farms and their employees. As a result of these contacts, cricket spread to many towns throughout Canterbury.

Australian Miners

Whilst the mid-nineteenth century saw cricket obtain a secure foundation in Canterbury, the situation in Otago was very different. Initially there was much enthusiasm and a club was formed in Dunedin in 1848 but, as the settlement came more under the influence of the Scottish Presbyterian Free Church, the game, along with all other sporting and leisure activities went into decline. Such pursuits were considered detrimental to the ideals of hard work and religious duty. Further, the Free Church encouraged the settlement of artisans, tradesmen and the self-employed which meant that there were few people in the city with sufficient money to act as patrons of cricket clubs. Cricket was therefore restricted to the so-called English faction until, in 1861, gold was discovered in central Otago, followed almost immediately by an influx of Australian miners, mainly from the gold fields of Victoria. Within two weeks of their arrival, cricket practices were held and in February 1862, a new Dunedin Cricket Club played its first match. The miners were instrumental in spreading the game throughout Otago so that by the mid 1860s, clubs existed in Port Chalmers, Dunstan, Alexandra, Arrowtown, Queenstown and Oamaru. Towards the end of the 1860s, gold mining declined and cricket resumed its struggle for survival against the Free Church.

Despite the constraints of finance, shortage of equipment, lack of grounds and difficulties of travel, there was sufficient enthusiasm to restart clubs and, from there, to progress to inter-provincial matches. These began in March 1860 when Wellington met Auckland in a one-day match. January 1864 saw the first three-day inter-provincial between Otago and Canterbury. Cricket was an important way of encouraging links between the various settlements. It also prevented the game from developing differently in the different centres particularly after round-arm and, eventually, over-arm bowling was introduced. These changes in bowling

action came in slowly and at different times in different places and, even by the 1870s, all forms of bowling were still in regular use.

Throughout the period of settlement, ties between New Zealand and England remained strong so that, even while inter-provincial cricket was in its infancy, there was an interest in getting an English side to visit New Zealand. Given the relative status of cricket in the various centres, it was perhaps surprising that the initiative for such a visit came from Dunedin. Shadrach Jones, an entrepreneur who was making his fortune from the gold discoveries, organised the sponsorship to attract George Parr's team, who were touring Australia at the invitation of Melbourne Cricket Club, to come to New Zealand and play matches in Dunedin and Christchurch. The results confirmed the very low standard of New Zealand cricket with the tourists winning three of the games easily and drawing with combined Otago-Canterbury side.

Thirteen years were to elapse before another overseas team came to New Zealand by which time local cricket had become more organised with Cricket Associations being established in Nelson (1874), Wellington (1875), Otago (1876) and Canterbury (1877). The last two were set up to help organise the matches against James Lillywhite's All England side which, in January 1877, was the first to tour the whole country. The following year, Arthur Shaw's side visited New Zealand. The matches against the English tourists again confirmed the low standard of local cricket. The game still suffered from the lack of grounds, money and players. Despite the growth of Wellington, Auckland, Canterbury and Dunedin, the country remained essentially rural. In 1891, only 23 per cent of the European population lived in the four main towns and there were only 36 other settlements with populations over 1,000. In most places the number of cricketers was below the critical mass required to sustain a cricket club. Even in the main towns the number of players was small because cricket could only be played regularly by the upper and middle classes. Members of the working class did not have sufficient leisure time and even the best players found it difficult to obtain leave from their employment to take part in interprovincial games. Rural labourers did not have even a half-day holiday per week until the early 1900s. Yet, despite this background, first-class cricket in New Zealand is considered to date from the game between Canterbury and Otago in February 1864, although only matches between these two teams were rated first-class until 1873 when Auckland sent a touring team to Wellington, Canterbury, Otago and Nelson. Taranaki acquired first-class in 1882/83 and Hawke's Bay in 1883/84 but their first-class rankings were short lived and, along with that of Nelson, did not last into the twentieth century.

First Formal Contact

The first formal contact with Australian cricket came in 1878 when D.W. Gregory's side stopped in New Zealand on their way to England via Fiji and North America. The Australians clearly felt they were superior in standard to the New Zealanders and when Canterbury requested a game on equal terms, it was refused. The Australians finally agreed to play a Canterbury XV instead of the normal XXII and, much to their chagrin, were beaten by six wickets. The New Zealanders were both surprised and embarrassed by the result, the Christchurch *Evening Post* describing it as one of those aspects of fortune by which the best teams are sometimes beaten. The *Sydney Mail,* however, attributed the result to a bad wicket, bad weather and bad umpiring. The progress of the New Zealanders attracted little interest in Australia and when, in the following year, Canterbury embarked on the first overseas tour by a New Zealand side and visited Victoria and Tasmania, few people came to the matches. As a result, the team ran into financial problems and had to send home for additional funds to cover the return journey.

Between 1864 and 1914, six English sides, fourteen Australian teams and Fiji made tours of New Zealand with itineries ranging from three to eighteen matches. The failure of the New Zealand teams to win more than seven per cent of the 174 fixtures is evidence of the continuing low standard of play. The best players were actually Australian born and had learned their cricket before migrating to New Zealand. The New Zealand cricket historian, T.W. Reese, attributed the problems of New Zealand cricket to a combination of insufficient practice, poor wickets and poor coaching. What little money was available was more often spent on hospitality so that touring teams would go away with good impressions of New Zealand as upholding the status of Britishness despite its geographical isolation. The result was to instill into New Zealand cricket an inferiority complex. This became even more pronounced as rugby union gradually won the battle with cricket to become the national sport. In taking up less time and not requiring much effort to produce a playable surface, rugby was cheaper and easier to organise. It was therefore more readily accessible to all classes of the population whereas cricket was sustained largely by the output of players from the elite public schools such as Christ's College, Christchurch, Wellington College, Auckland Grammar School and Otago Boys' High School. The national rugby side were also more successful. In 1905, New Zealand lost at cricket to Australia at Wellington by an innings and 358 runs whereas the 1905 New Zealand Rugby team on tour in Britain, France and North America amassed 976 points against 59 and lost only one match. In addition to being more open to all levels of European society, rugby union was also the preferred sport of the Maori for whom, being largely rural, it was cheaper to play and easier to fit into the pattern of daily life. Cricket was not generally taught in the leading Maori schools. The six Maoris to play first-class cricket before 1914 were all part of European urban society. No player of Maori ancestry played first-class cricket again until the 1980s and none played test cricket until Adam Parore in 1990.

With New Zealand cricket prior to 1914 imbued with the mores of Victorian England, it is not surprising that women's cricket was slow to develop. Indeed, it is perhaps surprising that it started at all, given that it was anathema to the male cricket administrators in the country throughout the nineteenth and early twentieth century. Whilst some sports were taught at girls' schools, cricket was confined to the elite public schools such as Wellington Girls' College, Wanganui Girls' College and Mount Eden College, Auckland. The first reference to women playing cricket in New Zealand is to a match at Greytown on 1 January 1867. A few matches seem to have been played in Waikato in the late 1880s and in Auckland in the early 1890s but interest was short-lived. Although teams existed in Greymouth and Westport in 1907, there were no competitions in the main urban centres before the First World War.

With the large number of sides touring New Zealand in the 1880s and early 1890s, the opportunity arose to test the strength of New Zealand cricket by selecting a national side to play the visitors. In February 1894, the Canterbury Cricket Association took the initiative, appointed A.M. Ollivier as the selector, and fielded a national team against New South Wales, a match which was lost by 160 runs. With complaints from both the Otago and Wellington Associations about selection combined with the financial loss sustained by Canterbury, there was a need to spread the decision-making about New Zealand cricket more widely. On 27 December 1894, the New Zealand Cricket Council was established with the aim of selecting a national side and coordinating the visits of overseas teams. All too quickly, the enthusiasm and idealism of the founders gave way to squabbles between the provincial representatives over selection of players and the choice of grounds for the international fixtures. The initial results, however, were good. New Zealand beat New South Wales by 142 runs in December 1895 and Queensland by 182 runs in December 1896. Later performances against Lord Hawke's side, the MCC and Australia ranged from disappointing to disastrous.

These international contacts led to an improvement in standard and when the MCC visited again in 1906/07, admittedly whilst the tourists were still adjusting to local conditions, Auckland and Wellington managed draws and Canterbury were victorious by seven wickets. In the latter game, the home side was helped by injuries to three of the visiting party and the fact that the match started only three hours after a rough sea voyage. In the last game of the tour, the New Zealand national side gained a five-run first innings lead over the MCC before losing by 56 runs. These performances prompted the Governor-General, Lord Plunket, to offer a trophy for interprovincial cricket. At first, the Plunket Shield did little to promote provincial matches because it was awarded only on a challenge basis on the home ground of the holder (Table 2.9). When it was introduced in 1907, there was an immediate controversy as to the first holder. The Shield was eventually awarded to Canterbury even though many observers, including members of the MCC considered Auckland to be the best team. Auckland immediately challenged for the trophy and beat Canterbury in Christchurch by an innings. The possibility of changing the Plunket Shield to a provincial league competition was raised in 1912 but dismissed as likely to lead to the bankruptcy of the provincial associations because of the costs of travel. It was not until 1921/22 that a league system was introduced involving Auckland, Canterbury, Otago and Wellington. For many years, each province played only three matches a season in the Shield, which meant that, in alternate years, only one first-class home match was played. Except when touring teams visited, the whole first-class season was completed over the Christmas holiday period and early January. Although this was inevitable because the players could not get leave for longer periods, the restricted nature of the competition did not provide the foundation needed to develop a strong national side. The Plunket Shield produced a limited number of good players but rarely any who could be rated as world class. The Shield was extended in 1950/51 with the appearance of the Central Districts, covering the minor associations of Taranaki, Wanganui, Hawke's Bay, Manawatu and Wairarapa in the North Island and Nelson and Marlborough on South Island, and again in 1956/57 with the inclusion of the Northern Districts, covering the minor associations of Northland, Waikato, Bay of Plenty and Poverty Bay in the north of the North Island (Table 2.10). In 1975/76, the Shell Oil Company sponsored the Shell Trophy for the domestic first-class competition. The Plunket Shield was allocated to the annual fixture between North and South Island.

During the First World War there were only two seasons without some first-class cricket in New Zealand (1915/16 and 1916/17). Yet, when first-class cricket

Table 2.9 Teams involved in New Zealand's first-class domestic competition: the Plunket Shield (1906/07–1920/21) contested on a Challenge basis

Team	Date of first appearance	Number of times challenges defeated
Auckland	1907/08	11
Canterbury	1906/07	13
Hawke's Bay	1914/15	0
Otago	1911/12	0
Wellington	1911/12	0

resumed in 1917/18, it took some time to return to its rather limited pre-War level of activity. A touring side came from Australia in 1920/21 and played matches against the major provinces as well as two fixtures against New Zealand. The first of these was drawn but the New Zealanders lost the second by an innings and 227 runs. The Plunket Shield did not restart until 1921/22. In 1922/23 the MCC sent an 'A' side, akin to one of the weaker first-class English counties in standard, but they proved too strong, winning two of the matches against New Zealand by an innings and drawing the third. Two international matches were played against New South Wales in 1923/24, both lost, and two against Victoria in 1924/25, with one loss and one draw. Although traditional wisdom has attributed the struggle of New Zealand's cricketers to the lack of batting experience on hard fast wickets, the results suggest that the main problem was the inability of the bowlers to dismiss the opposition for a low score. The status of cricket as a minority sport and the lack of leisure time to play or watch the game continued to pose financial problems. During the two-month long MCC tour, attendances were good only in the main cities and, even then, only on Saturdays. The up-country matches all lost money.

Following New Zealand's admission to the Imperial Cricket Conference in 1926, a decision was made to send a touring side to England. The NZCC set up a limited company to finance the trip. The touring party of fourteen players was captained by Thomas Lowry who had experience of English conditions from his time at Cambridge University in the early 1920s. The side had a long tour, playing 26 first-class matches. With over three months of continuous cricket, the players improved considerably. Although they won only five of their first-class matches, four of their five defeats came in May whilst the team were still adjusting to English wickets. The tour made a financial loss and the company shareholders received a mere ten shillings (50 pence) for every pound invested. The results encouraged the NZCC to organise a second tour in 1931. Based on the 1927 record, the New Zealanders were accorded test-match status and one three-day match was arranged at Lord's. Their performance in this drawn game led to two additional tests being arranged, one at The Oval which England won easily by an innings and 26 runs, and one at Old Trafford, Manchester, which was drawn after rain prevented any play until after lunch on the third (last) day.

Despite two successful tours of England and an encouraging start in test cricket, the impetus could not be maintained. Australia played two matches against New Zealand during a short tour in 1928, winning one and drawing one, but thereafter the Australian Board of Control ignored New Zealand throughout the 1930s and 1940s. Perhaps the ABC decided that New Zealand were just not of international standard. Whatever the reason, the neglect from the one country which, through relative geographical proximity, was best placed to exchange touring teams and generally help support the game, was certainly one factor responsible for the failure of New Zealand cricket to develop. The change in attitude seemed inexplicable given the regularity of contacts prior to the First World War and through the 1920s. As a result, New Zealand had no further international cricket until the MCC agreed to play three matches at the end of their Australian tour in 1936/37. However, no test match was played, further undermining the status of New Zealand cricket. The lack of external support gave no encouragement to young cricketers to take the game seriously and the best found themselves poached by the English counties. Thus Charles Dacre went to Gloucestershire, Stewart Dempster to Leicestershire and William Merritt and Kenneth James to Northamptonshire. When New Zealand returned to the international scene with their third tour of England in 1937, they were forced to select a largely young and inexperienced side. Considering the circumstances,

Table 2.10 Teams involved in New Zealand's first-class domestic competitions: the Plunket Shield (1921/22-1974/75) and the Shell Shield (1975/76-2006/07)		
Team	Date of first appearance	Number of times winners
Auckland	1921/22	20
Canterbury	1921/22	14
Central Districts	1950/51	6 + 1 shared
Northern Districts	1956/57	5 + 1 shared
Otago	1921/22	13
Wellington	1921/22	21

the team did well, losing one and drawing two of the test matches. Rather like the team of 1927, the side improved as the tour progressed but the results were very different from what might have been if the progress of the first two tours had been properly built-upon.

Women's cricket continued to make slow progress during the 1920s and early 1930s. The game was gradually adopted by an increasing number of girls' secondary schools, some of which made efforts to attain a reasonable standard of play. Development was strongest in Auckland where the game was taught in several schools and at Auckland Teachers' Training College. Inter-school matches and fixtures between schools and their old girls were organised on a fairly regular basis. A women's cricket association was formed in Auckland on 19 September 1928. Progress was slower in the other towns and it was not until the 1930s that girls' schools in Canterbury began to include cricket in their sporting curriculum. Even so, by 1932, Wellington, Otago and Canterbury had all formed women's associations and cricket was on the curriculum of Otago Girls High School. Once it was clear that the English women were to visit Australia in 1934/35, the four associations established the New Zealand Women's Cricket Council in 1934 with the aim of encouraging the English to visit New Zealand as well. They were successful in this and New Zealand played their inaugural women's test match against England at Christchurch in February 1935. Not surprisingly, given their very limited experience, the New Zealanders were outplayed, losing by an innings and 337 runs. In 1938, invited by the New South Wales Women's Cricket Board, New Zealand visited Australia as part of the 150th anniversary celebrations of the founding of New South Wales but the tour did not include a test match.

Although the Second World War prevented any international cricket and many cricketers served in the New Zealand forces, there were opportunities for cricket at home. When the New Zealand troops were not in the Middle East, they were stationed either in New Zealand or in the Pacific, so *ad hoc* matches could be arranged. At the end of the War, almost certainly with the aim of encouraging the resumption of their own cricket, Australia visited New Zealand and played a representative match at Wellington in March 1946 which was later granted test status by the ICC in March 1948. New Zealand's batsmen had no answer to the bowling of Ernie Toshack, Bill O'Reilly and Keith Miller and were defeated by an innings and 103 runs. The result confirmed the Australian view of the low standard of New Zealand's cricket and no further international matches between the countries were played until 1973/74. In 1947/48, the Australian women restarted their international programme by playing New Zealand at Wellington in March 1948, winning by an innings and 102 runs. It was to be January 1957 before the teams met again.

First Victory

New Zealand's first victory in test cricket came in March 1956 when, after 26 years and 44 matches, they overcame the West Indies by 190 runs. The test record to this point in their history, however, does not do justice to the ability of many of New Zealand's players. The 1949 tour of England is still considered by many to be a high point. New Zealand held their own in the four test matches, all of which were drawn. If they had been scheduled for five days each instead of three, New Zealand might well have won at least one match. Unfortunately, this promise was not maintained and throughout the 1950s New Zealand were regularly defeated. In March 1955, they were dismissed by a strong English side for 26, the lowest score ever recorded in test cricket. In 1958 they had a disastrous tour of England losing four out of the five test matches, three of them by an innings, and only drawing the fifth when rain intervened. It was not until the late 1960s that New Zealand began to win matches on a regular basis. They drew the test series against the West Indies in 1968/69 and against India in 1969/70. A period of consolidation followed during which they secured their first victory over England in February 1978. The foundation was laid for the most successful period in New Zealand's cricket history. They won two consecutive series against England, in 1983/84 and in 1986, two consecutive series against Australia in 1985/86, and the series against the West Indies in the Caribbean in 1979/80.

From the mid-1980s to the mid-1990s New Zealand were less successful and it was not until the late 1990s that a new set of world-class players emerged. Although the recent record is similar to that of the early 1980s, the results are not truly comparable because the opposition has been more varied in standard. Relatively easy wins have been obtained over Zimbabwe and Bangladesh. During this period, however, the management of New Zealand cricket has become more professional and, as a result, success on the cricket field is now an important indicator of national prestige. There is an increasing expectation that New Zealand can and will win against all opponents, including Australia.

The growth in New Zealand's population, which potentially provides a larger number of players, and the growth of many of the middle-sized towns, which has encouraged the NZCA to take the first-class game to more places, has made cricket increasingly accessible to all members of New Zealand society. In the 1935/36 season, there were very few first-class matches and they were confined to Auckland, Wellington, Christchurch and Dunedin. This situation changed in the 1950s with the inclusion of Central Districts and Northern Districts in the Plunket Shield, taking the first-class game to places like Napier, Rotorua, Palmerston North and New Plymouth. By 2003/04, first-class cricket was played in fourteen towns and Hamilton in the North Island had become more important as a test-match venue than Dunedin.

Changes also occurred in the geography of the itineraries of touring sides in New Zealand. When the MCC went to New Zealand in 1922/23, they had a relatively long tour involving 34 days of cricket. Since they played in centres from Auckland in the north to Invercargill in the south, a lot of travel was involved, covering 3,540km when measured in straight-line distances and, obviously, very much longer when accounting for the actual distances travelled by rail, road and sea. The most surprising feature of the tour was the amount of travel across the Cook Straits between North and South Island. Given how rough sea voyages can be in New Zealand waters, it might have been expected that one return journey across the Straits would have been sufficient. However, on 23 December 1922, the team played in Christchurch, having travelled from Wanganui in the North Island, presumably via Wellington. On 30 December, they

returned to Wellington, only for their following match on 5 January to be in Christchurch. This nonsense of an itinerary was repeated when, having travelled from Invercargill, they played in Wellington on 26 January before crossing the Cook Straits to play in Nelson on 30 January; their next game in 2 February was in Wellington. One wonders whether some board members of the NZCA had shares in the ferry company! Otherwise, by cricket tour standards, the visit was relatively gentle. There were 19 rest days so that the ratio of playing days to rest days was rather low (Table 2.11).

The 1950/51 tour by the MCC is typical of the short tours undertaken by teams as an add-on to a tour of Australia. Only a few centres were visited, in this case involving journeys from Auckland to Dunedin, Christchurch and Wellington. Although an order of Auckland, Wellington, Christchurch and Dunedin would have been more sensible for minimising travel, the tour probably satisfied the idea of combining cricket and some relaxation. The ratio of cricket to rest days was very low. The 2000/01 tour was clearly much harder in respect of the amount of cricket to rest days. This reflects the recognition of cricket as a profession and the inclusion of one-day matches into the itinerary with successive matches in different venues. Although the number of kilometres travelled per rest day increased, this largely reflects the greater ease of travel with journeys by air replacing those formerly made by sea. Even so, the itinerary has its oddities. Was it really necessary to play in Lincoln, just south of Christchurch, on 1 March 2001, play the next match, a five-day test, in Auckland starting on 8 March, and then return to Christchurch for a test match beginning on 15 March?

The history of women's cricket in New Zealand since the Second World War closely follows that of the men's

Table 2.11 Playing days, rest days and distances travelled on tours of New Zealand by the MCC (1922/23 and 1950/51) and Pakistan (2000/01)

Date	Playing days	Rest days	Ratio of cricket days to rest days	Kilometres travelled per rest day
1922/23	34	19	1.79	186
1950/51	13	8	1.63	208
2000/01	25	7	2.78	522

Notes: Rest days are days when no cricket is played and no travel takes place. The ratio of kilometres travelled per rest day is an underestimate because kilometres are based on straight-line distances between the venues and not the actual distance travelled.

game with one major exception. The first victory did not come until 1971/72 when, nearly fifteen years after the men won their first test match, Australia were defeated at St Kilda, Victoria, by 143 runs. This was, however, at only the seventeenth attempt because of the fewer number of matches. In the same season, New Zealand beat South Africa by 188 runs at Durban to record their first away win. To date these remain the only victories by New Zealand in women's test cricket. The reason is that since the three-match series against England in 1996, the women have played only one test match, also against England in 2004. In contrast to the men's game which has operated on a mixture of test and one-day cricket, the women's international game in New Zealand has been almost entirely one-day. New Zealand hosted the third women's World Cup competition in 1981/82 and finished third, a position they repeated when the contest was next held in 1988/89. They improved on this in 1993 when they had a superb run in the qualifying competition, beating both Australia and England, to reach the final. They then gave a disappointing performance and went down to England at Lord's by 67 runs. New Zealand hosted the women's World Cup in December 2000 and narrowly beat Australia in an exciting final by four runs. Although they remain one of the top four countries in women's cricket, they failed to make the final in the 2005 World Cup. Nevertheless, the playing record over the last decade has helped to establish women's cricket as a sport through which New Zealand women can acquire national recognition for sporting achievement.

Famous Victories
March 9, 10, 12 and 13, 1956 – Eden Park, Auckland
New Zealand 255 (J.R. Reid 84, T. Dewdney 5-21) and 157-9 dec (D. Atkinson 7-53)
West Indies 145 (H. Furlonge 64, H.B. Cave 4-22, A.R. MacGibbon 4-44) and 77 (H.B. Cave 4-21)
New Zealand won by 190 runs

Having lost the previous three test matches in the series, New Zealand lost their first five wickets for 87 runs and looked set to continue their dismal record. John Reid, the captain, then steadied the innings, batting freely and scoring eleven fours, adding 104 runs in partnership with John Beck (34). Play on the first day was halted forty

minutes early by bad light. Almost as soon as the players left the field, a tropical rainstorm occurred, producing wet conditions the following day which helped the seam bowlers. Tom Dewdney quickly finished off the New Zealand innings but, with the exception of a defensive display by Hammond Furlonge, the West Indies found Henry Cave and Tony MacGibbon too lively. Denis Atkinson also revelled in the conditions but again Reid (12) came to the rescue with Simpson Guillen (41), allowing New Zealand to set a formidable target of 268 runs in four hours. Cave and Donald Beard (3-22) exploited the conditions and the West Indies were in serious difficulties, losing six wickets for only 22 runs. Everton Weekes (31) and Alfred Binns (20) attempted a recovery but both fell to the leg spin of John Alabaster. Cave and Beard then returned to the attack to complete the rout. West Indies made their lowest total in test cricket to that date and New Zealand gained their first test match victory.

March 8, 9, 10, 12 and 13, 1974 – Lancaster Park, Christchurch
Australia 223 (I.R. Redpath 71) and 259 (K.D. Walters 65, I.R. Redpath 58, I.C. Davis 50, D.R. Hadlee 4-71, R.J. Hadlee 4-75)
New Zealand 255 (G.M. Turner 101, M.H.N. Walker 4-60) and 230-5 (G.M. Turner 110*)
New Zealand won by 5 wickets

Australia were sent in by Bev Congdon, the New Zealand captain, and through controlled seam bowling by Richard Hadlee (3-59) and Richard Collinge (3-70), supported by excellent fielding, were always under pressure. Only Ian Redpath and Rodney Marsh (38) who added 53 for the sixth wicket played with any freedom. New Zealand, in turn, struggled against good line and length seam bowling by Max Walker and Geoff Dymock (3-59). They owed their first innings lead to the persistence of Glenn Turner who played and missed regularly before scoring his century after four and three-quarter hours. Australia's second innings started abysmally with three wickets down for 33 before Ian Davis and Doug Walters added 106. Dayle Hadlee, bowling at a lively pace and gaining movement off the pitch, brought the innings to a close, leaving New Zealand to score 228 to win. John Parker and Turner opened with a partnership of 51 before Walker (2-50) struck with two quick wickets and Congdon was run out. Turner played a competent and near-faultless innings, adding 115 with Brian Hastings (46) in a stand marked by excellent running between the wickets. Hastings was dismissed in the last over of the fourth day which ended with New Zealand 177-4. Given the frailty of much of the batting in the match, the game could have gone either way. Australia only needed two quick wickets to gain the advantage. However, Turner found a reliable partner in Jeremy Coney (14) and completed his second century of the match, this time in five hours thirty-eight minutes. After Coney fell to Greg Chappell (1-38), Ken Wadsworth hit the winning runs to give New Zealand their first victory over Australia.

February 10, 11, 12, 14 and 15, 1978 – Basin Reserve, Wellington
New Zealand 228 (J.G. Wright 55, C.M. Old 6-54) and 123 (R.G.D. Willis 5-32)
England 215 (G. Boycott 77, R.J. Hadlee 4-74) and 64 (R.J. Hadlee 6-26)
New Zealand won by 72 runs

Geoffrey Boycott won the toss and with a gale force wind blowing down the pitch asked New Zealand to bat. Chris Old bowled splendidly into the wind and Bob Taylor made four superb catches behind the stumps. Only John Wright and Bev Congdon (44) offered resistance as New Zealand lost their fifth wicket at 191 and their eighth at 196. In reply, England batted very defensively with Boycott scoring ten, twelve and six in three successive hours. In all, he batted for seven hours and twenty-two minutes. Richard Hadlee and Richard Collinge (3-42) troubled all the English batsmen and Congdon, in a fill-in spell before a new ball became due, bowled seven successive maidens. Once Boycott became the sixth wicket to fall, England succumbed quickly. Wright and Robert Anderson made 54 for the first wicket, giving the impression that batting conditions had eased, but Bob Willis then produced some inspired bowling, taking four wickets for fourteen runs in 31 balls. Aided by Ian Botham (2-13) and Mike Hendrick (2-16), England came back into the match, requiring only 137 runs to win. When Boycott was bowled by Collinge off the twelfth ball, England performed like a beaten side and were soon 18 for four wickets. Botham

(19) attempted to hit England out of trouble but by the close of the fourth day, they were 53-8. On the last day, rain delayed the start by forty minutes before Hadlee took the last two wickets to complete a superb display of fast bowling, dismiss England for their lowest total against New Zealand, and give New Zealand their first test victory over England.

Women's match
December 23, 2000 – BIL Oval, Lincoln
New Zealand 184 (48.4 overs)
Australia 180 (49.1 overs) (B.J. Clark 91)
New Zealand won by 4 runs

New Zealand won the toss in this World Cup final and batted but against a competent Australia attack of Cathryn Fitzpatrick, Therese McGregor (2-26) and Charmaine Mason (2-30) found scoring difficult. Rebecca Rolls (34), Emily Drumm (21), Debbie Hockley (24) and Kathryn Ramel (41) all made starts but New Zealand finished at least twenty runs short of a defendable total. The New Zealand bowlers and fielders made up for the side's deficiencies in batting. Lisa Keightley was caught behind by Rolls on the fourth ball of the innings and Karen Rolton was run out at the non-striker's end by a direct hit from Helen Watson at extra-cover. From two runs for two wickets down, Belinda Clark and Cherie Bambury (14) took the score to 85, after which wickets fell regularly to take Australia to 115-6. Clark and McGregor then raised the total to 150 before Clark fell, sweeping the off-spin of Clare Nicholson (2-38), having scored 91 from 102 balls. Watson then made another direct hit at the stumps to run out McGregor. Fitzpatrick (6), Mason (11) and Avril Fahey (3*) took Australia closer and closer to their objective, reaching the final over with five runs to make and one wicket to fall. With the first delivery, Nicholson had Mason caught behind, to take New Zealand to a tense and exciting victory.

Player Profiles
Crowe, Martin David MBE. b Henderson, Auckland, 22 September 1962. rhb. rm. One of the greatest New Zealand batsmen of all time, he possessed a wide range of strokes which he executed with elegance. He headed the New Zealand batting averages on each of

his three tours of England. He also holds the record for the highest number of runs (1,676) scored in a New Zealand season (1986/87). He played county cricket for Somerset from 1984 to 1988. He was forced to retire with a serious knee injury in 1995/96. In 77 test matches, he made 5,444 runs (average 45.36) and took 14 wickets (average 48.28).

Dempster, Charles Stewart. b Wellington 15 November 1903. d Wellington 14 February 1974. rhb. One of the greatest batsmen to come from New Zealand in the Inter-War period, he was renowned for his powerful driving of the ball. After tours of England in 1927 and 1931 in which he made 1,430 runs and 1,778 runs respectively, he took up a business appointment with Sir Julian Cahn and had a successful career with Leicestershire (1935-1939). He also played for Scotland (1934). After the Second World War, he played three matches for Warwickshire. In 10 test matches, he scored 723 runs (average 65.72).

Donnelly, Martin Paterson. b Ngaruawahia, Auckland, 17 October 1917. d Sydney, New South Wales, Australia, 22 October 1999. lhb. Considered to be the best left-handed batsmen in the world immediately after the Second World War, he combined the complete range of strokes with superb footwork. He was chosen for the 1937 tour of England at the age of nineteen and scored 1,414 runs in first-class matches. He easily exceeded this on the 1949 tour, scoring 2,287 runs (average 61.81). Between the two tours, he served in the New Zealand forces in Egypt and Italy, reaching the rank of Major, graduated from University College, Canterbury and then read history at Oxford where he obtained blues for cricket and rugby union. He represented England at rugby against Ireland in 1947. He took up a business appointment in Australia in 1950 and gave up first-class cricket. In seven test matches, he scored 582 runs (average 52.90).

Downes, Alexander Dalziel. b Emerald Hill, South Melbourne, Victoria, Australia, 2 February 1868. d Dunedin 10 February 1950. rhb. rob. He would have been New Zealand's leading cricketer before the First World War if he could have obtained leave from his employment as a brass finisher more often. He turned the ball sharply from the off and was frequently

devastating on the rough pitches of his day. He played for New Zealand on 4 occasions, scoring 58 runs (average 8.28) and taking 14 wickets (average 23.57). He was a successful centre three-quarter in rugby union and played for Otago. He later became both a cricket umpire and rugby referee.

Drumm, Emily Cecilia. b Avondale, Auckland, 15 September 1974. rhb. rm/lb. One of the leading New Zealand women's cricketers of all time. In a test career limited to five matches, she has scored 433 runs (average 144.33) and taken 2 wickets (average 87.50). In 101 matches one day internationals she has made 2,844 runs (average 35.11) and taken 37 wickets (average 21.02) She captained the New Zealand team which won the World Cup in 2000/01.

Hadlee, Sir Richard John KBE. b St Albans, Christchurch, 3 July 1951. lhb. rfm. He is regarded by many as the greatest cricketer ever to represent New Zealand. He obtained speed, lift and outswing from a hostile classical side-on action. He became the first bowler in the world to obtain 400 test wickets which he achieved in his 79th test match. He was a professional cricketer with Nottinghamshire from 1978 to 1987 during which he became one of the top bowlers in English county cricket. His English experience made him shorten his run and concentrate on accuracy. In 86 test matches, he made 3,124 runs (average 27.16) and took 431 wickets (average 22.29). In 115 one-day internationals he scored 1,751 runs (average 21.61) and took 158 wickets (average 21.56). He was awarded the MBE in 1980 and the KBE in 1990.

Hockley, Deborah Ann. b Christchurch 7 November 1962. rhb. One of the leading batswomen of all time, in a test career of 19 matches, she has made 1,301 runs (average 52.04). She is the only woman to have played in over 100 one-day internationals. In 118 matches, she has scored 4,064 runs (average 41.89).

Reid, John Richard OBE. b Auckland 36 June 1928. rhb. rfm/rob. occ wk. The leading all-rounder in New Zealand cricket throughout the 1950s and early 1960s, at one time, he held records for the New Zealand cricketer who has scored most runs, scored most centuries, taken most wickets, made most catches and captained most times. In 58 test matches, he scored 3,428 runs (average 33.28) and took 85 wickets (average 33.35).

Sutcliffe, Bert MBE. b Ponsonby, Auckland, 17 November 1923. d Auckland 20 April 2001. lhb. sla. Arguably the best left-handed batsman of his generation in the world, his driving, hooking and pull strokes were played to text-book perfection. He is the only New Zealander to score two triple centuries in first-class cricket, 385 for Otago against Canterbury in 1952/53 and 355 for Otago versus Auckland in 1949/50. In 42 test matches, he made 2,727 runs (average 40.10). After retirement, he became a successful cricket coach.

Turner, Glenn Maitland. b Dunedin 26 May 1947. rhb. A sound opening batsman with an immaculate defence, he devoted himself to becoming a professional cricketer. He set himself to attain a high standard and expected the same of others. He played for Worcestershire between 1967 and 1982 and, through county cricket, changed from a largely defensive batsman to one with a wide range of strokes. As a result of his long county career, he is the only New Zealander to score more than 30,000 first class runs and to make 100 centuries. He has twice carried his bat in a completed test match innings. In 41 test matches, he scored 2,991 runs (average 44.64). In 41 one-day internationals he made 1,598 runs (average 47.00).

Vettori, Daniel Luca. b Auckland 27 January 1979. lhb. sla. He is New Zealand's leading spin bowler of all time and one of the leading left-arm spinners of his generation. When chosen against England at Wellington in 1996/97, he became the youngest person to play test cricket for New Zealand. In 72 tests, he has scored 2,242 runs (average 25.47) and taken 228 wickets (average 33.94). In 197 one-day internationals he has made 1,232 runs (average 14.32) and taken 195 wickets (average 33.38).

Other leading players: *1890-1914:* D. Reese (lhb. lsm). *1920-1940:* W.E. Merritt (rhb. lbg); K.C. James (rhb. wk); M.L. Page (rhb. rs); H.G. Vivian (rhb. sla). *1945-1960:* J. Cowie (rhb. rfm); W.M. Wallace (rhb). *1960-1980:* B.E. Congdon (rhb. rm); R.O. Collinge (rhb. lmf); B.R. Taylor (lhb. rfm); G.P. Howarth (rhb. rob). *1980-2000:* E.J. Chatfield (rhb. rmf); C.L. Cairns (rhb. rfm); A.C. Parore (rhb. wk); I.D.S. Smith (rhb.

wk). *Present day:* S.P. Fleming (lhb); N.J. Astle (rhb. rm); J.D.P. Oram (lhb. rm); J.E.C. Franklin (lhb. lfm). **Women:** *1960-1980:* J.A. Burley (rhb. rfm); J. Lord (rhb. lb); B.A. Brentnall (rhb. wk). *1980-2000:* S.L. Illingworth (rhb. wk); K.E. Flavell (rhb); B.L. Bevege (rhb). *Present day:* M.A.M. Lewis (rhb); R.J. Pullar (rhb. rfm); R.J. Rolls (rhb. wk).

Playing record
Test matches

	Won	Lost	Tied	Drawn
England	7	41	0	40
Australia	7	22	0	17
South Africa	4	18	0	11
West Indies	9	10	0	16
India	9	14	0	21
Pakistan	6	21	0	18
Sri Lanka	9	5	0	10
Zimbabwe	7	0	0	6
Bangladesh	4	0	0	0
Total	62	131	0	139

Internationals prior to test status*

0	9	0	4

* Matches against MCC and Australia

One-day matches

	Won	Tied	Lost	No Res
World Cup	35	0	26	1
Other ODIs	191	4	247	23

Twenty20

2	1	2	0

Highest team score

671-4 dec	v Sri Lanka, Wellington	1990/91

Lowest team score

26	v England, Auckland	1954/55

Highest individual score

299	M.D. Crowe	v Sri Lanka, Wellington	1990/91

Best bowling

9-52	R.J. Hadlee	v Australia, Brisbane	1985/86

Best wicket-keeping

7 (7c)	I.D.S. Smith	v Sri Lanka, Hamilton	1990/91

Women
Test Matches

	Won	Lost	Tied	Drawn
England	0	6	0	17
Australia	1	4	0	8
South Africa	1	0	0	2
India	0	0	0	6
Total	2	10	0	33

One-day matches

	Won	Lost	Tied	No Res
World Cup	40	17	2	3
Other ODIs	69	69	0	3

Twenty20

1	0	1	0

Highest team score

517-8 dec	v England, Scarborough	1996

Lowest team score

44	v England, Christchurch	1934/35

Highest individual score

204	K.E. Flavell	v England, Scarborough	1996

Best bowling

7-41	J.A. Burley	v England, Oval	1966

Best wicket-keeping

6 (4c 2st)	B.A. Brentnall	v South Africa, Johannesburg	
			1971/72

ODI

6 (4c 2st)	S.L. Illingworth	v Australia, Beckenham	1993

NICARAGUA

ALTHOUGH CRICKET has a somewhat tenuous hold amongst the expatriate community in Nicaragua, there was enough interest and a sufficient number of players in December 2002 to play two limited overs matches at home to Costa Rica. One match was won, the other lost.

NIGERIA

Associate Member of the ICC: elected 2002

EXACTLY WHEN cricket was first played in Nigeria is not known but it would not have been earlier than 1861 when the island of Lagos was annexed by the British. Before that no part of the country was under British rule although the British Navy was deployed from 1808 to help suppress the slave trade and missionaries started to arrive in 1842. By the end of the nineteenth century, however, the military and the civil administrative staff had introduced the game to Lagos and it is likely that the Army and staff of the Royal Niger Company organised *ad hoc* games in the north. Since the numbers of Europeans in the country remained small, it is probable that Nigerians were encouraged to play the game in

order to make up teams. Contacts between the military and civilian population in Lagos with their counterparts in the Gold Coast led to an international fixture in 1904. Played at the Racecourse ground in Lagos, the Gold Coast won by 22 runs in the first of what developed into an annual fixture. The matches in 1904, 1905 and 1906 were multiracial but the fourth encounter, in December 1906, was for Europeans only. Arrangements for the next European match were not made until 1910 but the fixture was first postponed because of the death of King Edward VII and then cancelled following an outbreak of yellow fever. In the meanwhile, the African cricketers had started their own international series in 1907.

International cricket stopped during the First World War and matches against the Gold Coast did not restart until 1925 for Europeans and 1926 for the Africans. Responsibility for organising and financing the European matches rested on wealthy patrons supported by enthusiastic public servants like Sir Shenton Thomas, Sir Selwyn Grier, Sir Charles Arden-Clarke and T.H. Wilson. The African matches were supported by similar patronage among the elite African community. Although Lagos was the focal point of Nigerian cricket, the game spread to all the main towns including Abeokuta, Ibadan, Benin, Kano, Zaria, Jos, Kaduna, Enugu, Port Harcourt, Onitsha and Calabar. Despite the distances and the slowness of transport, annual matches were held between the North and the South as trials for selecting the side to meet the Gold Coast. Roads were largely unsurfaced and it could take between two and three hours to travel 70 kilometres. Railways were slow and generally late; it could take over five hours to cover 150 kilometres. Only the military, government servants and the wealthy could afford the time to undertake the journeys and play matches which could last between three and five days. The Nigerian Cricket Association for Europeans was formed in 1932 at a meeting in Zaria and the following year, the Nigerian Cricket Association for Africans was founded. Although cricket remained racially organised until the two Associations merged in 1956, relationships between the two bodies were cordial and in 1951 they formed a joint Board of Control which was successful in obtaining government funding for the game.

In the 1920s and 1930s the standard reached in the

European matches against the Gold Coast was certainly at English minor county level and often close to first-class. Many of the leading players had first-class cricket experience before taking administrative positions in Nigeria. After a gap for the 1939-45 War, international cricket restarted in 1947 with a match against the Gold Coast by the Europeans. The African matches resumed the following year. Although there were still some European players with first-class experience, they were fewer in number and the overall standard was lower than that of the 1930s. In contrast, the quality of the African players improved. As the number of Europeans working in the country decreased, multiracial cricket became essential if international cricket was to continue. Matches against the Gold Coast were reduced to an annual multiracial fixture from 1956. Following independence in 1960 there was much support for cricket. Fixtures against Sierra Leone and The Gambia began in 1964. Through the late 1960s and early 1970s, these matches were evenly contested. In the late 1970s, the Nigerian economy suffered problems and the country became more successful in football and athletics. Less money was available for cricket and fewer young people showed interest in the game. Standards began to decline and when, in 1974, Tanzania visited Nigeria, two of the three international matches were lost and one drawn. Nigeria were also no match for the MCC in 1976, losing the three-day fixture by ten wickets. Along with much else in Nigeria, cricket suffered through the 1970s and 1980s from mismanagement, government interference, corruption, lack of money, lack of support for a sport with strong colonial associations and rivalries between the various ethnic groups. The only advantage that Nigeria possessed was that the number of players exceeded that of Ghana, Sierra Leone and The Gambia combined. Thus, it was difficult to kill cricket completely. Nigeria became the strongest side in West Africa and provided most of the players for the West African side on the few occasions that they competed in the ICC Trophy. These factors probably explain why Nigeria was granted associate rather than affiliate status by the ICC when the West African Cricket Conference ceased to exist in 2002. So far, the performance of the national side in various African competitions scarcely rates this status. In 2006, Nigeria finished last in Division 2 of the African Championships and were relegated to

Division 3. Fortunately, the reservoir of players and clubs remains sufficiently large to provide a basis for future development. It is up to the present administrators in the NCA and the Federal Ministry of Youth and Sport to which it is affiliated to bring this about; otherwise, after three decades of continuous decline, there is a risk that the game will become extinct.

Player Profiles

Butler, F.K. The leading all-round player for Nigeria in the series against the Gold Coast, he played from 1928 to 1939, the longest spell by any of the European cricketers. Before migrating to Nigeria, he played for Hertfordshire. He became Secretary of the Nigerian Cricket Association. In 12 matches against the Gold Coast, he scored 751 runs (average 37.55) and took 18 wickets (average 16.55).

Shirley, William Robert de la Cour. b Marylebone, London, 13 October 1900. d Bognor Regis, Sussex, 23 April 1970. rhb. rfm/rob. Having previously played first-class cricket for Cambridge University, where he obtained a blue in 1924, and Hampshire, he spent time in Nigeria between 1928 and 1938 during which he played 5 international matches against the Gold Coast, scoring 350 runs (average 43.75) and taking 21 wickets (average 15.00).

Other leading players: *1920-1940:* F.E.H. Godfrey (wk); N.D. Nuha (rhb. rfm); T.S.W. Thomas. *1945-1960:* R.E. Akpofure; O.A. Alakija; O.O. Coker. *Present day:* T. Okusanya (rhb. rm); A. Onikoyi (rhb. wk).

Playing record
International matches

	Won	Lost	Drawn
Europeans v Gold Coast*	12	8	7
Africans v Gold Coast†	5	10	3
Combined European and African v Gold Coast/Ghana‡	4	3	2

* matches played between 1904 and 1955
† matches played between 1907 and 1955
‡ matches played between 1956 and 1964

One-day matches

	Won	Lost	No Res
ICC African Six Nations Competition	1	5	0
African Championships Division 2	0	4	0

Highest team score
397-7 dec Nigeria (Europeans) v Gold Coast (Europeans), Lagos 1932

Lowest team score

| 37 | Southern Nigeria (Africans) v Gold Coast (Africans), Accra | 1912 |

ODI

| 30 | v Namibia, Lusaka | 2004 |

Highest individual score

| 166 | E. Henshaw | v Ghana, Lagos | 1982 |

ODI

| 166 | B. Olufawo | v Ghana, Freetown | 2001 |

Best bowling

| 7-65 | W.S. King | v Nigeria (Europeans) v Gold Coast (Europeans), Accra | 1952 |

Best wicket-keeping

| 6 (3c 3st) | C.J. Patterson | Nigeria (Europeans) v Gold Coast (Europeans), Lagos | 1938 |

NORFOLK ISLAND

THE AUSTRALIAN territory of Norfolk Island, 1610 kilometres from Sydney, originally served as a penal settlement. The soldiers who administered it established the Kingston Oval where cricket has been played since 1838. The ground was sited close to the gaol so that the military at leisure would not be too far away in case of an attempted break-out by the prisoners. It is also within 300 metres of the beaches of Slaughter Bay and Emily Bay which offer excellent swimming. Shortly after the penal settlement was closed, the inhabitants of the Pitcairn Islands came to Norfolk Island to escape problems of famine and water shortage. They arrived on 8 June 1856. Most stayed only three years before homesickness caused them to return but during that time they and the other Norfolk Island settlers were introduced to cricket by the Melanesian Mission which was established in 1857. It is tradition that on the anniversary of the Pitcairners' arrival, a cricket match is played between the descendants of the *Bounty* and an All-Comers team. It is not known when the first of these matches was played but the first recorded instance is in the diary of Elisabeth Colenso of the Melanesian Mission for 11 June 1876.

Since the 1870s cricket's fortunes on Norfolk Island have fluctuated. The greatest level of activity was in the 1920s and 1930s when up to six senior clubs existed and matches were played against Lord Howe Island. Activity was also high during the Second World War when some 1,000 servicemen were stationed on the island.

During the 1950s many young people left to pursue education and careers in Australia and the number of clubs declined. A revival occurred in the 1960s with the development of the tourist industry which encouraged Norfolk Islanders to return home. There was also an increase in the number of people coming to work on the island as bank staff, teachers and tradesmen. Despite this, cricket in the 1980s went into a slow decline and by the early 1990s only two teams remained and even the annual *Bounty* match had to be abandoned through a lack of players. The Norfolk Islands Cricket Association set about regenerating interest and in 1997, after a gap of four years, the *Bounty* match was resumed. The game, with many of the cricketers in period costume, was played following a re-enactment of the Pitcairners' arrival and a community picnic. The event was sufficient to re-establish cricket. With assistance from the New South Wales Cricket Association and Sportscare Australia a programme of coaching for senior and junior players has been instituted. The aim of the NICA is to obtain ICC recognition at affiliate status and to compete in the various competitions involving the Pacific islands.

NORWAY

Affiliate Member of ICC: elected 2000

CRICKET FIRST began in Norway in the 1960s when Asian immigrants started to organise matches. The first club, Oslo Cricket Club, now known as Sentrum Cricket Club, was founded in 1972, by Pakistanis. This was followed by Kampen Cricket Club, formed by Indian expatriates. Since that time the number of clubs has grown steadily so that there is now a 14-club league in the Oslo region and clubs in Trondheim, Bergen, Drammen, Asker and Stavanger. Initial growth was rather slow because the winter climate means that football is a competing summer sport both for players and space. In 1996 an advance was made when the Oslo Sports Council were persuaded to provide an artificial pitch and two practice wickets. However, as the number of clubs increased, a single ground quickly proved insufficient, particularly during wet summers when it was unusable for much of the time and it was impossible to complete the programme of league fixtures. In 2004, the first ground dedicated to cricket was opened at Stovner in Oslo. The national side competed for the first time in the Five Nations Representative Festival in Vienna, Austria, in 2000, winning the competition. Cricket was then immediately set back by disputes among the management of the Norwegian Cricket Board on the best way to promote the game. Unfortunately, the political and personal animosities in the top management of Norwegian cricket do not seem to have been resolved with some Board members believing that progress is not being made fast enough. This is somewhat surprising since Norway has twice won the European Affiliates competition which qualified them to play in Division 2 of the European Championships and in 2006 won promotion to Division 1. If the management issues can be sorted out, the future for Norwegian cricket looks good. Although some 90 per cent of the players are of Asian origin, most are either Norwegian citizens or nationals.

Leading players: *Present day:* Aamir Waheed; Munawar Ahmed (wk); Zeeshan Ali.

Playing record
One-day matches

	Won	Lost	No Res
ECC Trophy	6	0	0
European Affiliates Tournament	6	0	0
European Championships	2	3	0

Highest team score
ODI

341-7	v Malta, Mechelen	2003

Lowest team score
ODI

160	v Italy, Waterloo	2004

Highest individual score
ODI

131*	Shahbaz Butt	v Malta, Mechelen	2003

Best bowling
ODI

6-36	S. Chaudhry	v Austria, Vienna	2003

Best wicket-keeping
ODI

4 (4c)	Munawar Ahmed	v Portugal, Waterloo	2005
4 (4c)	Munawar Ahmed	v France, Paisley	2006

OMAN

Affiliate Member of ICC: elected 2000

CRICKET HAS made enormous strides in Oman since expatriates from the Indian sub-continent started to organise matches in the late 1970s. Although it is confined to Muscat and is not as popular as football, hockey or tennis, there were, by 2003, some sixty teams playing in a league of eight divisions. These included three teams of all-Omani nationals. The Oman Cricket Club, the body with responsibility for administering the game, has also insisted that every team in the league include at least one Omani or play with ten men. As a result of this encouragement to locals, Oman has more indigenous cricketers than any other Middle Eastern country. Oman made its international debut in the Asian Cricket Council Trophy in 2002, winning one match out of four. Two years later, the standard of the national team had improved so much that they won all their qualifying games and reached the final only to be defeated by 94 runs by the United Arab Emirates. This performance qualified them for the final stages of the ICC Trophy in 2005 and the next Asia Cup, originally scheduled for 2006 but postponed until 2008. They thus became the first affiliate country to participate at that level. In the ICC Trophy, they lost their first five games but salvaged their reputation by beating Uganda and the USA to finish ninth out of the twelve countries.

Cricket in Oman is seriously constrained by lack of finance. The Oman Cricket Club has yet to be recognised by the General Organisation for Youth, Sports and Cultural Activities and therefore receives no government support. No interest has been shown by the local business community in providing sponsorship. As a result, little progress has been made on developing cricket facilities. Lack of money may also explain why the number of clubs registering for the league in 2005/06 dropped to thirty-nine. Solving the financial issue is vital if Omani cricket is to build on its substantial achievements so far. The most consistent players all learnt the game on the Indian sub-continent and many are nearing the end of their careers which may explain why Oman failed to reach the quarter-finals of the 2006 Asian Cricket Council Trophy. The future depends on finding local replacements of comparable or higher standard.

Famous Victory
July 11, 2005 – Balrothery
USA 346 (50 overs) (G. Roopnarine 98, C.A. Reid 61*)
Oman 348-7 (49.1 overs) (Farhad Khan 94*, Mohammed Aslam 58)
Oman won by 7 wickets

In this play-off for ninth place in the ICC Trophy, the United States scored freely. Gowkaran Roopnarine and Leon Romero added 136 for the third wicket and Charles Reid and Hamish Anthony (39*) put on an unbeaten 97 for the seventh wicket. In reply, Oman started poorly, losing wickets to Howard Johnson (2-48) and Anthony (2-47). With five wickets down for 102, the Americans looked set to be easy winners but were then taken aback by Oman's demolition of the American support bowling. Richard Staple went for 85 runs off his seven overs and Steve Massiah conceded 30 runs in two overs. After Jitendra Redkar and Mohammed Aslam showed the way, Farhan Khan and Azhar Ali took the bowling apart in an unbeaten partnership of 137. In a remarkable match in which 694 runs were scored from 99.1 overs, Oman made one of the highest second-innings totals ever to win a one-day match.

Leading players: *Present day:* H.J. Mehta (lhb. sla); H.P. Desai (rhb. rfm); Adnan Ilyas (rhb. rm).

Playing record
One-day matches

	Won	Tied	Lost	No Res
Asian Cricket Council Trophy	7	0	6	0
ICC Trophy	2	0	5	0
Middle East Cup	3	1	1	0

Highest team score
ODI
348-7	v USA, Balrothery	2005

Lowest team score
ODI
41	v Papua New Guinea, Drummond	2005

Highest individual score
ODI
94*	Farhan Khan	v USA, Balrothery	2005

Best bowling
ODI
6-43	H.P. Desai	v Afghanistan, Kuala Lumpur	2004

Best wicket-keeping
5 (4c 1st) J.V. Redkar	v Uganda, Dublin	2005

PAKISTAN

Full Member of ICC: elected 1952

WHEN PAKISTAN was formed following the partition of India in 1947 it inherited a structure for cricket laid down first by the British Raj and then by the Indian Cricket Board of Control. The game had developed along communal lines with tournaments in Karachi and Lahore between sides representing Europeans, Muslims and Hindus. Multiracial cricket existed in so far as teams from Sindh, based in Karachi, Northern India, based at Lahore, and the North West Frontier Province, based in Peshawar, had taken part in the Ranji Trophy. Much cricket was played by the British military who were well represented in the NWFP team. Cricket was also well established amongst the elite in the public schools and universities, particularly in Punjab and Karachi. The area that was to become Pakistan had already supplied several cricketers to India, notably Wazir Ali, Nazir Ali, Naoomal Jeoomal, Jahangir Khan, Mohammad Nissar and A.H. Kardar. Despite this background, outside the military and the main towns of Lahore and Karachi, cricket had only a small presence. The departure of British troops, the political unrest associated with the move towards independence and the upheavals associated with the mass migrations of people across the sub-continent could have been disastrous for cricket. Fortunately, Muhammad Ali Jinnah, the first Governor-General of Pakistan, was a cricket enthusiast who encouraged the game at all levels as one of many factors that could help unify the new country. Thus, from its foundation, the Pakistan Cricket Board has always been closely associated with the government. Many of the Presidents of Pakistan, both civilian and military, have been keen on cricket and one, Nawaz Sharif, played first-class cricket for Punjab. One advantage of the relationship between the Cricket Board and the Government is that cricket has been allowed to develop largely free of religious influence from the mullahs. Although the Pakistan Board adopted the policy of the Indian Board in not choosing any player of European origin for the national team, there were no other ethnic or religious barriers to selection. Hindus and Christians have regularly played for Pakistan. More recently, the Board has been able to encourage women's cricket despite opposition from religious fundamentalists.

West Indies Visit

First-class cricket began almost immediately Pakistan was created with two matches in the 1947/48 season: West Punjab against Sindh, to raise funds for refugee relief, and Punjab University versus the West Punjab Governor's XI. The latter was a revival of an annual fixture which had started in 1929/30. The following season saw the West Indies visit Pakistan during their tour of the sub-continent. Pakistan then visited Ceylon where they won both international matches easily. The 1949/50 season saw a visit from the Commonwealth side touring India and a return series against Ceylon which Pakistan again won easily. After the visit of the MCC in 1951/52 in which Pakistan drew the first and won the second representative match, the ICC awarded Pakistan test status. The first tests were played in 1952/53 when Pakistan toured India and lost the five match series by two games to one. Victory came at the University Ground, Lucknow, by an innings and 43 runs. Fazal Mahmood took twelve wickets in the match and Nazar Muhammad carried his bat for 124 runs, becoming the first Pakistani to score a test century and the first player in test-match history to be on the field for an entire game. These performances led to a large following for cricket throughout the country which has continued to this day. Cricket is widely played by all sections of the community with government departments and private companies running teams alongside the more traditional clubs, schools and universities.

The Pakistan Cricket Board quickly realised that a strong first-class game was required to underpin the national side. In 1953/54, a national first-class championship was instituted for the Quaid-i-Azam Trophy, named in honour of Quaid-i-Azam Muhammad Ali Jinnah. The competition was organised on a knock-out basis and contested by seven provincial teams, Bahawalpur, Combined Services, Karachi, North Western Frontier Province, Pakistan Railways, Punjab and Sindh. Although it remains the premier first-class competition,

it has suffered from inconsistency in policy by the PCB regarding its format and the teams eligible for entry. The first changes attempted to address the problem of inequalities in standard and allowed the stronger sides of Karachi and the Punjab to enter two or even three teams. Later, experiments were made by forcing the weaker provincial sides to combine and allowing them to be assisted by one or more players on loan from the stronger teams. In the 1970s, banks, corporations and other institutions were allowed to enter teams. Policy fluctuated between the competition being only for banks and corporate bodies in some years, only for provincial sides in other years and, in some seasons, open to both types of team. Often the changes occurred from one season to the next. Sometimes the competition was restricted to the top ten first-class sides in the country, based on a qualifying contest. In 2005/06 it was reduced to seven teams. Compared to the first-class competition in other countries, the result can, at best, be described as a shambles, testing both player and spectator loyalties. Table 2.12 summarises the history of the competition.

Pakistan's international record began promisingly. Following their first test win against India, they shared the series against England in 1954, thereby becoming the first country to win a test match on their first tour of England. In a low-scoring game at The Oval, they gained a well-deserved victory by 24 runs but were fortunate to square the four match series since, in a very wet summer, they were saved by the weather from certain defeat at Manchester. Victories at home against New Zealand were followed by one against Australia on the matting wicket at Karachi in October 1956. By the late 1950s, however, many of the side were approaching retirement and there was a need to introduce new players. The team struggled on the tour of the West Indies in 1957/58, losing the series by three matches to one. The tour showed that Pakistan's batsmen and bowlers could not perform as well on grass wickets as on matting. When Australia visited Pakistan in 1959/60, the Australian captain, Richie Benaud, discussed this with President Ayub Khan during the presentation ceremony at the match in Karachi. Reflecting the close relationship between the Government and the PCB, all matches in the Quaid-i-Azam Trophy were played on turf wickets from 1959/60 on.

The change to turf wickets did not have an immediate

Table 2.12 Teams involved in Pakistan's first-class domestic competition: the Quaid-i-Azam Trophy (1953/54-2006/07)

Team	First appearance	Years of participation	Number of wins
Agricultural Development Bank of Pakistan	1985/86	5	1
Allied Bank	1982/83	5	0
Bahawalpur	1953/54	26	2
Bahawalpur-Multan-Lahore	1985/86	1	0
Bahawalpur-Multan-Sargodha	1966/67	1	0
Balochistan	1954/55	7	0
Combined Services	1953/54	8	0
Combined Universities	1958/59	10	0
Dadu	2002/03	1	0
Dhaka	1964/65	1	0
Dhaka University	1957/58	1	0
Dhaka University & Education Board	1964/65	1	0
East Pakistan	1954/55	8	0
East Pakistan A	1957/58	1	0
East Pakistan B	1957/58	1	0
East Pakistan Greens	1956/57	1	0
East Pakistan Whites	1956/57	1	0
Faisalabad	1990/91	17	2
Gujranwala	1997/98	6	0
Gujranwala-Sargodha-Faisalabad	1985/86	1	0
Habib Bank	1976/77	16	1
House Building Finance Corporation	1979/80	9	0
Hyderabad	1958/59	14	0
Hyderabad Blues	1969/70	1	0
Hyderabad Whites	1969/70	1	0
Hyderabad-Khairpur-Quetta	1966/67	1	0
Hyderabad-Sukkur-Quetta	1985/86	1	0
Industrial Development Bank of Pakistan	1979/80	3	0
Islamabad	1992/93	10	0
Kalat	1969/70	1	0
Karachi	1953/54	14	5
Karachi A	1957/58	3	1
Karachi B	1957/58	2	0
Karachi C	1957/58	1	0
Karachi Blues	1956/57	19	7
Karachi Greens	1956/57	2	0
Karachi Harbour	2006/07	1	0
Karachi Urban	2005/06	2	1
Karachi Whites	1956/57	19	4
Khairpur	1958/59	9	0
Khan Research Laboratories	1999/00	2	0
Lahore	1958/59	13	1
Lahore A	1961/62	4	0
Lahore B	1961/62	3	0
Lahore Blues	2001/02	3	0
Lahore City	1991/92	9	2
Lahore City Blues	2000/01	1	1
Lahore City Whites	2000/01	1	0
Lahore Division	1999/00	1	0
Lahore Greens	1963/64	2	0
Lahore Reds	1964/65	1	0
Lahore Shalimar	2005/06	2	0

effect because the pitches produced proved very slow, conducive neither to pace nor spin, and therefore gave little preparation for the batsmen to deal with faster pitches overseas. The 1960s and 1970s were a dire time for Pakistani cricket marked by disagreements between the members of the PCB and between the Board and the Government over selection, disputes between the Board and the players over financial terms for overseas tours, and a failure to find an inspiring captain to replace Abdul Kardar. It was not until Imran Khan took over the captaincy in the 1980s that the record improved. When injury forced Imran Khan to retire, squabbles over the captaincy resumed with no one able to unite the players and inspire them to function as a team. With the administrators and selectors also changing frequently there was nothing consistent about Pakistani cricket except inconsistency in performance and the presence of a number of excellent individual players. When Imran Khan returned to lead the team, they won the World Cup in 1991/92, beating England in the final at Melbourne by 22 runs.

The enthusiasm for cricket in Pakistan has been correctly reflected by the PCB in their decisions to take test cricket to many towns throughout the country. Although most test matches have been played in Karachi and Lahore, Faisalabad ranks third in terms of the number of matches staged. Other towns where tests have been played are Rawalpindi, Peshawar, Hyderabad, Sialkot, Multan, Sheikhupura, Gujranwala and Bahawalpur. With so many teams involved in the Quaid-i-Azam Trophy, it is not surprising that virtually every town of reasonable size has held first-class cricket matches. Whilst in the early days, when there were few first-class matches, they were restricted to the main towns, by the 1970s, first-class cricket had a greater reach across the country. Today, not only do many towns host first-class matches but they stage between four and seven a year. Thus, the PCB provides ample opportunities for the public to watch first-class cricket.

Another area where the PCB has acted with logic is the itinerary adopted for touring sides. Tours start either in the south or north of the country and then progress either north or south respectively from one centre to the next, thereby minimising both travel time and distance. The only exception was the one or two matches in East Pakistan, a requirement which disappeared once East Pakistan separated to become Bangladesh. When a team arrived in a given centre, all the matches scheduled for that centre were played with rest days between the games. On the more recent tours involving a combination of test, three-day and one-day matches, the number of rest days has increased (Table 2.13) although, unfortunately, many of these now seem to be taken up with practices held under tight security rather than providing an opportunity to see the country.

The late 1990s saw the start and very rapid development of women's cricket in Pakistan as a result of initiatives taken by Shaiza Khan and Sharmeen Khan. These sisters from Karachi had learnt the game from their brothers in the 1980s and developed it further whilst at boarding school in England. In the early 1990s, they returned to England as students at Leeds University where they played for and captained the University side as well as appearing for Middlesex women. When they returned to Pakistan in 1995,

Table 2.12 cont.

Team	First appearance	Years of participation	Number of wins
Lahore Whites	1963/64	4	0
Multan	1958/59	18	0
Muslim Commercial Bank	1978/79	10	0
National Bank	1970/71	18	5
North Western Frontier Province	1953/54	9	0
Pakistan Air Force	1969/70	2	0
Pakistan Automobiles Corporation	1983/84	5	0
Pakistan Customs	1999/00	2	0
Pakistan International Airlines	1964/65	21	6
Pakistan International Airlines A	1970/71	1	0
Pakistan International Airlines B	1970/71	1	0
Pakistan National Shipping Corporation	1987/88	4	0
Pakistan Railways	1953/54	28	2
Pakistan Railways A	1970/71	1	0
Pakistan Railways B	1970/71	1	0
Pakistan Reserves	1999/00	1	0
Peshawar	1956/57	27	2
Peshawar-Rawalpindi Combined	1966/67	1	0
Peshawar University & Education Board	1964/65	1	0
Public Works Department	1969/70	3	0
Punjab	1953/54	7	1
Punjab A	1956/57	4	1
Punjab B	1956/57	5	0
Punjab Greens	1977/78	1	0
Punjab University	1969/70	2	0
Punjab University & Lahore Education Board	1964/65	1	0
Punjab Whites	1977/78	1	0
Rawalpindi	1958/59	28	0
Rawalpindi A	1994/95	2	0
Rawalpindi B	1994/95	2	0
Rawalpindi Greens	1964/65	1	0
Rawalpindi Yellows	1964/65	1	0
Rawalpindi-Peshawar-Dera Ismail Khan-Hazara	1985/86	1	0
Reliable Efficient and Developing Company	1999/00	1	0
Rest of Balochistan	2001/02	1	0
Rest of North Western Frontier Province	2001/02	1	0
Rest of Punjab	2001/02	1	0
Rest of Sindh	2001/02	1	0
Quetta	1957/58	9	0
Sargodha	1961/62	17	0
Service Industries	2002/03	1	0
Sheikhupura	2000/01	3	0
Sialkot	2001/02	6	0
Sindh	1953/54	6	0
Sindh A	1957/58	4	0
Sindh B	1957/58	2	0
Sindh Blues	1975/76	2	0
Sindh Whites	1976/77	1	0
State Bank of Pakistan	1983/84	1	0
United Bank	1976/77	14	4
Water and Power Development Authority	1984/85	4	0
Zarai Taraqiati Bank Limited	2002/03	1	0

they founded the Pakistan Women's Cricket Control Association and managed to find a sufficient number of women interested in playing to form teams in the Punjab and Sindh. By the end of 1996, there was an adverse reaction from some of the Pakistani women players to the work of the so-called 'super-rich sisters', a term reflecting the amount of sponsorship provided by the United Carpets Group of Companies, run by their father. A rival organisation, the Pakistan Women's Cricket Association was formed but this quickly split into two factions, one of which was supported by the PCB. When all three bodies sent delegates to a meeting of the International Women's Cricket Council in Calcutta in 1997, a public squabble seemed certain until the IWCC resolved the issue by recognising the PWCCA. Unfortunately, this was too late to prevent the dispute from affecting the selection of the Pakistani team for the 1997 World Cup. The country was represented by a weakened side and lost all their matches. The dispute also affected Pakistan's entry to the International Women's Cricket Council Trophy in The Netherlands in 2003, a qualifying competition for the 2005 World Cup. The PCB insisted on their right to select and represent the Pakistani team. After the ICC again supported the PWCCA, the Dutch government refused entry visas to the PCB officials. The PCB then tried to prevent the PWCCA side from using the title of Pakistan but this was overruled by the IWCC.

In addition to these disputes over who runs women's cricket in Pakistan, the Pakistani women have had to overcome the expected opposition from the mullahs and that from male administrators both within the PCB and in provincial and national governments. Despite this there are now six sides competing annually in the domestic tournament for the Fatima Jinnah Trophy and cricket is now a compulsory sport in all-girls secondary schools throughout the country. Until 2001, the Pakistan women's team were prohibited from playing international matches at home. When the PWCCA invited the Netherlands to tour Pakistan in 2001/02 for a seven match series of one-day internationals, the PCB agreed to the National Stadium in Karachi being used but the promised support of television coverage did not happen. Since most of the sponsorship depended on the matches being televised the PWCCA were left to finance the venture with most of the funds coming from United Carpets. Pakistan won the series by four matches to three. The results since then have shown that they have already reached the standard of Scotland and the West Indies, as well as that of the Dutch. In accordance with ICC requirements laid down in 2005, the PCB now has the responsibility to run women's cricket and has had to recognise the work of the PWCCA in developing the game so far. It has established a women's wing but it may be some time before previous animosities are overcome. There is also concern as to whether the PCB will actively promote women's cricket or whether, in deference to the equivocal attitudes towards women's sport in the country, it will do no more than the minimum required to satisfy the ICC. A promising start was made when, in 2005/06, Pakistan hosted the women's Asia Cup, involving India, Pakistan and Sri Lanka. In the late 1990s and early 2000s, Pakistani cricket faced major problems. Spasmodic suicide bombings in Karachi and concerns over security in the north of the country meant that many countries were reluctant to send touring sides. The number of test matches played by Pakistan was temporarily reduced, being limited to away fixtures or matches on neutral grounds such as Sharjah. Although security issues remain, tours to Pakistan have resumed.

Pakistan cricket suffered a further set-back when they were eliminated in the first round of the 2007 World Cup, indicating that the present structure of the domestic game is not providing sufficient players with the skill and motivation required to perform consistently at international level.

Famous Victories
August 12, 13, 14, 16 and 17, 1954 – The Oval, London
Pakistan 133 (F.H. Tyson 4-35)

Table 2.13 Playing days, rest days and distances travelled on tours of Pakistan by India (1954/55) and England (2000/01)

Date	Playing days	Rest days	Ratio of cricket days to rest days	Kilometres travelled per rest day
1954/55	47	6	7.83	868
2000/01	31	16	1.94	180

Notes: Rest days are days when no cricket is played and no travel takes place. The ratio of kilometres travelled per rest day is an underestimate because kilometres are based on straight-line distances between the venues and not the actual distance travelled. The number of kilometres travelled per rest day for 1954/55 is reduced to 473 if the leg of the tour in East Pakistan is excluded from the calculations.

and 164 (J.H. Wardle 7-56)
England 130 (D.C.S. Compton 53, Fazal Mahmood 6-53, Mahmood Hussain 4-58) and 143 (P.B.H. May 53, Fazal Mahmood 6-46)
Pakistan won by 24 runs

England rested Alec Bedser and Trevor Bailey to give experience to Frank Tyson and Peter Loader prior to the winter tour of Australia. When Brian Statham, Tyson and Loader reduced Pakistan to 51 for seven wickets, the decision of the selectors seemed justified. The last two wickets added 56 runs, Shujauddin (16*), Zulfiqar Ahmed (16) and Mahmood Hussain (23) finding run-making surprisingly easy. Torrential rain prevented play on second day and on the following morning the uncovered wicket played appallingly. Fazal Mahmood and Mahmood Hussain made the ball rear awkwardly from a length and the English batsmen suffered terribly. Only Denis Compton made any attempt at survival but in a stay of two hours and twenty minutes he was dropped three times. With a lead of three runs, Pakistan's early batsmen again failed. The drying pitch now took spin and Johnny Wardle exploited it superbly. With Pakistan eight wickets down for 82 runs, an English victory was in sight. Wazir Muhammad (42*), who took thirty minutes to score his first run, and Zulfiqar Ahmad (34) added 58 for the ninth wicket, enabling Pakistan to set England a target of 168 runs. After Len Hutton (5) was dismissed with the score on 15, Reg Simpson (27) and Peter May (53) scored 51 runs for the second wicket. When May was caught by Kardar off the bowling of Fazal Mahmood, England needed only 59 runs with seven wickets in hand. They then collapsed to the superb fast-medium leg cutters of Fazal Mahmood, aided by wicket-keeper Imtiaz Ahmad who held seven catches in the match. Pakistan deserved to become the first touring side to beat England in a test match on their first visit.

October 11, 12, 13, 15 and 17, 1956 – National Stadium, Karachi
Australia 80 (Fazal Mahmood 6-34, Khan Muhammad 4-43) and 187 (R. Benaud 56, Fazal Mahmood 7-80)
Pakistan 199 (A.H. Kardar 69, Wazir Muhammad 67, I.W. Johnson 4-50) and 69-1
Pakistan won by 9 wickets

Pakistan had the satisfaction of not only beating Australia at the first attempt but doing so convincingly. Coming, after only a short break, from a disastrous tour of England, Australia were unable to adjust to the change from grass to a matting wicket without any acclimatisation to the new conditions. Pakistan took the initiative from the start with Fazal Mahmood bowling a mesmerising mixture of leg-cutters and break backs. He took the first six wickets to fall for 26 runs in only sixteen overs. He and Khan Muhammad bowled throughout Australia's first innings which ended shortly after tea on the first day. Pakistan lost wickets cheaply to the fast bowling of Ray Lindwall (1-42), Keith Miller (2-40) and Ron Archer (1-18) before Abdul Kardar and Wazir Muhammad hit their way out of trouble in a sixth wicket partnership of 104. This was sufficient to help secure a lead of 119 runs. Australia still had no answer to Fazal Mahmood and Khan Muhammad, though Richie Benaud and Ron Archer (27) made 64 for the sixth wicket whilst the strike bowlers were rested. At the end of the third day, Pakistan batted tediously towards their target of 69 runs and were still six runs adrift after two hours and forty minutes. With no play on the fourth day which was one of mourning for the first anniversary of the death of Liaqat Ali Khan, the first Prime Minister of Pakistan, victory was not obtained until early on day five.

March 25, 1993 – Melbourne Cricket Ground, Melbourne
Pakistan 249-6 (50 overs) (Imran Khan 72, Javed Miandad 58)
England 227 (49.2 overs) (N.H. Fairbrother 62)
Pakistan won by 22 runs

Pakistan owed much to the inspirational captaincy of Imran Khan in winning the final of the 1992 World Cup. Imran chose to bat on winning the toss but Derek Pringle dismissed both openers with only 24 runs on the board. Imran and Javed Miandad then batted slowly and after 25 overs the score was only 70; Javed also needed the assistance of a runner. The pair then accelerated the run-rate, setting an example which was followed by Inzamam-ul-Haq (42) and Wasim Akram (33). The last twenty overs produced 153 runs with 52 coming from the last six, even though Pringle conceded only two runs in the last over to give him an analysis of 10-2-22-3. England quickly lost Ian Botham, surprisingly promoted to open the innings, Alec Stewart, Graeme Hick and Graham Gooch, the last two failing to read the spin of Mushtaq Ahmed (3-41). Alan Lamb (31) and Neil Fairbrother added 72 runs but after Wasim Akram (3-49) bowled Lamb, Fairbrother, also batting with a runner, was unable to combine rapid scoring with protecting the tail. Fittingly, Imran Khan took the last wicket to take Pakistan to a comfortable victory.

Women
July 21, 2003 – Drieburg, Amsterdam
Pakistan 181-6 (50 overs)
Japan 28 (34 overs) (Sajjida Khan 7-4)
Pakistan won by 153 runs

Pakistan's women achieved their most convincing victory against an inexperienced Japanese side in their first game of the ICC Women's Cricket Council Trophy, a qualifying competition for the 2005 World Cup. Aided by some wayward bowling, Pakistan batted consistently with Kiran Baluch (31), Shaiza Khan (30*), Nazia Nazir (24) and Sajjida Shah (20) all making twenty or more runs. Japan batted with extreme caution at a rate of 0.82 runs per over but no one made double figures and six players failed to score. Having made 21 before the first wicket fell, they then lost ten wickets for only seven runs. Sajjida Shah's off-spin produced one of the more remarkable analyses in women's one-day cricket history of 8-5-4-7.

Player Profiles
Abdul Qadir Khan. b Lahore 15 September 1955. rhb. lbg. An outstanding bowler, his googly was difficult to read and he combined looping flight with prodigious spin at a pace on the slow side of medium. He was particularly effective on the wickets in Pakistan. He was the first bowler to take 100 wickets in a Pakistani season and the second Pakistani bowler to take 200 wickets in test cricket. In 67 test matches, he scored 1029 runs (average 15.59) and took 236 wickets (average 32.80). In 104 one-day internationals he made 641 runs (average 15.26) and took 132 wickets (average 26.16).

Fazal Mahmood. b Lahore 18 February 1927. d Gulberg, Lahore, 30 May 2005. rhb. rfm. The most successful strike bowler in the first ten years of Pakistani test cricket, he was, arguably, the best bowler ever produced by Pakistan. With his ability to cut the ball both ways off the pitch combined with unnerving accuracy, he was able to force most batsmen to offer catches to the wicket-keeper or the slip fielders. The others, he generally bowled out. He played first-class cricket for Northern India in the Ranji Trophy and was chosen by India for the 1947/48 tour of Australia, an offer which he declined following the creation of Pakistan as a country. In 34 test matches, he scored 620 runs (average 23.02) and took 139 wickets (average 24.70). After retiring from cricket, he became a Police inspector.

Hanif Muhammad. b Junagadh, India, 21 December 1934. rhb. occ wk. He developed into one of Pakistan's leading batsmen of all time. He was taken to Pakistan by his parents following the partition of India. The family settled in Karachi and Hanif quickly became a teenage prodigy. He made his first-class debut at sixteen and a year later, aged 17 years and 300 days, he was chosen for the test side on their tour of India. A small, compact player, he possessed a wide range of shots, but he was best known for his defence and power of concentration. His 337 runs against the West Indies at Bridgetown in 1957/58 took 970 minutes and is the longest innings ever recorded in test cricket. For a long time he held the record for the highest first-class score, 499 made in a mere 640 minutes before he was run out attempting the 500th run. In 55 test matches, he scored 3,915 runs (average 43.98).

Imran Khan Niazi. b Lahore 25 November 1952. rhb. rf. As well as being the leading all-rounder in Pakistani cricket, he was an outstanding captain. He was able to transform a match by an inspired batting or bowling performance. He was an exceptional cricketer whilst at Oxford University and he followed this with successful first-class careers with Worcestershire and Sussex. He was the first Pakistani to achieve 300 test wickets and the only Pakistani player to take 300 wickets and score 3,000 runs. On retirement, he entered public life, raising money for various charities, including a cancer hospital, and taking up politics in opposition to the government.

In 88 test matches, he scored 3,807 runs (average 37.69) and took 362 wickets (average 22.81). In 175 one-day internationals he made 3,709 runs (average 33.41) and took 182 wickets (average 26.61).

Inzamam-ul-Haq. b Multan 3 March 1970. rhb. With a wide range of strokes executed with great power, he was the leading batsman of the late 1990s and early 2000s. He has scored more test centuries than any other Pakistani and was the second Pakistani to exceed 7,000 test runs. Affectionately known as 'potato' because of a weight problem, he adjusted to this by scoring in fours rather than singles and in becoming a specialist slip fielder. He proved a charismatic captain able to get the best out of his players. In 118 tests he scored 8,812 runs (average 50.64). In 375 one-day internationals he made 11,701 runs (average 39.53).

Javed Miandad Khan. b Karachi 12 June 1957. rhb. lbg. The first Pakistani batsman to score over 8,000 test runs and the first Pakistani player to appear in over 100 test matches, he scored his first six test hundreds before his 22nd birthday. With his cover-driving and square-cutting, he became the leading Pakistani batsman of the 1980s; he was also one of the early exponents of the reverse sweep. He had a short but successful first-class career with Sussex before moving to Glamorgan for whom he was an outstanding player. He enjoyed being in the limelight and had a mixed success as captain. He was an effective leader on the 1992 tour of England but otherwise did not always gain the support and respect of his team. In 124 tests, he scored 8,832 runs (average 52.57) and took 17 wickets (average 40.11). In 233 one-day internationals he made 7,381 runs (average 41.70) and took 7 wickets (average 42.42).

Shaiza Said Khan. b Karachi 18 March 1969. rhb. lb. The leading female cricketer since Pakistan started playing international women's cricket, she became captain of the national side. In 3 test matches, she scored 69 runs (average 13.80) and took 19 wickets (average 24.05). In 40 one-day internationals, she scored 391 runs (average 11.17) and took 63 wickets (average 23.95), the latter being an exceptional performance for a leg spin bowler.

Wasim Akram. b Lahore 3 June 1966. lhb. lf. Able to swing the ball both ways and capable of intimidating most opposition, he was the first Pakistani to take 400 test wickets. As a batsman, he could rescue an innings by taking the opposing bowling apart. In 1996, he scored 257*, coming in at number eight. He had a successful first-class career with Lancashire. In 104 tests, he scored 2,898 runs (average 22.64) and took 414 wickets (average 23.62). In 356 one-day internationals he made 3,717 runs (average 16.52) and took 502 wickets (average 23.52).

Wasim Bari. b Karachi 23 March 1948. rhb. wk. Arguably the best ever wicket-keeper to come from Pakistan, he was generally undemonstrative though could be acrobatic when required. He was equally effective against pace or spin and considered to be one of the neatest and safest of keepers to spin bowling. He is the only Pakistani wicket-keeper to exceed 200 dismissals in test cricket. He shares the world record for the number of victims in a single innings (seven, all caught). In 81 test matches, he scored 1,366 runs (average 15.88) and made 201 catches and 27 stumpings. In 51 one-day internationals he scored 221 runs (average 17.00) and made 52 catches and 10 stumpings.

Zaheer Abbas, Syed. b Sialkot 27 July 1947. rhb. Able to dominate most attacks, he was a graceful player with an excellent judge of the line and length of the ball and the ability to score equally through the covers or the leg-side off both the front and back foot. He became an automatic selection for Pakistan in the 1970s. He was especially effective against England in England where he made 274 at Birmingham in 1971 and 240 at The Oval in 1974. He had a long and successful career with Gloucestershire. In 78 test matches, he scored 5,062 runs (average 44.79). In 62 one-day internationals he made 2,572 runs (average 47.62).

Other leading players: *1945-1960:* Imtiaz Ahmed (rhb. wk); Nazar Muhammad (rhb); Khan Muhammad (rhb. rfm). *1960-1980:* Mushtaq Muhammad (rhb. lbg); Asif Iqbal (rhb. rm); Saeed Ahmed (rhb. rob). *1980-2000:* Waqar Younis (rhb. rf); Saleem Malik (rhb. rm); Saeed Anwar (rhb). *Present day:* Muhammad Yousuf (formerly Yousuf Yohanna) (rhb); Younis Khan (rhb); Danish Kaneria (rhb. lb).

Women: *Present day:* Kiran Baluch (rhb. rob); Sajjida Shah (rhb. rob); Batool Fatima (rhb. wk).

Playing record
Test Matches

	Won	Lost	Tied	Drawn
England	12	19	0	36
Australia	11	24	0	17
South Africa	3	7	0	4
West Indies	15	14	0	15
New Zealand	21	6	0	18
India	12	8	0	36
Sri Lanka	15	7	0	10
Zimbabwe	8	2	0	4
Bangladesh	6	0	0	0
Total	103	87	0	140

One-day matches

	Won	Tied	Lost	No Res
World Cup	30	0	24	2
Other ODIs	320	6	261	13

Twenty20

Won	Tied	Lost	No Res
1	0	1	0

Highest team score
708   v England, The Oval   1987

Lowest team score
53   v Australia, Sharjah   2002/03

Highest individual score
337   Hanif Mohammed   v West Indies, Bridgetown   1957/58

Best bowling
9-56   Abdul Qadir   v England, Lahore   1987/88

Best wicket-keeping
7 (7c)   Wasim Bari   v New Zealand, Auckland   1978/79

Women
Test Matches

	Won	Lost	Tied	Drawn
Ireland	0	1	0	0
Sri Lanka	0	1	0	0
West Indies	0	0	0	1
Total	0	2	0	1

One-day matches

	Won	Lost	Tied	No Res
World Cup	0	5	0	0
World Cup Qualifying	2	3	0	0
Other ODIs	6	36	0	1
World Cup Qualifying - Asian region	3	0	0	0

Highest team score
426-7 dec   v West Indies, Karachi   2003/04

Lowest team score
53   v Ireland, Dublin   2000

ODI
23   v Australia, Melbourne   1996/97

Highest individual score
242   Kiran Baluch   v West Indies, Karachi   2003/04

Best bowling
7-59   Shaiza Khan   v West Indies, Karachi   2003/04

ODI
7-4   Sajjida Shah   v Japan, Amsterdam   2003

Best wicket-keeping
ODI
6 (2c 4st)   Batool Fatima   v West Indies, Karachi   2003/04

PANAMA

Affiliate Member of ICC: elected 2002

CRICKET WAS introduced to Panama by West Indian construction workers employed in the building of the Panama Canal between 1904 and 1914. The British Embassy also started a team which played against the crews and officers of British boats that stopped to refuel during their passage through the Canal. As the children of the Afro-Caribbean section of the West Indian community became more assimilated into Panamanian life, adopting Spanish as their first language, so cricket declined in favour of baseball. The game was kept alive, however, by the Caribbeans of East Indian origin. Reflecting their different backgrounds, the Hindus and Muslims developed separate leagues, not out of any ethnic or religious hostility but simply because scheduling of matches became difficult when Ramadan coincided with the dry season and the Muslims ceased sporting activities during the day. Cricket survived as a minority sport enjoyed at the weekends for recreation. In the absence of dedicated grounds, matches were played in either football or baseball stadiums.

The situation changed in 2000 when Panama were invited to participate in the South American Championships. The Panamanian Cricket Association was formed and, in preparation, a combined Muslim and Hindu representative side played two matches at home against Venezuela, winning one with the second being abandoned because of rain. Panama finished fourth in the Championships held in Buenos Aires.

Since then, a national league has been established with seventeen clubs playing in two divisions. Both Colombia and Costa Rica have been beaten and the national side has competed in the American Affiliates Tournament, finishing last in 2001 but improving to second place, behind the Bahamas, in 2004, when they hosted the competition at Howard.

Leading players: Irfan Tarajiya; Tarik Daya; A. Patel.

Playing record

ODI

	Won	Lost	No Res
American Affiliates Tournament	3	4	0
American Championships Division 2	2	2	0

Highest team score

ODI

275	v Turks and Caicos Islands, Howard (Panama)	2003/04

Lowest team score

ODI

93	v Bahamas, Howard (Panama)	2003/04

Highest individual score

ODI

61*	S. Chohan	v Belize, Buenos Aires	2005/06

Best bowling

ODI

6-40	I. Tarajiya	v Surinam, Buenos Aires	2005/06

PAPUA NEW GUINEA

Associate Member of ICC: elected 1973

MISSIONARIES INTRODUCED cricket to Papua in the 1890s and the local population took to the game with many villages forming teams and challenging their neighbours even though, in a country with few roads, players had to walk several kilometres to fulfil their away fixtures. Not all the games conformed to the MCC rules, with many matches being contested by teams of fifty or more men and women. Cricket did not arrive in New Guinea until the 1920s when Australia took over the administration of the territory from the Germans under the authority of a United Nations mandate. Whilst cricket developed as a rural game amongst the indigenous population, the Australians and the British started a competition for clubs in Port Moresby in 1937, thereby ensuring its position as an urban game among the expatriate community. The sport was encouraged by Sir John Guise, the first Governor-General. Following independence in 1975, many Australians left the country and the expatriate clubs in the towns were gradually taken over by locals, particularly as the urban centres grew through population migration from the rural areas. Although race was never a feature of cricket in Papua New Guinea, the migrants tended to associate with different clubs according to social background and language. Thus in Port Moresby, some clubs were dominated by Papuans and others by Motuans. In recent years, these distinctions have started to disappear as clubs have become open to all members of society. The difficulty of overland communication in the mountainous terrain has hindered the spread of the game, although air transport does allow contacts between clubs in Port Moresby, Lae, Rabaul, Bougainville, Mount Hagen, Goroka, Mendi and Madang. Many of Papua New Guinea's cricketers learn the game in village or beach competitions but there is little chance of good players in the villages being noticed unless they move to Port Moresby. The number of cricketers remains small, being just over 3,200 in the early 2000s.

Papua New Guinea played its first international match in 1973 when a team of nine Europeans and two indigenous cricketers met an Australian side. When the West Indies met Papua New Guinea at Port Moresby in 1975, the locals in the national side outnumbered the expatriates by six to five. Since that time, indigenous cricketers have dominated the national team. Not surprisingly, given the social history of the game as a recreational activity associated with much ceremony, eating, drinking and singing, one-day matches have been the norm and Papua New Guinea has yet to take part in a match of longer duration. Apart from two matches against Fiji in 1977, which were both won, and a tour of Hong Kong in 1980, almost all international matches have been played in major competitions like the ICC Trophy and the South Pacific Games. Their best performance in the ICC Trophy was in 1982 when they finished third. In 1986 and 1990, they were less successful but won just over half of their matches. In Nairobi in 1994 they should have contested the final of the Plate competition but, after poor performances earlier in the competition, had not expected to get that far and had already booked their flights home. One of the disadvantages of Papua New Guinea's location is that there are very few direct international flights and so, once made, travel arrangements are difficult to change. When competing in the Asian Cricket Council Trophy in Nepal in 1998, the team booked flights home after losing two of their first three matches, with one abandoned, rather than waiting a further week for the appropriate connections. As a result, they defaulted on their last match against the Maldives.

The promising performance of the national side in the 1980s culminated in winning the South Pacific Games in 1991 when this four-yearly event was staged in Port Moresby. Standards then declined through the 1990s much to the dismay of the local cricket administrators in Port Moresby and Lae. They held the Papua New Guinea Cricket Board responsible for failing to promote the game, allowing it to contract to the Port Moresby region, overseeing its decline in the smaller centres such as Mount Hagen, Goroka and Madang, letting grounds fall into disrepair, and not subjecting the accounts to open scrutiny. The action of the local associations led to a reform of the Board which then put in place promotional and development programmes and the upgrading of Amini Park which had been opened as a state-of-art cricket facility in 1999. Although this had little immediate effect on the country's performance at the ICC Trophy in Canada in 2001, where they won only one of the five matches played, they went on to win the Pacifica Cup in 2002 and the South Pacific Games in 2003, finishing both tournaments without defeat. By virtue of being the leading cricket country of the South Pacific, Papua New Guinea were given an exemption from the early rounds of the qualifying competition for the 2005 ICC Trophy and were allowed to go straight into the final qualifying contest in Kuala Lumpur in February 2005. They showed their improved standing by winning all their matches and become the twelfth and last country to qualify for the Trophy proper in Ireland. They struggled in the Irish conditions of grass wickets and damp atmosphere and found the opposition of the top associate countries too strong. In the play-off for last place, they beat Uganda in an exciting finish by 1 run off the last ball. A women's team made their debut in 2006 beating Japan to win the East Asia-Pacific regional qualifier for the 2009 World Cup. Many of the team are the sisters or wives of players in the men's team.

Famous Victory

July 5, 2003 – Grammar School, Suva
Papua New Guinea 502-9 (50 overs) (M.D. Dai 118, R. Leka 98, J. Maha 78, A. Uda 56, N. Kariko 56*, extras 59 including 39 wides)
New Caledonia 34 (10 overs) (M. Hobart 6-22, N. Kariko 4-9)
Papua New Guinea won by 468 runs

Papua New Guinea simply overwhelmed a hapless New Caledonia to achieve the highest score and the largest margin of victory in a one-day international. Mahuru Dai and Richard Leka started with a partnership of 216. James Maha and Arua Uda added 132 runs for the fourth wicket. New Caledonia tried nine bowlers but all were expensive and inaccurate. Their only consolation was that Clovis Wassingalu held four catches. Their batsmen fared no better with only Steven Selefen (15) reaching double figures. Noel Kariko and Maru Hobart bowled throughout the New Caledonian innings.

Leading players: *1960-1980:* N.R. Agonia; Karo Ao; A. Leka. *1980-2000:* V. Pala (lhb. lm); C. Amini (rhb. rm); T. Raka (rhb. rf). *Present day:* J.L. Brazier (rhb. rob); T. Gaudi (lhb. lm); R. Dikana (rhb. rm).
Women: *Present day:* K.R. Amini (rhb); H.A. Morea (rhb).

Playing record
One-day matches

	Won	Lost	No Res
ICC Trophy	25	25	3
South Pacific Games**	9	1	0
Asian Cricket Council Trophy	4	5	1
Pacifica Championships	7	2	0
ICC Qualifying Competition	5	0	0

* matches played in 1979 and 2003 competitions; detailed records of the 1987 and 1991 competitions have proved unobtainable.

Highest team score
ODI

502-9 dec	v New Caledonia, Suva	2003

Lowest team score
ODI

52	v Netherlands, Wolverhampton	1986

Highest individual score
ODI

162	B. Harry	v Israel, Worcester	1986

Best bowling
ODI

8-27	M. Stevens	v New Hebrides, Suva	1979

Best wicket-keeping
ODI

5 (5c)	N. Alu	v USA, Amsterdam	1990

Women
One-day matches

	Won	Lost	No Res
World Cup Qualifying East Asia-Pacific region	3	0	0

Highest team score
ODI

175-4	v Japan, Port Moresby	2006

Highest individual score
ODI

52	H.A. Morea	v Japan, Port Moresby	2006

Best bowling
ODI

3-17	K. Heagi	v Japan, Port Moresby	2006

PARAGUAY

CRICKET WAS played in Paraguay over a hundred years ago by British engineers involved in constructing the railways and by Australian immigrants who settled in Cosme and Nueva Australia. However, the game never took hold and has never had more than a tenuous existence. A small group of expatriates in Asunción have attempted to revive the sport, forming the Association of Paraguayan Cricket in 2000. A group of about 80 expatriates of Asian origin has also kept the game alive in Ciudad del Este near the Brazilian border.

PERU

THE LIMA Cricket Club was formed by British expatriates at the end of the nineteenth century. It still exists today with a playing strength of between 25 and 30 cricketers. Throughout its history, occasional international matches have been played by either Lima or Peru, the two being synonymous since Lima is the only cricket club in the country. The most important match is undoubtedly that of 6 February 1927 when the club met the MCC during the latter's 1926/27 tour of South America. The visitors were far too strong, winning by an innings and 81 runs. Since 1995 Peru have competed regularly in the South American Championships but with little success. The team is still largely expatriate though one Peruvian, Jorge Pancorvo, a wicket-keeper, has represented Peru for many years and played in the 2004 South American Championships at the age of 51.

Leading players: *1920-1940:* R.G. Brown; D. Thurmer. *1945-1960:* C. Maxwell.

PHILIPPINES

Affiliate Member of ICC: elected 2000
THE MANILA Nomads Cricket Club was formed in 1912 and has played matches for many years against visiting teams from Hong Kong. Hong Kong had already visited Manila in 1909 for what was intended as an extension of the Interport matches. Two single innings fixtures were played, Hong Kong winning the first and Manila the second. Although a series of Interport matches never materialised, regular games have been played between the Nomads and Hong Kong Cricket Club. In 1980 the Manila Anzacs Club was founded, followed by the Good Men Cricket Club in 1993. These are all largely expatriate clubs although a small number of Filipinos do play. The Philippine Cricket Association was formed in the late 1990s to promote the game.

Leading players: *1890-1914:* R. Thursfield.

PITCAIRN ISLANDS

DURING THEIR short stay on Norfolk Island between 1856 and 1859, the Pitcairn Islanders were introduced to cricket by the Melanesian Mission. Those who returned and their descendants continued to play the game on festive occasions. Until recently the presence of an occasional European visitor was usually enough to prevent the game from dying out. However, the game is now in serious danger of disappearing due to a severe shortage of male population between the ages of 15 and 45.

POLAND

CRICKET IS played in Poland by the Warsaw Cricket Club, Gorzów Cricket Club and Lubuskie Cricket Club based at Skwierzyna. The Warsaw Club is the oldest and comprises expatriates from a large number of Commonwealth countries, mostly on short-term contracts as accountants, teachers or computing specialists. The national team, known as the Polonia Cricket Club, draws players from all three clubs but only those who are qualified to play for Poland under ICC regulations. In 2002, they took part in a three-way tournament in Prague but lost to both the Czech Republic and Slovakia.

PORTUGAL

Affiliate Member of ICC: elected 1996

ON 12 July 1736 Admiral John Norris, Commander-in-Chief of His Majesty's Ships on board HMS *Pembroke* in the Tagus estuary, ordered the commanders of other ships in the Fleet to stop their men going ashore and upsetting the local population by playing cricket. This is the first reference to cricket being played in Portugal. The next reference is not until the 9 August 1810 when a certain Surgeon Boutflower FRCS, attached to British troops stationed in Portugal during the Peninsular War, mentioned in a letter that he and his fellows played cricket near Almeida. Neither of these instances led to cricket developing a permanent presence in Portugal. This had to wait until the 1850s when British merchants formed the Oporto Cricket Club at 1855. The club lasted only three years but was reformed in 1861 to meet a challenge put out by the Lisbon Cricket Club which was founded in 1860. The challenge was taken up on 17 October 1861. Nine of the Oporto players travelled to Lisbon by sea whilst the other two, who were prone to sea-sickness, travelled by horse-drawn carriage in a 33-hour journey to Carregado, the railhead 40 kilometres north of Lisbon. Surprisingly, after all this effort, Oporto won the match which was played at Campo Pequeno, now the site of the Lisbon bull ring. Clearly such a journey was not for the faint-hearted and Lisbon did not take-up the return fixture until 28 June 1867 by which time the railway between Lisbon and Oporto had been completed. Matches between Lisbon and Oporto have become an annual fixture.

During the 1870s and 1880s the Lisbon and Oporto clubs played matches against the officers of various British ships visiting the ports. The first combined team, representing Portugal, took the field at Oporto in April 1895 against T. Westray's XI, a privately-managed side, close to first-class in standard, got together in England to play cricket in Portugal in country-house style, whilst, at the same time, enjoying the local scenery and wine. Westray's side won the match against eighteen of Portugal by 91 runs. In April 1898, Westray brought an even stronger side, including two England cricketers, P.F. Warner and H.R. Bromley-Davenport, and several county players, and met Portugal on equal terms. Not surprisingly, the locals lost by an innings and 75 runs. Nevertheless, Westray started a fashion for British teams to visit Portugal. H.D. Swan brought a side in 1910. The Cryptics visited in 1924, 1925, 1930 and 1939, T. Westray's team again in 1928, a side raised by H.D.G. Leveson-Gower in 1934, the Gentlemen of Worcestershire in 1936 and Gibraltar in 1937 and 1939. None of these teams, however, met an all-Portugal side, although Gibraltar played against teams styled 'Oporto and Lisbon', drawing in 1937 and winning by eight wickets in 1939.

After the Second World War, the visits of sides from Britain continued but the local standard was in decline. Cricket suffered from being played by a small group of expatriates in rather exclusive clubs with high membership fees. At the same time, the number of British residents was falling and there was also a severe shortage of grounds. Following political upheavals in 1974, membership of the Lisbon Sports Club declined as the various multinational companies in Portugal stopped employing as many expatriates. With a decreasing and ageing membership at both Lisbon and Oporto, cricket seemed to have little future.

The overthrow of the Portuguese government and the establishment of democracy in 1974 was followed by the granting of independence to Portugal's colonies. This lead to the migration of Portuguese nationals from Goa and Mozambique, including many who had learned to play cricket. Many Portuguese expatriates in Mozambique and Angola also moved to Rhodesia and South Africa where their children were introduced to cricket. As the political situation in these countries changed, these people too migrated to Portugal so that by the late 1970s there was a reservoir of people interested in reviving the game. Portugal returned to the international scene in the European Cricketer Cup in 1992. In 1993, a three-day match was played against Spain at the newly-established cricket and sports facility of Barrington's in the Algarve. The Federação Portuguesa de Cricket was formed on 19 June 1994. Since that time the number of British expatriates representing Portugal has declined. The national team is now largely made-up of players of Asian origin, all of whom meet the ICC requirements of either citizenship or residence. Initially, the team in this form was particularly successful. Portugal won the ECF Nations Cup for European affiliate countries in 1995. The team contained ten players born in Portuguese territory, including six from Mozambique and three from Portuguese India. Portugal were runners-up in the same competition in 1996. In 1999 they finished second to Greece in the ECC Trophy in Corfu and thereby qualified for Division 2 of the 2000 European Championships. In their first competition at this level, they did reasonably well beating Israel and Greece. By winning the ECC Trophy in Vienna in 2001, Portugal again qualified for Division 2 and this time they fared even better, beating Austria, Israel and Gibraltar. As the team has aged and some players retired, performances have been disappointing. Today, Portuguese cricket suffers from two main problems: a shortage of players and a shortage of grounds. The two are related in that with few grounds it is difficult for clubs to organise regular matches and without the opportunity to get a regular game, players drift away to other sports.

Famous Victories

July 21, 2002 – Carrickfergus, Northern Ireland
Portugal 175 (49.4 overs)
Gibraltar 143-8 (50 overs)
Portugal won by 32 runs

Although Portugal had twice beaten Israel in the European Championships Division 2, this win over Gibraltar was easily their best performance against an affiliate country. Put in to bat, Portugal started badly losing four wickets for 40 runs including their best batsmen, Nadeem Butt, Inteshab Mehdi and Akbar Saiyad. However,

Ramesh Bhagvane Daia (43), Mohammed Nazir Usman (24) and Hussein Cheema (25) led a recovery and were able to post a reasonable total. With Humayun Shahzad (10-2-21-2) dismissing both openers, Gibraltar were also in difficulties early on and then found it surprisingly difficult to score against some tight bowling and keen fielding. In addition to Shahzad, Inteshab Mehdi (10-5-9-1), Bhagvane Daia (10-5-19-2) and Nadeem Butt (10-3-17-2) were especially effective in tying up Gibraltar's batting. Although Gibraltar used all their allotted overs and were still two wickets in hand, they rarely looked likely to reach the target.

Leading players: *1890-1914:* P. Barley; D. Rawes. *1920-1940:* G. White; M.C. Clodd. *1945-1960:* M. Rawes; E.S. Yeatman. *1960-1980:* A. Gouveia; G. Paine; R.P. Rankine. *1980-2000:* Intesab Mehdi (rhb. rob); Nadeem Butt (rhb. rm); Muntasir Mehdi. *Present day:* Tariq Aziz; Rizwan Khaliq; J. da Costa (rhb. wk).

Playing record

One-day matches

	Won	Lost	No Res
European Championships	5	5	0
ECC Trophy	12	3	0
European Affiliates Championships	2	4	0

Highest team score
ODI

381-3	v Greece, Zuoz	1997

Lowest team score

46	v Cryptics, Lisbon	1961

Highest individual score
ODI

173*	T. Rankine	v Greece, Zuoz	1997

Best bowling

6-52	N. Baxter	v Cryptics, Lisbon	1961

Best wicket-keeping

5 (4c 1st)	J. da Costa	v Norway, Waterloo	2005

PUERTO RICO

CRICKET IS played in Puerto Rico by a small group of expatriates from the other Caribbean islands. Although the Puerto Rico Cricket Federation is affiliated to the South-East Region of the United States Cricket Association, in practical terms the link is somewhat tenuous. In 2004 the Federation decided that Puerto Rico should have its own international team and accepted an invitation to enter the South American Championships, held in Chile. The team did surprisingly well beating Brazil, Chile and the Andean Masters to reach the final. They were then heavily defeated by 117 runs by the Guyana Masters.

Leading players: *Present day:* L. Brown; D. Africa; B. Douglas (wk).

QATAR

Affiliate Member of ICC: elected 1999

CRICKET STARTED in Qatar as an activity of the Asian expatriate population supported by leading Asian business executives. By 1980 twelve teams existed and their officials decided to form the Qatar Cricket Association to promote the game further. With the encouragement of the government's Youth and Sports General Authority, cricket was developed in schools where it has progressed rapidly at all age levels. The national side made its first appearance in the Asian Cricket Council Trophy in 2002 losing all four matches. With improved coaching Qatar were one of the surprises of the 2004 tournament, winning three of their four first round matches, including victory over Nepal, and finishing fourth overall. In 2006, they finished eighth.

Leading players: *Present day:* Omer Taj; Mohammed Jahangir; Saleem Akhtar.

Playing record
One-day matches

	Won	Lost	No Res
Asian Cricket Council Trophy	5	11	0
ICC Qualifying Competition	2	3	0
Middle East Cup	2	2	0

Highest team score
ODI

355-7	v Iran, Kuala Lumpur		2006

Lowest team score
ODI

64	v United Arab Emirates, Sharjah		2005/06

Highest individual score
ODI

178	Omer Taj	v Iran, Kuala Lumpur	2006

Best bowling
ODI

5-2	Saleem Akhtar	v Zambia, Kuala Lumpur	2004/05

ROMANIA

THE FIRST cricket match in Romania was played in Bucharest on 18 June 1893 between Bucharest and Brăila and won by the latter by 17 runs. The game developed as a pastime of the British community and survived up to the late 1920s when declining trade and political unrest caused a decline in the number of British residents. Teams existed in Bucharest, Ploieşti, Galaţi and Constanţa. One of the last matches played was between Bucharest and Constantinople (now Istanbul) in 1930, a game which involved twenty-one Englishmen and one Dane. Bucharest won the match which was notable for the attitude of the local British military authorities who charged the cricketers £25 for damage to the football pitch on which the game was played.

RUSSIA

CRICKET WAS being played by the British in St Petersburg in the 1870s. In 1875 the British residents challenged the officers and crew of the Prince of Wales's Royal Yacht, *Osborne,* during its visit to the city. By 1880 the game was reasonably well-established and, soon afterwards, an annual match was started between British diplomats and merchants and the British managers and foremen of the textile mills. In 1896 there were three clubs in the city, Nevski, Neva and Nevka, and a fourth at Schlüsselburg. The standard of cricket must have been high since many of the players had been educated in British public schools and some, such as A.L. Gibson of Essex, had first class experience. The game ceased after the Russian Revolution of 1917. Cricket did not return to Russia until the 1960s when occasional attempts to play were made by ambassadorial staff in Moscow. It was not until the late 1990s, however, that serious efforts were made to put the game on an organised footing. By this time there were enough players attached to the embassies of the United Kingdom, Australia, New Zealand, India and Pakistan. In the summer of 2000, the Moscow International Cricket

League was inaugurated with four teams with matches played at the Dynamo Sports Stadium.

RWANDA

Affiliate Member of ICC: elected 2003

CRICKET BEGAN in Rwanda in the 1990s when expatriate Indians and Pakistanis in Kigali and African students at the National University of Rwanda in Butare, who had learnt the game whilst in education in Uganda or Tanzania, started to organise matches. Occasional games were played between Kigali Cricket Club and the University but the distance of 126 km between the towns limited the number of matches. In 2001, a third club, Joban, was formed in Kigali by the Indian community and there is now a British community team. The Rwanda Cricket Association was founded in 2001. Rwanda played its first international matches in the ICC African Affiliates competition in South Africa in 2004. Not surprisingly, given their lack of experience, they lost all three games. The most serious constraint to the development of the game is finance. Industrial support has been forthcoming to cover the expenses of the annual league, involving four or five clubs. The game is being promoted in both boys and girls schools. Lack of finance, however, forced Rwanda to withdraw from the East African Women's Championships in Nairobi in January 2006.

Leading players: *Present day:* M. Jasat (rhb. rm); S. Vardhineni (rhb. rm).

Playing record

One-day matches

	Won	Lost	No Res
ICC African Affiliates Competition	0	3	0
African Championships Division 2	1	4	0

Highest team score

ODI

171	v Gambia, Benoni	2006

Lowest team score

ODI

60	v South African Country Districts, Benoni	2004

Highest individual score

ODI

69	S. Vardhineni	v Morocco, Benoni	2006

Best bowling

ODI

4-35	S. Vardhineni	v Mozambique, Benoni	2006

SAINT HELENA

Affiliate Member of ICC: elected 2001

CRICKET HAS been played on St Helena for more than 200 years. The St Helena Cricket League was started in 1903 and continues to this day with up to eight teams contesting one-day two-innings matches on Jamestown's ground at Francis Plain. The St Helena Cricket Club was founded in 1933 but has played very few matches against visiting teams because transport to the island is limited to one ship a month. Cricket balls are often lost in a waterfall on the side of the ground. In 1886, an Army officer, trying to prevent the ball from disappearing into the waterfall, slipped, fell over the cliff on to a protruding rock face and was killed.

Leading players: *1980-2000:* E. George (lhb. sla). *Present day:* G. George (lhb. lm).

SAMOA

Affiliate Member of ICC: elected 2000

THE INTRODUCTION of cricket to Samoa is attributed to William Churchward, the British Consul from 1881 to 1885. The first match was played in 1884 against the crew of HMS *Diamond*. Cricket was taken up enthusiastically by the local people who rapidly adapted it into a version involving whole villages with teams of 200 to 300 a-side playing matches lasting several days or even weeks. During these games, no work was done. The effect of match after match was so detrimental to the economy that in 1890, the King of Samoa, High Chief Malietoa I, was forced to issue a proclamation banning the game. Before cricket could be revived, it was banned again by the German administration between 1900 and 1914. Slowly, after 1914 under the administration of New Zealand, cricket began to be played again, both the local variety and that conforming to MCC rules. The local form is the more popular, played by teams of men and women, usually twenty-a-side, accompanied by much feasting and dancing. In contrast to the village base of the local game, the standard game is largely urban-based and has attracted fewer participants. Many of the best players learnt the sport at educational establishments in Fiji and New Zealand. One of the leading batsman in the side of the Central Medical School in Suva, Fiji, in the late 1930s was the Samoan, Ualesi Toelupe. The first Samoan to play first-class cricket was Sebastian Kohlhase, a left-handed batsman and right-arm medium pace bowler, who represented Northern Districts in New Zealand in 1963/64 and later played for Auckland. Samoa took part in the South Pacific Games in Suva in 1979 and finished fifth. Since the late 1990s, the Samoa Cricket Association has promoted the game with enthusiasm, establishing a local league and developing a dedicated cricket ground and facility. The effects of this were quickly seen in the performances in the Pacifica Cricket Championships. In the 2001 tournament Samoa lost four out of their five matches but in 2002, when they hosted the competition, they won three out of the five. They went on to win three out of their six matches in the 2003 South Pacific Games, including a surprising victory over Fiji. In 2005, their selection policy went awry and when the squad went to the East Asia Pacific Cup in Vanuatu, only nine of their team were allowed to play, the remainder being ruled ineligible for not meeting the ICC regulations on citizenship and residence. Not surprisingly, they lost all their matches and recorded one of the lowest team scores in one-day internationals.

Famous Victory

July 1, 2003 – Albert Park, Suva
Fiji 109 (25 overs) (F. Kolio 5-35)
Samoa 112-9 (29 overs) (N.D. Maxwell 5-26)
Samoa won by 1 wicket

Fiji's batsmen simply hit out and got out, wickets falling regularly to Fa'amatala Kolio and Niko Apa (3-25). Only Joeli Mateyawa (42) managed to stay long enough to make a reasonable score and he ended his innings by being run out. Samoa batted in the same vein with Taitoe Kaisara (41*) making most of the runs, supported by Geoffrey Clarke (13). The middle order fell to Neil Maxwell who looked likely to bowl Fiji to a close victory. In the end, however, Muamua Utu (4*) managed to scramble runs in an exciting finish, giving Samoa a surprise win in a match which had 46 overs to spare.

Leading players: *Present day:* G. Clarke (rhb. rm); S.M. Utu (lhb. lfm).

Playing record

One-day matches

	Won	Lost	No Res
Pacifica Championships	4	6	0
South Pacific Games (2003)	3	3	0
East Asia Pacific Cup	0	6	0

Highest team score

ODI

229	v Indonesia, Port Vila	2005

Lowest team score

ODI

19	v Cook Islands, Port Vila	2005

Highest individual score

ODI

87	S. Tua	v Vanuatu, Apia	2002

Best bowling

ODI

6-20	S.M. Utu	v New Caledonia, Suva	2003

SAUDI ARABIA

Affiliate Member of ICC: elected 2003

WITH INCREASING numbers of Indians and Pakistanis living and working in Saudi Arabia, cricket gradually became an important sport in the 1990s. Although it was difficult initially to get the game started because of the lack of grounds and equipment, the perseverance of a few dedicated cricketers led to the formation of the Saudi Cricket Centre as the administrative body. Once Royal patronage was obtained, financial support was forthcoming from both government and private sources. This has enabled a regional administrative structure to be established through which coaching camps can be run and the game promoted. Particular emphasis is being given to promotion in schools with the aim of two-thirds of the national team being Saudi nationals within about five years. At present, the team is largely expatriate with players meeting the ICC regulations to represent Saudi Arabia through residence.

Leading players: *Present day:* Fahad Sulaiman; Sarfraz Ahmed; K. Sohrab.

Playing record

One-day matches

	Won	Lost	No Res
Asian Cricket Council Trophy	2	4	0
Middle East Cup	3	5	0

Highest team score

ODI

499-6	v Brunei, Kuala Lumpur		2006

Lowest team score

ODI

166	v Bahrain, Doha		2005/06

Highest individual score

ODI

167	Sarfraz Ahmed	v Brunei, Kuala Lumpur	2006

Best bowling

ODI

5-22	Sarfraz Ahmed	v Kuwait Blues, Doha	2005/06

SCOTLAND

Associate Member of ICC: elected 1994

ALTHOUGH EARLY records of cricket in Scotland are sketchy, it seems clear that the game was played by soldiers of the English garrisons sent to quell the Jacobite rising led by Bonnie Prince Charlie in 1745. The game may well have been played earlier than that, however, because William Stephens, a planter in Georgia, USA, refers to cricket being played there by Scotsmen in 1737. This implies that cricket must have been known to those Scots who migrated to the American colonies in the early part of the eighteenth century. Cricket was certainly played by the military in Perth around 1750. The first recorded match in Scotland, however, was not until 3 September 1785 when a game was played on the estate of the Earl of Cathcart at Schaw Park, Alloa. The game is shown in the background of a painting of the Cathcart family by David Allan. By the end of the eighteenth century, cricket was being played by both the military and civilians but was largely restricted to Army officers and to gentlemen of leisure who used it as a basis for gambling rather than physical exercise. In the early 1800s, English immigrant workers in the paper, textile and iron industries brought the game to the Scottish borders and the central lowlands. The oldest cricket club for which records survive is that at Kelso, formed in 1820. The Grange Cricket Club in Edinburgh was founded a few years later. Cricket was also taken up in the elite public schools. Matches started between Edinburgh High School and the Edinburgh Academy in the 1820s and soon after cricket was taught in Fettes, Merchiston, Loretto and other leading boarding schools. Cricket remained, however, a game of the English, played separately by the aristocracy and by working-class immigrants.

Cricket was rather slow to develop even though matches between the early club sides could attract several thousand spectators. What Scotland lacked were large landowners or industrialists with sufficient interest to act as patrons or benefactors of clubs and as sponsors of the game at a national level. The first international match did not take place until 1849 when the All England XI met twenty-two of Scotland at Grove Street, Edinburgh. Other itinerant sides of professionals from England met Scottish teams against the odds during the 1850s and early 1860s but generally these matches were not lucrative and many of the English players barely broke even after they had covered their expenses. The first match played by Scotland on even terms was in 1865 when a side travelled to London, beating Surrey at The Oval and losing to the MCC at Lord's. In 1878, Scotland played England in the only recognised encounter between the two countries to date, losing by seven wickets. In 1880, the Australians beat Scotland in a two-day match in Edinburgh and set a pattern which continues today for the side touring England to make a visit north of the border.

The late nineteenth century saw another pattern of Scottish cricket established which continued until the 1980s, namely that the national side played two or three games only a year, one against Ireland and the others against English first-class counties. A regular fixture against the MCC was added in 1922. Given that the Scottish cricketers were all amateurs who played in their spare time, it was not surprising that they provided limited opposition to the county sides. Even the formation of the Scottish Cricket Union in 1909 made little difference. The work of the SCU was largely administrative and concentrated on representing Scottish cricket with the English authorities. A more enlightened administration might have sought to put Scottish cricket on a professional footing and pushed for Scotland to compete as an entity in the English county championship. Instead, Scottish cricket suffered a continuous 'brain drain' with its best players migrating to England. The most outstanding losses were Gregor Macgregor, Ian Peebles, Paul Gibb, Mike Denness, all of whom had successful county careers and went on to play for England. For a long time cricket remained a minority sport centred on the public schools and elite clubs. Apart from in the central lowlands, focused on Edinburgh and Glasgow, few clubs played matches outside of their local area because of the paucity of transport.

High Amateur Standard

Scottish cricket maintained itself at a high amateur standard from about 1900 to 1980 but with only three or four games a year, there was little opportunity for cricketers to gain from playing consistently against high class opposition. The opportunities were often reduced further by fixtures being curtailed by wet weather. It was not uncommon for all international matches in a season to be affected, with some being abandoned without a ball being bowled. One of the most successful periods in Scottish cricket history was in the late 1950s and 1960s. Although few matches were won, very few were lost and in many seasons Scotland were unbeaten. The 1970s witnessed a relative decline in the standard of Scottish cricket though this was due more to improvements in the first-class game in England rather than to any absolute decline in Scotland. After an unsuccessful season in 1973, the SCU decided to appoint a national coach. Almost immediately the SCU ran into financial problems and was forced to seek sponsorship. Initially, only small amounts of money were forthcoming, the small size of the international programme being unattractive to industry in terms of the benefits that would accrue. Yet it was difficult to increase the number of matches because many of the players could not obtain the extra leave from work. This seemingly intractable problem was partially resolved in 1980 when Scotland was accepted by the English authorities as a participant in the Benson and Hedges Cup and the NatWest Trophy. The number of fixtures in a season immediately increased by four but since these were all one-day matches, they could easily be accommodated by removing the three-day friendly

fixtures against the English counties.

The start of the 1980s marked a major change in the way Scotland's international programme was conducted. The majority of the matches were now one-day limited overs in the English domestic competitions in which Scotland was allowed to be assisted by a professional player, Brian Close, Desmond Haynes, Omar Henry, Clive Rice, John Love and Malcolm Marshall fulfilling that role in turn. Overall the results were disappointing with only three victories in twenty-three years. Although the increasing size of the international programme led to greater sponsorship, the costs of organisation escalated. The SCU was dependent on good weather and high attendances in the matches against the Australians, West Indians and other tourists in order to overcome a financial deficit. Clubs were particularly hard hit financially at this time by a rates burden which was some six times higher than that experienced by clubs in England. The financial difficulties of the clubs created an underlying problem for the future of Scottish cricket since, apart from the public schools, they are the main route through which youngsters learn the game. There is very little support from local authorities for cricket. Fortunately, during the 1980s, cricket became more popular. New clubs were formed, particularly in south-west Scotland and in the Shetland Isles. There was also an increase in the number of club players from Scottish-born members of the Asian community.

The biggest change in Scottish cricket took place in 1992 when the SCU severed its formal association with English cricket in order to seek associate membership of the ICC. This was finally achieved in 1994. Contemporary with this change was the formal appointment of a Director of Cricket with duties to coach the national team and promote the sport more generally. A more professional approach was adopted prior to the 1997 ICC Trophy with the naming of a national squad and the establishment of a training and preparation programme. The result was third place in the competition in Kuala Lumpur and, thereby, qualification for the 1999 World Cup. Scotland also participated regularly in the European Championships and the Triple Crown. Although these last two contests provided the chance for Scotland to meet opposition of similar status and standing, the results were somewhat disappointing. Scotland also took part in the 1998 Commonwealth Games but without success. More important for the future of Scottish cricket was the agreement of the clubs in 1996 to establish a national league, only 28 years after the idea was first proposed to the SCU, thereby ensuring that the top clubs meet each other competitively. The league now involves over thirty clubs in three divisions.

The 1999 World Cup was a further disappointment for Scotland. The matches against Australia, New Zealand, Pakistan and the West Indies only served to demonstrate the enormous gap in standards between the test-playing nations and the best of the associate countries. By losing to Bangladesh by 22 runs after taking their first five wickets for only 26, Scotland showed that they had much to learn about the ruthlessness required of cricket at the top level. Further disappointments occurred in the following year when Scotland obtained only one win in the Emerging Nations Tournament in Harare in 2000 and finished only third in the European Championships. In 2001, they lost the third-place play-off in the ICC Trophy to Canada and thus missed out on qualification for the 2003 World Cup.

The organisation of Scottish cricket was put on a professional basis in 2001 when the SCU was replaced by Scottish Cricket plc. In 2003, Scotland were admitted to the one-day league of the English counties, playing as Scottish Saltaires. After winning three of their first four matches, the results have mirrored those obtained in previous one-day encounters with English first-class counties, despite the assistance of Rahul Dravid, Sridharan Sriram and Yasir Arafat as professionals. However, the more professional outlook of the cricket administration has at last attracted a major sponsor to Scottish cricket and finance from SportScotland.

The early 2000s finally saw the appearance of a Scottish women's team in international cricket. Given that women in Scotland are likely to have played cricket for as long as those in England and Ireland, it is perhaps surprising that women's cricket took so long to develop. With cricket not forming part of the sports curriculum in Scottish state schools or girls schools, very few women learnt the game. Further, those that did were content to play in clubs within their local area so that there was no incentive to organise the game on a national basis. The standard was very low as was shown when a women's team undertook a short tour of Ireland in 1978 and were outplayed by South Leinster and North Leinster. Once Scottish Cricket was formed, it took on the responsibility for developing women's cricket and in 2001 Scotland entered the women's European Championships. Not surprisingly, considering the small number of players from which to choose and their lack of experience at international level, the women have yet to achieve much success. In eight matches, their sole victory has been over Japan.

Three-day international cricket returned to Scotland in 2004 with the Intercontinental Cup. Scotland won the European leg of the competition, beat a weakened Kenya side in the semi-final and then gained a surprisingly easy victory over Canada to acquire their first international trophy. Their second was gained in 2005 when they beat Ireland in the final of the ICC Trophy and qualified for the 2007 World Cup. Thus Scotland became the leading associate country in both the three-day and the one-day game, a position they lost in 2006 when they finished second to Ireland in the European Championships. Scotland's ambition is to obtain permanent one-day international status from the ICC. However, they may have to overcome the problem of having seven of their current squad attached to English counties which means that they must be released from county duties in order to play in international matches. The only way round this dilemma would be for Scotland to establish a professional structure for its players.

Famous Victories
November 21 and 22, 2004 – Sharjah Cricket Association Stadium, Sharjah
Canada 110 and 93 (Asim Butt 4-10, J.A.R. Blain 4-28)
Scotland 287-8 dec (G.M. Hamilton 115, D.R. Lockhart 64, R.R. Watson 56, Umar Bhatti 4-49)
Scotland won by an innings and 84 runs

The final of the inaugural ICC Intercontinental Cup was surprisingly one-sided. Canada chose to bat after winning the toss but were soon in difficulties against John Blain (3-27) and Asim Butt (1-40). Only Ian Billcliff provided any opposition and he fell to Ryan Watson (4.1-3-1-3) who took the last three wickets to fall. After Fraser Watts (2) went quickly, Dougie Lockhart and Cedric English took the score to 53. Lockhart and Gavin Hamilton then added 101 for the third wicket. Hamilton and Watson put on 118 for the fourth wicket, Hamilton going on to his first century for Scotland. Scotland then lost some quick wickets to Umar Bhatti whilst trying to push the score to a declaration. Canada found Blain and Asim Butt unplayable, losing eight wickets for 24 runs. With Sunil Dhaniram retiring hurt, it was left to Umar Bhatti and Ashok Patel (25*) to restore some respectability in a last wicket partnership of 69. This, however, only delayed the inevitable.

Player Profiles

Aitchison, Reverend James. b Kilmarnock 26 May 1920. d Glasgow 13 February 1994. rhb. An automatic selection for Scotland in a long career between 1946 and 1963, he combined good footwork with an ability to concentrate for long periods. Despite his limited experience in first-class cricket, he scored three centuries against Ireland and hundreds against the Australians, South Africans, Lancashire and Yorkshire. He played each ball on its merit and was quite content to take advantage of any luck that came his way. In 69 matches for Scotland, he scored 3,669 runs (average 32.76).

Brown, James MBE. b Perth 24 September 1931. rhb. wk. The finest of the many excellent wicket-keepers to play for Scotland, he was unobtrusive but extremely efficient, keeping particularly well to the Scottish spin bowling. At his peak he was chosen to represent the Gentlemen against the Players at the Scarborough Festival. He took four catches and made three stumpings in an innings against Ireland at Dublin in 1957. In 85 matches for Scotland, he scored 1,730 runs (average 19.01), made 119 catches and 40 stumpings.

Leading players: *1860-1890:* D.C.R. Buchanan (lhb. lf(r)/sla); L.M. Balfour-Melville (rhb. wk). *1890-1914:* W. Ringrose (lhb. rfm); R.W. Sievwright (lhb. sla). *1920-1940:* J. Kerr (rhb); W.K. Laidlaw (rhb. lbg); A.D. Baxter (rhb. rfm). *1945-1960:* J.M. Allan (rhb. sla); W. Nichol (lhb. sla); R.H.E. Chisholm (rhb). *1960-1980:* T.B. Racionzer (rhb); B.R. Hardie (rhb); G.F. Goddard (rhb, rob). *1980-2000:* I.L. Philip (rhb. occ wk); B.M.W. Patterson (rhb); A.G. Davies (rhb. wk). *Present day:* G.M. Hamilton (lhb. rmf); J.A.R. Blain (rhb. rfm); R.R. Watson (rhb. rm).

Women: *Present day:* K. Anderson (rhb. rm); V.S.C. Maxwell (rhb. rm).

Playing record
International matches

	Won	Lost	Tied	Drawn	Ab
Ireland (first class 1909-2000)	20	19	0	36	2
ICC Intercontinental Cup	3	1	0	5	0
Other first-class matches	4	40	0	40	1
Other internationals (*)	2	0	0	7	0

* Matches against Philadelphia, Canada; Denmark, Netherlands and Bangladesh

One-day matches

	Won	Lost	Tied	No Res
World Cup	0	8	0	0
Commonwealth Games	0	2	0	1
Other ODIs	7	8	0	0
English domestic competitions	21	135	1	8
ICC Trophy	20	5	0	1
European Championships	17	10	0	0
Triple Crown	20	6	0	0
Emerging Nations Tournament	1	4	0	0
Six Nations Tournament	3	2	0	0

Highest team score
537-5 dec	v MCC, Glasgow	1991

Lowest team score
23	v MCC, Lord's	1865
23	v Lancashire, Edinburgh	1895

Highest individual score
234	I.L. Philip	v MCC, Glasgow	1991

Best bowling
8-32	R.H. Scott	v Parsis, Edinburgh	1886

Best wicket-keeping
7 (4c 3st)	J. Brown	v Ireland, Dublin	1957

Women
One-day matches

	Won	Lost	Tied	No Res
European Championships	0	7	0	0
World Cup Qualifying	1	4	0	0

Highest team score
ODI
145	v Netherlands, Arbroath	2004

Lowest team score
ODI
24	v England Under 19, Reading	2001

Highest individual score
ODI
61*	K. Anderson	v Netherlands, Arbroath	2003

Best bowling
4-25	F. Campbell	v Japan, The Hague	2003

SEYCHELLES

THE SEYCHELLES Cricket Association play on a small ground at Victoria on Mahé Island and have managed to keep cricket going for many years, despite the small number of players and limited finance. Home and away fixtures are played each year against Maurindia Cricket Club in Mauritius. Although cricket was brought to the island by the British, its survival depends on the Asian communities, particularly expatriates from Sri Lanka.
Leading player: *Present day:* D. Patel.

SIERRA LEONE

Affiliate Member of ICC: elected 2002
THE ROYAL Artillery brought cricket to Sierra Leone in 1898, setting up a ground at the Tower Hill Parade in the centre of Freetown. Thereafter the game was played by the military, colonial civil servants and other British residents, particularly traders and teachers. However, the game was slow to develop because the total number of players remained small. It was not until the 1920s that cricket started to prosper. International matches with The Gambia began in 1927 and, with a break for the Second World War, lasted into the late 1960s. For most of this time the national side was expatriate British. Although cricket was taught in the Sierra Leone Grammar School, the Methodist Boys High School and other leading schools from the early twentieth century few Africans kept up the game after leaving school. It was not until the 1950s that Sierra Leoneans started to play regularly. By the 1960s, however, they made up the bulk of the national side, following the departure of many of the British after the country's independence in 1961. During the 1960s it looked as though the game would prosper, albeit as a minority sport. International fixtures were started with Ghana and Nigeria and, in 1968, J. Lister brought his international team to the country. In a two-day fixture, Sierra Leone were overwhelmed by an innings and 118 runs. The MCC beat Sierra Leone by 115 runs during their West African tour of 1976. It was to be 2003 before the MCC visited again. Like other West African countries, Sierra Leone has suffered from being ignored by touring parties from the leading test-playing countries. Without external interest, it is difficult

to attract local people to play the game, especially when this situation is accompanied by limited facilities and lack of finance. Since the mid 1970s, the game has declined both in standard and the numbers playing. Those who supported the game did so with dedication, however, and cricket survived the civil war of the late 1990s. Despite the disturbances, Sierra Leone never missed sending a team to the West African Championships. They won the title in 2004 and 2005. With recent financial support from industry and the state lottery, the Sierra Leone Cricket Association has been able to organise a cricket league for schools in Freetown. There is a need, however, for a dedicated cricket ground and for training programmes to raise the overall standard.
Leading players: *1960-1980:* M. Turay; S.A. Fraser (rhb. rfm). *Present day:* G. Kpundeh (rhb. rfm).

Playing record
One-day matches
	Won	Lost	No Res
ICC African Affiliates Competition	1	2	0
African Championships Division 3	3	2	0

Highest team score
221	v Nigeria, Freetown	1966

ODI
231-7	v Rwanda, Benoni	2006

Lowest team score
88	v MCC, Freetown	1976

Highest individual score
97	M. Turay	v Ghana, Freetown	1961

Best bowling
7-34	S.A. Fraser	v Nigeria, Lagos	1965

Best wicket-keeping
ODI
4 (2c 2st)	M. Mansaray	v Mozambique, Benoni	2006

SINGAPORE

Associate Member of ICC: elected 1974
THE FIRST record of cricket in Singapore was in a letter to the *Singapore Free Press* on Thursday 23 March 1837 from a Mr 'Z' complaining of Europeans playing cricket the previous Sunday near the New Church, on the site of the present cathedral, in violation of the Sabbath. Since many of the leading Europeans at the time were of Scot-

tish Presbyterian background, the complaint resulted in cricket being banned on Sundays, a prohibition which lasted into the 1930s. Nevertheless, the game survived this set-back, despite there being only about 100 Europeans in the country at the time. Cricket was an important recreational activity and sides were got together to play against the officers and crews of visiting ships. The next mention of cricket is just such a game on 20 April 1843 against the *Dido*, an anti-pirate gunboat under the command of Admiral Sir Henry Keppel who acted as one of the umpires. The Singapore Cricket Club was formed in October 1852 by British businessmen and those working in trade as clerks and junior assistants and in that month the club's first fixture was played. Although billed as 'a picked eleven' versus 'the club', the match was between sides of six and nine respectively. It was probably a very short affair since the club scored 14 and 12 to the opponent's 11 and 1. Along with other sporting and recreational clubs, the SCC provided the basis for Europeans to engage in a way-of-life isolated from the dominantly Chinese community. By 1880 the Europeans numbered 3,000 compared to some 86,000 Chinese residents. Cricket was one of the most important recreational activities which relieved the boredom of life, provided exercise and the opportunity for social contact. Cricket matches were arranged between the club and the military and matches against visiting ships continued. The original pitch on the Singapore Padang was almost certainly extremely poor since military drill, athletics and horse- and pony-racing were carried out on it. Once the padang was enclosed with posts and a chain, improvements to the pitch were possible and led to better batting conditions; the players also became more skilled. Thus whilst it took until 1865 before the first team total over 100 was recorded, it was only two further years before the first individual century in Singapore was made when Louis Glass scored 118 not out for the SCC against a combined Army and Navy side. As the size of the European population on the Malay Peninsula increased in the 1880s and trading contacts were developed, the SCC started to play matches against Penang, the Selangor Club in Kuala Lumpur and Perak. The Straits Settlements also sent teams to Ceylon in 1893, Jakarta in 1895, Yangon in 1906 and Bangkok in 1910. In the late nineteenth century other ethnic groups started to emulate the Europeans by taking up cricket

and establishing their own clubs. By 1883, the Singapore Recreation Club had been formed for the Eurasian Community, providing a rival to the SCC since they played cricket on the opposite side of the Padang. The Straits Chinese Recreation Club was established at Hong Lim Green in 1885.

As trading contacts widened, Singapore accepted an invitation from the Hong Kong Cricket Club to visit Hong Kong. In January 1890, a team representing the Straits Settlements of Singapore, Penang and Malacca, sailed to Hong Kong and lost by 147 runs. The long sea voyage probably had a deleterious effect on the result because, the following January, Hong Kong undertook the return fixture and lost by an innings and 166 runs. These matches were the start of Singapore's involvement in Interport fixtures with Hong Kong, played alternately home and away. When in Hong Kong, the Straits also met Shanghai but the latter never ventured as far as Singapore. Many of those who represented the Straits Settlements did so because of their membership of the SCC. Their work often took them outside of the Straits Settlements and into the Federated Malay States. Thus Frederic Talbot was the State Auditor in Negeri Sembilan, Henry Talbot was the Commissioner of Police in the FMS and based in Kuala Lumpur, and Theodore Hubback was the Government Architect in Selangor; he was also an authority on large fauna, particularly elephant and seladang, and became an honorary game warden in Perak.

Growth Of The Game

The early 1900s represented a period of consolidation in Singapore's cricket. Matches against Hong Kong continued until 1909, after which the Straits Settlements gave way to an All-Malaya side. This change reflected the growth of the game in Malaya which was undoubtedly encouraged by the regular series of matches between the Straits Settlements, often called The Colony, and the Federated Malay States which started in 1905. With an interruption for the 1914-18 War, the series continued until 1940 by which time the Straits had won eight of the 36 matches played to the FMS's twenty. It was surprising that the Straits did so poorly because they fielded a number of players with first-class cricket experience in England or were close to first-class standard but the players attached to the military generally stayed only two or three years in the country.

Cricket only just managed to survive the effects of the First World War. Many young British cricketers left the country to fight and did not return, either dying in action or deciding, when the War ended, to make a life elsewhere. Whilst the number of British residents had declined, the Chinese population reached 400,000 by the 1920s. The British also led a rather isolated existence. There was little opportunity for competitive cricket, matches being limited to those between the SCC and either the military or the SRC. Nevertheless, among the expatriates who remained, cricket was taken seriously. Matches against the FMS restarted in 1919. With fewer British cricketers to choose from there was an opportunity for good players from the other communities to make the Straits team. This coincided with a period when the European dominance of Singaporean sport began to be more generally questioned. Although cricket was slower than football or rugby union to respond to the idea of multiracial sides, by the late 1920s Theo Leijssius and Evan Wong, both Asian cricketers, were regular selections for the national team. In the 1930s, Fu Chow Teik, the leading batsman from Penang, was also a regular choice. By the mid 1920s there was considerable enthusiasm for cricket across the elite society of all ethnic groups. When the Australians, captained by Charles Macartney and including Bertie Oldfield, Bill Woodfull and Thomas Andrews in the side, came to Singapore in 1927 on a private venture, the interest generated was such that the *Straits Times* suggested that there should be a two-day public holiday for the match played in Singapore against All-Malaya. In addition to this game, which the tourists lost by 39 runs, fixtures were played against SCC and Singapore, both of which the Australians won easily. Singapore was also the venue for the All-Malaya matches against Sir Julien Cahn's XI in 1937 and Ceylon in 1938. Even though the FMS generally provided the majority of the players in the Malayan side, Singapore, and in particular the ground of the SCC, was viewed as the focal point of Malayan cricket.

Immediately prior to the Second World War, the standard of Singaporean cricket rapidly declined as many of the cricketers in the military returned to Eu-

rope. Asian players made up the greater proportion of the Straits and FMS teams in the final match between the two sides in 1940. Cricket continued on the padang until a few months before the Japanese invasion, sport being viewed as a welcome diversion from the perils of war. As the fall of Singapore approached, the cricket ground became a place for the remaining Europeans to dump cars and other bulky possessions before rushing to obtain places on the last few ships to leave the country. The surrounding area was also bombed during a Japanese air raid and the club house was hit and damaged. After a short period as a temporary hospital, the club was requisitioned by the Japanese and used as a tea room and meeting place, known as the Syonan-ko Tonan Club. Attempts were made to revive sport and in March 1943 a cricket match was organised at the Jalan Besar Stadium between Evan Wong's XI (Singapore) and Lall Singh's XI (Federated Malay States). This and some local matches were organised by the Syonan Sports Association as part of an attempt to gain the support of the local population for the Japanese administration. As the Japanese hold on the country became increasingly less secure, however, enthusiasm for sport disappeared and many of the leading Asian cricketers were sent into exile to work on farms in southern Malaya. Following the Japanese surrender, it took a surprisingly short time to repair the damage to the pitch and get cricket restarted. Matches were played again on the padang in 1947 and the first overseas visitors, the Hong Services, were received in 1948. The SCC was opened to members of all ethnic communities and in 1949 the Singapore Cricket Association was formed to organise inter-club cricket, tours and representative matches and to promote the game amongst youth.

Rapid Development

The 1950s were a time of rapid development in Singaporean sport generally and, although cricket suffered from being denounced by nationalists as a relic of British imperialism, the game prospered, particularly at club level where, in addition to the SCC and SRC on the padang, there were the SCRC, the Ceylon Sports Club and the Indian Association on grounds on the Balestier Plain. Ceylon visited in 1957 and in 1958, when Singapore became a self-governing territory, matches were renewed against Federation of Malaya. These continued until 1963 when, for two years, Singapore became part of the Malaysian Federation. In the 1950s and 1960s, Singapore had a dual status in terms of representative cricket. When they competed in the Malaysian Cricket Association's inter-state championships, they were on a par with Selangor, Perak and the other Malaysian states. Once Singapore left the Malaysian Federation in 1965 and became an independent country, they also played as a national team. For several years in the late 1960s they played matches against the Malaysian states and international matches against Malaysia in the same season. During this time, Singapore were able to include players attached to the British, Australian and New Zealand Forces, stationed in the country. The 1960s was also the period when Malaysia and Singapore were popular venues for touring sides, giving the opportunity for the local cricketers to play against first-class and, often, test-class opposition. A strong Commonwealth XI came in 1962, followed by E.W. Swanton's XI in 1964, Worcestershire in 1965, J. Lister's International XI in 1968, the Hyderabad Blues in 1969 and the MCC in 1970. Interport fixtures with Hong Kong resumed in 1968 and continued until 1987.

Cricket suffered a major set-back in the 1970s with the departure of the British troops. Not only had they supplied players to the national side, the military teams had maintained as many as nine cricket grounds. These were returned to the Singapore government and, in a period when urban development and the economy were considered greater priorities than sport, many were lost to housing estates and industry. Despite this, the SCA continued to promote the game and eventually gained government support because of its role in furthering multiracial contacts. Yet it remains a minority sport because, in a dominantly Chinese society, it is played mainly by Eurasians and Indians.

Since the 1970s Singapore has been one of the most active of the associate countries in terms of the number of international matches played. Unfortunately, the high level of activity has not been matched by success. Singapore has won only seven matches out of the 37 played against Malaysia in the Saudara Cup and 14 out of the 36 played in the Stan Nagaiah Trophy, a one-day competition against Malaysia which started in 1995 and is played annually as the best of three matches. Since 1991 Singapore has played in the annual one-day competition with Malaysia, Hong Kong and Thailand for the Tuanku Ja'afar Cup but has won the tournament only once.

With access to cricket on satellite television, the sport has become more popular over the last decade. In April 1996, Singapore made a bid to become a regular venue for top-class one-day international cricket when it hosted the Singer Cup between India, Pakistan and Sri Lanka on the padang. The high heat, humidity and heavy rainfall with the absence of a dry season do not make ideal conditions, however, and it was not until September 1999 that another attempt to promote Singapore was made. This time the West Indies, Zimbabwe and India met at the new cricket centre at Kallang. Again rain marred the tournament which was otherwise successful. Singapore hosted the Asian Cricket Council Trophy in 2002. With increased interest in the game, more of Singapore's schools are offering it as one of their sports and there is some evidence that the standard of play is rising. They won the Plate competition in the 2006 Asian Cricket Council Trophy. Singapore's status as a cricket nation may well improve over the next decade. A women's squad was assembled in 2006 but their only international to date, against Malaysia, was lost by 58 runs.

Famous Victory
November 20, 1994 – Wong Chung Nai Gap, Hong Kong
Hong Kong 234-8 (50 overs) (S.J. Brew 73)
Singapore 236-8 (49 overs) (M. Naushad 53, K.M. Deshpande 50)
Singapore won by 2 wickets

With Hong Kong being unbeaten in the preliminary rounds of the 1994 Tuanku Ja'afar Cup in which they had already gained a victory over Singapore by 107 runs, they were clearly favourites to take the trophy. This looked the likely outcome after Hong Kong reached a competitive total in their fifty overs with Stewart Brew and Mark Eames (49) putting on 100 for the third wicket. Although Kiran Deshpande picked up three wickets, his eight overs went for 51 runs. Despite a valiant effort from Zubin Shroff (40), Hong Kong had six Singaporean wickets down for 127 runs. Deshpande and Mohammed Naushad then decided to attack the bowling and were surprisingly successful in a partnership of 84 in just six overs. With Narayanan Balasubramaniam (27*) and Graham Wilson (23), continuing in the same vein Singapore went to an incredible victory and Stewart Brew's analysis went from 7-1-16-2 to 9-1-48-2.

Player Profiles

McKenzie, R.M. rhb. rm. He was the most successful cricketer for the Straits Settlements in Interport matches prior to the First World War. For a short while he was based in Perak where he was Clerk to the Land Department in Taiping, and thus, during his career, he represented both the Straits and the Federated Malay States. In 24 matches for the Straits, FMS and All-Malaya, he scored 455 runs (average 13.38) and took 123 wickets (average 11.37) including ten or more wickets in the match on four occasions.

Muruthi, Sreerangam. b Singapore 31 May 1952. rhb. rob. A regular choice for Singapore from his debut in 1970 until he retired in 2000. He was highly commended for his bowling by the Pakistanis when they visited Singapore in 1973 as the local player who would most likely succeed in first-class cricket. He captained Singapore in Interport matches against Hong Kong in the 1980s but developed a reputation for a rather negative approach. In 64 matches he scored 760 runs (average 14.90) and took 109 wickets (average 18.99). In 43 limited overs matches he scored 245 runs (average 12.89) and took 44 wickets (average 24.86).

Other leading players: *1890-1914:* S.C.G. Fox; R.T. Reid; J.A. Scharenguivel. *1920-1940:* A.S.A. Jansen; A.C. Growder (rhb. lbg); E. Wong. *1945-1960:* R.C.K. da Silva; J. Martens. *1960-1980:* M.K. Mehta (rhb. rm); Pritam Singh (wk). *1980-2000:* Z.A. Shroff (rhb. rm); J.E. Dearing (rhb. rm); K.M. Deshpande (lhb. lm/sla). *Present day:* C. Ruwan (rhb. rf); Y.O.B. Mendis (rhb. rob); Pramodh Raja (rhb. rfm).

Playing record

International matches

	Won	Lost	Drawn
Interport*	9	9	9
Straits Settlements v Federated Malay States (1905-1940)	8	20	8
Singapore v Malaysia (Saudara Cup) (1970-2006)	7	12	18
ACC Fast Track Tournament/Premier League	2	6	4

* Matches played as Straits Settlements against Hong Kong, Shanghai and Ceylon (1890-1909) and as Singapore against Hong Kong (1957-1987)

One-day matches

	Won	Lost	No Res
ICC Trophy	8	22	6
Asian Cricket Council Trophy	10	13	2
Tuanku Ja'afar Trophy (1991-2004)	15	22	5
Stan Nagaiah Trophy (1995-2006)	14	19	3

Highest team score

413	Straits Settlements v Hong Kong, Hong Kong	1897

ODI

440-2	v Thailand, Singapore	2002

Lowest team score

28	Straits Settlements v Federated Malay States, Penang	1909

Highest individual score

163	R.M. McKenzie	Straits Settlements v Hong Kong-Shanghai, Hong Kong	1897/98

ODI

191	K. Mendis	v Thailand, Singapore	2002

Best bowling

8-8	M.K. Mehta	v Malaysia, Kuala Lumpur	1979

Best wicket-keeping

5 (5c)	Pritam Singh	v Malaysia, Singapore	1973

ODI

6 (4c 2st)	C. Suryawanshi	v Malaysia, Kuala Lumpur	2005

SLOVAKIA

THE SLOVAK Cricket Club was formed in 2000 in the village of Hajske near Nitra by Vladimir Chudáčik who learned the game playing club cricket in England. All the members are Slovak. In 2002 they played their first international match in Prague and lost to the Czech Republic by 56 runs. In 2004, they returned to Prague for a three-nation tournament in which they beat Poland but again lost to the Czech Republic. With few players, limited equipment and restricted to the use of a football ground, it will be a test of the enthusiasm for the founding members of the club as to whether they can establish the game in the country.

Leading players: *Present day:* J. Somorovský; V. Chudáčik.

SLOVENIA

Affiliate Member of ICC: elected 2005

CRICKET WAS started in Slovenia in the small town of Mežica near the Austrian border in 1974 by Borut Čegovnik. He was then aged thirteen and had learnt the game in England when staying with his pen friend. He managed to get as many as twenty-four of his friends interested and they played regularly amongst themselves until 1982 when several of them moved to Ljubljana to further their careers. Ljubljana Cricket Club was not formed until 1997 when a team of expatriates and one Slovene came together to answer a request from the Royal Hague Cricket Club in The Netherlands for a fixture during an east European tour. The club increased its playing strength, recruiting expatriates from England and Canada, as well as some of the Slovenes from Mežica. After two years playing friendly matches against teams from Austria and Italy, the club entered the Austrian League in 1999. The first internationals were played in 2000 in the ECC Representative Festival in Vienna where Slovenia beat Finland but lost to Austria, Croatia and Norway. In the equivalent Festival two years later they lost to Finland but beat Croatia. Ljubljana CC is still the only club in Slovenia. In 2004, they hosted the European Representative Championships which was used as a qualifying competition for the 2005 European Affiliate Championships. Fielding a team which met the ICC qualification regulations, they beat Luxembourg and Bulgaria but lost their other three matches. They finished second in Division 4 of the European Championships in 2006.

Leading players: *Present day:* B.J. Eve (rhb, rfm); R.M. Crawford (wk); M.H. Oman (rhb. rf).

Playing record

One-day matches

	Won	Lost	No Res
European Representative Championships	2	3	0
European Championships Division 4	1	2	0

Twenty20

	0	1	0

Highest team score

230-9 dec	v Czech Republic, Ljubljana	2001

Lowest team score
ODI

46	v Finland, Antwerp	2006

Highest individual score
ODI

90*	M.H. Oman	v Finland, Vienna	2000

Best bowling

7-36	M.H. Oman	v Czech Republic, Ljubljana	2001

SOLOMON ISLANDS

CRICKET HAS been played intermittently in the Solomon Islands since missionaries first introduced the game in the 1870s. Initially it was played enthusiastically between the villages but, over time, enthusiasm waned. The isolation of the islands meant virtually no opportunity for visiting teams and the Solomon Islanders showed little interest in organising the sport, even though some learnt to play the game to a reasonable standard whilst in Fiji for further education. The Central Medical School team in Suva in 1940 included two Solomon Islanders, Ezekiel Kopana and John Wesley Kere. The Solomon Islands played a match at Honiara against Fiji in 1977 which was drawn but the game declined in the 1980s when many expatriate teachers left. An attempt at revival was made in the early 1990s and a team was sent to the 1991 South Pacific Games after which interest again declined. The amount of cricket played depends on the number of expatriates, mainly from Australia and New Zealand. A resurgence of interest in early 2000 led to the formation of the Solomon Islands Cricket Association and an attempt to establish a league in Honiara. Following a political coup in June of that year, however, many expatriates left and by 2001 the future of the Association was in doubt. With cricket not being taught in schools, there is no incentive for Solomon Islanders to play although, those who do sometimes reach a higher standard than the expatriates. In the early 2000s, there were only some twenty Islanders who were active players.

Leading players: *Present day:* G. Talaqua; H. Vaho.

SOUTH AFRICA

Full Member of ICC: elected 1909; ceased membership 1961; re-elected 1991

A BRITISH garrison was posted on the Cape of Good Hope between 1795 and 1802 during the early part of the Napoleonic Wars. Since the British military generally played cricket wherever they were stationed and among the garrison's officers was Charles Anguish, a well-known cricketer who had represented Surrey, it is probable that cricket was played in South Africa at this time. However, interest may have been short-lived because Anguish died at Cape Town, aged only 28, in May 1797. The first reference to cricket in South Africa occurs soon after the British began to control the area around the Cape from 1806. An announcement of a forthcoming game on 5 January 1808 between officers of the artillery mess and officers of the colony was published in *The Cape Town Gazette and African Advertiser*. Another announcement in the same newspaper occurred in 1810 in respect of a game on 13 January at Green Point Common between a side comprising the Ordnance Department and the officers of the 87th Regiment and a side drawn from the officers of the rest of the army. From these beginnings the game spread from the military to British civilians settling in the area and by 1840 both groups were playing the game in the Cape. As other settlements were established in South Africa, so cricket followed. What is regarded as the first formalised cricket club was founded in Port Elizabeth, then a town of some 3,000 inhabitants, on 15 January 1843. The town's administrators set aside an area of land at St George's Park for the club and the ground is still used today for both test cricket and first-class matches. The Cape Town and Wynberg Cricket Club was formed in 1844. By 1848 the game was being played in Pietermaritzburg and by 1850 in Bloemfontein, even though the town's population was then only about 100. The game must also have been known in Durban around that time since, in 1852, the players in Bloemfontein challenged them to a match, a challenge which was not taken up until 1860. Problems of transport undoubtedly limited such contests since it took three days to travel between Durban and Bloemfontein, a straight-line distance of some 475 kilometres. By the early 1850s, cricket was being introduced into such elite schools as the Diocesan College, the South African College at Cape Town and the Port Elizabeth Academy.

During the 1860s and early 1870s cricket became established as an important recreational activity among the military and civilian populations of all the main coastal towns under strong British influence.

As the British extended their control inland, new towns were developed and contacts were established with the indigenous Xhosa population. Schools were established by missionaries at stations such as Lovedale, Healdtown and Zonnebloem in the eastern Cape where African children were given a basic education focused on Christianity and European cultural values. Sport, including cricket, was encouraged. The boys educated at these schools not only developed into an elite African society but also spread the game of cricket wherever they went. The diffusion of cricket within South African society took on a characteristic pattern, pioneered by the British settlers and then repeated by the African community about a generation later. The pattern began with the take-up of the game by the elite schools in the 1850s, the formation of cricket clubs in the 1860s, and then, in the late nineteenth century, the start of inter-town competitions and the inauguration of provincial competitions. The first African cricket club was formed in Port Elizabeth in 1869. Whilst Cape Town may be considered the heartland of British cricket in South Africa, that for African cricket was in the Eastern Cape centred on King William's Town and later on Alice, the home of Lovedale College and Fort Hare University, both of which became nurseries for African cricketers. Cricket also spread in the 1860s beyond the British colonies into Transvaal where the first recorded match took place in 1861 at Potchefstroom. In April 1874 the first of a series of nine matches over eleven years took place between Potchefstroom and Pretoria and in 1888 President Kruger granted an area of land for use by the Wanderers Cricket Club in Johannesburg.

'The Champion Bat'

Although various inter-town contests took place in the 1860s and 1870s, they were on an *ad hoc* basis. In January 1876, the municipality of Port Elizabeth offered a trophy, known as 'The Champion Bat' for a contest between European teams from towns of the Cape Colony. The tournament was won by King William's Town against teams from Port Elizabeth, Cape Town and Grahamstown. The second tournament was not held until 1880 when King William's Town retained the trophy. Further tournaments in 1884/85,

1887/88 and 1890/91 were won respectively by Port Elizabeth, Kimberley and Cape Town. The first inter-town competition for Africans took place at Grahamstown in December 1884 with King William's Town winning against Grahamstown, East London and Port Elizabeth. Port Elizabeth won the tournaments in 1886/87 and 1890/91. Further tournaments continued into the 1890s, played for the Jabavu Cup, a trophy presented by John Tengu Jabavu, the editor of *Imvo Zabantsundu,* one of the leading African newspapers in King William's Town.

The 1880s were marked by an increasing number of matches between the leading African and European clubs, such games becoming a feature of public holidays. In King William's Town, the Champion Cricket Club, the leading African side which had represented the settlement in the 1884/85 inter-town tournament, beat the Alberts Cricket Club, the leading European side, on the first innings in a drawn game in early 1885. In the same year, the Port Elizabeth Africans beat Cradock, one of the European clubs in the town, but were then comprehensively defeated by the Port Elizabeth CC, the leading European side. These fixtures were short-lived, however, because by the early 1890s, the Europeans were increasingly concerned about economic and social competition between themselves and the Africans. Their response was to promote policies of community segregation in an effort to ensure that they obtained political and commercial control, consigning the other communities to the working class.

Discovery of Diamonds

Thus, segregation began to appear in cricket just at the time it was spreading beyond the British and African populations to other communities. The area around Cape Town had a large population of Christians and Muslims who were the descendants of political prisoners and slaves brought from Asia in the late seventeenth and early eighteenth centuries. The Christians formed the basis of the Cape Coloured community and the Muslims were generically but largely erroneously termed 'Malays'. Both groups were now forming their own cricket clubs. In 1888/89, the Malays organised their own inter-town tournament involving Cape Town, Port Elizabeth and

Johannesburg. In the following year, they were joined by Kimberley. With the discovery of diamonds, Kimberley was growing rapidly at this time and all communities there had their leading clubs.

Although, clubs were established by the British in the Afrikaner territories of the South African Republic (ZAR) and the Orange Free State, the development of cricket there was slower than in the British colony. Inter-town tournaments were held at Boshef in the Orange Free State in 1880, involving teams from Boshef, Bloemfontein and Kimberley, and at Pretoria in 1888, with clubs from Pretoria, Johannesburg, Barberton and Potchefstroom. The game was less popular amongst the Afrikaners and, although there were several good players in the 1880s, notably Arthur Ochse and Nicolaas Theunissen, it suffered a set back during the Anglo-Boer South African Wars when activities associated with the British were shunned. Segregationist policies were entrenched in the constitution of the ZAR which stated that there was no equality between black and white inhabitants in either church or state. However, the playing of cricket by the black communities was not prohibited even though it was not encouraged. There were also fewer mission schools in which black children could be educated and cricket was not generally on their curriculum. Nevertheless, the African, Coloured, Malay and Indian communities formed their own clubs in Johannesburg and in the main towns of the Orange Free State during the 1890s and early 1900s.

Cricket was also late to establish in Natal. Whilst the British were playing in Durban with matches against Pietermaritzburg being resumed in 1888, the Zulu-speaking inhabitants did not develop the same enthusiasm for the game as the Xhosa-speaking peoples of the Cape. Many of the mission schools were run by Americans, Germans and Norwegians who were not familiar with cricket. Further, the British operated a system of indirect rather than direct rule which allowed the Zulu administrative structures to remain in place and more of their traditional culture to survive. The greatest interest in cricket was shown by the Indian community of whom some 150,000 were brought to Natal as indentured labourers between 1860 and 1911 to work on the sugar estates. They were followed by traders, other businessmen, teachers and clerks, mainly from Gujarat, and it was these people who formed cricket clubs from 1889 onwards.

There is some evidence that, particularly in Cape Province, women were starting to the take up the game in the late 1880s and 1890s. Cricket was more popular amongst the African and Coloured women than the Europeans. A women's cricket club was formed at Port Elizabeth in 1884 as a sub-section of the Ladies' Croquet Club. African women formed at least three clubs in Kimberley in 1909. A women's team also existed at Pietersburg in the Transvaal in 1894. However, the number of women involved was very small at this time and most clubs lasted only a few years.

English Struggled

The latter part of the nineteenth century thus saw cricket spread to most of the settled parts of South Africa. As inter-town contacts became more common, ideas began to be expressed about testing the strength of South African cricket against teams from England. In 1884, J.T. Jabavu proposed that an African team, representing the best players in the inter-town tournament, should make a tour of England. The proposal was then modified to make the side an Anglo-African one. Although there was reputedly some interest in England at the idea, no tour took place. The first external contact was the 1888/89 tour of South Africa by an English team managed by Major Gardner Warton. Warton, who had served for five years in South Africa on the General Staff, was a cricket enthusiast and keen to bring a party of English cricketers to the country. He chose seven players, two amateurs and five professionals, who had played regular county cricket in 1888 and supplemented them with one professional and five amateurs of good club standard. The tourists met only European sides, mostly against the odds of eleven against either fifteen or twenty-two players. Initially, the English struggled against the conditions and the surprising strength of the opposition and lost four of their first six games. After that, performances improved. Towards the end of the tour, two matches were played, at Port Elizabeth and Cape Town, against representative South African all-white teams and which are now regarded as the inaugural test matches between the two coun-

tries. England won both matches easily largely due to the superior bowling of C. Aubrey Smith, the English captain later to become a Hollywood actor, in the first game and Johnny Briggs in the second.

Before the 1888/89 tour started, Sir Donald Currie, the head of Castle Mail Packets Ltd, the company which provided the boat service between England and South Africa, donated a trophy to be first awarded to the team which did best against the English tourists and thereafter to be contested in an all-white inter-provincial competition. Kimberley were awarded the trophy for the ten wicket victory of their eighteen over Warton's side. Known as the Currie Cup, the trophy then formed the basis of the first-class domestic competition between the provinces (Table 2.14). Transvaal challenged for and won the cup from Kimberley in 1889/90 only to lose it again when Kimberley returned the challenge the following year. The competition then opened up to other provinces, initially three and later five, with teams meeting each other during a festival held over a few weeks at one centre. This arrangement had the advantage of reducing to a minimum the number of days leave required by the cricketers for playing and travel. Starting in 1903/04 the tournament changed to matches played throughout the season in all the main towns. With gaps for the two World Wars, it was played for every season, although until 1966/67, whenever a touring team came to South Africa, it was replaced by a series of friendly matches between the provinces. The competition soon established itself as involving seven provincial teams: Transvaal, Western Province, Eastern Province, Border, Orange Free State (later Free State), Natal (later KwaZulu-Natal) and Griqualand West (formerly Kimberley). Rhodesia entered in 1904/05 but did not compete again until 1930/31. In 1937/38, in an attempt to prevent domination of the trophy by Transvaal, the province was divided into two and North Eastern Transvaal created. In 1951/52, the competition was split into two divisions with Eastern Province, Natal, Transvaal and Western Province forming Division A, the rest Division B, and a system of promotion and relegation instituted. The two-tier arrangement was abandoned for the 1960/61 season but reverted to in 1962/63 when the competition was next held. From the 1970s on, the trophy appeared under a variety of names, reflecting sponsorship. In 1970/71, North Eastern Transvaal was replaced by

Northern Transvaal (later renamed Northerns) and in 1980/81, Boland was created by splitting Western Province. The 1990s saw further changes with the formation of Western Transvaal (later renamed North West) and Eastern Transvaal (later renamed Eastern); Transvaal became Gauteng. From 1977/78, the stronger provinces were allowed to enter B teams into the two divisional structure. Rhodesia, who played as Zimbabwe-Rhodesia in 1979/80, withdrew from the competition in 1980 when Zimbabwe became independent. The various changes represented an attempt by the cricket authorities to balance the need to raise the standard of first-class cricket by having the best teams competing against each other with the desire to spread first-class cricket throughout the country. Following dissatisfaction with the standard of the first-class game in the early 2000s, the competition was completely restructured for 2004/05. Six teams were formed by amalgamating the provinces as follows: Dolphins (KwaZulu-Natal), Eagles (Free State and Griqualand West), Lions (Gauteng and North West), Titans (Northerns and Eastern), Warriors (Eastern Province and Border) and Western Province Boland (Western Province and Boland) which became Cape Cobras in 2005/06. It remains to be seen whether the anticipated rise in standards will occur and whether the players and spectators will develop the same degree of loyalty to these artificially contrived teams as they had to the provinces. Perhaps in recognition of this problem, an additional first-class competition at provincial level was started in 2006/07.

The South African Cricket Association (SACA) was formed in 1890 to promote cricket amongst the white community throughout South Africa. In addition to organising the Currie Cup competition, it took responsibility for tours to and from the country. In 1891/92 a second tour by England was arranged. Again most matches were against provincial sides with between fifteen and twenty-two players, the only eleven a-side game being against South Africa at Cape Town which the English won easily. After this match, the tourists met a Malay XVIII at Cape Town, the only time until the 1990s that England played a non-white side. The match was important because it was a precursor of problems and attitudes to come. First, whether in deference to SACA or because of their personal views is not known, the amateurs in the English touring party refused to play. Later some of the amateurs tried to justify their action by claiming that the match was organised for the benefit of the professionals. Secondly, two of the Malays impressed, L. Samoodien who scored 55 out of their side's first innings total of 113, and J. (Krom) Hendricks, a fast-bowler who took four wickets for 50 in 25 overs in England's innings. Although he played for the Malays in this fixture, he was strictly a Cape Coloured, being a Christian rather than Muslim.

When the touring party was being chosen for the South Africa's first visit to England in 1894, some of the players in both South Africa and England lobbied for Hendricks to be included. This was met by strong resistance from SACA. The *Cape Times* insultingly suggested that he might be allowed to accompany the side as a baggage man. One of the top South African white players, who eventually decided not to tour, made it clear that there was no way that Hendricks could travel as

Table 2.14 Teams involved in South Africa's first-class domestic competitions: the Currie Cup (1889/90-1989/90), Castle Cup (1990/91-1995/96) and the SuperSport Series (1996/97-2006/07)

Team	Date of first appearance	Number of times winners
Boland	1980/81	0
Border	1897/98	0
Cape Cobras (Western Province-Boland)	2005/06	0
Dolphins (Kwazulu-Natal)	2004/05	1 shared
Eagles (Free State and Griqualand West)	2004/05	0
Eastern	1995/96	1
Eastern Province	1893/94	2 + 1 shared
Free State (also played as Orange Free State)	1903/04	3
Gauteng (also played as Transvaal)	1889/90	25 + 4 shared
Griqualand West (also played as Kimberley)	1889/90	1
KwaZulu-Natal (also played as Natal)	1893/94	21 + 3 shared
Lions (Gauteng and North West)	2004/05	0
Northerns (also played as North East Transvaal and Northern Transvaal)	1970/71	0
North West (also played as Western Transvaal)	1991/92	0
Titans (Northerns and Easterns)	2004/05	1 + 1 shared
Warriors (Eastern Province and Border)	2004/05	0
Western Province	1892/03	18 + 3 shared
Western Province Boland	2004/05	0

Until 1990/91 the trophy was contested only by 'all-white' provincial teams attached to the South African Cricket Association

an equal. After consulting with Cecil Rhodes, the Prime Minister of the Cape, the chairman of the selectors, William Milton, formally vetoed Hendrick's inclusion, a decision which effectively cemented the racial structure of South African cricket. Milton also ensured that H.G. Cadwallader, the proposed manager and a supporter of Hendricks, did not tour and was replaced by W.V. Simkins. It should be noted that these initial decisions promoting white domination in cricket were taken by the English and not the Afrikaners. That the tour took place at all was somewhat surprising since it was in the middle of the South African Wars. Financially it was a disaster with expenses exceeding £3,600 against receipts of just under £500. The balance was largely met by the Hon J.D. Logan, a patron of the game who had paid for George Lohmann to come and coach in South Africa in the early 1890s and who later supported the development of the game in Rhodesia. Despite the South African Wars, a further tour of England took place in 1901, this time underwritten by J.D. Logan as a private venture. SACA was not involved in the team selection which received much criticism since it was felt by many that only six of the fourteen players would have made an objectively selected representative South African squad.

By the 1890s, in addition to its strength in European cricket, Kimberley had become the focus of the African and Coloured game. In November 1897, Sir David Harris, chairman of De Beers, donated the Barnato Memorial Trophy, named in honour of the mining magnate, Barney Barnato, for an inter-provincial tournament involving non-European sides. A tournament was staged in Port Elizabeth in 1898 and was won by Western Province over teams from Griqualand West, Southern Border (based on King William's Town), Queenstown and Eastern Province. The South African Wars prevented any further tournaments being played. The trophy was then adopted by the South African Coloured Cricket Board (SACCB), formed in 1904 as a non-racial organisation. Since it was ignored by the Europeans, however, it was effectively responsible for non-white cricket. As with the initial years of the Currie Cup, the Barnato Trophy competitions (Table 2.15) were held in single centres as festivals.

The early twentieth century was marked by considerable progress in European cricket which owed much to the financial patronage provided by Sir Abe Bailey who supported tours to England in 1904 and 1906, funded the Australians to visit South Africa in 1902/03 and initiated the Triangular Tournament held in England in 1912. Bailey, a good enough cricketer to captain Transvaal in the Currie Cup, supported the proposal for a Union of South Africa, uniting the British and Afrikaner communities but was opposed to rights being granted to the non-white communities. Surprisingly, during his period of influence over South African cricket, one Coloured but very pale-skinned player, C.B. Llewellyn, represented South Africa in tests.

No First-class Matches

During the First World War most cricket in South Africa ceased. There were no first-class matches between 1913/14 and 1919/20, no Currie Cup games from 1913/14 to 1920/21 and no Barnato Trophy games from 1913/14 to 1922/23. Once cricket resumed, the racial structure of its organisation became further entrenched. SACA adopted policies which reflected a general view of the white population that sport was a unifying force between the British and Afrikaner and that, with the whites forming a minority in comparison with the non-white population, developing contacts with overseas countries sympathetic to the white South Africans was a priority. Ties with England and Australia were strengthened. Unfortunately, South African cricket was stagnating. South Africa had not produced a new generation of bowlers to take over the mantle of the pre-war stars who were world-class exponents of the art of the googly. Whilst the matting wickets of South Africa had perhaps helped the art of spin bowling in the early 1900s, they were now considered a stultifying factor. Once overseas, South African batsman and bowlers found it difficult to adjust to grass wickets whereas it seemed that English and Australian cricketers, brought up on grass, adjusted more rapidly to the matting surfaces in South Africa. Starting in Natal in 1926/27, grass wickets were introduced for Currie Cup matches and were in general use by the late 1930s. Unfortunately, they proved to be somewhat bland and easy-paced which resulted in high scores and drawn games. Although the results of the national side were disappointing, white cricket flourished during the Inter-War period. It was

Table 2.15 Teams involved in South Africa's inter-provincial competition organised by the South African Coloured Cricket Board and the South African Malay Cricket Board for the Barnato Trophy (1904-1957/58)

Team	Number of wins
Border	0
Eastern Province	1
Griqualand West	1
Transvaal	2
Western Province	12

No tournaments were held during the two World Wars or between 1933 and 1944 when the SACCB was dormant as an organisation

encouraged in the English language schools. Facilities were good and the country was highly regarded as an ideal one to tour by English and Australian cricketers. The sympathy and understanding of the white South African viewpoint amongst the English and Australian cricket hierarchy was illustrated when, either out of deference to or respect for SACA and the South African government, the MCC chose not to select K.S. Duleepsinhji for the test matches against South Africa in 1929 or the South African tour of 1930/31.

The contrast in the 1920s and 1930s between white and non-white cricket was stark. Even on the main grounds used by non-whites, such as Green Point in Cape Town, Natalspruit in Johannesburg and Curries Fountain in Durban, facilities were poor and nowhere approaching international standards. Non-white cricket was held back by being an activity of the middle class, a group which was kept small in size by the segregationist policies of the all-white South African government. Further, the attitudes of segregation began to pervade the non-whites. There were concerns within the African and Indian communities that their players were not receiving the same level of recognition from the SACCB as the Coloureds. The first expression of disunity came in 1922 when a team of South African Indians acted independently and sent a side to visit the Mohun Bagan Cricket Club in Kolkata. In 1926, the South African Independent Coloured Cricket Board (SAICCB) broke away and set up a separate organisation for Coloured cricketers. It has been suggested that the break arose because of religious differences between Christians and Muslims and unhappiness by Coloured cricketers in the Cape that the organisation's headquarters remained

in Kimberley. The South African Bantu Cricket Board (SABCB) was established in 1932, leaving the SACCB with responsibility for the game amongst the Indian and Malay communities. When the South African Indian Cricket Union (SAICU) was established in 1940, the SACCB became defunct before reviving in 1945 and then changing its name to the South African Malay Cricket Board (SAMCB) in 1953. Unified non-white cricket effectively ceased and each board ran its own inter-provincial competitions. Sir David Harris presented a new trophy for the SAICCB (Table 2.16), the Native Recruiting Corporation (NRC) provided a trophy to the SABCB (Table 2.17) and the SAICU played for the Christopher Trophy (Table 2.18), presented by Albert Christopher, a lawyer who was involved in the passive resistance movement promoted by Mahatma Gandhi. The overall standard of non-white cricket was undoubtedly lower than that of the white players, a difference that largely reflected the lack of facilities and the lack of opportunity to play against top-class opposition. There were some outstanding cricketers.

Although the Second World War saw the temporary cessation of Currie Cup matches, the policies adopted by SACA meant that the game flourished in white schools. When cricket restarted, the basic pattern of Currie Cup matches and international contests with England and Australia was soon in place again. By the early 1950s the standard of cricket, relative to these other countries, was rising and there was more interest in the game amongst Afrikaners. The main problem was that, since all cricket was amateur, the players tended to retire in their early thirties and there was a continuous need to replace them. Up until 1960, however, white cricket was able to continue much as it had in the 1930s, segregated and isolationist, a condition reinforced by the policies of the Nationalist Government. The tour of England in 1960 marked the start of public demonstrations against white South African cricketers, expressing opposition to the *apartheid* policies of the South African government. Anti South African feeling was sufficiently strong before the tour that the MCC gave SACA the option of cancelling it but the offer was rejected. Small numbers of people staged protests at London's Heathrow Airport on the South African's arrival and outside most of the grounds where they played. With the tour plagued by a wet summer and controversy over the bowling action of Geoff Griffin, one of their fast bowlers, attendances at the matches were low and the tour made a loss financially.

By the 1950s there was an increasing realisation among non-white cricketers that the existence of four separate boards of control was inhibiting rather than encouraging the recognition of non-white cricket both within South Africa and by cricket authorities overseas. The officials of SAICU were most strongly affected because they had problems establishing a nationwide organisation since the majority of the South African Indian population was in Natal and Transvaal. At a SAICU meeting in January 1945 it was agreed that an attempt should be made to establish a coordinating multiracial body for non-white cricket. In July 1947, the South African Cricket Board of Control (SACBOC) was founded, initially with a federal structure within which the different race-based boards retained their identities. Although the SABCB tried to resist the move towards inter-racial cricket, arguing that it too closely matched the aspirations of the *apartheid* policies of the South African government, they failed to prevent an inter-racial tournament being established. In 1951 the first of four tournaments for the Dadabhay Trophy took place on the Natalspruit grounds near Johannesburg between teams representing the best of South Africa's Coloured, Malay, Indian and Bantu cricketers. The tournament was won by SAICU who also won in 1955. The 1953 and 1958 tournaments went to the Coloureds, represented by the South African Coloured Cricket Association, the renamed SAICCB. However, SACBOC did have a broader view of South African cricket than these racially-based tournaments and envisaged international matches in which South Africa were represented by a multiracial side. Government policy and the attitude of SACA meant that white cricketers had to be excluded and, indeed, SACA generally ignored the activities of SACBOC, the exceptions being a few invitation matches arranged between European and non-white teams.

International non-white cricket began in 1956 when SACBOC organised a visit by the Kenya Asians who were potentially a strong side containing six players with first-class cricket experience in India and Pakistan. The tourists played multiracial non-white provincial sides. South Africa won the first two test matches and the

Table 2.16 Teams involved in South Africa's inter-provincial competition organised by the South African Independent Coloured Cricket Board for the Sir David Harris Trophy (1926/27-1957/58).

Team	Number of wins
Eastern Province	2 + 2 shared
Griqualand West	1 + 1 shared
Natal	1
Transvaal	1 shared
Western Province	6 + 2 shared

Shared tournaments involved a triple tie in 1946/47 between Western Province, Eastern Province and Griqualand West.

Table 2.17 Teams involved in South Africa's inter-provincial competition organised by the South African Bantu Cricket Board for the NRC Trophy (1933-1958.

Team	Number of wins
Border	2
Eastern Province	2
Griqualand West	0
Transvaal	6
Western Province	3

Table 2.18 Teams involved in South Africa's inter-provincial competition organised by the South African Indian Cricket Union for the Christopher Trophy (1941-1957).

Team	Number of wins
Eastern Province	0
Griqualand West	0
Natal	4 + 1 shared
Transvaal	4 + 1 shared
Western Province	0

third was drawn when rain intervened. In August and September 1958, SACBOC went on their first overseas tour, visiting East Africa, beating Kenya in two test matches and East Africa in one.

The success of these ventures encouraged SACBOC to restructure as a united multiracial organisation. At a meeting on 27 January 1958, the individual racial boards were given three years in which to disband and arrange for multiracial boards to be set up in each of the provinces. In 1961/62, the Dadabhay Trophy was awarded to the winners of the provincial tournament (Table 2.19). SACBOC made further attempts at international cricket. A proposal to invite the West Indies to tour in

1959 fell through because the overriding non-white South African Sports Association believed that non-white representative teams furthered *apartheid* policies and were therefore unhelpful to the long-term cause of non-white cricketers. A tour of India was prevented by shortage of finance. In 1955 SACBOC applied to join the ICC. Although the request was rejected, the move drew the position of non-white cricket in South Africa to the attention of the cricket authorities in India, Pakistan and the West Indies, thereby causing differences of view within the ICC regarding the status of SACA and the future of test matches involving South Africa. Unfortunately, SACBOC had difficulties maintaining its multiracial structure. By the mid 1960s the SABCB developed a strong belief that SACBOC was dominated by the interests of the South African Indians and Coloureds and that African cricket was being sidelined. The Africans therefore reconstituted the SABCB as the South African African Cricket Board (SAACB) to promote African cricket outside of the framework of SACBOC.

The late 1960s was a critical period in South African cricket. Just at the time that South Africa produced arguably their best white team of all time, it was forced out of the international arena. South Africa had left the ICC in 1961 when the country ceased to be a member of the Commonwealth. However, the MCC, representing England, and the boards of Australia and New Zealand made it clear that they would continue to play South Africa. A conflict of interest arose between the increasing political opposition within these countries against maintaining contacts and the desire of many cricket enthusiasts to see players of the calibre of Barry Richards and Graeme Pollock in action. Eventually, a selection issue involving the MCC tour to South Africa in 1968/69 resolved the situation. Unable to realise his full potential as a non-white cricketer within South Africa, Basil D'Oliveira had moved to England where he played for Worcestershire and, from 1966, for England. He had a particularly good season in 1968 and when he was not selected for the South African tour, there was a public outcry which effectively accused the MCC of acting in deference to SACA and the South African government. When one of the chosen players withdrew, however, D'Oliveira was named as the replacement.

Table 2.19 Teams involved in South Africa's inter-provincial competition organised by the South African Cricket Board of Control (SACBOC) for the Dadabhay Trophy (1961/62-1973/74) and the SFW Trophy (1975/76) and by the South African Cricket Board (SACB) for the Howa Bowl (1977/78-1990/91).	
Team	*Number of twirs*
Eastern Province	3
Natal	1 shared
Transvaal	2 + 2 shared
Western Province	16 + 3 shared

Immediately the South African government accused the MCC of responding to the pressure of the anti-apartheid movement and making selections for political reasons. The South African government stated that the chosen team was unacceptable and the MCC were forced to cancel the tour. The focus then shifted to the proposed South African tour of England in 1970. Despite a movement within the MCC led by the Reverend David Sheppard and Mike Brearley to cease all cricketing contacts with South Africa, the MCC decided that the tour should go ahead. A national 'stop-the-tour' campaign was mounted amongst the general public by Peter Hain which threatened to disrupt the tour by organising demonstrations at all the matches. Amid concerns for the safety of the South African team and the costs of providing security, the British government intervened and the tour was cancelled.

SACA were increasingly concerned about the likely isolation of white South African cricket and approached SACBOC and SAACB with offers of assistance and an understanding, which with government policy would have been difficult to fulfil, that all future South African sides should be selected on merit. However, with the white South African team being so strong at the time, there was little likelihood that any non-white players would be good enough for selection. Whilst SACBOC rejected the offer as a token gesture to non-white cricket, the SAACB responded positively. Coaching sessions by white players for African cricketers were initiated. The Africans were invited to take part in the International Datsun Double Wicket competition in 1973/74, where they were represented by Edmund Ntikinca and Edward Habane. They were also given fixtures against the touring sides of Derrick Robins and the International Wanderers and, in March 1975, made a tour of Rhodesia. The cricketing bodies recognised, however, that the future of South African cricket lay in unity and in January 1976, SACBOC, SACA and SAACB set out a vision for cricket involving competitions between players regardless of race, creed or colour. Following a relaxation of *apartheid* in sport by the government in 1973, multiracial teams were allowed to represent South Africa internationally but by October 1976, the government had still not permitted such teams at provincial or club level. Nevertheless in September 1977, SACBOC, SACA and SAACB were dissolved and the South African Cricket Union (SACU) formed. Two months later, however, a group from SACBOC, which had refused to join on the basis that government policy still meant that the unity was only in name rather than practice, formed the South African Cricket Board (SACB). Thus two rival boards now existed, both committed in principle to multiracial cricket. Domestic cricket declined in standard. Teams in the Currie Cup competition were weakened by the departure of many of the top white players who joined the World Series Cricket venture organised by Kerry Packer in Australia. The non-white provincial competition continued as the Howa Bowl, named after Hassan Howa, the President of the SACB, but without those players attached to SACU who, unfortunately, did not get much high level competitive cricket due to SACU's failure to organise any provincial tournament in which non-whites could participate. Indeed, much of SACU's efforts seemed to be devoted to the support of white cricketers.

Not Recognised by the ICC

DESPITE A general ban on contact with South Africa for any sporting activity, there were still individuals who were prepared to play in South Africa. During the 1980s SACU managed to arrange for tours by teams from England (twice), Australia (twice), West Indies (twice) and Sri Lanka (once) even though the respective Cricket Boards banned the players involved, either temporarily or permanently, from any further involvement in cricket. The matches were not recognised by the ICC though SACU accepted the tests and the other two-innings

matches as first class and awarded caps to the South African players in the tests and one-day internationals. None of these touring sides met non-white teams.

The 1989/90 tour by an English side was the subject of demonstrations within South Africa. The English were viewed as upholding the South African government policy of racial segregation. The tour coincided with a sudden and substantial change in government attitudes. The ban on the African National Congress was lifted and its leader, Nelson Mandela, released from prison. The tour became the subject of a power struggle between SACU and the South African Council on Sport on the one hand and the newly-formed National Sports Congress on the other. When this was won by the latter, the tour had to be abandoned. SACU had no alternative but to enter into negotiations with the SACB which resulted, in May 1991, in the formation of the United Cricket Board of South Africa (UCB). In June that year, South Africa were welcomed back into the ICC and in November, now free to play test cricket against all countries, toured India. The UCB immediately faced the problem of meeting the expectation that South Africa should field a multiracial cricket team whilst, at the same time, choosing the best team possible. The challenge was not only to bring non-white players up to the same level as the best white cricketers but to ensure that, among the non-whites, the Africans were given equal chances along with the Coloureds and Indians. Initially progress was slow. Omar Henry became the first Coloured player to be selected for South African since C.B. Llewellyn in 1912/13 when he played against India in 1992/93. However, by becoming South Africa's oldest debutant in test cricket at the age of 40 years and 295 days, his inclusion was not a foundation for the future. In 1995/96, Paul Adams, a slow-left arm spinner with a highly unorthodox action, became the next non-white cricketer to make the national side, at the same time becoming South Africa's youngest ever debutant at 18 years 340 days. Since both Henry and Adams were from middle class Coloured families, their selection did not meet the demands of those people in government with aspirations to advance the status of the African community.

In 1996/97 the UCB adopted a policy of affirmative action. Whilst insisting that the national side and the

A teams of the provincial sides should be picked on merit, they instituted a requirement that all provincial B sides and club teams must include non-white players. In 1998/99 the UCB proposed that the national side should always include one 'player of colour'. The following season, all provincial A teams were required to do the same. This was extended to two such players in 2000/01 and three in 2001/02. For the latter season, the requirement for provincial B teams and clubs was increased so that fifty per cent of the team had to be 'players of colour' and had to include at least one African. Although there is no doubt that this policy encouraged non-white cricketers and helped to raise their standard of play, it was by no means universally accepted. Whilst he was captain of the national team, Hansie Cronje tried to uphold the principle of selection on merit. This only fuelled controversy over selection since the performances of the black players in the national side generally matched that of their white counterparts. Resistance to affirmative action also came from some of the African players and administrators who disliked the stigma attached to being selected as the 'quota player'. Responding to these concerns, the UCB dropped the quota system in July 2002 and replaced it with a set of guidelines. For 2004/05, these resulted in targets for each of the first-class teams in the new domestic structure of having a squad that contains at least 40 per cent black players and that in any match, a side should include at least four such players. At present it is difficult to tell whether the policies will lead to equal opportunities for all players, regardless of colour, to reach the highest standards and play for the national side or whether it will be aimed solely at producing a national team whose composition reflects the proportions of the different communities within the South African population.

Unified Structure

The unified structure of South African cricket has made little difference to the distribution of the first-class game. Rather than improving the grounds used by non-white players to first-class standard, the emphasis has been on upgrading the existing first-class grounds to international standard. Although this has given those non-white cricketers good enough to make the provincial squads access top-class facilities, it has done little to increase the accessibility of first-class cricket to the general public. The only obvious change between the pattern of first-class cricket in the 1930s and 1950s and the present day is the greater number of games played at each ground. What has altered is the pattern of touring itineries (Table 2.20). When England visited South Africa in 1891/92, the itinerary was fairly straightforward. After arrival in Cape Town, the team progressed eastwards and northwards to Johannesburg and Pretoria before moving southeast to Durban and then back westwards to Cape Town for the boat journey home. Consecutive matches were often played in one centre where the cricketers would sometimes spend six or more days. Although the travel distances seem relatively small, many of the journeys would have taken more than one day because of the slowness of the transport. A similar itinerary occurred on the 1948/49 tour, except that after the return to Cape Town, a further journey to Johannesburg took place to allow an onward trip to Bulawayo and Harare, before returning again through Johannesburg, Durban and Port Elizabeth to Cape Town. Although the number of rest days more than doubled, so did the distance travelled from 4,490 to 10,220 kilometres based on straight-line distances between the towns. The 2004/05 tour is typical of modern touring patterns in which the need to separate the test matches from one-day internationals and to take both to the main centres outweighs any logic of geography. Thus, starting at Randjesfontein, near Pretoria, the itinerary moved south-east to Durban, then to Cape Town and then, via Johannesburg,

Table 2.20 Playing days, rest days and distances travelled on tours of South Africa by England

Date	Playing days	Rest days	Ratio of cricket days to rest days	Kilometres travelled per rest day
1881/92	61	15	4.07	299
1948/49	70	33	2.12	310
2004/05	37	17	2.18	511

Notes: Rest days are days when no cricket is played and no travel takes place. The ratio of kilometres travelled per rest day is an underestimate because kilometres are based on straight-line distances between the venues and not the actual distance travelled.

back to Centurion, near Pretoria. A second circle was then undertaken in the reverse direction, moving from Centurion through Kimberley, Johannesburg and Port Elizabeth to Cape Town, followed by matches in East London, Durban and then Centurion. Although the tour is shorter than that of 1948/49, with only 37 days of cricket compared to 70, the number of kilometres travelled is some 8,685, again based on straight-line distances. Even though many of the journeys are made by air, an unnecessary travel effort seems to be involved.

One of the more positive aspects of unified cricket is that is has allowed the women's game to become established and flourish. The activity of the early twentieth century was not maintained after the First World War and the game virtually died before a revival was attempted in the early 1930s when Winifred Kingswell formed the Peninsular Ladies' Cricket Club in Cape Province. But whilst the game was played by small numbers locally, no effort was made to develop it nationally by either whites or non-whites. Women's cricket ceased during the Second World War and it was not until the late 1940s that further efforts were made to promote the game. Enthusiasts founded the Southern Transvaal Women's Cricket Association in 1947/48. Other provincial bodies followed in Border, Eastern Province, Natal and Northern Transvaal. These were all run by white cricketers as was the South African and Rhodesian Women's Cricket Association, founded as the national body in 1952. Little progress was made, however, and no encouragement was forthcoming from any of the men's cricketing organisations. The first international matches were not played until 1960/61 when the English women toured South Africa; four tests were played with England winning the third and the other matches drawn. Despite these encouraging performances, it was another ten years before a further international series took place and by the 1980s women's cricket was struggling for survival and the SARWCA was largely dormant.

Reached Quarter-finals

The UCB decided in 1995/96 to promote women's cricket and founded the South African Women's Cricket Association to replace the SARWCA. In December 1995 a provincial tournament was staged as a pilot in Johannesburg involving four teams and the following year a full inter-provincial competition was organised. The aim was to send a team to the 1997/98 World Cup and make a reasonable showing. A tour of England was arranged for 1997 by way of preparation and, with the help of this experience, the team reached the quarter-finals. The pattern was repeated in 2000 with a tour of England prior to the 2000/01 World Cup. This time South Africa made the semi-finals. By now South African women's cricket was becoming well-established and the organisation was confident enough to host the women's World Cup in 2005. However, South Africa were heavily defeated by England in February 2004 and the results in the World Cup were equally disappointing. South Africa finished seventh, gaining only one victory, over Ireland.

South Africa played its first test match in 1891/92 but did not achieve its first victory until 1905/06 during the first of three successful periods in South Africa's cricket history. This lasted until about 1910 and was based on proficiency in spin bowling. South Africa's record in the 1920s, 1930s and 1940s was relatively poor though this was in part due to their cricket being restricted to matches against England and Australia. What is sometimes described as the 'second golden age' of South African cricket came in the early 1950s but it was followed by a decline from the mid-1950s to mid-1960s. The late 1960s saw South Africa produce what is probably their strongest side ever when, such was the quality of their all-round game, they attracted many spectators to see their outstanding fielding alone. Politics cut this team off from world cricket in its prime. Few of the players who represented South Africa in the unofficial tests during the period of isolation reached the same standards. It took a surprisingly short period for South Africa to become a world-class team following their return to test cricket in 1991/92 and by the late 1990s, under the inspirational captaincy of Hansie Cronje, they promised to become one of the top teams in the world. The momentum was not maintained, however, and over the last two years, fewer victories have been obtained; hence, the concern over declining standards.

There is also concern regarding possible long-term effects of the bribery scandal involving Cronje. Allegations of match-fixing by South African players were made in April 2000 by the Indian police authorities.

Soon after Judge Edwin King was appointed by the South African Minister of Sport and Justice to investigate, Cronje admitted to taking four bribes to fix the result of one-day internationals and test matches. Apart from one match in which two other players were involved, Cronje appeared to have acted alone and without the knowledge of his team. Since Cronje was highly regarded as an honest, upright individual with a strong sense of Christian values, his admission of guilt came as a shock. He had a fantastic record as captain with South Africa winning 51 per cent of their matches played whilst he was in charge, a record which demonstrated his ability in leadership and which produced great loyalty from his players. He was banned from any future involvement in cricket at any level, a punishment which most people accepted as inevitable. When he was killed in a plane crash on 1 June 2002, however, his loss was strongly felt by many of those who knew him.

With both the men's and women's teams less successful than in the late 1990s, the challenge is for the domestic first-class game to produce the quality of players necessary to keep South Africa amongst the top countries in the world. The challenge is more demanding than that facing the other test-playing countries since it must do this whilst producing a population of top-class cricketers which matches the ethnic distribution of the population as a whole.

Famous Victories

January 2, 3 and 4, 1905 – Old Wanderers, Johannesburg
England 184 and 190 (P.F. Warner 51, G.A. Faulkner 4-26)
South Africa 91 (W.S. Lees 5-34) and 287-9 (A.W. Nourse 93*, G.C. White 81)
South Africa won by 1 wicket

The team chosen by the MCC for the first South African tour after the Boer War was rated no better than a moderate first-class county side. However, on winning the toss, England batted competently with John Crawford (44) making the highest score and Schwarz being the best of the bowlers with three wickets for 72 runs. South Africa found Walter Lees and Colin Blythe (3-33) difficult to deal with and none of their batsmen reached twenty. With Warner, Crawford (43) and David Denton

(34), England got the better of the local bowlers, aided by 23 byes conceded by Percy Sherwell, standing up to the spinners on a turning wicket. With six wickets down for 105 and Lees (3-74) again bowling well, England looked set for an easy victory. Dave Nourse, on his test debut, and Gordon White then contrived a stand of 121. They were aided by Schofield Haigh being unable to bowl for England because of illness. After White was bowled by Albert Relf, further wickets fell and 45 runs were still required when the last man and captain, Sherwell, joined Nourse. In front of an excited crowd, these two scored the runs needed for South Africa's first test match victory.

June 29, July 1 and 2, 1935 – Lord's, London
South Africa 228 (H.B. Cameron 90) and 278-7 dec (B. Mitchell 164*)
England 198 (R.E.S. Wyatt 53, X.C. Balaskas 5-49) and 151 (A.B.C. Langton 4-31, X.C. Balaskas 4-54)
South Africa won by 157 runs

Having had the best of the draw in the first test match at Nottingham when rain saved South Africa from a likely defeat, England entered the match at Lord's with confidence. South Africa made a no more than an adequate score on winning the toss due largely to Horace Cameron who hit three sixes and six fours in an innings of only 110 minutes. Only Eric Rowan (40) and Bruce Mitchell (30) made worthwhile supporting contributions whilst Hedley Verity picked up three wickets for 61 runs. Xenophon Balaskas then spun South Africa to a first innings lead. Mitchell batted superbly in his second innings which lasted 330 minutes. He put on 104 with Ivan Siedle (13) for the second wicket and 101 with Arthur Langton for the seventh wicket, enabling Herbie Wade, the South African captain to declare, setting England a competitive target of 309 runs in 285 minutes. Both Herbert Sutcliffe and Leslie Ames had to bat with a runner. With Balaskas and Langton bowling well and Cameron keeping wicket superbly (one catch, one stumping and no byes), England offered little resistance allowing South Africa their first test victory on English soil.

March 12, 2006 – New Wanderers Stadium, Johannesburg
Australia 434-4 (50 overs) (R.T. Ponting 164,

**M.E.K. Hussey 81, S.M. Katich 79, A.C. Gilchrist 55)
South Africa 438-9 (49.5 overs) (H.H. Gibbs 175, G.C.
Smith 90, M.V. Boucher 50*, N.W. Bracken 5-67)
South Africa won by 1 wicket**

Australia reached 97 in 15.2 overs before Gilchrist, who had reached 50 off 35 balls, was dismissed. Whilst Simon Katich played the anchor role, Ricky Ponting played an innings which has since been described as 'cultured slogging'. Together they added 119. Mike Hussey then partnered Ponting in a stand of 158, Hussey's 81 coming from 51 balls. Ponting's innings lasted only 105 balls and contained nine sixes and thirteen fours. All the South African bowlers were treated with disdain as Australia posted the highest score ever recorded in an official one-day contest. Jacques Kallis conceded 70 runs in six overs and Roger Telemachus went for 19 runs off four no-balls. After the loss of Bocta Dippenaar with only three runs scored, Herschelle Gibbs and Graeme Smith responded with a magnificent partnership of 187 runs from 121 balls. Mick Lewis went for 113 runs off his ten overs, the most expensive one-day analysis ever. Once Smith departed, Gibbs scored runs so briskly that South Africa were 229 for two after only 25 overs. Although Nathan Bracken took five wickets, he aided South Africa's cause by dropping Gibbs at mid-off when he was on 130. When Gibbs finally fell, having faced 111 balls and hit seven sixes and twenty-one fours, Kallis (20) and Mark Boucher kept up the scoring rate with 28 in six overs. Justin Kemp (13), Johan van der Wath (35) and Telemachus (12) all gave support and South Africa reached the final over with six runs needed and two wickets in hand. Andrew Hall (7) hit the first ball bowled by Brett Lee for four but then holed out to mid-on. Makhaya Ntini scrambled a single to third-man to tie the scores. Mark Boucher then settled the outcome by lofting Lee over mid-on for four. One of the most exciting finishes in one-day history ended with South Africa now holding the record for the highest one-day score after a remarkable match had produced 872 runs.

Player Profiles

D'Oliveira, Basil Lewis OBE. b Signal Hill, Cape Town, 4 October 1931. rhb. rm/rob. The most successful all-rounder ever in non-white South African cricket, his batting was noted for his back-foot play, reflecting an incredible ability to read the ball off the pitch, a prerequisite for success on matting wickets. Added to this were his calmness, determination and power of concentration. His bowling was based on a classic side-ways action from which he could swing the ball either way. He was selected for Western Province in the Sir David Harris tournament at the age of sixteen. He represented South Africa in the SACBOC sides which played East Africa, Kenya and the Kenya Asians. In 1960 he joined Middleton in the Lancashire League and in 1965, after completing the period of residential qualification, began his county career with Worcestershire. The following year, he was chosen for England, the start of an international career for his adopted country which lasted seven years. It was his selection for England in the touring party to South Africa in 1968/69 which led to the cancellation of the tour and the isolation of South African from test cricket for twenty-one years. In 5 matches for SACBOC, he scored 447 runs (average 55.87) and took 7 wickets (aver 15.85); in 44 matches for England, he scored 2,484 runs (average 40.06) and took 47 wickets (average 39.55). In 5 one-day internationals for England he made 30 runs (average 10.00) and took 3 wickets (average 46.66). He was awarded the OBE in 1969.

Donald, Allan Anthony. b Bloemfontein 20 October 1966. rhb. rf. Capable of generating frightening pace, he was one of the few top-class cricketers to emerge during the period when South Africa was barred from test cricket. He chose to earn his living from cricket by playing for Warwickshire and soon established himself in the South African team on their readmission to test cricket. He bowled with passion for his country and was particularly successful against England in 1998 and 1999/00. He became the first South African to achieve 300 test wickets. In 72 test matches, he scored 652 runs (average 10.68) and took 330 wickets (average 22.25), including five or more wickets in an innings on 20 occasions. In 164 one-day internationals he scored 95 runs (average 4.31) and took 272 wickets (average 21.78).

Nourse, Arthur Dudley. b Durban 12 December 1910. d Durban 14 August 1981. rhb. An automatic choice for South Africa between the mid 1930s and early

1950s, he scored 1,000 runs on tours of England in 1935 and 1947 but a broken thumb in his fifth match prevented him from repeating the feat in 1951. He batted with it pinned and in pain when he scored 208 against England in the first test. Known for his fighting qualities, he survived a bout of pneumonia which nearly killed him whilst serving in the Western Desert campaign of the Second World War. In 34 test matches, he scored 2,960 runs (average 53.81) including double centuries against England and Australia.

Ntini, Makhaya. b Mdingi, near King William's Town, 6 July 1977. rhb. rfm. An aggressive but sometimes wayward and expensive bowler, he became the most successful African cricketer to represent South Africa and his country's leading strike bowler. He was first spotted playing for Mdingi village on a bumpy outfield with grazing cows near King William's Town; his promise led to a UCB scholarship to attend Dale College. Bowling from wide of the crease, he angles the ball awkwardly across the batsman. In 2003, he became the first African to appear in the top ten of the bowlers in the Price Waterhouse rankings and the first African to achieve both 100 and 200 test wickets. In 75 test matches, he has scored 619 runs (average 9.98) and taken 308 wickets (average 27.48). In 150 one-day internationals, he has made 173 runs (average 9.10) and taken 236 wickets (average 23.54).

Pollock, Robert Graeme. b Durban 27 February 1944. lhb. He was considered by many as the best batsman in the world in the 1970s, scoring runs attractively, quickly and profusely with a mixture of drives, cuts and pulls. Such was his timing and power that he made batting seem effortless. He was acknowledged as a master of swing, seam and spin bowling. When politics forced South Africa out of the test arena, he was only 26 years of age but had already made seven test hundreds, including two double hundreds, playing only against England and Australia. Recognised for his ability when still a schoolboy, he became the youngest person to make a century in the Currie Cup and the youngest to score 1,000 test runs. In 23 test matches, he scored 2,256 runs (average 60.97).

Richards, Barry Anderson. b Morningside, Durban,

21 July 1945. rhb. In the early 1970s, he was the best opening batsman in the world. Politics prevented him from playing more than one test series, that against Australia in 1969/70, but rather than stay in his own country, he chose to take his talents overseas. He played for Hampshire between 1968 and 1978, South Australia in 1970/71 and joined World Series Cricket in 1977/78 and 1978/79, all with great success. With very quick reactions, he was rarely caught misjudging the line or length of the ball; he had a high backlift, allowing him to use the full swing of the bat. His quick footwork meant that he was invariably in the perfect position to play the most appropriate shot to whatever ball was delivered. He was equally proficient in one-day cricket as in the three- or five-day game. He was devastating as a slip fielder. In 4 test matches, he scored 508 runs (average 72.57).

Roro, Frank. b Kimberley, 1908. rhb. With perfect footwork and a quick eye, he became known in non-white South African cricket as the 'dusky Bradman'. Sound in defence, he made his runs with graceful drives, hooks and glances. After education in Kimberley, he moved to Johannesburg and played his provincial cricket for Transvaal and the South African Bantu Cricket Board. He was the greatest non-white batsman of the 1930s but the true extent of his achievements will never be known because the necessary records have not survived. Between 1934 and 1951, he scored over 3,000 runs for the Transvaal Bantu team, including 20 centuries and a highest score of 228 against the Transvaal Coloureds. In the first Dadabhay Trophy in 1951 he scored 192 runs (average 48.00) including a century (116) in his first innings. He was less successful in his last and second tournament in 1953, when aged 45, his reactions at the crease were starting to slow.

Tayfield, Hugh Joseph (Toey). b Durban, South Africa, 30 January 1929. d Hillcrest (in hospital), Durban, 24 February 1994. rhb. rob. He was among the best in the world of his generation and the best spin bowler ever to come from South Africa. He was exceptionally accurate and could bowl all day without wavering. He was known for his flamboyant and unorthodox field placings with a large tempting gap at extra cover and two straightish silly mid-ons waiting for the mistimed shot. He was known as 'Toey' because he stubbed his toes into the ground before every delivery. He was the first South African to take 100 test wickets. He had a reputation as a playboy and was married and divorced five times. In 37 tests he took 170 wickets (average 25.91) and scored 862 runs (average 16.90).

Vogler, Albert Edward Ernest. b Startwater, Queenstown, 28 November 1876. d Fort Napier, Pietermaritzburg, 9 August 1946. rhb. lbg. He was considered the best bowler in the world during the 1907 tour of England when he formed part of a four-person spin attack with Reggie Schwarz, Aubrey Faulkner and George White. He bowled a mixture of leg spin, top spin and googlies and was extremely difficult to read. His deliveries appeared to come very fast off the pitch and his slow yorker was sparingly used but generally deadly. He could also bowl fast medium swing with the new ball. He came to England in 1906 to qualify for Middlesex as a professional cricketer but, after one season, decided to revert to amateur status and return to South Africa. In 15 test matches, he took 64 wickets (average 22.73) and scored 340 runs (average 17.00).

Other leading players: *1860-1890:* A. Ngcumbe (rhb. rf); N.H.C.D. Theunissen (rhb. rf). *1890-1914:* J. Hendricks (rhb. rf); G.A. Faulkner (rhb. lbg); R.O. Schwarz (rhb. rob/rm); S.J. Pegler (rhb. rmlb). *1920-1940:* B. Mitchell (rhb. lb); M.I. Yusuf; H.W. Taylor (rhb); H.B. Cameron (rhb. wk). *1945-1960:* S. Abed (wk); T.L. Goddard (lhb. lfm); D.J. McGlew (rhb); N.A.T. Adcock (rhb. rf). *1960-1980:* E.J. Barlow (rhb. rm); M.J. Proctor (rhb. rf/rob); P.M. Pollock (rhb. rf); G.N. Kirsten (rhb). *1980-2000: Present day:* H.H. Gibbs (rhb); S.M. Pollock (rhb. rfm); J.H. Kallis (rhb. rfm); G.C. Smith (lhb).

Women: *1960-1980:* L.G. Ward (fm); Y. van Mentz. *1980-2000:* L. Olivier (rhb; rm); H.A. Davies (rhb. rm). *Present day:* M. Terblanche (rhb. wk); C.Z. Brits (rhb; rmf); C.E. Eksteen (rhb. rfm).

Playing record

Test Matches

	Won	Lost	Tied	Drawn
England	26	54	0	50
Australia	15	44	0	18
West Indies	12	2	0	5
New Zealand	18	4	0	11
India	9	4	0	6
Pakistan	7	3	0	4
Sri Lanka	8	4	0	5
Zimbabwe	6	0	0	1
Bangladesh	4	0	0	0
Total	105	115	0	100

Unofficial Tests*

	Won	Lost	Tied	Drawn
England	2	0	0	2
Australia	2	0	0	5
West Indies	2	3	0	1
Sri Lanka	2	0	0	0

SACBOC Tests

	Won	Lost	Tied	Drawn
East Africa	1	0	0	0
Kenya	2	0	0	0
Kenya Asians	3	0	0	0

One-day matches

	Won	Lost	Tied	No Res
World Cup	25	13	2	0
Other ODIs	209	118	3	11

Unofficial one-day internationals*

	Won	Lost	Tied	No Res
	25	11	0	1

Twenty20

	Won	Lost	Tied	No Res
	2	3	0	0

* matches against 'rebel' touring sides during the period that sporting contacts with South Africa were banned.

Highest team score

682-6 dec	v England, Lord's	2003

Lowest team score

30	v England, Port Elizabeth	1895/96
30	v England, Birmingham	1924

Highest individual score

277	G.C. Smith	v England, Birmingham	2003

Best bowling

9-113	H.J. Tayfield	v England, Johannesburg	1956/57

Best wicket-keeping

6 (6c)	D.T. Lindsay	v Australia, Johannesburg	1966/67
6 (6c)	M.V. Boucher	v Pakistan, Port Elizabeth	1997/98
6 (6c)	M.V. Boucher	v Sri Lanka, Cape Town	1997/98
6 (6c)	M.V. Boucher	v Zimbabwe, Centurion	2004/05

ODI

6 (6c)	M.V. Boucher	v Pakistan, Cape Town	2006/07

Women
Test Matches

	Won	Lost	Tied	Drawn
England	0	2	0	4
New Zealand	0	1	0	2
India	0	1	0	0
Total	0	4	0	6

One-day matches

	Won	Lost	Tied	No Res
World Cup	8	11	0	2
Other ODIs	15	21	0	3

Highest team score

316	v England, Shenley	2003

Lowest team score

89	v New Zealand, Durban	1971/72

ODI

80	v India, Patna	1997/98
80	v India, Pretoria	2004/05

Highest individual score

105*	Y. van Mentz	v England, Cape Town	1960/61

Best bowling

6-39	J.F. McNaughton	v England, Durban	1960/61

Best wicket-keeping
ODI

5 (5c)	S. Pillay	v England, Port Elizabeth	2003/04

SPAIN

Affiliate Member of ICC: elected 1992

CRICKET HAS traditionally been a minority sport in Spain played spasmodically in different places by expatriates. It was first played in 1809 in and around Ciudad Rodrigo, Lugo and Orense by soldiers serving the Duke of Wellington during the Peninsular War. In 1813, the British Mediterranean Fleet played in Menorca. In 1891, a merchant seaman called Thomas Ingles tried to introduce the game at San Sebastián. A.T. Kemble took a touring side, including A.H. Hornby and H.G. Garnett, to the Canary Islands in 1898 and played three matches against expatriates in Las Palmas, winning all three games. In the first of these, W. Tonge took seven wickets for 43 runs in the visitor's first innings, easily the best performance by a local player. In 1913, British residents in Barcelona were involved in matches against the crews of visiting British ships.

It was not until the 1970s that the game began to be played more regularly. British and Indian expatriates formed the Madrid Cricket Club in 1976 and very quickly West Indians and even some Spaniards became members. After some years of playing matches against touring sides or teams from the various embassies, internal competition became possible with the founding of Barcelona Cricket Club in 1982. During the 1980s cricket clubs were formed in Malaga followed by an expansion of the game on the Costa del Sol and the Costa Blanca. These clubs were generally formed by British residents wanting to stage friendly matches with more emphasis on social contact and after-match drinking than development of the sport. Most clubs had little interest in promoting cricket amongst the Spanish. Some either excluded Spanish membership or preferred to field only nine or ten players rather than include a Spaniard in the team. However, other expatriates, keen to further the game in Spain founded the Asociación Española de Cricket in 1987 to coordinate cricket throughout the country. Spain made its first international appearance in the European Cricketer Cup in Guernsey in 1990, finishing in ninth place. In 1992, a dedicated cricket facility was opened at the Catarma Oval near Malaga.

Hopes were raised in 1995 when the AEC was recognised by the Spanish government, making it eligible for federal funding. In 1996, however, the government failed to approve the budgets for many of the country's sports federations and, despite a three-year agreement with the government made in 1998, finance has not been forthcoming. Nevertheless with company support, the AEC has been able to invest in youth training programmes in clubs and schools. International results have also been promising. Spain won four out of its six matches in the European Affiliates competition in 2005.

There is the possibility that women's cricket will also develop in Spain. Several matches were held in the 1980s on Ibiza between ladies teams from San Antonio and Ibiza-Santa Eulalia. In November 2005, a fourteen a-side match was staged at the Catarma Oval between Cádiz and Malaga, the first women's match to be played in mainland Spain. As the AEC's youth programme is targeting both boys and girls, it can be expected that more women will play cricket in the future.

Leading players: *1980-2000:* L. Rivero. *Present day:* G. Howe; P. Venus; Wasim-ur-Rehman.

Playing record

One-day matches

	Won	Lost	No Res
ECC Trophy	5	5	0
European Affiliates Championships	4	2	0

Highest team score

ODI

247-8	v Croatia, Vienna	2003

Lowest team score

ODI

85	v Isle of Man, La Manga	2006

Highest individual score

120	G. Headon	v Portugal, Barringtons	1993

Best bowling

5-52	D. Le Geyt	v Portugal, Barringtons	1993

SRI LANKA

Associated Member of ICC: elected 1965
Full Member of ICC: elected 1981

CRICKET PROBABLY started in Sri Lanka or Ceylon, as it was known until 1972, soon after the island became a British colony in 1815. British troops were stationed at garrisons in Colombo, Kandy and Galle and they undoubtedly played the game for recreation. By the 1830s, British administrators, businessmen and teachers were settling in the country and many of these came from public schools and universities with a strong tradition of sport, including cricket. The first record of the game in Ceylon was in 1832 when a match was played in November that year by the 97th Regiment. The Colombo Cricket Club was formed by the European residents soon after. Although very few records exist, it seems likely that the game became firmly established in the 1840s and 1850s in Colombo, Kandy and Galle and that it spread into the rural areas up-country as individuals opened up, first, coffee estates and, later, tea plantations. Cricket was also taken up by the local population. In the rural areas it was necessary for the plantation owners to encourage the locals to play in order to have enough people to make up teams for matches. In the towns, particularly in Colombo, the game was taught in the newly-established schools which were attended by the children of elite Ceylonese as well as those of the European residents.

In 1879, the Colombo Academy (later to become the Royal College) challenged St Thomas's College to a match and thus initiated a fixture, the local equivalent of Eton versus Harrow, which continues to attract large crowds and excitement today.

The 1870s and 1880s saw the formation of many of the clubs which still exist and make-up the first-class domestic competition today. In 1872, the Malay Cricket Club was founded by Malay soldiers recruited from Java to serve in the Ceylon Rifle Regiment. In the following year the first Ceylonese club, Colts Cricket Club, was founded and soon attracted the best Ceylonese players in the country. By 1887 the standard of the Colts CC was sufficient to challenge the Colombo CC to a match which became the precursor of an annual fixture between the Ceylonese and the Europeans. Known locally as the 'test' match, it had the status of the Presidency Matches in Bombay and Madras, until it ceased in 1933 by which time European cricket was in decline. The initiative taken by the Ceylonese in challenging the Europeans encouraged local cricket generally and with increasing numbers coming through the elite school system, the Nondescripts Cricket Club was formed in 1888. In 1900 the Sinhalese Sports Club was founded. With one European, three Ceylonese and one Malay club now in existence, the other communities in Colombo developed their own clubs, resulting in the formation of the Tamil Union Cricket and Athletic Club, the Moors Sports Club and the Burgher Recreation Club. Thus cricket became a game which was organised along racial lines although there was considerable enthusiasm for the various clubs to play each other. In July 1901, the Colts CC provided recreation for prisoners from the South African Wars. They met and beat a Boers PoW side by 141 runs. Cricket clubs were also formed by both Europeans and Ceylonese outside of Colombo. Those in Kandy, Galle and Kalutara reached a reasonable standard. European clubs established in more rural areas by the plantation owners included Dimbulla-Agrapatna and Dikoya-Maskeliya. These provided players for another annual fixture of high standard, Colombo versus Up-Country. Among the plantation owners and managers with first-class cricket experience were the tea planters, Vivian Crawford (Surrey), Archibald Gibson (Essex) and Algernon Whiting (Oxford University), the coffee planter, Alfred Tabor (Middlesex) and the tea and rubber estate manager, Walter Greswell (Somerset).

The first international matches played by Ceylon were organised by the Colombo CC and therefore involved European sides. Initial contacts were with Madras to which the Europeans sent a touring side in 1876. Between then and 1910, a further five tours were made and European teams from Madras made three visits to Ceylon. In 1889, a three day match was played against G.F. Vernon's side who visited Colombo before embarking on their tour of India. Since Vernon's team beat an all-European side, representing Ceylon, by an innings and 77 runs and then defeated Colombo CC by an innings and 10 runs in a two-day fixture, the standard of local cricket was clearly no better than good English club level; Vernon's team included only three players of first-class standing. In 1891, a side visited Singapore where they beat Hong Kong but lost to the Straits Settlements by an innings and 18 runs. A Straits team returned the visit in October 1893 and won in Colombo by 10 wickets. Despite these contacts, Ceylon did not become part of the Interport matches with Singapore and Hong Kong. There was no need since the geography of Ceylon's location gave sufficient opportunity for international fixtures. These started by accident, literally, in October 1882, involving the Hon Ivo Bligh's side on its way to Australia. The Colombo CC tried to persuade them to play a match in Ceylon but the invitation was declined, the English preferring to spend their stop-over sightseeing. However, two days after their ship, the *Peshawar,* left Colombo for Australia, it was in collision with the *Glenroy* and had to return to Colombo for repairs. The opportunity was then taken to arrange two one-day games against a Colombo side drawn mainly from the garrison. The matches were drawn but very much in the visitor's favour. Thereafter, most MCC and Australian sides travelling between England and Australia played a one-day match in Colombo until sea travel gave way to air travel and a stop-over in Ceylon was no longer necessary.

Won all their Matches

Given the number of European cricketers of first-class standing in the country prior to the First World War, it was surprising that Ceylon did not perform better in its international matches. They were generally the equal of the Madras Presidency sides but by 1912 had fallen behind Myanmar who beat them by an innings and 37 runs in Yangon in 1912. In January 1914, the Reverend E.F. Waddy brought a side from New South Wales for a tour of nine matches, including several up-country. Even though the team had only two players who had represented New South Wales in that year's Sheffield Shield competition, they still won all their matches, including that against All-Ceylon. Ceylon were themselves weakened because the Ceylon Europeans had organised a conflicting tour of Bengal in December 1913 and on their return, neither Vivian Crawford nor Walter Greswell could afford the time to play.

No international matches were played by Ceylon between 1914 and 1920. As cricket resumed after the First World War, it was recognised by the leading players and administrators that the standard of play would remain low as long as cricket was restricted to friendly matches of four hours duration between club sides on Saturday afternoons and the occasional one-day match against an English or Australian team whilst their ship was refuelling in Colombo harbour. The leading administrator and promoter of the game, Dr John Rockwood, proposed the formation of a national body to promote and govern cricket. Thus, in July 1922, the Ceylon Cricket Association was formed. Rockwood was also instrumental in arranging for some short tours of Ceylon by first-class overseas teams which, in addition to fixtures against European and Ceylonese sides, met an All-Ceylon team combining the best of the European and Ceylonese cricketers. In February 1926, J. Rockwood's All-Ceylon team played a team from Bombay, chosen by W.E. Lucas in what is now recognised as the first first-class fixture played by and in Ceylon. Ceylon won by seven wickets.

The highlight of the 1920s was the visit of the MCC in 1926/27 during their tour of the Indian sub-continent. Four matches were played, all now considered first-class. After draws against the Europeans, the Ceylonese and an Up-Country XI, the visitors had a surprisingly easy victory over an All-Ceylon side by an innings and 91 runs. This tour set a second precedent to the pattern of Ceylon's cricket. In addition to receiving English, Australian and, later, New Zealand teams on their stop-overs between

England and the Antipodes, Ceylon was now on the itinerary for sides touring India. Together, these meant that there was a visiting team from overseas virtually every year. Usually only between one and four matches were played, however, which meant that Ceylon did not benefit from dedicated tours. One exception to this was the visit in December 1930 for a programme of eight games by a side raised by the Maharaj Kumar of Vizianagram to fulfil some of the fixtures of the cancelled MCC tour of India and Ceylon. The visitors included many top Indian players supplemented by Jack Hobbs and Herbert Sutcliffe. The tour marked the change-over point where the standard of the Ceylonese players exceeded that of the Europeans. The Europeans were comprehensively beaten by an innings and 259 runs whereas the Ceylonese and the All-Ceylon sides drew their matches.

Sufficient Confidence

With the improvement in the standard of cricket, sufficient confidence existed to undertake the first overseas tour by a representative national side. Under the captaincy of Dr Churchill Gunasekara, fifteen players embarked on a ten-match tour of India. The team were unfortunate in that Cecil de Saram was at Oxford University and therefore unavailable and that Gunasekara, who was the Chief Medical Officer of Health in Colombo, had to return home after seven matches to deal with an outbreak of cholera. Although only two matches were won, the side remained undefeated until their last game when they succumbed to Madras by five wickets. Ceylon lost seven wickets for 34 runs in their first innings before recovering to 72 all out; M.J. Gopalan achieved the remarkable analysis of 11-7-16-6, including four wickets in five balls. He followed this with 7-57 in Ceylon's second innings. It was to commemorate this performance that V. Pattabhiraman and D.L. Narasimha Raju presented the M.J. Gopalan Trophy in 1952 for a competition between Madras and Ceylon. The match was played in most years until 1977 by which time Sri Lanka had become too strong and the trophy was contested between Madras and a Sri Lanka Under 23 side.

The 1930s saw visits from the MCC (1933/34), the Indian University Occasionals (1935/36), an Australian team organised by the Maharaja of Patiala (1935/36) and Sir Julien Cahn's side (1936/37). The matches played demonstrated that the standard of Ceylon's national side was equivalent to that of a moderate English county or an Indian state team. Although not yet at test-playing standard, they were clearly the strongest of the non-test countries as shown by their easy victories over the Federated Malay States and All-Malaya on their Malayan tour of 1938. This remained the situation throughout the 1940s and 1950s. A second tour of India was made in 1940/41 with India winning the single 'test' by an innings and 110 runs. Ceylon's performances in the two decades after the Second World War were characterised by inconsistency. With representative matches being limited to only two or three games a year, some of the best players decided to pursue their cricket overseas.

Ceylon's cricketers had a good reputation in the first-class game in England. Churchill Gunasekara played 39 matches for Middlesex between 1919 and 1922, impressing with his medium-pace bowling and fielding. De Saram had an excellent record whilst at Oxford University, scoring a century against the Australians in 1934 and 208 against H.D.G. Leveson-Gower's XI. Gamini Goonesena pursued a career with Nottinghamshire, Stanley Jayasinghe and Clive Inman had long spells with Leicestershire and Ladislaus Outschoorn was a regular in the Worcestershire side. Patrick McCarthy emigrated to Perth where he played Sheffield Shield cricket for Western Australia. Thus Ceylon's inconsistent performance partly reflected their inability always to field their best side.

By the early 1960s there was a general realisation within the CCA that Ceylon's cricket was stagnating relative to that of the other main cricketing countries with the national side being easily defeated in unofficial 'test' matches by India and Pakistan. The CCA recognised that the traditional strength of the country's cricket lay in the schools. The *Daily News* offered a trophy for the schoolboy cricketer of the year and the decision was taken to develop a national side at schoolboy level. In December 1959, a party of fifteen schoolboys toured Western Australia. In 1963/64, an Indian Schools team came on tour and Ceylon schools defeated them by 14 runs. As the leading school cricketers progressed through the domestic game to the national side, standards at the top began to improve and Ceylon gained their first international victory over a test-playing country when they beat India in January 1975. A tour of England was proposed for 1968 but after a squad was selected, it was called off when the government was unable to release the necessary foreign exchange. Some authorities believe that this was the diplomatic way the government used to express their dissatisfaction with the selectors for choosing themselves.

Narrow Margins

The first team to suffer from Ceylon's newly emerging side was the unfortunate Malaysians who were completely outplayed during their tour in April 1972. In the international fixture, the Malaysian bowlers were powerless as the home team amassed 736 for the loss of four wickets. They then dismissed Malaysia twice to win by an innings and 483 runs. Throughout the 1970s, Ceylon were competitive against most opposition. In matches against India and Pakistan, they often had the advantage in drawn games and the defeats were by narrow margins such as 6 runs by India and 17 runs by Pakistan in 1974. In 1975 they were invited to participate in the first World Cup. Following a tour of Bangladesh in 1978 where they won all three 'tests' by an innings, Sri Lanka returned to England in 1979 to take part in the ICC Trophy. Sri Lanka won the competition with ease, beating Canada in the final by 60 runs. They therefore qualified to take part in the second World Cup where they gained an unexpected victory over India by 47 runs.

Sri Lanka were granted test-match status in 1981 and the CCA immediately began a programme to upgrade the grounds in Colombo, Kandy and Galle. Unfortunately, the ground on the Galle Esplanade was destroyed during the Boxing Day tsunami in 2004. With an estimated cost for repair at £2.25 million, it is by no means certain that the ground will be reinstated. Sri Lanka's inaugural test match occurred against England at Colombo in February 1982, resulting in a loss by seven wickets. Sri Lanka came close to avenging this in 1984 when, on their first appearance in a test match at Lord's, they gained a first innings lead of 121 runs before the match petered out into a draw. Sri Lankan cricket then

suffered a serious setback when fourteen of their players, under the captaincy of Bandula Warnapura, accepted the financial inducements offered to undertake a tour of South Africa. Since the Sri Lankan government, in common with the majority of world governments at the time, had banned all sporting contacts with South Africa to express opposition to that country's *apartheid* policy, the Board of Control for Cricket in Sri Lanka had no option but to ban the players for life, thereby reducing the squad of top players available for selection by half. From that time, the government has exerted a strong influence over the way cricket has developed. All team selections, for example, must be approved by the Ministry of Sport.

The first test win was gained at the fourteenth attempt in September 1985 but Sri Lanka then struggled to build on this performance. Concern about the slow progress at test level prompted the BCCSL to invest more funding at Under 15, Under 17 and Under 19 levels and to upgrade the main domestic competition to first-class in 1988/89. The rules for the competition have been subject to many changes since that date. Until 2003/04, clubs could qualify for entry through a preliminary non first-class section, so that the list of clubs competing was different each year (Table 2.21). Since 2003/04, the competition has been between the same sixteen clubs which has meant that teams in Kandy and some other up-country towns where the game is long established are excluded from first-class cricket. As a result, cricket is not being promoted across the whole country. In 2003/04, 66 per cent of first class matches were staged at grounds in Colombo. Three per cent were held in Kandy with the remainder at various centres in the south-west of the country. Although part of the reason clearly relates to security problems posed by the Tamil Tiger movement in the north and east, very little effort has ever been made to promote the game in these areas. Only two touring sides have played in Jaffna, Madras in 1970 and the Malaysians in 1972; neither of these matches were first class. No first-class matches or fixtures against touring sides have been played at any town along the east and south coast between Jaffna and Galle. The concentration of cricket in the south west of the country has meant that Sri Lanka has not experienced the same problems of producing sensible touring itineries that other countries have faced. First, tours have generally been very short. Secondly, they can be completed by being based on Colombo for most of the time with short periods, either before or after, in Galle and Kandy.

The 'golden age' of Sri Lankan cricket occurred in the late 1990s. The major difference between the Sri Lankan side at this time and its predecessors was that it now contained a world-class spin bowler in Muttiah Muralitharan. The importance of Muralitharan is illustrated by the year 2003 when he took 44 per cent of Sri Lanka's test wickets. It was very clear throughout this period that with Muralitharan in the side, Sri Lanka could dismiss the opposition and win matches whereas, without him, they could not. Sri Lanka's greatest achievement came in 1996 when they won the World Cup, surprisingly beating Australia in the final by seven wickets.

It was not until the 1990s that Sri Lankan women started to take a serious interest in playing cricket. It has been suggested that cultural issues inhibited women from taking up the game but whilst this might be true for other South Asian countries, it is difficult to apply this argument to a country where Buddhism is the major religion and which has elected two women as Presidents. Whatever the reasons, it was not until 1997 that Sri Lanka made an appearance in women's international competition. To date, only one test match has been played. Although the side has won more one-day internationals than it has lost, this partly reflects matches played against Pakistan and The Netherlands. The foundation for women's cricket needs to be improved, however, since the national domestic competition involves only three or four teams.

Since 2004 Sri Lanka has been less successful. It is doubtful whether a domestic competition of sixteen club teams is an appropriate base from which to develop new cricketers with the skills to succeed anywhere in the world. There has been a marked contrast in recent years between achievements at home and abysmal performances overseas. With Kandy being excluded from first-class domestic matches and the need to rebuild the stadium at Galle, there is a risk that cricket will become concentrated even more on Colombo. Since the late 1990s, the BCCSL, now restyled Sri Lanka Cricket, has

been bedevilled with internal administrative problems often ending in disputes between the Board and the government and constant changes in the selection committee. These need to be resolved so that Sri Lanka Cricket can concentrate on promoting the sport rather than on its own internal arguments. Throughout its history, Sri Lanka has consistently produced exciting cricketers and the enthusiasm and talent exist for this to continue. The players need the support of the administration which needs to invest in cricket throughout the country, regardless of gender.

Table 2.21 Teams involved in Sri Lanka's first-class domestic competitions: the Lakspray Trophy (1988/89-1990/91), the P.Saravanamuttu Trophy (1991/92-1997/98) and the Premier Trophy (1998/99-2006/07)

Team	Date of first appearance and no. of years of participation	Winners
Air Force CC	1988/89 (8)	0
Antonians SC	1991/92 (11)	0
Baduraliya SC	2005/06 (2)	0
Bloomfield C & AC	1994/95 (13)	3 + 1 shared
Burgher RC	1988/89 (15)	0
Chilaw Marians CC	2001/02 (6)	0
Colombo CC	1988/89 (17)	2
Colts CC	1988/89 (19)	4
Galle CC	1988/89 (15)	0
Kalutara Physical Culture Club	1991/92 (1)	0
Kalutara Town CC	1996/97 (1)	0
Kandy CC	1992/93 (3)	0
Kandy Youth Club	1991/92 (1)	0
Kurunegala SC	1992/93 (1)	0
Kurunegala Youth CC	1991/92 (14)	0
Lankan SC	2005/06 (1)	0
Matara SC	1997/98 (3)	0
Moors SC	1988/89 (17)	1
Moratuwa SC	1988/89 (9)	0
Navy SC	2000/01 (1)	0
Nomads SC	1988/89 (2)	0
Nondescripts CC	1988/89 (18)	2 + 1 shared
Old Cambrians	1989/90 (2)	0
Panadura SC	1988/89 (17)	0
Police SC	1995/96 (10)	0
Ragama CC	2001/02 (6)	0
Rio SC	1992/93 (2)	0
Saracens SC	1990/91 (2)	0
Sebastianites C and AC	1990/91 (17)	0
Singha SC	1989/90 (10)	0
Sinhalese SC	1988/89 (19)	5 + 2 shared
Tamil Union C and AC	1988/89 (18)	0

Famous Victories
January 2, 3, 4 and 5, 1965 – Sardar Vallabhai Patel Stadium, Ahmedabad
India 189 (R. Saxena 63*, S. Jayasinghe 6-38, N. Frederick 4-85) and 66
Ceylon 141-7 dec (A. Polonowita 53, U.N. Kulkarni 4-43) and 115-6 (R. Goel 4-33)
Ceylon won by 4 wickets

Ceylon's first victory over a test-playing country, on a wicket which favoured the bowlers, was due largely to an enterprising declaration by their captain, Michael Tissera. Batting first on winning the toss, India, already 2-0 up in the three-match series, lost Dilip Sardesai (9), Farokh Engineer (17), Abbas Ali Baig (10) and Hanumant Singh (30) for only 79 runs. Mansur Ali Khan (28) and Ramesh Saxena then added 42 before the former became Norton Frederick's fourth victim. Saxena continued to bat sensibly whilst Stanley Jayasinghe ran through the tail with his off-spin. Ceylon were in greater trouble with left-armer Umesh Kulkarni making the ball swing and bounce awkwardly. After the fifth wicket fell at 25, Tissera (28) batted attractively before Anurudda Polonowita and Herbert Fernando (38*) put on 85 for the seventh wicket. Shortly after Polonowita fell to the spin of Srinivasagan Venkataraghavan, Tissera declared with a deficit of 42 runs. Frederick (3-24), Jayasinghe (3-14) and Polonowita (slow left-arm) (3-7) took advantage of the conditions to dismiss India cheaply. Much credit was due to the deftness of wicket-keeper Fernando, who caught four and stumped three batsmen in the match off Ceylon's spin bowlers. Despite the left-arm spin of Rajinder Goel, who exploited the wicket well, Abu Fuard (40) laid the foundation to enable Tissera (15*) and Polonowita (3*) to take Ceylon to a well-deserved but surprising win.

March 17, 1996 – Gaddafi Stadium, Lahore
Australia 241-7 (50 overs) (M.A. Taylor 74)
Sri Lanka 245-3 (46.2 overs) (P.A. de Silva 107*, A.P. Gurusinha 65)
Sri Lanka won by 7 wickets

Australia started this World Cup Final confidently after being asked to bat first by Arjuna Ranatunga. Thanks to Mark Taylor and Ricky Ponting (45) they reached 137

for the loss of only one wicket by the 27th over. Both then fell to the off-spin of Aravinda de Silva (3-42) attempting to raise the run-rate further. Thereafter, though they took only one wicket each, Muttiah Muralitharan, Kumar Dharmasena and Sanath Jayasuriya succeeded in constraining the Australians. After losing Jayasuriya and Romesh Kaluwitharana quickly, de Silva and Asanka Gurusinha batted beautifully, first consolidating and then increasing the scoring rate so that Sri Lanka needed only 51 runs from the last ten overs. De Silva and Ranatunga (47*) quickly reduced this to ten runs from five overs and took Sri Lanka to a surprisingly easy but convincing victory with nearly four overs to spare. De Silva's innings off 124 balls contained 13 fours.

August 27, 28, 29, 30 and 31, 1998 – The Oval, London
England 445 (J.P. Crawley 156*, G.A. Hick 107, M.R. Ramprakash 53, M. Muralitharan 7-155) and 181 (M. Muralitharan 9-65)
Sri Lanka 591 (S.T. Jayasuriya 213, P.A. de Silva 152, A. Ranatunga 51) and 37-0
Sri Lanka won by 10 wickets

Having been asked to bat by Arjuna Ranatunga, England took nearly two days over the first innings and compiled what seemed to be an impregnable total. Only John Crawley batted with any fluency even though Muttiah Muralitharan's spin was negated by a slow pitch. The English bowlers also found the pitch unresponsive and Sri Lanka replied with some entertaining batting. Sanath Jayasuriya's innings lasted 346 minutes and 278 balls; he hit one six and 33 fours. He added 243 for the third wicket with Aravinda de Silva. A tenth wicket partnership of 59 between Suresh Perera and Muralitharan added to England's woes and gave Sri Lanka a lead of 146 runs. Instead of adopting a positive approach, the English batsmen set themselves the task of survival but, apart from Mark Ramprakash who spent more than four hours compiling 42 runs, they had no answer to the spin and dip of Muralitharan who, but for the run-out of Alec Stewart in a mix-up with Ramprakash, might have taken all ten wickets. As it was he obtained his 200th test wicket in only his 42nd match. He finished with match figures of 113.5-41-220-16. Sri Lanka had no difficulty making the runs required for their first test victory over England in England.

Player Profiles

De Saram, Frederick Cecil (Derrick). b Colombo 5 September 1912. d Colombo 11 April 1983. rhb. He was considered a complete batsmen, with all the strokes and a strong defence. Although he could bat aggressively, he scored many of his runs in ones and twos between mid-on and mid-wicket, purposely placing the ball to avoid the fieldsmen. On going to Oxford University in 1932, he gained blues in 1934 and 1935. After completing his university education, he played regularly for Ceylon and was the captain from 1949 to 1954. He had a career with the Ceylon Garrison Artillery and Ceylon Defence Force, retiring with rank of Full Colonel. In 1962 he was jailed for being a political activist but acquitted on appeal. In 9 first-class matches for Ceylon he scored 448 runs (average 24.88). He was an all-round sportsman: in lawn tennis he won Ceylon's men's doubles title in 1930 with his father, Fred de Saram, and in 1940, 1941, 1946-1949 with his brother F.J. de Saram – he also gained an Oxford blue; in golf, he represented Ceylon in the 1971 World Championships and gained an Oxford half-blue.

De Silva, Pinnaduwage Aravinda. b Colombo 17 October 1965. rhb. rob. He was the most successful and attractive batsman to play for Sri Lanka during the 1980s and 1990s. With good footwork and a wide range of strokes, he used his wrists to place the ball so as to evade whatever field placing the opposition set. He liked to score runs quickly and had the ability to demolish the best bowling but with elegance rather than savagery. He was also a useful off-break bowler. He played for Kent in 1995. In 93 test matches, he scored 6,361 runs (average 42.97) and took 29 wickets (average 41.65). In 308 one-day internationals he scored 9,284 runs (average 34.90) and took 106 wickets (average 39.40).

Greswell, William Territt. b Cuddalore, India, 15 October 1889. d Wedcombe House, Bicknoller, Somerset, 12 February 1971. rhb. rsm. He was the best European player to appear in Ceylonese cricket. In addition to managing tea and rubber estates, he appeared regularly for Ceylon between 1909 and 1926. He also captained Ceylon at hockey and soccer and was Ceylon's 880 yards champion.

When on leave he played cricket for Somerset, the Gentlemen of England and the Free Foresters and hockey for Somerset and the West of England. He became President of Somerset CCC (1962-1965). In local cricket in Ceylon between 1909 and 1923 he took 1,016 wickets (average 8.72).

Gunasekara, Conroy Ievers. b Colombo 14 July 1920. rhb. lbg. Ceylon's leading all-rounder in the 1950s and early 1960s, he was somewhat ungainly at the crease with a crouching stance but had powerful forearms and a good eye. When set, he savaged the bowling with straight drives, hooks and square cuts. In bowling, he had a short run but used his power to deliver the ball at near medium pace. He could spin his leg break and googly on most surfaces but his most deadly ball was a fizzing top spinner. In 14 first-class matches for Ceylon he scored 718 runs (average 31.21) and took 30 wickets (average 27.73). He was the Ceylon men's doubles lawn tennis champion with Walter Rutnam (1946) and the mixed doubles champion with Ruth Wijewardene (1949).

Jayawardene, Denagamage Proboth Mahela de Silva. b Colombo 27 May 1977. rhb. The most exciting of the new generation of Sri Lankan players, he combines calm temperament with high technical skill and has the ability and concentration to compile high scores. He took over the captaincy in 2005. In 85 tests he has scored 6,289 runs (average 48.37); in 245 one-day internationals he has made 6,681 runs (average 32.91).

Jayawickreme, Sagaradaththa Sudirikku (Sargo) MBE. b Walawwe 10 January 1911. d Colombo 15 February 1983. rhb. rsm. Ceylon's leading batsman of his generation and a dependable all-rounder, bowling swing and cutters, he was a powerful and majestic scorer of runs, best known for the strength and beauty of his cover drives. During the tour of India in 1932/33, he became the first batsman to score a century (130) on the Feroz Shah Kotla ground, New Delhi. He worked as a Manager with the Rubber Control Department. In 21 first-class matches for Ceylon he scored 977 runs (average 25.05) and took 22 wickets (average 39.36). He was awarded the MBE in 1953 for services to cricket.

Muralitharan, Muttiah. b Kandy 17 April 1972. rhb. rob. He has turned modern spin bowling into a mixture of art and alchemy. He loves to entertain and does this best by the enjoyment he receives from consistently outwitting the best batsmen in the world with a mixture of spin, flight and dip. Determined to keep ahead of whatever defence the batsmen can offer, he first developed his top spinner and then invented the 'doosra', the off-spinner's googly, so well-disguised that the batsman has no idea which way the ball will turn. Since he cannot be played off the pitch on the back foot, the only method is to move to the pitch of the ball but he makes this difficult by his ability to vary the point at which the ball will suddenly dip from its flight and reach the ground. He delivers the ball with his right-arm bent, a result of a deformity present at birth, and his wrist action is more flexible than that of other spin bowlers. Together, these have led many pundits to question the validity of his action and accuse him of 'throwing'. On Boxing Day 1995, in a test match in Australia, he was no-balled for throwing and in a one-day international, ten days later, he was repeatedly no-balled. His action has been investigated by the ICC on at least two occasions, using the most up-to-date technology and filming his delivery from at least 27 different angles. Following extensive scrutiny, the ICC has declared his action to be legal. He is easily Sri Lankan's most successful bowler. In 109 test matches, he has scored 1,115 runs (average 11.98) and taken 669 wickets (average 21.66); in 290 one-day internationals he has scored 491 runs (average 5.84) and taken 444 wickets (average 22.65).

Sathasivam, Mahadevan. b Kitiyakara 18 October 1915. d Colombo 9 July 1977 (heart attack at seaside restaurant). rhb. Probably the most flamboyant cricketer produced by Ceylon, he combined perfect poise and power with his own batting style. With a good eye and footwork, he entertained the crowd with his finesse in cuts, glances and drives. He seemed to rise to the occasion, with his best performances coming on difficult wickets or against the best opposition. He was at his best in the 1940s when he became the first Ceylonese to score a double century in international cricket and made two other

centuries. Towards the end of his career, he went to coach in Singapore and Malaysia, and played for both countries. He thus has the unique distinction of captaining three different countries in cricket against visiting English and Australian teams. His career was limited by the 1939-45 War so that he played for Ceylon in only 6 first-class matches. In these, he scored 366 runs (average 30.50). He had a reputation for a Bohemian lifestyle. He was implicated in the murder of his wife but acquitted on all charges.

Tennekoon, Anura Punchi Banda b Anuradhapura 29 October 1946. rhb. An outstanding schoolboy cricketer, he developed into one of Sri Lanka's greatest players. He was a regular choice for Sri Lanka in the late 1960s and 1970s and impressed in matches against Pakistan and India before Sri Lanka obtained test-match status. He was among the most successful of Sri Lanka's captains. In 61 matches for Ceylon and Sri Lanka, he scored 3,481 runs (average 36.26). In 34 one-day internationals, he scored 2,163 runs (average 40.81). He later became Secretary to the Board of Control for Cricket in Sri Lanka.

Other leading players: *1890-1914*: V.F.S. Crawford (rhb. rf); C. Horan (lhb. sla); J.L.S. Vidler (rhb. rm). *1920-1940*: A.M.H. Kelaart (lhb; rm); L.E. Bakelman (lhb. lm/sla); E.G.S. Kelaart (lhb. rob); Dr C.H. Gunasekara (rhb. rm). *1945-1960*: B. Navaratne (rhb. wk); S. Jayasinghe (rhb. rob); A.C.M. Lafir; V.G. Prins. *1960-1980*: H.I.K. Fernando (wk); S. Wettimuny (rhb); L.R.D. Mendis (rhb); D.S. de Silva (rhb. lbg). *1980-2000*: S.T. Jayasuriya (lhb. sla); A. Ranatunga (lhb. rm); R.S. Mahanama (rhb); H.P. Tillakaratne (lhb. occ wk). *Present day*: W.P.U.J.C. Vass (lhb. lfm); M.S. Atapattu (rhb); K.C. Sangakkara (lhb. wk); W.U. Tharanga (lhb).

Women: *Present day*: W.R.P. Fernando (rhb. rob); C. Seneviratne (rhb. rm); S. Sivanantham (rhb. rob).

Playing record
Test Matches

	Won	Lost	Tied	Drawn
England	5	8	0	5
Australia	1	11	0	6
South Africa	4	8	0	5
West Indies	5	2	0	3
New Zealand	5	9	0	10

India	3	10	0	13
Pakistan	7	15	0	10
Zimbabwe	10	0	0	5
Bangladesh	7	0	0	0
Total	47	63	0	57

Unofficial Tests*

India	1	6	0	7
Pakistan	1	9	0	3
Bangladesh	3	0	0	0
East Africa	1	0	0	0

One-day matches

	Won	Lost	Tied	No Res
World Cup	25	30	1	1
Other ODIs	216	234	2	19
ICC Trophy	4	1	0	1

Twenty20

2	1	0	0

* Matches played before being granted test-match status

Highest team score

952-6 dec	v India, Colombo	1997

Lowest team score

71	v Pakistan. Kandy	1994

ODI

55	v West Indies, Sharjah	1986/87

Before test match status

39	Ceylon XVIII v Australians, Colombo	1884
42	Ceylon President's XI v International XI, Colombo	1968

Highest individual score

374	D.P.M.D. Jayawardene v South Africa, Colombo	2006

Best bowling

9-51	M. Muralitharan v Zimbabwe, Kandy	2001/02

Best wicket-keeping

6 (6c)	S.A.R. Silva v India, Colombo	1985/86

Women

Test Matches

	Won	Lost	Tied	Drawn
Pakistan	1	0	0	0
Total	1	0	0	0

One-day matches

	Won	Lost	Tied	No Res
World Cup	4	12	0	3
Other ODIs	25	15	0	0

Highest team score

305-9 dec	v Pakistan, Colombo	1997/98

Lowest team score

ODI

57	v Australia, Pretoria	2004/05

Highest individual score

105*	C.R. Seneviratne	v Pakistan, Colombo	1997/98

Best bowling

5-31	C.R. Seneviratne	v Pakistan, Colombo	1997/98

ODI

5-2	S. Sivanantham	v Pakistan, Colombo	2001/02

Best wicket-keeping

ODI

4 (2c 2st)	E.M.T.P. Ekanayake	v West Indies, Kingstown	2002/03

SUDAN

A CRICKET club was established in Khartoum in the early part of the last century by British residents and officials attached to the Sudanese government under the Anglo-Egyptian mandate. The game was also introduced to Gordon College, the leading school of the expatriate community. No international fixtures were ever played but, up to the start of the Second World War, the best players often represented All-Egypt and, when on leave, played for a combined Egypt and the Sudan in occasional matches at Lord's against the MCC. Some cricket continued at the club until the early 1980s but it now seems to be either defunct or dormant and no cricket has been played in Sudan for nearly two decades.

SURINAM

Affiliate member of the ICC: elected 2002

CRICKET WAS first played in Surinam by Indians brought in as indentured labourers in the 1890s to work on the sugar estates. The first cricket club, Royal Scott's, was established in 1885. Since then the game has been variously supported by migrants from British Guiana (later Guyana) and other English-speaking Caribbean countries, and by expatriates from The Netherlands. A national association was formed in 1931. The game flourished in the 1950s and 1960s but then went into decline. The early 2000s have witnessed a revival with at least seven clubs in Paramaribo and a further eight in Nickerie District in the west on the Guyanan border. Surinam made its first international appearance in the American Affiliates Tournament in 2004 but with no success. In 2006 they hosted Division 3 of the American

Championships, winning the tournament and qualifying for promotion to Division 2.

Leading players: *Present day:* S. Meghoe; D. Sewanan; S. Oemraw.

Playing record

One-day matches

	Won	Lost	No Res
American Affiliates Tournament	0	4	0
American Championships Division 3	3	0	0
American Championships Division 2	1	3	0

Highest team score

ODI

252-4	v Brazil, Paramaribo	2006

Lowest team score

ODI

106	v Panama, Howard (Panama)	2003/04

Highest individual score

ODI

103*	S. Meghoe	v Brazil, Paramaribo	2006

Best bowling

ODI

5-31	S. Mangal	v Turks and Caicos, Paramaribo	2006

SWAZILAND

THE BRITISH introduced cricket into Swaziland in the early 1900s when the game was played by settlers in the north-west of the country working in mining and forestry. A cricket team existed in the small settlement of Piggs Peak in 1904 and a club was started in Mbabane in 1910. Thereafter, the game survived as a minority sport, played mainly by the British and white South African residents in a small number of exclusive country clubs. Matches were played against South African clubs and district teams. Following independence in 1967, the game became multiracial involving the British and Indian communities with a small number of African players. International matches were played with some success against Zambia and Lesotho in the 1980s. Swaziland hosted the Zone VI African one-day tournament in 1992 but have not competed since. The Swaziland Cricket Association is attempting to revive the game by concentrating on schools. International cricket has been restarted at youth level. Swaziland beat Mozambique in an Under 17 match at Malkerns in December 2005 and matches are proposed at Under 19 level against South Africa.

SWEDEN

Affiliate Member of ICC: elected 1997

ERIK BLIDBERT, who learnt his cricket in London, formed the Lyckans Samfund Cricket Club in Göteborg in 1883. Exactly how long it lasted is uncertain but it could only have been a few years. An attempt to introduce cricket in the early 1920s at the international boarding school at Lundsberg in Värmland was similarly unsuccessful. A more permanent footing for the game was established in 1948 when staff at the British Embassy formed the Stockholm Cricket Club. Fluctuations in staff numbers with an interest in playing soon forced the club to open its membership which now includes expatriates from many Commonwealth countries, in addition to Swedes. Early matches were played against crews of visiting ships and Helsinki CC but with the formation of clubs elsewhere in Sweden during the 1970s and 1980s, more local matches became a possibility. The Svenska Cricketförbundet was established in 1989 to promote the game. Sweden made its international cricket debut at the ECF Nations Cup in 1993 and participated in European competitions throughout the rest of the 1990s but with little success. In the ECC Trophy in 2001, all five matches were lost and the country has not competed internationally since. The early 2000s saw Swedish cricket bedevilled by an internal dispute between the SCF and a faction led by Guttsta Wicket Cricket Club, based in Kolsva, who proposed establishing a new governing body which would give greater emphasis to encouraging Swedish participation in the sport. Guttsta Wicket CC boycotted the Swedish national league for three seasons in protest at SCF policies. In 2001 a compromise was discussed with the SCF agreeing a reform which required that clubs participating in the national league must include at least four players who are Swedish citizens, two of whom must be Swedes. Unfortunately, at the Annual General Meeting of the SCF in that year, the proposal was rejected. Swedish cricket suffered a further setback in 2003 when Malmö CC and Malmöhus CC decided to play in the Danish league. At present, individual clubs are thus pursuing their own interests rather than the national cause. Guttsta Wicked CC has established its own Swedish Cricket Academy and runs both junior and ladies teams. However, the future of Swedish cricket depends on more than one club. There is a need to promote the game nationally among young Swedes and this will require a more sympathetic approach from the expatriate community and a more active approach on the part of SCF.

Playing record
One-day matches

	Won	Lost	No Res
ECC Trophy	0	5	0

Highest team score
ODI

200-9	v Portugal, Corfu	1999

Lowest team score
ODI

43	v Croatia, Vienna	2001

Highest individual score
ODI

90*	P. Rehman	v Finland, Vienna	2001

Best bowling
ODI

3-21	E. Folker	v Malta, Oxford	1995

SWITZERLAND

Affiliate Member of ICC: elected 1985

A WATERCOLOUR by Giovanni Salucci entitled *Vue de la Ville de Genève et de Plein-Palais* and painted in 1817 shows cricket being played in Geneva. Cricket was again being played in Geneva by British and Commonwealth expatriates attached to the League of Nations in 1919. It is unlikely, however, that there was any continuity for the game between these dates or between those who played before the First World War and those who founded the Geneva Cricket Club in 1951. Continuity for cricket in Switzerland lies in the mediaeval village of Zuoz, situated at an altitude of 1,700 metres in the Upper Inn valley of the Engadine. Here in 1923, Gordon Spenser, the

sports teacher at the Lyceum Alpinum, an international school founded at the end of the nineteenth century, introduced cricket to the curriculum. With the help of a succession of cricket assistants from Cambridge during the 1920s and 1930s, the game acquired a degree of permanence with matches played against visiting teams from England and The Netherlands. Very soon it was possible to establish an annual fixture between the School and its Old Boys. In 1985, the School organised a Zuoz Cricket Festival which has since become an annual event. The facilities are good with the ground being large enough to accommodate four matches simultaneously on well-prepared grass wickets. In 1997, the Lyceum Alpinum hosted the European Cricket Federation Nations tournament.

During the 1970s cricket clubs were established by expatriates in Bern, Baden, Basel and Zurich and by staff working at CERN. Representatives of four of these clubs met in Bern in March 1980 and set up the Swiss Cricket Association. Switzerland played its first international matches in the European Cricketer Cup in Guernsey in 1990, where they finished sixth. The country has taken part in the various European competitions for affiliate countries ever since, with moderate success.

Since 1988, Switzerland has staged a cricket-on-ice tournament during the winter on the frozen lake at St Moritz. The event has attracted teams from England, India, South Africa and Hong Kong, as well as Swiss clubs and the Lyceum Alpinum. Unlike ice-cricket played in other countries, such as Estonia and Sweden, and that played at various centres in England in the winter of 1878-79, the St Moritz version is more sophisticated with matting being placed on the ice to form a pitch.

Leading players: *1980-2000:* N. Burrell; J. Boshoff; N. Hamirani. *Present day:* A. Gerrard-Röthlisberger; R. Baleri.

Playing record
One-day matches

	Won	Lost	No Res
ECC Trophy	4	7	0
European Representative Championships	3	2	0

Highest team score
ODI

330	v Austria, Zuoz	1997

Lowest team score

ODI

61	v France, Geneva		2000

Highest individual score

ODI

135	N. Burrell	v France, Geneva	2000

Best bowling

ODI

6-55	M. Barone	v France, Château-Thoiry	2001

SYRIA

SYRIA HAS the honour of the first reference to cricket being played outside England. According to the diary of Henry Tonge, who was attached to the British mission in Aleppo which was then part of Turkey, on the 6th May 1676 some forty English persons on holiday left the city, found a place at which to pitch a tent for dinner and then engaged in a number of sports, including cricket. They returned at 6.00 p.m. The event had no lasting effect as there is no record of cricket having been played in Syria since.

TAIWAN

THERE ARE three main cricket clubs in Taiwan: the Taipei Cricket Association and the Formosa Cricket Club, based in Taipei, and the Kaohsiung Community Cricket Club in the south of the island. All are run by expatriates from Commonwealth countries. They compete annually in a 15 overs-a-side competition for the Taiwan Cup. With most of the expatriates being employed on contracts, there is a high turnover of players. This is hindering the establishment of the game on a more permanent basis.

TANZANIA

Associate Member of ICC: elected 2001
THE EARLIEST cricket in East Africa was played in Zanzibar, the island off the east coast which became part of Tanzania in April 1964. From there it spread slowly to the mainland throughout Tanganyika, Kenya and Uganda. The first matches were played in 1890 by the British Navy as recreation for the officers and crew but very soon fixtures began between the Navy and British settlers. British forces were posted at Lushoto, near Tanga, bringing cricket with them, in 1916. After the First World War when the British took over Tanganyika from Germany under the mandate of the League of Nations, they moved their headquarters to Dar es Salaam. In the early 1920s the British military and civilian officials established the Government Service Sports Club, the Railways Sports Club and the Dar es Salaam Gymkhana. The Indian Sports Club was founded by traders and railway workers. In 1923, the Satchu Pira brothers, Indian businessmen, presented the Satchu Pira Shield for a league competition. This was followed in 1933 by the KJ Cup, offered by the Directors of Karimjee Jivanjee to the winners of a knock-out competition. Thus, by the 1930s, cricket was well established in Dar es Salaam and on 20 March 1935 the leading clubs formed the Dar es Salaam Cricket Association to promote and organise the game. Although the Association was multiracial, the individual clubs were generally representative of separate ethic communities.

In addition to the Gymkhana, which was a European but largely British club, and the Indian SC, there were the Muslim Sports Club, the Goan Sports Club and the Sinhalese Sports Club. The majority of the players in Dar es Salaam were from the Indian sub-continent with Europeans forming a small but important minority. There was little interest in the sport from the African community. Cricket continued in Zanzibar with occasional matches against the Royal Navy and the Dar es Salaam Gymkhana. In 1938 Zanzibar met a combined Dar es Salaam side for the first of a series of matches for the Pardhan Ladak Memorial Shield. Matches between Zanzibar and Tanga began in 1949. The 1930s and 1940s saw the British and Indian communities take cricket to most other areas of the country. Clubs were formed in Moshi, Arusha, Mwanza, Lindi and Mtwara. Since the large distances and the slowness of transport prevented matches between these towns, however, cricket never developed the same hold as it did on the coast.

Distance also inhibited contacts between Tanganyika and Zanzibar and the other countries of East Africa.

The first international fixture was not played until 1951 when Tanganyika went to Nairobi and lost to Kenya by an innings and 27 runs. As the 1950s progressed, a regular series of matches with Kenya and Uganda evolved, leading in 1967 to an annual Triangular and later Quadrangular Tournament. Tanganyika won the tournament in 1968. This was the period when many touring sides visited East Africa and matches were played against the Pakistan Cricket Writers (1956), Sunder Cricket Club (1957), MCC (1957 and 1963), South Africa (SACBOC) (1958), Gujarat (1959), F.R. Brown's XI (1961), a Commonwealth XI (1962), Pakistan International Airlines (1964) and India (1967). Zanzibar met the Pakistan Cricket Writers, Sunder, SACBOC, Gujarat and F.R. Brown's XI. Since many of these sides contained players with test-match experience, it was not surprising that no games against the visitors were won. Tanganyika (later Tanzania) drew four and lost six games and Zanzibar drew one and lost four.

Tanzanian cricket underwent a major change in the early 1970s. Following the nationalisation of the banks and other businesses in 1971, many of the British and Indian communities left the country. Among the cricketers, R.D. and C.D. Patel moved to Zambia. One of the promising young players, John Solanky, had already gone to England in 1967 and did not return, choosing instead to play county cricket for Glamorgan. Cricket standards began to decline and the game contracted in its geographical spread to become concentrated in Dar es Salaam. This did not prevent Tanzania from undertaking their first and only tour outside of East Africa. In February and March 1974, they went to Nigeria and won two and drew one of the three-match series. Since the 1970s, the Tanzanian Cricket Association has concentrated on preventing further declines in the game and on promoting it amongst the Africans. To some extent, both have been successful. In the one-day international competitions for African associate countries, Tanzania finished runners-up in 1994 and 1995. They fell away in the early 2000s, losing all four matches in the 2002 Africa Cricket Association Cup and winning only one match out of five, against Zambia, in the African Associates competition in 2004. But in 2006 they won Division 2 of the African Championships. Africans now comprise some 20 to 25 per cent of the players in the national team.

In contrast to the men's side, Africans make up about half of the Tanzanian women's team. They have also been more successful. Having lost both matches in the inaugural East African Championships in 2002, they hosted the African Championships in 2004 and won all their games to give Tanzania their first trophy in women's cricket.

In 2005, the Tanzania Cricket Association began a development programme designed to increase the number of Africans playing cricket and to re-introduce the sport across the whole country. Particular effort is being given to cricket demonstrations and coaching sessions for boys and girls in schools to encourage teachers to adopt the game as part of the sports curriculum. Such initiatives should ensure that cricket has a strong future in Tanzania for both men and women.

Famous Victories
September 15, 16 and 17, 1968 – Nairobi
Zambia 287 (R. Patterson 90, Pranlal Divecha 5-113) and 248 (B. Ellis 75, Vasant Tapu 4-59)
Tanzania 304 (Zulfiqar Yusuf Ali 69, Jamalu Nanji 60, B. Horton 5-98) and 235-4 (R.D. Patel 73, Badru Bhamji 65*, Taher Ali Amijee 50)
Tanzania won by 6 wickets

Tanzania's victory over Zambia in the last game of the 1968 East African Quadrangular Tournament secured them their first trophy in international competition. On a good matting wicket, several Zambian batsman made starts, notably Daniel Wilson (48), H.G. McLeod (31), S.B. Naik (23) and C.D. Patel (22) but only Roy Patterson converted his into a sizeable score. Pranlal Divecha picked up wickets regularly and was well supported by Vasant Tapu (3-57) and Suresh Rawal (2-64). Tanzania's innings was a similar story with R.D. Patel (37), Praful Mehta (37) and Taher Ali Amijee (23) getting out to Bernard Horton's fast-medium just when they looked set. It was left to Jamalu Nanji and Zulfiqar Yusuf Ali in a fifth wicket partnership of 117 runs to ensure a first innings lead. Zambia's batsmen again fell victim to Vasant Tapu, Divecha (3-100) and Rawal (3-79). Despite contributions from Barry Ellis, C.D. Patel (42) and Patterson (33), Zambia failed to set a challenging target, particularly as Tanzania produced the best batting of the match to ensure a surprisingly easy win.

Women
April 12, 2004 – Annadil Burhani Ground, Dar es Salaam
Uganda 50 (25.1 overs) (Extras 34, F. Omary 3-9)
Tanzania 51-2 (12.4 overs)
Tanzania won by 8 wickets.

Tanzania won the final of the Africa Women's Cricket Tournament quite easily. None of the Uganda side reached double figures against the medium-pace of Fatuma Omary (3-9), Anneth Banali (2-9) and Hawa Salum (2-12). Only a contribution of 29 wides enabled the half-century to be reached. In reply, Hadija Nasibu (10) and Anjelina Mwabalulu (21) took Tanzania close to the target. Once they were out, Anneth Banali (5*) and Monica Pascal (1*) had no difficulty making the remaining runs required.

Leading players: *1945-1960:* R.D. Patel (rhb. wk); C.D. Patel (rhb. rob); A. Fernandes (rhb. rfm). *1960-1980:* Pranlal Divecha (rhb. rf); Vasant Tapu (lhb. lf); Babu Chohan. *1980-2000:* M. Dhirani; V. Kamanya (rhb. rob/lb). *Present day:* A. Kakonzi (rhb. sla); B. Mwita (rhb. rm).
Women: *Present day:* A. Banali (rhb. rm); S. Hamisi (rhb, rob)

Playing record
One-day matches

	Won	Lost	No Res
African Cricket Association Cup	0	4	0
African Six-Nations Tournament	1	4	0
African Championships Division 2	4	0	0

Highest team score
406-8 dec	v Uganda, Nairobi	1968	

Lowest team score
53	Tanganyika v Uganda, Entebbe		1953

Highest individual score
195	S. Rawal	v Kenya, Kampala	1970

Best bowling
7-5	Shashikant Patel	v Tanganyika v Kenya, Dar es Salaam	1960

Best wicket-keeping
4 (3c 1st)	R.D. Patel	v Tanganyika v Uganda, Kampala	1957
4 (3c 1st)	R.D. Patel	v Tanganyika v Uganda, Kampala	1957
4 (4c)	Nazir Hussein	v Tanganyika v Pakistan International Airlines, Dar es Salaam	1964

R.D. Patel's dismissals were in the first and second innings of the match

Women
One-day matches
	Won	Lost	Tied	No Res
East African Championships	0	2	0	0
African Championships	4	0	0	0
World Cup qualifying – African region	2	1	0	0

Highest team score
ODI
207	v Kenya, Nairobi		2006/07

Lowest team score
ODI
63	v Zimbabwe, Nairobi		2006/07

Highest individual score
ODI
56	S. Hamisi	v Uganda, Nairobi	2006/07

Best bowling
5-18	A. Banali	v Kenya, Dar es Salaam	2004

THAILAND

Affiliate Member of ICC: elected 1995
Associate Member of ICC: elected 2005

AT THE end of the nineteenth century many elite families in Thailand sent their children to England for school and university education. They learnt cricket and, on their return, founded the Bangkok City Cricket Club in 1890 and played the first game of cricket recorded in Thailand at the Pramane ground in November that year. An invitation was extended to Singapore Cricket Club to visit Bangkok but it was rejected because of the fear of a cholera epidemic. Cricket as a sport played by Thais, however, failed to develop and by the early 1900s, the game was virtually confined to expatriate residents. The Royal Bangkok Sports Club established cricket facilities in July 1904 and played their first matches in December 1905. Contacts were remade with Singapore and in January 1909, a team, entitled Siam, visited Singapore and, somewhat surprisingly, beat a Straits Settlements side by an innings and 39 runs. A return match was played in Bangkok in 1910 for a trophy offered by Sir Ralph Paget, a British minister in Bangkok, which Siam also won, this time by 39 runs. In December 1911, the Straits Settlements returned to Bangkok to take the cup. No further matches were played.

Cricket survived in Thailand as a recreational activity for members of the Royal Bangkok SC with occasional matches being played against the crews of visiting ships of the British Navy, Penang Sports Club and Hong Kong Cricket Club. In the 1960s Thailand became an exciting and exotic place to visit and the Royal Bangkok SC was able to entice several overseas teams to the city as part of their tours of South East Asia. The club's team, however, were no match for E.W. Swanton's side (1964), Worcestershire (1965), J. Lister's International XI (1968) or the MCC (1970), all of which comprised first-class cricketers, many with test-match experience. Nevertheless, their visits did much to publicise the game amongst the expatriate community and encourage them to form additional cricket clubs. New grounds were developed at the Polo Club and the Asian Institute of Technology and at Chiengmai, in the north of the country. Two players who did much to keep cricket going were Anton Perera, the sports editor of the *Bangkok Post*, and Ronald Endley, who worked for Volvo in Bangkok and persuaded the company to offer the Volvo Trophy for matches against Hong Kong. The first of these, marking Thailand's first international appearance, took place as a two-day fixture at the Polo Ground in January 1990 and was drawn. This is the only two innings match played by Thailand. In 1991, the trophy was contested as a one-day international. In 1992, it formed the basis of a three-way contest with Malaysia. No further matches were played since it was superseded by the Tuanku Ja'afar Cup.

The early 1990s was the most successful period to date in Thai cricket. They won two matches out of three in the 1992 Volvo Cup, losing to Hong Kong, the winners of the tournament and won one of their three matches in each of the Tuanku Ja'afar Cup contests in 1994 and 1995. As the ICC tightened its regulations regarding qualifications, Thailand was forced to field weaker teams. This period also coincided with a decline in overall standard and problems of finance which prevented Thailand from taking part in the 1998 and 1999 Tuanku Ja'afar Cup contests. The early 2000s have seen an increase in activity with promotion of the game at Under 19, Under 17, Under 15 and Under 13 levels, a greater interest in the sport by Thais and a new generation of players. In 2005 and 2006 Thailand hosted the Asian Cricket Council Emerging Nations Tournament, taking over the role from Nepal. This resulted in wins over

Brunei and Bhutan but consistent defeats by the Maldives, thereby placing Thailand among the weaker group of Asian nations. One of the highlights of the Thai season is the annual six-a-side tournament held in Chiengmai which attracts many teams from overseas.

Leading players: *1980-2000:* Luke Buathong Thongyai; Larn Kathatong Thongyai; Zeeshan Hasib. *Present day:* Zeeshan Khan; A. Tanwani.

Playing record
One-day matches

	Won	Lost	No Res
Asian Cricket Council Trophy	1	12	1
Tuanku Ja'afar Trophy	4	24	2
ACC Emerging Nations	3	4	1

Highest team score
ODI
247	v Malaysia, Bangkok	1992

Lowest team score
36	v Malaysia, Kuala Lumpur	1996

Highest individual score
ODI
132	Luke Thongyai	v Malaysia, Singapore	1996

Best bowling
9-26	N. Sutton	Siam v Singapore, Singapore	1909

Best wicket-keeping
4 (3c 1st)	W.H.R. Taylor	Siam v Singapore, Singapore	1909

TIMOR-LESTE

CRICKET STARTED in Timor-Leste shortly after the country achieved its independence from Indonesia in 1999 and expatriates arrived to assist with aid programmes and help with reconstruction. Some Australians formed the Dili Cricket Club which now includes four Timorese among its playing members. Occasional matches are played against expatriate Indian sides, mainly local tradesmen. The sport is played as a friendly recreational activity. The players face problems of security, shortage of equipment and the lack of a ground. Matches take place on a very rough soccer field. In 2001, Timor-Leste took part in the Bali six-a-side tournament at Denpasar in Indonesia.

TOKELAU

AS IN several of the South Pacific islands, a local version of cricket is played by both men and women with teams of twenty or more on each side. Wickets are coconut matting laid on compacted bare earth. Matches are usually social occasions accompanied by feasting. The standard MCC version of the game is not played even though the territory is administered by New Zealand. The opportunities for its development are limited because only about 1,500 people live on the three coral atolls which comprise the territory and there is a shortage of land. However, since some 7,500 Tokelauans are resident overseas, many in New Zealand, it would be feasible to produce a national side if enough of them were sufficiently interested to take up the sport.

TONGA

Affiliate Member of ICC: elected 2000

DR MOLITONI, a missionary, introduced cricket to Tonga in 1874 after which further missionaries and teachers taught the game to youth groups attached to local churches. The local people were enthusiastic and soon started matches between various villages. Cricket thus developed as a rural recreational activity in addition to taking hold in Nuku'alofa, the capital. The Tonga Cricket Association was formed in 1930 by which time the game was being spread by Tongans who had moved temporarily to Fiji and New Zealand for their education. Several Tongans played for the Central Medical School in Suva whilst it was one of Fiji's stronger sides. Despite this long history, cricket was a sport of the minority and well behind rugby union, rugby league and soccer in popularity. International matches did not start until 1979 when Tonga finished fourth in the South Pacific Games. Tongan cricket has suffered from the lack of visiting sides and thereby the limited opportunity to play against good class opposition. It is only since the ICC started organising tournaments for the Pacific and East Asian countries that much international cricket has been played. This has also boosted domestic cricket. Eight teams from the main island of Tongatapu now contest the main domestic competition. There are also two teams on Eua, the country's second largest island. Tonga finished second in the 2002 Pacifica Cricket Championships and in the 2004 East Asia Pacific Challenge.

Leading players: *1980-2000:* S. Tupou. *Present day:* M. Faivakimoana (rhb. rm); F.H. Latu (rhb. wk); V. Tupouniua (rhb. rm).

Playing record
One-day matches

	Won	Lost	No Res
Pacific Championships	6	4	0
South Pacific Games	2	2	0
East Asia Pacific Challenge	2	2	0
East Asia Pacific Cup	4	2	0

Highest team score
ODI

352-7	v New Caledonia, Apia	2002

Lowest team score
ODI

64	v New Hebrides, Suva	1979

Highest individual score
ODI

144*	M. Faivakimoana	v Indonesia, Fuji	2004

Best bowling
ODI

8-26	Kolatau	v Western Samoa, Suva	1979

TRISTAN DA CUNHA

ALTHOUGH CRICKET has been played on Tristan da Cunha since late Victorian times when the game was introduced by British missionaries, the small size of the population, the limited accessibility and the lack of space have prevented it from being any more than an occasional recreational activity. Matches were played on matting laid at Hottentot Fence. The game ceased in 1961 following the volcanic eruption which caused the evacuation of the whole population. When the islanders returned in 1963, the same constraints prevailed and despite having spent much of their exile in Hampshire, England, they had not developed sufficient interest in the sport as to want to promote it more actively. Some matches were played in the 1970s when the British administrator on the island, S.G. Trees, was enthusiastic but when a game was organised in 1996, it was the first on the island for ten years.

TURKEY

THE BRITISH influence on the Bosporus in the late nineteenth century was sufficiently strong to support expatriate cricket. The Hansons, a banking family, formed a club at Kandilli, on the eastern side of the Bosporus some six kilometres north of Uskūdar (Scutari), in the 1870s but it did not survive the collapse of the family's fortunes. The Mediterranean fleet played local residents at Moda, close to the ancient city of Kaldiköy (Chalcedon) in 1879 and for some years in the 1880s there was a local league comprising teams from Moda, Bebek, Therapia and Istanbul (Constantinople). In 1923, I Zingari visited and played Constantinople Cricket Club at Şişli (Chichli) and the Dardanelles at Cannakale, winning both matches easily. Flight-Lt Cecil Wigglesworth, who played one first-class match for the RAF in 1927, scored 128 for Constantinople. Occasional matches were organised with Odessa and between Turkey and Romania. By the end of the 1920s, the British presence declined and the game became extinct. Cricket was not played again in Turkey until the mid 1990s when students from the Indian sub-continent at the Middle Eastern Technical University in Ankara formed a club. Matches were organised against teams from various Commonwealth embassies and against Bilkent University where Indian students had also formed a team. By 1999 there were enough teams to organise a tournament for the Faisal Khalid Memorial cup.

TURKS AND CAICOS ISLANDS

Affiliate Member of ICC: elected 2002
CRICKET IS played on at least three of the eight islands which make up the territory, namely Grand Turk, Salt Cay and South Caicos. These compete annually for the Goldblatt Cup. Although there is considerable enthusiasm for the sport, the geographical position of the islands to the south-east of the Bahamas has kept them isolated from the influence of the West Indies. The territory took part in two tournaments for affiliate countries in the Americas with limited success but finished second in Division 3 of the American Championships in 2006.
Leading players: *Present day:* M. Baptiste (wk).

Playing record
One-day matches

	Won	Lost	No Res
American Affiliates Tournament	2	5	0
American Championships Division 3	2	1	0

Highest team score
ODI
290-8	v Chile, Paramaribo		2005/06

Lowest team score
ODI
58	v Belize, Howard (Panama)		2003/04

Highest individual score
ODI
125*	E. Ceasear	v Chile, Paramaribo	2005/06

Best bowling
ODI
5-4	C. Saunders	v Brazil, Paramaribo	2005/06

Best wicket-keeping
4 (4c)	M. Baptiste	v Belize, Howard (Panama)	
			2003/04

TUVALU

MISSIONARIES BROUGHT cricket to Tuvalu in the late nineteenth century but the local population has shown only limited interest in the game. Occasional matches are played against Kiribati. In 1979 a team competed in the South Pacific Games in Suva but their lack of experience and practice was all too apparent. They finished seventh and last.

UGANDA

Associate Member of ICC: elected 1998
CRICKET WAS probably first played in Uganda around 1900 as the game spread inland to the territories of East Africa from Zanzibar where it was played in 1890. The Entebbe Sports Club is known to have existed in 1901 but its foundation could be a year earlier. As a club for British residents, officials and visiting military, its early years were hampered by small numbers and the lack of any opposition. Fixtures were largely scratch matches between the 'club eleven'

and 'the rest'. In 1907, the Kampala Sports Club was formed, probably based on an earlier foundation, the Mengo Cricket Club whose precise origins are not known. These two British-based teams combined in 1914 to form a Ugandan side to play against a team from Nairobi, also British, representing the British East African Protectorate. The Ugandans won the match by 5 wickets. The 1914-18 War brought a temporary halt to cricket and it was not until 1920 that the return match was played, the British East African Protectorate winning by 48 runs in Nairobi.

Although no international cricket was played during the Inter-War years, the period saw the consolidation of the game in the country. The British established a cricket club at Jinja in the 1920s, regular fixtures were resumed between Kampala SC and Entebbe SC and an annual match began between Kampala SC and a Planters side. The 1920s also saw clubs founded in Kampala by the Indian and Goan communities. Although these clubs reflected the social structure of the period, organised according to ethnic groups, club tournaments provided the opportunity for frequent contacts between the different communities. The Kampala Goan Institute was the leading club for much of the 1930s, generally winning the Lowis Cup, a trophy provided for inter-club competition by Louis Gerald Sequeira of Messrs. Lowis and Company, a sports shop. Negotiations were started in 1930 for a tour of Uganda by the Incogniti Cricket Club from England, but they collapsed before the arrangements could be finalised. The first overseas team from outside East Africa to play in Uganda was the officers and crew of HMS *Effingham* who travelled up from Mombasa to take part in various sports against local opposition in Entebbe. Following a suggestion made in a letter to the *Uganda Herald* in September 1935, it was agreed at a meeting attended by representatives of various clubs in Entebbe, Kampala and Jinja to establish an annual Triangular Tournament between representative European, Indian and Goan teams. The tournament started in 1936 and lasted into the 1960s. In 1949 the tournament became Quadrangular with the inclusion of an African team. The enthusiasm of all communities to work together and promote the game was expressed in 1952 by the formation of the Uganda Cricket Association.

As in much of East Africa, the Africans started playing cricket much later than the immigrant communities who brought the game with them from Britain, India and Ceylon. Africans came in contact with the game in two ways. Those from the wealthier families sent their children to schools established by the British where they were taught the game as part of the sporting curriculum. Others found employment as ground staff and net bowlers at the clubs. It was not until the 1940s that the Africans were playing in sufficient numbers and at a high enough standard that they could compete against teams of the other communities. Nevertheless, the Africans in Uganda took to cricket earlier and more enthusiastically than those in the other East African countries. The leading African player of the time, O.G. Mawanda, was selected for Uganda when they played its first international against Kenya in 1952. Although they were beaten comprehensively by 254 runs, the following year they achieved their first international victory, beating Tanganyika by 5 wickets. From the mid 1950s to the mid 1970s, Ugandan international fixtures mirrored those of Kenya and Tanganyika, with matches in the East African Triangular competition, later Quadrangular with the entry of Zambia, and games against visiting touring sides. These included the Pakistan Cricket Writers (1956), Sunder Cricket Club (1957), MCC (1958, 1963), South Africa (SACBOC) (1958), Gujarat (1960), F.R. Brown's side (1961), Pakistan International Airlines (1964), India (1967), Warwickshire (1968), J. Lister's International XI (1968) and Hyderabad Blues (1971). All matches against the tourists were lost except for draws against Warwickshire and the Hyderabad Blues.

Major Problems

Cricket suffered major problems in the mid 1970s and the early 1980s as a result of the policies adopted by the Ugandan government under Idi Amin. Many Asians and Europeans left the country, never to return, and with them went many cricketers. Although the game was strong enough amongst the Africans to survive, the government considered cricket to be an elitist sport, introduced by foreigners. Cricket was starved of funding and, if that was not sufficient to prevent Uganda playing international matches overseas, passports were either not released or permission to travel simply not granted. Uganda's appearances in the East African Quadrangular became intermittent and, when they did appear without their best players and without much practice, they were easily defeated. It was not until the mid 1990s that Ugandan cricket recovered sufficiently for the country to appear regularly again in international cricket. With a team drawn from the African and, by now, a much smaller Asian community, experience was gained by playing in various East African and pan-African competitions. Standards improved surprisingly quickly. When Uganda left the East and Central African Cricket Conference in 1998, efforts were concentrated on producing as good a team as possible for the ICC Trophy competition in 2001. So successful were they that Uganda were one of the surprise teams of the tournament. They finished top of their group, winning all five matches, before losing the qualifying play-off for the final stages against the United Arab Emirates. They qualified for the 2005 ICC Trophy by finishing second to Namibia in the African Associates competition but then disappointed, winning only one game in the tournament to finish last of the twelve competing countries. Nevertheless, Uganda has established itself as the fifth best African country at cricket and the only one in which Africans form the majority of the players.

Uganda's women were also successful in the early 2000s. They won the East African Championships in 2002 and were second to Tanzania in the African Women's Tournament in 2004.

Famous Victory
April 23, 24 and 25, 2004 – Wanderers Ground, Windhoek
Namibia 165 and 289 (D. Keulder 67, D.B. Kotze 60, K. Kamyuka 5-83)
Uganda 274 (N.K. Patel 74, F. Nsubuga 62) and 183-5 (B. Musoke 72)
Uganda won by 5 wickets

Namibia were clear favourites to win this ICC Intercontinental Cup match on their own ground but, on winning the toss, their batting surprisingly failed against a consistent all-round bowling attack of Kenneth Kamyuka (2-32), Richard Okia (2-32), Franco Nsubuga (2-27) and Joel Olweny (2-26). Uganda also found run-scoring dif-

ficult, the early order falling to Deon Kotze (3-30). A sixth-wicket partnership of 56 by Nand Kishore Patel and Junior Kwebiha (23) secured first innings lead. Nsubuga then supported Kishore in ensuring the lead was substantial. Namibia responded with an opening partnership of 111 by Danie Keulder and Johannes van der Merwe (48) and with night-watchman Kola Burger (33), Deon Kotze and Gerrie Snyman (32) all contributing they were able to set Uganda a challenging target. Kamyuka bowled well for his five wickets. After losing three wickets for 33 runs, Ben Musoke, Nsubuga (41) and Kwebiha (25*) ensured a reasonably comfortable victory.

Leading players: *1920-1940:* H. Davidson; S. Hooper; D.P. Khetani. *1945-1960:* J.V. Wild (rhb. rs). *1960-1980:* Salaudin Khan; Kishore Vasani (lhb. sla); Upendra Patel. *1980-2000:* S. Walusimbi (rhb. lm); N. Bibodi (rhb. rob); B. Musoke (rhb. rm). *Present day:* K. Kamyuka (rhb. rfm); J. Kwebiha (rhb. rm); F. Nsubuga (rhb. rob). **Women:** *Present day:* F. Najjumba (rhb. rm); M. Ayato (rhb. rm).

Playing record
International matches

	Won	Lost	Drawn
ICC Intercontinental Cup	1	3	0

One-day matches

	Won	Lost	No Res
ICC Trophy	6	6	1
African Cricket Association Cup	2	2	0
African Six-Nations Tournament	4	1	0

Highest team score

436	v Kenya, Nairobi		1968

Lowest team score
ODI

41	v South African Development XI, Pretoria		1996/97

Highest individual score

201	V. Noordin	v Zambia, Kampala	1970

Best bowling

7-54	J. Nagenda	v Kenya, Kampala	1975

ODI

7-29	J. Kwebiha	v Nigeria, Lusaka	2004

Best wicket-keeping

5 (1c 4st)	Nazir Awan	v Tanzania, Ndola	1969

Women

One-day matches

	Won	Lost	Tied	No Res
East African Championships	4	0	0	0
African Championships	2	2	0	0
World Cup qualifying – African region	1	2	0	0

Highest team score

ODI

201	v Namibia, Dar es Salaam	2004

Lowest team score

ODI

50	v Tanzania, Dar es Salaam	2004

Highest individual score

ODI

42*	R. Akwenyu	v Namibia, Dar es Salaam	2004

Best bowling

5-12	C. Namugenyi	v Kenya, Nairobi	2006/07

UKRAINE

CRICKET WAS first played in the Ukraine by British residents at Odessa in 1881. The game continued as a recreational activity until the end of the nineteenth century with occasional fixtures against Constantinople. As far as is known, no further cricket took place until the late 1990s when a number of expatriates, mostly from the Indian sub-continent and the Middle East, started to organise matches in Vinnitsa. There are now some nine teams in the city which form the basis of a Ukrainian league launched in 2002.

UNITED ARAB EMIRATES

Affiliate Member of ICC: elected 1989
Associate Member of ICC: elected 1990

IT IS not surprising that cricket should be a major sport of the United Arab Emirates when about half of the resident population are of Pakistani, Indian or Sri Lankan origin. However it was not until the 1970s that these communities became sufficiently numerous for clubs to be formed and the game established on a firm foundation. Before that, cricket had been played by the Royal Air Force and troops of the British Commonwealth stationed in what was then the Trucial States during the 1939-45 War. The cricket pitches they installed around the air base in Sharjah were then used by British and other foreign nationals for occasional matches. Just about the time that there was a danger that the game would not survive, Asians began settling in the country as tradesmen and businessmen in the 1960s. Towards the end of that decade, Arabs in Sharjah and Dubai, returning from their education in India and Pakistan, established clubs. The 1970s then witnessed the arrival of many more immigrants from the Indian sub-continent as workers in a wide range of service industries. Domestic tournaments were established and, on 20 February 1976, the first international fixture took place, a one-day match at Sharjah against Pakistan International Airlines. After the visitors had made 345 for the loss of five wickets from their 50 overs, the game was abandoned with the UAE on 88 for four after 28 overs because of rain! In 1980, Cricket Associations were set up in Sharjah and Dubai to ensure the expansion of the game.

Although there is little doubt that cricket would have developed anyway, the rapid rise of the game in the Emirates owes much to the patronage of Sheikh Abdul Rehman Bukhatir. The son of a wealthy Arab sheikh, he was educated at the BVS Parsi School in Karachi where he obtained an infectious enthusiasm for cricket. As he acquired wealth from his interests in oil and banking, he invested some of it in constructing a cricket stadium at Sharjah with a grass wicket which could be used for international cricket. Opened in 1981 and costing US$10 million, it hosted its first major international competition in 1984 when India, Pakistan and Sri Lanka contested the Asia Cup. Numerous one-day tournaments involving the test-match countries have been staged there since. First used for the game between Pakistan and the West Indies in January 2002, it has also proved a useful neutral venue for test matches when security problems have prevented countries from playing at home. Four test matches have been held there to date. The presence of cricket involving the best countries and the best players in the world has been a stimulus to the local game which is now based on league and knock-out competitions involving teams in Sharjah, Dubai, Abu Dhabi and Ajman.

The Emirates Cricket Board was established by

Government decree in 1989 to promote and regulate the sport. Following the country's admission to the ICC in 1990, the immediate aim was to develop a strong national side for the 1994 ICC Trophy in Kenya. Two heavy defeats by The Netherlands in Sharjah in March 1990 showed that much work needed to be done. The approach adopted by the ECB was to attract a number of good players from India, Pakistan and Sri Lanka to take up employment and residence in the country so that they would satisfy the ICC regulations regarding eligible players by the time of the competition. Those attracted included Riaz Poonawala, who had represented India at Under 25 level, Mazher Hussain, who had toured Zimbabwe with Pakistan B, and Johanne Samarasekara, who had played for Sri Lanka B. An impression of the resulting assemblage being a national team was created by selecting an Arab, Sultan Muhammad Zarawani, who learnt cricket during his education in Pakistan, as captain. Whatever the ethics of this approach, it was extremely successful. The Emirates won the ICC Trophy, beating Kenya in the final, and the victory undoubtedly encouraged more youngsters, particularly amongst the immigrant communities, to take up the game. The result was not without controversy, however. The Kenyan players and cricket authority were angry at being defeated by what some observers described as a team of 'imported mercenaries'. Although the ICC disassociated itself from this and similar criticism, the regulations concerning citizenship and residence were tightened for future ICC-sanctioned competitions.

Major Programme

By winning the ICC Trophy, the UAE qualified to take part in the 1996 World Cup. A major programme of preparation was followed with the Emirates returning to Kenya in December 1994 for a tripartite tournament with Kenya and The Netherlands in which, surprisingly, they finished last. In January 1996, the UAE took part in the Pakistani domestic one-day competition but, after beating Peshawar in the first game, lost their other three matches. The contrast in standard between that required to beat the associate level countries and that needed to compete with teams of first-class status was now all too apparent. The problem of relying on a team of former

first-class cricketers near the end of their careers is that the average age of the team is high. The players no longer have the agility in the field nor the speed of reaction in batting required to cope with top-class bowling. The Emirates were outclassed by South Africa, England, New Zealand and Pakistan in the World Cup but managed one victory, over The Netherlands. It was clear that if cricket in the Emirates was to progress they would have to find some new and preferably younger players and that they would have to promote the game more strongly among its nationals.

The team that played in the Asian Cricket Council Trophy matches in December 1996 and the ICC Trophy in March and April 1997 contained many new players. The policy of having a national citizen as captain was retained, Saeed Al-Saffar replacing Zarawani. Few of the newcomers did well and the team still relied on the performances of Saleem Raza, Azhar Saeed and Arshad Laeeq. Whilst they were the second-best associate side within Asia they were no match for the best associate countries of Europe and North America, a position that continues to this day. With the promotion of Bangladesh to full membership of the ICC, the UAE won the Asian Cricket Council Trophy in 2000, 2002, 2004 and 2006. Results in the ICC Trophy have been mixed, however, and the Emirates have not finished high enough to qualify for the World Cup again. In the two-innings matches of the ICC Intercontinental Cup, they have twice won the Asian leg of the competition but then lost in the semi-finals to Canada in 2004 and Ireland in 2005. The team is still strongly reliant on cricketers either born in Pakistan or born in the Emirates to Pakistani parents. It is the latter group on whom the future of Emirates cricket depends. If 2005 is an indicator, the outlook is not promising. The sixth place in the ICC Trophy was a disappointment but, in the ICC Intercontinental Cup, the comprehensive and unexpected loss by 172 runs to Nepal and the failure of the bowling to contain Ireland as they scored 794 runs in two innings for the loss of eleven wickets were even more worrying.

Famous Victory
**March 6, 1994 – Ruaraka Sports Club, Nairobi
Kenya 281-6 (50 overs) (M.O. Odumbe 87, S.O. Tikolo 54)**

United Arab Emirates 282-8 (49.1 overs) (R.H. Poonawala 71, Azhar Saeed 59, Mohammed Ishaq 51, M.A. Suji 4-61)
United Arab Emirates won by 2 wickets

Kenya were the favourites to win this final of the ICC Trophy on their home ground. Being asked to bat on losing the toss, they lost their first wicket quickly whereupon, in difficult conditions following rain on the previous afternoon, Kennedy Otieno and Maurice Odumbe put on 98 runs. After Otieno was caught and bowled by Azhar Saeed, Odumbe and Steve Tikolo increased the scoring rate in a partnership of 112. The Emirates' bowlers continued to bowl line and length and, well-supported by keen fielding, were able to restrict Kenya to a manageable target, despite the efforts of Tom Tikolo (42 not out off 24 balls) and Edward Odumbe (25 off 22 balls). In reply, Riaz Poonawala and Azhar Saeed were impressive in an opening stand of 141 runs in 28 overs. When Edward Odumbe dismissed both in quick succession and Martin Suji bowled Mazher Hussain (9), three wickets were down and over 100 runs were still needed. Muhammad Ishaq and Vijay Mehra took some time to settle against a freshly-inspired Kenyan attack and the required scoring rate rose to over eight runs per over. Nevertheless, both batsmen gained in confidence and 30 runs suddenly came in only three overs. Ishaq reached his fifty off 36 balls. A hostile spell of pace bowling by Martin Suji and two run-outs, both direct hits, took the game to an exciting finish but Arshad Laeeq (20) mustered enough runs before being dismissed to enable the Emirates to secure victory in the final over with two new batsmen at the crease. The Emirates thus won a major trophy at their first attempt.

Player Profiles

Ali Asad Abbas. b Lahore, Punjab, Pakistan, 6 December 1976. rhb. rfm. He had a remarkable debut in first-class cricket, taking 9 wickets for 74 and 4 for 52 against Nepal in an ICC Intercontinental Cup match in Sharjah in March 2004. He has been the Emirates' leading strike bowler ever since. He played limited overs cricket for Lahore City (1995/96) before migrating to the UAE. In 15 international matches he has scored 295 runs (average 16.38) and taken 83 wickets (average 16.63). In 2 one-day internationals he has made 21 runs (average 21.00) and taken 2 wickets (average 36.50). In 22 other limited overs matches he has scored 75 runs (average 8.33) and taken 28 wickets (average 23.21).

Azhar Saeed, Syed. b Lahore, Pakistan, 25 December 1970. lhb. sla. The leading all-rounder for the Emirates during the 1990s, he played first-class cricket for Lahore City Whites and Lahore City before taking up residence in the UAE. In 22 limited overs internationals he made 672 runs (average 35.36) and took 24+2 wickets (average 24.20).

Other leading players: *1980-2000:* Mohammed Ishaq (rhb. rm); Arshad Laeeq (rhb. rfm); Saleem Raza (rhb. rob). *Present day:* Khurram Khan (lhb. sla); Arshad Ali (rhb. rm); Mohammed Nadeem (rhb. wk).

Playing record
International matches

	Won	Lost	Drawn
ICC Intercontinental Cup	2	3	4
ACC Fast Track Tournament/			
Premier League	9	1	2

One-day matches

	Won	Lost	No Res
World Cup	1	4	0
Other ODIs	0	4	0
Pakistan domestic competition	1	3	0
ICC Trophy	22	9	1
Asian Cricket Council Trophy	32	2	1
Six Nations Challenge	3	2	0

Highest team score

356-8 dec	v Scotland, Sharjah		2006/07

ODI

459-4	v Brunei, Kuala Lumpur		2006

Lowest team score

76	v Nepal, Kathmandu		2005

ODI

54	v The Netherlands, Toronto		2001

Highest individual score

143	Arshad Ali	v Nepal, Sharjah	2003/04

ODI

213*	Arshad Ali	v Brunei, Kuala Lumpur	2006

Best bowling

9-74	Ali Asad	v Nepal, Sharjah	2004/05

Best wicket-keeping

7 (7c)	Mohammed Taskeen	v Hong Kong, Hong Kong	2005

UNITED STATES OF AMERICA

Associate Member of ICC: elected 1965

ALTHOUGH MANY of the early settlers in the American Colonies in the late seventeenth and early eighteenth centuries were escaping from conditions in Great Britain, they did not discard all aspects of British culture in their new environment. They took cricket with them. The earliest record of the game in America is contained in the diary of William Byrd II of Virginia who noted playing cricket with his family and friends on the front lawn of his estate at Westover on the banks of the James River on 25 April 1709. In 1737, William Stephens, a plantation owner on the Oglethorpe colony in Georgia mentioned cricket being played on the main square. The first recorded match was between eleven New Yorkers and eleven Londoners, played on the site of the Fulton Fish Market in Manhattan on 29 April 1751. The New Yorkers won, scoring 80 and 86 to the Londoners' 43 and 47. The game that all these people played was, of course, that which had been brought from England characterised by two stumps, underarm bowling and curved bats. Changes to this style of game had to wait for them to be imported by new settlers from Britain. As a result, the American game was often a decade behind that in England. It is not entirely clear who was playing cricket in the first part of the eighteenth century. Certainly it was played by British soldiers stationed in the Colonies and by expatriate English residents. However, there is evidence that American soldiers in South Carolina and Boston also played and that cricket was introduced into American colleges. Before cricket could take a firm hold among those born in America, however, the American Revolution led to a move to boycott goods and activities associated with Britain. After the Colonies obtained their independence, cricket had to be restarted. Hence there was little continuity between the early games on colonial plantations and where cricket eventually obtained a stronghold.

Once the United States had achieved its independence, cricket underwent a slow revival. For many years the game survived through informal matches, largely involving English immigrants but increasingly including Americans who had played the game as college students. There is evidence from diaries and newspaper reports that cricket existed in this way in Connecticut, South Carolina, Massachussetts and New York. A major impetus occurred in the 1820s with the arrival of mill workers from Sheffield and Nottingham who brought with them updated versions of the game with straight bats and length bowling. By the late 1830s, round-arm bowling had been introduced. The geographical distribution of the American textile industry meant that cricket began to develop more rapidly in New England, New York and Pennsylvania than elsewhere. It is likely that a club had existed at Brooklyn in New York as early as 1789.

First Organised Fixture

The match generally recognised as the first organised fixture in the USA took place in New York near the Ferry House Tavern in Brooklyn on 20 September 1838 when English residents from Sheffield played English residents from Nottingham for a wager of US$100. A return game was arranged for 22 October for US$400 but with the teams called New York and Long Island. Many of the players seem to have been working-class immigrants. On 23 April 1840, a group of wealthy English traders and businessmen established a ground in Manhattan on the corner of Bloomingdale Road and 42nd Street and founded the St George Cricket Club. The club employed a Yorkshire professional, Sam Wright, as groundsman, the father of George and Harry Wright who went on to combine careers as professional cricketers with success in baseball. The name, St George, seems to have been chosen as a way of indicating a degree of exclusivity in its membership which, following the tradition of many clubs in England, was open only to the society's elite. Thus, despite the egalitarian aspirations of American independence, cricket in the USA developed the same class structure as that prevailing at the time in England. There was considerable antipathy towards the club in its early years and no other side would play them. Eventually St George's were forced to offer a challenge with a $100 prize to any club that could beat them. Even this produced no opponents and the club started to look to Toronto, Canada, for matches. At the invitation of a 'Mr Phillpots', St George's club travelled to Toronto in 1840 to play the local club but found they were the victims of a hoax (see Country Profile for Canada). Nevertheless, Toronto honoured the match. Attempts to organise a return fixture failed in 1841, 1842 and 1843 but, eventually, agreement was reached for a match at St George's in 1844, played for a stake of US$1,000. The size of the wager led to St George's deciding to enrol as 'honorary members' some players from the Union Cricket Club in Philadelphia, a move which the Canadians strongly criticised as unethical, a criticism which was dampened somewhat after Toronto won the match by 33 runs. This game is now recognised as an official match between the United States and Canada and the first international cricket match in the world.

The move to include players from Philadelphia was a reflection of the spread of organised cricket from New York to that city. Cricket was first played there by immigrant mill workers from England. Lindley Fisher, who was taught cricket at Haverford College, organised a club for the English workers in the Wakefield Mills. Other Englishmen attached themselves to clubs organised by Tom Senior, a Yorkshireman who ran the Cricketer's Arms on Bank Street, and William Jarvis, who hailed from Leicestershire and ran the Star Hotel. In 1831 Robert Waller, an Englishman who ran an import business, brought together some of the English mill owners and a group of cricketers who played at the ground of George Tichnor on the west bank of the River Schuykill, near Fairmount Bridge, to form the Union Cricket Club with a base at Harding's Tavern. The club was promoted as a rival to St George's, both being largely English in their memberships, but disbanded in the early 1840s when Waller moved to New York. Unlike the situation in New York, however, there was a strong interest in cricket in Philadelphia among the American-born. In 1845, William Rotch Wister founded a cricket club in Germantown with his friends, mostly students at the University of Pennsylvania. Wister went on to form the Philadelphia Cricket Club on 10 February 1854 and some of his friends founded the Germantown Cricket Club on 10 August 1854. On 19 November the following year, some younger cricketers who were denied membership of these clubs, formed the Young America Club. By the late 1850s, cricket was becoming established at Haverford College. Founded in the 1820s and later to become an important nursery for cricketers

in Philadelphia, it is not clear when the game was first played there. Wister refers to it being introduced in 1834 by William Carvill, an Englishman employed by the College to landscape the gardens but the college's records do not mention Carvill's appointment until 1842. Fisher's initiatives at the Wakefield Mills imply that cricket must have been established at the College well before Carvill's appointment although the extent and popularity of the activity amongst the pupils is uncertain. The College closed in 1845 and re-opened in 1848 when Dr Lyon, an English teacher in a nearby school, helped to revive the game.

'Ungentlemanly Behaviour'

By the mid-1850s cricket in New York and Philadelphia was firmly established and there was a strong interest in testing the strength of the American game against international opposition. Matches against Canada had come to a halt after a dispute in the game in 1846 and were not resumed until 1853. The incident occurred when Canada had lost three wickets in their second innings and were still sixteen runs behind. Samuel Dudson was about to take a caught-and-bowled when the Canadian batsman, T. Helliwell, charged the bowler and prevented him from taking the catch. In his anger, Dudson picked up the ball and threw at it the Canadian. When the umpires called for the game to restart, the Canadians left the field in protest, criticising the Americans for 'ungentlemanly behaviour'. It appeared that Helliwell, citing the Laws of Cricket for 1702, believed his action was legal. Unfortunately, the entitlement of the batsman to hinder a bowler from taking a catch between the wickets had been made illegal in 1787. The incident illustrates the length of time that it can take to implement changes made to the laws in England through person-to-person contact overseas.

The suggestion that some of England's best cricketers should visit America was proposed by William Pickering after the USA–Canada match in 1856. It took the efforts of Robert Waller, now with St George's club in New York, to secure the necessary sponsorship and in September 1859, the first overseas tour took place. George Parr's team, which included John Wisden, John Jackson and Tom Lockyer, played against the USA XXII at Hoboken NJ and Camac Woods PA. Since the best teams in England were generally playing against local sides of eighteen or twenty-two at that time, the concept of matches against the odds was not a slight on the standard of the local cricket. However, the local players were no match for the Englishmen and lost both games easily. The best of the local cricketers was Tom Senior who took six wickets for 20 runs, including the hat-trick, in the Englishmen's first innings of the second game. Despite the defeats and the poor timing of the tour which meant that in the last game at Rochester against a combined USA-Canada XXII the weather was so cold that the Englishmen fielded in coats and gloves, there is no doubt that the tour would have been a stimulus to the local game had not the United States succumbed to civil war in 1861 and cricket ceased. When it resumed in 1865, the USA had lost one of their most promising cricketers, Walter L. Newhall, believed to be the first American-born player to score a century and the only local batsman to play the bowling of Senior successfully; he was drowned trying to ford the Rappahannock River in Virginia in flood.

The late 1860s and 1870s were a period of growth in American cricket in New York and Philadelphia. Although a few English professionals had migrated to America in the 1850s, there was now a major influx. They were employed as coaches and groundsmen and the result was a marked improvement in the standards of play and wickets. This was helped by the experience of playing against further visiting teams from England under E. Willsher (1868), R.A. Fitzgerald (1872) and R. Daft (1879), and Ireland (1879). Fitzgerald's side included W.G. Grace and A. Appleby, Daft's included Arthur Shaw and Frederick Morley, both bowling combinations which were too strong for the Americans. These visits were the precursors of a regular pattern of tours during the 1880s, 1890s and early 1900s. Visits were organised either as business ventures for the professional players or as cricketing holidays for the amateurs. Whilst some teams combined both amateurs and professionals, amateur visits began to dominate as the business interests of English cricketers switched to Australia where the standard of play was higher.

The growth of cricket among the American-born owed much at this time to the Newhalls, a great cricketing family. In addition to Walter, mentioned above, there were his brothers, Charles, a fast round-arm bowler who dismissed

W.G. Grace more often than any other American bowler, Daniel, a stubborn batsman at his best in a crisis, George, a reliable batsman and wicket-keeper, Robert, arguably the best Philadelphian batsman of the period, and Harrison. They were the basis of the Philadelphian side throughout the 1870s. Charles, Daniel, Robert and George were in the side which represented Philadelphia in the Halifax Cup, a competition organised in Halifax, Nova Scotia, at the initiative of Norman Wallace to bring together the best cricketers from North America in teams (twelve-a-side) representing Canada, Philadelphia and officers of the English military. Philadelphia won the competition and took the Halifax Cup home where it became the trophy for the major inter-club competition from 1880 until 1926. The same four Newhalls played for Philadelphia against the Australians in October 1878, a game which is now regarded as Philadelphia's first first-class match. Philadelphia gained a first innings lead of 46 over D.W. Gregory's side which contained Charles Bannerman, Fred Spofforth, Billy Murdoch and John Blackham. The match ended in a draw, the first time that Philadelphia had not been defeated by a team from outside North America. The Australians would probably have won the game if they had not wasted 70 minutes of play on the third and last day by refusing to play after disputing an umpiring decision, one of several made by H.W. Brown, the Philadelphian umpire, which they had disagreed with. The Australians asked that he be replaced to which the Philadelphians agreed provided that H.F.J. Freeman, the Australian umpire was also replaced. The match eventually resumed with the same umpires. Whatever the correctness or otherwise of Brown's decisions, the Australian protest might have carried more weight if they had not already gained a reputation for disputing umpiring decisions whilst on tour in England.

Pleasing Aberration

The fixture against Australia was a pleasing aberration in Philadelphia's records against visiting teams. Philadelphia averaged 11.4 runs per batsman against the bowling of Spofforth and Frank Allan whereas the averages against English teams between 1859 and 1881 ranged from 2.6 to 7.4; against the Australians in 1882, they averaged only 4.2. Whilst it could be suggested that such results were inevitable whilst cricket remained an amateur game for wealthy Americans, educated in private schools and at university, the records of the local professionals were no better. Most turned out for New York who were easily defeated by the same visiting sides. The best of the professionals was undoubtedly George Lane, a left-handed batsman and left-arm medium pace bowler who had played for Nottinghamshire. It was soon being suggested that, in addition to the professional coaching, Philadelphian cricket would benefit from a tour of England. At the end of 1883, one representative from each of the leading five clubs in Philadelphia formed a committee to raise the necessary funds. A total of $8,200 was obtained from public subscription. Although some of the best players, notably George and Daniel Newhall, were unable to go, an all amateur team of fourteen players was selected. Eighteen matches were played, all against amateur sides of varying strength, the team winning eight and losing five.

Great Boost

The 1884 tour gave a great boost to cricket in Philadelphia which was further strengthened by visits from sides raised by E.J. Sanders in 1885 and 1886 and a second visit by Ireland in 1888. In December 1887 and January 1888, a United States team, chosen mainly from Philadelphia, toured the Caribbean, playing eleven matches. They defeated the West Indies in a low-scoring game at Georgetown by nine wickets. Philadelphia undertook a second tour of England in 1889, playing twelve matches, winning three and losing three. Although the record of the 1884 and 1889 tours looks similar, the 1889 side played stronger opposition. They also averaged 25.2 runs per wicket compared to their predecessor's 17.8. By now Philadelphia was being recognised as first-class in standard. Although the game did not reach that level elsewhere in the country, it continued to flourish in New York and Boston and clubs were formed in many other cities. By the 1880s cricket was established in Baltimore, Detroit (where the Peninsular Cricket Club also attracted players from Canada), Pittsburgh, Chicago (where the Canadian player, Edward Ogden, settled and Tom Armitage, a Yorkshireman played professionally), St Louis and San Francisco (where the British diplomatic

community had started the game before the American Civil War). Through the initiatives of English settlers, the game also spread to a number of rural communities in New York, New Jersey, Illinois and Wisconsin. In the early 1850s cricket was played in Hawaii but the game declined after the Americans took over administration of the islands in 1900.

In 1878 the Cricketers' Association of the United States was formed in Philadelphia, initially to select the team to play the Australian tourists. Intended as a national body, the Association became attached to Philadelphia, largely because the clubs in other cities, like St George's in New York, were dominated by English society and resented any proposals made about the game by the Philadelphia's Americans. Similarly, the Philadelphians viewed any suggestions made by the other clubs as challenges by foreign residents to the American view of the game. After the Association became defunct, the Associated Cricket Clubs of Philadelphia was established to control club and international cricket in the city, including the arrangements for the 1897 tour of England. Philadelphia differed from the other parts of the United States where cricket was played in being the only centre with a well-established upper or leisured class with sufficient wealth and time to take part in cricket tournaments and overseas tours. Although professionals were employed as coaches, umpires and groundsmen, Philadelphia shunned professionalism amongst its players. Arthur Wood, the former Derbyshire player who emigrated to the United States as a professional and settled in Philadelphia, had to regain his amateur status before he could represent Philadelphia and become one of their leading players.

During the 1890s some attempts were made to get women's cricket started. The Seabright Lawn Tennis and Cricket Club in New Jersey organised several cricket matches for its lady members in 1888. By the late 1890s there were women's teams in Staten Island and at several clubs in Philadelphia. Cricket was also introduced into two private girls schools, Mrs John Cunningham Hazen's school in Pelham Manor, New York, and Rosemary Hall in Wallingford, Connecticut. These efforts never prospered, however, and lawn tennis soon became the dominant summer sport for women whilst cricket died.

Philadelphia's greatest achievements in international cricket were their two victories over the Australians, by an innings and 69 runs in 1893 and an innings and 60 runs in 1896, and their performances on the three tours of England (1897, 1903 and 1908) where they were accorded first-class status and held their own against the county sides. Their best players could easily have commanded places in the top county teams. Yet, by the end of the first decade of the 1900s, there were signs that Philadelphian cricket was declining in standard. As economic conditions changed, fewer people were able to maintain the life-style of the leisured class and had less time to devote to cricket. Lawn tennis and baseball were taken up instead as activities which required less time and less expensive equipment. The younger players who should have been the next generation of Philadelphian cricketers were clearly not of the same standard. The tour to England of 1908 marked the end of matches between Philadelphia and top-class English teams. The visit of the MCC in 1907 was the last by an English first-class side. It is questionable whether more effort by the MCC to retain contacts could have provided the necessary stimulus to prevent the decline. The three further tours that took place before the First World War, one by Ireland in 1909 and two by the Australians in 1912 and 1913, had no lasting effect. The 1913 tour is important because the Australians played against a West Indian black team in New York. Although the latter were beaten easily, the match indicates that West Indians were settling in New York in the early 1900s and that they were continuing to play the game that they had learnt in the Caribbean. The first West Indian black cricket club in New York dates to 1893 and by the time of the Australian fixture there were at least twelve such clubs in the New York area.

Very Low Standard

After the 1914-18 War, cricket in Philadelphia suffered from a lack of interest and a decline in ability. Visits by Incogniti and Free Foresters confirmed that the standard had fallen to below that of the best English club sides. Most clubs in Philadelphia folded between 1920 and 1930. The conditions which allowed cricket to develop in Philadelphia in the 1880s and 1890s no longer existed and the clubs were unable to replicate the more egalitarian environment which enabled cricket to survive elsewhere in the country, albeit as a minority sport played to a very low standard. The leisured and wealthy classes were badly hit by the Wall Street crash and the Great Depression. Between the Wars the focus of American cricket shifted to Chicago where Karl Auty, an Englishman by birth, promoted the game, St Louis, and Los Angeles, where C. Aubrey Smith, who had captained England in South Africa in 1888/89, organised the game in Hollywood.

According to Tom Melville, an American sports historian, cricket failed in the USA largely because those who supported it and played it retained too much of its exclusivity as an English game. No attempt was ever made to promote and develop it as a mass sport with an American character. This situation still remains. The only difference between the present day and a hundred years ago is that instead of being played in accordance with English traditions, it is now played to Caribbean and Indian sub-continental traditions. Its development is hindered by a combination of its continued amateur status and the geography of the United States. Although there are some 600 clubs and over 10,000 players across the country, they play in some 40 separate league competitions. Contact between clubs in different leagues is inhibited by the great distances between the main cricketing centres. For a side in New York to meet one in California would require players to obtain leave from work for at least three days to cover travel and playing time. Without sponsorship to cover the costs, this is just not possible on a regular basis.

Some efforts have been made to organise the game nationally, notably by John Marder who was instrumental in establishing the United States Cricket Association in 1961 and in restarting the annual fixture with Canada in 1963 with American sides chosen from clubs across the country. In 1968, a United States team toured England although only two of the eighteen players were American. By the late 1970s a sizeable section of the cricket community in the United States became increasingly critical of the USCA (renamed the USA Cricket Association in 1981), accusing it of failing to promote the game amongst Americans, administrative incompetence and sloppy accounting. They established the United States Cricket Federation as an alternative body to run the game. Clearly, having two bodies working in opposition to each other was not a sensible way of promoting a minority sport and the two organisations agreed to merge in 1998. In 2004 the ICC developed a plan, known as Project USA, to promote cricket throughout the country. They appointed an American businessman with experience in sport development to run the project. Some members of the USACA, however, opposed the plan, seeing the project as encroaching on its territory and possibly diverting funds from the national body. When the ICC became concerned about the USACA's commitment to cricket as a national sport and its financial management they withdrew the proposal and wrote formally to the USACA questioning whether, in its current form and with its current officers, it could play any constructive role in developing the sport within the USA. Such blunt language had never before been used by the ICC in its dealings with any national association, but it was not entirely clear whether the approach just reflected the ICC's exasperation with the USACA or whether there was a political element of anti-Americanism in the decision.

ICC's frustration was compounded by the poor performance of the American national side which is now almost entirely expatriate and reliant on cricketers who have migrated to the United States at the end of first-class careers in their own countries. Some of the West Indians, notably Faoud Bacchus, Colin Lambert and Hamish Anthony, are former test or one-day international players but they seem unable to reproduce the form that brought them success in their home countries. It is almost as though their main interest is playing for fun and relaxation rather than the honour of representing their adopted country. Notwithstanding their generally poor record, the national team is capable of springing surprises. In 2000, in the West Indies domestic one-day competition, a sensational two-wicket victory was obtained over Barbados. A five wicket victory over Scotland in the Six Nations Challenge in 2004 enabled them to win the tournament and qualify as the associate country participant in the 2004 ICC Champions Trophy where, as expected, they lost their matches against New Zealand and Australia as well as acquiring the unenviable distinction of being the oldest side ever to take part in an official one-day tournament.

In 2003 the United States of America Women's Cricket Association was formed to promote cricket amongst women throughout the mainland state of the US and the Caribbean territories of St Thomas and St Croix. The organisation combined with its counterpart in Canada to send a North American team to the West Indies Women's Cricket Championships in Grenada in July that year. Although no matches were won, the side was by no means outclassed. No further international appearance has been made.

The future of American cricket remains uncertain. The immediate requirement is for the USACA to reform, look to the future rather than to tradition and work with the ICC to promote cricket to Americans at all levels for men and women. It is noticeable that on the official web-site of the USACA there is no mention of women's cricket, yet following the merger of the ICC and the IWCC the national bodies of each country have a formal requirement to promote the women's game.

Famous Victory
September 29, 30 and October 2, 1893 – Belmont Ground, Elmwood PA
Philadelphia 525 (F.H. Bohlen 118, W.W. Noble 77, H.I. Brown 59*, G.S. Patterson 56)
Australians 199 (G. Giffen 62, J.B. King 5-78) and 258 (A.C. Bannerman 79*, G.H.S. Trott 58)
Philadelphia won by an innings and 68 runs

The Australians were ill-prepared for this match. They had arrived late in New York from their sea-crossing of the Atlantic and were transported immediately from the docks to Belmont by a private railway train on the Pennsylvanian Railroad. George Patterson chose to bat on winning the toss for Philadelphia and the Australians without sleep and still with their sea-legs, fielded and bowled appallingly. When Philadelphia had reached 124 for three, eight catches had already been dropped. Frank Bohlen and William Noble had a partnership of 180 for the fifth wicket but Bohlen was dropped three times. As the Australian bowlers tired, Henry Brown and Frank Ralston (47) added 90 for the ninth wicket to be followed by a partnership of 61 for the last wicket between Henry Brown and Bart King (36). With the exception of George Giffen, the Australians were unable to deal with the inswing of King who was well-supported by Henry Brown (3-41) and three good catches by Arthur Wood. Forced to follow-on, Alex Bannerman carried his bat in a stay of three hours but Henry Trott was the only one to offer much support as Philadelphia alternated their bowlers. The wickets were shared by King (2-90), Henry Brown

(1-28), Patterson (1-48), Walter Scott (3-41), John Muir (2-14) and Reynolds Brown (1-10). This was Philadelphia's first victory over the Australians and their highest team score in first-class cricket.

Player Profiles

King, John Barton (Bart). b Philadelphia 19 October 1873. d Philadelphia 17 October 1965. rhb. rf. Acknowledged as the finest American cricketer in history and one of the best fast bowlers of all time, he was an expert baseball pitcher and he used this experience to develop his 'swerver' or 'angler', a fast ball that swerved in the air and then dipped in late from leg towards the batsman – he adapted this ball to bowl both a fast good-length break-back and a faster inswinging yorker. He took 42 per cent of the wickets taken by Philadelphia in international matches during the time he played for them. No bowler in first-class cricket has exceeded his strike rate of 1 wicket per 23.34 balls. He was also an effective batsman who often opened the innings; he had good eyesight, long reach and powerful shoulders but also a very sound defence. In 64 first-class matches for Philadelphia he scored 2,102 runs (average 20.40) and took 415 wickets (average 15.65). In 17 other international matches he made 531 runs (average 24.13) and took 116 wickets (average 9.55).

Patterson, George Stuart. b Philadelphia, 10 October 1868. d Penn Hospital, Philadelphia, 7 May 1943. rhb. rm. One of the finest cricketers produced by the USA, arguably ranking second to J.B. King, he was a reliable stylish batsman with a wide range of strokes and a strong defence. He was also a bowler of quality with a very high delivery and good command of length and direction. Dubbed the 'W.G. Grace of American cricket', he holds the record for the highest individual score made by an American (271), the only double-century recorded in first-class American cricket. He was an attorney in the legal department of the Pennsylvania Railroad. In 33 first-class matches for Philadelphia he scored 1,598 runs (average 33.29) and took 58 wickets (average 24.08). In 13 other international matches he made 466 runs (average 24.52) and took 46 wickets (average 17.13).

Other leading players: *1835-1860:* W. Comery; W.R. Wister; W. Crossley (rhb. rmob). *1860-1890:*

C.A. Newhall (rhb. rf(r)); S. Meade (lhb. lfm(r)); D.S. Newhall (rhb. rs(r)/lobs); W.C. Lowry (lhb. sla(r)/sla). *1890-1914:* J.A. Lester (rhb. rs); F.H. Bohlen (rhb); P.H. Clark (rhb. rfm); J.H. Scattergood (rhb. wk). *1920-1940:* W.P. O'Neill (lhb. lm/sla); C.C. Morris (rhb). *1960-1980:* O. Durity; D.R. Weekes; B.B. Ramnanan. *1980-2000:* K.R. Khan (rhb. wk); A.D. Texeira (lhb); N.S. Lashkari. *Present day:* S.J. Massiah (rhb); M.R. Johnson (lhb. wk); H.R. Johnson (rhb. rmf).

Playing record
International matches

	Won	Lost	Drawn
ICC Intercontinental Cup	1	1	2
Other first class*	25	43	10
International Series+	32	23	10

* Matches played by Philadelphia between 1878 and 1913
+ Matches against Canada between 1844 and 1995

One-day matches

	Won	Lost	No Res
ODI	0	2	0
West Indies domestic competitions	1	8	4
ICC Trophy	26	24	6
Americas Cup	12	4	2
ICC Six-Nations Challenge	3	2	0

Highest team score
541 Philadelphia v Bermuda, Haverford 1923
The highest score by Philadelphia in a first-class match is 525 against the Australians at Belmont in 1893. The highest score in Philadelphian first-class cricket is 689 by G.S. Patterson's XI against A.M. Wood's XI at Elmwood in 1894.

Lowest team score
32 v Canada, Toronto 1854
ODI
32 v Kenya, Kuala Lumpur 1996/97

Highest individual score
164 C.C. Morris Philadelphia v Nottinghamshire, Nottingham 1903
Two higher scores have been recorded in Philadelphian first-class cricket: 271 by G.S. Patterson for G.S. Patterson's XI v A.M. Wood's XI at Elmwood in 1894 and 182 by A.M. Wood for the Gentlemen of Philadelphia v Players (USA) at Manheim in 1892.

Best bowling
10-54 J.B. King Philadelphia v Ireland, Haverford 1909
King also bowled G.A. Morrow, the not out batsman, with a no-ball.

Best wicket-keeping
6 (5c 1st) J.H. Scattergood Philadelphia v P.F. Warner's XI, Belmont 1897
6 (6c) M.R. Johnson v Canada, Fort Lauderdale 2004

URUGUAY

CRICKET BEGAN in Uruguay in the 1860s when the British started to settle in and around Montevideo to run cattle ranches, set up meat processing and packing plants and invest in the railways. Although cricket was essentially a recreational and social activity, the first international match took place in April 1868 when a group of players from Montevideo played host to the Buenos Aires Cricket Club. The fixture then became a regular event up to the Second World War (see Country Profile for Argentina). Several clubs were formed during the late nineteenth century, the most important being the Montevideo Cricket Club, founded in 1871, and the Central Uruguay Railway Cricket Club, founded in 1891 as an association for British workers attached to the various Uruguayan railroad companies. The latter club eventually evolved into Peñarol, one of the best-known soccer clubs in the country. Cricket never extended outside the capital city and, after the First World War, most matches involved players only from Montevideo CC. The standard was low which was not surprising since the British population was much smaller in numbers than that in Buenos Aires and the country did not attract players with first-class cricket experience. Montevideo were beaten by the MCC by an innings and 204 runs in 1926, by Brazil by 10 wickets in 1928, and by Sir Theodore Brinckman's XI by 475 runs in 1938. Most of the British residents left the country during or soon after the Second World War and cricket died out. Efforts are now being made by to revive the game and a Uruguayan Cricket Association has been formed.

Leading player: *1920-1940:* H.L. Pennock.

UZBEKISTAN

A SMALL number of expatriate Indians attached to an Indo-Uzbeki health care company began organising cricket as a recreational activity on Sunday afternoons in 1997. Since 1999 they have also arranged an annual fixture, 30 overs a-side, between a Commonwealth XI, comprising expatriates from India, Pakistan, Bangladesh and Malaysia, and a British Embassy XI.

VANUATU

Affiliate Member of ICC: elected 1995

THE EARLY history of cricket in Vanuatu remains undocumented. The game may well have been brought to the country by missionaries early in the twentieth century but, at best, it remained an unorganised minority sport. It was not until the end of the Second World War that the game became more firmly established as a result of the initiatives of P. Colley, Commander of the British Police, J. Lançon, a French engineer and J.C. Stegler from the Burns Philp Company. The Vila Cricket Club was founded in 1945 and this evolved into the New Hebrides Cricket Association in 1978, renamed the Vanuatu Cricket Association in 1980 when the country changed its name on independence. Today there are some 4,000 cricketers of which 75 per cent are ni-Vanuatu, the remainder being expatriate residents from Australia, New Zealand and the United Kingdom. International fixtures started in March 1977 with a match against Fiji. Since then Vanuatu has competed regularly in the South Pacific Games and the various Pacific and East Asian competitions organised by the ICC. In 2005, the country hosted the East Asia-Pacific Cup, playing matches at Independence Park and the Kazaa Field in Port Vila. With wins over Indonesia and Samoa, Vanuatu played Tonga for in the third-place play-off and gained a surprising six wicket victory.

In common with some of the other South Pacific Islands, 'traditional' cricket is popular, particularly amongst women. It is organised by the South West Efate Traditional Cricket Association which is affiliated to the VCA. Since 1997, seven women's clubs from the villages around Port Vila have taken part in an annual competition. This has spurned an increasing interest by women in the normal version of the game and there are now six women's clubs in the Port Vila area.

Leading players: *Present day:* A. Mansale (rhb. rob); A. Nasak (rhb. rfm); R. Tatwin (lhb. wk).

Playing record
One-day matches

	Won	Lost	No Res
Pacifica Championships	3	7	0
South Pacific Games*	2	6	0
East Asia Pacific Cup	3	3	0

* matches played in the 1979 and 2003 competitions; detailed records of the 1987 and 1991 competitions have proved unobtainable.

Highest team score

ODI

284-7	v New Caledonia, Auckland		2000/01

Lowest team score

ODI

53	New Hebrides v Papua New Guinea, Suva		1979

Highest individual score

ODI

90	Kaipaba	v New Caledonia, Nouméa	1991

Best bowling

ODI

6-42	Rezel	v New Caledonia, Nouméa	1991

Best wicket-keeping

ODI

4 (4c)	R. Tatwin	v Indonesia, Port Vila	2005
4 (4c)	R. Tatwin	v Japan, Port Vila	2005

VENEZUELA

CRICKET HAS been played in Venezuela ever since Caracas Cricket Club was founded in 1952. The game is largely expatriate consisting of players from Britain and the Caribbean. Occasional matches are played against club sides from Miami, Trinidad, Belize, Colombia and Panama. In 1999 and 2000 Venezuela sent sides to the South American Championships. In five matches, the only victory was over the Guyana Masters in Lima in 1999. Lack of finance has prevented further participation in this competition.

Leading player: *1980-2000:* Fazal Mathura.

VIETNAM

VIETNAMESE CRICKET is focused on Hanoi Cricket Club, founded in 1993, which organises a 30 overs-a-side tournament between teams representing Australia, India and the Rest of the World, played on football pitches at the Air Force grounds. So far attempts to organise fixtures with Phnom Penh Cricket Club and clubs in Thailand have come to nought. The club is keen to increase its forty to fifty strong playing membership and to encourage Vietnamese to take up the sport. So far, only one Vietnamese who learnt the game when studying in Melbourne, is involved. Since membership is partly based on embassy staff, there is quite a high turnover.

Leading players: *Present day:* N. Sellathurai; S. Kalra; Arvinder Singh.

WALES

AN ANNOUNCEMENT in the *Hereford Journal* for 6 May 1785 referring to the first meeting of the season of Swansea Cricket Club in accordance with the previous year's resolution implies that cricket was already established in the Swansea area in the early 1780s. It is likely that in the early nineteenth century, cricket was played throughout the Principality as a recreational activity by the landed gentry, many of whom copied the way-of-life of their English compatriots. Wealthy landowners would have provided patronage for newly-formed clubs and had the time to organise them. Through them cricket spread to the artisans and farmers in the rural areas as they were needed to augment the numbers of players in the village teams. Records of early Welsh cricket are sparse and it is not until well into the nineteenth century that definite dates can be assigned to the formation of clubs. County sides organised by the landowners were the first to emerge with Monmouthshire being formed in 1823, Breconshire in 1825, Pembrokeshire in 1830 and Montgomeryshire in 1853. By the 1840s and 1850s, the growth of towns associated with the industrialisation of South Wales led to the formation of many cricket clubs so that, in this part of Wales, cricket became an urban game played by factory workers and miners. The large number of clubs and the larger population meant that South Wales became the focal area for Welsh cricket. This was where professionalism and league cricket emerged among the clubs run by the steelworks and coalmines in contrast to the more amateur approach of the north and centre of the country. Here, in the clubs of both the towns and the villages, the attitudes of the players and organisers were more akin to those of the village clubs in England with players from public schools and universities. Near Conwy the McAlpine family developed a private ground at Marchwiel and in the 1920s and 1930s ran cricket weeks in the country-house style.

Organised cricket was developed first in the south. The first representative match was played in 1855 when twenty-two of Wales met the All England XI at Cardiff. All England made further visits in 1856, 1858 and 1859 and the United England XI undertook a fixture in 1857. *Ad hoc* county matches were arranged in the 1860s throughout the Principality but standards and interest were highest in the south. The South Wales Cricket Club was founded at Newport in 1859. Its most important activity before its demise in 1887 was the annual tour it organised to London for matches against the MCC and the Gentlemen of Surrey. For a short period in the mid 1860s, the club seemed to contain more Gloucestershire players than Welshmen and managed to obtain the services of W.G., E.M. and H. Grace. Although it did not survive, the South Wales club provided the inspiration for the officials of the Cardiff and Swansea Cricket Clubs to form Glamorgan County Cricket Club in 1888. Along with Monmouthshire and Carmarthenshire, Glamorgan played in the English Minor Counties Championships prior to 1914. The development of county cricket in Wales thus became associated, at its highest level, with English County Cricket. Carmarthenshire dropped out of the Minor Counties competition after 1911 and Glamorgan after 1914. When cricket resumed after the First World War, Monmouthshire continued in the Minor Counties until 1934 but Glamorgan achieved first-class status and entered the English County Championships in 1921. Based on the urban centres of South Wales and bound into English cricket, Glamorgan never developed the status of a Welsh national side. Indeed, the county drew many of its players from outside Wales, yet, at the same time, became a focus for the best Welsh players who wanted to become professional cricketers.

Sydney Barnes Recruited

In 1923 a Welsh Cricket Union was founded to develop cricket at the national level. Between 1923 and 1930, Wales played fixtures against Ireland, Scotland, the MCC and some of the overseas teams on tour of England. Many of these matches were considered first class. The team was chosen from the best professional and amateur players available at the time and so included those from Glamorgan if they did not have a county fixture. They also included residents and so Wales were able to recruit Sydney Barnes, the ex-England and Staffordshire player, for a few matches towards the end of his career. When the Principality stopped playing international cricket after the 1930 season, Welsh cricket constituted Glamorgan at first-class level, the club competitions of the South Wales and North Wales leagues and various friendly matches between club sides. It continued in this format until 1968 when the Welsh Cricket Association was formed as the governing body for Welsh amateur cricket.

Under the auspices of the WCA, Wales resumed international fixtures with Ireland in 1972 and Scotland in 1975. In 1979 they were invited to play in the inaugural ICC Trophy, replacing Gibraltar who withdrew before the start of the tournament. Wales returned to Minor Counties cricket in 1988, competing as Wales Minor Counties Cricket Club. The complicated administrative structure of Welsh cricket poses problems for deciding when a match can be truly described as an international. The overriding responsible body is the England and Wales Cricket Board. The presence of this body means that the only first-class cricket in Wales is played by Glamorgan which has the same status as an English county. Cricketers who play for Glamorgan can be considered for the English national side. Similarly, as seen above, Wales Minor Counties has the same status as an English Minor Counties side. However, their players do not qualify automatically to play for English Cricket Board elevens but can play for their Welsh counterpart instead. This is essentially the national side which represented Wales in the Triple Crown competition. The umbrella body coordinating cricket in Wales is the Cricket Board of Wales (Bwrdd Cricet Cymru) which is affiliated to the England and Wales Cricket Board and comprises the Welsh Cricket Association, Glamorgan County Cricket Club, Wales Minor Counties Cricket Club, the Welsh Schools Cricket Association, the Sports Council for Wales and the Welsh Women's Cricket Association. The status of Welsh matches was further confounded between 2002 and 2004 when Wales played an annual one-day match against England as practice for the English team. For these matches, the Welsh team comprised Welsh-born professional players with Glamorgan and the English counties, the top Welsh amateurs and an overseas professional.

The same issues of status affect matches played by the Welsh women's team. Although women in Wales have played cricket at club level for some fifty years or more, it is only in the last few years that the women's game has become organised nationally. The Welsh women made their international debut in 2005 when they played in Division 3 of the English County Cup against Worcestershire, Warwickshire and Northamptonshire. Also in that year they hosted the European Women's Championships in which they beat Ireland and Scotland but lost to England and The Netherlands.

There can be no doubt that in both men's and women's cricket Wales could be one of the top six countries in Europe if its administrative structure could be adjusted to enable proper national sides to be fielded and official international fixtures to be played. More drastic changes would be needed to allow Wales to become an Associate member of the ICC since the links to the England and Wales Cricket Board would need to be changed for either the CBW or the WCA to be recognised as the official governing body. If Wales is serious about international cricket on a par with Scotland and Ireland, however, these issues will need to be addressed.

Leading players: *1920-1940:* J. Mercer (rhb. rfm); N.V.H. Riches (rhb); J.T. Bell (rhb). *1980-2000:* M.H. Davies (rhb. wk); G.P. Ellis (rhb. rm); A.C. Puddle (lhb). *Present day:* J.P.J. Sylvester (rhb. rob).
Women: *Present day:* H.J. Lloyd (rhb. rm); M.J. Davies.

Playing record

International matches

	Won	Lost	Tied	Drawn	Ab
First-class matches	5	4	0	5	0
Other internationals*	3	9	0	13	1

* Matches against Ireland, Scotland and Zimbabwe.

One-day matches

	Won	Lost	Tied	No Res
ICC Trophy	2	2	0	0
Triple Crown	5	19	3	0

Highest team score

555-6 dec	v Sussex, Hove	1929

Lowest team score

48	v Scotland, Colwyn Bay	1977

Highest individual score

258*	D.L. Hemp	v MCC, Lord's	1991

Best bowling

9-24	J. Mercer	v Scotland, Perth	1923

Best wicket-keeping

4 (3c 1st)	S.C. Wilcox	v Minor Counties, Colwyn Bay	1930

ODI

4 (2c 2st)	A.D. Shaw	v West Indians, Brecon	1991

Women

One-day matches

	Won	Lost	Tied	No Res
European Championships	2	2	0	0

Highest team score

ODI

320-5	v Scotland, Cardiff	2005

Lowest team score

ODI

88	v England, Cardiff	2005

Highest individual score

ODI

121*	H.J. Lloyd	v Scotland, Cardiff	2005

Best bowling

3-16	M.J. Davies	v Ireland, St Fagans	2005

WALLIS AND FUTUNA ISLANDS

TRADITIONAL SOUTH Pacific cricket has long been played in the Wallis and Futuna Islands, particularly by women. Matches between the villages form important social occasions. The Wallis and Futuna Cricket Association is attempting to promote the standard version of the game and is being assisted by the New Caledonia Cricket Federation. The immediate aim is to compete as soon as possible in the South Pacific Games.

WEST AFRICA

Associate Member of ICC: elected 1976
MEMBERSHIP CEASED in 2002 when the cricket associations of the individual countries were recognised separately by the ICC.

The first attempts at uniting the various cricketing countries of West Africa occurred in the late 1930s when a proposal was made for Sir Julien Cahn to bring a team on tour. A fixture was arranged against a combined West African side and a multiracial team was chosen from Nigeria, the Gold Coast and Sierra Leone. Unfortunately the tour fell through. No further attempt at unity was made until 1975 when the West African Cricket Conference was formed. The MCC toured West Africa in 1976, playing two matches against a combined West African side, in Freetown and Lagos, and winning both easily. The WACC suffered from the fact that the governments of Nigeria, Ghana, Sierra Leone and The Gambia looked with disfavour on cricket as a game inherited from their colonial past and invested very little money in it. The fifth member, Liberia, was largely inactive because of its internal political problems. As a result the WACC was perpetually short of finance. It also had difficulty coordinating the activities of the cricket organisations in the member countries. West Africa competed in only three of the ICC Trophy competitions. The Conference was unable to prevent a serious decline in cricket in West Africa. Its major achievement was to inaugurate a West African Quadrangular competition in 1991 and to establish it as an annual event which still continues.

Playing record
One-day matches

	Won	Lost	No Res
ICC Trophy	6	10	6

Highest team score
ODI

249	v Bermuda, Olton	1982

Lowest team score

54	v MCC, Lagos	1976

Highest individual score
ODI

106	O.E. Ukpong	v Singapore, Nairobi	1993/94

ODI

5-57	S.A. Fraser	v MCC, Freetown	1976

ODI

5-31	P.D. Vanderpuje-Orgle	v Israel, Kuala Lumpur	1996/97

WEST INDIES

Full Member of ICC: elected 1926

THE FIRST reference to cricket in the West Indies is an item in the *Barbados Mercury and Bridgetown Gazette* on 10 May 1806 related to a meeting of the St Ann's Garrison Cricket Club which must already have been in existence. Two years later the same newspaper gives notice of a proposed cricket match between the Officers of the Royal West Indies Rangers and the Officers of the Third West Indian regiment for a stake of 55 guineas per side. The result of the game has not survived. The first match for which a result is known is that in May 1838 when the 78th Regiment beat the Garrison by 91 runs to 53. In contrast to the 1808 fixture, the Garrison side is known to have included soldiers from the lower ranks. Although it is clear that the earliest cricket was played by the British military, the game soon spread to the plantation owners, financiers, clergy, lawyers, doctors, teachers and others who settled in the West Indies, particularly after the abolition of slavery in 1833. Many of these people were public school and Oxford or Cambridge educated and reasonably wealthy as were those attached to the colonial civil service. They laid the foundation for organised cricket by forming cricket clubs. By 1849 in the parish of St Michael on Barbados, there were the City and the St Michael Clubs. In Jamaica, the St Jago, Vere and Clarendon clubs were established in 1857 and the Kingston Cricket Club in 1863. A club was formed in Antigua in 1840. The Georgetown Cricket Club in Guyana was in existence by 1857.

Cricket was quickly established in the leading schools particularly in Barbados where it was played at The Lodge School and Codrington College in the 1850s and at Harrison College, where a club was formed in 1877. These were essentially schools for the sons of the British well-to-do, modelled in the English public school system, but by the 1890s they were taking the children of wealthy West Indians of African descent. As the numbers of non-white businessmen, teachers, clerks and other professions increased, they chose to emulate the British by playing cricket and setting up their own clubs. They were followed by the West Indians of lower class who worked as labourers on the plantations and in the main towns. Some of the better cricketers were employed at the

British clubs as groundstaff and net bowlers. The clubs formed by the British adopted a policy of exclusivity which was easily enforced by a combination of charging a high joining fee and annual subscription and by requiring new members to be proposed and seconded by existing members. The clubs formed by the West Indians followed similar policies so that membership could be restricted to people of similar class. Thus, there were middle class West Indian clubs and working class ones. Since class also strongly related to skin colour, a hierarchy of clubs was established so that, by the 1890s in Barbados, there was the Wanderers Club, founded in 1877, for the white elite, Pickwick, formed in 1882, for middle class whites, Spartan, for the non-white middle class, and Empire for the working class. In Trinidad the club for the white elite was Queen's Park, founded in 1891, followed by Shamrock, largely for white Catholic families, Maple for brown-skinned middle class, Shannon for black-skinned lower middle class and Stingo for the black working class. In Trinidad and Guyana (then British Guiana), the situation was more complicated because separate clubs also existed for people of Indian and Chinese ancestry.

Racially Structured

Although cricket thus became racially structured, the small size of the white population and the small number of whites-only clubs meant that exclusivity could not be applied to fixture lists, otherwise the white clubs would have played only matches between teams of their own members. The clubs of all races and classes in each of the West Indian territories played each other, a situation which undoubtedly resulted in rapid improvements in standard, particularly among the black players. Despite this, the racial structure of cricket had profound effects on the way domestic and international cricket evolved.

The first match between different countries within the West Indies took place in 1865 when Barbados met Demerara from British Guiana at the Garrison ground in Bridgetown on 15 and 16 February, Barbados winning by 138 runs. A return game was played on the Parade Ground in Georgetown in September that year, the victors this time being Demerara. After the conclusion of the return game, the visitors were invited by the hosts to a river trip on the Essequibo which ended in disaster.

One of the boats capsized whilst 'shooting the rapids' of the Koestabraek Falls. Seven people were drowned, including R.D. Stewart and H.S. Beresford, two of the leading cricketers from Demerara. It was six years before the teams met again. In the meanwhile, Trinidad had begun its inter-territorial matches with a fixture against Demerara in 1869. These early matches involved only all-white teams, partly because the whites were the only ones able to afford the time and the expense and partly because the matches were organised by the leading white clubs. Trinidad, Barbados and Demerara established a Triangular tournament for the Inter-Colonial Cup in 1893. Played in each territory in turn, the tournament lasted until 1939 (Table 2.22). Although the Garrison Club from Barbados visited Kingston in 1891, contacts between Jamaica and the other territories were limited and Jamaica did not take part in the Inter-Colonial tournament. Jamaica was just too distant from the other countries. There were no direct sailings. All shipping services went via Panama and, in the late nineteenth century, the journey could take nine to ten days. Encouragement for cricket in Jamaica came from tours arranged separately from those to the rest of the Caribbean. Philadelphia visited in 1909 and Hon H.L. Tennyson organised private tours in 1926/27, 1927/28 and 1931/32. Sir Julien Cahn's team visited in 1928/29 and Yorkshire in 1935/36. Some matches were played between Trinidad, Barbados and the smaller islands in the Leewards and Windwards but, except for a short period in the early 1900s when J.S. Udal organised cricket in Antigua after moving from Fiji to take up the post as Chief Justice, they were not of the same standard and they were not invited to participate in the Inter-Colonial tournament.

The first time a team was chosen to represent the West Indies was in 1886 when George Wyatt of the Georgetown CC organised a tour of North America. The all-white team, captained by Wyatt and with L.K. Fyfe of Jamaica as vice-captain, comprised six Jamaicans, two Barbadians and four Guyanese. It had been intended to select some players from Trinidad but none could afford the individual cost of US$350. No representative international fixture was organised, the team playing club sides only, winning six, losing five and drawing two games. The first international match occurred at

Table 2.22 Teams involved in Inter-Colonial Tournament (1893-1939)

Team	winners
Barbados	10
British Guiana (formerly Demerara)	5
Trinidad	11

Georgetown on 5 January 1888 when the West Indies were dismissed in their first innings for 19 by the USA and lost the match by nine wickets. This was the only international fixture during what was the first tour to the West Indies by another country. The USA played matches in St Kitt's, Barbados, Grenada, Trinidad, Demerara and Jamaica. The white West Indians now started to look to England for overseas contact and both Wyatt and Fyfe attempted to organise tours to England. Both approached the MCC but neither succeeded with their proposals.

Instead the first contact came in 1895 when arrangements for a side to visit the West Indies were made by Lord Stamford, N. Lubbock, Dr R.B. Anderson and Lord M.B. Hawke. It was hoped that Hawke would captain the side. Unfortunately he withdrew and it was Slade Lucas who led the party of English amateurs on a tour of eighteen matches encompassing Barbados, Antigua, St Kitt's, St Lucia, St Vincent, Trinidad, Demerara and Jamaica. No representative match was played but the matches against Barbados, Trinidad, Demerara and Jamaica are rated as first class. Even though the English side was little better than a poor county side, the results showed West Indian white cricket to be of good standard. Barbados, Trinidad, Jamaica and, most surprisingly of all, St Vincent all beat the tourists.

Having had to forego the 1895 tour, Lord Hawke accepted an invitation from the Governor of British Guiana to bring a touring party in 1897. His telegram of acceptance was never received, however, so the organisers in British Guiana, Barbados and Trinidad went along with the invitation made by Jamaica to Arthur Priestley to bring a team. By the time Hawke and Priestley realised the situation, arrangements for both tours were well advanced and neither would give way. As a result, two English teams toured the Caribbean simultaneously. Since both sides were all amateur, the financial implications of the competing tours were minimal. Both sides were beaten by Trinidad who included two black professional fast

bowlers, Joseph Woods and Archie Cumberbatch. The West Indies were captained by Aucher Warner, brother of Sir Pelham Warner who was a member of Hawke's touring party. Both Warners were critical of local selection policies, particularly in Barbados and British Guiana, in which the best black players were excluded.

From this time it became inconceivable that the West Indies could field a representative side without including black players. The questions were always how many and what status they should have, given that they were often professional whilst the whites were amateurs. Selection was further complicated by rivalries between the authorities in the four leading territories of Jamaica, Barbados, Trinidad and British Guiana which meant that all had be more or less equally represented. It also meant that players from the smaller islands in the Windwards and Leewards had to be exceptionally good to be considered. As a result of Lord Hawke's visit to the Caribbean in 1897, an invitation was made for a West Indies side to tour England in 1900. The team comprised ten whites and five black players. The regional balance was three from British Guiana, four from Barbados, three from Trinidad, two from Jamaica and one each from Grenada and St Vincent. The financial arrangements for the tour placed the black cricketers at a disadvantage since each player had to pay his own way. The white players, being part of West Indian society's elite, could afford to do this but the non-white players, dominantly middle class, could not and had to raise their fares and expenses by public subscription. As a result, some of the best black players were unable to go. Under the captaincy of Aucher Warner of Trinidad, all team members were treated as equals and socially the tour enhanced the acceptance of black cricketers at a national level.

The period between 1900 and the First World War was marked by a continuous improvement in the standard of the black players relative to the whites. As a result the proportion of non-white to white players in the national side increased to fifty-fifty when the team was selected for the next tour of England in 1906. The tour of twenty matches was very demanding and the team played below expectations. The West Indies played five matches against visiting MCC sides in 1911 and 1913 but, for various reasons, the team was never properly representative. Jamaican players were excluded from some matches, a quarantine restriction prevented players from Trinidad playing in one match in Barbados and a selection dispute caused two Barbadian players to withdraw from the team for one of the matches in Georgetown. Arrangements were put in place for a third West Indian tour of England in 1914 but the First World War intervened and it did not take place.

Although the Inter-Colonial tournament and other first-class cricket stopped during the 1914-18 War, club cricket continued. Cricket was therefore able to regain its pre-war level of activity quickly in the 1920s. The proposed tour of England was rescheduled and took place in 1923. Although the touring party was fifty-fifty white to black players, the selection was not without controversy. Winston St Hill and Herman Griffith, considered by many to be among the best of the non-white cricketers, were omitted. It has been suggested that this was for reasons other than cricketing ability. Both held strong views about the opportunities available for black players and the way cricket was administered and it seems likely they were seen as potential troublemakers. Further, the team was chosen entirely from the four main territories with each being represented by a set proportion. This was another reason why St Hill and Griffith were not selected since their associations would then have exceeded their quota. Despite the disadvantage of a selection which was both regionally and colour coded, the side, under the captaincy of Harold Austin, performed well. By the time of their next tour of England in 1928, the West Indies had been granted test-match status.

The early test record of the West Indies was mixed partly because all their matches were against England and Australia. When these were played away the West Indies came up against those countries' best teams. Only when England visited the Caribbean did they meet opposition slightly below full strength. Nevertheless, these matches established what became the typical pattern of West Indian cricket, namely exciting batting and aggressive fast bowling. The problem with the West Indies in the 1930s was simply that there were not enough top class players. There were also concerns about the captaincy. Harold Austin was now too old and Karl Nunes, Jack Grant and Rolph Grant, all individuals of great integrity, lacked the inspiration required to lead successfully a team chosen

according to regional quotas. Team building was difficult because many of the players did not know each other before overseas tours began and, indeed, the captain often did not know them either. Further, the chosen captains were often poor tacticians, an issue which reflected their limited experience. Three or four first-class matches a season was not enough to build a tactical appreciation of the game. Throughout the 1930s, the selectors followed a traditional view that since the political administration of the separate territories was the responsibility of members of the elite white community, these were the people with the necessary skills of leadership in other fields too. Even though by 1939 the proportion of black players in the West Indies touring party to England had risen to 61 per cent, there was never any question that the captain of the side would be anything other than white. Thus Learie Constantine who, through his experience in the Lancashire League had developed a superb tactical understanding of the game, was ignored as a possible leader.

World Class Ability

After the 1939-45 War, the West Indies demonstrated their world-class ability for the first time. Initially their success was built on batting strength as Everton Weekes, Clyde Walcott and Frank Worrell, known collectively as the three Ws, constructed large totals against a somewhat moderate English team in the Caribbean in 1947/48 and, without Worrell, against India in 1948/49. Worrell, who rejected the terms offered by the West Indies Board of Control for the tour of India as amounting to exploitation of the black professional cricketer, measured his worth by what he could earn in the Lancashire League and expected the Board to offer a similar rate. The Board considered this impertinent and refused to negotiate. Fortunately the issue was resolved before the team was chosen for the tour of England in 1950. After losing the first test, the West Indies went on to humiliate England partly through their strong batting but also because they possessed two young spin bowlers, Alf Valentine and Sonny Ramadhin, who adapted well to the conditions. In the late 1950s and early 1960s, as the three Ws got older and the spin duo became less effective, West Indian cricket entered a lean period. Lack of success resurrected the question of the West Indian captaincy. John Goddard had led the victorious team in 1950 whilst just performing well enough as an all-rounder to justify his inclusion in the side. When asked to lead young sides to New Zealand in 1956 and England in 1957, he carried out the task conscientiously but with little inspiration. Gerry Alexander took over from Goddard after the English tour but was never more than a stand-in appointment which he, also, undertook with dignity whilst showing considerable skill as a wicket-keeper.

The successes of late 1940s and early 1950s helped to mask some underlying problems of West Indian cricket. First, any player who wanted to make cricket their career had to leave the Caribbean and seek employment with an English county or in the English or Scottish leagues. The Inter-Colonial tournament was not renewed after the Second World War and so there was hardly any domestic first-class cricket. Second, little money was invested in facilities. Even the major test-match grounds lacked investment and offered the spectators little value for their entrance fees. Territorial rivalries pervaded the administration affecting the distribution of money, the choice of selectors and selection of the team. Some historians consider this period to be the most chaotic in West Indian cricket history with respect to the organisation of the game. It was not unusual for the tenth and eleventh players in home test matches to vary game by game according to the territory in which it was played. Each territory also chose the umpires for the test matches on its own ground, resulting in many complaints by visiting teams because of the discrepancy in standards. Occasionally umpiring decisions resulted in riots, notably in matches against England at Georgetown in February 1954, Port of Spain in January 1960 and Kingston in February 1968. Although contemporary reports, particularly in English newspapers, were critical of the West Indian crowds and of the West Indian authorities for failing to control what was described as hooliganism, they were written solely in the context of the cricket. More considered appraisals by social historians now view the incidents as a trigger for sections of the crowd to express their feelings on wider issues such as the status of black people in West Indian society in the 1950s and the demand for independence of the West Indian territories from the colonising power. No

longer are the disturbances viewed as aimed specifically at the English cricketers.

The first attempt at reviving a first-class domestic competition came in 1956/57 when a quadrangular tournament was staged in Georgetown involving British Guiana, Barbados, Jamaica and Trinidad. The venture was not repeated, however, until 1961/62 when Georgetown staged a Pentangular Tournament, a combined side from the Leeward and Windward Islands being admitted to the competition. A regional tournament was also held in 1963/64, this time without the Leewards and Windwards. Matches were played in Bridgetown, Port of Spain and Georgetown. In the middle 1960s the West Indies Board obtained sponsorship for a first-class domestic competition. Apart from 1967/68, the competition has been held annually since 1965/66 (Table 2.23).

Most Momentous Decision

The revival of West Indies cricket came in the mid 1960s with the emergence of Garfield Sobers and, arguably the most momentous decision in West Indian cricket, the appointment of a black cricketer as captain. The choice of Frank Worrell was widely applauded and he proved an inspirational leader as well as an excellent tactician. Under his leadership in Australia in 1960/61, he became the first captain to command loyalty to the concept of playing for the West Indies over that of being a Barbadian, Jamaican, Trinidadian or Guyanan. The appointment was timely in coinciding with the transfer of political power from the white elite to a black elite as the individual territories gained their independence. It also coincided with moves towards some form of Caribbean federation. The West Indies thus gained a national identity. After Worrell's retirement the team had a short run of success under Sobers, followed, after a short lull, by another highly successful period as the captaincy passed in the mid 1970s to another inspiring leader, Clive Lloyd. The West Indies were the best side in the world at this time and won the World Cup in 1975 and 1979. After a lull in the early 1980s, Lloyd was still captain for a resurgent West Indies in England in 1984 when all five test matches were won.

Just as in the early 1950s, the achievements of the

West Indies side were a function of the skill of the individual players and occurred despite rather than because of the policies of the West Indies Cricket Board of Control. Inconsistency in policy was most obvious in the late 1970s when many of the best players signed with Kerry Packer for his World Series Cricket. Unlike the administrative authorities in Australia and England who tried to ban their cricketers who played for Packer, the WICBC continued to select them. Packer even arranged his schedules to enable the West Indians to play for their country. The issue came to a head in 1978 during the Australian tour of the Caribbean. Having lost the first two tests easily, Australia, minus their Packer players, were unhappy with the situation. Whether the Australian Board of Control approached the WICBC or not is uncertain but, for the third test, the West Indies inexplicably dropped three of their Packer players. This brought the players into conflict with the Board. The captain, Clive Lloyd resigned and the remaining Packer players withdrew from the team in support. The West Indies fielded weak sides for the remainder of the series. They lost the third test and drew the fourth. The fifth at Kingston also ended in a draw when crowd disturbances in protest against the WICBC prevented the game from being completed. There was much public support in the Caribbean for Packer's venture and the financial rewards it brought to the players who signed with him. Whilst a weakened West Indies side was struggling in India where the series of six matches was lost, large crowds attended the five matches in the Caribbean between the WSC West Indies and WSC Australia. Eventually the WICBC decided it would be better to recognise the strength of West Indian public and player opinion and negotiate with Packer. The Packer players were reinstated for the 1979/80 tour of Australia.

The 1960s also marked by the start of women's cricket. Unlike their counterparts in England, Australia and New Zealand white women in the Caribbean in the late nineteenth and first half of the twentieth century did not attempt to organise women's matches. The white cricket administrators viewed the sport as a male preserve and white Caribbean society retained gender consciousness about

the appropriate roles for men and women until well into the 1950s. West Indian women's cricket had to wait until the political administration of the various territories had passed from whites to the black community. Black women cricketers then felt able to formalise the game which many had undoubtedly played informally with their fathers and brothers for many years. Jamaica was the first territory to establish a Women's Cricket Association on 26 January 1966. That Jamaica was the pioneer reflected the major role that women there had played in the anti-colonial and nationalist movement. Although there were only some thirty to forty women interested in playing at a national level, under Monica Taylor, the Jamaican WCA established the infrastructure for women's cricket and organised a tour of Trinidad in 1967. This was the trigger for establishing the Trinidad and Tobago Women's Cricket Association in October that year. Jamaica then invited England to tour in January 1970. The visit was repeated the following year when Jamaica, Trinidad and England took part in a triangular competition in Trinidad. By 1970, women's cricket was being organised in Barbados, Grenada, St Vincent, St Lucia and Guyana. Jamaica hosted the Australian women's team in 1973 on their way to England for the Women's World Cup in which both Jamaica and Trinidad participated. In 1975 the Caribbean Women's Cricket Federation was formed with the objective of promoting the game at West Indies level. The annual Caribbean tournament was started and the first test matches were played against Australia in 1976. The two matches were both drawn. A tour of

Table 2.23 Teams involved in West Indies's first-class domestic competitions: the Shell Shield (1965/66-1986/87), Red Stripe Cup (1987/88-1996/97), President's Cup (1997/98), Busta Cup (1998/99-2001/02) and Carib Beer Cup (2002/03-2006/07)

Team	Date of first appearance	Winners
Barbados	1965/66	19 + 1 shared
Combined Islands	1969/70	1
Guyana (formerly British Guiana)	1965/66	5 + 1 shared
Jamaica	1965/66	7
Leeward Islands	1981/82	3 + 1 shared
Trinidad and Tobago	1965/66	4 + 1 shared
West Indies B	2001/02	0
Windward Islands	1981/82	0

The Combined Islands competed until 1981/82. An overseas side was invited to compete between 2000/01 and 2003/04 but none won the competition. The teams invited were: England A (2000/01), Bangladesh A (2001/02), India A (2002/03), Kenya (2003/04). West Indies B competed between 2001/02 and 2003/04.

India followed in 1976/77 in which the West Indies came from behind to draw the six-match series (one game each) by winning the sixth test in Jammu by an innings. In 1979, the West Indies toured England, losing one test match and drawing the other two.

As regards the men's game, it is arguable whether the mid 1970s or the mid 1980s, when Viv Richards replaced Lloyd as captain, represents the greatest period in West Indian cricket history. Both Lloyd and Richards commanded one of most aggressive pace attacks in the history of the game, often comprising four first-class bowlers plying a succession of yorkers and bouncers without respite. Such was their dominance that many questioned whether the tactics were within the spirit of the game. There was concern about the safety of the players. Helmets became part of the standard dress and the ICC passed regulations relating to the number of bouncers above shoulder height that could be bowled in any one over and the number permitted against tail-end batsmen who, often, did not have the skills to cope. World dominance was not to last, however. No more World Cups were won after 1979 and by the 1990s, weaknesses were beginning to show in the national side. The side maintained its supremacy in fast bowling through Curtly Ambrose and Courtney Walsh but the support bowling was inconsistent, however, and prone to injury. The batting too was less reliable and increasingly reliant on one man, Brian Lara. Poor performances by the national side in the 2000s clearly demonstrate that the West Indies faces serious problems for the future.

Revive Interest

Whilst from the 1950s to the 1970s cricket was the national sport of the former British Caribbean countries, by the 1990s, basketball, athletics and soccer were competing for this status in men's sport and athletics and netball in women's sport. As social ties strengthen with overseas West Indians in the USA and Canada and weaken with those in Britain, cricket no longer commands the same level of interest. Attendances at test matches and first-class domestic games are in decline and investment is clearly needed to upgrade the major grounds to international standard. Much of this happened for the 2007 World Cup but it may not be enough to revive

interest. One positive feature of the first-class game is that it is now spread widely throughout the Caribbean. No longer is top-class cricket confined to the four main territories as it was in the 1930s and 1970s. Matches are now played on the smallest of the islands, such as Tobago and Anguilla, and even in St Maarten, a Dutch territory, and the United States Virgin Islands.

This wider spread of first-class cricket has not been extended to touring teams. Indeed, the itineraries of tours have not changed much over the years (Table 2.24). When England visited in 1934/35, matches were confined to Bridgetown, Port of Spain, Kingston and Georgetown, each being visited in turn. With transport between the centres being by ship and taking several days, there was no opportunity to visit each town more than once. Thus, the matches against the territory and the test against the West Indies were played during a stay of ten days in each centre. A large number of rest days was provided to enable players to recover from the sea journey and to see the tourist sites. By 1973/74, the itinerary was harder. Matches were played in seven centres, there were fewer rest days and the total distance travelled was much longer. There was little difference in the time spent travelling, however, because most journeys were made by air. The 2003/04 tour, an example of a recent itinerary, was theoretically the more leisurely. Compared to 1973/74, fewer days were spent playing cricket, the distance travelled was less and there were more rest days. Eight centres were visited but many for only a few days at a time. This, combined with more of the rest days being used for practice, meant fewer opportunities to enjoy the Caribbean as a tourist. Overall, however, tours of the Caribbean seem to be less arduous than those to many of the other test-playing countries.

West Indies cricket now provides the opportunity for players of all classes and ethnic backgrounds to participate in the sport. The priorities must be to encourage the game at all ages in schools and clubs, improve coaching and provide the top players with appropriate experience. There is an urgent need to regenerate interest in the game as a national sport and to prevent the standard of West Indian cricket declining. Cricket is now virtually the only activity to happen regularly at Caribbean level so the Board needs to be even more sensitive to regional rivalries than in the past. Sponsorship arrangements also need to be rationalised. At present the Board and the individual players seek separate sponsorships and, in order to maximise the monies made available, enter into restrictive agreements. This has led to some of the top players being unable to represent the West Indies because the contracts with their individual sponsors prohibit them from being associated with any other sponsor, including that of the national side. Clearly in the interests of West Indian cricket this is a situation which cannot be allowed to continue. Another issue for the Board is the promotion of women's cricket for which, following the merger of the ICC and the IWCC, it now has responsibility. Previously there was little communication between the WICBC and the CWFC. The CWFC viewed the WICBC as a male preserve and the WICBC did nothing to change that perception. Since the end of the 1970s women's cricket has struggled. No further tests against Australia or England have taken place. Shortage of funds has limited the CWFC in its promotion of the game and efforts have concentrated mainly on the participation of the West Indies in the World Cup competitions. Not surprisingly, the standard of women's cricket has fallen. How the WICBC responds to the various challenges will determine whether cricket retains its position as fundamental to the social and political life of the Caribbean or whether it will become just one of many sports with only tenuous links to the evolution of West Indian society and culture.

Famous Victories

June 24, 26, 27, 28 and 29, 1950 – Lord's, London
West Indies 326 (A.F. Rae 106, E.D. Weekes 63, F.M. Worrell 52, R.O. Jenkins 5-116) and 425-6 dec (C.L. Walcott 168*, G.E. Gomez 70, E.D. Weekes 63, R.O. Jenkins 4-174)
England 151 (S. Ramadhin 5-66, A.L. Valentine 4-48) and 274 (C. Washbrook 114, S. Ramadhin 6-86)
West Indies won by 326 runs

Having won the first test match of the series at Manchester easily, England entered this game with confidence despite being without Denis Compton, Reg Simpson and Trevor Bailey through injury. By four o'clock on the first day,

however, the West Indies were on top with a score of 233 for two wickets thanks to a patient innings by Allan Rae and an exhibition of batsmanship from Frank Worrell and Everton Weekes. A fine spell of leg spin bowling by Roly Jenkins enabled England to recover and Alec Bedser bowled well without luck to obtain three wickets for 60 runs from 40 overs. Len Hutton and Cyril Washbrook took England to 62 but once they were gone, the side crumbled to some masterful spin by Sonny Ramadhin. On a pitch which gave little assistance, he bowled straight at the wicket, on a teasing length and imparted sufficient spin to turn the ball either way and beat the bat. England's score was their lowest to that date in a home test against the West Indies. Jenkins pinned down the West Indies batsman until the score reached 199 for five after which Clyde Walcott and Gerry Gomez took the bowling apart in a stand of 211. Set to score 601 to win in nearly two days, England were never in danger of reaching the target despite the efforts of Washbrook, who resisted for five and a half hours, and Gilbert Parkhouse (48), playing in his first test. Ramadhin and Alfred Valentine (3-79) bowled the West Indies to their first test victory in England.

July 8, 9, 10, 12 and 13, 1976 – Old Trafford, Manchester
West Indies 211 (C.G. Greenidge 134, M.W.W. Selvey 4-41) and 411-5 dec (I.V.A. Richards 136, C.G. Greenidge 101, R.C. Fredericks 50)
England 71 (M.A. Holding 5-17) and 126 (A.M.E. Roberts 6-37)
West Indies won by 425 runs

On an unpredictable pitch, England folded against one of the world's fastest bowling pairs whilst the West Indies batsmen adapted to the conditions and completely

---

Table 2.24 Playing days, rest days and distances travelled on tours of the West Indies by England

Date	Playing days	Rest days	Ratio of cricket days to rest days	Kilometres travelled per rest day
1934/35	39	30	1.30	107
1973/74	51	15	3.40	397
2003/04	35	24	1.46	209

Notes: Rest days are days when no cricket is played and no travel takes place. The ratio of kilometres travelled per rest day is an underestimate because kilometres are based on straight-line distances between the venues and not the actual distance travelled.

mastered the English attack. England started well taking the first four West Indies wickets for 26 with Mike Selvey particularly impressive on his debut. Gordon Greenidge batted with skill to reach his second century in test cricket in two hours fifty minutes and found support from Collis King (32) in a stand of 111. Greenidge was the ninth man out but, despite his efforts, the total looked too small. This view was rapidly changed by some aggressive bowling from Michael Holding, Andy Roberts (3-22) and Wayne Daniel (2-13). England's last eight wickets fell in just one hour as balls lifted dangerously from the wicket at great speed. Much of the bowling was unplayable and the batsmen did well to avoid serious injury. Surprisingly, the English attack got little help from the wicket and Roy Fredericks and Greenidge made 116 for the first wicket, the latter going on to his second century of the match in four and three-quarter hours. He and Vivian Richards put on 108 for the second wicket. When Clive Lloyd declared, England were set to score 552 in thirteen and a quarter hours. John Edrich (24) and Brian Close (20) defended grimly in an opening stand of 54 against extremely hostile bowling. Umpire Bill Alley warned Holding for intimidation and a sequence of bouncers. Despite hold-ups for rain which took the game into the fifth day, England never looked like preventing the West Indies from obtaining their largest runs victory in their history.

May 9, 10, 11, 12 and 13, 2003 – St John's
Australia 240 (J.J.C. Lawson 7-78) and 417 (M.L. Hayden 177, J.L. Langer 111, M. Dillon 4-112)
West Indies 240 (B.C. Lara 68) and 418-7 (R.R. Sarwan 105, S. Chanderpaul 104, B.C. Lara 60, B. Lee 4-63)
West Indies won by 3 wickets

As Australia already led the series by three matches to none, the final game was destined to be without interest. On the first day Jermaine Lawson exploited a pitch which favoured pace bowling and found that the hitherto fault-less Australian batting had some weaknesses. Even so, scores from Justin Langer (42), Martin Love (36), Steve Waugh (41), Adam Gilchrist (33) and Andy Bichel (34) enabled a competitive total to be obtained. The umpires asked for video evidence of Lawson's bowling and, after careful viewing, reported him to the ICC for a suspect action. Whether this had an effect on captain Brian Lara

is uncertain but he adopted a very aggressive attitude towards the Australians whilst batting to which they responded with unwanted comments and general chatter. The umpires were forced to intervene to prevent a major incident. Through Lara's efforts, the West Indies tied the first innings. With Lawson unable to bowl more than six overs, supposedly a result of a back injury, Langer and Matthew Hayden made an opening stand of 242 to put the Australians in an apparently impregnable position. The West Indies fought back and restricted the Australians to a further 175 runs. Set 418 to win, the West Indies started badly losing three wickets for 74 runs. When Lara became the fourth wicket to fall at the total of 165, an Australian victory looked certain. Ramnaresh Sarwan and Shivnarine Chanderpaul, who batted with a broken finger, had other ideas and performed responsibly in a partnership of 123 runs. On field behaviour was far from mature, however. As the Australians sensed that victory was becoming less sure, they resorted to verbal exchanges with the batsmen. After the dismissal of Sarwan, Ridley Jacobs was given out first ball, caught behind the wicket, though television replays suggested the ball hit his elbow rather than his bat. The crowd expressed their view of the Australians and the umpires by throwing bottles on to the pitch. Despite a delay to clear the litter and a further delay through rain, Chanderpaul maintained concentration in a stand with Omari Banks (47*). By the start of the final day, the West Indies needed only 47 more runs. Chanderpaul was quickly out but Banks and Vasburn Drakes (27*) took the West Indies to a sensational victory and the highest ever fourth innings score to win a test match.

Player Profiles

Constantine, Baron Learie Nicholas. MBE. b Petit Valley, Diego Martin, Trinidad, 21 September 1901. d Brondesbury, Hampstead, London, 1 July 1971. rhb. rf/rm. Recognised as the best West Indian all-rounder of his generation, he was renown for his outstanding fielding. Wherever he played, crowds came to see him. An unorthodox batsman with powerful drives and pulls, he was especially severe on the leg side. His bowling was characterised by a lithe, smooth action. He played for both Rochdale and Nelson in the Lancashire League where, through his dynamism and his personality, he did much to bring about the acceptance of black cricketers in England and the acceptance of black people in Britain in general. After retiring from cricket, he became an MP and the Minister for Works in the Trinidad Government before returning to England as High Commissioner for Trinidad and Tobago. He was knighted in 1962 and made a life peer in 1969. Posthumously, he was awarded the Trinity Cross, Trinidad's highest honour. In 18 test matches, he made 635 runs (average 19.24) and took 58 wickets (average 31.10).

Cumberbatch, Archibald Belford. b Four Hills Estate, St Andrews, Barbados, 1 June 1879. Presumed dead. rhb. rfm. He was one of the first black West Indian fast bowlers to make an impression in top-class cricket. Moving from Barbados to Trinidad where it was easier for a black player to gain recognition, he was the one bowler who troubled all the English teams to the Caribbean in the 1890s. In 14 representative matches for West Indian sides he scored 256 runs (average 12.19) and took 37 wickets (average 24.86).

Headley, George Alphonso. MBE. b Colón, Panama, 30 May 1909. d Meadowbridge, Kingston, Jamaica, 30 November 1983. rhb. The outstanding West Indian batsman of the 1930s, he was a compact player, able to execute every shot but especially strong off the back foot. He was notably successful on 'sticky' wickets affected by rain. Born in Panama, his mother took him to Jamaica when he was ten years of age so that he could have his education in English. He headed the English batting averages on both his tours to England in 1933 and 1939 when he scored 2,320 (average 66.28) and 1,745 (average 72.70) respectively. He also scored 1,066 runs (average 44.41) on the 1930/31 tour of Australia. In 22 test matches, he scored 2,910 runs (average 60.83).

Lara, Brian Charles. b Cantaro, Santa Cruz, Trinidad, 2 May 1969. lhb. The outstanding Caribbean cricketer of the 1990s and 2000s, he is a determined and dedicated player with the ability to concentrate for long periods and execute the complete range of shots. Although in the record books for his ability to accumulate large scores, his batting is always entertaining. He came to world attention during the 1992/93 tour of Australia when he made 277 in the third test at Sydney. The following season, he obtained the then record test score of 375 against England at St John's. In 1994, during a season with Warwickshire, he amassed the world record individual first-class score of 501 not out against Durham from only 427 balls. He lost his test record to Matthew Hayden in 2003/04 but later in the same season showed his liking for St John's and for the English bowling by reclaiming it with a score of 400 not out. In 130 test matches, he has scored 11,912 runs (average 53.17). In 295 one-day internationals he has made 10,398 runs (average 40.90).

Marshall, Malcolm Denzil. b Bridgetown, Barbados, 18 April 1958. d Bridgetown, Barbados, 4 November 1999 (cancer). rhb. rfm. Considering both the total number of test wickets and bowling average, he is arguably the greatest bowler ever to represent the West Indies. His hostile action made the ball skid off the wicket to which he added the ability to make the ball move late off the pitch both to leg and off. Combining dedication, skill and ambition, he played fourteen seasons for Hampshire for whom he developed great affection and loyalty. He was a more than useful late order batsman. After retirement, he became a successful coach. In 81 test matches he scored 1,810 runs (average 18.85) and took 376 wickets (average 20.94). He was the first West Indian to take 350 wickets in a test-match career. In 136 one-day internationals he made 955 runs (average 14.92) and took 157 wickets (average 26.96).

Ramadhin, Sonny. b Esperance Village, Trinidad, 1 May 1929. rhb. rob/lb. For a short period, he was one of the best spin bowlers in the World with a story-book start to his cricket career. An orphan, he was helped in his youth by a Barbadian inter-colonial cricketer resident in Trinidad. He was chosen for the 1950 visit to England after having played only two first-class matches which were the trial games for the tour. One of the boldest selections in test history, made by John Goddard and Jeffrey Stollmeyer, proved one of the most successful. He took 138 wickets during the season (average 14.88) including 26 in the test matches (average 23.23). His command of flight, length and changes of pace combined with the ability to deliver both off breaks and leg breaks from the back of the hand so as to conceal which way the ball would turn. He also bowled with his shirt-sleeves buttoned down round his wrist, thereby hiding his wrist action from the batsman. In 43 test matches, he scored 361 runs (average 8.20) and took 158 wickets (average 28.98).

Sobers, Sir Garfield St Aubrun. b Chelsea Road, Bay Land, Bridgetown, Barbados, 28 July 1936. lhb. lfm/sla. The greatest all-round cricketer of all time, he combined natural ability with determination and enthusiasm. Throughout his career, he was the player the crowd came to see and the one the opposition most feared. He batted with great freedom, being especially strong on the off and straight drive. He made his test-match debut at the age of seventeen. Within four years he had progressed to a being a great player, a transition which was marked by making the then record individual score of 365 not out against Pakistan at Kingston in 1958. He had seasons with South Australia from 1961/62 to 1963/64 and with Nottinghamshire from 1968 to 1974 for whom, in his first season, he hit six sixes in a six-ball over against Glamorgan at Swansea off the bowling of Malcolm Nash. Always competitive, regardless of the class of cricket, he responded to being bowled first ball when playing for E.W. Swanton's XI against Malaysia in 1964 by taking five wickets in five balls. He had the unenviable task of following Frank Worrell as captain of the West Indies, a position he upheld with dignity. He was widely respected for his sportsmanship and unselfishness. He was knighted in 1975 for his services to cricket. In 93 test matches, he scored 8,032 runs (average 57.78) and took 235 wickets (average 34.03), as well as holding 109 catches. He played only one one-day international, scoring no runs and taking one wicket (average 31.00). An all-round sportsman, he represented Barbados at golf, soccer and basketball.

Weekes, Everton de Courcy. MBE. b Pickwick Gap, Westbury, St Michael, Barbados, 26 February 1925. rhb. An attacking batsman, excelling in powerful cuts, drives and hooks, he endeavoured to dominate the bowling. A defensive stroke seemed to be an unorthodox improvisation. He was easily the leading batsman in the world in the late 1940s and early 1950s. In India in 1948/49, he scored hundreds in four innings in succession and looked in line to make it five until he was run out for 90 at Madras. An immensely popular person, he played league cricket in England and was in demand for various touring international and Commonwealth sides. After retiring, he became a coach in Barbados, a cricket summariser on radio, and an international bridge player. In 48 test matches he scored 4,455 runs (average 58.61).

Worrell, Sir Frank Mortimore Maglinne. b Bank Hall, Bridgetown, Barbados, 1 August 1924. d Mona, Kingston, Jamaica, 13 March 1967 (leukaemia). rhb. lfm/sla. A prolific scorer of runs wherever he played, he displayed superb footwork and timing and possessed an immaculate late cut. He bowled with sufficient skill to open the bowling with the new ball. He showed his ability as captain when he took over from Leslie Ames to lead a Commonwealth side in India in 1949/50. When he gained the honour of captaining the West Indies, he carried out his duties with a mixture of dynamism and diplomacy and gained the respect of all his players. He was calm in a crisis and it was his judgement and coolness that enabled the West Indies to tie the match against Australia at Brisbane in 1961 and draw the match against England at Lord's in 1963 with England six runs short of victory and the last pair at the wicket. He captained the West Indies fifteen times and won nine matches, a remarkable success rate of 60 per cent. After retirement from first-class cricket, he became Warden of the University of the West Indies and a senator in the Jamaican Parliament. He was knighted for his services to cricket in 1964. His death three years later ended what promised to be a distinguished second career as an administrator and statesman. In 51 tests he scored 3,860 runs (average 49.48) and took 69 wickets (average 38.72).

Other leading players: *1890-1914:* C.E. Goodman (rhb. rf); J. Woods (rhb. rf); G. Challenor (rhb. rm); S.G. Smith (lhb. sla); C.A. Ollivierre (rhb). *1920-1940:* G.N. Francis (rhb. rf); G. John (rhb. rfm); E.A. Martindale (rhb. rf); W.H. St Hill (rhb). *1945-1960:* C.L. Walcott (rhb. rfm. wk); A.L. Valentine (rhb.

sla); A.F. Rae (lhb); J.B. Stollmeyer (rhb. lbg); F.C.M. Alexander (rhb. wk). *1960-1980:* C.C. Hunte (rhb); R.B. Kanhai (rhb. occ wk); W.W. Hall (rhb. rf); A.I. Kallicharran (lhb); L.R. Gibbs (rhb. rob). *1980-2000:* I.V.A. Richards (rhb. rob/rm); D.L. Haynes (rhb); C.G. Greenidge (rhb); C.A. Walsh (rhb. rf); C.E.L. Ambrose (lhb. rf). *Present day:* S. Chanderpaul (lhb); D.J. Bravo (rhb. rfm); R.R. Sarwan (rhb); C.H. Gayle (lhb. rob). **Women:** *1960-1980:* L.P. Browne (rhb); V. Latty-Scott (rhb. rob); P. Whittaker (rhb. rmf). *1980-2000:* N.A. George (lhb. wk). *Present day:* V.M. Felician (rhb. rob); N.A. Williams (rhb. rm).

Playing record

Test Matches

	Won	Lost	Tied	Drawn
England	52	38	0	44
Australia	32	48	1	21
South Africa	2	12	0	5
New Zealand	10	9	0	16
India	30	11	0	41
Pakistan	14	15	0	15
Sri Lanka	2	5	0	3
Zimbabwe	4	0	0	2
Bangladesh	3	0	0	1
Total	149	138	1	148

One-day matches

	Won	Tied	Lost	No Res
World Cup	35	0	21	1
Other ODIs	278	5	213	16

Twenty 20

0	1	0	0

Highest team score

790-3 dec	v Pakistan, Kingston	1957/58

Lowest team score

47	v England, Kingston	2003/04

Highest individual score

400*	B.C. Lara	v England, St John's	2003/04

Best bowling

9-95	J.M. Noreiga	v India, Port of Spain	1970/71

Best wicket-keeping

7 (7c)	R.D. Jacobs	v Australia, Melbourne	2000/01

Women

Test Matches

	Won	Lost	Tied	Drawn
England	0	2	0	1
Australia	0	0	0	2
India	1	1	0	4
Pakistan	0	0	0	1
Total	1	3	0	8

One-day matches

	Won	Lost	Tied	No Res
World Cup	5	11	0	3
World Cup Qualifying	4	1	0	0
Other ODIs	8	15	0	0

Highest team score

440	v Pakistan, Karachi	2003/04

Lowest team score

67	v England, Canterbury	1979

ODI

52	v Ireland, Amstelveen	2003

Highest individual score

118	N.A. George	v Pakistan, Karachi	2003/04

Best bowling

5 48	V. Latty Scott	v Australia, Montego Bay	1975/76

ODI

5-36	C.A. Singh	v Ireland, Dorking	1993

Best wicket-keeping

ODI

4 (2c 2st)	S.J. Power	v Ireland, Dorking	2003

YEMEN

CRICKET WAS played by British servicemen stationed in Aden up until 1967 when the territory became independent as part of the People's Democratic Republic of South Yemen. With the departure of the British troops, the game survived through expatriates from the Indian sub-continent. At least two representative matches have been played. In 1964 Aden were narrowly defeated by one wicket in a low-scoring one-day fixture against Pakistan International Airlines during a stop-over on their way to a tour of East Africa. In 1971, South Yemen were defeated by Hyderabad Blues by an innings and 92 runs. In recent years, with the formation of the Yemen Cricket Association, the focus of the game has moved to Sana'a where eight teams take part in a national league.

ZAMBIA

Associate Member of ICC: elected 2003

CRICKET SPREAD into Zambia (then Northern

Rhodesia) from neighbouring Zimbabwe (then Southern Rhodesia) in the early 1900s as the British began to settle in small numbers following the extension of the railway from Bulawayo across the Victoria Falls to Livingstone in 1904 and then northwards to the Copperbelt in 1909. The sport was slow to develop because the number of settlers was never large and the long distances along the railway line between the north and south of the country restricted contact between the clubs that were formed. Even at their peak in the early 1960s, Europeans represented only 3 per cent of the country's population and only in Kitwe and Lusaka did their numbers exceed 10,000. Organised cricket at a national scale did not occur until after the Second World War when the Northern Rhodesia Cricket Union was formed. Nevertheless, the MCC travelled to Livingstone during their tour of South Africa in 1929/30 and played a Northern Rhodesian side, beating them easily by nine wickets. By the late 1930s, Northern Rhodesian cricket was being partially integrated with that in Southern Rhodesia so that when a combined Rhodesian side was selected to meet the MCC in 1938/39, Tommy and Frank Davidson were included and made a round trip of some 2,500 kilometres from the Copperbelt to Bulawayo to play. Born in South Africa, the Davidsons had settled in the Copperbelt where Tommy worked in the Police Force.

Completely Bemused

In October 1948, the series of matches between Northern and Southern Rhodesia was inaugurated, originally as a trial to aid selection of a Rhodesian side to play the MCC in January and February 1949. The match was played at Nkana on the Copperbelt which was now the centre of Northern Rhodesian cricket. The series continued until 1954 by which time it had become too one-sided in the Southerners' favour to produce a worthwhile contest. Out of seven matches played, the Northerners won only once, in 1952; five matches were lost and one drawn. The next representative match was not until 1957 when the Australians opened their South African tour with a two-day match at Kitwe. The local batsmen were completely bemused by Richie Benaud who took nine wickets for 16 runs but, following on,

managed to hold out for a draw. No further international matches were played by Northern Rhodesia. With the Federation of Rhodesia and Nyasaland coming into being in 1954, cricket became officially integrated with that of Southern Rhodesia but, because of the lower playing standards, received less investment and encouragement as the game focused increasingly on Harare and Bulawayo. Rhodesia's formal association with South Africa for cricket purposes also meant that the game remained, as it had started, a white person's activity.

The 1950s also witnessed the peak of the women's game in the country. Occasional matches were played against Southern Rhodesia and in 1959 the country entered the Simon Trophy, South Africa's domestic competition but lost all their matches easily. In other years, Northern Rhodesia combined with Northern Transvaal and competed as a Northerns side. Unlike their male counterparts, Northern Rhodesia's women were the leading component of the Rhodesian Women's Cricket Union. They were strongly aided by the fact that Sheila Nefdt, South Africa's captain in the their first test match, had settled in Lusaka.

The situation changed when Zambia gained its independence in 1964. The Zambia Cricket Union was formed immediately as the national association and the game encouraged as a multiracial activity although this meant effectively as a minority sport for the European and Asian populations. Separated now from Rhodesia and South Africa, the true strength of Zambian cricket could be tested against other opposition. Zambia joined the East African Cricket Conference and participated in the annual tournaments for the Robert Menzies Trophy, hosting it in 1969 and 1973. The early 1970s were the most successful period in Zambia's cricket history. For a short time, Zambia was on the favoured country list for tours by English county sides. Gloucestershire visited in 1971 and Glamorgan in 1972. The MCC came in 1974.

By the end of the 1970s, declining economic conditions resulted in many Europeans leaving the country. This not only affected men's cricket but also led to the decline of the women's game which had become restricted to a very small section of the white community. Less money was available for investment in sport and the government gave cricket a low priority. With reduced finance, there was little chance of popularising cricket amongst the African population for whom soccer and athletics were the favoured sports. Visits from the MCC in 1981, the Minor Counties in 1982 and the transfer of the headquarters of the East African Cricket Conference to Lusaka provided enough stimulus to enable cricket to survive through the 1980s and 1990s but not sufficient to prevent it from dying in several of the towns on the Copperbelt. By the mid 1990s, cricket was almost entirely confined to Lusaka.

As economic conditions improved, the ZCU was able to invest in a schools development programme. There are now some 5,000 schoolchildren across government, private and community schools involved in the game. The national team has participated regularly in the African Zone VI tournaments. In 2004, Zambia hosted the African Associates competition, finishing third. They then played in the ICC Trophy qualifying tournament in Malaysia but disappointed, losing all their matches and finishing last. The ZCU remains constrained by shortage of finance and has recently had difficulty meeting the participation fees for ICC Under 15 and Under 19 competitions.

Leading players: *1920-1940:* T.M. Davidson (rhb. sla); F. Davidson (rhb. occ wk). *1945-1960:* W.B. Hitzeroth (rhb. rob). *1960-1980:* Baloo Vashee; B. Ellis; B. Horton (rhb. rfm). *1980-2000:* K. Cummings. *Present day* G. Geldenhuys; K.H. Frick; S. Malama.
Women: *1945-1960:* S.N. Nefdt.

Playing record
One-day matches

	Won	Lost	No Res
African Cricket Association Cup	2	2	0
African Six-Nations Tournament	2	3	0
ICC Qualifying Competition	0	5	0
African Championships Division 2	1	3	0

Highest team score

449-5 dec	v Uganda, Kitwe	1969

Lowest team score

66	Northern Rhodesia v Southern Rhodesia, Harare	1953

ODI

58	v Tanzania, Dar es Salaam	2006

Highest individual score

183	B. Vashee	v Uganda, Kitwe	1969

Best bowling

7-76	R.C. Wilson	v Kenya, Nairobi	1968

ZIMBABWE

Associate Member of ICC: elected 1981
Full Member of ICC: elected 1992

THE PIONEER Corps which trekked into the area which is now Zimbabwe from South Africa and claimed Fort Salisbury for the British on 12 September 1890 included among its troops, Monty Bowden. A former Surrey cricketer, he went to South Africa with Gardner Warton's side in 1888/89 and captained England in the second test match against South Africa at Cape Town. It was not surprising therefore that the troops took cricket equipment with them and played several games whenever they were camped. On 16 August one of these took place at Fort Victoria (now Masvingo) when, after a morning visit to the ruins of Great Zimbabwe, the A Troop, which included Bowden, played a combined team from the B and C Troops. Thus the first cricket match in Zimbabwe took place even before the country, in its present boundaries, existed. Bowden died of fever and an epileptic fit the following year in Umtali but there were several other cricket enthusiasts among the Pioneers. As a result the game quickly became established. The Police played at least two matches in Harare in 1891 and on the 10th October that year, the Salisbury Cricket Club was founded. Cricket was also played in Umtali and by 1894, three clubs had been formed in Bulawayo. That year saw Bulawayo challenge Salisbury to a match and in 1892, under the captaincy of Henry Taberer, at that time considered the best amateur cricketer in South Africa, Salisbury undertook the round trip of some 960 kilometres only to be beaten by an innings and 83 runs. The difficulties of organising cricket in the 1890s were shown by the events of the return journey during which there were many delays. Rivers were in flood and the coaches frequently got bogged down in muddy conditions. When they were still 30 kilometres south of Fort Charter two of the team decided to walk and they arrived in Salisbury several days before the rest of the party.

In 1896, William Milton, who later became the Administrator of Southern Rhodesia, settled in Harare. An English rugby international and a South African international cricketer, he favoured cricketers for appointments to the Civil Service. He granted Salisbury CC title to the land which forms the present Harare Sports Club ground. In September 1897 he organised a Sports Carnival to celebrate the Diamond Jubilee of Queen Victoria and the end of the Mashona War. Within nine years of the Pioneers arriving in Harare, cricket was firmly established in Zimbabwe. In 1898 the Rhodesian Cricket Union was formed and immediately they invited Lord M.B. Hawke's English side to visit during their tour of South Africa. Two matches were played in Bulawayo, the English first meeting a Bulawayo XVIII and then a Rhodesia XV. For the Rhodesian game, five players travelled from Harare. Heavy rain had increased the journey time to Bulawayo from four days to ten or twelve. The players allowed fourteen and arrived only on the morning of the first day of the match, having had to pull themselves across the flooded Hunyani river on a makeshift rope pulley and then wait for the coach from Bulawayo to arrive and turn round because the coach from Harare was unable to cross. In recognition of their determination, J.D. Logan, the legislator from Cape Province and patron of the tour, offered a cup for an inter-town competition. The Logan Cup is now the trophy for the inter-provincial first-class competition.

Rhodesia's cricketers continued their pioneering spirit when they went to Johannesburg in March 1905 to take part in South Africa's Currie Cup competition. The team travelled by train from Bulawayo to Mafeking and then by coach to Potchefstroom where they caught the train to Johannesburg. The coach journey consisted of twenty-six hours in wind and rain, crossing rivers in spate; for most of that time the players went without sleep and sat, permanently drenched, with their feet in water. Whether this effort dampened enthusiasm or not, another 25 years elapsed before Rhodesia again competed in the Currie Cup.

By the early 1900s cricket was established in the private schools set up for the European population. Cricket was introduced at St George's College, Bulawayo, in the 1897/98 season. In November 1907, the first inter-school contest took place between Plumtree and St John's College which later became Milton School. Plumtree and Milton in Bulawayo and Prince Edward School in Salisbury supplied many of Rhodesia's cricketers from the 1920s through to the 1970s.

With no matches during the First World War and distance and cost preventing Rhodesia from playing in South Africa, matches between 1906 and 1930 were restricted to visiting teams. Two matches were played against the English team, captained by H.D.G. Leveson-Gower, which visited South Africa in 1909/10. They became the first visiting team to travel to Harare as well as Bulawayo. Transvaal came in 1923 and 1928 and an England side assembled by Solly Joel in 1924. Hosting these visiting sides was expensive. The South African Cricket Union asked for a guarantee of £800 for the visit of Leveson-Gower's side which there was no chance of the Rhodesians raising. With the visit about to be cancelled, Leveson-Gower offered to accept £450 but the inhabitants of Bulawayo raised only £100 and those of Salisbury £50. The Chartered Company and Sir Abe Bailey, who was a patron of much cricket in South Africa, agreed to make up the difference. With Rhodesia effectively coming under the wing of the South African Cricket Association, cricket became a game of the white minority. No attempt was made to encourage Africans to take up the game and, although it was played by expatriate Indians, their numbers were too small for their cricket to reach a standard comparable to that of the whites.

Incorrect Procedure

Rhodesia returned to the Currie Cup in 1929/30 and in 1931/32 finished runners-up when they were assisted by George (Jackie) Grant, the former captain of the West Indies, whose experience and skill vitalised the side. Rhodesia took no further part in Currie Cup matches before the Second World War. First-class representative games were restricted to matches against Australia in 1935/36, Transvaal in 1936/37 and the MCC in 1938/39. The first Rhodesian cricketers to gain selection for South Africa were Bob Crisp, a fast-bowler, and Denis Tomlinson, an all-rounder who bowled leg spin. Both were chosen to tour England in 1935. That honour should have fallen to Leo Robinson who took part in the trials to select the South African side for England in 1907. Although not selected, he travelled to England anyway and during the tour the selection committee wanted to add him to the party. He was actually chosen for one of the test matches but his brother, the Reverend (later Canon) C.D. Robinson, vice-captain of the touring party, advised that selecting him in this way was an incorrect procedure, so he did not play.

During the Second World War, the Rhodesian Air Training Scheme kept cricket alive by organising matches against local sports clubs. These included women's games with a team captained by Lila Franklin. When the War ended, Rhodesia returned to the Currie Cup competition as soon as it resumed and remained in it until the country gained independence as Zimbabwe in 1980. During that time Rhodesia functioned effectively as a provincial side in the South African domestic cricket with the same status as Western Province, Natal or Transvaal. At this level cricket remained the preserve of the minority white population which in the early 1960s amounted to only 5 per cent of the country's total population. With Asian numbers being even smaller, cricket was easily viewed as a privileged sport which had no connexion with the majority of the people. Few Africans played and there was little opportunity for them to do so.

Although Rhodesia never won the Currie Cup, they produced some excellent cricketers who became regular choices for South Africa, most notably Percy Mansell, Colin Bland, Joe Partridge, Godfrey (Goofie) Lawrence, Tony Pithey and John du Preez. The team also benefited from South Africans who spent periods working in Rhodesia, particularly Paul Winslow. The period 1960-65 is sometimes termed the 'golden years' when the country was one of the strongest sides in South Africa. Rhodesia's second period as a major cricketing force is known simply as the 'Mike Proctor era'. As a professional cricketer, he took up the position of Rhodesia's coach in 1970 and immediately marked his appointment with the following sequence of scores in the Currie Cup: 119, 129, 107, 174, 106 and 254. Six consecutive first-class centuries equalled the record set by C.B. Fry in 1901 and Don Bradman in 1938/39.

On independence, Zimbabwe immediately became one of the strongest cricketing countries among the associates with excellent facilities, professional coaches, a good club structure and cricket played in the leading private schools. In addition, following the move towards multiracial cricket in South Africa, Asian cricket was gaining strength at club level. Offsetting this was the still urgent need to spread the game among the African population and to prevent the decay of women's cricket. The women's game was administered by the South African and Rhodesian Women's Cricket Association but few women in Rhodesia played and the standard was low. With few players, there was little money to invest and the women's game virtually died.

Potentially World-class

Great efforts were made to maintain the standard of men's cricket in the period after the links with South Africa were severed. Zimbabwe played hosts to at least two touring sides a season which provided valuable experience of both three-day and one-day international cricket. They won the ICC Trophy in 1982, 1986 and 1990 and were unbeaten in all three tournaments. March 1986 marked the arrival of Graeme Hick as a potentially world-class batsman. His 309 represented 60 per cent of Zimbabwe's total against the Irish tourists in a match which was won by an innings and 67 runs. Unfortunately for Zimbabwe, which did not have test-match status at that time, Hick decided to follow his profession in England. He had a long and successful first-class career with Worcestershire and an inconsistent record as an England international. In 1980, Ali Omar Shah became the first player of Indian descent to play for Zimbabwe, although perhaps that honour should be given to Kishore Desai who played for Rhodesia B in South Africa's Castle Bowl competition in 1977. Several other Asians were selected for Zimbabwe during the 1980s but only Omar Shah commanded a regular place.

Success in the ICC Trophy qualified Zimbabwe for the World Cup. They made a sensational start, beating Australia by 13 runs in their very first match at Nottingham in 1983. However, they lost their remaining five matches that year, all their matches in the 1987 competition and their first seven matches in 1992. They then took England by surprise. With Eddo Brandes taking four for 21, Zimbabwe were victorious by nine runs. These performances combined with good records on tours of England in 1985 and 1990 and an effective administrative structure led to Zimbabwe being granted full membership of the ICC in 1992. This admission to test status ignored the obvious weakness in the game in Zimbabwe, namely its concentration on a small proportion of the population with increasingly limited political clout.

One of the first tasks of the ZCU was to underpin the test status by establishing a structure for domestic cricket at first-class level. This was achieved by upgrading the Logan Cup into a first-class provincial competition. The problems in so doing were the small number of players, their concentration in the main towns of Harare and Bulawayo and, within those, the dominance of Harare, the centre of Mashonaland, in terms of standard. It was thus difficult to provide a competition with enough teams to create a worthwhile first-class season and avoid a one-sided contest. In the first year of the competition in 1993/94 this was achieved by splitting Mashonaland into three teams, Mashonaland, Mashonaland Under 24 and Mashonaland Country Districts with Matabeleland, based on Bulawayo, as the fourth side. In 1995/96, the competition was reduced to just Mashonaland and Matabeleland who played each other three times. For the next two years, a third side, Mashonaland A was added. In 1999/00 the competition was extended by admitting Manicaland, based at Mutare, and the Midlands, based at Kwekwe, reflecting successful efforts by the ZCU to revive the game in these centres, and the CFX Academy, a team designed to bring on young cricketers. Despite these changes and recent moves to second players from Harare to the other provincial centres, Mashonaland have remained the dominant side (Table 2.25).

Table 2.25 Teams involved in Zimbabwe's first-class domestic competition: the Logan Cup (1993/94-2004/05)

Team	Dates of appearances	Winners
CFX Academy	1999/00-2001/02	0
Manicaland	1999/00-to date	0
Mashonaland	1993/94-to date	8
Mashonaland A	2000/01-2001/02	0
Mashonaland Under 24	1993/94-1994/95	1
Matabeleland	1993/94-to date	2
Midlands	1999/00-to date	0
Young Mashonaland	1995/96	0

No competition was held in 2005/06 or 2006/07.

Zimbabwe's record in test matches has been disappointing. The only teams they have beaten are Bangladesh (four times), India (twice) and Pakistan (twice). Their first victory, which came in their eleventh match, was a convincing innings defeat of Pakistan but since then they have struggled through not having enough world-class players. By the late 1990s, Zimbabwean cricket started to suffer from problems arising both directly and indirectly from the country's declining economy and its governance. Shortage of money reduced the investment that could be made in young players and the payments made to the national team. Many of the best players who wanted to follow their career as professional cricketers found that they could make more money in England or Australia. As high inflation and declining living standards hit Zimbabwe, they also found that these countries offered a more attractive living environment for themselves and their families.

In 2000, under political pressure from the government, the ZCU set up a task force to examine the future of Zimbabwean cricket. Their report concluded that racism lay at the heart of Zimbabwe's cricket and that this culture should change so that by 2005, Africans would be in the majority in every aspect of the game. Exactly how much political pressure was exerted is unclear but many whites left the administration of the ZCU and many white players either left the country or decided on early retirement. A new committee was appointed to run the ZCU under chairman, Peter Chingoka, who had played cricket in South Africa under the South African African Cricket Board during the years of *apartheid*. Concerns were expressed over other appointments to the Board, particularly those of people with little or no experience of cricket and who looked very much like representatives of the government. An immediate aim of the new Board was to include a minimum of three African players in the national side with increasing representation over the following few years. Ironically, government mismanagement of the country's economy meant that the ZCU had less money to invest in the development of African cricket. A dispute arose between the Board and many of the players as to whether the national side was being selected on merit. The Board took the view that Zimbabwean cricket was multiracial and that the complaints were coming from white players whose places in the national side were marginal. Some of the players took the view that few of the Africans merited a place in the team.

By 2004, the dispute between the Board and the players had worsened. The players grievances had extended to payments to the national team, monies owed to individuals because of the Board's failure to honour previous payments and the Board's interference in the selection of teams at provincial and club level. The Board responded by removing Heath Streak as captain of the national side even though he had been a leader in the coaching of young African cricketers. It looked very much as though Africanisation was for a select group of cricketers and that non-Shona and those Shona who expressed views in opposition to the government were not to be included. Streak is a fluent Ndebele speaker.

The ZCU could not, however, ignore the effect of their policies on the performance of the national side. On 25 April 2004, Zimbabwe were dismissed for 35 by Sri Lanka, the lowest total ever recorded in official one-day internationals and in May 2004, a team with only one white player were defeated by an innings and 240 runs by Sri Lanka; with two white players, they then lost the second test by an innings and 254 runs. Concerns about the effect of such mismatches on test cricket records and whether or not Zimbabwe should be suspended from test status were complicated by the fact that Zimbabwe were still capable of beating Bangladesh who were promoted to test status by the ICC in 2000. The ZCU spared the ICC's embarrassment by unilaterally withdrawing from test cricket for the foreseeable future. Politically the ZCU remains astute particularly regarding its relations with the ICC. It has responded to concerns about mismanagement of finance by disbanding and establishing a new body, Zimbabwe Cricket, in its place. There are now no whites or Asians involved in cricket administration at national level. Despite this, Zimbabwe Cricket can claim that it is multiracial; the team selected for a one-day series against Kenya in 2006 contained a majority of white players. Also in 2005, Zimbabwe Cricket, in accordance with ICC policy, attempted to revive the women's game. Seven sides competed in a 15-overs aside tournament in Bulawayo. The international debut

was made in 2006 when Zimbabwe won the African region tournament, a first stage qualifying competition for the 2009 women's World Cup. Nevertheless, the underlying issues remain. In early 2006, Tatenda Taibu, Zimbabwe's captain and best young player at the age of 22, resigned to seek a career overseas. Zimbabwe Cricket still faces the issue that, despite its best efforts, the best cricketers in the country are still mostly white, even though the standard is now much lower. Domestic cricket is now well below first class, a fact recognised by Zimbabwe Cricket who, in 2006, cancelled the Logan Cup.

The recent history of Zimbabwean cricket demonstrates that whilst it can take many years and far longer than the government is prepared to accept to raise the standard of cricket in an ethnic community which has long been excluded from the game, national standards can fall very quickly if an encouraging environment for the best players is not maintained. The problems at the heart of Zimbabwean cricket are racial but not at a simplistic level between African and European. They also reflect a long standing rivalry between Shona and Ndebele which has been exploited politically by an elite section of Shona society. The effect has been compounded by mismanagement of the country's economy which has starved cricket of the necessary funds for its development. Zimbabwean cricket will remain in crisis at least until there is a change in national government. The hope must be that the present generation of young players, African, European and Asian men and women, will still want to play the game when a new government is in place.

Famous Victories
June 9, 1983 – Trent Bridge, Nottingham
Zimbabwe 239-6 (60 overs) (D.A.G. Fletcher 69*)
Australia 226-7 (60 overs) (K.C. Wessels 76, R.W. Marsh 50*, D.A.G. Fletcher 4-42)
Zimbabwe won by 13 runs

Zimbabwe's first appearance in the World Cup produced a sensational result. After being asked to bat and losing five wickets for 94 runs, Duncan Fletcher added 70 in fifteen overs with Kevin Curran (27) and an unbeaten 75 with Iain Butchart (34*) in twelve overs. Australia missed five catches. In reply Graeme Wood and Keith

Wessels made 61 before the first wicket fell but against keen fielding and some tight bowling, Australia were always behind the required run-rate. Whilst Fletcher took four wickets in his eleven overs, credit must also go to Vince Hogg (6-2-15-0), Iain Butchart (10-0-39-1) and John Traicos (12-2-27-0) for some economical bowling.

January 31, February 1, 2 and 4, 1995 – Harare Sports Club
Zimbabwe 544-4 dec (G.W. Flower 201*, A. Flower 156*, G.J. Whittall 113*)
Pakistan 322 (Inzamam-ul-Haq 71, Ijaz Ahmed 65, Aamir Sohail 61, H.H. Streak 6-90) and 158 (Inzamam-ul-Haq 65)
Zimbabwe won by an innings and 64 runs

Zimbabwe gained their first test victory in spectacular fashion. They started slowly, scoring 42 and losing three wickets before lunch on the first day. After the interval, Wasim Akram bowled seven consecutive maidens. Then Grant and Andy Flower took control in a partnership of 269, the best in test cricket by two brothers, from which Pakistan never recovered. Even after Andy Flower departed there was no respite, Grant Flower adding a further 233 with Guy Whittall. The declaration came late on the second day by the end of which Pakistan had already lost a wicket, Saeed Anwar (8) being caught behind by Andy Flower to give Henry Olonga his first test wicket on his debut, the first African to play test cricket for Zimbabwe. Accurate bowling by Heath Streak kept Zimbabwe on top with only Inzamam-ul-Haq, batting number eight because of a damaged shoulder, offering much resistance. Pakistan performed even worse in the follow-on when Streak (11-5-15-3) was supported by David Brain (3-50) and Whittall (3-58). Inzamam added 96 in a sixth-wicket stand with Rashid Latif (38) but Wasim Akram (19) was the only other player to make double figures. Pakistan succumbed with a day to spare.

Player Profiles

Flower, Andrew. b Fish Hoek, Cape Town, South Africa, 28 April 1968. lhb. wk. A fine player of fast bowling, he scores many of his runs off the back foot square of the wicket. During a tour of India he developed into one of the best players of spin bowling and perfected the reverse sweep. He shares the world record of seven consecutive test match fifties and holds the record for the highest individual test score by a wicket keeper and the only wicket-keeper to score centuries in both innings of a test. He remained loyal to Zimbabwe until the 2003 World Cup during which he led a protest with his team colleague Henry Olonga against the loss of democracy in Zimbabwe. He then retired from international cricket and moved permanently to England to continue a successful career with Essex which had started in 2002. In 76 matches for Zimbabwe he scored 5,378 runs (average 46.76) and made 169 catches and 10 stumpings; 63 of these have been test matches in which he scored 4,794 runs (average 51.54), took 151 catches and made 9 stumpings. In 213 one-day internationals for Zimbabwe he scored 6,786 runs (average 35.34) and made 141 catches and 32 stumpings.

Gardiner, Howard Arthur Bruce. b Bulawayo 3 January 1944. rhb. wk. At 1.96 metres, one of the tallest-ever wicket-keepers, his consistency behind the stumps in the late 1960s and early 1970s contributed much to the potency of Godfrey Lawrence and Joe Partridge as new-ball bowlers. He was also adept standing up to the wicket and made several good stumpings off the spin bowlers. A useful lower middle order batsman, in 54 matches for Rhodesia he scored 1,700 runs (average 22.97) and had the remarkable return of 137 catches and 19 stumpings, with four or more victims in an innings on seven occasions. He became the Managing Director of BOC Zimbabwe Ltd in 1989.

Houghton, David Laud. b Bulawayo 23 June 1957. rhb. wk. The leading Zimbabwean cricketer immediately prior to and after the country obtaining test-match status, he first played for Rhodesia in 1978 and continued in international cricket until 1997. He scored a century in Zimbabwe's inaugural test match. A renowned player of spin bowling, he could both bat aggressively and play a long defensive innings. In 87 matches for Rhodesia and Zimbabwe he scored 5,270 runs (average 36.34) and made 130 catches and 9 stumpings; 22 of the matches were tests in which he made 1,464 runs (average 43.05) and 17 catches. In 63 one-day internationals he made 1,530 runs (average 26.37), 29 catches and 2 stumpings. In 109 other limited overs matches he scored 2,985 runs (average 33.53) and made 99 catches and 10 stumpings. He played hockey for Zimbabwe as goalkeeper, an experience which undoubtedly helped his wicket-keeping.

Kaschula, Richard Herbert. b Gwelo 9 November 1946. ed Chaplin HS Gwelo. rhb. sla. A recognised number eleven batsman, he is arguably the most successful spin bowler to come from Rhodesia. Were it not for his 122kg weight which restricted his nimbleness in the field, the fact that he combined cricket with farming and that his best years coincided with South Africa's isolation from international cricket, he might well have played at test level. He first played for Rhodesia in 1970 but dropped out of the game for four years in 1973. In 48 matches he took 196 wickets (average 25.71) and scored 273 runs (average 7.37). He became a national selector for Zimbabwe but was removed by Zimbabwe Cricket in 2006.

Lawrence, Godfrey Bernard (Goofy). b Salisbury 31 March 1932. rhb. rfm. He formed an effective new ball partnership with Joe Partridge in the 1950s and early 1960s. At 1.96 m, he was the tallest player in South African cricket at that time. If his peak had not coincided with Neil Adcock and Peter Heine, he might well have played more test cricket for South Africa. In 66 first-class matches for Rhodesia, he scored 908 runs (average 12.61) and took 296 wickets (average 17.29) with five or more in an innings on 13 occasions. In five test matches for South Africa, he scored 141 runs (average 17.62) and took 28 wickets (18.28). A Civil Servant by profession, he later left Rhodesia and played for Natal.

Mansell, Percy Neville Frank MBE. b St George's, Oakengates, Shropshire, 16 March 1920. d Somerset West, Cape Province, 9 May 1995. rhb. rm/lb. Slightly-built and bespectacled, he was a forceful right-hand batsman, a safe slip field, a skilful right-arm leg spinner and, in emergency, a useful seam bowler. Making his debut in 1936, he became the leading all-rounder for Rhodesia in the late 1940s and 1950s. He made two tours of England and one of Australia for South Africa but was never chosen

by South Africa at home. Not one for personal glory, he is reputed to have been in a position where he needed to score two runs for victory and three for his hundred; he settled for two. In 55 matches for Rhodesia, he scored 3,027 runs (average 36.46) and took 203 wickets (average 22.00). In 13 test matches for South Africa he scored 355 runs (average 17.75) and took 11 wickets (average 66.90). An accountant, he was awarded the MBE and a Freeman of Bulawayo for services to cricket.

Partridge, Joseph Titus (Joe). b Bulawayo 9 December 1932. d Harare 6 June 1988 (suicide). rhb. rfm. Relying on accuracy, stamina and swing rather than pace, his stock ball was an inswinger which he straightened off the pitch and occasionally cut away to slips; months of practice also gave him an outswinger. Bespectacled, strongly built, he was always a willing competitor, even on the hottest days. He first played for Rhodesia in 1952 but was not chosen by South Africa for test cricket until 1963. In 56 matches for Rhodesia he scored 419 runs (average 9.10) and took 281 wickets (average 19.01). In 11 test matches for South Africa he scored 73 runs (average 10.42) and took 44 wickets (average 31.20). He was a Bank Official by profession.

Streak, Heath Hilton. b Bulawayo 16 March 1974. rhb. rfm. Noted for his stamina, he virtually led the Zimbabwean attack in the late 1990s and early 2000s. He bowled mainly outswing but with excellent control of line and length. At his peak, he was one of the best opening bowlers in the world. Although he batted mainly in the lower middle order, as selection policies began to weaken the Zimbabwean side, his batting became ever more important, frequently rescuing his team from an early order collapse. A keen supporter of the game amongst the African population, he did much to help African cricket and was highly regarded by the young players in his charge. As captain of the national side, he led his colleagues in their dispute over selection policy and playing conditions with the Zimbabwe Cricket Union. As a result, he was relieved of the captaincy. Loyal to his country, he later returned to play for them in one-day internationals. He played county cricket for Warwickshire and was appointed their captain for 2006. In 65 test matches he has scored 1,990 runs (average 22.35) and taken 216 wickets (average 28.14). In 187 one-day internationals he has scored 2,901 runs (average 28.44) and taken 237 wickets (average 29.81).

Taibu, Tatenda. b Harare 14 May 1983. rhb. rm. wk. Seemingly destined to become the best African cricketer ever to play for Zimbabwe, his potential caused the selectors to rush him into positions of responsibility. He was chosen as vice-captain for the 2003 tour of England aged only nineteen. Following the resignation of Heath Streak, he was appointed captain in April 2004, becoming the youngest ever captain in test cricket. Leading a team which was woefully inadequate at test level, he all too often made the only score of any substance. In one-day matches, he was frequently forced to hand over the wicket-keeping duties to a colleague in order to bowl. In some matches, he was not only captain but also the highest scorer, the leading bowler and wicket-keeper. As captain, he found himself leading his players in dispute with Zimbabwe Cricket in the autumn of 2005. Following threats to himself and his family, he resigned the captaincy and retired from international cricket. He is unlikely to play for Zimbabwe again until there is a change in the leadership of both the Zimbabwe Cricket Board and his country. In 2006/07 he assisted Namibia in South African domestic competitions. In 24 test matches he scored 1,273 runs (average 29.60) and made 48 catches and 4 stumpings. In 83 one-day internationals for Zimbabwe he has scored 1,400 runs (average 25.45) and made 73 catches and 8 stumpings.

Other leading players: *1890-1914:* J. Bissett; L.G. Robinson (rhb. rm(u)); W.S. Taberer (rhb. rm). *1920-1940:* R.J. Crisp (rhb. rf); J.C. Campbell-Rodger (rhb. rm); J.D. Thompson (rhb. wk); D.S. Tomlinson (rhb. lbg). *1945-1960:* A.J. Pithey (rhb. rob); R. Ullyett (rhb. rm); D.J. Lewis (rhb); C. Harris (rhb. wk); D. O'Connell-Jones (rhb). *1960-1980:* R.A. Gripper (rhb); B.F. Davison (rhb. rob/rm); D.A.G. Fletcher (lhb. rfm); K.C. Bland

(rhb. rm); J.H. du Preez (rhb. lbg). *1980-2000:* A.J. Traicos (rhb. rob); A.J. Pycroft (rhb. rob); G.W. Flower (rhb. sla); E.A. Brandes (rhb. rfm); A.H. Omar Shah (lhb. rm). *Present day:* E.C. Rainsford (rhb. rfm); H. Masakadza (rhb).
Women: *Present day:* Y. Rainsford (rhb. rfm); J. Chibhabha (lhb. sla).

Playing record
Test Matches

	Won	Lost	Tied	Drawn
England	0	3	0	3
Australia	0	3	0	0
South Africa	0	6	0	1
West Indies	0	4	0	2
New Zealand	0	7	0	6
India	2	7	0	2
Pakistan	2	8	0	4
Sri Lanka	0	10	0	5
Bangladesh	4	1	0	3
Total	8	49	0	26

One-day matches

	Won	Tied	Lost	No Res
World Cup	8	1	33	3
Other ODIs	71	4	195	6
ICC Trophy	23	0	0	2

Highest team score

| 570-6 dec | Rhodesia v Griqualand West, Bulawayo | 1955 |

The highest test match score by Zimbabwe is 563-9 declared against the West Indies at Harare in 2001.

Lowest team score

| 47 | Rhodesia v North-Eastern Transvaal, Pretoria | 1963 |

The lowest test match score by Zimbabwe is 54 against South Africa at Cape Town in 2004/05.

ODI

| 35 | v Sri Lanka, Harare | 2004 |

Highest individual score

| 309 | G.A. Hick | v Ireland, Harare | 1986 |

The highest individual test match score by Zimbabwe is 266 by D.L. Houghton against Sri Lanka at Bulawayo in 1994/95.

Best bowling

| 9-71 | M.J. Procter | Rhodesia v Transvaal, Bulawayo 1972 |

The best individual test match bowling for Zimbabwe is 8-109 by P.A. Strang against New Zealand at Bulawayo in 2000/01.

Best wicket-keeping

5 (3c 2st) C. Harris	Rhodesia v MCC, Salisbury	1949
5 (4c 1st) C. Harris	Rhodesia v Border, East London 1951
5 (4c 1st) C. Harris	Rhodesia v North-Eastern Transvaal, Pretoria 1951

5 (4c 1st)	H.A. B. Gardiner	Rhodesia v Griqualand West, Kimberley	
			1971
5 (5c)	S.D. Robertson	Rhodesia v Northern Transvaal, Pretoria	
			1973
5 (4c 1st)	H.A.B. Gardiner	Rhodesia v International Wanderers, Salisbury	1974
5 (5c)	H.A.B. Gardiner	Rhodesia v Natal, Durban	1976
5 (5c)	W.R. James	Zimbabwe B v Pakistan B, Harare South	
			1987
5 (5c)	D.L. Houghton	v New South Wales, Harare	1987
5 (5c)	W.R. James	v Sri Lanka, Bulawayo	1994/95
5 (5c)	A. Flower	v England, Nottingham	2000

ODI

5 (5c)	D.L. Houghton	v Young India, Harare	1984
5 (4c 1st)	D.L. Houghton	v Young New Zealand, Harare	1988
5 (5c)	A. Flower	v South Africa, Harare	1995/96
5 (5c)	A. Flower	v England, Harare	1996/97

Women

	Won	Tied	Lost	No Res
World Cup qualifying – African region	3	0	0	0

Highest team score

ODI

189	Zimbabwe v Kenya, Nairobi	2006/07

Lowest team score

ODI

189	Zimbabwe v Kenya, Nairobi	2006/07

Zimbabwe have not been dismissed in their other ODIs

Highest individual score

ODI

46	T. Milo	v Kenya, Nairobi	2006/07

Best Bowling

ODI

3-10	J. Chibhabha	v Uganda, Nairobi	2006/07
3-10	J. Chibhabha	v Tanzania, Nairobi	2006/07

CHAPTER 3

TOURNAMENTS AND TROPHIES

TEST MATCHES

TEST MATCHES represent the highest standard of cricket. They comprise matches between full member countries of the International Cricket Council. At present ten countries have such status: England, Australia, South Africa, West Indies, India, New Zealand, Pakistan, Sri Lanka, Zimbabwe and Bangladesh. The first test match is recognised as that between England and Australia at Melbourne in March 1876, this being the first time that a representative Australian side played England on equal terms. Since then – up to 30 April 2007 – 1830 test matches have been played, with Australia easily the most successful country.

	Date of first match	Won	Tied	Lost	Drawn	Percentage matches won	Win/Loss Ratio
Australia	1877	320	2	178	187	46.6	1.80
England	1877	298	0	250	309	34.8	1.19
West Indies	1928	149	1	138	148	34.2	1.08
South Africa	1889	105	0	115	100	32.8	0.91
Pakistan	1952	103	0	87	140	31.2	1.18
Sri Lanka	1982	47	0	63	57	28.1	0.75
India	1932	89	1	131	182	22.1	0.68
New Zealand	1930	62	0	131	139	18.7	0.47
Zimbabwe	1992	8	0	49	26	9.6	0.16
Bangladesh	2000	1	0	39	4	2.3	0.03

Match records

Highest team score

952-6 dec	Sri Lanka v India, Colombo	1997

Lowest team score

26	New Zealand v England, Auckland	1954/55

Highest individual score

400*	B.C. Lara	West Indies v England, St John's	2003/04

Best bowling in an innings

10-53	J.C. Laker	England v Australia, Manchester	1956

Best wicket-keeping in an innings

7 (7c)	Wasim Bari	Pakistan v New Zealand, Auckland	1978/79
7 (7c)	R.W. Taylor	England v India, Bombay	1979/80
7 (7c)	I.D.S. Smith	New Zealand v Sri Lanka, Hamilton	1990/91
7 (7c)	R.D. Jacobs	West Indies v Australia, Melbourne	2000/01

The majority of test matches are played as a series of two to six games between two countries, taking place home or away every three to five years. Only seven of these series involve competitions for a trophy of which the most famous is The Ashes.

The Ashes

ALTHOUGH, AS noted above, England first played Australia in March 1877, four series of matches were to take place before a trophy was inaugurated for contests between the two countries. The trophy arose by happenstance rather than by design. After England were beaten by Australia by seven runs at The Oval in August 1882, the *Sporting Times* carried a mock obituary on the death of English cricket, noting that the 'body will be cremated and the ashes taken to Australia'. In 1882/83, the Hon Ivo Bligh led an English side to Australia, saying, in the spirit of the obituary, that his intention was to recover 'those ashes'. The cricket historian, Rowland Bowen, believes that Bligh's team proposed to play three games against the Australians led by W.L. Murdoch, the Australian captain in The Oval game, and possibly two more against a Combined Australian side. The comments relating to 'the ashes' referred only to the matches against Murdoch's team. After the third of these was completed, with Bligh's team winning the series by two matches to one, some ladies from Melbourne burnt a bail and placed its ashes in an urn on which was written the inscription, 'The Ashes of English Cricket'. The urn was then presented in a velvet bag to Ivo Bligh. One further match was played which the Australians won but although this levelled the

series, it is not considered part of the matches between the teams of Bligh and Murdoch. One of the ladies involved in the scheme to present the urn, Miss Florence Rose Morphy, married Ivo Bligh and, after his death in 1900, she presented the urn and bag to the MCC.

It was not until the 1890s that the term 'ashes' was used again when Clarence Moody referred to the matches between England and Australia as being contests for 'the Ashes'. The next mention was not until 1903 when, prior to the MCC tour to Australia in 1903/04, the captain, Pelham Warner, stated that his aim was to 'recover the Ashes'. Since then each series of matches between the two countries has been described as a contest for The Ashes. The unwritten competition rules require that in order for The Ashes to change hands, one side must beat the other in the series. If the series is drawn, the holder retains The Ashes. In reality, the trophy changes hands only metaphorically since the urn is considered too fragile to undergo regular journeys between England and Australia. Australia have won or retained The Ashes on 35 occasions to England's 29. The highest number of consecutive series in which The Ashes have been either won or retained is eight: by England from 1882/83 to 1890 and by Australia from 1989 to 2002/03.

Season	Location	Trophy held by	Results
1882/83	Australia	England	2-2
1884	England	England	1-0 with 2 drawn
1884/85	Australia	England	3-2
1886	England	England	3-0
1886/87	Australia	England	2-0
1887/88	Australia	England	1-0
1888	England	England	2-1
1890	England	England	2-0
1891/92	Australia	Australia	2-1
1893	England	England	1-0 with 2 drawn
1894/95	Australia	England	3-2
1896	England	England	2-1
1897/98	Australia	Australia	4-1
1899	England	Australia	1-0 with 4 drawn
1901/02	Australia	Australia	4-1
1902	England	Australia	2-1 with 2 drawn
1903/04	Australia	England	3-2
1905	England	England	2-0 with 3 drawn
1907/08	Australia	Australia	4-1
1909	England	Australia	2-1 with 2 drawn
1911/12	Australia	England	4-1
1912	England	England	1-0 with 2 drawn
1920/21	Australia	Australia	5-0
1921	England	Australia	3-0 with 2 drawn
1924/25	Australia	Australia	4-1
1926	England	England	1-0 with 4 drawn
1928/29	Australia	England	4-1
1930	England	Australia	2-1 with 2 drawn
1932/33	Australia	England	4-1
1934	England	Australia	2-1 with 2 drawn
1936/37	Australia	Australia	3-2
1938	England	Australia	1-1 with 2 drawn
1946/47	Australia	Australia	3-0 with 2 drawn
1948	England	Australia	4-0 with 1 drawn
1950/51	Australia	Australia	4-1
1953	England	England	1-0 with 4 drawn
1954/55	Australia	England	3-1 with 1 drawn
1956	England	England	2-1 with 2 drawn
1958/59	Australia	Australia	4-0 with 1 drawn
1961	England	Australia	2-1 with 2 drawn
1962/63	Australia	Australia	1-1 with 3 drawn
1964	England	Australia	1-0 with 4 drawn
1965/66	Australia	Australia	1-1 with 3 drawn
1968	England	Australia	1-1 with 3 drawn
1970/71	Australia	England	2-0 with 4 drawn

1972	England	England	2-2 with 1 drawn
1974/75	Australia	Australia	4-1 with 1 drawn
1975	England	Australia	1-0 with 3 drawn
1977	England	England	3-0 with 2 drawn
1978/79	Australia	England	5-1
1981	England	England	3-2 with 2 drawn
1982/83	Australia	Australia	2-1 with 2 drawn
1985	England	England	3-1 with 2 drawn
1986/87	Australia	England	2-1 with 2 drawn
1989	England	Australia	4-0 with 2 drawn
1990/91	Australia	Australia	3-0 with 2 drawn
1993	England	Australia	4-1 with 1 drawn
1994/95	Australia	Australia	3-1 with 1 drawn
1997	England	Australia	3-2 with 1 drawn
1998/99	Australia	Australia	3-1 with 1 drawn
2001	England	Australia	4-1
2002/03	Australia	Australia	4-1
2005	England	England	2-1 with 2 drawn
2006/07	Australia	Australia	5-0

Notes: Matches prior to 1882/83 and the single matches played in 1976/77, 1979/80, 1980 and 1987/88 are not considered part of The Ashes series.

Tournament records

Highest team score
903-7 dec   England v Australia, The Oval   1938

Lowest team score
36   Australia v England, Birmingham   1902

Highest individual score
364   L. Hutton   England v Australia, The Oval   1938

Most wickets in an innings
10-53   J.C. Laker   England v Australia, Manchester   1956

Best wicket-keeping in an innings
6 (6c)   R.W. Marsh   Australia v England, Brisbane   1982/83
6 (6c)   R.C. Russell   England v Australia, Melbourne 1990/91
6 (6c)   I.A. Healy   Australia v England, Birmingham   1997
6 (6c)   A.J. Stewart   England v Australia, Manchester   1997

Frank Worrell Trophy

AUSTRALIA FIRST played the West Indies in a test series in 1930/31. Two further series occurred before the West Indies embarked on their tour of Australia in 1960/61. This series, which included the first tied match in test cricket, was so entertaining that the Australian and West Indies Cricket Boards decided to commemorate the contest by instituting the Frank Worrell Trophy. The Trophy honours the achievements of Frank Worrell, the first black cricketer to be appointed captain of the West Indies side (see Chapter 2 – Country Profile for the West Indies) and the most successful West Indian captain

of all time. The Trophy has been held by Australia and the West Indies nine times each. The most consecutive series for which the trophy has been held is eight by the West Indies between 1977/78 and 1992/93. Australia held it for five consecutive series between 1994/95 and 2002/03.

Season	Location	Trophy held by	Results
1960/61	Australia	Australia	2-1 with 1 tied and 1 drawn
1964/65	West Indies	West Indies	2-1 with 2 drawn
1968/69	Australia	Australia	3-1 with 1 drawn
1972/73	West Indies	Australia	2-0 with 3 drawn
1975/76	Australia	Australia	5-1
1977/78	West Indies	West Indies	3-1 with 1 drawn
1979/80	Australia	West Indies	2-0 with 1 drawn
1981/82	Australia	West Indies	1-1 with 1 drawn
1983/84	West Indies	West Indies	3-0 with 2 drawn
1984/85	Australia	West Indies	3-1 with 1 drawn
1988/89	Australia	West Indies	3-1 with 1 drawn
1990/91	West Indies	West Indies	2-1 with 2 drawn
1992/93	Australia	West Indies	2-1 with 2 drawn
1994/95	West Indies	Australia	2-1 with 1 drawn
1996/97	Australia	Australia	3-2
1998/99	West Indies	Australia	2-2
2000/01	Australia	Australia	5-0
2002/03	West Indies	Australia	3-1

Tournament records

Highest team score
650-6 dec   Australia v West Indies, Bridgetown   1964/65

Lowest team score
51   West Indies v Australia, Port of Spain   1998/99

Highest individual score
277   B.C. Lara   West Indies v Australia, Sydney   1992/93

Most wickets in an innings
8-71   G.D. McKenzie   Australia v West Indies, Melbourne   1968/69

Best wicket-keeping in an innings
7 (7c)   R.D. Jacobs   West Indies v Australia, Melbourne   2000/01

The Wisden Trophy

ON 19 April 1963, *Wisden Cricketers' Almanack* published its 100th edition. The firm of John Wisden and Company Limited decided to mark this event, with the approval of the MCC and the West Indies Cricket Board of Control, by offering The Wisden Trophy to be played for by England and the West Indies who were the tourists in that centenary year. Like The Ashes, the Trophy is housed permanently in the International

Cricket Museum at Lord's in London. The Trophy has been held by the West Indies on fifteen occasions compared to England's five. Between 1973 and 1997/98 the West Indies held the Trophy for thirteen consecutive series. For six of those series, from 1976 to 1988, England did not win a single test match.

Season	Location	Trophy held by	Results
1963	England	West Indies	3-1 with 1 drawn
1966	England	West Indies	3-1 with 1 drawn
1967/68	West Indies	England	1-0 with 4 drawn
1969	England	England	2-0 with 1 drawn
1973	England	West Indies	2-0 with 1 drawn
1973/74	West Indies	West Indies	1-1 with 3 drawn
1976	England	West Indies	3-0 with 2 drawn
1980	England	West Indies	1-0 with 4 drawn
1980/81	West Indies	West Indies	2-0 with 2 drawn
1984	England	West Indies	5-0
1985/86	West Indies	West Indies	5-0
1988	England	West Indies	4-0 with 1 drawn
1989/90	West Indies	West Indies	2-1 with 1 drawn
1991	England	West Indies	2-2 with 1 drawn
1993/94	West Indies	West Indies	3-1 with 1 drawn
1995	England	West Indies	2-2 with 2 drawn
1997/98	West Indies	West Indies	3-1 with 2 drawn
2000	England	England	3-1 with 1 drawn
2003/04	West Indies	England	3-0 with 1 drawn
2004	England	England	4-0

Tournament records

Highest team score

751-5 dec	West Indies v England, St John's	2003/04

Lowest team score

46	England v West Indies, Port of Spain	1993/94

Highest individual score

400*	B.C. Lara	West Indies v England, St John's	2003/04

Most wickets in an innings

8-45	C.E.L. Ambrose	West Indies v England, Bridgetown	1989/90

Best wicket-keeping in an innings

5 (5c)	D.L. Murray	West Indies v England, Leeds	1976
5 (5c)	P.J.L. Dujon	West Indies v England, Bridgetown	1985/86
5 (5c)	R.C. Russell	England v West Indies, Bridgetown	1989/90
5 (5c)	C.O. Browne	West Indies v England, Nottingham	1995

Trans-Tasman Trophy

THE TRANS-TASMAN Trophy was instituted in 1985/86 for contests between Australia and New Zealand. The establishment of the trophy was a recognition by the Australians that in the 1980s the two countries were able to meet each other on more or less equal terms. Prior to that Australia had largely ignored New Zealand as far as test cricket was concerned. Since the Trophy was inaugurated, Australia have held it for seven series and New Zealand for four.

Season	Location	Trophy held by	Results
1985/86	Australia	New Zealand	2-1
1985/86	New Zealand	New Zealand	1-0 with 2 drawn
1987/88	Australia	Australia	1-0 with 2 drawn
1989/90	Australia	Australia	1 drawn
1989/90	New Zealand	New Zealand	1-0
1992/93	New Zealand	New Zealand	1-1 with 1 drawn
1993/94	Australia	Australia	2-0 with 1 drawn
1997/98	Australia	Australia	2-0 with 1 drawn
1999/00	New Zealand	Australia	3-0
2001/02	Australia	Australia	3 drawn
2004/05	Australia	Australia	2-0

Tournament records

Highest team score

607-6 dec	Australia v New Zealand, Brisbane	1993/94

Lowest team score

76	New Zealand v Australia, Brisbane	2004/05

Highest individual score

215	J.L. Langer	Australia v N Zealand, Adelaide	2004/05

Most wickets in an innings

9-52	R.J. Hadlee	N Zealand v Australia, Brisbane	1985/86

Best wicket-keeping in an innings

5 (5c)	I.A. Healy	Australia v N Zealand, Brisbane	1993/94

Border-Gavaskar Trophy

NAMED AFTER Alan Border and Sunil Gavaskar, leading cricketers of the 1970s and early 1980s for Australia and India respectively, the trophy was first contested in 1996/97 when a single match was arranged in New Delhi to coincide with a festival designed to strengthen political and economic links between the two countries. Unfortunately it also coincided with a period of poor relationships between the respective cricket boards. India won the inaugural game by seven wickets. Since then the Trophy has been held by India on four occasions to Australia's two.

Season	Location	Trophy held by	Results
1996/97	India	India	1-0
1997/98	India	India	2-1
1999/00	Australia	Australia	3-0
2000/01	India	India	2-1
2003/04	Australia	India	1-1 with 2 drawn
2004/05	India	Australia	2-1 with 1 drawn

Encyclopedia of World Cricket

Tournament records

Highest team score
705-7 dec | India v Australia, Sydney | 2003/04

Lowest team score
93 | Australia v India, Mumbai | 2004/05

Highest individual score
281 | V.V.S. Laxman | India v Australia, Kolkata | 2000/01

Most wickets in an innings
8-84 | Harbhajan Singh | India v Australia, Chennai | 2000/01

Best wicket-keeping in an innings
4 (4c) | M.S.K. Prasad | India v Australia, Adelaide | 1999/00
4 (4c) | A.C. Gilchrist | Australia v India, Mumbai | 2000/01
4 (4c) | P.A. Patel | India v Australia, Nagpur | 2004/05

Sir Vivian Richards Trophy

THE SIR Vivian Richards Trophy was instituted for matches between the West Indies and South Africa during the South African tour of the Caribbean in 2000/01. The Trophy is dedicated to the cricketer who has played in more test matches (121) and, at the time, had scored more test match runs (8,540) than any other West Indian. The establishment of the Trophy coincided with a decline in the standard of West Indian cricket so that, to date, it has been held only by South Africa.

Season	Location	Trophy held by	Results
2000/01	West Indies	South Africa	2-1 with 2 drawn
2003/04	South Africa	South Africa	3-0 with 1 drawn
2004/05	West Indies	South Africa	2-0 with 2 drawn

Tournament records

Highest team score
747 | West Indies v South Africa, St John's | 2004/05

Lowest team score
140 | West Indies v South Africa, Port Elizabeth | 2000/01

Highest individual score
317 | C.H. Gayle | West Indies v South Africa, St John's | 2004/05

Most wickets in an innings
7-37 | M. Ntini | South Africa v West Indies, Port of Spain | 2004/05

Best wicket-keeping in an innings
5 (5c) | M.V. Boucher | South Africa v West Indies, Kingston | 2000/01

Basil D'Oliveira Trophy

THE BASIL D'Oliveira Trophy was established by the United Cricket Board of South Africa in 2004/05 for matches between England and South Africa. The Trophy honours the greatest coloured cricketer to play for South Africa. He represented the South African Cricket Board of Control (SACBOC) against Kenya and East Africa before migrating to England where he had a successful test match career. The UCBSA has proposed that the Trophy be restricted to series played in South Africa. England hold the trophy, winning the only series contested to date by two matches to one with two drawn.

Tournament records

Highest team score
570-7 dec | England v South Africa, Durban | 2004/05

Lowest team score
139 | England v South Africa, Durban | 2004/05

Highest individual score
180 | M.E. Trescothick | England v South Africa, Johannesburg | 2004/05

Most wickets in an innings
7-61 | M.J. Hoggard | England v South Africa, Johannesburg | 2004/05

Best wicket-keeping in an innings
4 (4c) | A.B. de Villiers | South Africa v England, Durban | 2004/05
4 (4c) | G.O. Jones | England v South Africa, Cape Town | 2004/05
4 (4c) | M.V. Boucher | South Africa v England, Johannesburg | 2004/05

ICC Test Championships

THE IDEA of ranking the performance of the test-cricketing countries so as to determine who is the World Champion has long attracted the interest of both cricket statisticians and the general public. The Triangular Series between England, Australia and South Africa, held in England in 1912, was intended to decide just that issue. In the event, a wet summer, the hapless performance of the South Africans, an Australian side weakened by a boycott by six of their best players who were in dispute with the Australian Cricket Board over selection policy, and the boorish and drunken behaviour of the Australians who did tour, all mitigated against the venture. Attendances were poor and the cricket authorities of all three countries agreed that such a tournament should never be repeated. Nevertheless, over time, the concept of some form of world championship regained popularity.

In 1996 Wisden Cricketers' Almanack proposed an unofficial World Championship based on the ideal situation that each test-playing country would play one another in a series at least every four years. Two points would be awarded for a series win, one point for a draw and no points for losing. A series could be any number of matches, including a one-off game. The country rankings would be continuously updated every time a series was played. In reality, the countries did not all play each another in the first years of the calculations, so the results were based instead on the difference between the number of points achieved and the number of series played.

In 2001, the ICC adopted the principle of a World Test Championships by inaugurating a ten-year programme of fixtures in which the countries meet each other, home and away, over two five-year cycles, with each series comprising at least two matches. Each side receives points according to the results of the matches played from which the team's rating is calculated. The rating equals the total points scored divided by the number of matches played. For each series, a side is awarded 1 point for a match win, ½ point for a match draw, 1 bonus point for a series win and ½ bonus point for a series draw. The series score is converted into a rating by whichever of the following applies:

(1) if the gap between the ratings of the two teams at the start of the series is less than 40 points, the rating (R) for each team is calculated as follows:

$$R = [(A) \times (X + 50)] + [(B) \times (X - 50)]$$

(2) if the gap between the ratings of the two teams at the start of the series is 40 points or more, the rating for the stronger team is calculated as:

$$R = [(A) \times (Y + 10)] + [(B) \times (Y - 90)]$$

and the rating for the weaker team as:

$$R = [(A) \times (Y + 90)] + [(B) \times (Y - 10)]$$

where A = the team's series score; B = the opponent's series score; X = the opponent's rating prior to the start of the series; and Y = the team's rating prior to the start of the series.

The rating points for each team are then added to the total rating points already achieved and the new total divided by the new number of total matches played. In addition, when the recalculations are made the points obtained for a series played two or three years previous are halved, therefore giving more weight to the most recent series. Series results older than three years are removed from the calculations. The table below shows the team rankings as at April 2007.

There is no trophy for these championships and, since the rankings are continually updated, there is no specific time of the year when a trophy could be awarded. Although the results are probably meaningful as a statement of the relative strengths of the test-playing countries, the ratings suffer from the different number of matches that constitute a series, which can range from two to six.

Rank	Team	Matches	Points	Rating
1	Australia	43	5807	135
2	England	47	5344	114
3	Pakistan	38	4092	108
4	India	38	4056	107
5	Sri Lanka	36	3686	102
6	South Africa	42	4274	102
7	New Zealand	28	2602	93
8	West Indies	33	2378	72
9	Zimbabwe	15	415	28
10	Bangladesh	22	48	2

World Elevens official and unofficial tests

THE FIRST time an eleven under the title 'World' appeared in a match considered first class was 1 March 1862 at the start of a three-day exhibition game at Melbourne between Surrey and The World. The match was organised during the 1861/62 tour of Australia by H.H. Stephenson's side. There were enough Surrey players in the touring party and resident in Melbourne at the time for a county eleven to be raised. The remaining tourists and some Australians comprised the World eleven. Since the English tourists were not representative of the best cricketers in England at the time and test-match cricket did not begin until 1876, there is no way this game can be rated as equivalent to test standard. Indeed, it was the only game of the fourteen played on the tour to rate as first class. Over one hundred years were to elapse before another World team was involved in first-class cricket. In September 1965 two matches were played between an England XI and a Rest of the World XI. Although the English side was of test-match standard and the World team comprised eleven test cricketers from Australia, West Indies, South Africa and Pakistan, the teams were chosen by the sponsors. These matches and a number of similar games arranged in subsequent years are not therefore classified as test matches.

The first matches involving a World eleven which might be considered test matches were those organised in 1970 between England and the Rest of the World to replace the test series against South Africa which was cancelled. Five matches were played with the Rest of the World winning the series by four matches to one. The English Test and County Cricket Board stated in advance that the series would have the status of tests and that the players chosen for England would receive their international caps. The TCCB set up separate selection committees to choose the two teams. Since the matches did not come under the jurisdiction of the ICC, they were given the status of unofficial tests although the players and the general public at the time treated the games as equivalent to test matches. Further, Garfield Sobers is reputed to have agreed to captain the World eleven on the understanding that the fixtures were recognised test matches. Wisden Cricketers' Almanack included the games in their test-match statistics from 1971 to 1979. The ICC ruled in 1972 that the matches were not official tests, thereby disregarding the way they were advertised to the public.

A World team toured Australia in 1971/72, playing twelve games including five representative matches against Australia. This tour was also a replacement for a cancelled visit by South Africa. The Australian and Rest of World sides were both selected by the Australian Cricket Board. Unlike the 1970 series in England, this one was never marketed as comprising test matches. The World XI won the series by two games to one with two matches drawn. The Australian side was certainly of test standing and might well have been the one chosen had the South African tour have gone ahead. All of the Rest of the World team consisted of test cricketers.

The Pakistani cricket season of 1973/74 began with

two matches between Pakistan and a World XI. Pakistan won both. Since both sides included players who had no test-match experience, the matches cannot be considered the same standard as those of the 1970 and 1971/72 series.

The next major fixture involving a World team was that played at Sydney in October 2005 between Australia and an ICC World XI. The game was organised as part of a Super Series which included three one-day internationals between the same sides. A proportion of the proceeds went towards the Joint United Nations Programme on HIV/AIDS (UNAIDS) and the Australian Red Cross Appeal for earthquake relief in Pakistan. It was scheduled as a six-day game and classified by the ICC as an official test match. As it included the best players in the world at the time, there can be no doubt about the 'test' quality of the two teams. The decision to award the game test-match status was undoubtedly influenced by the greater sponsorship that would result through the sale of television rights and other forms of publicity, thereby increasing the amount of money that would go to the charities. Unfortunately the World XI performed poorly and the game ended on the fourth day with Australia winning by 210 runs. The major criticism to classifying the match as an official test is the inconsistency of the ICC in applying its own rules. There is no obvious difference in the standards of the games and the teams between the 2005 fixture and the matches in the 1970 and 1971/72 series.

Match records

Opponent	Status	Won	Lost	Drawn
England	Unofficial	4	1	0
Australia	Unofficial	2	1	2
Australia	Official	0	1	0
Total		6	3	2

Highest team score

563-9 dec	Rest of the World v England, Birmingham	1970

Lowest team score

59	Rest of the World v Australia, Perth	1971/72

Highest individual score

254	G.S. Sobers	Rest of the World v Australia, Melbourne 1971/72

Most wickets in an innings

7-64	E.J. Barlow	R of World v England, Leeds	1970

Best wicket-keeping in an innings

4 (4c)	D.L. Murray	R of World v England, Leeds	1970

Commonwealth Elevens unofficial tests

A SIDE under the title of a Commonwealth eleven first appeared in 1949/50 when an all-professional team, mostly from the Lancashire League, visited India, Pakistan and Ceylon following a decision of the MCC not to go ahead with their proposed tour. Altogether twenty-one matches were played including five against India which were described as unofficial tests. Such was the success of the tour that a much stronger team repeated the venture to India and Ceylon in 1951/52. A third tour was made, to India only, in 1953/54. These tours did much to develop interest in cricket in India who fielded their best representative sides in all the unofficial tests. Similar ventures aimed at promoting cricket and filling gaps the country's international programme were undertaken in November 1963 and February-March 1968 when Commonwealth sides toured Pakistan.

Match records

Opponent	Status	Won	Lost	Drawn
India	Unofficial	4	4	7
Pakistan	Unofficial	0	1	5
Total		4	4	12

Highest team score

630-9 dec	Commonwealth v Pakistan, Lahore	1963/64

Lowest team score

132	Commonwealth v Pakistan, Multan	1967/68

Highest individual score

285	F.M. Worrell	Commonwealth v Ceylon, Colombo	1950/51

Most wickets in an innings

6-47	J. Iverson	Commonwealth v India, Kolkata	1953/54

Best wicket-keeping in an innings

4 (4c)	H. W. Stephenson	Commonwealth v India, Kolkata	1950/51

Women's Test Matches

WOMEN'S TEST cricket started in 1934/35 when England visited Australia for a series of three matches before continuing on to New Zealand where one match was played. Financial constraints have meant that women have played far fewer test matches than men. Over the last two decades one-day matches rather than test matches have dominated the women's game. Women's cricket has also been held back by a general lack of interest from the men's cricket authorities and the general public. In some countries, particularly but not exclusively in the Indian sub-continent, religious and cultural traditions have also stifled the development of women's cricket and these are only slowly being overcome. Thus whilst the women's game is now reasonably well-established in England, Australia and New Zealand, it is still developing in India and in its infancy in Sri Lanka and Pakistan. The game is now played at test-match level by eight of the ten full-member countries of the ICC. Most recently Ireland has been accepted as having test-match status but, so far, they have played only one match. Now that the ICC has merged with the International Women's Cricket Council, it is up to the ICC to ensure that the women's game is properly supported. They need to institute a Women's Test Match Championship, actively publicise the game, ensure that it has equal coverage on satellite television and, through the respective country authorities, ensure that matches get properly recorded, with full scores and reports, in the national press. At present, equality of the men's and women's game still seems a long way off. The events of the England–Australia series in 2005 provide an example of the gap which exists. England won both the men's and women's series. All of the men's team received awards in the Queen's honours list but only the captain of the women's team was similarly recognised. Yet it is difficult to see how the achievements of the men's and women's teams were in any way different in magnitude.

Australia have the most successful overall record with England the next best. The percentage of games won, however, is much lower than in the men's matches which is a reflection of the larger number of drawn games. If women's test cricket is to prosper there is a need to make it more attractive and, in particular, to increase the scoring rate so that more matches produce a result. The records to date suggest that women are more determined not to lose a game than to win one.

	First match	Won	Tied	Lost	Drawn	% won
Australia	1934	18	8	40	27.3	2.25
England	1934	18	11	57	20.9	1.64
India	1977	3	6	25	8.8	0.50
West Indies	1976	1	3	8	8.3	0.33
New Zealand	1935	2	10	33	4.4	0.20
South Africa	1960	0	4	6	0.0	0.00
Pakistan	2000	0	2	1	0.0	0.00

Match records

Highest team score

| 569-6 dec | Australia v England, Guildford | 1998 |

Lowest team score

| 35 | England v Australia, Melbourne | 1957/58 |

Highest individual score

| 242 | Kiran Baluch | Pakistan v West Indies, Karachi | 2003/04 |

Best bowling in an innings

| 8-53 | N. David | India v England, Jamshedpur | 1995/96 |

Best wicket-keeping in an innings

| 8 (6c 2st) | L. Nye | England v New Zealand, New Plymouth |
| | | 1991/92 |

The Women's Ashes

THE ONLY women's tests for which there is a trophy are those between England and Australia. Although contests between the two countries were often described as being for the 'Women's Ashes', the trophy has only existed since 1998 when an autographed bat was burned before the first test match at Lord's. The trophy was shared in the inaugural series when all three test matches were drawn. Since then it has been held for two consecutive series by Australia and then by England.

Season	Location	Trophy held by	Result
1998	England	England and Australia	0-0 with 3 drawn
2001	England	Australia	2-0
2002/03	Australia	Australia	1-0 with 1 drawn
2005	England	England	1-0

Tournament records

Highest team score

| 569-6 dec | Australia v England, Guildford | 1998 |

Lowest team score

| 78 | Australia v England, Brisbane | 2002/03 |

Highest individual score

| 209* | K.L. Rolton | Australia v England, Leeds | 2001 |

Most wickets in an innings

| 7-51 | L.C. Pearson | England v Australia, Sydney | 2002/03 |

Best wicket-keeping in an innings

| 4 (4c) | J.C. Price | Australia v England, Brisbane | 2002/03 |

ONE DAY INTERNATIONALS

THE FIRST international match under one-day rules was a 40-over game between Australia and England at Melbourne on 5 January 1971. It attracted some 40,000 spectators and resulted in a win for Australia by 5 wickets. Since then to 30 April 2007 2,581 matches have taken place varying in length from 40 to 60 overs per side. The majority of the contests are now standardised at 50 overs. South Africa and Australia have been the most successful countries in one-day cricket.

	Won	Tied	Lost	Drawn	% won	Win/Loss Ratio
Australia	406	8	227	18	61.6	1.79
South Africa	234	5	131	11	61.4	1.79
West Indies	313	5	234	17	55.0	1.34
Pakistan	350	6	285	15	53.3	1.22
England	226	4	222	15	48.4	1.02
India	304	3	312	27	47.0	0.97
Sri Lanka	241	3	264	20	45.6	0.92
New Zealand	226	4	273	24	42.8	0.83
Scotland	7	0	16	0	30.4	0.43
Kenya	27	0	65	2	28.7	0.41
Netherlands	8	0	20	1	27.5	0.40
Zimbabwe	79	5	228	9	24.6	0.34
Ireland	4	1	11	1	23.5	0.36
Bangladesh	36	0	120	2	22.8	0.30
Bermuda	5	0	17	0	22.7	0.29
Canada	7	0	25	0	21.8	0.28
UAE	1	0	8	0	11.1	0.13
Namibia	0	0	6	0	0.0	0.00
East Africa	0	0	3	0	0.0	0.00
Hong Kong	0	0	2	0	0.0	0.00
USA	0	0	2	0	0.0	0.00

Match records

Highest team score

| 443-9 | Sri Lanka v Netherlands, Amstelveen | 2006 |

Lowest team score

| 35 | Zimbabwe v Sri Lanka, Harare | 2004 |

Highest individual score

| 194 | Saeed Anwar | Pakistan v India, Chennai | 1996/97 |

Best bowling in an innings

| 8-19 | W.P.U.J.C. Vaas | Sri Lanka v Zimbabwe, Colombo | 2001/02 |

Best wicket-keeping in an innings

| 6 (6c) | A.C. Gilchrist | Australia v South Africa, Cape Town | 1999/00 |

6 (6c)	A.J. Stewart	England v Zimbabwe, Manchester	2000
6 (5c 1st)	R.D. Jacobs	West Indies v Sri Lanka, Colombo	2001/02
6 (5c 1st)	A.C. Gilchrist	Australia v England, Sydney	2002/03
6 (6c)	A.C. Gilchrist	Australia v Namibia, Potchefstroom	2002/03
6 (6c)	A.C. Gilchrist	Australia v Sri Lanka, Colombo	2003/04

Unlike test matches, one-day internationals are mostly played as one-off series involving two or three countries for a trophy presented by a sponsor. Apart from the World Cup and the Asia Cup, there are only two trophies for specific repeatable series. These are the recently-established Chappell-Hadlee Trophy and the ICC Champions Trophy.

Chappell-Hadlee Trophy

DEDICATED TO the most famous cricketing family in each country (the brothers G.S., I.M. and T.M. Chappell in Australia and the brothers R.J. and D.R. Hadlee and their father, W.A., in New Zealand), the Chappell-Hadlee Trophy is awarded to the winners of a regular three-match series of one-day internationals between Australia and New Zealand. Three series have been played to date.

Season	Location	Trophy held by	Result
2004/05	Australia	Australia and New Zealand	1-1 with 2 drawn
2005/06	New Zealand	Australia	2-1
2007/07	New Zealand	New Zealand	3-0

Tournament records

Highest team score

350-9	New Zealand v Australia, Hamilton	2006/07

Lowest team score

105	New Zealand v Australia, Auckland	2005/06

Highest individual score

181*	M.L. Hayden	Australia v New Zealand, Hamilton 2006/07

Most wickets in an innings

4-55	S.R. Clark	Australia v New Zealand, Christchurch 2005/06

Best wicket-keeping in an innings

3 (3c)	A.C. Gilchrist	Australia v New Zealand, Christchurch 2005/06

ICC Champions Trophy

STARTED AS a Mini World Cup in 1998/99, the ICC Champions Trophy is held approximately every two years. Two of the four competitions to date have been staged in Kenya and Bangladesh which has provided an opportunity to promote the game in those countries. The first two competitions were held on a knock-out basis which had the advantage of a short tournament progressing rapidly to the semi-final stages. The competition was then extended by allowing entry to a qualifying associate country and having the first stage as a league competition with four divisions, each of three teams. This has lengthened the competition, resulting in many pointless matches where the outcome is a foregone conclusion since the winner of each division and therefore the potential semi-finalists is usually easily predicted in advance. It does, however, guarantee that each team plays at least two games, therefore making the time and expense of travel to the competition more worthwhile. One of the surprising aspects of this competition is that Australia and South Africa have each won it only once. The results provide a contrast to the more general records in one-day competitions noted above.

Year	Location	Winner	Runner-up	Semi-finalists	Others
1998/99	Bangladesh	S Africa	W Indies	India/ Sri Lanka	Australia England N Zealand Pakistan Zimbabwe
2000/01	Kenya	N Zealand	India	Pakistan/ S Africa	Australia Bangladesh England/Kenya/ Sri Lanka W Indies Zimbabwe
2002/03	Sri Lanka	India/ Sri Lanka		Australia/ S Africa	Bangladesh England Kenya Netherlands N Zealand Pakistan/W Indies/ Zimbabwe
2005	England	W Indies	England	Australia/ Pakistan	Bangladesh India/Kenya N Zealand Sri Lanka S Africa/USA Zimbabwe

2006	India	Australia	W Indies	N Zealand	Bangladesh
				S Africa	England/India
					Pakistan/Sri Lanka
					Zimbabwe

In 2002/03, two attempts were made to play the final but rain prevented a result in both games; the trophy was therefore shared.

Tournament records

Highest team score

347-4	New Zealand v USA, The Oval	2005

Lowest team score

65	USA v Australia, Southampton	2005

Highest individual score

145*	N.J. Astle	New Zealand v USA, The Oval	2005

Most wickets in an innings

5-29	M. Dillon	West Indies v Bangladesh, Southampton 2005

Best wicket-keeping in an innings

4 (2c 2st)	D.O. Obuya	Kenya v South Africa, Colombo 2002/03
4 (3c 1st)	K.C. Sangakkara	Sri Lanka v Netherlands, Colombo 2002/03
4 (3c 1st)	C.O. Browne	West Indies v Pakistan, Southampton 2005

ICC World ODI Championship

SIMILAR TO the ICC World Test Championships, the World One-Day International Championships is a notional competition based on matches played over a three-year period. Each country is awarded points for the result of each match played and these are converted into a rating based upon the relative strengths of the teams involved and how recently the match took place. Only matches played in the last three years are counted and these are weighted so that the results of matches played in the previous year count fully, those of matches played two years ago count only as two-thirds and those of matches played three years ago count as one-third.

A team's rating after a particular match is calculated according to whichever of the following applies:

(1) If the difference between the ratings of the two teams before the match is less than 40 points, the winner scores the opponent's rating +50 points and the loser scores the opponent's rating -50 points; if the match is tied, each team scores the opponent's rating.

(2) If the difference between the ratings of the teams

before the match is equal to or greater than 40 points, the winner scores its own rating +10 points if it is the higher rating team or its own rating +90 points if it is the lower rating team; the loser scores its own rating -90 points if it is the higher rating team or its own rating -10 points if it is the lower rating team; in the event of a tie, the stronger team scores its own rating -40 points and the weaker team scores its own rating +40 points. The match points are added to the points already scored and a new rating calculated by dividing the total points scored by the number of matches played. The table below shows the rankings as at 30 April 2007. The table is continually recalculated to provide a ranking of current one-day international performance. No trophy is awarded.

Rank	Team	Matches	Points	Rating
1	Australia	54	7038	130
2	South Africa	43	5313	124
3	New Zealand	45	5103	113
4	Sri Lanka	53	5879	111
5	Pakistan	36	3950	110
6	India	50	5320	106
7	England	43	4457	104
8	West Indies	47	4666	99
9	Bangladesh	42	1892	45
10	Ireland	11	317	29
11	Zimbabwe	36	779	22
12	Kenya	11	0	0

ICC World One-Day Elevens

THE ICC has selected World Elevens to play in matches organised to support charitable causes. The match at Melbourne on 10 January 2005 against an Asian Cricket Council XI was in support of the Boxing Day 2004 Asian Tsunami Relief Fund. The three games in Melbourne in October 2005 against Australia supported the United Nations HIV/AIDS programme and the Australian Red Cross Pakistan earthquake relief appeal. These matches were controversially classified by the ICC as official one-day internationals which means that such matches are no longer restricted to contests between individual countries. A player's career record now encompasses matches played for his country and those for multinational elevens. The results of the ICC World XIs have been mixed. They defeated the Asian side easily but then lost all three matches against Australia.

Opponent	Won	Lost	No Res
Asian Cricket Council XI	1	0	0
Australia	0	3	0

Highest team score

344-8	ICC World XI v Asian Cricket Council XI, Melbourne	
		2004/05

Lowest team score

137	ICC World XI v Australia, Melbourne	2005/06

Highest individual score

115	R.T. Ponting	ICC World XI v Asian Cricket Council XI, Melbourne	
			2004/05

Most wickets in an innings

4-33	D.L. Vettori	ICC World XI v Australia, Melbourne	
			2005/06

Afro-Asian Cup

THE FIRST international cricket involving continents instead of countries took place in August 2005 when an eleven selected by the Asian Cricket Council played an eleven chosen by the Africa Cricket Association in a three-match series in South Africa. The aim was to raise money to promote cricket development and support charity. Selection panels were established by each association and the availability of the top players was assured by the respective national bodies. In the event, the teams were not necessarily the best possible since it was decided to include players from all the countries with one-day international status. Thus Asia included one player from Bangladesh alongside those from India, Pakistan and Sri Lanka. Africa included two cricketers from Zimbabwe and two from Kenya during the series. Somewhat surprisingly, given that the Asian team came from three strong countries and the African side from only one such country, the series was drawn, one game each, with the remaining match abandoned because of rain.

Tournament records

Highest team score

267	Asia v Africa, Durban	2005

Lowest team score

106	Africa v Asia, Durban	2005

Highest individual score

78	J.L. Ontong	Africa v Asia, Centurion	2005

Most wickets in an innings

3-21	Zaheer Khan	Asia v Africa, Durban	2005

Best wicket-keeping in an innings

4 (4c)	M.V. Boucher	Africa v Asia, Centurion	2005
4 (3c 1st)	M.V. Boucher	Africa v Asia, Durban	2005

World Cricket League

THE WORLD Cricket League is the newly-established one-day competition instituted by the ICC for associate and affiliate countries. It comprises five divisions. Scheduled to take place every two years, the first competition will be in 2007. The next, in 2009, will also form the qualifying route for the 2011 World Cup. For 2007, countries have been allocated to divisions based on their finishing position in the 2005 ICC Trophy, and various qualifying competitions held in Europe, Asia, Africa, the Americas and the East Asia-Pacific region. Promotion and relegation will take place between the divisions. The make-up of the Divisions for 2007 is as follows:

Division 1: Kenya, Scotland, Ireland, Canada, Bermuda and The Netherlands.

Division 2: United Arab Emirates, Namibia, Denmark, Oman and the top two countries from Division 3.

Division 3: Argentina, Papua New Guinea, Uganda, Italy, Hong Kong, Tanzania, Cayman Islands and Fiji.

Division 4: To be contested in 2008 with the top two countries from Division 5 and the bottom four countries from Division 3.

Division 5: Norway, Afghanistan, Argentina, Botswana, Cook Islands, Jersey, Nepal and Singapore.

Kenya won the Division 1 tournament held in Nairobi in 2007. The USA were originally placed in Division 3 but were forced to withdraw and were replaced by Argentina following the suspension of the USA Cricket Association from the ICC. Should the USA be readmitted they will join Division 5.

WOMEN'S ONE-DAY INTERNATIONALS

THE FIRST one-day international matches played by women were in the 1973 World Cup. Since then some 605 matches have taken place, the majority of which have been in the World Cup or regional competitions in Europe and Asia. There are no women's tournaments equivalent to the ICC Champions Trophy for men and, so far, the ICC has not produced a ratings table for women's one-day matches. Australia has been easily the most successful country winning 80 per cent of its matches and having a very high win to loss ratio. New Zealand, England, India and Sri Lanka have also won more matches than they have lost. A large difference in standard exists between these countries and the others which is reflected in the international records, most of which result from games between strong and weak opponents.

	Won	Tied	Lost	No Res*	% won	Win/Loss ratio
Australia	158	1	34	4	80.2	4.64
New Zealand	109	2	86	4	54.2	1.26
India	80	1	67	3	52.9	1.19
England	104	2	88	4	52.5	1.18
Sri Lanka	29	0	27	1	50.8	1.07
South Africa	23	0	32	4	38.9	0.71
West Indies	17	0	27	1	37.8	0.63
Ireland	30	0	62	3	31.6	0.48
Netherlands	18	0	57	0	24.0	0.32
Denmark	6	0	27	0	18.2	0.22
Pakistan	8	0	44	1	15	0.18
Scotland	1	0	7	0	12.5	0.14
Japan	0	0	5	0	0.0	0.00

Excludes all matches abandoned without a ball being bowled, including those in the Women's World Cup. The latter are counted as 'no result' games in the World Cup records in Chapter 2 and Chapter 4 because they resulted in competition points being awarded. Records as at 30 April 2007.

Match records

Highest team score
455-5   New Zealand v Pakistan, Christchurch   1996/97

Lowest team score
23   Pakistan v Australia, Melbourne   1996/97

Highest individual score
229*   B.J. Clark   Australia v Denmark, Mumbai   1997/98

Best bowling in an innings
7-4   Sajjida Shah   Pakistan v Japan, Amsterdam   2003

Best wicket-keeping in an innings
6 (4c 2st) S.L. Illingworth   N Zealand v Australia, Beckenham   1993
6 (1c 5st) V. Kalpana   India v Denmark, Slough   1993
6 (2c 4st) Batool Fatima   Pakistan v West Indies, Karachi   2003/04

ICC INTERCONTINENTAL CUP

THE INTERCONTINENTAL Cup was introduced by the ICC in 2004 as a competition for the leading associate countries based on two-innings matches scheduled over three or four days. For the first two years of the competition, the top three rated countries in each of Africa, the Americas, Asia and Europe played each other in a league to determine a winner for each continent. These four teams progressed to the semi-finals, decided on a knock-out basis, and the winners to the final. Perhaps the most surprising outcome has been the failure of Kenya to win the trophy. European teams have dominated with Scotland winning in 2004 and Ireland in 2005 and 2006. Unfortunately, the matches have been affected by the inability of some countries to field their strongest team because their players are contracted to first-class teams in the English or Australian domestic competitions and requests for their release have been refused. In the final stages of the 2004 competition, Kenya's best players withdrew from the national side in a dispute over terms with the Kenya Cricket Association.

Year	Winner	Runner-up	Semi-finalists	Other participants
2004	Scotland	Canada	Kenya / UAE	Bermuda/Ireland Malaysia/Namibia Nepal/Netherlands Uganda/USA
2005	Ireland	Kenya	Bermuda / UAE	Canada/Cayman Islands Hong Kong/Namibia Nepal/Netherlands Scotland/Uganda
2006	Ireland	Canada	None Played	Scotland/UAE Namibia/Kenya Bermuda/Netherlands

Tournament records

Highest team score
620   Bermuda v Netherlands, Pretoria   2006/07

Lowest team score		
76	United Arab Emirates v Nepal, Kathmandu	2005

Highest individual score		
259*	R.N. ten Doeschate	Netherlands v Canada, Pretoria 2006/07

Best bowling in an innings		
9-74	Ali Asad	United Arab Emirates v Nepal, Sharjah 2004

Best wicket-keeping in an innings			
6 (6c)	M.R. Johnson	USA v Canada, Fort Lauderdale	2004
6 (6c)	D.R. Lockhart	Scotland v United Arab Emirates	2006/07

OTHER WORLD COMPETITIONS

Olympic Games

CRICKET WAS included in the original list of Olympic Sports when the proposals were drawn up by the International Olympic Committee for the first of the modern Olympic Games. There were insufficient entries to support a viable competition in the 1896 Games in Athens but the sport remained on the list for the 1900 Games in Paris. It was expected that England, France, Belgium and The Netherlands would compete but, in the event, only England and France sent teams. The side raised by the French Sports Association comprised players from the Albion and Standard Athletic Clubs in Paris. The English team consisted of players from Blundell's School and Castle Cary CC and went under the title of the Devon and Somerset County Wanderers. At the last moment it was agreed to play the match as twelve-a-side. Since the 1900 Olympics were not officially ratified by the IOC until 1912, it seems that several of the players were unaware that the fixture was part of the Olympic Games. No medals were awarded. Devon and Somerset County Wanderers won the two-innings game by 158 runs. Cricket was dropped from the list of sports for subsequent Games.

Commonwealth Games

CRICKET WAS accepted as an official sport for the Commonwealth Games held in Kuala Lumpur, Malaysia in 1998. Some full member countries chose not to field their best sides which was undoubtedly a factor causing the sport to be removed from the Games before they were next held in Manchester, England, in 2002. England, refused to take part. The English Cricket Board were only prepared to send a second-string team whilst the English Commonwealth Games authorities insisted it had to be the best team or none at all. The impasse was never resolved. The Commonwealth Games structure also meant that the West Indies were unable to compete as a team and had to be represented by the separate countries. Jamaica, Barbados and Antigua and Barbuda participated. Similarly, the all-Ireland side were ineligible but Northern Ireland sent a team.

Since the West Indies and Ireland could not be represented in accordance with their ICC status, the ICC refused to classify the matches as official one-day internationals. With the Commonwealth Games being second to the Olympic Games as an international sports festival and cricket being a leading sport among the Commonwealth countries, the ICC should perhaps show a little more pragmatism in what is and is not classified as an official international. The experience of 1998 also shows that the Commonwealth Games have much more meaning as an international event than many of the one-day tournaments supported by the ICC. Unfortunately the attitude of the ICC and some of the national cricket authorities is unlikely to encourage the Commonwealth Games Committee to reinstate cricket as an official sport in the foreseeable future. It has been suggested that were cricket to be included, the Twenty20 format would be adopted. This might allow more teams to compete but no other sport in the Games is played in anything other than its traditional form. The results of the 1998 tournament are summarised below.

Year	Gold	Silver	Bronze	Other participants
1998	Australia	South Africa	New Zealand	Sri Lanka (fourth place)/Antigua and Barbuda Bangladesh Barbados/Canada India/Jamaica Kenya/Malaysia Northern Ireland/Pakistan Scotland/Zimbabwe

Tournament records

Highest team score

| 309 | Zimbabwe v Malaysia, Kuala Lumpur | 1998 |

Lowest team score

| 45 | Canada v India, Kuala Lumpur | 1998 |

Highest individual score

| 107 | D.A. Gunawardene | Sri Lanka v Jamaica, Kuala Lumpur | 1998 |

Best bowling in an innings

| 5-24 | D.W. Fleming | Australia v Antigua and Barbuda, Kuala Lumpur | 1998 |

Best wicket-keeping in an innings

| 5 (5c) | Javed Qadeer | Pakistan v Kenya, Kuala Lumpur | 1998 |
| 5 (4c 1st) | Khaled Mashud | Bangladesh v Northern Ireland, Kuala Lumpur | 1998 |

World Series Cricket

ORGANISED BY Kerry Packer, the Australian Television Station Channel 9 and J.P.Sport, an Australian sports promotion agency, World Series Cricket comprised teams representing Australia, West Indies and a World XI who played each other in a series of three-day two-innings internationals and one-day internationals in 1977/78 and 1978/79. The venture was initiated by Packer after his failure to gain the broadcasting rights for test cricket from the Australian Cricket Board. By offering better financial terms than the players could obtain from their national authorities, he signed up sixty-eight top class cricketers, invariably bringing them into dispute with their own boards. Whilst his dispute with the Australian Board, the Australian Broadcasting Corporation, the International Cricket Council and the English Cricket Board went through the courts, Packer organised the matches. Thwarted by being rejected from the main Australian grounds, he set about acquiring other locations in the main cities and pioneered the concept

of preparing 'slot-in' wickets in greenhouses in large concrete trays which could be inserted in the ground where and when required. Since many of the grounds had floodlights, he was able to inaugurate day-night matches for the one-day games, using white balls. He also introduced coloured clothing. The players were given training programmes in 'professionalism' which covered how to obtain and deal with personal sponsorship. In the first season all the matches were played in Australia but attendances were initially poor with little interest shown in games where the result hardly mattered. Through improved television presentation and by taking many of the one-day games to the smaller towns up-country interest increased. Television audiences increased as did attendances at the day-night matches. The second season saw World Series Cricket taken to New Zealand and the West Indies, in what was sometimes described disparagingly as the 'Packer Circus'. The venture ceased when the English High Court ruled that the players were entitled to seek as good remuneration as possible in their profession as cricketers and that the ICC and the national boards were guilty of restraint of trade in banning them from international cricket. Rather than appeal the decision, the ICC and the cricket boards sought a compromise with Packer. The ICC has never recognised any of the matches as first-class or as official one-day internationals. The table below summarizes the results of the three-day games.

Team	Won	Lost	Drawn	% matches won	Win/Loss ratio
WSC Australian XI	5	8	4	29.4	0.63
WSC West Indies XI	3	3	4	30.0	1.00
WSC World XI	5	2	0	71.4	2.50

Match records

Highest team score

| 625 | WSC World XI v WSC Australian XI, Perth | 1977/78 |

Lowest team score

| 85 | WSC World XI v WSC Australian XI, Auckland | 1978/79 |

Highest individual score

| 246 | G.S. Chappell | WSC Australian XI v WSC World XI, Melbourne | 1977/78 |

Best bowling in an innings

| 7-23 | D.K. Lillee | WSC Australian XI v WSC West Indies XI, Sydney | 1978/79 |

Best wicket-keeping in an innings

| 5 (5c) | R.W. Marsh | WSC Australian XI v WSC World XI, Melbourne | 1977/78 |

AFRICAN TOURNAMENTS

INTERNATIONAL CRICKET tournaments involving African countries have a rather chequered history regarding status and continuity. The first tournament occurred in 1966, a Triangular Competition between Kenya, Uganda and Tanzania. These countries had been playing three-day matches against each other since the early 1950s and it was decided to formalise these into an annual competition. The competition became Quadrangular in 1968 with the entry of Zambia. During the 1970s, Uganda's participation was irregular because the government, under Idi Amin, either did not allow the team to compete or did not release funds for travel. The winners of each tournament were awarded the Robert Menzies Trophy. Some cricket statisticians and commentators do not treat the matches as true internationals because they were played under the auspices of the East African Cricket Association and East Africa was the effective 'international body' of the period. According to this view, the matches have a similar status to Jamaica versus Barbados or Yorkshire versus Lancashire, i.e. they are part of 'domestic' cricket. For the first decade the matches were of a high standard but by the late 1970s, socio-economic changes throughout East Africa resulted in the departure of many European and Asian cricketers and the standard of play began to decline. The tournament is generally considered to have a history from 1966 to 1980, although the Robert Menzies Trophy was still contested in the 1990s in occasional tournaments involving Zambia, Tanzania, Uganda and Malawi. In the 1966-1980 period, Kenya won the competition nine times, Zambia four times and Uganda and Tanzania once each.

The West African Cricket Conference initiated an annual Quadrangular competition in 1991 between Nigeria, Ghana, Sierra Leone and The Gambia, played in each country in turn. As with the East African tournament, some commentators consider the matches as a West African 'domestic' competition. Since the disbandment of the WACC in 2002, however, the matches must be classified as proper international games. Nigeria won the competition every year for the first ten years and again in 2002 since when they have taken part

only intermittently. Sierra Leone won in 2001, 2004 and 2005 and Ghana in 2003 and 2006. The standard of play is low, facilities are poor, funding is limited and the countries often have difficulty in raising a team. It is a tribute to the respective cricket associations and their players that the tournament survives.

From 1991 to 1997 the Africa Cricket Association organised an annual one-day international tournament. The number of participants varied but included most of the associate and affiliate countries from eastern, central and southern Africa as well as development elevens from South Africa and Zimbabwe. Since the competition involved teams of different status, it cannot be recognised as a true 'international' tournament with each country represented by its best possible team. Most of the affiliate countries proved no match for those of associate standing and the associates were generally outclassed by the South African Development side. In 1998 the tournament evolved into the African Cricket Association Cup which was held every two years until 2002. Kenya won the first two tournaments and the South African Development XI won in 2002.

Africa Cup

IN 2004 the Africa Cup was formalised within the qualifying competitions for the ICC Trophy and the World Cup. An associates competition was held in Lusaka in August 2005 preceded by a qualifying affiliates tournament in Benoni in March 2005. Eight countries were scheduled to compete in the affiliates competition but Morocco withdrew before the start of the competition and the South African Country Districts replaced them. The SACD won the tournament easily but were not allowed to proceed to the associates competition since they were not a recognised 'national' side. The runners-up, Botswana, went forward to the associates competition and did extremely well in finishing fourth. The competitions were repeated in 2006 when they became Division 2 and Division 3 of the African Championships.

Division Two

Year	Winner	Runner-up	Other participants
2004	Namibia	Uganda	Botswana/Nigeria/ Tanzania/Zambia
2006	Tanzania	Botswana	Mozambique/Zambia Nigeria (relegated)

Division Three

Year	Winner	Runner-up	Other participants
2004	South African Country Districts	Botswana (promoted)	Gambia/Ghana Malawi/Mozambique Rwanda Sierra Leone
2006	Mozambique	Sierra Leone	Gambia/Ghana Lesotho/Malawi Morocco/Rwanda

Tournament records

Division Two

Highest team score

270	Botswana v Nigeria, Lusaka	2004

Lowest team score

30	Nigeria v Namibia, Lusaka	2004

Highest individual score

102	A.J. Burger	Namibia v Botswana, Lusaka	2004

Best bowling in an innings

5-15	G. Snyman	Namibia v Nigeria, Lusaka	2004

Best wicket-keeping in an innings

4 (4c)	A. Onikoyi	Nigeria v Botswana, Dar es Salaam	2006

Division Three

Highest team score

418-6	South African Country Districts v Rwanda, Benoni	2003/04

Lowest team score

18	Ghana v South African Country Districts, Benoni	2003/04

Highest individual score

143	A. Galloway	South African Country Districts v Botswana, Benoni	2003/04

Best bowling in an innings

7-25	P.K. Ananya	Ghana v Malawi, Benoni	2005/06

Best wicket-keeping in an innings

5 (5c)	M. Kamara	Gambia v Mozambique, Benoni	2003/04

African Women's Tournaments

TO DATE three women's international one-day tournaments have been held. The first, in Uganda in 2002, was an East African Championships which Uganda won with Kenya second and Tanzania third. An attempt was made to repeat the competition in Kenya in February 2006 but only Uganda and Kenya sent teams. Uganda won. In 2004 an African competition took place in Tanzania, involving the three East African countries and Namibia. Tanzania beat Uganda by 8 wickets in the final. The African qualifying tournament for the 2009 World Cup, held in Nairobi in December 2006, was won by Zimbabwe over Tanzania, Uganda and Kenya.

Tournament records

Highest team score

201	Uganda v Namibia, Dar es Salaam	2004

Lowest team score

29	Namibia v Tanzania, Dar es Salaam	2004

Highest individual score

56	S. Hamisi	Tanzania v Uganda, Nairobi	2006/07

Best bowling in an innings

5-22	M. Ayato	Uganda v Namibia, Dar es Salaam	2004

AMERICAN TOURNAMENTS

THE OLDEST international competition on the American continent is between Canada and the United States. First played in 1844, making it the oldest such competition in the world, the match has been played irregularly since. The American cricket historian, John Marder, lists the games in three periods: 1844-1865, 1879-1912 and those from 1963. Matches since 1963 have been played for the K.A. Auty Trophy. In 1970, the United States started matches with Bermuda for the Sir Henry Tucker Trophy but these only lasted three years; Bermuda won one match and the other two were drawn. The South American Championships were inaugurated in 1995 and are held every two years. The first tournament under ICC regulations was organised in 2000 for the Americas Cup. This has since been held every two years, most recently as a qualifying competition for the ICC Trophy and World Cup. A separate tournament for affiliate countries began in

2001 with the winners being allowed to compete in the following Americas Cup. March 2006 saw the first Central American Championships.

Americas Cup

Canada have been the most successful, winning the competition twice and finishing runners-up on the third occasion. An affiliates competition was introduced in 2001 and used as a qualifying tournament for the senior competition. The two competitions are now integrated into the American section of the World Cricket League, forming two divisions with promotion and relegation between them. A third division was introduced in 2006.

Division One

Year	Winner	Runner-up	Other participants
2000	Canada	Bermuda	USA/Argentina/Cayman Islands
2002	USA	Canada	Bermuda/Cayman Islands Argentina/Bahamas
2004	Canada	USA	Bermuda/Cayman Islands Argentina/Bahamas
2006	Bermuda	USA	Cayman Islands/Canada Argentina (relegated)

Division Two

2001	Cayman Islands	Bahamas	Panama, Turks & Caicos
2004	Bahamas	Panama	Belize, Turks & Caicos, Surinam
2006	Argentina	Bahamas	Panama, Surinam Belize (relegated)

Division Three

2006	Surinam	Turks & Caicos	Brazil, Chile

Tournament records

Division One

Highest team score
346-8	Bermuda v Argentina, King City	2000

Lowest team score
59	Bermuda v Cayman Islands, Hurlingham	2001/02

Highest individual score
164	C.M. Marshall	Bermuda v Argentina, King City	2000

Best bowling in an innings
6-33	Nasir Islam	USA v Bermuda, Toronto	2000

Best wicket-keeping in an innings
5 (4c 1st)	A. Ferguson	Argentina v Bahamas, Hurlingham 2001/02

Division Two

Highest team score
289-4	Belize v Surinam, Howard (Panama)	2003/04

Lowest team score
58	Turks & Caicos Islands v Belize, Howard (Panama)	2003/04

Highest individual score
118	C. Young	Belize v Surinam, Howard (Panama) 2003/04

Best bowling in an innings
6-12	N. Ekanayake	Bahamas v Panama, Corimayo 2005/06

Best wicket-keeping in an innings
5 (1ct 4st)	G. Taylor jnr	Bahamas v Surinam, Hurlingham 2005/06

Division Three

Highest team score
290-8	Turks & Caicos Islands v Chile, Paramaribo	2005/06

Lowest team score
88	Brazil v Chile, Paramaribo	2005/06

Highest individual score
180*	S. Shalders	Chile v Turks & Caicos Islands, Paramaribo 2005/06

Best bowling in an innings
6-35	D. Randolph	Brazil v Turks & Caicos Islands, Paramaribo 2005/06

K.A. Auty Trophy

WHEN THE annual series of matches between the United States and Canada was revived in 1963, the cricket associations of the two countries decided to offer a trophy, dedicated to Karl André Auty. Auty was born in England in July 1878 and emigrated to Vancouver in 1909 to become the Power and Contract Manager for the British Columbia Railway Company. He moved to Chicago in 1918 as a Sales Manager for the Commonwealth Edison Company. He did much to keep the game of cricket alive throughout the 1930s and 1940s, turning Chicago into a leading centre for the sport. He was President of the Chicago Cricket Club and the Illinois Cricket Association. He died in 1959, aged 81.

Matches were played regularly as two innings over three days between 1963 and 1980, the venue alternating between Canada and the USA. Canada dominated the event in the 1960s but the competition became more even in the 1970s. There was a two-year gap after the 1980 fixture and when the series resumed in 1983 it became a two-yearly fixture. Another gap occurred after 1991 but matches were played in 1994 and 1995. The trophy is no longer contested. With the increasing commitments of both countries to the ICC Trophy and the Americas Cup, there is no room in the calendar for the fixture. Whilst the ICC is to be applauded for increasing the amount of international competition for associate and affiliate countries, it seems a pity that this has to be achieved without a sense of history. Surely some way could have been found of allowing the oldest international fixture to continue.

Year	Trophy held by	Result
1963	Canada	Innings and 164 runs
1964	Canada	Innings and 94 runs
1965	Canada	Drawn
1966	USA	58 runs
1967	Canada	7 wickets
1968	Canada	Drawn
1969	Canada	Drawn
1970	Canada	Drawn
1971	Canada	1 wicket
1972	USA	Innings and 34 runs
1973	USA	Drawn
1974	USA	176 runs
1975	Canada	3 wickets
1976	USA	2 wickets
1977	Canada	Innings and 187 runs
1978	USA	25 runs
1979	Canada	6 wickets
1980	Canada	136 runs
1983	Canada	Innings and 28 runs
1985	Canada	Drawn
1987	Canada	Drawn
1989	Canada	7 wickets
1991	USA	107 runs
1994	Canada	5 runs
1995	Canada	128 runs

Tournament records
Highest team score
437-8 dec	Canada v USA, North York		1985

Lowest team score
42	Canada v USA, Philadelphia		1976

Highest individual score
176	R. Nascimento	Canada v USA, Toronto	1963

Best bowling in an innings
7-29	R.J. Stevens	Canada v USA, Toronto	1977

Best wicket-keeping in an innings
4 (2c 2st)	L. Balgobin	USA v Canada, Philadelphia	1976
4 (3c 1st)	K. Mars	USA v Canada, Staten Island	1978

Central American Championships

THE FIRST Central American Championships were held in Belize City 2006 with Belize, Mexico and Costa Rica as the competing countries. Being modelled on the South American Championships, it was not necessary for the teams to satisfy the ICC eligibility requirements. Belize won the tournament easily.

South American Championships

STARTING IN December 1995, the South American Championships have been staged approximately every other year. Initially the competition was between Argentina, Brazil, Chile and Peru, the four countries in South America where the game took hold in the late nineteenth and early twentieth century. After winning the first four contests, Argentina have since been represented by their A-team, thereby giving their younger players some international exposure. The A-side won the tournament in 2000 and 2002. In 1999, a team of Guyanese cricketers based in Miami, Florida, some with first-class experience, were allowed to participate. The competition has since been opened up to the Andean Masters, a side based on Asian cricketers resident in Paraguay supplemented by the reserves of some of the other competing teams. In 2004, Puerto Rico entered for the first time. The geographical concept of South America is now seriously challenged by the origins of the competing teams, particularly as, in 2004, the Guyana Masters won the championship by beating Puerto Rico in the final.

American Women's Championships

INAUGURATED AS the preliminary round qualifying competition for the 2009 Women's World Cup, the first American Women's Championships were held in Toronto, Canada, in September 2006. Only two countries took part with Bermuda victorious over Canada by two matches to one.

Tournament records

Highest team score

| 203-5 | Canada v Bermuda, Toronto | 2006 |

Lowest team score

| 124 | Canada v Bermuda, Toronto | 2006 |

Highest individual score

| 86* | B. Marshall | Bermuda v Canada, Toronto | 2006 |

Best bowling in an innings

| 5-32 | C. Fulbert | Bermuda v Canada, Toronto | 2006 |

ASIAN TOURNAMENTS

THE FIRST trophy for a cricket competition in Asia was donated by Sir Ralph Paget, a British Minister in Bangkok, for the match between Siam and Singapore in 1910. The competition lasted only two years. Surprisingly neither of the two long-established contests prior to the Second World War, those between Hong Kong and Shanghai and between the Straits Settlements and the Federated Malay States, had a trophy attached.

Today, Asia has the most active programme of international cricket tournaments of any continent. Although the premier event, the Asian Test Championships, has proved ill-fated, it remains the only test-match competition with more than two countries. The one-day competition for the Asia Cup has been more successful and there is now a similar one-day competition for women. The Asia Cup involves the full-member countries and the top associate countries, qualification being through the Asian Cricket Council Trophy, a two-yearly event open to all associate and affiliate countries. Instead of relying on ICC rankings to determine which Asian teams can compete in the ICC Intercontinental Trophy, the Asian Cricket Council has set up its own Premier League to establish the rankings based on performance in three-day two-innings matches between the associate countries. The ACC also runs a one-day tournament for affiliate countries. Known as the Emerging Nations tournament, it has provided the route through which Nepal has progressed from an affiliate country of moderate standard to one of the leading associate countries in Asia. Regional tournaments are held in south-west Asia for the Middle East Cup and in south-east Asia for the Tuanku Ja'afar Trophy. In addition there is a long-established annual series of two innings matches between Malaysia and Singapore and a somewhat more recent one-day competition.

Asian Test Championships

THE FIRST Asian Test Championships took place in February and March 1999 involving India, Pakistan and Sri Lanka. Three matches were played on a league basis with the top two teams contesting a final. Apart from the first match, that between India and Pakistan in Kolkata, which was attended by an estimated 465,000 people, the games attracted little interest. Even this match, however, finished in a near empty stadium when some 65,000 spectators were forcibly removed by the police after a riot ensued when Sachin Tendulkar was given run out, with India already close to defeat. Despite the delay of three hours whilst the evacuation was effected, Pakistan found time to win the match by 46 runs. The crowd's reaction probably reflected wider political ill-feeling between India and Pakistan as much as dissatisfaction with the umpire's decision.

If the first tournament failed to uphold the ideals of test cricket, the second tournament, in 2001/02, was a disaster. Matches were spread over seven months, giving players and spectators alike the opportunity to forget that a tournament was in progress. India withdrew one week before the start, the Indian government and the Indian Cricket Board refusing to have any sporting contact with Pakistan until political relationships between the two countries were 'normalised'. Bangladesh were admitted to the tournament but performed so poorly against both Pakistan and Sri Lanka that the tournament finalists became immediately obvious. The scheduled 'league' game between Pakistan and Sri Lanka was therefore dispensed with. Sri Lanka beat Pakistan by eight wickets in another one-sided final. The two tournaments held to date have done so little to promote the image of Asian test cricket that it seems unlikely the event will be staged again.

Year	Winner	Runner-up	Other participant
1998/99	Pakistan	Sri Lanka	India
2001/02	Sri Lanka	Pakistan	Bangladesh

Tournament records

Highest team score

594	Pakistan v Sri Lanka, Dhaka	1998/99

Lowest team score

90	Bangladesh v Sri Lanka, Colombo	2000/01

Highest individual score

242	D.P.M.D. Jayawardene Sri Lanka India, Colombo	1998/99

Best bowling in an innings

8-86	J. Srinath India v Pakistan, Kolkata	1998/99

Best wicket-keeping in an innings

5 (5c)	N.R. Mongia India v Pakistan, Kolkata	1998/99

Asia Cup

THE SENIOR one-day international competition for the Asia Cup was first held in Sharjah in April 1984 and has since been staged approximately every two years. India was the leading country in the first decade, winning four out of the first five competitions. Since then, Sri Lanka have the best record. The poor performance of Pakistan is somewhat surprising considering that their cricketers are responsible for most of the team and individual tournament records. The inaugural contest was restricted to India, Pakistan and Sri Lanka. From 1986, the winner of the Asian Cricket Council Trophy for associate countries provided an additional competitor. This slot was occupied by Bangladesh until that country also became a full ICC member at which point the number of associate countries taking part was increased to two. Although the intention of providing the associate country with the experience of top-class opposition was met, the outcome only served to emphasize the gap in standard between the associate and full member countries. Bangladesh were easily beaten in all their matches. The United Arab Emirates and Hong Kong took part in the 2004 tournament and were also easily defeated. The UAE and Oman qualified for the 2006 tournament but now that this has been postponed until 2008 it is not clear whether Oman will participate or be replaced by Hong Kong, the runner-up in the 2006 ACC Trophy.

Year	Winner	Runner-up	Other participants
1984	India	Sri Lanka	Pakistan
1986	Sri Lanka	Pakistan	Bangladesh
1988	India	Sri Lanka	Pakistan/Bangladesh
1991	India	Sri Lanka	Bangladesh
1994	India	Sri Lanka	Pakistan/Bangladesh
1998	Sri Lanka	India	Pakistan/Bangladesh
2000	Pakistan	Sri Lanka	India/Bangladesh
2002	Cancelled		
2004	Sri Lanka	India	Pakistan/Bangladesh United Arab Emirates Hong Kong

Note: India withdrew from the 1986 contest. Pakistan withdrew in 1990 because of safety concerns following inter-communal violence in Indian cities. The competition scheduled for 2006 has been postponed until 2008.

Tournament records

Highest team score

343-5	Pakistan v Hong Kong, Colombo	2004

Lowest team score

87	Bangladesh v Pakistan, Dhaka	1999

Highest individual score

143	Shoaib Malik Pakistan v India, Colombo	2004

Best bowling in an innings

5-38	Saqlain Mushtaq Pakistan v Bangladesh, Colombo	1997

Best wicket-keeping in an innings

5 (4c 1st)	R.S. Kaluwitharana Sri Lanka v Pakistan, Sharjah	1994

Asian Cricket Council Trophy

THE ASIAN Cricket Council Trophy is the one-day international competition open to all countries within Asia which are not full members of the ICC. It started in 1984 as a South East Asian Tournament held in Bangladesh. Originally, Bangladesh, Hong Kong, Singapore and Malaysia were to take part but Malaysia withdrew for financial reasons just before the tournament began and Bangladesh fielded an Under 25 side in their place. Further tournaments were held in Hong Kong in 1988 and Singapore in 1992. By the time of the 1996 tournament in Malaysia, external sponsorship was forthcoming and the competing countries had been extended to include the United Arab Emirates, Fiji and Papua New Guinea. The tournament is now staged every two years and has become the qualifying competition for the Asia Cup, the ICC Trophy and the World Cup. Bangladesh won the trophy in the first five tournaments and since their promotion first to full one-day status and later to full membership of the ICC, the United Arab Emirates have been victorious. With seventeen countries of highly varying standards taking part in the 2006 tournament, the competition was not only extremely large but the opportunities for mismatches were very great (see Chapter 2 – Country Profile for Nepal). A league system with promotion and relegation between divisions will be instituted for the 2008 contest.

Year	Winner	Runner-up	Other participants
1984	Bangladesh	Hong Kong	Singapore
			Bangladesh Under 25
1988	Bangladesh	Hong Kong	Singapore/Hong Kong
			President's XI
1992	Bangladesh	Hong Kong	Singapore/Malaysia
1996	Bangladesh	United Arab Emirates	Brunei/Fiji/Hong Kong
			Japan/Maldives
			Malaysia/Nepal
			Papua New Guinea
			Singapore/Thailand
1998	Bangladesh	Malaysia	Hong Kong/Maldives
			Nepal/Papua New
			Guinea/Singapore/
			Thailand/ UAE
2000	UAE	Hong Kong	Japan/Kuwait
			Malaysia/Maldives
			Nepal/Singapore
2002	UAE	Nepal	Hong Kong/Kuwait
			Malaysia/Maldives
			Oman/Qatar
			Singapore/Thailand
2004	UAE	Oman	Afghanistan/Bahrain
			Bhutan/Hong Kong
			Iran/Kuwait/Maldives
			Malaysia/Nepal/Qatar
			Saudi Arabia
			Singapore/Thailand
2006	UAE	Hong Kong	Afghanistan/Nepal
			Singapore/Bahrain
			Malaysia/Qatar
			Saudi Arabia/Oman
			Kuwait/Thailand
			Brunei/Bhutan
			Maldives/Iran/Myanmar

Tournament records

Highest team score

469-7	Fiji v Japan, Kuala Lumpur	1996

Lowest team score

10	Myanmar v Nepal, Kuala Lumpur	2006

Highest individual score

213*	Arshad Ali	UAE v Brunei, Kuala Lumpur	2006

Best bowling in an innings

7-3	M. Alam	Nepal v Myanmar, Kuala Lumpur	2006

Best wicket-keeping in an innings

6 (5c 1st)	Mohammed Nadeem	United Arab Emirates v Kuwait, Singapore	2002

Asian Cricket Council Premier League

STARTED IN 2004 as the Asian Cricket Council Fast Track Tournament and renamed the Premier League in 2006, the tournament aims to give the associate countries of Asia the opportunity to meet each other competitively in three-day two-innings matches. The competition is on a league basis with each country playing one another over the course of one year. The United Arab Emirates won the first two tournaments but, with the abandonment of their match against Singapore without a ball being bowled, they failed to secure sufficient points to overtake Nepal in 2006.

Year	Winner	Runner-up	Other participants
2004	UAE	Hong Kong	Nepal/Singapore
			Malaysia
2005	UAE	Nepal	Malaysia/Singapore
			Hong Kong
2006	Nepal	UAE	Malaysia/Singapore
			Hong Kong

Tournament records

Highest team score

426-8 dec	Hong Kong v UAE, Sharjah	2006/07

Lowest team score

64	Nepal v UAE, Kathmandu	2004

Highest individual score

218*	Khalid Hussain Butt	Hong Kong v UAE, Sharjah	2006/07

Best bowling in an innings

8-50	Afzaal Haider	Hong Kong v Malaysia, Kuala Lumpur	2006/07

Best wicket-keeping in an innings

7 (7c)	Mohammed Taskeen UAE v Hong Kong, Hong Kong 2004	

Emerging Nations Tournament

DESIGNED AS a tournament in which the lesser cricketing countries of Asia could meet each other on more equal terms instead of being outclassed by stronger teams, it has produced some spectacularly one-sided contests (see Chapter 2 – Country Profiles for Maldives and Nepal). Four tournaments have been held to date.

Year	Winner	Runner-up	Other participants
2003	Nepal	Maldives	Bhutan
2003	Nepal	Maldives	Bhutan
2005	Maldives	Thailand	Bhutan, Brunei
2006	Maldives	Thailand	Bhutan

Tournament records

Highest team score
486-5	Maldives v Brunei, Bangkok	2004/05

Lowest team score
34	Maldives v Nepal, Kathmandu	2002/03

Highest individual score
217	Moosa Kaleem	Maldives v Brunei, Bangkok	2004/05

Best bowling in an innings
8-23	M. Alam	Nepal v Maldives, Kathmandu	2002/03

Middle East Cup

THE MIDDLE East Cup was first staged in Kuwait in 2004 and seems destined to become a regular competition, held every two years, for the lower level countries of south-west Asia. The United Arab Emirates are excluded. In the first tournament Kuwait, encouraged by their performance in the 2004 ACC Trophy, decided to enter two teams. Instead of making these a first and second eleven, the Kuwait Cricket Association decided to distribute their best players equally between the Reds and the Blues. The policy was not a success since the teams occupied the last two places. In 2006 neither Oman nor Qatar took part, being replaced by Iran and Afghanistan.

Year	Winner	Runner-up	Other participants
2004	Oman	Bahrain	Kuwait Reds/Kuwait Blues/Qatar/Saudi Arabia
2006	Bahrain	Afghanistan	Iran/Kuwait/Saudi Arabia

Tournament records

Highest team score
401-5	Bahrain v Iran, Ahmadi	2005/06

Lowest team score
122	Iran v Kuwait, Doha	2005/06

Highest individual score
154*	Asghar Bajwa	Bahrain v Iran, Ahmadi	2005/06

Best bowling in an innings
5-22	Sarfraz Ahmed	Saudi Arabia v Kuwait Blues, Doha	2005/06

Saudara Cup

THE SAUDARA Cup was established in 1970 for international matches between Malaysia and Singapore. Unlike the earlier fixtures between the Straits Settlements and the Federation of Malaya before the Second World War and the matches between Malaya and Singapore in the late 1950s, only national citizens were eligible for team selection for this competition. The decision of the cricket authorities of the two countries to start an international series for citizens only was remarkably farsighted. It was some nine years in advance of the move by the ICC to establish qualifying criteria for players representing national teams. By offering a trophy for an annual two-innings match, the cricket authorities also stood out against the trend towards one-day international cricket. The Saudara Cup is now the longest running two-innings international contest still extant outside of the test-playing countries. The name 'Saudara' was chosen to promote friendship between the two countries, it being the Malay word for 'brother', 'sister', 'cousin' or any close relative. The early matches produced somewhat unexciting cricket with seven out of the first nine games ending in draws. One of the surprising features of the contest has been that when one side wins, it does so easily. The only close result was the win by one wicket by Malaysia in 1982. The dominance of Malaysia owes more to their bowling than their batting. Only two centuries have been scored by Malaysian batsmen compared to seven by Singapore's. In addition to the ten wickets in an innings achieved by Krishnan Saker in 1983, Malaysian bowling performances have included hauls of seven wickets in an innings in consecutive matches by Suresh Navaratnam in 2004 and 2005 and the only hat-trick in the competition by Arul Suppiah in 1999. Singapore's best bowling was the 8-8 (match return of 14-40) by Mahesh Mehta when Malaysia were dismissed for 33 in 1979.

Year	Holder	Result
1970	Malaysia & Singapore	Draw
1971	Malaysia	Malaysia won by an innings and 76 runs
1972	Malaysia	Draw
1973	Malaysia	Draw
1974	Malaysia	Draw
1975	Malaysia	Draw
1976	Malaysia	Draw
1977	Singapore	Singapore won by 151 runs
1978	Singapore	Draw
1979	Singapore	Singapore won by an innings and 80 runs
1980	Singapore	Singapore won by 107 runs
1981	Singapore	Draw
1982	Malaysia	Malaysia won by 1 wicket
1983	Malaysia	Malaysia won by 10 wickets
1984	Malaysia	Malaysia won by 3 wickets
1985	Malaysia	Malaysia won by 8 wickets
1986	Malaysia	Malaysia won by 127 runs
1987	Malaysia	Draw
1988	Singapore	Singapore won by 51 runs
1989	Singapore	Draw
1990	Singapore	Draw
1991	Malaysia	Malaysia won by 132 runs
1992	Singapore	Singapore won by 5 wickets
1993	Malaysia	Malaysia won by 7 wickets
1994	Malaysia	Draw
1995	Malaysia	Malaysia won by 7 wickets
1996	Malaysia	Draw
1997	Malaysia	Draw
1998	Malaysia	Draw
1999	Malaysia	Malaysia won by 149 runs
2000	Malaysia	Malaysia won by 3 wickets
2001	Malaysia	Draw
2002	Singapore	Singapore won by 10 wickets
2003	Singapore	Singapore won by 7 wickets
2004	Malaysia	Malaysia won by 3 wickets
2005	Malaysia	Draw
2006	Malaysia	Draw

Tournament records
Highest team score
| 394 | Malaysia v Singapore, Singapore | 1971 |
Lowest team score
| 33 | Malaysia v Singapore, Kuala Lumpur | 1979 |
Highest individual score
| 152 | Gurcharan Singh Malaysia v Singapore, Singapore | 1971 |
Best bowling in an innings
| 10-25 | K. Saker | Malaysia v Singapore, Kuala Lumpur | 1983 |
Best wicket-keeping in an innings
| 5 (5c) | Pritam Singh | Singapore v Malaysia, Singapore | 1973 |

Stan Nagaiah Trophy

MATCHES FOR the Stan Nagaiah Trophy between Malaysia and Singapore began in 1995. The competition is held annually, alternately in each country, as a series of three one-day internationals. The trophy is dedicated to Stanley Nagaiah, a leading cricketer from Singapore in the late 1950s who was also a regular choice for All-Malaya. Malaysia has the better record in the competition, having won nineteen of the matches played against Singapore's fourteen. The most remarkable series was that of 1999 when Zubin Shroff scored 124 in the second game to create the highest individual score in the competition and help Singapore to a 41-run win, levelling the series at one game each. In the next game, Rakesh Madhavan equalled that score in helping Malaysia to a 38-run victory and the trophy.

Year	Winner	Result
1995	Singapore	2-1
1996	Malaysia	2-1
1997	Malaysia	3-0
1998	Singapore	2-1
1999	Malaysia	2-1
2000	Malaysia	2-0 with 1 no result
2001	Malaysia	2-1
2002	Singapore	3-0
2003	Malaysia	2-1
2004	Malaysia	3-0
2005	Singapore	2-0 with 1 no result
2006	Malaysia / Singapore	1-1 with 1 no result

Tournament records
Highest team score
| 268-8 | Malaysia v Singapore, Singapore | 1999 |
Lowest team score
| 80 | Singapore v Malaysia, Singapore | 1999 |
Highest individual score
| 124 | Z.A. Shroff | Singapore v Malaysia, Singapore | 1999 |
| 124 | R. Madhavan | Malaysia v Singapore, Singapore | 1999 |
Best bowling in an innings
| 5-13 | J. Nair | Malaysia v Singapore, Singapore | 1997 |
Best wicket-keeping in an innings
| 6 (4c 2st) | C. Suryawanshi | Singapore v Malaysia, Kuala Lumpur | 2005 |

Tuanku Ja'afar Cup

THE TUANKU Ja'afar Cup was inaugurated in 1991 for competition between Hong Kong, Malaysia and

Singapore to help these countries prepare for the ICC Trophy. Thailand became the fourth competing country the following year. The competition was proposed by Tuanku Imran who had played cricket at King's School, Canterbury, and Nottingham University and was a reserve wicket-keeper for Malaysia on their tour of Hong Kong in 1971. He represented Malaysia on the International Cricket Council and for many years was one of the two representatives of the associate countries on the ICC Executive Board. He dedicated the Tuanku Ja'afar Cup to his brother, Tuanku Ja'afar ibni Al-Marham Tuanku Abdul Rahman, who became the tenth Yang Di-Pertuan Besar of Negeri Sembilan in 1967 and was elected the tenth Yang Di-Pertuan Agong (King) of Malaysia in April 1994, a position which is held for five-year periods in rotation by the Heads of the Royal Families in the Malay States. Along with Tuanku Imran, Tuanku Ja'afar was a leading supporter of cricket in Malaysia.

For the first three years the competition was decided on an all-play-all basis and was dominated by Hong Kong. Since 1994, the top two teams in the league have contested a final. In 1994 Hong Kong were surprisingly beaten by Singapore (see Chapter 2 - Country Profile for Singapore) even though they had already beaten Singapore in the league stage. Since then the Cup has been won by either Hong Kong or Malaysia. The competition was last held in 2004. With the increase in the number of fixtures following inauguration of the ACC Premier League, there has been no space in the calendar for the tournament in recent years. A surprising feature is that all the tournament records have been set when it has been held in Singapore.

Year	Winner	Runner-up	Other participants
1991	Hong Kong	Singapore	Malaysia
1992	Hong Kong	Malaysia	Singapore, Thailand
1993	Hong Kong	Singapore	Malaysia, Thailand
1994	Singapore	Hong Kong	Malaysia, Thailand
1995	Malaysia	Hong Kong	Singapore, Thailand
1996	Hong Kong	Singapore	Malaysia, Thailand
1997	Malaysia	Singapore	Hong Kong, Thailand
1998	Hong Kong	Singapore	Malaysia
1999	Hong Kong	Malaysia	Singapore
2000	Malaysia	Hong Kong	Singapore, Thailand
2001	Hong Kong	Singapore, Malaysia	Thailand
2002	Hong Kong	Singapore	Malaysia, Hong Kong A
2003	Hong Kong	Malaysia	Singapore, Thailand
2004	Malaysia	Hong Kong	Singapore, Thailand

Tournament records

Highest team score

415-5	Hong Kong v Thailand, Singapore	1996

Lowest team score

63	Thailand v Malaysia, Singapore	2004

Highest individual score

178	M.R. Farcy	Hong Kong v Thailand, Singapore 1996

Best bowling in an innings

7-15	J.P.R. Lamsam	Hong Kong v Singapore, Singapore 2004

Best wicket-keeping in an innings

5 (3c 2st)	R.D. Brewster	Hong Kong v Singapore, Singapore 2000
5 (5c)	M. Cheruparambil	Hong Kong v Singapore, Singapore 2004

Women's Asia Cup

THE INAUGURAL Women's Asia Cup, a competition under one-day international rules, was staged in Karachi, Pakistan in late December 2005 and early January 2006. The trophy was decided on a league basis with each country playing each other twice. As expected, India dominated, Sri Lanka finished second and Pakistan third a result repeated in the second contest in December 2006. More important than the results, however, is the encouragement given to the women's game throughout Asia. The intention is to hold the competition every two years and to increase the number of participants by holding qualifying tournaments among the other countries. To date, Bangladesh, Malaysia, Singapore and the United Arab Emirates have expressed interest in taking part.

Tournament records

Highest team score

289-2	India v Pakistan, Karachi	2005/06

Lowest team score

93	Pakistan v Sri Lanka, Karachi	2005/06
93	Sri Lanka v India, Jaipur	2006/07

Highest individual score

138*	J. Sharma	India v Pakistan, Karachi	2005/06

Best bowling in an innings

5-62	Qanita Jalil	Pakistan v India, Jaipur	2006/07

Best wicket-keeping in an innings

4 (2c 2st)	Sana Javed	Pakistan v Sri Lanka, Karachi	2005/06

EUROPEAN TOURNAMENTS

WITH ENGLAND being the dominant European country and the other leading countries like Scotland, Ireland, The Netherlands and Denmark being equal, at best, to the weaker first-class counties, there was no interest until the 1990s in holding a European cricket competition. The longest standing European international series between Scotland and Ireland was never contested for a trophy. The first European tournament was the Cricketer Cup organised in Guernsey in May 1990 for teams from countries which were not already associate members of the ICC or, like Scotland and Ireland, attached to the English Cricket Board. The competition was won by Guernsey who defeated Belgium in the final. Apart from Guernsey and Greece, most of the teams comprised expatriates from the United Kingdom or the Indian sub-continent. The event was therefore snubbed by the European Cricket Federation which had been formed in 1988 to promote indigenous cricket across the continent of Europe. Nevertheless the event showed that it was possible to organise a European event which, at that time, the ECF seemed reluctant to do. When the Cricketer Cup was successfully repeated in England in 1992 it forced the ECF into action so that the pioneer work of The Cricketer was eventually superseded by the ECF's own competition, the ECF Nations Cup, first held in Berlin in 1993. Further tournaments were staged in 1995, 1996 and 1997. The competition was largely ignored by the ICC but its success finally encouraged the ICC to promote the game in Europe and provide sufficient funding to do so. As a result, the ECF Nations Cup became a tournament which made itself redundant by laying the foundation for the European Championships.

A quadrangular tournament was organised in 1994 and 1995 between Denmark, Scotland and The Netherlands with The Netherlands B and Scotland B making up the fourth team in respective years. The European Championships for associate countries was first held in 1996 with Scotland, Ireland, The Netherlands, Denmark, Gibraltar and Italy being joined by an English amateur team chosen mainly from the English Minor Counties, and Israel. With the admission of France and Germany to associate status, the competition was expanded in 1998 to two divisions, ostensibly with promotion and relegation although this has been applied in practice somewhat intermittently. The ECF Nations Cup was replaced by the European Cricket Championships Trophy which effectively became a European Division 3 with the two finalists qualifying to play in Division 2 in the following European Championships. In 2004, a European Representative Championships was held from which the winner qualified to take part in the next ECC Trophy. Thus, by the time of the 2006 European Championships, a European structure of four divisions existed. This has now been formalised as the European section of the ICC World Cricket League with promotion and relegation.

The other major European international competitions are the Women's European Cup which was first held in 1989, preceding the men's competition by seven years, and the Triple Crown, a contest involving Scotland, Ireland, Wales and an English Cricket Board XI.

European Championships

THE EUROPEAN Championships is a one-day limited overs international competition staged every other year. Ireland won the inaugural contest in 1996 after which the Dutch won two consecutive tournaments. Since a Division 2 was established in 1998, the competition has been marked by an inconsistent policy of promotion and relegation, seemingly designed to protect the status of the five top countries. Italy won Division 2 in the 1998 tournament but were not promoted automatically. They had to play-off against the England amateur side who had finished last in Division 1. When Italy won the play-off they were promoted but, instead of England being relegated, the number of countries in Division 1 was increased to six so that England held their place. England then chose stronger sides and, after finishing runners-up in 2000, won the competition in 2002 and 2004. Denmark finished last in Division 1 in 2000 but were not relegated and there was no promotion from Division 2. In 2002, Italy finished last and were relegated but, again there was no promotion from Division 2 so that only five teams took part in Division 1 in 2004. Italy were promoted again, after winning the Division 2 Championships in 2004 but, since the England Board no longer competed, the 2006 tournament still involved only five teams. Although Italy finished last, they were not demoted. Norway, winners of Division 2, were promoted to bring the number of teams in Division 1 up to six for the 2008 contest.

Protectionism has featured just as strongly in Division 2. From 2000 to 2004 the top teams from what was effectively a Division 3 competition were allowed to take part in the next Division 2 championships but there was no promotion or relegation so that, even if they did not finish last, they did not retain their position in Division 2 but had to qualify again next time. In contrast, the position of Israel, the weakest of the associate countries in Division 2 seemed to be sacrosanct. Proper promotion and relegation systems were instituted for the 2006 tournament but the play-off for relegation between Israel and Greece never took place. After winning their first three games Greece were penalised for fielding two ineligible players. With all their points deducted, they decided not to contest the relegation play-off match, allowing Israel to retain their place in Division 2 by default.

Division One

Year	Winner	Runner-up	Other participants
1996	Ireland	Netherlands	England NCA/Scotland Israel/Gibraltar/Denmark Italy
1998	Netherlands	Denmark	England Cricket Board XI Scotland/Ireland
2000	Netherlands	England CB	Scotland/Ireland/Italy Denmark
2002	England CB	Scotland	Ireland/Netherlands Denmark/Italy
2004	England CB	Ireland	Scotland/Netherlands Denmark
2006	Ireland	Scotland	Netherlands/Denmark/Italy

Division Two

1998	Italy	Germany	France/Gibraltar/Israel
2000	Gibraltar	Germany	France/Portugal/Israel Greece
2002	Germany	Gibraltar	France/Portugal/Israel Austria
2004	Italy	France	Germany/Gibraltar/Norway Israel

2006	Norway	Jersey	Germany/Gibraltar Guernsey/France/Israel Greece (relegated)

Division Three

1999	Greece	Portugal	Austria/Switzerland/ Belgium/Malta/Sweden
2001	Portugal	Austria	Greece/Croatia/Belgium Switzerland/Malta, Finland/Sweden/Spain
2003	Norway	Austria	Greece/Switzerland Luxembourg/Malta Belgium/Spain/Croatia Portugal
2005	Norway	Greece	Belgium/Malta/Spain Portugal/Croatia/Isle of Man Finland (relegated)

Division Four

2004	Croatia	Finland	Switzerland/Luxembourg Slovenia/Bulgaria
2006	Finland	Slovenia	Cyprus/Luxembourg

Tournament records

Division One

Highest team score

359-9	Denmark v Gibraltar, Glostrup	1996

Lowest team score

38	Israel v England NCA, Glostrup	1996

Highest individual score

171*	D.F. Watts	Scotland v Denmark, Glasgow	2006

Best bowling in an innings

5-19	S.J. Foster	England CB XI v Scotland, Glasgow	2000

Best wicket-keeping in an innings

6 (6c)	N.J. O'Brien	Ireland v Italy, Glasgow	2006

Division Two

Highest team score

358-6	Germany v France, The Hague	1998

Lowest team score

46	Israel v Gibraltar, Paisley	2000

Highest individual score

136	L. Savident	Guernsey v France, Glasgow	2006

Best bowling in an innings

6-24	Farooq Ahmed	Germany v Gibraltar, Bready	2002

Best wicket-keeping in an innings

7 (7c)	P. Amit	Israel v France, Glasgow	2000
7 (7c)	G. Passaretti	Italy v France, Mechelen	2004
7 (6c 1st)	R. Buzaglo	Gibraltar v France, Waterloo	2004

Division Three

Highest team score

| 377-5 | Greece v Luxembourg, Vienna | 2003 |

Lowest team score

| 43 | Sweden v Croatia, Vienna | 2001 |

Highest individual score

| 150 | Sadiq Mehmood | Greece v Croatia, Vienna | 2001 |

Best bowling in an innings

| 6-24 | V. Zanko | Croatia v Sweden, Vienna | 2001 |

Best wicket-keeping in an innings

| 5 (2c 3st) | R. Webber | Isle of Man v Finland, Mechelen | 2005 |
| 5 (4c 1st) | J. da Costa | Portugal v Norway, Waterloo | 2005 |

Division Four

Highest team score

| 322-5 | Switzerland v Bulgaria, Valburga | 2004 |

Lowest team score

| 38 | Bulgaria v Croatia, Ljubljana | 2004 |

Highest individual score

| 137* | M.P. Moilanen | Finland v Bulgaria, Ljubljana | 2004 |

Best bowling in an innings

| 5-8 | S. Mayland | Slovenia v Bulgaria, Ljubljana | 2004 |

Best wicket-keeping in an innings

| 4 (2c 2st) | A. Govorko | Croatia v Finland, Valburga | 2004 |

Triple Crown

THE TRIPLE Crown was started in 1993 as a one-day competition between Scotland, Ireland, Wales and the English amateur side. Since 2001, the increasing size of the fixture list for Scotland and Ireland has made it impossible to fit the tournament into the calendar. Scotland dominated the competition.

Year	Winner	Runner-up	Other participants
1993	England Board XI	Ireland	Wales/Scotland
1994	Scotland	England Board XI	Ireland/Wales
1995	Scotland	England Board XI	Ireland/Wales
1996	Ireland	England Board XI	Scotland/Wales
1997	Scotland	England Board XI	Ireland/Wales
1998	England Board XI	Ireland	Scotland/Wales
1999	Scotland	England Board XI	Wales/Ireland
2000	Scotland	Ireland	Wales/England Board XI
2001	England Board XI	Scotland	Wales/Ireland

Tournament records

Highest team score

| 351-5 | England Board XI v Wales, Old Hill | 1997 |

Lowest team score

| 109 | Ireland v England Board XI, Stirlands | 2001 |

Highest individual score

| 130 | S.J. Dean | England Board XI v Ireland, Glasgow | 1994 |
| 130 | S.J. Foster | England Board XI v Wales, Old Hill | 1997 |

Best bowling in an innings

| 5-34 | P.J.C. Hoffmann | Scotland v England Board XI, Arundel | 2001 |

Best wicket-keeping in an innings

| 5 (5c) | C.J.O. Smith | Scotland v Wales, Skerries | 1999 |

Women's European Championships

THE FIRST European Championships for women was held in Denmark in 1989. Six further tournaments have been held at intervals ranging from one to four years. England dominated the first four championships and have since chosen to use the tournament to give experience to young players. They have been represented respectively by the A side (1999), Under 19 (2001) and a Development Squad (2005). Denmark ceased to participate after staging the 1999 tournament.

Year	Winner	Runner-up	Other participants
1989	England	Denmark	Netherlands/Ireland
1990	England	Ireland	Netherlands/Denmark
1991	England	Denmark	Netherlands/Ireland
1995	England	Ireland	Netherlands/Denmark
1999	England A	Ireland	Netherlands/Denmark
2001	Ireland	England Under 19	Netherlands/Scotland
2005	England Development Squad	Ireland	Wales/Netherlands Scotland

Tournament records

Highest team score

| 323-5 | England Development Squad v Scotland, Miskin Manor | 2005 |

Lowest team score

| 24 | Scotland v England Under 19, Bradfield College | 2001 |

Highest individual score

| 121 | H.J. Lloyd | Wales v Scotland, Swansea | 2005 |

Best bowling in an innings

| 7-8 | J.M. Chamberlain | England v Denmark, Haarlem | 1991 |

Best wicket-keeping in an innings

| 4 (4c) | E. Donnison | England v Denmark, Nykøbing Mors | 1999 |

PACIFIC ISLANDS TOURNAMENTS

CRICKET IS an accepted sport in the charter of the South Pacific Games, held every four years. Since all the participating countries do not play cricket, the sport is only included when one of the countries where it is well-established hosts the Games. So far a cricket tournament has been staged on four occasions. No other international tournaments in the Pacific were held until the early 2000s, since when there has been considerable activity. The Pacifica Cricket Championships were started in 2001 with the expectation that they would subsequently be held every two years. Only one further tournament took place, however, and they have been superseded by competitions involving the Pacific countries and East Asia within the framework of qualifying competitions for the World Cup and ICC Trophy. A women's competition was held for the first time in 2006.

South Pacific Games

THE FIRST cricket tournament in the South Pacific Games was staged in Suva, Fiji, in 1979. Three further tournaments have taken place since: in Nouméa, New Caledonia, in 1987; Port Moresby, Papua New Guinea, in 1991; and Suva, again, in 2003. Papua New Guinea and Fiji have dominated, winning the gold medal and silver medal respectively on all four occasions. The tournaments have served to demonstrate the enormous range in standards across the Pacific with many games being horrendous mismatches. New Caledonia's loss to Papua New Guinea in 2003 by 468 runs represents the greatest difference between two teams ever recorded in a one-day international competition (see Chapter 2 - Country Profile for Papua New Guinea). Detailed records of all but the most recent tournament do not seem to have been kept so it is not possible to present tournament records.

Pacifica Cricket Championships

THE PACIFICA Championships were initiated by the ICC as part of their East Asia and Pacific Development Programme started in 1999. The first competition was held in Auckland, New Zealand, in 2001. Samoa hosted the second in 2003. In 2001 a New Zealand Maori side was allowed to compete and they proved too strong for the Pacific Island countries, winning the trophy with ease, beating Fiji in the final by three wickets. In 2003 the competition was rigged to avoid a final between Papua New Guinea and Fiji. These two countries played in one division whereas the other countries played each other in a separate division. The winners of the two divisions met in the final. As a result, the final was very one-sided with Papua New Guinea beating Tonga by seven wickets.

Tournament records

Highest team score
433-5	Fiji v New Caledonia, Auckland	2000/01

Lowest team score
25	New Caledonia v Tonga, Auckland	2000/01

Highest individual score
156*	T. Nukunuku	New Zealand Maori v Cook Islands, Auckland 2000/01

Best bowling in an innings
9-16	D. Eliaba	Cook Islands v New Caledonia, Apia 2002

Best wicket-keeping in an innings
4 (4c)	F.H. Latu	Tonga v Cook Islands, Apia	2002
4 (3c 1st)	C. Rika	Fiji v Cook Islands, Apia	2002
4 (4c)	C. Rika	Fiji v Papua New Guinea, Apia	2002

East Asia–Pacific Challenge

THE EAST Asia–Pacific Challenge was held in Fujigawa, Japan, in May 2004 to determine which country from the region in addition to Papua New Guinea, who were given automatic qualification, would participate in the ICC Trophy Qualifying tournament in Malaysia in 2005. Surprisingly, only four countries participated, two from East Asia (Japan and Indonesia) and two from the Pacific (Fiji, the winners, and Tonga).

Tournament records

Highest team score

| 362-7 | Fiji v Indonesia, Fujigawa | 2004 |

Lowest team score

| 122 | Indonesia v Fiji, Fujigawa | 2004 |

Highest individual score

| 144* | M. Faivakimoana | Tonga v Indonesia, Fujigawa | 2004 |

Best bowling in an innings

| 5-22 | M.M. Langi | Tonga v Indonesia, Fujigawa | 2004 |

East Asia–Pacific Cup/ East Asia–Pacific Trophy

THE FIRST East Asia–Pacific Cup was held in Vanuatu in September 2005. The competition formed Division 2 of the East Asia–Pacific region within the World Cricket League. Six countries participated: Japan and Indonesia represented East Asia and the Cook Islands, Tonga, Samoa and Vanuatu the Pacific. Unfortunately some of the Samoan squad were declared ineligible because they failed to meet the ICC's citizenship and residential qualifications, so Samoa were forced to play all their matches with only nine players. Apart from a disaster against the Cook Islands, they were not totally disgraced and narrowly lost to Indonesia by 39 runs. Japan beat Cook Islands in the final by 6 runs. Both qualified for Division 1, a three-way tournament with Fiji, held in Brisbane, Australia, in late June and early July 2006. Fiji won this tournament to become the East Asia–Pacific qualifier for Division 3 of the World Cricket League. Although the objective of the ICC is to encourage international competition between the countries, organising a tournament for six countries to enable two to qualify for a further tournament with one other country seems to be creating tournaments for the sake of them. Surely Fiji could have played in the tournament in Vanuatu thereby giving countries like Tonga and Indonesia the experience of playing one of the stronger teams in the South Pacific?

Tournament records

Division 1 - East Asia–Pacific Trophy

Highest team score

| 189-2 | Fiji v Japan, Brisbane | 2005/06 |

Lowest team score

| 74 | Cook Islands v Japan, Brisbane | 2005/06 |

Highest individual score

| 59* | N.D. Maxwell | Fiji v Japan, Brisbane | 2005/06 |

Best bowling in an innings

| 4-15 | G. Beath | Japan v Cook Islands, Brisbane | 2005/06 |

Best wicket-keeping in an innings

| 4 (4c) | I. Cakacaka | Fiji v Japan, Brisbane | 2005/06 |

Division 2 - East Asia–Pacific Cup

Highest team score

| 268-8 | Indonesia v Samoa, Port Vila | 2005 |

Lowest team score

| 19 | Samoa v Cook Islands, Port Vila | 2005 |

Highest individual score

| 92 | S. Sampath | Japan v Tonga, Port Vila | 2005 |

Best bowling in an innings

| 5-19 | C.M. Brown | Cook Islands v Japan, Port Vila | 2005 |

Best wicket-keeping in an innings

| 5 (5c) | J. Kairua | Cook Islands v Japan, Port Vila | 2005 |
| 5 (5c) | I. Tangimetua | Cook Islands v Tonga, Port Villa | 2005 |

Women's East Asia Pacific Cup

THE FIRST women's competition in the East Asia-Pacific area was held in Port Moresby, Papua New Guinea, in September 2006. Only two countries, Papua New Guinea and Japan, took part, Papua New Guinea winning all three of the one-day matches.

Tournament records

Highest team score

| 175-4 | Papua New Guinea v Japan, Port Moresby | 2006 |

Lowest team score

No team has been all out. The lowest 50-over total is 109-9 by Japan against Papua New Guinea at Port Moresby in 2006.

Highest individual score

| 67* | E. Kuribayashi | Japan v Papua New Guinea, Port Moresby 2006 |

Best bowling in an innings

| 3-17 | K. Heagi | Papua New Guinea v Japan, Port Moresby 2006 |

CHAPTER 4

WORLD CUPS

WOMEN'S WORLD CUP

THE IDEA of a women's international one-day competition came from discussions in June 1971 between Rachael Heyhoe-Flint, the then captain of the English women's team, and the benefactor and millionaire from the Bahamas, James Hayward OBE. Hayward had previously given financial support to the International Women's Cricket Council and the English Women's Cricket Association. He was so impressed by the efforts of these bodies to promote the sport that he offered to finance the whole of the first competition, held in England in 1973. A proposal was put to the IWCC in 1971 and received with enthusiasm. Thus women cricketers got the first World Cup underway two years before the ICC and the men's cricket associations decided to copy the initiative. Despite this pioneering work, the men's World Cup has always generated much greater interest and publicity.

1973 TOURNAMENT

THE 1973 tournament was staged in England from 20 June to 28 July. Seven teams participated in which England, Australia and New Zealand were joined by Jamaica, Trinidad and Tobago, Young England and an International XI. India applied too late to be accepted. South Africa should have taken part but they were barred from international sporting contacts at the time because of their government's policy of *apartheid*. The aim of the International XI was to enable some of the leading South African cricketers to play but the five individuals chosen were also barred. Had they taken part, it was clear that several countries, Jamaica and Trinidad in particular, would have been prevented by their governments from competing. The International XI was therefore made up of players who just failed to make the squads of the competing countries. Young England comprised promising young players with a view to providing them with international experience.

All the countries played each other in a league from which the top two teams contested the final. League matches were played on club grounds in the south and midlands of England. The final was held at Edgbaston, Birmingham. England finished top of the league, winning five out of their six matches, losing only to New Zealand. Australia ended in second place, their only defeat being by England. The International XI came third as a result of a somewhat charmed existence, leaving it until the final over to beat both New Zealand and Jamaica. If

Final qualifying table				
	Played	*Won*	*Lost*	*No result*	*Points*
England	6	5	1	0	20
Australia	6	4	1	1	17
International XI	6	3	2	1	13
New Zealand	6	3	2	1	13
Trinidad and Tobago	6	2	4	0	8
Jamaica	6	1	4	1	5
Young England	6	1	5	0	4

Final

England (273-3) beat Australia (187-9) by 92 runs.

they had not given Young England their only victory of the tournament, they, instead of Australia, might have reached the final. New Zealand disappointed by losing to the International XI and Australia. Jamaica and Trinidad gained valuable experience, Trinidad finishing above Jamaica in the league as a result of their two-wicket victory in the match between the two sides.

The final resulted in a surprisingly easy win for England. Their score of 273 for 5 from their 60 overs was the highest team total of the tournament. Enid Bakewell and Lynne Thomas had an opening partnership of 101 which was followed by a second-wicket stand of 117 runs between Bakewell and Rachael Heyhoe-Flint. Australia made a promising start but once the openers, Bev Wilson and Jackie Potter, were dismissed, they struggled against some tight bowling and excellent fielding. England provided the outstanding players of the tournament. Enid Bakewell made two centuries and Lynne Thomas and Rachael Heyhoe-Flint one each. No player from any other team reached three figures. The best bowling was six for 20 by Glenys Page of New Zealand against Trinidad.

1978 TOURNAMENT

THE DISAPPOINTMENT of India's women cricketers in not being able to take part in the first World Cup was partially offset by India's hosting of the second tournament in January 1978. Unfortunately between the time of India offering to hold the event and it actually taking place, there was a change in the management structure in the Indian Women's Cricket Association which resulted in considerable problems with the organisation. The competing teams found it difficult to extract information on the preparations for the tournament. When The Netherlands and the West Indies withdrew for a combination of political and financial reasons, it was far from clear that the event would go ahead.

Australia, England, New Zealand and India played each other in a league over a period of two weeks. There was no separate final although the last game at Hyderabad on 14 January between Australia and England, both unbeaten to that point, decided the outcome. England batted poorly reaching only 96 runs for the loss of eight wickets from their 50 overs, with Sharon Tredrea taking four wickets for 25. Australia reached their target in 31.3 overs for the loss of only two wickets with Margaret

Jennings and Janette Tredrea scoring 57 not out and 37 not out respectively. The opening game between India and England was played at Eden Gardens, Kolkata, and all the remaining matches took place at major cricket grounds in Jamshedpur, Patna and Hyderabad. All the visiting players found Indian conditions difficult whilst the Indian side suffered from lack of experience. As a result, scoring rates were low, the highest total being Australia's 177 all out against New Zealand. No one scored a century and no one took more than four wickets in an innings, Tredrea's return against England being the best in the tournament. Sharon Tredrea was easily the outstanding player with scores of 56 and 31 against India and New Zealand respectively and a return of six wickets at an average of 7.00 and a strike rate of one wicket every 25 balls. The highest individual score was 67 not out by Barbara Bevege of New Zealand.

Final table					
	Played	Won	Lost	No result	Points
Australia	3	3	0	0	6
England	3	2	1	0	4
New Zealand	3	1	2	0	2
India	3	0	3	0	0

1982 TOURNAMENT

FIVE TEAMS took part in the 1982 tournament held in New Zealand in January and early February. Australia, England, New Zealand and India were joined by an International XI comprising players who did not make the squads of the four participating countries and two cricketers from The Netherlands. The tournament lasted far longer than was necessary with the teams meeting each other three times in a league. The matches were played at a large number of venues spread across the North and South Islands. Australia ended the league unbeaten but a tie in their third match against England prevented them gaining maximum points. England had rather a charmed life, being involved in two ties. Nevertheless, their record of seven wins in twelve games, one more than New Zealand achieved, was enough for them to reach the final. The four main countries finished in the same order as in 1978. In the final, at Lancaster Park, Christchurch, England did not make enough runs in their 60 overs against a tight but unpenetrative Australian attack. Australia struggled equally in reply with three of their side falling to run-outs as England's enthusiastic fielding

provided excellent support to the bowlers. After losing their first three wickets for 28, Australia, in an exciting finish, won with one over to spare.

Two centuries were made during the tournament. The highest was 138 not out by Janette Brittin for England. Barbara Bevege of New Zealand scored 101. New Zealand also produced the outstanding bowler in Jaqueline Lord who took six wickets for 10 runs in helping to dismiss India for 37 runs at Auckland. Her liking for the Indian opposition continued when she returned four for 12 against them at Christchurch. Australia's Lynette Fullston was the tournament's leading wicket taker with 23 victims to Lord's 22. India's star performer was their wicket-keeper, Fowzieh Khalili, who, in ten matches, achieved seven catches and thirteen stumpings.

Final qualifying table

	Played	Won	Tied	Lost	No result	Points
Australia	12	11	1	0	0	46
England	12	7	2	3	0	32
New Zealand	12	6	1	5	0	26
India	12	4	0	8	0	16
International XI	12	0	0	12	0	0

Final

Australia (152-7) beat England (151-5) by 3 wickets.

1988 TOURNAMENT

SIX YEARS rather than four elapsed before the fourth women's World Cup was held. Although this allowed time for the various national associations to find sponsorship, it allowed interest in international women's cricket to decline. Australia hosted the tournament which should have comprised six teams. However, India withdrew which meant that Australia, England and New Zealand were joined by Ireland and The Netherlands, both making their first international appearance at this level. The league stage was reduced with the teams playing each other twice instead of three times but the results were of limited value in deciding which countries would meet in the final. Many of the games involving Ireland and The Netherlands were mismatches and served only to contribute to tournament

records. The opening games of the league were played in Perth, after which all the teams moved to Sydney and then to Melbourne. In each of these cities the games were played on club or school grounds. One match, Australia against New Zealand, was staged at the Manuka Oval in Canberra. The final was held at the Melbourne Cricket Ground, Australia following the precedent of staging it at a major international venue. As in the previous tournament, England batted first in the final and did not score sufficient runs. Only Janette Brittin survived both the difficult batting conditions and a very economical Australian attack. Australia lost two wickets for 14 runs but Lindsay Reeler and Denise Annetts then remained unbeaten as they reached their target in 44.5 overs.

Australia dominated the individual performances in the tournament. Lindsay Reeler (143*) and Ruth Buckstein (100) both scored centuries in the first game against the Dutch and Buckstein (105*) scored another century when the countries met the second time. Reeler made a further century (108*) against New Zealand and finished the tournament with an aggregate of 448 runs and an average of 149.33. The fifth century of the competition was made by Nicki Turner of New Zealand. Although she did not score a hundred, Debbie Hockley (New Zealand) achieved the highest run aggregate, 446 runs, at an average of 63.71. Lyn Fullston returned the best bowling performance with 5-28 against The Netherlands. She also took 4-21 against Ire-

land and finished with sixteen wickets for an average of 11.87. Karen Brown (Australia), Carole Hodges (England) and Caroline Barrs (England) all took four wickets in an innings. All these bowling performances were achieved against either The Netherlands or Ireland.

Final qualifying table

	Played	Won	Lost	No result	Points
Australia	8	7	1	0	28
England	8	6	2	0	24
New Zealand	8	5	3	0	20
Ireland	8	2	6	0	8
Netherlands	8	0	8	0	0

Third place play-off

New Zealand (208-6) beat Ireland (138-7) by 70 runs.

Final

Australia (129-2) beat England (127-7) by 8 wickets.

1993 TOURNAMENT

THE WORLD Cup returned to England in 1993 but not without difficulty as the English Women's Cricket Association struggled to obtain the necessary finance. Almost at the point where the tournament was in danger of being cancelled, funding was obtained from the Foundation for Sports and the Arts, the Sports Council and the MCC. The tournament proved the largest and most successful so far with eight countries participating. India returned to the competition and the West Indies and Denmark took part for the first time. Each country played each other in the league and the top two teams contested the final. No play-off was held for third place. Matches were staged at club grounds throughout the midlands and south of England with the final again being held at Lord's. As in 1988, there was a major difference in standard between the top four countries and the rest. All teams, however, achieved at least one victory. The surprise of the tournament was the poor performance of Australia who lost to England and New Zealand and failed to reach the final. New Zealand

finished the league unbeaten. England finished second, losing only to New Zealand but, in what was almost the shock result of the tournament, they only just managed to defeat India. India required four runs from the last two balls but, in a desperate attempt to get them, their last batswoman was run out with one ball remaining to give England a three run victory. Some 4,500 people attended the final which saw England asked to bat after New Zealand had won the toss. A competitive total was achieved against somewhat disappointing bowling and fielding. Reaching their first final and playing at Lord's seemed to frighten the New Zealanders who played

Final qualifying table

	Played	Won	Lost	No result	Points
New Zealand	7	7	0	0	28
England	7	6	1	0	24
Australia	7	5	2	0	20
India	7	4	3	0	16
West Indies	7	2	5	0	8
Ireland	7	2	5	0	8
Denmark	7	1	6	0	4
Netherlands	7	1	6	0	4

Final

England (195-5) beat New Zealand (128) by 67 runs.

below par throughout. Their batting never got going against tight bowling and some excellent fielding. Karen Smithies bowled her twelve overs for 14 runs.

In their home conditions, England produced the only century makers. Janette Brittin scored two centuries and was the tournament's leading run-maker with 410 at an average of 51.25. She became the first player to score 1,000 runs in World Cup matches. Carole Hodges also made two centuries and Helen Plimmer one. Smithies

finished with 15 wickets (average 7.93) and conceded only 1.54 runs per over. New Zealand's Julie Harris also took 15 wickets (average 9.33) including a hat-trick, all leg-before-wicket, against the West Indies. Sarah Illingworth achieved a World Cup record of six victims in an innings (4 caught and 2 stumped) for New Zealand against Australia only for it to be equalled some 16 minutes later by India's Ventacher Kalpana (1 caught and 5 stumped) against Denmark.

1997 TOURNAMENT

ELEVEN COUNTRIES participated in the December 1997 tournament hosted by India, making it the largest World Cup to date. There should have been twelve contestants but Canada withdrew. Again finance was a problem with the Indian Women's Cricket Association unable to find a sponsor until Hero Honda came to the rescue. A sensible decision was made to play the qualify-

ing league stage in two groups but, instead of proceeding from here to the semi-finals or even directly to a final, the top four teams in each group played some rather pointless quarter-finals. Again there was a clear difference in standard between the top four countries of Australia, New Zealand, England and India and the rest. South Africa, Sri Lanka and Pakistan took part for the first

time. Matches were played at major first-class grounds all over India which led to a large amount of travelling by all teams. Most games were well-attended and the tournament attracted a great deal of interest.

Australia won Group A of the league easily. After their opening match against Ireland was washed out, they defeated all their other opponents. England also won their first four matches but then succumbed rather tamely to Australia, losing by eight wickets. Australia dismissed Pakistan for 27 runs, the lowest team total ever in the World Cup, in only 13.4 overs and scored the winning runs off the first ball of the seventh over, losing only one wick-

Final qualifying tables

Group A

	Played	Won	Tied	Lost	No result	Points	Net run rates
Australia	5	4	0	0	1	27	4.62
England	5	4	0	1	0	24	2.56
South Africa	5	3	0	2	0	18	1.22
Ireland	5	2	0	2	1	15	−0.58
Denmark	5	1	0	4	0	6	−2.85
Pakistan	5	0	0	5	0	0	−3.58

Group B

	Played	Won	Tied	Lost	No result	Points	Net run rates
New Zealand	4	3	1	0	0	21	2.46
India	4	2	1	0	1	18	1.19
Netherlands	4	1	0	2	1	9	−0.77
Sri Lanka	4	1	0	2	1	9	−1.16
West Indies	4	0	0	3	1	3	−2.43

Ninth place play-off

West Indies (229-5) beat Denmark (128) by 101 runs.

Quarter-finals

Australia (223-4) beat Netherlands (108-6) by 115 runs.
England (105-1) beat Sri Lanka (104) by 9 wickets.
India (81-5) beat South Africa (80) by 5 wickets.
New Zealand (244-3) beat Ireland (105-9) by 139 runs.

Semi-finals

Australia (123-7) beat India (104-9) by 19 runs.
New Zealand (175-6) beat England (155) by 20 runs.

Final

Australia (165-5) beat New Zealand (164) by 5 wickets.

et. At 19.5 overs the match was the shortest ever in the World Cup. Australia batted first against Denmark and made 412 for 3 from their 50 overs with Belinda Clark becoming the first woman to make a double century (229*) in one-day international cricket. She obtained her first hundred off 64 balls, the fastest century ever by a woman in top-class cricket and her complete innings lasted only 157 balls. In Denmark's reply only extras reached double figures as they fell for 49 in 25.5 overs. Group B was more closely contested. New Zealand and India tied their match and both finished the group stage unbeaten. India had fewer points because their match against Sri Lanka was abandoned without a ball being bowled whereas New Zealand's itinerary was unaffected by the weather.

The quarter-finals went as expected with Australia, England, India and New Zealand all progressing against weaker opposition. The semi-finals were closer contests but not without controversy since both India and England were both penalised, two overs and one over respectively, for slow over-rates. England protested that the umpires had failed to allow for two five-minute drinks breaks and for time lost whilst ground staff cleared dogs from the outfield. The final, staged at Eden Gardens, Kolkata, was dominated by Australia. Only three New Zealanders reached double figures and the second highest scorer in their innings was extras at 23. Opening the innings, Debbie Hockley was not dismissed until the 47th over when she became the eighth wicket to fall with the score on 155, having scored 51 per cent of her team's runs to that point. Australia reached their target without difficulty with 14 balls to spare to obtain their fourth title in six tournaments whilst New Zealand again found themselves overawed by the occasion.

Debbie Hockley was the outstanding player of the tournament. She scored two centuries and finished with the highest run aggregate of 456 and an average of 76.00. She became the leading World Cup run scorer with 1,351 surpassing Janette Brittin's 1,314. The highest batting average was achieved by Belinda Clark. Aided by the not out double century against Denmark, she finished with an aggregate of 445 runs at an average of 148.33. Charlotte Edwards, Barbara Daniels and Janette Brittin all hit hundreds for England, Brittin and Daniels attaining theirs against Pakistan when the pair added 203 for the second wicket. The best match bowling was 5-21 by Purnima Chowdhury for India against the West Indies but she only took one other wicket during the tournament. The highest aggregate was the 13 wickets of Katrina Keenan of New Zealand (average 8.84).

2000 TOURNAMENT

IN ORDER to avoid the mismatches of previous tournaments, the International Women's Cricket Council limited participation in the 2000 tournament to the eight quarter-finalists of the 1997 competition. The event, staged in November and December in New Zealand, resulted in a more sensible itinerary. The countries all played each other in a qualifying league and the top four went straight into the semi-finals. In contrast to previous tournaments, the whole competition was staged in one centre, Christchurch, Canterbury, in the South Island with matches played at Hagley Park and at Lincoln University, some 30 kilometres to the southwest. Australia finished the league unbeaten and New Zealand, after losing the opening game of the tournament to Australia by six wickets, won all their remaining matches to finish in second place. India continued to improve and overturned their close defeat by England in the previous tournament by securing a narrow eight runs win in a low-scoring game. South Africa were the surprise of the tournament. Their victory over England was achieved largely through the batting of Dalene Terblanche and Sunette Viljoen but before the end of the tournament, Linda Olivier had become their leading run-scorer. Overall, the league finished extremely logically with each country having lost to all the countries above them in the table and beaten all those below them. The semi-finals produced convincing wins for Australia and New Zealand.

On their home ground and in the final at their third attempt, New Zealand again looked as though they would be unable to rise to the occasion. Despite seven of their side getting into double figures, none went on to make a substantial score and the total of 184 was clearly well within the capabilities of Australia. Whether through complacency or simply because New Zealand's bowlers and fielders rallied superbly, Australia found themselves in trouble, losing two wickets for two runs. Belinda Clark attempted to keep up the run-rate and take Australia to victory but she lacked support; only four other players got into double figures and none exceeded the 20 extras which was the second highest score. Nevertheless, Clark's magnificent innings brought Australia very close but it was not enough to prevent New Zealand achieving victory (see Chapter 2 - Country Profile for New Zealand).

Karen Rolton was the leading player of the tournament. With two centuries, 154 not out against Sri Lanka and 107 not out against South Africa, she finished with an aggregate of 393 runs and an average of 131.00. Two other players, Lisa Keightley (375) and Belinda Clark (351), both from Australia, exceeded 350 runs though neither made a century. The next highest aggregate was 339 runs by New Zealand's Emily Drumm which included 108 not out against South Africa. Other century makers were Linda Olivier of South Africa

against Ireland and Charlotte Edwards of England who made 139 not out against South Africa. Australia's Charmaine Mason led the bowling with 17 wickets at 10.76, followed by England's Clare Taylor with 14 at 10.85. The best individual performance was Sarah Collyer's 5 for 32 for England against The Netherlands. The tournament was sponsored by the internet site, Cricinfo, whose officials created controversy by questioning the actions of four bowlers, two from India and one each from New Zealand and The Netherlands. Neither the players nor the umpires raised concerns, however, and it was suggested that the complaints were a misguided attempt by the sponsors to gain publicity.

Final qualifying table

	Played	Won	Lost	No result	Points	Net run rates
Australia	7	7	0	0	14	1.98
New Zealand	7	6	1	0	12	2.00
India	7	5	2	0	10	0.71
South Africa	7	4	3	0	8	−0.40
England	7	3	4	0	6	0.44
Sri Lanka	7	2	5	0	4	−1.57
Ireland	7	1	6	0	2	−0.98
Netherlands	7	0	7	0	0	−2.09

Semi-finals

Australia (181-1) beat South Africa (180-8) by 9 wickets.
New Zealand (121-1) beat India (117) by 9 wickets.

Final

New Zealand (184) beat Australia (180) by 4 runs.

2005 TOURNAMENT

THE INTERNATIONAL Women's Cricket Council decided that only the top six countries in the 2000 tournament should have automatic qualification for the 2005 competition. A qualifying competition was therefore held in 2003 which all other member countries of the IWCC could enter, the top two teams going forward to the main tournament.

Qualifying Competition

THE QUALIFYING competition for the IWCC Trophy was held in The Netherlands in July 2003 with Ireland, The Netherlands, West Indies, Pakistan, Scotland and Japan participating. The last two countries were competing internationally for the first time. The tournament was held on a league basis. As expected

Ireland won the trophy and finished the tournament unbeaten. The Dutch were disappointed not to qualify. They were surprisingly defeated by the West Indies by seven wickets in their second game. They had easily the best batting side in the tournament but were let down by their bowlers. In Pauline te Beest, they had the outstanding player. The only person to score a century, she made two and finished with an aggregate of 317 runs for an average of 63.40. The second highest average was 55.50 by Maartje Köster and the second highest aggregate was 140 runs by Caroline Salomons, both from The Netherlands. Ireland had easily the best bowling side. Barbara McDonald with her seam bowling and Catherine O'Neill with her off-spin each took 11 wickets in the tournament with averages of 5.54 and 9.00 respectively. The top bowling aggregate belonged to Pakistan's Sajjida Shah who took 12 wickets at

8.00 but she was aided by her seven wickets for four runs against a very weak Japanese side. For the West Indies, Nadine George scored 114 runs in the tournament and Indomatie Goordial and Verena Felician each took eight wickets.

Final qualifying table

	Played	Won	Lost	No result	Points	Net run rates
Ireland	5	5	0	0	10	1.72
West Indies	5	4	1	0	8	1.20
Netherlands	5	3	2	0	6	2.13
Pakistan	5	2	3	0	4	0.16
Scotland	5	1	4	0	2	−2.04
Japan	5	0	5	0	0	−3.64

Main Competition

SOUTH AFRICA hosted the eighth Women's World Cup in March and April 2005. All the matches were played at grounds in and around Pretoria. Lack of finance hindered the preparations and only ICC sponsorship of some $400,000 saved the tournament from being transferred to Australia. There was limited advance publicity and, as a result, little interest locally until the semi-final stage. The poor performance of the South Africans who dropped from fourth to seventh in the rankings did not help. They were badly served by their bowlers who contributed 109 wides in their five league games. The scoring system was made unnecessarily complicated by the addition of bonus points to those gained from winning a match. One point was awarded to the winning team if their run rate was 1.25 times greater than that of the losing team, or to the losing team if they prevented the winners from obtaining their bonus. The system worked against the hosts who would have finished sixth if places had been decided by net run rate. Eight matches were affected by rain, four being washed out completely and the remainder being abandoned before a result could be obtained. The league stage produced the 'standard' World Cup results. Australia were undefeated and India, New Zealand and England occupied the other three places in the top four. The gulf in standard between these countries and the rest remained. Of the qualifying teams, Ireland disappointed and lost five

matches but the West Indies were the surprise of the tournament beating Ireland and Sri Lanka, the latter by an eight-wicket margin, and losing to South Africa by only one run. It was the failure of South Africa that allowed England to return to the top four. India were the most improved side. In the league their only defeat was by New Zealand but their match against Australia was a victim of the weather. With England and New Zealand both uninspired in the semi-finals, Australia and India moved to the final with relative ease.

The final again showed how the combination of reaching this stage of the competition and playing Australia can intimidate and undermine a team's confidence. India were completely overcome by the occasion. Their bowlers, having formed the most impressive attack in the competition, performed poorly and allowed Karen Rolton to make her third World Cup hundred and put on 139 for the fourth wicket with Australia's Indian-born Lisa Sthalekar. India panicked when faced with a target over 200 and tight Australian bowling and lost four wickets to run-outs. The excitement of 2000 proved an aberration as, once again, the final produced a one-sided contest.

Only Clare Taylor (England) and Karen Rolton and Lisa Keightley (Australia) scored centuries. The highest tournament run aggregates belonged to England's Charlotte Edwards (280 at 46.66) and Claire Taylor (265 at 53.00) but this largely reflected their achievements against Sri Lanka when they enjoyed a second-wicket partnership of 128. Rolton was clearly the best batswomen in the competition with 246 runs for an average of 61.50. The best bowling performances were 5 for 25 by Louise Milliken for New Zealand against India and 5 for 32 by Neetu David for India against New Zealand, achieved in the same match in which Anju Jain, the Indian wicket-keeper made three catches and two stumpings. David took the most tournament wickets (20 at 8.35), followed by the Indian seamers, Amita Sharma (14 at 14.85) and Jhulan Goswami

(13 at 13.53). India's slow left-armer, Deepa Marathe, produced the remarkable analysis of 6-5-1-4 against South Africa.

Final qualifying tables

	Played	Won	Lost	No result	Points	Net run rates
Australia	7	5	0	2	35	2.04
India	7	4	1	2	30	1.06
New Zealand	7	4	1	2	29	0.87
England	7	3	2	2	26	1.49
West Indies	7	2	3	2	19	−0.22
Sri Lanka	7	1	4	2	12	−1.93
South Africa	7	1	4	2	11	−1.07
Ireland	7	0	5	2	6	−2.62

Semi-finals

Australia (159-5) beat England (158) by 5 wickets.
India (204-6) beat New Zealand (164) by 40 runs.

Final

Australia (215-4) beat India (117) by 98 runs.

The top seven teams qualify automatically for the 2009 World Cup. A qualifying competition for the eighth place will be held in Ireland in 2008, involving Ireland, The Netherlands, Scotland and the winners of regional competitions in Asia (Pakistan), East Asia-Pacific (Papua New Guinea), the Americas (Bermuda) and Africa (Zimbabwe).

Tournament Records

Highest team score

412-3   Australia v Denmark, Mumbai   1997/98

Lowest team score

27   Pakistan v Australia, Hyderabad   1997/98

Highest individual score

229*   B.J. Clark   Australia v Denmark, Mumbai   1997/98

Best bowling in an innings

6-10   J. Lord   New Zealand v India, Auckland   1981/82

Best wicket-keeping

6 (4c 2st)   S.L. Illingworth   New Zealand v Australia, Beckenham   1993
6 (1c 5st)   V. Kalpana   India v Denmark, Slough   1993

	Played	Won	Lost	Tied	No result	Percentage matches won	Win/Loss Ratio
Australia	64	54	6	1	3	84.4	9.00
New Zealand	62	40	17	2	3	64.5	2.35
England	60	37	19	2	2	61.7	1.95
India	45	21	20	1	3	46.7	1.05
South Africa	21	8	11	0	2	38.1	0.73
Trinidad & Tobago	6	2	4	0	0	33.3	0.50
West Indies	19	5	11	0	3	26.3	0.46
Sri Lanka	19	4	12	0	3	21.1	0.33
Ireland	35	7	26	0	2	20.0	0.27
Jamaica	6	1	4	0	1	16.7	0.25
International XI	18	3	14	0	1	16.7	0.21
Young England	6	1	5	0	0	16.7	0.20
Denmark	13	2	11	0	0	15.4	0.18
Netherlands	27	2	24	0	1	7.4	0.08
Pakistan	5	0	5	0	0	0.0	0.00

WORLD CUP & ICC TROPHY

A PROPOSAL to organise a World Cup for men's cricket was first discussed by the Public Relations and Promotion Sub-Committee of the English Test and County Cricket Board in 1970. The idea was to develop a competition based on five-day test matches played in the various participating countries and finishing with a final at Lord's. The proposal was put to a meeting of the International Cricket Conference in July 1971 but it met with little support. Concerns were expressed about the likely cost, the time that such a competition would take and the conflict with the programme of test matches and tours already agreed by the ICC. The TCCB was also approached in 1970 by Ben Brocklehurst of *The Cricketer* magazine with an alternative proposal for a limited-overs competition for which he offered the prospect of supporting sponsorship of some £50,000. The TCCB turned this down, most probably because it interfered with their own proposal and because it was felt that external sponsorship might compromise their position as the body solely responsible for the organization of cricket in England and Wales. Of course, these reasons were not publicly stated. Instead the argument presented was that there was no room in the international programme for such a competition, a view which the TCCB conveniently ignored when, in 1973, they presented their own proposal to the ICC for a competition based on one-day matches. By this time the International Women's Cricket Council had proved that such an event was both feasible and viable. The ICC finally accepted the proposal in 1974 and went ahead to seek their own industrial sponsor.

The idea of a competition between the non test-playing countries was first made by Philip Snow, the former Fijian cricketer, to a meeting of the ICC in 1966 where it was supported by Gamini Goonesena of Sri Lanka and John Marder of the USA. The original suggestion was a contest involving two- or three-day matches but this would have been too time-consuming for the amateur cricketers of the participating countries. A competition based on the one-day format was therefore proposed. This was accepted by the ICC who donated the trophy. By the time the first competition was held in 1979, it had also become a qualifying contest for the World Cup, as well as being an event in its own right. The biggest obstacle to the ICC Trophy was finance. Whilst sponsorship could be obtained for the World Cup, no private company was likely to be interested in funding a competition between the minor countries of the cricketing world. Each country was given the responsibility of providing their own finance which, surprisingly, most managed to do. A key feature of the ICC Trophy from the outset was to encourage indigenous cricket. Strict qualification rules were established as to which cricketers could represent their countries in order to avoid teams being comprised solely of short-term expatriate residents. These have gradually become more stringent over time. The competition has proved so successful that by 2005 it was necessary to limit the number of countries that can take part. Qualifying competitions are now held to determine which twelve sides can contest the ICC Trophy. At the same time, the World Cup proper has expanded and the number of minor countries which can qualify from the ICC Trophy to take part has increased from one to five.

1975 TOURNAMENT

THE FIRST World Cup, staged in England in June 1975, was marked by some exciting cricket played in superb weather. Aided by the long daylight hours in the weeks immediately prior to the summer solstice, all matches were 60 overs per side and none suffered from poor light conditions or rain. The final, played at Lord's on 21 June, went on until 8.43 p.m. With South Africa banned from international cricket for political reasons, the contest was between the six test-playing countries of England, Australia, West Indies, New Zealand, India and Pakistan, supplemented by Sri Lanka and East Africa, the two associate members of the ICC with recent first-class experience. The eight teams were arranged in two groups of four with the top two in each group progressing to the semi-finals. When preparing the draw for the groups, Australia and

England were seeded to keep them apart and Sri Lanka and East Africa were placed in different groups. Failure to employ any further seeding meant that Pakistan and the West Indies had to compete with Australia for the semi-final places, whereas England seemed to be in a somewhat easier group with India and New Zealand. The simple structure, however, meant that, unlike in many future tournaments, most of the group matches had some purpose and there was real competition for the semi-final places. By moving from the groups direct to the semi-finals, the tournament was kept short and public interest was sustained throughout. The only surprising feature of the scheduling was the playing of all twelve group matches on just three days. With four matches on each day, it was not possible to have ball-by-ball television and radio coverage of every match and press coverage of some games was somewhat limited.

As expected, England topped their group, winning all their matches easily. In their first match they scored 334 for four at which point India effectively admitted defeat and, instead of attempting the target, laboriously worked their way through 60 overs to 132 for three, a rate of 2.2 runs per over, with Sunil Gavaskar batting throughout for 36 runs off 174 balls. Fortunately, most of the other matches were more entertaining. The West Indies were unbeaten in their group after a surprisingly easy victory over Australia, aided by the sheer brilliance and audacity of Alvin Kallicharran who, in ten balls

from Lillee, scored 4, 4, 4, 4, 4, 1, 4, 6, 0 and 4. Although they did not win a match, the Sri Lankans became one of the tournament's crowd favourites for their display against the Australians. Despite having Sunil Wettimuny and Duleep Mendis taken to hospital after being struck by some spiteful balls from Jeff Thomson, Sri Lanka's batsmen got behind the line of the ball and cut and hooked any short-pitched deliveries with some skill, to reach 276 for four in reply to Australia's 328 for six. The semi-finals produced an easy wins for Australia over England and the West Indies over New Zealand.

The final was one of the most entertaining one-day games of all time. Put into bat, the West Indies lost three wickets for 50 runs before Clive Lloyd gave one of the best batting displays ever seen. He reached a century off 82 balls, hitting two sixes and twelve fours. Australia set about the task in a convincing manner but they did not allow for the inspired West Indian fielding, in particular, Viv Richards, who was responsible for three of Australia's five run-outs, two with direct hits. The game swung continuously, first in favour of the Australians, then back to the West Indies who achieved victory with eight balls still to be bowled. The match demonstrated that good fielding can win matches whilst bad running between the wickets can lose them.

Glen Turner of New Zealand was the outstanding batsman of the tournament. With centuries against India and East Africa, his aggregate of 333 runs (average 166.50) was the highest by a margin of 90. Other centuries were scored by Dennis Amiss and Keith Fletcher (England), Clive Lloyd (West Indies) and Alan Turner (Australia). The best bowling performance was Gary Gilmour's six for 14 against England. With a further five for 34 against Pakistan, he finished with the highest tournament aggregate of eleven wickets at an average of 5.63. Bernard Julien and Keith Boyce, both of the West Indies, obtained the next highest aggregate with ten wickets each.

Final qualifying tables
Group A

	Played	Won	Lost	No result	Points
England	3	3	0	0	12
New Zealand	3	2	1	0	8
India	3	1	2	0	4
East Africa	3	0	3	0	0

Group B

West Indies	3	3	0	0	12
Australia	3	2	1	0	8
Pakistan	3	1	2	0	4
Sri Lanka	3	0	3	0	0

Semi-finals
Australia (94-6) beat England (93) by 4 wickets.
West Indies (159-5) beat New Zealand (158) by 5 wickets.

Final
West Indies (291-8) beat Australia (274) by 17 runs.

1979 TOURNAMENT

ALTHOUGH THERE was some interest from India in hosting the 1979 World Cup, the ICC decided to stage the competition in England. With South Africa still barred from international sport, the contest was again between six test-playing countries and two associates. A preliminary competition was held among the associate countries for the ICC Trophy with the two finalists going forward to the World Cup. As a result the only change from 1975 was that Canada replaced East Africa.

Qualifying Competition – ICC Trophy 1979

THE DREAM of Philip Snow that there should be an international competition to test the relative playing strengths of the minor cricketing countries came to fruition on 22 May 1979 when the first matches were played in England for the ICC Trophy. There were some disappointments before the tournament started. Hong Kong were unable to compete since they could not field a team which met the residential qualifications. West Africa failed to submit their application on time. Gibraltar withdrew because the dates clashed with an international hockey tournament for which several of their players were required. Wales replaced Gibraltar but, since the Principality was not a member of the ICC, they were not allowed officially to gain points. Had they progressed to the final they would not have been permitted to win the trophy or play in the World Cup. Nevertheless, it was a major achievement of the organisers to attract fifteen countries from across the world. The teams were divided into three groups with the winners of each group and the country with the highest number of points finishing second contesting the semi-finals. All matches except the final took place on leading club grounds in the English Midlands. The tournament coincided with the coldest and wettest May since 1722 and six of the matches were abandoned, four without a ball being bowled. The game between Israel and Sri Lanka was also abandoned because Sri Lanka, under instructions from their government, refused to play against the Israeli team. Fortunately, none of the governments of the other countries in that group had a policy of boycotting contacts with Israel.

Bermuda won all the matches that they played to finish top of their group, ahead of a somewhat dis-appointing East African side which contained only two players from their 1975 World Cup squad. Denmark won all their matches to head their group but, by winning three out of their four games, Canada finished as the highest ranking runners-up. As expected, Sri Lanka won their group but, by giving a walkover to Israel and having one match abandoned, they had to rely on a faster run-rate to do so. Canada improved as the tournament progressed. Having lost to Denmark by 46 runs in the group stage, they beat Bermuda in the semi-final. Sri

Final qualifying tables

Group A

	Played	Won	Lost	No result	Points
Bermuda	4	3	0	1	14
East Africa	4	2	1	1	10
Papua New Guinea	4	1	2	1	8
Singapore	4	1	2	1	6
Argentina	4	0	3	1	2

Group B

	Played	Won	Lost	No result	Points
Denmark	4	4	0	0	16
Canada	4	3	1	0	12
Bangladesh	4	2	2	0	8
Fiji	4	0	3	1	2
Malaysia	4	0	3	1	2

Group C

	Played	Won	Lost	No result	Points
Sri Lanka	4	2	1	1	10
USA	4	2	1	1	10
Wales	4	2	1	1	10
Netherlands	4	1	2	1	6
Israel	4	1	3	0	4

Note: Israel won over Sri Lanka on a walkover.

Semi-finals

Sri Lanka (318-6) beat Denmark (110) by 208 runs.
Canada (186-6) beat Bermuda (181) by 4 wickets.

Final

Sri Lanka (324-8) beat Canada (264-5) by 60 runs.

Lanka overwhelmed Denmark in the other semi-final. The final took place after Sri Lanka and Canada had completed their matches in the World Cup. Held on the County Ground at Worcester, the match was notable for its high scoring. Having already beaten India in the World Cup, Sri Lanka batted with confidence and posted a virtually unassailable target as Canada's bowlers conceded 5.4 runs per over. After a shaky start, Canada's batsmen showed up the weaknesses in the Sri Lankan attack and, for a time, a Canadian victory seemed possible but they were unable to maintain the scoring rate.

The wet weather meant that there were few outstanding performances. No batsman scored a century. The highest run aggregates belonged to two Sri Lankans and one Canadian, reflecting that with their semi-final and final games, they played more matches than the other countries. Duleep Mendis and Roy Dias (both Sri Lanka) finished with 221 runs (average 55.25) and 214 runs (average 71.33) respectively with John Vaughan (Canada) on 211 runs (average 70.33). The highest average (153.00) was obtained by Anton Bakker of The Netherlands who was dismissed only once in three innings. Vaughan, with 14 wickets (average 16.21), was the highest wicket-taker. The best match bowling was seven wickets for 23 runs by Bangladesh's Syed Ashraf-ul-Haque against Fiji. He, Øle Mortensen and Carsten Morild of Denmark, Winston Trott of Bermuda and Lawrence Young Keng Sim of Singapore all took ten wickets during the tournament.

Main Competition 1979

DESPITE CONCERNS in 1975 that one group was easier to qualify from than the other, the organisers decided against any seeding when making the draw. The only constraint was to keep the two associate countries apart. Thus England and Australia found themselves in the same group with Pakistan whilst the holders, the West Indies, were in what seemed an easier group with New Zealand and India. All group matches were again held on three days so that four games were always taking place simultaneously, at least in theory. In practice, the weather was less kind than in 1975 and three matches continued into the second or reserve day. The match between the West Indies and Sri Lanka was abandoned completely. As in 1975, only test match grounds were used.

England won all their matches to head their group. They made a sensational start against Australia who were weakened by the loss of their key players in the dispute between World Series Cricket and the Australian Cricket Board. Australia proved their players were still a bad judge of a run. Four of them were run out as they crawled their way to 159 for nine in 60 overs. England achieved the total required with six wickets and 23 balls to spare. From being finalists in 1975, Australia failed to make the semi-finals. Their only victory was over Canada who, despite considerable enthusiasm, were outclassed. The West Indies were untroubled in the second group. New Zealand finished second with victories over India and Sri Lanka. India still seemed to have much to learn about one-day cricket and were surprisingly beaten by Sri Lanka who thus improved on their performance in 1975.

The semi-final between England and New Zealand produced the most exciting game of the tournament with the likely result continually fluctuating throughout the day. England scraped home by 9 runs. Gordon Greenidge and Desmond

Final qualifying tables

Group A

	Played	Won	Lost	No result	Points
England	3	3	0	0	12
Pakistan	3	2	1	0	8
Australia	3	1	2	0	4
Canada	3	0	3	0	0

Group B

	Played	Won	Lost	No result	Points
West Indies	3	2	0	1	10
New Zealand	3	2	1	0	8
Sri Lanka	3	1	1	1	6
India	3	0	3	0	0

Semi-finals

England (221-8) beat New Zealand (212-9) by 9 runs.
West Indies (293-6) beat Pakistan (250) by 43 runs.

Final

West Indies (286-9) beat England (194) by 92 runs.

Haynes started with a superb opening stand of 132 runs at over four runs an over for the West Indies in the other semi-final against Pakistan. The score of 293 look insurmountable but Majid Khan and Zaheer Abbas responded with a brilliant partnership of 156 runs and complete mastery over the West Indies' pace attack. Pakistan tried heroically to keep the run-rate going but finished 43 runs short.

The final proved disappointingly one-sided. With only four front-line bowlers because of injuries, England lost the initiative allowing the West Indies to recover from 99 for four through a partnership of 139 by Viv Richards and Collis King for the fifth wicket. England decided that the best way to win was to obtain a steady start without losing wickets and then accelerate from that base. Brearley and Boycott achieved exactly that with an opening partnership of 129 runs but the scoring rate was too slow. Boycott batted for seventeen overs before reaching double figures and after 25 overs the score was only 79. England still needed 103 runs with twelve overs remaining and, attempting the near-impossible, lost their last eight wickets in 26 balls for 11 runs.

The West Indians Viv Richards with 217 runs (average 108.50) and Gordon Greenidge with 253 runs (average 84.33) were the batsmen of the tournament. Only two centuries were scored in the competition and they managed one each. The only other run aggregate over 200 was 210 (average 52.50) by Graham Gooch of England. The best bowling belonged to Alan Hurst whose 5 wickets for 21 ensured that Australia were not embarrassed by Canada. Joel Garner's five wicket haul for 38 runs for the West Indies against England in the final was arguably the more impressive performance. Mike Hendrick (England) led the tournament aggregate with 10 wickets for an average of 14.90.

1983 TOURNAMENT

AFTER THE 1979 tournament the ICC decided that the World Cup should become a permanent feature of the cricket calendar and staged every four years. They agreed that the third competition should again be held in England in 1983. The ICC Trophy would also become a four-yearly event with the winner qualifying to play in the main competition. With Sri Lanka being admitted as a full member of the ICC in 1981, there was room for only one associate country in the main competition. This was a disappointment to the associate countries who had hoped that the existing arrangement of two qualifiers would continue. The ICC also decided to hold the ICC Trophy in the year prior to the World Cup. Whilst this had the advantage of allowing the qualifying country time to prepare for competition at a higher level, it took away the immediacy of qualification and meant that the qualifying country had to find the finance to come to England in two consecutive years.

Qualifying Competition – ICC trophy 1982

THE 1982 event was again held in England but in an effort to avoid a repeat of the problems posed in 1979 by a wet May, the tournament was scheduled for the second half of June. Unfortunately, the first two weeks of the competition coincided with one of the wettest and coldest summer periods in the English Midlands for more than a century and fifteen matches were abandoned without a ball being bowled. West Africa suffered particularly in being able to play only two of their seven games. The USA, Gibraltar and Singapore also had more games abandoned than they managed to play. Apart from the final, all matches were again played on leading club grounds. Sixteen countries took part with Zimbabwe, Hong Kong, Gibraltar and West Africa competing for the first time. Kenya also played in their own right having previously been part of East Africa who, therefore, were weaker than in 1979. Denmark were unable to participate for financial reasons and Argentina were prevented from playing by the dispute between the British and Argentinian governments over the sovereignty of the Falkland Islands. The teams were divided into two groups which, if the weather had been better, would have allowed each country to play seven matches instead of only the four of the previous tournament. The top two teams in each group contested the semi-finals. A play-off for third place was introduced. Although, arguably, the best four teams reached the semi-finals, the final tables did not necessary represent the relative strengths of the competing countries. Since the points for abandoned matches were shared, several of the weaker sides gained points which they might not otherwise have achieved.

With a team that included several players with experience of first-class cricket in South African domestic competition prior to the country's independence, Zimbabwe were easily the classiest team of the tournament. They were unbeaten, never bowled out within their 60 overs and finished with the fastest scoring rate. As expected, they won their group. The

surprise of the competition was Papua New Guinea. Their four victories enabled them to finish above Canada who were unfortunate to have three matches abandoned. Israel again failed to win a match and finished last in the group. Their participation meant that extra security had to be provided and the draw had to be fixed in order to ensure that they were in a group with no countries where Islam is the dominant religion. They repaid this special treatment by having a dispute between several members of their team and the management which led to some of their players walking out before the end of the tournament. They were unable to fulfil their last fixture which was awarded to Canada by default. Bermuda were the victors of the second group. Although their bowling was a shade weaker than in 1979, their batting, aided by Colin Blades, an import from Barbados with first-class experience, was particularly strong and aggressive. They were the only team other than Zimbabwe to score at more than five runs per over. Bangladesh were a little fortunate to finish above The Netherlands in second place. They had a slower run rate but lost one match fewer to the weather. The semi-finals produced easy wins for Zimbabwe and Bermuda.

Bermuda batted well in the final showing that Zimbabwe's pace attack was not to be feared. John Traicos with his off-spin was the only bowler to slow the run-rate; his analysis was 12-3-25-0. When Zimbabwe were two wickets down for 30 runs, it looked as though Bermuda might create an upset but Kevin Curran, Andy Pycroft and Craig Hodgson overpowered all the bowling apart from Winston Trott (11.3-1-27-1). Zimbabwe thus went forward to the World Cup without having been seriously challenged.

Despite the weather, the overall standard of play showed considerable improvement. Ten centuries were made. The highest was an undefeated 155 by Robert Lifmann for The

Final qualifying tables

Group A

	Played	Won	Lost	No result	Points	Scoring rate
Zimbabwe	7	5	0	2	24	5.5
Papua New Guinea	7	4	2	1	18	3.8
Canada	7	3	1	3	18	4.0
Kenya	7	3	2	2	16	3.4
Hong Kong	7	2	3	2	12	3.0
USA	7	1	2	4	12	3.6
Gibraltar	7	0	3	4	8	2.4
Israel	7	0	5	2	4	2.6

Group B

	Played	Won	Lost	No result	Points	Scoring rate
Bermuda	7	6	0	1	26	5.2
Bangladesh	7	4	1	2	20	3.2
Netherlands	7	3	1	3	18	3.6
Singapore	7	1	2	4	12	3.0
Fiji	7	1	3	3	10	3.6
East Africa	7	1	3	3	10	2.8
West Africa	7	0	2	5	10	2.8
Malaysia	7	0	4	3	6	3.0

Note: Canada won over Israel on a walkover.

Semi-finals
Zimbabwe (126-2) beat Bangladesh (124) by 8 wickets.
Bermuda (155-4) beat Papua New Guinea (153) by 6 wickets.

Third place play-off
Papua New Guinea (225-7) beat Bangladesh (224) by 3 wickets.

Final
Zimbabwe (232-5) beat Bermuda (231-8) by 5 wickets.

Netherlands against Malaysia, beating his compatriot, Ron Elferink (154* against Fiji) by one run. Other century makers were David Houghton and Kevin Curran of Zimbabwe, Rudi Schoonheim of The Netherlands, Winston Reid and Gladstone Brown of Bermuda, Yousuf Rahman of Bangladesh, Farouk Kirmani of Canada and Vavine Pala from Papua New Guinea. The highest run aggregate was 310 by Bermuda's Colin Blades. David Houghton (308) was the only other player to exceed 300 tournament runs. The best bowling was by Elvin James who achieved the remarkable figures of 7.1-5-2-5 against Malaysia. La'a Aukopi (Papua New Guinea) and Mohan Rajalingam (Singapore) were the other bowlers to achieve five wickets in an innings. James' performance helped him take the most tournament wickets (15 at an average of 12.46). Peter Rawson (Zimbabwe) and K. Kalo (Papua New Guinea) each obtained fourteen wickets.

Main competition 1983

THE 1983 World Cup differed from its predecessor in 1979 in three respects. Among the eight competing countries, Canada were replaced by Zimbabwe. The umpires were asked to be strict about wides and bouncers which meant that, from this tournament on, the definition of a wide in one-day international cricket was much more severe than that used in test matches. The tournament was increased in length by having the teams in each group play each other twice. This change was justified by the ICC as minimising the chance that a team would be eliminated if bad luck with the weather forced it to share points with a weaker opponent which it would otherwise have beaten. Although the ICC clearly had the experience of the previous year's ICC Trophy in mind, it had to be admitted that the problem had not arisen in either of the previous World Cup competitions; nor had the weather produced an injustice in the outcome of the ICC Trophy. It seemed clear that this reasoning was cosmetic and that the change was really made to increase the financial returns on the competition. However, the change did allow the matches to be spread to more venues and therefore gave more people the opportunity to witness top-class one-day international cricket. In addition to the test match grounds of London (Lord's and The Oval), Manchester, Birmingham, Nottingham and Leeds, matches were played at Bristol, Chelmsford, Derby, Leicester, Southampton, Swansea, Taunton, Tunbridge Wells and Worcester, giving an even stronger southern and midlands bias to the competition. Again the group matches were arranged so that four took place on each scheduled day, making it impossible for television and radio to give full ball-by-ball coverage.

England won their group with convincing victories in five of their six matches and a surprise defeat by New Zealand by two wickets with one ball to spare. New Zealand's victory was not sufficient to take them to the semi-finals. Despite having same record of three wins and three defeats, they finished behind Pakistan on run-rate. Sri Lanka were unable to repeat their performances of the previous tournaments; their solitary win against New Zealand confined them to bottom position in the group. The West Indies won the second group despite losing their first match to India. For the first time in a World Cup competition, India, under the captaincy of Kapil Dev, looked a competent one-day side. Australia had a poor time for the second successive tournament. On a good day they were unbeatable but both their batting and bowling were too inconsistent. They began the competition with a surprise defeat by Zimbabwe, dropping five catches and, unable to match the required run rate, finishing 13 runs adrift (see Chapter 2 – Country Profile for Zimbabwe). Zimbabwe were unable to repeat their heroics, however, and, as expected, finished last in the group.

India were never in difficulty in their semi-final against England. Their six wicket victory was achieved with 5.2 overs to spare. The West Indies pace attack was too powerful for Pakistan whose total of 184 for six was surpassed in 48.4 overs with Viv Richards and Hilary Gomes in an unbeaten partnership of 132 runs. The West Indies began their third consecutive World Cup final as firm favourites to retain the title. The pace attack of Andy Roberts, Joel Garner, Malcolm Marshall and Michael Holding was unrelenting in dismissing India for

183. West Indies reached 50 for one but then it all went wrong. Whether they suddenly remembered from their opening game how difficult it was to score runs against the Indian medium-pacers or whether there was a degree of complacency, the run-rate fell dramatically and the wickets started to fall regularly. They were dismissed 43 runs short in 52 overs to give India an unexpected victory (see Chapter 2 – Country Profile for India).

Eight centuries were scored during the tournament. Kapil Dev's 175 not out for India against Zimbabwe was the highest individual score in the World Cup to date. The other centuries were David Gower and Alan Lamb (England), Viv Richards and Gordon Greenidge (West Indies), Zaheer Abbas and Imran Khan (Pakistan) and Trevor Chappell (Australia). Gower obtained the most tournament runs of 384 for an average of 76.80. Richards (367 at 73.40) and Graeme Fowler (England) (360 at 72.00) had the next highest aggregates. Winston Davis became the first bowler to take seven wickets in an innings in the World Cup with his 7-51 against Australia. Australia's Ken MacLeay

took six for 39 against India and there were twelve instances of bowlers taking five wickets in an innings, an achievement which Asantha de Mel (Sri Lanka) and Abdul Qadir (Pakistan) managed twice. The highest tournament aggregate was 18 wickets (average 18.66) by India's Roger Binny. De Mel and Madan Lal (India) each took 17 wickets at averages of 15.58 and 15.76 respectively.

Final qualifying tables

Group A

	Played	Won	Lost	No result	Points	Runs per over
England	6	5	1	0	20	4.67
Pakistan	6	3	3	0	12	4.01
New Zealand	6	3	3	0	12	3.93
Sri Lanka	6	1	5	0	4	3.75

Group B

	Played	Won	Lost	No result	Points	Runs per over
West Indies	6	5	1	0	20	4.31
India	6	4	2	0	16	3.87
Australia	6	2	4	0	8	3.81
Zimbabwe	6	1	5	0	4	3.49

Semi-finals

India (217-4) beat England (213) by 6 wickets.
West Indies (188-2) beat Pakistan (184-8) by 8 wickets.

Final

India (183) beat West Indies (140) by 43 runs.

1987 TOURNAMENT

WITH THE World Cup now firmly established as cricket's major four-yearly event, considerable kudos was to be gained from hosting it and there was increasing pressure on the ICC to stage the tournament outside England. By the autumn of 1983, the ICC therefore requested tenders to host the next competition, resulting in a decision to award the 1987 tournament to India and Pakistan as joint hosts. The ICC Trophy, however, remained in England.

Qualifying Competition – ICC Trophy 1986

AS WITH the 1983 tournament, the ICC Trophy was held the year before the World Cup. The matches were again staged at various club grounds in the English Midlands, except for the final which, for the first time, was held at Lord's. At the time of the competition there were eighteen associate countries in the ICC and all were invited. They were divided into two groups with the top two in each group going forward to the

semi-finals. Before the competition started, West Africa were barred because of the failure of the West African Cricket Conference to respond to requests for information about their entry by the necessary deadlines. Singapore withdrew at the last moment when several of their squad were unable to get leave. These withdrawals meant that one group was left with only seven countries. Compared with 1982, Denmark and Argentina returned. Israel were again placed in a group without Islamic countries.

Zimbabwe won all their matches in their group with ease and, as in 1982, showed the benefits of having played first-class cricket. Denmark lost only to Zimbabwe. Malaysia were the surprise of the group, winning their first three matches against East Africa, Argentina and Bangladesh. The second group was more closely contested with The Netherlands, Bermuda and the USA all finishing on the same number of points and the first two progressing to the semi-finals on run rate. The USA were the surprise team. Wins over Canada and Bermuda looked to have qualified them for the semi-finals until Bermuda's surprise defeat of the Dutch. The semi-finals produced easy victories for Zimbabwe and The Netherlands. The final saw Zimbabwe tested for the only time in the competition and they needed a certain amount of luck to win the trophy. The Dutch bowlers exploited a damp pitch following morning rainfall. With four wickets down for 101, the impetus seemed to be with the Dutch but they then dropped several catches and Zimbabwe made 73 runs from the last nine overs. The Netherlands made steady progress to reach 109 for 1 but a middle-order collapse occurred before Steve Lubbers and Ron Elferink put on 67 for the seventh wicket. Lubbers then damaged the ligaments in his ankle and with Elferink finding running difficult following an injury sustained when fielding, the runs came too slowly. If Lubbers and Elferink had remained fully fit, there is a chance that the Dutch would have provided the upset of the tournament instead of falling short by 25 runs.

After the dismal weather of the two previous tournaments, this one took place in dry, sunny conditions, at least until rain caused the final to extend into its reserve day. As a result, batsmen prospered. Twenty centuries

were made. Canada's Paul Prashad scored three of them to finish with the highest run aggregate (533) and the highest average (88.83). Steve Atkinson and Rupert Gomes both made two hundreds for The Netherlands to finish second (508 average 72.57) and third (499 average 83.16) in the run aggregate. Simon Myles (Hong Kong) (408) was the fourth player to score more than 400 runs. The best bowling return was six for 11 by Bharat Goel for Hong Kong against Fiji. Ron Elferink took six for 14 and six for 22 against Fiji and Israel respectively. Other bowlers to achieve six wickets were A. Kumar (6-28 for East Africa against Argentina) and Anthony Edwards (6-38 for Bermuda against Fiji). Elferink had the highest wicket aggregate with 23 at an average of 9.82 but he was closely followed by Denmark's Øle Mortensen with 22 at 9.40 and Paul-Jan Bakker (The Netherlands) with 21 at 13.19.

Final qualifying tables

Group A

	Played	Won	Lost	No result	Points	Scoring rates
Zimbabwe	6	6	0	0	24	4.92
Denmark	6	5	1	0	20	3.68
Malaysia	6	3	3	0	12	2.85
Kenya	6	3	3	0	12	2.73
East Africa	6	2	4	0	8	3.07
Bangladesh	6	2	4	0	8	2.82
Argentina	6	0	6	0	0	2.52

Group B

	Played	Won	Lost	No result	Points	Scoring rates
Netherlands	8	7	1	0	28	5.03
Bermuda	8	7	1	0	28	4.62
USA	8	7	1	0	28	4.21
Canada	8	5	3	0	20	4.42
Papua New Guinea	8	4	4	0	16	5.08
Hong Kong	8	3	5	0	12	3.58
Fiji	8	2	6	0	8	3.23
Gibraltar	8	1	7	0	4	2.58
Israel	8	0	8	0	0	2.78

Semi-finals

Zimbabwe (205-0) beat Bermuda (201-7) by 10 wickets.
Netherlands (225-5) beat Denmark (224-6) by 5 wickets.

Third place play-off

Denmark (158-4) beat Bermuda (155) by 6 wickets.

Final

Zimbabwe (243-9) beat Netherlands (218) by 25 runs.

Main competition 1987

WITH ZIMBABWE occupying the single qualifying place from the associate countries, the 1987 World Cup had the same countries and the same format as 1983. The eight countries were split into two groups within which each country played the others twice. There were, however, several important differences between this and the previous tournament. First, the shorter daylight hours in India and Pakistan meant that all games had to be 50 overs per side instead of 60. With playing conditions less conducive to seam bowling, all teams except Australia played two specialist spin bowlers. No more than two matches took place on any one day, allowing for better coverage by the broadcasting services. The hosts continued with the policy of spreading the games across many venues. Altogether, twenty-one were used. The larger geographical area of the Indian sub-continent compared to England resulted in the teams covering much greater travel distances between matches, many involving two-day journeys. The Sri Lankans were the worst affected with consecutive games in Peshawar (Pakistan), Kanpur (India), Faisalabad (Pakistan) and Pune (India). In contrast, the itinerary for the Indians followed a relatively logical path from the south-east to north-west of the country in a series of relatively short hops. Starting in Chennai, they moved to Bengaluru,

Mumbai, New Delhi, Ahmedabad, Nagpur. Similarly, Pakistan stayed in their own country and moved from Hyderabad to Rawalpindi, Lahore, Karachi, Faisalabad and back to Karachi. With allowances for reserve days in case of bad weather, the tournament took 32 days to complete compared with the 17 needed in 1983. With matches scheduled to begin at 09.00 hours local time, there was concern that, particularly in the north of both Pakistan and India, the team batting first would be at a disadvantage because of morning dew on the pitch. This proved not to be the case and nineteen of the twenty-seven matches were won by the side batting first. The teams batting second found it difficult to score at the high run-rates required after having fielded in the heat for some three and a half hours.

India and Australia finished equal on points in their group with India occupying the top position on run-rate. Both teams won five out of their six matches and their defeats came against each other. Although Zimbabwe failed to win a match, they were regarded by many as the best fielding side in the competition. Pakistan won their first five matches to head the second group before surprisingly succumbing to the West Indies. England's only defeats were their two games against Pakistan. Overall, England were somewhat fortunate to occupy the second spot and the West Indies somewhat unlucky not to do so, especially as they had the highest run-rate in the group. Pakistan were in their third consecutive semi-final but, despite being on home ground, they failed to progress further. Australia put up a highly professional performance and, although winning by only 18 runs, were always in control. England had the best of the second semi-final from the start. The Indian spinners proved unable to trouble the English batsmen and Graham Gooch played one of the greatest ever World Cup innings. His 115 was made off 136 balls and contained eleven fours.

Final qualifying tables

Group A

	Played	Won	Lost	No result	Points	Runs per over
India	6	5	1	0	20	5.39
Australia	6	5	1	0	20	5.19
New Zealand	6	2	4	0	8	4.88
Zimbabwe	6	0	6	0	0	3.76

Group B

	Played	Won	Lost	No result	Points	Runs per over
Pakistan	6	5	1	0	20	5.01
England	6	4	2	0	16	5.12
West Indies	6	3	3	0	12	5.16
Sri Lanka	6	0	6	0	0	4.04

Semi-finals

Australia (267-8) beat Pakistan (249) by 18 runs.
England (254-6) beat India (219) by 35 runs.

Final

Australia (253-5) beat England (246-8) by 7 runs.

Before a crowd estimated at 70,000, Australia chose to bat first in the final and posted 52 in the first ten overs. The last eleven overs produced 65 runs and Australia finished with a total that no side batting second in the tournament had exceeded. England were undeterred. Graham Gooch and Bill Athey made 65 runs in 17 overs, and Athey and Mike Gatting 69 in thirteen overs. Seventeen runs were needed from the last over. England came very close but could not prevent Australia from winning the World Cup for the first time.

England's Graham Gooch scored the most runs in the tournament, 471 at an average of 58.87. He was followed by David Boon (Australia) with 447 (average 55.87) and Geoff Marsh (Australia), 428 (average 61.14). Marsh was the only player to make two centuries, 126 not out against New Zealand and 110 against India. The highest individual score was 181 by Viv Richards for the West Indies against Sri Lanka. Craig McDermott was the only bowler to take five wickets in an innings. His five for 44 against Pakistan, alongside 4-56 against India, helped him to the highest tournament aggregate of 18 wickets (average 18.94). Imran Khan (Pakistan) achieved 17 (average 13.05), twice taking four in an innings, against the West Indies and England, both times conceding 37 runs.

1992 TOURNAMENT

AUSTRALIA AND New Zealand were joint hosts for the 1992 tournament which, with South Africa competing for the first time, was the largest competition to date in terms of the number of matches played. Zimbabwe were again the representative of the associate countries having won the ICC Trophy in 1990.

Qualifying Competition – ICC Trophy 1990

THE ICC Trophy was held outside of England for the first time. The Netherlands acted as hosts which meant that all the matches were played on coconut matting. Fixtures were held at ten different club grounds in The Hague, Amsterdam, Rotterdam, Haarlem, Nijmegen and Deventer, all within a two-hour drive of The Hague where the teams and central organisation were based. Singapore returned to the competition and East Africa became East and Central Africa with the addition of Malawi to the countries from which the squad was chosen. Again West Africa were barred because of their failure to communicate with the organisers or to provide the necessary deposits for the hotel accommodation. An additional stage was added to the competition. The seventeen countries were initially arranged in four groups with the first two teams in each group progressing to a second round. Here, the qualifying teams were placed into two groups from which the top two in each group moved to the semi-finals. The teams which did not qualify for the second round entered a Plate Competition. These changes were designed to ensure that the most consistently successful teams reached the semi-finals rather than a team which happened to have

one 'giant-killing' day. The downside was that with only four or five teams in each of the first round groups, the two qualifying countries could usually be predicted in advance, thereby rendering many of the games pointless. The introduction of a Plate competition allowed the weaker teams to meet each other and ensured that they all played a sufficient number of games to make their participation worthwhile.

Zimbabwe won all the first round matches in their group with ease. Canada finished in second place with comfortable victories over Malaysia and Singapore. The second group was more closely contested. Bangladesh, a much improved side on that of 1986, won all their games but Kenya, Fiji and Bermuda finished with identical records. Bermuda lost both their opening matches and were a poor side compared to that which had represented them in previous tournaments. However, in their last game, they rallied to beat Kenya and scored their runs fast enough to ensure they finished above Fiji on run-rate. The USA were unbeaten in the third group despite being the victim of the strange rule which prevailed in both the ICC Trophy and the World Cup at the time, that if a match

Final qualifying tables
Group A

	Played	Won	Lost	No result	Points	Scoring rates
Zimbabwe	3	3	0	0	12	3.79
Canada	3	2	1	0	8	3.18
Singapore	3	1	2	0	4	2.06
Malaysia	3	0	3	0	0	2.08

Group B

Bangladesh	3	3	0	0	12	3.17
Kenya	3	1	2	0	4	3.45
Fiji	3	1	2	0	4	3.31
Bermuda	3	1	2	0	4	3.15

Group C

USA	3	3	0	0	12	4.08
Denmark	3	2	1	0	8	3.45
Gibraltar	3	1	2	0	4	2.52
East and Central Africa	3	0	3	0	0	2.23

Group D

Netherlands	4	4	0	0	16	5.49
Papua New Guinea	4	3	1	0	12	3.27
Hong Kong	4	2	2	0	8	3.81
Israel	4	1	3	0	4	2.29
Argentina	4	0	4	0	0	1.96

Second round
Group E

Zimbabwe	3	3	0	0	12	3.72
Kenya	3	1	2	0	4	2.98
Papua New Guinea	3	1	2	0	4	2.70
USA	3	1	2	0	4	2.68

Group F

Netherlands	3	2	1	0	8	3.68
Bangladesh	3	2	1	0	8	3.62
Denmark	3	1	2	0	4	2.93
Canada	3	1	2	0	4	2.72

Plate competition
Group G

Bermuda	3	3	0	0	12	5.19
Gibraltar	3	2	1	0	8	3.48
Singapore	3	1	2	0	4	2.26
Israel	3	0	3	0	0	2.58

Group H

Fiji	4	4	0	0	16	4.77
Hong Kong	4	3	1	0	12	3.33
East and Central Africa	4	1	3	0	4	3.12
Malaysia	4	1	3	0	4	3.00
Argentina	4	1	3	0	4	2.85

Semi-finals
Netherlands (205-5) beat Kenya (202) by 5 wickets.
Zimbabwe (231-7) beat Bangladesh (147) by 84 runs.

Final
Zimbabwe (198-4) beat Netherlands (197-9) by 6 wickets.

was started but could not be completed because of the weather, it was abandoned and the match replayed the following day. This happened after the USA had made 404 for eight from 60 overs with Errol Peart and Hugh Blackman scoring centuries. The game was abandoned when East and Central Africa were 41 for two after 20 overs. Although the USA won the replay by 5 wickets, the rules stated that the abandoned match did not count in official records. This ruling was later rescinded and the two centurions now have their achievements included in the all-time tournament statistics. As expected Denmark finished second. The Netherlands were clearly the strongest side in the fourth group. Papua New Guinea finished second beating Hong Kong by 36 runs in the match which effectively decided which of those two teams progressed to the next stage.

The second round saw Zimbabwe progress without being troubled whilst Kenya, Papua New Guinea and the USA fought for the second place which was decided, in Kenya's favour, on run-rate. The Kenyan team were tactically astute. Knowing that they could not score 260 runs to beat Zimbabwe, they calculated the target required for second place and ensured that they made it. Not everyone was supportive of this clinical approach which resulted in a boring game for all but the Kenyan players. The Netherlands finished first in the second group of the second round by virtue of a faster run-rate than Bangladesh. The Plate competition saw Bermuda and Fiji unbeaten in their groups but no attempt was made to schedule a play-off match or award a trophy. Fiji could consider they were the default winners by virtue of their victory over Bermuda in the first round.

The Dutch had the advantage of the

conditions in the first semi-final. Kenya who chose to bat despite the rather damp atmosphere lost five wickets for 52 runs. Only a sixth-wicket stand of 115 by Aasif Karim and Muslim Kanji helped them to a reasonable total. In reply an unbeaten sixth wicket partnership of 85 by Tim de Leede and Steven Lubbers took The Netherlands to a comfortable victory. Zimbabwe were made to fight by Bangladesh. Asked to bat, they were undone by the left-arm pace of Golam Nowsher who took three quick wickets to leave them on 37 for four. The rest of the bowling was not as penetrative, however, and Zimbabwe recovered. A stronger batting side might have got close to Zimbabwe's 231 for seven but only two players reached double figures and Zimbabwe had a relatively easy victory. There was no play-off for third place which was therefore shared by Kenya and Bangladesh. Zimbabwe and The Netherlands again met in the final but this time there was scarcely a contest. Reckless batting by the middle order meant that the Dutch failed to set Zimbabwe a challenge.

Nolan Clarke, who had previously played first-class cricket for Barbados, was the outstanding batsman of the tournament. His two centuries meant that he topped the runs aggregate with 523 for an average of 65.37. Roland Lefebvre (The Netherlands), with one century, tied for second place in the total tournament runs with Hong Kong's John Marsden. Both made 315 and both had an average of 45.00. Zimbabwe's Andy Flower was the only other player to exceed 300 runs. He did not make a century but with his 311 runs he topped the averages at 77.75. Other centurions were Peart and Blackman of the USA, Rupert Gomes (Netherlands) whose 169 not out against Israel was the highest individual score of the tournament, Nurul Abedin (Bangladesh), Asgari Stevens (Malaysia) and Ricky Hill (Bermuda). Bakker's 6-14 against Kenya was the best bowling performance but since he played only two matches, he was not among the leading wicket-takers on aggregate. Eddo Brandes (Zimbabwe) took the most wickets, 18 at 12.77 with a best performance of 5-27 against the USA. The next highest wicket aggregates were 16 by Salauddin Tariq (Hong Kong) and 14, achieved by Roland Lefebvre and Kevin Duers (Zimbabwe). Nasir Ahmed, Bangladesh's wicket-keeper, twice obtained four victims in an innings. In seven matches, he caught sixteen batsmen and stumped seven.

Main Competition 1992

THE FIFTH World Cup took place in February and March 1992. The basic structure was sensible. With nine countries participating, they played each other in a league with the top four teams progressing to the semi-finals. This should have ensured that the best four teams in the competition went forward but the arrangement was not without problems. With 39 matches to fit into 33 days, there was no possibility of reserve days except for the semi-finals and final. Where rain intervened in the league matches, a strange rule was introduced to help decide the target for the team batting second, replacing the previous method of deciding the winner on net run-rate. The latter was generally considered unsatisfactory since it invariably favoured the team batting second who were always able to calculate the run-rate required. The new rule worked by determining how many overs were lost to the team batting second and reducing the target by the number of runs made, in the equivalent number of the lowest-scoring overs, by the side batting first. When England played South Africa in the league, they lost nine overs to the weather but had their target reduced by only eleven runs since that was the number of runs made by South Africa in their lowest-scoring nine overs. Despite the much harder target, England reached it with one ball and three wickets to spare. The farcical nature of the rule did not become truly apparent until the semi-final between the same two teams. This time South Africa, batting second, lost 12 minutes to rain late in their innings when only 22 runs were needed from 13 balls. When the game restarted, the target became 21 runs from one ball! If the rain had come earlier and South Africa had not completed 25 overs, the match would have been abandoned and the game replayed the following day. Since the match was a day/night fixture, no one understood why the two lost overs could not have been played under floodlights.

For the first time in the World Cup, the teams played in coloured clothing. Ten of the 25 matches staged in Australia were day/night affairs with a white ball and floodlights. New Zealand hosted 14 matches but did not have floodlight facilities. Both countries took the opportunity to hold matches in the smaller towns. In Australia, Mackay (Queensland), Ballarat (Victoria), Berri (South Australia), Albury (New South Wales) and Canberra each hosted one game. All were successful except for the game at Mackay which was ruined by torrential rain. After a delay of five hours, India and Sri Lanka began a 20 overs-a-side match, but after two balls, further rain flooded the ground. New Zealand played all their league matches on home grounds; Australia's only 'away' fixture was that against New Zealand.

Australia had a disappointing time after starting the tournament as favourites. They lost their first two games to New Zealand and South Africa before scraping home against India by 1 run after India fell victim to the rain-rule. Playing in the competition for the first time, South Africa had a mixed record but did enough to qualify for the semi-finals. New Zealand topped the league, their sole defeat coming in their last match, against Pakistan. This match was one of two vital games which decided the fourth country to make up the semi-finals. New Zealand, South Africa and England were already certain of places. Pakistan would qualify if they beat New Zealand and Australia beat the West Indies. The West Indies would qualify if they beat Australia. Australia would qualify if they beat the West Indies and Pakistan lost to New Zealand. The first situation prevailed. The last day of the league saw England, who had been beaten only by New Zealand thus far, put in a dismal batting display against Zimbabwe. On a pitch helpful to bowlers but chasing a target of only 135, England succumbed without a fight to lose by 9 runs to

give Zimbabwe their only win of the tournament. India and Sri Lanka never adjusted to the conditions.

The semi-finals were high-scoring affairs. New Zealand relied on a fourth wicket partnership of 107 by Martin Crowe and Ken Rutherford to post a challenging target of 263 runs. With 15 overs remaining, Pakistan still required 123 runs. Unfazed by run rate of 8.2 per over, Inzamam-ul-Haq hit 60 from 37 balls, 87 runs were added in ten overs and Pakistan completed their task with an over to spare. The second semi-final ended in the farcical victory for England over South Africa. Before rain and the tournament rules produced an impossible target, South Africa required only 47 runs from five overs.

Pakistan chose to bat first in the final. After losing both openers for 24 in nine overs, their batsmen gained an increasing mastery over the English attack. Imran Khan and Javed Miandad put on 139 to provide the base from which Inzamam-ul-Haq (42 in 35 balls) and Wasim Akram (33 in 18 balls) could accelerate the scoring. The last 20 overs produced 153 runs. England were in considerable difficulty at 69 for four. Neil Fairbrother and Alan Lamb added 72 but once Lamb was bowled by Wasim and Fairbrother was reduced to batting with a runner, the run-rate required became too high and England finished 22 runs short. Thus Pakistan won the World Cup for the first time whilst England failed for the third time in their third final.

Eight scores of 100 or more were made during the competition, two by Rameez Raja (Pakistan) and two by David Boon (Australia). Andy Flower (Zimbabwe), Aamer Sohail (Pakistan), Phil Simmons (West Indies) and Martin Crowe (New Zealand) were the other century makers. Crowe had the highest run aggregate with 456 at an average of 114.00. Others who scored over 400 runs were Javed Miandad (Pakistan) (437 at 62.42) and Peter Kirsten (South Africa) (410 at 68.33). No bowler took five or more wickets in an innings, the best performance being 4-11 by Meyrick Pringle for South Africa against the West Indies. Eddo Brandes' four for 21 against England was the second best. The most tournament wickets was 18 by Wasim Akram (average 18.77), followed by three players on 16, Ian Botham (England), Mushtaq Ahmed (Pakistan) and Chris Harris (New Zealand).

Final qualifying table

	Played	Won	Lost	No result	Points	Net run rate
New Zealand	8	7	1	0	14	0.59
England	8	5	2	1	11	0.47
South Africa	8	5	3	0	10	0.13
Pakistan	8	4	3	1	9	0.16
Australia	8	4	4	0	8	0.20
West Indies	8	4	4	0	8	0.07
India	8	2	5	1	5	0.14
Sri Lanka	8	2	5	1	5	−0.68
Zimbabwe	8	1	7	0	2	−1.14

Semi-finals

Pakistan (264-6) beat New Zealand (262-7) by 4 wickets.
England (252-6) beat South Africa (232-6) by 19 runs.

Final

Pakistan (249-6) beat England (227) by 22 runs.

1996 TOURNAMENT

THE 1996 event returned to the Indian sub-continent with India, Pakistan and Sri Lanka acting as joint hosts. The largest and longest competition to date was undertaken with the number of participants expanding to twelve, following the decision of the ICC to allow the top three countries in the ICC Trophy to take part. The latter was held two years earlier in Kenya, the first time the competition had moved outside of Europe. This too was the largest to date with all twenty associate countries sending

teams. The two year gap between the ICC Trophy and the World Cup did the associate countries no favours. Two of the qualifying teams, the United Arab Emirates and The Netherlands, relied on players towards the end of their cricketing careers who had played first-class cricket in the countries of their birth and then qualified for their adopted countries by residence. Being two years older and facing test-class opponents they were unable to reproduce the form shown in the ICC Trophy.

Qualifying Competition – ICC Trophy 1994

THE 1994 ICC Trophy was held in Nairobi, Kenya. All the games were played on grass wickets on grounds within a fifteen minute drive of the city centre. Two controversies marred the otherwise extremely successful competition in which Ireland, United Arab Emirates and Namibia took part for the first time. The major problem concerned the status of the team from the United Arab Emirates which comprised seven Pakistanis, two Indians, one Sri Lankan and only one Emirate by birth, Sheikh Zarawani, who was given the captaincy. Although all the players satisfied the ICC regulations, there was a general feeling that the UAE had effectively 'bought' a team from the Indian sub-continent by offering various incentives to players with first-class experience (see Chapter 2 – Country Profile for United Arab Emirates). The second topic of dispute related to the lack of adequate rules for the outcome of matches affected by rain. As long as the innings of the team batting second lasted 30 overs, the outcome was decided on run-rate. The problems arose where the game was abandoned before this could be achieved. They were exacerbated by a rule that matches had to finish by 5.40 p.m. on the second day. Not surprisingly, some bizarre situations emerged. There was no play on the first day in the match between Singapore and Canada. The umpires then decided that since no play had occurred, the second day must effectively be the first day which meant that there was no time limit to the finish on that day. The umpires therefore invoked the first-day rule that a match could continue after the proposed finishing time if an outcome looked possible. In the

end, rain brought the match to its conclusion after only 20 overs of Singapore's innings. The match was officially abandoned and the points shared. With the precedent set, the umpires of the match between Papua New Guinea and Ireland, two days later, again decreed that the second day was the first day, after there had been no play on the official first day. On the second day, Papua New Guinea were forced to continue batting into the night with no indication of how many overs the innings would last. The game was eventually stopped after 32 overs and Ireland declared the winners on run-rate. Papua New Guinea protested that the umpires had breached tournament regulations but the result was allowed to stand. In reality, no injustice was done because Papua New Guinea had been completely outplayed and their score of 88 for seven was a poor reply to Ireland's 230 for eight.

The tournament followed the format of that in 1990 with a first round in which the twenty teams were split into four groups. The top two in each group entered the second round with the first two teams of the two second round groups progressing to the semi-finals. The third- and fourth-placed teams in the first round groups entered a Plate competition where they were divided into two groups, the winners of each contesting the Plate final. The outcome was a farce because the top teams, Papua New Guinea and the USA, had both booked their flights home not expecting to qualify. As a result, the runners-up in each group played the final. The bottom teams in each of the first round groups entered what the organisers chose

Final qualifying tables

Group A

	Played	Won	Lost	No result	Points	Scoring rates
Netherlands	4	4	0	0	16	4.71
Ireland	4	3	1	0	12	4.02
Papua New Guinea	4	2	2	0	8	3.66
Malaysia	4	1	3	0	4	3.03
Gibraltar	4	0	4	0	0	2.37

Group B

United Arab Emirates	4	4	0	0	16	4.60
Bangladesh	4	3	1	0	12	3.90
USA	4	2	2	0	8	4.82
Argentina	4	1	3	0	4	3.27
East and Central Africa	4	0	4	0	0	2.32

Group C

Kenya	4	4	0	0	16	4.84
Canada	4	2	1	1	10	4.50
Namibia	4	2	2	0	8	3.31
Israel	4	1	3	0	4	2.58
Singapore	4	0	3	1	2	2.12

Group D

Bermuda	4	4	0	0	16	3.93
Hong Kong	4	3	1	0	12	4.95
Denmark	4	2	2	0	8	3.95
Fiji	4	1	3	0	4	3.06
West Africa	4	0	4	0	0	2,57

Second round

Group E

Kenya	3	3	0	0	12	5.16
Netherlands	3	2	1	0	8	4.83
Bangladesh	3	1	2	0	4	4.23
Hong Kong	3	0	3	0	0	4.06

Group F

United Arab Emirates	3	3	0	0	12	5.38
Bermuda	3	2	1	0	8	4.59
Canada	3	1	2	0	4	4.43
Ireland	3	0	3	0	0	4.17

Plate competition

Group G

Papua New Guinea	3	3	0	0	12	4.03
Namibia	3	2	1	0	8	3.78
Argentina	3	1	2	0	4	3.32
Fiji	3	0	3	0	0	3.26

Group H

USA	3	3	0	0	12	5.01
Denmark	3	2	1	0	8	4.09
Malaysia	3	1	2	0	4	3.34
Israel	3	0	3	0	0	2.36

to call a 'wooden spoon deluxe' contest. There is no evidence that the winner of this received any trophy or that the team finishing last, Gibraltar, was formally awarded a 'wooden spoon'.

There were few surprises in the first round. The biggest was the failure of Denmark to go through. They finished below a much improved Hong Kong, a position which was determined by the outcome of the game between the two countries. With the scores level, Hong Kong were declared the winners by losing fewer wickets. The USA could not repeat their 1990 performance and they failed to progress after allowing Bangladesh to contrive a victory from almost certain defeat. The second round also produced the expected results with Kenya and The Netherlands progressing from the first group and the UAE and Bermuda from the second. The UAE were perhaps a shade fortunate in that their victories over Canada and Bermuda were both achieved by the narrow margin of one wicket.

Kenya dominated their semi-final against Bermuda with Maurice Odumbe hitting one six and eleven fours in what was regarded as the best innings of the tournament. The UAE won the other semi-final surprisingly easily. Some 10,000 people came to watch the final, most hoping to see a Kenyan victory. Asked to bat, Kenya did well. Kennedy Otieno and Maurice Odumbe made 98 for the second wicket and a partnership of 102 for the third wicket followed between Odumbe and Steve Tikolo. However, Kenya could not raise the scoring rate sufficiently to take their total beyond 300. When Riaz Poonawala and Azhar Saeed opened with a stand of 141 in 28 overs, the Kenyan total looked to be in easy reach but a collapse in the middle order caused the run-rate to rise to more than 8 an over and the game became quite evenly poised. Mohammed Ishaq then struck 50 off 36 balls and it was a relatively easy task for the Emirates to make the single needed for victory in the last over (see Chapter 2 – Country Profile for the United Arab Emirates).

During the tournament, seventeen centuries were scored, three by Nolan Clarke (The Netherlands) and two by Maurice Odumbe (Kenya). Clarke scored the most tournament runs with 517 (average 86.16), well ahead of the next highest of 392 by Dexter Smith (Bermuda). Maurice Odumbe and Clay Smith (Bermuda) both finished with 391 runs. The best bowling was the 7-19 by Øle Mortensen of Denmark against Israel, who were dismissed for 45, in the Plate competition. Bhowan Singh also took seven wickets (7-21) in an innings for Canada against Namibia. Benefiting from the matches in the Plate competition, the highest wicket aggregate of 19 was achieved by Gavin Murgatroyd (Namibia) and Fred Arua (Papua New Guinea). Øle Mortensen, Stewart Brew (Hong Kong) and Anthony Edwards (Bermuda) each took 18 wickets. Mohammed Saddique (Denmark) took six catches as wicket-keeper for Denmark in the match against Israel.

Wooden spoon deluxe competition

Group 1

West Africa	3	3	0	0	12	3.26
East and Central Africa	3	2	1	0	8	3.28
Singapore	3	1	2	0	4	3.12
Gibraltar	3	0	3	0	0	2.87

Plate final – Philip Snow Plate

Namibia (262-8) beat Denmark (221) by 41 runs. The final was contested by the runners-up in each group of the Plate competition. The winners of each group, Papua New Guinea and the USA had already booked their flights home.

Semi-finals

Kenya (318-5) beat Bermuda (254-9) by 64 runs.
United Arab Emirates (195-4) beat Netherlands (194) by 6 wickets.

Third place play-off

Netherlands (306-2) beat Bermuda (203) by 103 runs.

Final

United Arab Emirates (282-8) beat Kenya (281-6) by 2 wickets.

Main Competition 1996

THE 1996 World Cup will be remembered as the event in which the ICC lost control of the cricket to commercial interests. They handed over the organisation of the tournament to an independent World Cup Committee known as Pilcom. A large amount of sponsorship was obtained for the supply of official merchandise and the organisation of the opening ceremony. The efforts made in these areas seemed to be at the expense of providing adequate practice facilities for the players or arranging a sensible match itinerary. The organisers set out with the laudable aim of staging matches in as many venues as possible throughout India, Pakistan and Sri Lanka. This invariably resulted in some very early starts for the players since most internal flights in India take place just after dawn or just before dusk. Where a change of flights was required, a long wait ensued in the middle of the day, often at a regional airport with limited facilities. More matches were played than in previous tournaments because of the decision of Pilcom to introduce a quar-ter-final stage. The twelve teams were divided into two groups of six with the top four teams progressing to the quarter-finals. The qualifying league stage was therefore largely meaningless since it served only to eliminate the three associate countries, Kenya, United Arab Emirates and The Netherlands, and the newest and weakest of the full member countries, Zimbabwe. The local public was not fooled by these arrangements and attendances for many of these early games were low, particularly in Pakistan. The arrangement did, however, provide a cushion enabling Australia and the West Indies to forfeit their matches against Sri Lanka after refusing to play in Colombo where there had been a bomb blast a fortnight before the tournament started. Both teams were concerned about security arrangements and feared further attacks which were part of the long-term dispute between the Tamil Tigers and the Sri Lankan government. When the opening ceremony at the Eden Gardens, Kolkata, flopped with a failure of the laser extravaganza, there was a demand from a section of the public for the local government to arrest the head of Pilcom for wasting public money. Typical of the organisation was the fact that having assembled all the teams in Kolkata for the opening ceremony, none of the first round matches was played there. Instead of the tournament starting with a high-profile fixture involving either India or Pakistan, which could have attracted a lot of interest, the first game was between England and New Zealand in the industrial city of Ahmedabad. When the accounts of the tournament became available and showed only a small surplus, the competence of the organising committee was severely questioned.

Aided by points from the two walkovers, Sri Lanka topped Group A with Australia beating India for second place on net run-rate after obtaining the same number of points. The West Indies had a decidedly lack-lustre tournament. Their low point was their 73-run defeat by Kenya (see Chapter 2 – Country Profile for Kenya). South Africa dominated Group B with five convincing wins. Playing all their matches at home, Pakistan lost only to South Africa

and, on paper, had the better all-round team. New Zealand occupied third place by virtue of winning the tournament's opening game against England by 11 runs. England gave a poor demonstration of one-day cricket; even their victories over the United Arab Emirates and The Netherlands were unconvincing.

With their captain, Wasim Akram, unavailable because of injury and their bowlers contriving such a slow over rate that they were fined one over, Pakistan always seemed destined to lose their quarter-final against India. Australia met little resistance from New Zealand and England were never serious contenders against Sri Lanka. The surprise of the quarter-finals was the defeat of South Africa by the West Indies. The South Africans omitted Alan Donald and played two specialist spinners, Paul Adams and Pat Symcox. Brian Lara relished what the bowlers offered and produced a superb innings of 111 from 94 balls with sixteen fours, 42 per cent of the West Indian total.

The first semi-final, at Eden Gardens, Kolkata, ended disgracefully when a section of the crowd began bottle-throwing and lighting fires as India moved to defeat. The Indian cricket authorities and most of those watching were embarrassed by the behaviour. After Clive Lloyd, the match referee, awarded the game to Sri Lanka by default the Indian Cricket Board of Control tried, unsuccessfully, to get the result changed to a victory to Sri Lanka on run-rate. Although the disturbances followed India losing seven wickets for 22 runs, they seemed as much a protest against the tournament organisers as a demonstration directed at the individual Indian players. The second semi-final saw the West Indies dominate much of the game against Australia, set themselves up for an inevitable victory and then plunge to a spectacular defeat by five runs.

In the final, a day/night match at Lahore, Australia failed to capitalise on the good fortune of their semi-final victory. For once, their fielding was abysmal with catches dropped and the ground fielding

Final qualifying tables

Group A

	Played	Won	Lost	No result	Points	Net run rate
Sri Lanka	5	5	0	0	10	1.60
Australia	5	3	2	0	6	0.90
India	5	3	2	0	6	0.45
West Indies	5	2	3	0	4	−0.13
Zimbabwe	5	1	4	0	2	−0.93
Kenya	5	1	4	0	2	−1.00

Group B

	Played	Won	Lost	No result	Points	Net run rate
South Africa	5	5	0	0	10	2.04
Pakistan	5	4	1	0	8	0.96
New Zealand	5	3	2	0	6	0.55
England	5	2	3	0	4	0.08
United Arab Emirates	5	1	4	0	2	−1.83
Netherlands	5	0	5	0	0	−1.92

Quarter-finals

Sri Lanka (236-5) beat England (235-8) by 5 wickets.
India (287-8) beat Pakistan (248-9) by 39 runs.
West Indies (264-8) beat South Africa (245) by 19 runs.
Australia (289-4) beat New Zealand (286-9) by 6 wickets.

Semi-finals

Sri Lanka (251-8) beat India (120-8) by default after a crowd riot.
Australia (207-8) beat West Indies (202) by 5 runs.

Final

Sri Lanka (245-3) beat Australia (241-7) by 7 wickets.

marred by errors. They were not helped by fielding second. Dew formed quickly after dusk and made both the ball and the outfield slippery. With Aravinda da Silva scoring a masterly 107 runs from 124 balls with 13 fours, Sri Lanka won their first major cricket trophy (see Chapter 2 – Country Profile for Sri Lanka) and became the first team to win the World Cup when batting second, a performance that was viewed as a victory for the spirit of cricket over the commercialism of the tournament.

Sachin Tendulkar (India) scored the most tournament runs with 523 at an average of 87.16. Mark Waugh (Australia) made 484 (average 80.66) and Aravinda da Silva (Sri Lanka) 448 (average 89.60). Waugh scored three centuries in his seven innings. Tendulkar and da Silva made two centuries each. The highest individual score was 188 not out by Gary Kirsten for South Africa against the United Arab Emirates. The leading wicket-taker was Anil Kumble (India) whose 15 wickets came at an average of 18.73. He was followed by Waqar Younis (Pakistan) with 13 (average 19.46). Paul Strang (Zimbabwe), Roger Harper (West Indies), Damien Fleming (Australia) and Shane Warne (Australia) all achieved 12 wickets. Strang's 5-21 for Zimbabwe against Kenya was the best individual bowling.

1999 TOURNAMENT

THE SEVENTH World Cup saw England act as hosts for the fourth time. In line with the policy of the ICC to promote cricket as widely as possible, some of the preliminary round matches were held in Scotland, Ireland and The Netherlands. This move would have been even more successful if these three countries had qualified from the ICC Trophy held in Malaysia in 1997. Unfortunately, only Scotland did so.

Qualifying Competition – ICC Trophy 1997

CRICKETERS FROM twenty-two countries gathered in Kuala Lumpur, Malaysia, in late March and early April 1997 for the sixth ICC Trophy. Scotland and Italy took part for the first time. Eight grounds in and around Kuala Lumpur were used. Surprisingly, in an area where the annual rainfall is about 2,700mm and the leading clubs have a long history of grass wickets, all the matches were played on newly-laid artificial surfaces which resulted in inconsistent bounce. The timing of the tournament was also questionable. Kuala Lumpur has no dry season but is generally driest in February and early March. By holding it a month later, the first round matches generally benefited but thereafter the games were often seriously affected by rain. Reserve days had to be used for both semi-finals and the final. The Dutch were particularly badly affected by the weather, losing one second-round match to Ireland by the Duckworth-Lewis method and having another, against Hong Kong, abandoned so that the points were shared. The Dutch also had their first round match against Canada abandoned, the victim of a political demonstration. As hosts, the Malaysians courageously accepted the presence of the Israeli team but Islamic fundamentalists threatened to disrupt Israel's match against Gibraltar. The organisers tried to combat this by making a late and unpublicised switch of venues with the match between The Netherlands and Canada. Unfortunately, the demonstrators refused to accept that the Israelis were not at the originally scheduled ground, occupied the pitch and set fire to advertising hoardings. As a result, the Netherlands–Canada encounter had to be abandoned whilst that between Gibraltar and Israel went ahead. The other main change from the 1994 tournament was the stricter citizenship and residential qualifications demanded of the players. Every country's team had to contain at least seven citizens although countries could claim a special dispensation if this new rule was considered too stringent. Seemingly ignorant of the ill-feeling generated by the composition of their side in 1994, the United Arab Emirates was the only country to apply for dispensation and they were permitted to field a team with only six citizens. They thus played under different rules to the other countries although the ICC did allow Italy to include Benito Giordano in their side through the route of temporary registration. Giordano

Final qualifying tables

Group A

	Played	Won	Lost	No result	Points	Net run rate
Kenya	5	5	0	0	10	2.71
Ireland	5	4	1	0	8	1.68
USA	5	3	2	0	6	0.74
Singapore	5	2	3	0	4	−1.07
Gibraltar	5	1	4	0	2	−2.13
Israel	5	0	5	0	0	−1.83

Group B

	Played	Won	Lost	No result	Points	Net run rate
Bangladesh	5	5	0	0	10	1.91
Denmark	5	4	1	0	8	0.93
United Arab Emirates	5	3	2	0	6	0.32
Malaysia	5	2	3	0	4	0.05
West Africa	5	1	4	0	2	−1.10
Argentina	5	0	5	0	0	−2.35

Group C

	Played	Won	Lost	No result	Points	Net run rate
Netherlands	4	3	0	1	7	2.93
Canada	4	3	0	1	7	0.85
Fiji	4	2	2	0	4	0.18
Namibia	4	1	3	0	2	−1.29
East and Central Africa	4	0	4	0	0	−0.98

Group D

	Played	Won	Lost	No result	Points	Net run rate
Scotland	4	4	0	0	8	1.65
Hong Kong	4	3	1	0	6	0.71
Bermuda	4	2	2	0	4	0.70
Papua New Guinea	4	1	3	0	2	−0.72
Italy	4	0	4	0	0	−2.36

Second round

Group E

	Played	Won	Lost	No result	Points	Net run rate
Kenya	3	2	0	1	5	2.03
Scotland	3	1	1	1	3	0.05
Denmark	3	1	1	1	3	−0.38
Canada	3	0	2	1	1	−1.62

Group F

	Played	Won	Lost	No result	Points	Net run rate
Bangladesh	3	2	0	1	5	0.97
Ireland	3	2	0	1	5	0.47
Netherlands	3	0	2	1	1	−0.42
Hong Kong	3	0	2	1	1	−1.03

Plate final – Philip Snow Plate

Bermuda (214-8) beat United Arab Emirates (158) by 56 runs.

Semi-finals

Kenya (215-8) beat Ireland (208-9) by 7 runs.
Bangladesh (243-7) beat Scotland (175) by 72 runs.

Third place play-off

Scotland (187-8) beat Ireland (141) by 51 runs.

Final

Bangladesh (166-8) beat Kenya (214-7) by 2 wickets
(Duckworth-Lewis method).

was born in England but his parents were Italian. He did not meet the ICC rules but under Italian national law he qualified as an Italian citizen and the Italians were contemplating legal action against the ICC if he was excluded.

The format of the tournament followed that adopted in 1990 and 1994 with a preliminary round of four groups from which the top two in each group progressed to a second round and the rest entered the Plate competition. As expected, Kenya and Ireland finished in the top two in Group A. Even so, Kenya were given a fright when, having dismissed Singapore for 89 they lost eight wickets whilst struggling to 90 in 30 overs. Bangladesh were unbeaten in Group B with Denmark as runners-up by virtue of their victory over the United Arab Emirates by one wicket. With only five of the squad which won the competition in 1994, the Emirates never looked likely to retain the Trophy. The Netherlands and Canada finished top of Group C, sharing the points. After the fixture between the two countries was abandoned, The Netherlands occupied first place on run-rate. Scotland won Group D in which Hong Kong surprisingly finished second above both Bermuda and Papua New Guinea.

The second round matches were badly affected by rain with the risk that the outcome would become a lottery rather than a result of good competitive cricket. Kenya benefited most from the weather in their group which enabled them to finish top. Scotland and Denmark ended with identical records but Scotland progressed to the semi-finals by virtue of their 45 run win over Denmark. In the second group Bangladesh headed Ireland on net run-rate after both countries finished with identical records and the match between them was abandoned with the points shared. The Dutch were particularly unlucky with all three of their matches affected by rain, resulting in two defeats under Duckworth-Lewis regulations and one game abandoned. The teams which failed to make the second round played a series of games designed to determine the relative rankings between the ninth and twenty-second position. The play-off for ninth place constituted the match for the Philip Snow Plate. This was won by Bermuda on the strength of superior batting.

The first semi-final was closely-fought. A wet outfield delayed the start until 2.14 p.m. at which point the Irish asked Kenya to bat and then proceeded to bowl so poorly that, after 30 overs, Kenya had reached 108 with the loss of only three wickets. After that, they found scoring more difficult. Ireland were always behind the required run-rate in reply until Derek Heasley decided to abandon caution and struck 50 from 46 balls but it was not quite enough and they finished seven runs short. In the second semi-final, Scotland, after a promising start, proved no match for Bangladesh; their batsmen did not have the technique to deal with some top-class spin bowling.

The final was one of the most exciting matches of the tournament probably because of rather than despite the weather which, overall, dominated the proceedings. Play did not begin until 1.45 p.m. on the first day when Kenya lost the toss and were asked to bat first, a decision of Akram Khan, the Bangladeshi captain, which looked justified when Kenya were 15 for two and then 58 for three. Steve Tikolo then hit three sixes and twelve fours in his innings of 147, made off 152 balls. He and Maurice Odumbe added 138 for the fourth wicket, allowing Kenya to make what looked like a winning total. Rain

then prevented play until 3.30 p.m. on the second day causing Bangladesh's innings to be reduced to 25 overs with a revised target of 166 set by the Duckworth-Lewis method. With Bangladesh just keeping to the run-rate but losing wickets, a victory for either side always seemed possible. With one ball remaining, Bangladesh had reached 165. For some reason, Martin Odumbe, Kenya's captain, thought that 166 was the equivalent of the revised Kenyan total and that the target was therefore 167; he therefore set a field to prevent two runs. Hasibul Hussain swung at the last ball but down the wrong line and missed; the ball hit his pads and the batsmen scrambled a leg bye. Bangladesh celebrated winning their first major trophy whilst Odumbe, in disbelief, came to recognise that the match had been lost and not tied (see Chapter 2 – Country Profile for Bangladesh).

During the tournament, six batsmen scored centuries, the highest being 148 not out by Maurice Odumbe for Kenya against Canada. Odumbe had the highest run aggregate with 493 at an average of 98.60. Steve Tikolo, also of Kenya, was second with 399 runs at 44.33. Although Bangladesh won the competition, none of their batsmen reached a hundred or finished in the top six on run aggregate. The best individual bowling was seven for 9 by Asim Khan for The Netherlands when they dismissed East and Central Africa for 26. Asim Khan, Aasif Karim (Kenya), Ian Bevan (Scotland) and Mohammed Rafique (Bangladesh) all obtained 19 tournament wickets. Asim Khan took four or more wickets in an innings on three occasions whereas no other bowler achieved this feat more than twice.

Main Competition 1999

THE 1999 World Cup returned to England but was nowhere near as successful as the previous tournaments which England hosted. The English Cricket Board looked for eight corporate sponsors but struggled to find four, a clear indication of the reluctance of companies to invest in sporting events if the publicity from doing so has to be shared. They then brought in an external consultant as tournament director instead of organising the event themselves. For reasons which presumably the appointee understood but the general public did not, there was no elaborate opening ceremony with the twelve teams parad-

ing in front of the pavilion at Lord's and either royalty or a cricketing celebrity formally opening the proceedings. Instead there was a low-key event without most of the teams, held in a typical English mid-May cold drizzle, culminating in a poor display of fireworks which would have shamed most school or village displays on November 5th. For the second consecutive World Cup, the opening ceremony was a shambles. The complete tournament lasted 37 days which, in order to take advantage of the Saturday closest to the summer solstice for the final, meant ignoring the problems associated with English early summer weather and beginning the competition in mid-May. By disregarding basic geographical knowledge, the organisers clearly showed that they had learnt nothing from previous experience; otherwise it would have been obvious not to repeat the mistakes of the 1997 ICC Trophy. Fortunately, the weather was kind, at least regarding rainfall. Only one of the 42 matches was abandoned and only one other extended into its reserve day. Nevertheless, low temperatures and a lack of sunshine made cricket in the first round quite unpleasant for players and spectators alike. The most miserable weather was in Dublin where, in a bitterly cold wind, accompanied by squally showers, the West Indies manager, Clive Lloyd wrapped himself in blankets to watch his side play Bangladesh, and the drinks cart served hot soup to the players on the field.

Another problem which the organisers failed to tackle, despite the experience of 1996, was the idiocy of having a stage between the preliminary round and the semi-finals. Having realised that using the preliminary round to reduce twelve teams to eight and hold quarter-finals was unsatisfactory, the decision was made to reduce the teams to six and introduce a stage known as the Super Six. For the preliminaries, the teams were divided into two groups of six with the top three in each group progressing to the Super Six. In order to reduce the number of games in the tournament, the teams going forward took with them their record against the other teams from their group who also went forward. They therefore played new matches only against the teams qualifying from the other group. The top four teams in the Super Six then progressed to the semi-finals. As a result, Pakistan, Australia, South Africa and New Zealand contested the semi-finals. If the semi-finals had been played directly from the top two in each of the preliminary round groups, they would have comprised Pakistan, Australia, South Africa and India, a combination which some observers felt would have better reflected the abilities of the competing countries. India suffered badly in the Super Six because they carried with them their only two defeats of the preliminary round which meant they were always going to struggle to progress further. In contrast, Zimbabwe, who finished below India in their group, took two victories into the Super Six and, even though they did not win any further games, would have qualified for the semi-finals if their batsmen had managed a slightly higher run-rate.

South Africa looked the strongest side in Group A, winning their first four games easily before falling to an up-beat Zimbabwe in one of the surprises of the tournament. India were easily beaten by South Africa by four wickets and surprisingly lost to Zimbabwe by three runs. Zimbabwe gained a third win over Kenya to record their best performance to date in the World Cup, finishing above England who performed poorly. Neither England's batsmen nor their bowlers were consistent in conditions which should have been familiar to them. Pakistan were

Final qualifying tables

Group A

	Played	Won	Lost	No result	Points	Net run rate
South Africa	5	4	1	0	8	0.85
India	5	3	2	0	6	1.28
Zimbabwe	5	3	2	0	6	0.01
England	5	3	2	0	6	−0.33
Sri Lanka	5	2	3	0	4	−0.80
Kenya	5	0	5	0	0	−1.19

Group B

	Played	Won	Lost	No result	Points	Net run rate
Pakistan	5	4	1	0	8	0.52
Australia	5	3	2	0	6	0.73
New Zealand	5	3	2	0	6	0.57
West Indies	5	3	2	0	6	0.49
Bangladesh	5	2	3	0	4	−0.54
Scotland	5	0	5	0	0	−1.92

Super Six

	Played	Won	Lost	No result	Points	Net run rate
Pakistan	5 (2)	3 (2)	2 (0)	0 (0)	6 (4)	0.65
Australia	5 (2)	3 (0)	2 (2)	0 (0)	6 (0)	0.35
South Africa	5 (2)	3 (1)	2 (1)	0 (0)	6 (2)	0.17
New Zealand	5 (2)	2 (1)	2 (1)	1 (0)	5 (2)	−0.51
Zimbabwe	5 (2)	2 (2)	2 (0)	1 (0)	5 (4)	−0.78
India	5 (2)	1 (0)	4 (2)	0 (0)	2 (0)	−0.15

Figures in parentheses show the positions at the start of the Super Six.

Semi-finals

Pakistan (242-1) beat New Zealand (241-7) by 9 wickets.
Australia (213) beat South Africa (213) on a superior run-rate in the Super-Six.

Final

Australia (133-2) beat Pakistan (132) by 8 wickets.

the outstanding team of Group B until, sure of qualifying for the Super Six, they inexplicably lost to Bangladesh. So surprising was the outcome that, over the next few years, questions were raised about match-fixing but no firm evidence has yet been produced to show that the result was other than genuine. Australia, New Zealand and the West Indies fought for the remaining two places in the Super Six and, in a series of matches with fluctuating fortunes, all finished with three wins and two losses. New Zealand upset the expected outcome when they beat Australia by five wickets. It was the West Indies who missed out, pushed into fourth position on net run-rate.

With England eliminated, the Super Six began with fears that public interest in the tournament would decline. With the points taken forward from the preliminary round, Pakistan and Zimbabwe headed the table with four points each whilst India and Australia were in difficult positions at the bottom with no points. Australia responded brilliantly, winning all three matches. Zimbabwe and Pakistan fared badly, South Africa beating both to secure their semi-final place. Although New Zealand's win over Australia was sufficient to give them passage to the semi-finals, they were unlucky to finish fourth. Their match against Zimbabwe was the sole victim to the weather, so that New Zealand gained one point instead of two and missed the chance to increase their net run-rate.

New Zealand's bowlers were unable to defend their total of 241 for seven in the semi-final against Pakistan. Saeed Anwar and Wajahatullah Wasti gave a superb display of controlled hitting in an opening partnership of 194 which was not broken until the 41st over. Pakistan found the ecstatic crowd more trouble than the New Zealand bowlers. Fireworks were ignited and the pitch invaded with six runs still to make. After a delay of ten minutes, the game restarted but trouble returned when, with two runs needed, the crowd again invaded and the New Zealand players ran for the safety of the pavilion. The final two runs were never technically scored but were awarded to Pakistan by the umpires. The second semi-final was closely-contested throughout and ended in an exciting finish with any one of three results possible before the match ended in confusion following a disastrous misjudgement by the batting side. Australia, asked to bat first, never mastered the South African attack and fell for 213 runs in 49.2 overs. South Africa began their reply convincingly before

becoming increasingly bogged down by the spin of Shane Warne. Lance Klusener then struck 31 runs from 14 balls in a daunting display of hitting, bringing South Africa to the point of victory with one run needed from three balls. Klusener hit the ball back past the bowler, called for a run and set off immediately. His partner, Alan Donald, taken completely by surprise, dropped his bat and set off with no chance of reaching the other end. Klusener's moment of madness when two balls still remained is something for sports psychologists to consider in their studies of how pressure can lead to misjudgements. The match was tied and Australia proceeded to the final because they had a superior net run-rate in the Super Six.

The final was a huge disappointment for the 27,800, largely disinterested, crowd. The policy of selling tickets for the final at high cost well in advance rather than reserving a proportion of the tickets for sale to fans of the competing teams once the finalists were known, resulted in a game without passion. An announcement in Urdu just before the finish to warn spectators not to invade the pitch seemed superfluous given the small number of Pakistanis in the crowd. Responding to the situation with good humour, however, they made a half-hearted attempt at invasion immediately. Australia brought the ruthlessness of their test-match cricket to the one-day arena and Pakistan were completely outplayed.

Eleven centuries were scored during the tournament with Rahul Dravid (India) and Saeed Anwar (Pakistan) each making two. Dravid had the highest tournament aggregate 461 runs (average 65.85) followed by Steve Waugh (398 runs, average 79.60, for Australia), Saurav Ganguly (379 runs, average 54.14, for India) and Mark Waugh (375 runs, average 41.66, for Australia). The most exciting player of the tournament, Lance Klusener (South Africa), headed the averages with 281 runs at 140.50, aided by being six times not out in his eight innings. The best bowling performance was five for 14 by Glen McGrath for Australia against the West Indies. Five other bowlers took five wickets in an innings, once each. Geoff Allott (New Zealand) and Shane Warne (Australia) took most tournament wickets. Each had 20 for respective averages of 16.25 and 18.05. Glen McGrath (Australia) took eighteen wickets (average 20.38). The most economical bowler was Courtney Walsh (West Indies) who conceded only 2.29 runs per over.

2003 TOURNAMENT

THE 2003 World Cup and the qualifying ICC Trophy 2001 both moved to new venues. The World Cup was staged in Africa, hosted by South Africa with some matches being played in Zimbabwe and Kenya. An opportunity was missed by not extending the tournament into Namibia. The ICC Trophy moved to the American continent with Canada as hosts. The experience of previous tournaments was again ignored with the result that the World Cup was seriously affected by problems of both sponsorship and politics. The ICC Trophy continued to suffer from issues related to the eligibility of players. Further, not only did the organisers of the World Cup retain the Super Six stage but an equivalent was introduced into the ICC Trophy with even more bizarre rules whereby one team entered that stage taking with it, not its own record, but that of a completely different country.

Qualifying Competition – ICC Trophy 2001

CANADA HOSTED the 2001 ICC Trophy with matches at seven grounds in and around Toronto. The ICC decided to address the issue of the enormous diversity in standard of the associate level countries by arranging them into two divisions, based on their finishing position in the previous tournament. Those countries competing for the first time, namely France, Germany, Nepal and Uganda, were placed in Division 2. The twelve sides in Division 1 were arranged in two groups with the top three in each group progressing to an equivalent of the Super Six stage. The ICC were then faced with the problem of how to allow teams in Division 2 to progress. They provided a route whereby the winners of the two groups in Division 2 met the fourth-placed countries from the groups of Division 1 in play-offs with the winners qualifying for the next stage, which became a Super Eight. This created a problem when a team from Division 2 qualified for the Super Eight because they could not take with them a playing record against any of the other teams reaching that stage. They therefore 'inherited' the record of the Division 1 side that they beat in the play-offs. Despite the complexity and, what seemed to many, the obvious stupidity of this procedure, it provided the highlight and surprise of the competition. Namibia, who had finished fifteenth in 1997, not only qualified for the Super Eight from Division 2 but went on from there to reach the final without being beaten.

Problems of player eligibility arose again and showed that, despite having had two years to address the issue, the ICC had failed to resolve the conflict between its regulations and those of Italian law. The ICC refused to sanction the participation of four players in the Italian squad who were considered Italian citizens under Italian law but not under ICC rules. The Italian cricket authorities objected and, rather than include alternative players, withdrew from the competition. Nepal, the United Arab Emirates and West Africa all experienced visa problems with the Canadian immigration service. Nepal and the Emirates were forced to replace players when they were refused visas. The West African applications for visas arrived late and were rejected en masse, thereby causing their late withdrawal. Even though Italy and West Africa had been placed in the same group in Division 2, the organisers did not readjust the groups. Instead, the other teams were awarded points for victories by default. This meant that Nepal, Germany and Gibraltar travelled all the way to Canada to play only three matches.

In the first round, the Dutch topped Group A in Division 1 with maximum points. The only country to come close to challenging them was Scotland who won all their other matches relatively easily. Canada qualified for the Super Eight through their victory over the United Arab Emirates by two wickets. In Group B of Division 1, Denmark surprised probably even themselves by heading the group. After losing their opening game against Bermuda, they won all their remaining matches. Against the United States, Søren Vestergaard performed the hat-trick to complete the American's dismissal for 80 in a miserable 24.4 overs, finishing with the analysis of 6-2-11-3. Despite this set-back, the United States performed well in some games, notably when beating Ireland by six wickets and Bermuda by 57 runs, and finished second in the group, above Ireland and Bermuda. All three countries had the same number of points but, instead of using net run-rate to separate them, placings were determined on the basis of the results of the matches between the teams. Thus, by losing to both the USA and Ireland, Bermuda failed to benefit from their victory over Denmark and were forced into the play-offs. In Division 2, Namibia proved far too strong for the other teams in the depleted Group A. Group B had the makings of a close contest after Argentina and Uganda both won their first three games and Malaysia won three of their first four but, in the end, Uganda were untroubled and headed the group. In the play-offs for places in the Super Eight, Uganda's batting failed. The Emirates passed the Ugandan score easily with five wickets and eight overs in hand. Namibia batted inconsistently against Bermuda but secured a total which proved remarkably easy to defend. Namibia were allocated Bermuda's record as they moved into the Super Eight, namely one win and two defeats.

Namibia continued their form in the Super Eight, winning all four games, including a convincing 41 run victory over The Netherlands. The Dutch won all their other games and therefore finished above Namibia in the table with six wins and one defeat. Scotland lost to The Netherlands and Namibia but won their other games without difficulty to finish third, equal on points with Namibia and a clear four points above Canada and the United Arab Emirates. For the first time in the ICC Trophy's history, there were no semi-finals. There was also no competition for the Philip Snow Plate. The final always promised to be closely

Final qualifying tables
First round
Division 1
Group A

	Played	Won	Lost	No result	Points	Net run rate
Netherlands	5	5	0	0	10	1.37
Scotland	5	4	1	0	8	1.03
Canada	5	3	2	0	6	0.72
United Arab Emirates	5	2	3	0	4	−0.29
Fiji	5	1	4	0	2	−1.36
Singapore	5	0	5	0	0	−1.85

Group B

	Played	Won	Lost	No result	Points	Net run rate
Denmark	5	4	1	0	8	1.64
USA	5	3	2	0	6	0.19
Ireland	5	3	2	0	6	0.53
Bermuda	5	3	2	0	6	0.03
Hong Kong	5	1	4	0	2	−1.06
Papua New Guinea	5	1	4	0	2	−1.49

Division 2
Group A

	Played	Won	Lost	No result	Points	Net run rate
Namibia	5	5	0	0	10	3.15
Nepal	5	4	1	0	8	−0.38
Germany	5	3	2	0	6	−0.77
Gibraltar	5	2	3	0	4	−1.63
Italy	5	0	5	0	0	0.00
West Africa	5	0	5	0	0	0.00

Group B

	Played	Won	Lost	No result	Points	Net run rate
Uganda	5	5	0	0	10	1.97
Argentina	5	4	1	0	8	−0.70
Malaysia	5	3	2	0	6	0.93
East and Central Africa	5	2	3	0	4	0.47
France	5	1	4	0	2	−1.52
Israel	5	0	5	0	0	−1.01

Where teams had the same number of points, placings were determined by the results of the matches played between them.

Play-offs for Super Eight
Namibia beat Bermuda by 75 runs, United Arab Emirates beat Uganda by 5 wickets.
Namibia progressed but carried the first round record of Bermuda into the Super Eight.

Super Eight

Netherlands	7 (3)	6 (3)	1 (0)	0 (0)	12 (6)	0.68
Namibia	7 (3)	5 (1)	2 (2)	0 (0)	10 (2)	0.74
Scotland	7 (3)	5 (2)	2 (1)	0 (0)	10 (4)	0.72
Canada	7 (3)	3 (1)	4 (2)	0 (0)	6 (2)	0.67
United Arab Emirates	7 (3)	3 (0)	4 (3)	0 (0)	6 (0)	0.01
USA	7 (3)	2 (2)	5 (1)	0 (0)	4 (4)	−0.51
Ireland	7 (3)	2 (1)	5 (2)	0 (0)	4 (2)	0.18
Denmark	7 (3)	2 (2)	5 (1)	0 (0)	4 (4)	0.39

Figures in parenthesis show the positions at the start of the Super Eight.

Third place play-off
Canada (177-5) beat Scotland (176-9) by 5 wickets.

Final
Netherlands (196-8) beat Namibia (195-9) by 2 wickets.

contested and the finish did not disappoint. Namibia had yet to be beaten in the tournament whilst the Dutch were out to avenge their defeat by Namibia in the Super Eight stage. Namibia chose to bat first but their batsmen could not exert their authority over the Dutch attack in which there seemed to be no weak link. Six bowlers were used and all bowled accurately and economically. The Namibian bowlers placed their side in a strong position before Jacob-Jan Esmeijer and Roland Lefebvre put on 52 very quickly in a seventh wicket partnership. With Namibia placed under pressure for the first time in the competition, their bowling and, more particularly, their fielding wilted. With four overs to go, the Dutch still required 38 runs but Esmeijer, not previously known for his batting ability, continued the onslaught to reduce the target to ten runs from the last over. In partnership with Asim Khan this became three runs from the last ball, a position which would normally just favour the fielding side. However, Riaan Walters produced a spectacular misfield at short fine leg and, in the confusion, the runs were scrambled (see Chapter 2 – Country Profile for The Netherlands).

Namibia's Danie Keulder scored the most runs in the tournament, finishing on 366 at an average of 45.75. Ed Joyce of Ireland made 359 (average 71.80), Vikram Harris of Canada, 329 (average 41.12), Colin Smith of Scotland, 326 (average 46.57) and Ahmed Nadeem (United Arab Emirates, 318 (average 45.42). No one else scored over 300 runs. Ten centuries were made but no player scored more than one. The highest was 118 by Shankar Retinam for Malaysia against France. The best individual bowling was six for 43 by Burton van Rooi for Namibia against Scotland. There were eleven performances of five wickets in an innings, the best being 5-10 by Neil Maxwell for Fiji against Singapore and 5-11 by Asim Butt for Scotland against Fiji. The highest wicket aggregate was 20 obtained by Roland Lefebvre (The Netherlands) and Søren Vestergaard (Denmark). Burton van Rooi (Namibia), Khurram Khan (United Arab Emirates) and Sanjay Thuraisingham (Canada) each took 19 wickets.

Main competition 2003

THE 2003 World Cup was beset with political and sponsorship problems months before it took place. Sponsorship became an issue as soon as the ICC secured exclusive contractual arrangements with the Global Cricket Corporation. Sponsorship arrangements between individual players and other sponsors were therefore prohibited and a dispute immediately arose between the Indian cricket authorities, who had to conform to what the ICC had secured, and several individual Indian players. At one time it looked as though India would either have to withdraw or be represented by a second-string team. With the issue unresolved, India participated with their best team but the ICC withheld India's share of the revenue from the tournament.

There were two major political problems which affected the ability of the tournament organisers to make the tournament pan-African in scope by playing some matches in Kenya and Zimbabwe. Following terrorist incidents in Nairobi and Mombasa aimed particularly at nationals from countries which were supporting American government policy in Iraq, the New Zealand players were concerned about security for their game against Kenya in Nairobi. Although the ICC sent independent consultants to report on the situation and they declared it safe, the New Zealand Cricket Board undertook discussions with the players and supported their decision not to play. The ICC awarded the match to Kenya by default and withheld US$2.5 million of New Zealand's tournament revenue. The second issue related to the matches played in Zimbabwe where, under the increasingly autocratic rule of Robert Mugabe, economic and social conditions of the people were deteriorating rapidly and there was a moral issue of whether agreeing to play in Zimbabwe constituted *de facto* support for the Mugabe regime. The English players were particularly concerned because of threats made against people connected with Great Britain, the former colonial power. The ICC refused to intervene and sent their security consultants to investigate who declared the country was safe to visit. They then threatened to fine the English Cricket Board if they did not play but gave a caveat that if the British government were to rule that England should not play in Zimbabwe, the ICC would acquiesce.

The British government refused to make any appropriate declaration and hid from the issue by stating it was a matter for the ECB and the individual players. Concerned about the possibility of a substantial fine, the ECB prevaricated but eventually had to submit to the wishes of the players and withdraw from the game.

At one stage it looked as though the Australian players might also decide not to play in Zimbabwe. The Australian Cricket Board and the Australian government also refused to intervene but the cricketers were eventually persuaded to play when the Australian Board agreed they could fly in and out of Zimbabwe for the game without having to stay in the country. The overall outcome was completely unsatisfactory because none of the official bodies involved showed any leadership. An opportunity was missed by the ECB whilst the Australian players were still uncertain about how to proceed. If the ECB and the ABC had taken a firm line at that stage and told the ICC that they were not going to sanction matches in Zimbabwe under any circumstances, the ICC would have been forced to take alternative action and rearrange the matches in alternative venues. Any other action such as imposing fines would have led to a public outcry. Through their failures to take strong action, the ICC, the ECB and the British government mishandled the situation and gave no support to the individual cricketers. In the end, the greatest public support was provided by two Zimbabwean cricketers with a conscience and a willingness to express it. Andy Flower and Henry Olonga took the field against Namibia wearing black armbands to commemorate the 'death of democracy' in Zimbabwe.

These pre-tournament events overshadowed many of the preparations made by South Africa and the ICC. Anxious not to repeat the fiascos of the opening ceremonies of the two previous World Cups, the South Africans organised an Olympic style occasion, in the evening, at Newlands, Cape Town, followed the next day by the opening game, South Africa against the West Indies. The ICC invested US$1 million in helping Namibia, The Netherlands, Canada and Kenya prepare for the event. The work of the ICC's Anti-Corruption Unit ensured that there was no hint of match-fixing. With fourteen countries taking part, the event was the biggest ever, involving 54 matches spread over 43 days. By arranging the countries into two groups for the first round with the

top three in each group progressing to the Super Six, the outcome was far from predictable and public interest was maintained to end of the group stage. Before the tournament started, few people would have listed Kenya and Zimbabwe in the teams most likely to proceed. As in the previous tournament, the Super Six was a waste of time. It resulted in Australia, India, Kenya and Sri Lanka as the semi-finalists. If, instead of the Super Six, the semi-finalists had come from the top two teams in each of the first round groups, they would have been Australia, India, Sri Lanka and Kenya.

Clinical Efficiency

Australia dominated Group A in the first round, winning six of their seven games easily. They performed with clinical efficiency, no more so than against Namibia when they recorded the biggest win in World Cup history. England's defeat by Australia meant that, yet again, they failed to go beyond the first round. Following victories over The Netherlands, Namibia and Pakistan, they lost to India. India lost only to Australia and therefore finished second in the group. They were clearly one of the best-equipped teams of the tournament. England's refusal to play in Zimbabwe led to Zimbabwe progressing to the Super Six. If England had played and beaten Zimbabwe, they would have qualified instead. Group B produced more surprises than had occurred in any previous World Cup beginning with the first match of the tournament which South Africa lost to the West Indies by three runs during which Brian Lara gave a masterful display of limited-overs batting to reach 116 off 134 balls with two sixes and twelve fours. South Africa then failed to defend a total of 306 for six against New Zealand. They might still have qualified for the Super Six if they had beaten Sri Lanka. As they chased 269 to win, rain began to fall heavily with the prospect that the match would be abandoned at almost any moment. It was important that the run-rate kept up with what would be needed for victory under the Duckworth-Lewis calculations whenever the umpires decided to call the match off. With Mark Boucher and Lance Klusener together word was obtained from the dressing-room that at the end of the 45th over, South Africa would win if they reached 229 and did not lose any more wickets. With the score at 223 for six, Boucher hit the penultimate ball of that over for six and then blocked the last ball. The umpires decided the rain was now too heavy to continue and the South African batsmen left the field believing they had won only to find that those consulting the Duckworth-Lewis tables in their dressing room had misread them. The total of 229 was only sufficient to tie, a result which ensured that Sri Lanka finished top of the group and that South Africa went out of the competition. After the events of Sydney in 1992 and Birmingham in 1999, South Africa had now developed a reputation for the most incompetent and unusual ways of exiting a cricket tournament.

Sri Lanka and New Zealand were both fortunate to reach the Super Six. After a 47-run victory over New Zealand, Sri Lanka failed by 53 runs to overhaul Kenya's 210 for nine (see Chapter 2 – Country Profile for Kenya) and were then somewhat fortunate to beat the West Indies by six runs in a match which went to the last ball. New Zealand qualified largely as a result of a 20-run win over the West Indies which offset their decision not to play in Nairobi and give Kenya a walkover. Kenya added to the excitement of Group B by beating Bangladesh and Canada to finish second in the group and become unexpected qualifiers for the Super Six. After their heroics of 1999, Bangladesh had an appalling tournament, the ignominy reaching its peak in a 60-run defeat by Canada (see Chapter 2 – Country Profile for Canada).

The Super Six scarcely looked representative of world cricket with the West Indies and South Africa notable absentees. The failure of South Africa to reach this stage was a major disappointment to the local organisers and public, particularly as the two other African participants qualified. The scoring system for the Super Six was also amended. In addition to taking forward the points obtained in matches against the other qualifiers, the teams carried bonus points related to the matches against the non-qualifiers. As a result, the final points score in the Super Six table was biased towards the results of the first round matches. What purpose this served in unclear. Australia were never severely tested in their three additional matches and thus topped the table. Arguably the most interesting moment of opposition came in the game against Kenya. Australia destroyed the start of the Kenyan innings as a hat-trick by Brett Lee reduced them to three for three. Although Kenya recovered to reach 174 for eight, Australia responded ag-

Final qualifying tables

Group A

	Played	Won	Lost	No result	Points	Net run rate
Australia	6	6	0	0	24	2.05
India	6	5	1	0	20	1.11
Zimbabwe	6	3	2	1	14	0.50
England	6	3	3	0	12	0.82
Pakistan	6	2	3	1	10	0.23
Netherlands	6	1	5	0	4	−1.45
Namibia	6	0	6	0	0	−2.96

Group B

	Played	Won	Tied	Lost	No result	Points	Net run rate
Sri Lanka	6	4	1	1	0	18	1.20
New Zealand	6	4	0	2	0	16	0.99
Kenya	6	4	0	2	0	16	−0.69
West Indies	6	3	0	2	1	14	1.10
South Africa	6	3	1	2	0	14	1.73
Canada	6	1	0	5	0	4	−1.99
Bangladesh	6	0	0	5	1	2	−2.05

Super Six

	Played	Won	Lost	No result	Points	Net run rate
Australia	5 (2)	5 (2)	0 (0)	0 (0)	24 (12)	2.01
India	5 (2)	4 (1)	1 (1)	0 (0)	20 (8)	1.34
Kenya	5 (2)	3 (2)	2 (0)	0 (0)	14 (10)	−0.36
Sri Lanka	5 (2)	2 (1)	3 (1)	0 (0)	11.5 (7.5)	0.03
New Zealand	5 (2)	1 (0)	4 (2)	0 (0)	8 (4)	−0.02
Zimbabwe	5 (2)	0 (0)	5 (2)	0 (0)	3.5 (3.5)	−0.57

Figures in parentheses show the positions at the start of the Super Six. Where teams finished equal on points, placings were decided first on the results of the matches between the teams. Points gained in the Super Six include points added for results against teams in the first round which did not qualify on the basis of 1 point for a win and 0.5 for a no result.

Semi-finals

Australia (212-7) beat Sri Lanka (123-7) by 48 runs (Duckworth-Lewis method).
India (270-4) beat Kenya (179) by 91 runs.

Final

Australia (359-2) beat India (234) by 125 runs.

gressively in reply and, after twelve overs, were 98 for one. Kenya turned to Aasif Karim, their 39-year old, slow left-arm spinner brought out of retirement for this tournament. He took three wickets in his first two overs and obtained complete control over the run-rate. Australia made runs at the other end and passed the Kenyan total for the loss of five wickets but Karim finished with the analysis of 8.2-6-7-3. In a judgement recognising the romance of unexpected achievement over clinical professionalism, Karim received the man-of-the-match award over Brett Lee. Aided by their points inherited from the first round which included their walkover victory against New Zealand, Kenya ensured they were surprise qualifiers for the semi-finals by a seven-wicket win over Zimbabwe.

The early stages of the semi-final between Australia and Sri Lanka were keenly contested but, on a wicket where the bounce was far from true, Sri Lanka's batsmen never adjusted to the conditions. When rain intervened to end the match, Sri Lanka were 48 runs short of what the Duckworth-Lewis system required. India defeated Kenya easily in the other semi-final.

Australia dominated the final from the moment that the Indian captain, Saurav Ganguly, won the toss and asked them to bat. India's bowlers gave their worst display of the tournament. The first over went for 15 runs and after nine overs, Adam Gilchrist and Matthew Hayden had made 94. A partnership of 234 between Ricky Ponting and Damien Martyn, became increasingly aggressive the longer it lasted. The last ten overs produced 109 runs with 64 of those coming in the last five. A somewhat surreal episode occurred when it looked as though rain might prevent the game from being completed. Australia needed to bowl 25 overs for there to be a result; otherwise the match would be declared void and replayed the following day. Ponting quickened the Australian over-rate by bowling Brad Hogg and Lehmann, occasional purveyors of spin, taking the risk of providing India with easy runs. Once the required minimum number of overs had been bowled, the pace attack returned. A 25-minute break for rain took place when India had made 103 for three but the game restarted without any reduction in the number of overs. Australia completed their task in a most efficient manner, the last five wickets falling for only 26 runs, the floodlights shining brightly against a background of dark grey rain clouds interspersed with flashes of lightning.

In a tournament remarkable for its batting, twenty-one individual scores over 100 were made, three by Saurav Ganguly (India) and two each by Ricky Ponting (Australia) and Marvan Atapattu (Sri Lanka). The highest individual score was 172 not out by Craig Wishart for Zimbabwe against Namibia. Sachin Tendulkar (India) scored the most tournament runs with 673 at an average of 61.18. This was well ahead of the next highest aggregate, 465 by Ganguly (average 58.12). Ricky Ponting (415) and Adam Gilchrist (408) were the only others to exceed 400 runs. The best individual bowling was the 7-15 by Glen McGrath (Australia versus Namibia), followed by Andy Bichel's 7-20 for Australia against England. Chaminda Vaas (Sri Lanka) took the most tournament wickets, 23 at an average of 14.39. Australia's Brett Lee (22 at 17.90) and Glen McGrath (21 at 14.76) were the others who exceeded twenty wickets. The most economical bowlers were Andrew Flintoff (England) who conceded only 2.87 runs per over and Aasif Karim (Kenya), 2.95. No one else was below three runs per over.

2007 TOURNAMENT

THE ICC set out to make the 2007 World Cup the biggest ever exhibition of high level one-day international cricket. For the main competition, hosted for the first time by the West Indies, the number of participants was increased to sixteen. The ten test-playing countries and Kenya were given automatic entry to be joined by five associate Countries qualifying through the 2005 ICC Trophy. The two-division structure of the ICC Trophy used in 2001

was abandoned and the event limited to twelve countries, all of which had to qualify through a series of structured regional competitions. Based on recent rankings of the Associates, the twelve countries were allocated as two from Asia, two from Africa, three from the Americas and four from Europe with the final place going to the winners of a Division 2 competition. Division 2 consisted of eight countries, namely Papua New Guinea, three from Asia, one from Africa, one from the Americas, one from Europe and one from East Asia-Pacific. This approach opened up the World Cup to every member country of the ICC . The existing competitions for the Asian Cricket Council Trophy,

the Americas Cup and the European Championships were used as the regional tournaments. Equivalent contests were initiated for Africa and the East-Africa Pacific.

Regional Qualifying Rounds

Preliminary Round 2003

EUROPE WAS the only region in which a preliminary round was required. Eleven countries participated in a competition in Vienna, Austria, on 10-16 August, 2003, with the winner progressing to the European section of the First Qualifying Round which doubled as the European Championships Division 2.

First Round
Group A

	Played	Won	Lost	No res	Points
Malta	2	2	0	0	4
Finland	2	1	1	0	2
Portugal	2	0	2	0	0

Group B

	Played	Won	Lost	No res	Points
Greece	3	3	0	0	6
Austria	3	2	1	0	4
Switzerland	3	1	2	0	2
Luxembourg	3	0	3	0	0

Group C

	Played	Won	Lost	No res	Points
Norway	3	3	0	0	6
Spain	3	2	1	0	4
Belgium	3	1	2	0	2
Croatia	3	0	3	0	0

Championship Round

	Played	Won	Lost	No res	Points
Norway	3	3	0	0	6
Austria	3	1	2	0	2
Malta	3	1	2	0	2
Greece	3	1	2	0	2

Norway progressed to the First Qualifying Round (European Group).

First Qualifying Round 2004

This round comprised three tournaments. The African and American competitions involved affiliate countries of the ICC. The European competition comprised largely associate countries.

African Group

Eight countries participated in the competition, held in Benoni, South Africa, from March 21 to 26, 2004.

Morocco withdrew at a late stage and were replaced by the South African Country Districts who were not permitted to qualify for the next round.

First Round
Group A

	Played	Won	Lost	No res	Points
Botswana	3	3	0	0	6
Malawi	3	2	1	0	4
Sierra Leone	3	1	2	0	2
Gambia	3	0	3	0	0

Group B

	Played	Won	Lost	No res	Points
South African Country Districts	3	3	0	0	6
Ghana	3	2	1	0	4
Mozambique	3	1	2	0	2
Rwanda	3	0	3	0	0

Semi-finals

Botswana beat Ghana by 4 wickets.
South African Country Districts beat Malawi by 10 wickets.

Final

South African Country Districts beat Botswana by 235 runs.
Botswana progressed to the Second Qualifying Round.

American Group

The American affiliates competition was held in Howard, Panama, from March 23 to 27, 2004.

	Played	Won	Lost	No result	Points
Bahamas	4	4	0	0	24
Panama	4	3	1	0	18
Belize	4	2	2	0	12
Turks and Caicos Islands	4	1	3	0	6
Surinam	4	0	4	0	0

Bahamas progressed to the Second Qualifying Round.

European Group

The European competition, the European Championships Division 2, was staged in Belgium from July 18 to 23, 2004.

	Played	Won	Lost	No result	Points
Italy	5	5	0	0	10
France	5	3	2	0	6
Germany	5	3	2	0	6

	Played	Won	Lost	No result	Points
Norway	5	2	3	0	4
Gibraltar	5	2	3	0	4
Israel	5	0	5	0	0

Italy progressed directly to the ICC Qualifying Tournament Division 2.

Second Qualifying Round 2004

This stage of the competition was made up of five tournaments.

East Asia-Pacific Group

Matches in this Group took the form of the East Asia-Pacific Challenge held in Japan from 25 to 29 May 2004.

First Round

	Played	Won	Lost	No result	Points
Fiji	3	3	0	0	6
Tonga	3	2	1	0	4
Indonesia	3	1	2	0	2
Japan	3	0	3	0	0

Final

Fiji (304-6) beat Tonga (123) by 181 runs.
Fiji progressed to the ICC Trophy Qualifying Tournament Division 2.

Asian Group

The biennial Asian Cricket Council Trophy, held in Malaysia from 12 to 22 June 2004, was used as the qualifying competition. In contrast to the other qualifying contests, this was a substantial event involving fifteen countries.

First Round
Group A

	Played	Won	Lost	No result	Points
United Arab Emirates	3	3	0	0	6
Qatar	3	2	1	0	4
Singapore	3	1	2	0	2
Thailand	3	0	3	0	0

Group B

	Played	Won	Lost	No result	Points
Kuwait	3	3	0	0	6
Malaysia	3	2	1	0	4
Saudi Arabia	3	1	2	0	2
Maldives	3	0	3	0	0

Group C

	Played	Won	Lost	No result	Points
Oman	3	3	0	0	6
Afghanistan	3	1	2	0	2
Bahrain	3	1	2	0	2
Hong Kong	3	1	2	0	2

Group D

	Played	Won	Lost	No result	Points
Nepal	2	2	0	0	4
Bhutan	2	1	1	0	2
Iran	2	0	2	0	0

Quarter-finals

Kuwait beat Afghanistan by 49 runs.
Oman beat Bhutan by 10 wickets.
Qatar beat Nepal by 4 wickets.
United Arab Emirates beat Malaysia by 61 runs.

Semi-finals

United Arab Emirates beat Kuwait by 120 runs.
Oman beat Qatar by 4 wickets.

Final

United Arab Emirates beat Oman by 94 runs.
The United Arab Emirates and Oman qualified to play in the ICC Trophy, Oman becoming the first affiliate country to do so.
Kuwait and Qatar progressed to the ICC Trophy Qualifying Tournament Division 2.

American Group

THE AMERICAS Cup, held in Bermuda from 6 to 11 July 2004, formed the qualifying competition.

	Played	Won	Lost	No result	Points
Canada	5	5	0	0	20
USA	5	4	1	0	16
Bermuda	5	3	2	0	12
Cayman Islands	5	2	3	0	8
Argentina	5	1	4	0	4
Bahamas	5	0	5	0	0

Canada, the USA and Bermuda qualified for the ICC Trophy. The Cayman Islands progressed to the ICC Trophy Qualifying Tournament Division 2.

European Group

THE EUROPEAN Championships Division 1, held in The Netherlands from 18 to 24 July 2004, doubled as the qualifying competition though in this respect it was somewhat pointless since it comprised five teams, one of which, the English Cricket Board, was not permitted to progress, leaving four teams to fill four qualifying places.

	Played	Won	Lost	No result	Points
England Cricket Board	4	4	0	0	8
Ireland	4	3	1	0	6
Netherlands	4	2	2	0	4
Scotland	4	1	3	0	2
Denmark	4	0	4	0	0

Ireland, The Netherlands, Scotland and Denmark qualified for the ICC Trophy.

African Group

IN ORDER to provide a qualifying competition at the associate level, the African Cricket Championships were held in Zambia from 1 to 8 August 2004.

	Played	Won	Lost	No result	Points
Namibia	5	5	0	0	25
Uganda	5	4	1	0	20
Zambia	5	2	3	0	10
Botswana	5	2	3	0	10
Nigeria	5	1	4	0	5
Tanzania	5	1	4	0	5

Namibia and Uganda qualified for the ICC Trophy and Zambia progressed to the ICC Trophy Qualifying Tournament Division 2.

ICC Trophy Qualifying Tournament Division 2 2005

THE COMPETITION was held in Malaysia between 21 and 27 February 2005. It brought together eight countries with the winners progressing to the ICC Trophy proper. This simple structure was far preferable to the complicated arrangements for promotion from Division 2 adopted in 2001. Unfortunately, it did not restore the Philip Snow Plate which no longer seems to be awarded. Since the objective of the Plate had been to provide an award for the best of the second tier of countries competing in the ICC Trophy, it would be appropriate for the Philip Snow Plate to become the ICC Division 2 Trophy.

First round

Group A

	Played	Won	Lost	No result	Points
Papua New Guinea	3	3	0	0	6
Nepal	3	2	1	0	4
Kuwait	3	1	2	0	2
Italy	3	0	3	0	0

Group B

	Played	Won	Lost	No result	Points
Fiji	3	3	0	0	6
Qatar	3	2	1	0	4
Cayman Islands	3	1	2	0	2
Zambia	3	0	3	0	0

Semi-finals

Papua New Guinea beat Qatar by 35 runs.
Fiji beat Nepal by 3 runs.

Final

Papua New Guinea beat Fiji by 30 runs.
Papua New Guinea qualified for the ICC Trophy.

ICC Trophy 2005

IRELAND HOSTED the 2005 ICC Trophy from 1 to 13 July. The twelve teams were divided into two groups with all the group matches being played on grounds in Northern Ireland. The top two teams in each group contested the semi-finals, with all four qualifying for the 2007 World Cup. The teams in third and fourth place played a separate knock-out phase to determine the fifth qualifier. These matches along with play-offs for the other places took place in the Republic of Ireland on grounds in and around Dublin. With no Super Six and with so much depending not just on winning the group but also on which place a team finished in, the group stage held its interest to the end. With eight teams as possible contenders for the five World Cup places and at least three others capable of surprising any one of those, the outcome of any part of the tournament was never obvious. Only the USA seemed misplaced in terms of ability and enthusiasm. The simple arrangement of a group stage, semi-finals and final was a model of efficiency which could well be copied for other tournaments. There was not a single match which was pointless.

Ireland finished Group A unbeaten and were unfortunate to have to share points with the USA in an abandoned fixture. Bermuda lost only once which was surprising since their leading batsman, Clay Smith, was injured in their first game. The United Arab Emirates beat Denmark for third place on run-rate, their head-to-head match being abandoned after 15 overs. Overall, the Emirates were disappointing. They struggled to adjust to the combination of grass wickets, low temperatures and damp atmosphere. Group B saw Scotland finish first without being extended in any match. Canada took advantage of some good fortune to finish second. In their opening game against Namibia they gained victory by two runs. After the game evidence was produced that the scorers had missed two runs in the 45th over of Namibia's innings and that the match should have ended in a tie. Unfortunately, the camera which was fitted to the sightscreen in every match to record every ball failed on the ball before the one in question so that the organising committee, aided by an independent member of the ICC, had no alternative but to reject Namibia's appeal against the result. The outcome did not affect Namibia's final position in the Group Table which, after their performance in the 2001 competition, was disappointing. They lost the chance of finishing higher by an inept bowling display against The

Netherlands. Canada's second piece of luck was against The Netherlands. In a match reduced by rain to 35 overs per side, Canada were struggling at 116-6 in reply to the Dutch total of 187-9. A further rain delay of 19 minutes, however, led to a revised target of 160 from 30 overs, a proposition which was just within reach and obtained in an exciting finish with one ball and two wickets to spare. As a result, the Dutch missed out on a semi-final place despite seeming to have one of the best all-round sides in the competition.

The first round phase of the play-offs for fifth place saw The Netherlands reach a total well beyond the ability of the Danes. Namibia began disastrously against the United Arab Emirates who achieved an easy victory with three overs and four wickets to spare. The Dutch continued their batting form into the vital play-off for fifth place. The Netherlands lost two early wickets for fifteen runs to Ali Asad but Bas Zuiderent (116*) and Tim de Leede (65) added 122 to place the Dutch in a comfortable position. Zuiderent then added a further 144 in an unbeaten stand for the fourth wicket with Ryan ten Doeschate (65*). Against accurate, penetrating bowling none of the Emirates' batsmen displayed any degree of permanence and The Netherlands completed a relatively easy victory. The semi-final between Canada and Ireland was a close contest until about half-way through the Irish innings when Canada struggled to find a fifth containing bowler and Ireland finished comfortable winners. Scotland were in command against Bermuda for most of the game and finished convincing winners with three overs remaining.

The final was a decidedly one-sided affair from the start. Asked to bat on a pitch which might have assisted the Irish pace attack, Scotland exerted their dominance, passing the 100 mark in the fourteenth

over. From this point on, the Irish were always in the process of catching-up. Their bowling lacked consistent length and direction and the faster Scotland scored, the more wayward it became. After losing two wickets for 11, Jeremy Bray and Ed Joyce attempted to bring Ireland back into the match with a partnership of 137 but when both got out to mistimed shots, the middle order was unable to maintain the momentum. An unbeaten last wicket stand of 55 between Paul Mooney (22*) and Geoff Cooke delayed the inevitable by ensuring that Scotland had to field the full fifty overs.

Bas Zuiderent (The Netherlands) was the leading batsman of the tournament with three centuries and the highest run aggregate (474 at an average of 118.50). He was closely followed by Ireland's Ed Joyce with two centuries and a total of 399 runs (average 99.75). Joyce played in two fewer matches since he was called away for county

Final qualifying tables
First round
Division 1 – Group A

	Played	Won	Lost	No result	Points	Net run rate
Ireland	5	4	0	1	9	1.49
Bermuda	5	3	1	1	7	0.69
United Arab Emirates	5	2	2	1	5	0.43
Denmark	5	2	2	1	5	−0.21
Uganda	5	1	3	1	3	−1.04
USA	5	0	4	1	1	−1.38

Group B

Scotland	5	5	0	0	10	2.06
Canada	5	4	1	0	8	0.78
Netherlands	5	3	2	0	6	1.45
Namibia	5	2	3	0	4	0.41
Papua New Guinea	5	1	4	0	2	−2.20
Oman	5	0	5	0	0	−2.72

Semi-finals for fifth-place
United Arab Emirates (242-6) beat Namibia (240-7) by 4 wickets.
Netherlands (314-6) beat Denmark (225) by 89 runs.

Fifth-place play-off
Netherlands (284-7) beat United Arab Emirates (142) by 145 runs.

Third-place play-off
Canada (197-5) beat Bermuda (195) by 5 wickets.

Semi-finals
Ireland (241-6) beat Canada (238-9) by 4 wickets.
Scotland (224-4) beat Bermuda (219-9) by 6 wickets.

Final
Scotland (324-8) beat Ireland (277-9) by 47 runs.

duty with Middlesex for part of the time. Other scorers of more than 300 runs were Ian Billcliff (Canada) with 315 and Jim Davison (Canada) with 312. The best individual bowling was Paul Hoffmann's six for 12 for Scotland against Oman. Thomas Hansen took six for 30 for Denmark against Uganda. Hoffmann topped the wicket aggregate with 17 (average 10.17), a total shared with Edgar Schiferli (The Netherlands) whose average was 14.64. Two players took 15 tournament wickets: Ryan ten Doeschate and Thomas Hansen.

MAIN COMPETITION 2007

THE 2007 World Cup was staged in the West Indies between 12 March and 28 April. Prior to the event taking place, the individual countries of the West Indies were invited to bid for the right to host matches. Bermuda, the USA and Canada were also hopeful of staging one or two fixtures but their bids were rejected. Canada would have been too distant, Bermuda and the USA did not have appropriate facilities. There was also uncertainty over whether all the players could have gained visas for entry to the United States under their current immigration policies. Matches were therefore restricted to Antigua, Barbados, Grenada, Guyana, Jamaica, St Kitts, St Lucia and Trinidad. Hurricane damage in 2004 led to concerns as to whether the facilities in Grenada could be rebuilt in time so that the ground in Trinidad was held as an additional reserve. Much adverse publicity was given to the high prices of tickets and accommodation, the likely problems of local air travel between the individual countries and the somewhat chaotic procedure for issuing special visas to visitors, allowing them entry to all the different countries. Visa application centres were set up in London, Toronto, New York, Miami, New Delhi and Sydney but they were not staffed until very close to the deadline for application. The procedure was also somewhat insensitive in that New Zealanders had to apply to the centre in Australia and Pakistanis, Sri Lankans and Bangladeshis to the one in India. In the end, in traditional Caribbean fashion, last minute organisation was effective. All the facilities were completed to a satisfactory standard and local good humour made up for deficiencies in the transport systems which generally worked. Attendances, however, were, with few exceptions, generally poor. The ICC invested a lot of time and money in providing pre-tournament coaching and match practice for the cricketers from the associate countries.

In contrast to some previous World Cups, the opening ceremony at the newly-built Trelawny Stadium in northern Jamaica, provided a superb spectacle of local carnival, reggae and fireworks, with a parade of all sixteen teams to hear Sir Garfield Sobers formally open proceedings. Unfortunately, the carnival atmosphere was not continued into the individual matches. Restrictions imposed by the ICC and the tournament sponsors which prohibited spectators from taking their own food and drink into the grounds, the need to register musical instruments with the ground authorities in advance, the failure to provide exit and re-entry passes so that people could buy lunch outside the ground instead of paying two to three times local prices inside, and the pricing of tickets in relation to the tourist market instead of local disposable incomes, all meant that locals largely ignored the competition. Until the semi-final stage, most matches were played to small crowds although special arrangements for parties of schoolchildren and free entry after a certain hour at some grounds helped to increase attendances for the afternoon sessions. The impression was created that the priority of the ICC, local organisers and sponsors was to maximise income rather than promote a major international cricket contest to the local population and thereby help to renew interest in the game in the West Indies. Attempts to create a gala atmosphere were further muted by the suspected murder of Bob Woolmer, the Pakistani coach, early in the tournament.

The ICC continued to ignore the experience of the two previous tournaments and retained a Super Eight stage. The first round consisted of placing the sixteen teams in four groups with the expectation that two weeks of pointless matches would ensue to eliminate eight teams, the names of which were eminently predictable in advance. No one anticipated the victories of Ireland and Bangladesh over India and Pakistan respectively which led to the failure of the latter two countries to qualify for the Super Eight. If the first round had consisted of two groups of eight with the top two in each group progressing to the semi-finals, the chances of any of the major sides going out following one upset result would have been prevented. Also, the associate countries would have played more games, with the opportunity for Scotland and The Netherlands to demonstrate their abilities relative to other countries more generally instead of having the unenviable task of playing only Australia and South Africa. The differences in standard between the sixteen countries was reflected in the very low number of close matches; only eight per cent resulted in wins by one wicket, less than 5 runs or a tie, whereas twenty-five per cent of the matches resulted in victories by either more than 200 runs or eight, nine or ten wickets. Although the associate countries were involved in 69 per cent of these mismatches, it should be noted that Australia accounted for 39 per cent of the mismatch wins. Mismatches were as much a reflection of Australia's dominance as an inability of the associate countries to perform. All the associate sides had their 'champagne' moments and all had to be treated seriously by the test-playing countries.

As expected, Australia, South Africa, the West Indies, New Zealand, Sri Lanka and England qualified for the Super Eights, where they were surprisingly joined by Ireland and Bangladesh. Australia ruthlessly demolished all opposition to confirm their reputation as tournament favourites although Sri Lanka looked to have the best all-round side, combining efficient and attractive run-scoring with an effective mixed pace and spin bowling attack. In contrast, the performances of the West Indies and England were unconvincing. Ireland produced the first excitement of the tournament by holding their nerve whilst a young and inexperienced Zimbabwe team panicked; requiring ten runs to win, they lost four wickets in the last 15 balls and finished one run short. Ireland followed this with an even more surprising result, a three-wicket victory over Pakistan on St Patrick's Day (see Chapter 2 – Country Profile for Ireland). Bangladesh overcame an uninspired Indian side as Mashrafe Mortaza made the ball seam prodigiously off the pitch to take four wickets for 38 runs; despite an innings of 66 runs

from 129 balls by Sourav Ganguly, India were throttled by accurate left-arm spin from Mohammad Rafique, Aftab Ahmed and Saqibul Hasan before Tamim Iqbal, Mushfiqur Rahim and Saqibul exuberantly punished the Indian bowling to secure a convincing win by 5 wickets. Although out of the tournament, India salvaged some of their reputation against Bermuda by recording the highest ever world-cup innings. The Netherlands became the second associate country to achieve a victory producing a highly polished and clinical performance to overwhelm Scotland by eight wickets.

Domination

Australia continued their domination in the Super Eight, finishing unbeaten and being responsible for three out the six mismatches in this stage. They reached the semi-finals without losing more than six wickets in any match. New Zealand and Sri Lanka each lost two matches. Both were beaten by Australia, although Sri Lanka chose to rest Muttiah Muralitharan and Chaminda Vaas in their game. Australia savaged the New Zealand bowlers, scoring 348 runs for the loss of six wickets in their 50 overs and gaining a 215-run victory. After Glen McGrath and Shaun Tait took two wickets each, Brad Hogg disposed of the lower order, taking four wickets with his left-arm spin. New Zealand's second defeat was by Sri Lanka. South Africa were somewhat fortunate to progress to the semi-finals. They tried very hard to build on their previous world cup disasters when, needing four runs to win with five wickets in hand against Sri Lanka, they lost four wickets in four balls to Lasith Malinga before scrambling home by one wicket. They were then outplayed by Bangladesh, being undone by a three-pronged left-arm spin attack and having no effective spin-bowler of their own with which to retaliate. Bangladesh won by 67 runs. South Africa's nine wicket win over England ensured their semi-final place. Neither England nor the West Indies had the confidence or the consistency required to progress further. England were, however, involved in two close finishes, losing to Sri Lanka by two runs and beating the West Indies by 1 wicket. Bangladesh also showed their inconsistency. They followed their performance against South Africa by losing to Ireland. On a wicket which started with plenty of bounce but became slower as the game progressed, Ireland batted slowly at first but reached 92 before losing a wicket. They then accelerated, using short singles to tease the Bangladeshi fielding which deteriorated badly. In turn, Ireland bowled and fielded superbly as Bangladesh showed no understanding of the concepts of anchorage or caution and ended up 74 runs short of Ireland's total of 243 for seven.

The first semi-final between New Zealand and Sri Lanka was closely contested for the first thirteen overs but after their second wicket fell in the fourteenth over with the score on 67, Sri Lanka were always in control. Mahela Jayawardene gave a masterclass in the art of one-day batting by building an innings and then gradually accelerating. He took 47 balls to score his first 17 runs; his next 23 runs came from 23 balls, the next 60 from 30 balls and the last 15 from 5, to give a total of 115 not out from 109 balls with ten fours and three sixes. He was superbly supported by Upul Tharanga's 73 from 74 balls. Replying to 289 for five, New Zealand lost two wickets for 32 runs in the first ten overs as Lasith Malinga and Chaminda Vaas troubled the batsmen with swing and pace. Muttiah Muralitharan's four wickets for 31 in eight overs reduced New Zealand to 116 for seven after which a win for Sri Lanka was inevitable. South Africa confirmed their position as the weakest of the semi-finalists. Their attempt to overpower the Australian bowling with aggressive batting was ill-conceived and by the end of the tenth over they had lost five wickets for only 27 runs. Although they recovered to 149 all out, none of their batsmen were at ease against the pace attack of Glen McGrath, Shaun Tait and Nathan Bracken and the spin of Brad Hogg. In contrast, South Africa had no spinner and chose to leave out Makhaya Ntini, their most attacking bowler. Not surprisingly, Australia cruised to victory in the thirty-second over.

Rain ruined any possibility of the final becoming the spectacular contest which everyone had hoped for. The match was reduced to 38 overs per side before it started whereupon Adam Gilchrist treated the crowd to an audacious display. In an opening stand of 172 runs in 22.5 overs with Matthew Hayden, he made 119, reaching his century in only 72 balls. He was eventually dismissed for 149 with 100 of his runs coming in boundaries (8 sixes and 13 fours). Whilst Lasith Malinga conceded

only six runs in his first four overs, no other Sri Lankan bowler could stem the deluge and Australia's total of 281 for four wickets was certainly more than competitive. Sri Lanka lost an early wicket but Sanath Jayasuriya (63 runs from 67 balls) and Kumar Sangakkara (54 from 52 balls), in a partnership of 116 runs, began to build the foundation for a counter-attack. As the threat of rain returned, it was no longer sufficient to build the innings. As soon as the mandatory 20 overs had been completed, it was also necessary to be ahead of the required target according to the Duckworth-Lewis method in order to be certain of victory should the match be abandoned. The rapid increase in the run-rate required was beyond Sri Lanka's ability against a four-pronged pace attack in increasingly dull conditions. After 33 overs, Sri Lanka's batsmen admitted defeat and accepted the offer of bad light. Both sides assumed the match had finished but chaos reigned as the umpires and match referee failed to interpret the match regulations correctly. Inexplicably ignoring the fact that the innings had lasted more than 20 overs, they insisted that the 38 overs should be completed and that the players would have to return the following day to do this. Fortunately, the two captains showed sense and agreed to complete the match in the dark that evening, with the Australians using their spin bowlers. Further delays followed whilst the pitch was remarked and a new target of 269 runs from 36 overs recalculated. What should have been a showpiece for international cricket, with Australia extending their unbeaten run in World Cup matches to 39 and securing their third successive World Cup title, thus ended in farce; the only consolation being that it was so dark that no one could see what was going on anyway.

Twenty Centuries

Matthew Hayden (Australia) was the leading batsman of the tournament, scoring 659 runs (average 73.22). Mahela Jayawardene (Sri Lanka) with 548 runs (average 60.88) and Ricky Ponting (Australia) with 539 runs (average 67.37) were the others to exceed 500 runs. Altogether, twenty centuries were made with Hayden scoring three and Sanath Jayasuriya (Sri Lanka), two. The highest individual score was 160 by Imran Nazir for Pakistan against Zimbabwe. Glen McGrath (Australia) was the leading bowler with 26 wickets (average 13.73). Others who took over twenty wickets were Muttiah Muralitharan (Sri Lanka), 23 at 15.26, Shaun Tait (Australia), 23 at 20.30 and Brad Hogg (Australia), 21 at 15.80. The best individual performances were 5 for 18 by Andrew Hall (South Africa against England) and 5-39 by Charl Langeveldt (South Africa against Sri Lanka). Two one-day records were broken during the tournament. Herschelle Gibbs (South Africa) scored 36 runs in one over; Daan van Bunge (The Netherlands) was the unlucky recipient. Lasith Malinga took four wickets in four balls for Sri Lanka against South Africa.

What started so promisingly at the opening ceremony ended in embarrassment for the ICC. The incompetence of supposedly ICC-trained umpires in the final was, for many, a fitting end to a tournament in which the maximising of profit and the rigid application of exclusive sponsorship rights stifled what should have been a tournament played before large crowds in a carnival atmosphere. Even recognising that cricket is a business and that the ICC needs finance to undertake it global promotion work, there is also a need to appreciate that cricket is an entertainment and this World Cup failed to entertain. Further, the ICC were culpable in ignoring basic geography. For most countries of the Caribbean, February and early March are the driest time of year. The decision to hold the tournament in late March and April was inexplicable and meant that 18 per cent of the matches were affected by rain and several others were played in dull cloudy conditions. Perhaps for future tournaments the ICC will learn some geography, give priority to the need to entertain, allow the organisers to reflect their local culture and shorten the competition by progressing straight from a league phase to the semi-finals.

Final qualifying tables

Group A

	Played	Won	Lost	No result	Points	Net run rate
Australia	3	3	0	0	6	3.433
South Africa	3	2	1	0	4	2.403
Netherlands	3	1	2	0	2	-2.527
Scotland	3	0	3	0	0	-3.793

Group B

	Played	Won	Lost	No result	Points	Net run rate
Sri Lanka	3	3	0	0	6	3.493
Bangladesh	3	2	1	0	4	-1.523
India	3	1	2	0	2	1.206
Bermuda	3	0	3	0	0	-4.345

Group C

	Played	Won	Lost	No result	Points	Net run rate
New Zealand	3	3	0	0	6	2.138
England	3	2	1	0	4	0.418
Kenya	3	1	2	0	2	-1.194
Canada	3	0	3	0	0	-1.389

Group D

	Played	Won	Tied	Lost	No result	Points	Net run rate
West Indies	3	3	0	0	0	6	0.764
Ireland	3	1	1	1	0	3	-0.092
Pakistan	3	1	0	2	0	2	0.089
Zimbabwe	3	0	1	2	0	1	-0.886

Super Eight

	Played	Won	Lost	No result	Points	Net run rate
Australia	7 (1)	7 (1)	0 (0)	0	14 (2)	2.40
Sri Lanka	7 (1)	5 (1)	2 (0)	0	10 (2)	1.48
New Zealand	7 (1)	5 (1)	2 (0)	0	10 (2)	0.25
South Africa	7 (1)	4 (0)	3 (1)	0	8 (0)	0.31
England	7 (1)	3 (0)	4 (1)	0	6 (2)	-0.39
West Indies	7 (1)	2 (1)	5 (0)	0	4 (0)	-0.57
Bangladesh	7 (1)	1 (0)	6 (1)	0	2 (0)	-1.51
Ireland	7 (1)	1 (0)	6 (1)	0	2 (0)	-1.73

Figures in parentheses show the positions at the start of the Super Eight; the two teams qualifying from each first-round group took forward the result of the match played between them.

Semi-finals

Sri Lanka (289-5) beat New Zealand (208) by 81 runs.
Australia (153-3) beat South Africa (149) by 7 wickets.

Final

Australia (281-4) beat Sri Lanka (215-8) by 53 runs (Duckworth-Lewis method).

TOURNAMENT RECORDS

ICC Trophy

	Played	Won	Lost	No res	% won	Win/Loss Ratio
Zimbabwe	25	23	0	2	92.0	∞
Scotland	26	20	5	1	76.9	4.00
Netherlands	64	43	15	6	67.2	2.87
Sri Lanka	6	4	1	1	66.6	4.00
UAE	33	22	10	1	66.6	2.20
Nepal	3	2	1	0	66.6	2.00
Kenya	39	24	12	3	61.5	2.00
Bermuda	57	35	18	4	61.4	1.94
Bangladesh	41	25	14	2	61.0	1.79
Namibia	30	18	12	0	60.0	1.50
Canada	59	33	20	6	55.9	1.65
Denmark	52	29	21	2	55.8	1.38
Ireland	33	18	13	2	54.5	1.39
USA	55	26	23	6	47.3	1.13
Papua New Guinea	53	25	25	3	47.2	1.00
Uganda	13	6	6	1	46.2	1.00
Hong Kong	42	16	23	3	38.1	0.70
Germany	3	1	2	0	33.3	0.50
Fiji	43	13	26	4	30.2	0.50
Oman	7	2	5	0	28.6	0.40
East & Central Africa	41	11	25	5	26.9	0.44
Malaysia	43	11	28	4	25.6	0.39
Singapore	35	8	21	6	22.9	0.38
West Africa	22	5	11	6	22.7	0.45
Argentina	36	8	27	1	22.2	0.30
France	5	1	4	0	20.0	0.25
Gibraltar	38	6	27	5	15.0	0.22
Israel	45	3	40	2	6.7	0.07
Italy	5	0	4	1	0.0	0.00

Highest team score
455-9   Papua New Guinea v Gibraltar, Cannock   1986

Lowest team score
26   East & Central Africa v Netherlands, Kuala Lumpur   1996/97

Highest individual score
172   S.D. Myles   Hong Kong v Gibraltar, Bridgnorth   1986

Best bowling in an innings
7-9   Asim Khan   Netherlands v East & Central Africa, Kuala Lumpur   1996/97

Best wicket-keeping
6 (6 ct)   M. Saddique   Denmark v Israel, Nairobi   1994

World Cup

	Played	Won	Lost	No res	% won	Win/Loss Ratio
Australia	69	51	17	1	0	73.9	3.00
South Africa	40	25	13	2	0	62.5	1.92
West Indies	57	35	21	0	1	61.4	1.67
England	59	36	22	0	1	61.0	1.64
New Zealand	62	35	26	0	1	56.5	1.35
India	58	32	25	0	1	55.1	1.28
Pakistan	56	30	24	0	2	53.5	1.25
Sri Lanka	57	25	30	1	1	43.9	0.83
Kenya	23	6	16	0	1	26.0	0.37
Bangladesh	20	5	14	0	1	25.0	0.36
Ireland	9	2	6	1	0	22.2	0.33
UAE	5	1	4	0	0	20.0	0.25
Zimbabwe	45	8	33	1	3	17.7	0.24
Netherlands	14	2	12	0	0	14.2	0.16
Canada	12	1	11	0	0	8.3	0.09
Bermuda	3	0	3	0	0	0.0	0.00
East Africa	3	0	3	0	0	0.0	0.00
Namibia	6	0	6	0	0	0.0	0.00
Scotland	8	0	8	0	0	0.0	0.00

Highest team score
413-8   India v Bermuda, Port of Spain   2006/07

Lowest team score
36   Canada v Sri Lanka, Paarl   2002/03

Highest individual score
188*   G.N. Kirsten   South Africa v United Arab Emirates, Rawalpindi   1995/96

Best bowling in an innings
7-15   G.D. McGrath   Australia v Namibia, Potchefstroom   2002/03

Best wicket-keeping
6 (6 ct)   A.C. Gilchrist   Australia v Namibia, Potchefstroom   2002/03

CHAPTER 5

THE FUTURE

NOW THAT cricket is played in nearly 150 countries and the ICC is implementing major development programmes to spread the game further, there is a need to ensure that it is self-sustaining. History has shown that where the game has relied on an immigrant population to survive, it has struggled as soon as that section of the population, for whatever reason, moves away. The situation in Africa is of particular concern. Only in South Africa is the game played to a high standard by all communities and is the international side truly multiracial. For various reasons, attempts to promote cricket among the dominant African population in other countries have not been very successful. In Zimbabwe, government interference to reduce the influence of the white minority and increase that of a particular ethnic group of the African community has resulted in a substantial decline in standards, a loss of key players from all communities, and a breakdown in the structure of the game at provincial and club level. In Kenya, the initial development programmes among the African community were successful and produced some excellent cricketers, notably Steve Tikolo and Maurice Odumbe, but there seem to be few replacements of comparable standard.

Very Few African Players

In Namibia, the international side remains all-white and there are very few African players, even at club level; if any future government were to pursue a policy of Africanisation, the game would almost certainly die. In Ghana and The Gambia, the number of people playing cricket may already be below that which is necessary for the game to pass successfully to the next generation. The only exception to this depressing picture is Uganda where the game is dominantly African but the best Asian cricketers are still selected for the national side. A more active policy by the ICC to promote cricket with equal opportunity to all communities will be essential if the game's contraction is to be avoided.

Another challenge facing the ICC and the national cricket authorities is to provide further encouragement to women's cricket. The ICC lists some 47 countries where women's cricket is played which is less than half of those countries that are members of the ICC. Of those 47, only twenty have been involved in women's international cricket. In some countries where the women's cricket was once established, notably Denmark, it is in danger of dying. Many countries have development programmes in schools and at Under-13 level girls but there is a need to ensure that they are truly open, regardless of social, religious or ethnic background, and the adverse attitudes to women's cricket that may prevail more widely in the community. More opportunities must also be provided for girls to continue playing as they get older. At present a professional aspiration for women's cricket does not exist. Yet, a professional status for the top players would probably do more to encourage women to remain in the sport than almost any other incentive.

Over the last two decades men's cricket has become more commercialised and the amount of international cricket played has increased. Not only are there more test matches and more official one-day internationals but there are now nearly 200 matches a year involving the associate and affiliate countries. Since most of the players in these countries are amateurs, sponsorship becomes ever more important in order to cover the costs of transport, accommodation and time away from work. Company sponsorship is now the main source of finance for the test-match countries. It enables their national bodies to enter into central contracts with players, run cricket academies and engage in tours by A-teams and youth teams. The ICC and the national bodies have recognised that cricket can attract large sums of money in sponsorship provided that they involve the best players in the world and that the national sides are successful. Sponsors can be fickle, however, and will withdraw their support to teams which lose regularly and for matches which will not attract high attendances. The corollary is that the best players are being asked to play much more cricket. Although in the 1930s, '50s and '60s, English cricketers in particular played many more games than their counterparts today, they were largely first-class county matches. The number of games played out of season was small. Overseas tours were not undertaken every winter and those that did take place did not always involve the best players. Second-class teams were often selected for tours of India and, before the Second World War, the West Indies and New Zealand too. The top cricketers of today are asked to play a lot more international matches with much higher levels of expectation. Further, the match programme lasts all year with the majority of the games overseas. Tours have become more stressful with fewer rest days, more time spent travelling and less opportunity to see and enjoy the country being visited. The pressure on players at the top level is likely to increase further as Twenty20 competitions develop as a third form of international cricket along side test and one-day matches.

Largely Oblivious

Yet the ICC and the national cricket authorities seem largely oblivious to any effects of these changes on the health of the players and their families. There is an urgent need for research on the effects of current cricket regimes on the physical and mental health of the top players. The responsibilities of the national bodies to players on central contracts should be no different to those of major companies towards their employees in relation to sickness, holidays and general duty of care. The players' associations could and should act more strongly to ensure that notice is taken over these issues. Unless action is taken there is a real danger that the standard of top-class cricket will decline as cricketers increasingly become unavailable through injury or decide to retire

early from the game. The present level of sponsorship will then become unsustainable.

The health issue is just one of many where the role of the ICC is made difficult by potential conflicts of interest. Others noted elsewhere in the book include the conflict between exclusive sponsorship arrangements made by the ICC and sponsorship contracts entered into by the national boards and individual players; the aim of promoting cricket world-wide with equal opportunities for all who want to play but the inability of the ICC to act where obvious interference by national governments prevents this from being the case; the grey area between the ICC's responsibility for regulations on how the game is played and the role of the MCC as custodians of the laws of the game; and the classification of test matches. Much of what the ICC does is excellent, particularly its work in promoting the game, raising the standards of umpiring, encouraging international cricket generally, and, albeit after a period of inaction, dealing with match-fixing. Unfortunately what gets more publicity is ICC's attempts to continually alter the regulations of the game, such as introducing 'power play' and 'super subs' into one-day internationals and its inconsistency in addressing political issues. To its credit, the ICC is prepared to withdraw its regulations where they have not worked; hence the demise of 'super subs' after only about one year. On the political side, the contrast in action is enormous. In its dealings with the United States Cricket Association, the ICC acted firmly by insisting on improved corporate management and transparency in accounts, whilst introducing sanctions which included preventing the USA from participating in some tournaments. In contrast, there has been no intervention, apart from some gentle cajoling, in Zimbabwe, where the effect of politics on the future of cricket is much more serious. Similarly, the ICC has ignored the possible government interference in Sri Lanka which has affected who holds the key administrative posts of the Sri Lankan Board of Control for Cricket, who are chosen as selectors and, indeed, who the selectors can choose to represent their country. If the ICC is to be respected as the body responsible for world cricket, it needs to be more consistent in how it deals with issues over which it has no direct control.

The ICC has been widely criticised for its decisions to grant test-match status to Bangladesh, not to rescind the test-match status of Zimbabwe, to assign first-class status to matches between associate level countries in the Intercontinental Cup and to accord temporary official one-day status to the top six associate countries. All the criticisms relate to whether teams from these countries are of sufficient standard to merit their status. Such criticism seems to assume, however, that great equality between sides has always been the case in the past. When India lost their first four wickets for no runs against England at Leeds in 1952 and when New Zealand were dismissed for 26 by England at Auckland in 1955, they were accorded much sympathy by the general public but their right to test-match status was not questioned. There is a danger that making decisions on match status and on which countries should be promoted to full membership of the ICC on the basis of some statistical ideal would hinder the development of the game in the associate and affiliate countries.

If cricket is to continue its progress as a world game, the objective should be to promote more countries to full membership when they meet the criteria of a well-established domestic game with three- or four-day matches, an effective and professionally-run administrative structure and a reasonable level of public interest which demonstrates that cricket is recognised as a national sport. The objective should not be to restrict full membership to the current members. More needs to be done to ensure that the associate countries field their best sides for major tournaments. The ICC needs to legislate to give international matches by associate countries the same priority as test matches and one-day internationals by the full member countries, thereby making it compulsory for the English first-class counties and Australian state sides to release players to represent these countries in the same way that they have to release players required by England or Australia. If the associate countries are to aspire to test-match or permanent one-day status, they need to show their strengths by fielding their strongest teams. At present, the ICC's regulations regarding player eligibility prevent this.

Designed to ensure that countries are properly represented by nationals or, in some cases, long-term residents, the ICC's regulations have been successful in preventing the rise of a transfer market and in stopping countries effectively 'buying' a team of mercenaries. Problems arise where they take priority over government definitions of national citizenship. It is not sufficient to have been born in a country and recognised by that country's laws as a *bona fide* citizen in order to represent it in an ICC-recognised tournament. In addition you must have resided in that country for 100 or more days over the previous five years and, further, have spent that time supporting cricket in some way, for example through coaching or administration. Since most cricketers from associate and affiliate countries are amateurs they would need to obtain leave of absence from work to fulfil this requirement. The regulations for non-citizens are even stricter and impact on those who have committed themselves to permanent residence, for example after marriage to a local. These people must have spent a minimum of 183 days in that country in each of the four preceding years. This effectively rules out individuals working in, for example, that country's overseas development work or in overseas branches of that country's national companies. In recent tournaments, Italy, Greece and Samoa have all had players declared ineligible by the ICC and therefore not been able to field their strongest sides. It is not clear what legal right the ICC has to prevent *bona fide* citizens from representing their country but the ruling has never been challenged in an international court. The regulations seem particularly harsh since they apply only to associate and affiliate members of the ICC and not to countries which are full members.

Generally Welcomed

The work of the ICC in increasing the competence of the umpires has been generally welcomed. In addition to the international panel of umpires for test matches, similar panels have been set up amongst the associate and affiliate countries to provide the umpires for tournaments at these levels. There is no reason, however, why an umpire from one of the associate countries should not be as competent as one from any of the full-member countries. Hopefully, it will not be too long before the talent of one or more umpires on the associate panel is recognised by promotion to the full panel. The prospect of a test match being officiated by an umpire from Bermuda, Kenya or Indonesia cannot be too far distant.

One area where improvement and greater consistency is necessary is in the archiving of statistics. The test and first class-game is well recorded through the various editions of *Wisden Cricketers' Almanack* and its equivalent in other countries, although the accuracy of some of the statistics is questionable. The cricket archive and the cricinfo internet sites (www.cricketarchive. co.uk; www.cricinfo.com) and the publications of the Association of Cricket Statisticians and Historians provide a consistent and, usually, more accurate record. The two internet sites also include some non first-class matches played by associate and affiliate countries but these depend on what information is available and rarely give a complete record for a particular country. The cricket europe website (www.cricketeurope4.net) includes full scores of all the representative matches ever played by Scotland and Ireland. The official web-site of the Nederlandsche Cricket Bond attempts to do the same for The Netherlands but many scorecards are missing, some are incomplete and the list has not been updated since 2002. Potentially, the internet is a valuable source of information but in practice it is often of limited value. The late 1990s and early 2000s saw a flurry of activity in the establishment of websites by the cricket associations of the associate and affiliate countries but only a few of these are regularly updated. Some have disappeared. It is possible to obtain full scores of matches involving Denmark from the Danish Cricket Association site but only if you are quick; old scorecards are not permanently stored on an archive. Instead anything older than about two years seems to be automatically removed. The website of the Singapore Cricket Association was reorganised in early 2005 since when much archival material has disappeared whereas the old site contained full scorecards of Singapore's international matches from the 1970s. Some sites are set up for specific tournaments but disappear shortly after. The ICC should take the initiative and require all national bodies, as part of their requirement for membership, to adopt a proper policy on archiving.

With cricket now played in more countries than ever before, there are more opportunities for countries of similar standard to play each other in one-day matches and for those whose standards are improving relative to others to gain promotion to a higher level through the various divisions of the newly-formed World Cricket League. The Intercontinental Cup allows the best of the associate countries to meet each other in two-innings matches. Perhaps in the future a way will be found to develop a parallel structure to the World Cricket League for the two-innings version of the game. This would leave the full member countries playing test match cricket in a protected structure. Although the countries are ranked by the ICC and the table regularly updated, perhaps the time will come when they too are integrated into a league structure with promotion and relegation. If one of the present associate countries were to gain promotion to the highest division through such a league system, their right to test-match status would have been truly demonstrated and not open to criticism. Similarly, a country could forfeit its position among the top countries if its standards fell to a level where it was relegated. There are no obvious reasons why similar structures could not be developed for women's cricket. The fact that these heretical thoughts are not so fanciful is tantamount to the strength of cricket as a truly global game.

INTERNATIONAL STATISTICS

The following statistics cover international matches played as test matches, official one-day internationals and international fixtures between non full-member countries of the ICC. Matches between non full-member countries and sides such as the England Cricket Board and South African Country Districts, which are not the official representative teams of their countries, are excluded. Similarly, matches between associate and affiliate countries and first-class domestic teams from the full-member countries are excluded.

Men

Highest team totals

Test matches

952-6 dec	Sri Lanka v India, Colombo	1997/98
903-7 dec	England v Australia, The Oval	1938
849	England v West Indies, Kingston	1929/30
790-3 dec	West Indies v Pakistan, Kingston	1957/58
758-8 dec	Australia v West Indies, Kingston	1954/55

The highest total involving non test-playing countries is 736-4 dec by Ceylon v Malaysia, Colombo, 1972.

Official one-day

443-9	Sri Lanka v Netherlands, Amstelveen	2006
438-9	South Africa v Australia, Johannesburg	2005/06
434-4	Australia v South Africa, Johannesburg	2005/06
413-8	India v Bermuda, Port of Spain	2006/07
398-5	Sri Lanka v Kenya, Kandy	1995/96

Other one-day

502-9	Papua New Guinea v New Caledonia, Suva	2003
499-6	Saudi Arabia v Brunei, Kuala Lumpur	2006
486-5	Maldives v Brunei, Bangkok	2004/05
469-7	Fiji v Japan, Kuala Lumpur	1996
467-1	Germany v Switzerland, Zuoz	1997

Lowest team totals

Test matches

26	New Zealand v England, Auckland	1954/55
30	South Africa v England, Port Elizabeth	1895/96
30	South Africa v England, Birmingham	1924
35	South Africa v England, Cape Town	1898/99
36	Australia v England, Birmingham	1902
36	South Africa v Australia, Melbourne	1931/32

Other matches

23	Belgium v Netherlands, Antwerp	1905
25	Ireland v Scotland, Dublin	1965
28	Canada v USA, New York	1846
28	Straits Settlements v Federated Malay States, Penang	1909
29	Belgium v Netherlands, Antwerp	1905

Official one-day

35	Zimbabwe v Sri Lanka, Harare	2004
36	Canada v Sri Lanka, Paarl	2002/03
38	Zimbabwe v Sri Lanka, Colombo	2001/02
43	Pakistan v West Indies, Cape Town	1992/93

45	Canada v England, Manchester	1979
45	Namibia v Australia, Potchefstroom	2002/03

Other one-day

10	Myanmar v Nepal, Kuala Lumpur	2006
18	Japan v Hong Kong, Kathmandu	1998
19	Samoa v Cook Islands, Port Vila	2005
20	Myanmar v Hong Kong, Kuala Lumpur	2006
21	Ghana v Nigeria, Freetown	1993

Highest individual innings

Test matches

400*	B.C. Lara	W Indies v England, St John's	2003/04
380	M.L. Hayden	Australia v Zimbabwe, Perth	2003/04
375	B.C. Lara	W Indies v England, St John's	1993/94
365*	G.S. Sobers	W Indies v Pakistan, Kingston	1957/58
364	L. Hutton	England v Australia, The Oval	1938

The highest total involving non test-playing countries is 309 by G.A. Hick, Zimbabwe v Ireland, Harare, 1986.

Official one-day

194	Saeed Anwar	Pakistan v India, Chennai	1996/97
189*	I.V.A. Richards	West Indies v England, Manchester	1984
189	S.T. Jayasuriya	Sri Lanka v India, Sharjah	2000/01
188*	G. Kirsten	South Africa v UAE, Rawalpindi	1995/96
186*	S.R. Tendulkar	India v New Zealand, Hyderabad	1999/00

Other one-day

217	Moosa Kaleem	Maldives v Brunei, Bangkok	2004/05
213*	Arshad Ali	UAE v Brunei, Kuala Lumpur	2006
209*	Saeed Al-Saffar	UAE v Thailand, Kathmandu	1998
203*	A.N. French	Hong Kong v Maldives, Singapore	2002
200*	Shamasuddin Khan	Germany v Switzerland, Zuoz	1997

Best bowling in an innings

Test matches

10-53	J.C. Laker	England v Australia, Manchester	1956
10-74	A. Kumble	India v Pakistan, New Delhi	1998/99
9-28	G.A. Lohmann	England v S Africa, Johannesburg	1895/96
9-37	J.C. Laker	England v Australia, Manchester	1956
9-51	M. Muralitharan	Sri Lanka v Zimbabwe, Kandy	2001/02

Other matches

10-17	T.S. Gilbert	Bermuda v Philadelphia, Hamilton 1907
10-25	K. Saker	Malaysia v Singapore, Kuala Lumpur1983
10-54	J.B. King	Philadelphia v Ireland, Haverford 1909
9-7	J. Bradbury	Canada v USA, Toronto 1854
9-10	A.J. Bostock-Hill	Malaya v Hong Kong, Singapore 1926

Official one-day

8-19	W.P.U.J.C. Vaas	Sri Lanka v Zimbabwe, Colombo 2001/02
7-15	G.D. McGrath	Australia v Namibia, Potchefstroom 2002/03
7-20	A.J. Bichel	Australia v England, Port Elizabeth 2002/03
7-30	M. Muralitharan	Sri Lanka v India, Sharjah 2000/01
7-36	Waqar Younis	Pakistan v England, Leeds 2001

Other one-day

9-16	D. Eliaba	Cook Islands v New Caledonia, Apia2002
8-23	M. Alam	Nepal v Maldives, Kathmandu 2003
8-26	Kolatau	Tonga v Western Samoa, Suva 1979
8-27	M. Stevens	Papua New Guinea v New Hebrides, Suva 1979
7-3	M. Alam	Nepal v Myanmar, Kuala Lumpur 2006

Wicket-keeping: most dismissals in an innings

Test matches

7 (7c)	Wasim Bari	Pakistan v N Zealand, Auckland1978/79
7 (7c)	R.W. Taylor	England v India, Bombay 1979/80
7 (7c)	I.D.S. Smith	N Zealand v Sri Lanka, Hamilton 1990/91
7 (7c)	R.D. Jacobs	W Indies v Australia, Melbourne 2000/01

Other matches

| 7 (4c 3st) | J. Brown | Scotland v Ireland, Dublin 1957 |
| 7 (7c) | Mohammed Taskeen | UAE v Hong Kong, Hong Kong 2005 |

Official one-day

6 (6c)	A.C. Gilchrist	Australia v South Africa, Cape Town 1999/00
6 (6c)	A.J. Stewart	England v Zimbabwe, Manchester 2000
6 (5c 1st)	R.D. Jacobs	West Indies v Sri Lanka, Colombo 2001/02
6 (5c 1st)	A.C. Gilchrist	Australia v England, Sydney 2002/03
6 (6c)	A.C. Gilchrist	Australia v Namibia, Potchefstroom 2002/03
6 (6c)	A.C. Gilchrist	Australia v Sri Lanka, Colombo 2003/04
6 (6c)	M.V. Boucher	South Africa v Pakistan, Cape Town 2006/07

Other one-day

7 (7c)	P. Amit	Israel v France, Uddingston 2000
7 (7c)	G. Passaretti	Italy v France, Mechelen 2004
7 (6c 1st)	R. Buzaglo	Gibraltar v France, Waterloo 2004

Fielding: most catches in an innings

Test matches

5	V.Y. Richardson	Australia v S Africa, Durban 1935/36
5	Yajurvindra Singh	India v England, Bengalooru 1976/77
5	M. Azharuddin	India v Pakistan, Karachi 1989/90
5	K. Srikkanth	India v Australia, Perth 1991/92
5	S.P. Fleming	N Zealand v Zimbabwe, Harare1997/98

Other matches

| 5 | Gurucharan Singh | Malaya v Hong Kong, Kuala Lumpur 1961 |

Official one-day

| 5 | J.N. Rhodes | S Africa v W Indies, Mumbai 1993/94 |

Other one-day

| 5 | F. Jansen | Netherlands v Denmark, Utrecht 1992 |

Women

Highest team scores

Test matches

569-6 dec	Australia v England, Guildford	1998
525	Australia v India, Ahmedabad	1983/84
517-8 dec	New Zealand v England, Scarborough	1996
503-5 dec	England v New Zealand, Christchurch	1934/35
497	England v South Africa, Shenley	2003

One-day

455-5	New Zealand v Pakistan, Christchurch	1996/97
412-3	Australia v Denmark, Mumbai	1997/98
397-4	Australia v Pakistan, Melbourne	1996/97
376-2	England v Pakistan, Vijayawada	1997/98
375-5	Netherlands v Japan, Schiedam	2003

Lowest team scores

Test matches

35	England v Australia, Melbourne	1957/58
38	Australia v England, Melbourne	1957/58
44	New Zealand v England, Christchurch	1934/35
47	Australia v England, Brisbane	1934/35
53	Pakistan v Ireland, Dublin	2000

One-day

23	Pakistan v Australia, Melbourne	1996/97
24	Scotland v England, Reading	2001
26	India v New Zealand, St Saviours	2002
27	Pakistan v Australia, Hyderabad	1997/98
28	Japan v Pakistan, Amsterdam	2003

Highest individual scores

Test matches

242	Kiran Baluch	Pakistan v West Indies, Karachi	2003/04
214	M. Raj	India v England, Taunton	2002
209*	K.L. Rolton	Australia v England, Leeds	2001
204	K.E. Flavell	New Zealand v England, Scarborough1996
204	M.A.J. Goszko	Australia v England, Shenley	2001

One-day

229*	B.J. Clark	Australia v Denmark, Mumbai	1997/98
173*	C.M. Edwards	England v Ireland, Pune	1997/98
156*	L.M. Keightley	Australia v Pakistan, Melbourne	1996/97
156*	S.C. Taylor	England v India, Lord's	2006
154*	K.L. Rolton	Australia v Sri Lanka, Christchurch	2000/01

Best bowling in an innings
Test matches

8-53	N. David	India v England, Jamshedpur	1995/96
7-6	M.B. Duggan	England v Australia, Melbourne	1957/58
7-7	E.R. Wilson	Australia v England, Melbourne	1957/58
7-10	M.E. Maclagan	England v Australia, Brisbane	1934/35
7-18	A. Palmer	Australia v England, Brisbane	1934/35

One-day

7-4	Sajjida Shah	Pakistan v Japan, Amsterdam	2003
7-8	J.M. Chamberlain	England v Denmark, Haarlem	1991
7-24	S. Nitschke	Australia v England, Kidderminster	2005
6-10	J. Lord	New Zealand v India, Auckland	1981/82
6-10	M. Maben	India v Sri Lanka, Kandy	2003/04

Wicket-keeping: most dismissals in an innings
Test matches

8 (6c 2st)	L. Nye	England v N Zealand, New Plymouth	1991/92
6 (2c 4st)	B.A. Brentnall	N Zealand v South Africa, Johannesburg	1971/72
5 (2c 3st)	S.A. Hodges	England v New Zealand, Christchurch	1968/69
5 (2c 3st)	S.A. Hodges	England v New Zealand, Auckland	1968/69
5 (3c 2st)	B.A. Brentnall	New Zealand v England, Auckland	1968/69
5 (1c 4st)	F. Khalili	India v Australia, Perth	1976/77
5 (4c 1st)	C. Matthews	Australia v India, Adelaide	1990/91
5 (5c)	C. Matthews	Australia v India, Melbourne	1990/91
5 (3c 2st)	A. Jain	India v England, Shenley	1999

One-day

6 (4c 2st)	S.L. Illingworth	New Zealand v Australia, Beckenham	1993
6 (1c 5st)	V. Kalpana	India v Denmark, Slough	1993
6 (2c 4st)	Batool Fatima	Pakistan v West Indies, Karachi	2003/04

BIBLIOGRAPHY

Beckles HM and Stoddart B. 1995. *Liberation cricket. West Indies cricket culture.* Manchester University Press, Manchester.

Birley D. 1999. *A social history of English cricket.* Aurum, London.

Bose M. 1986. *A maiden view. The magic of Indian cricket.* Allen and Unwin, London.

Bose M. 1990. *A history of Indian cricket.* André Deutsch, London.

Bowen R. 1970. *Cricket: a history of its growth and development throughout the world.* Eyre and Spottiswoode, London.

Bridger KE. 1976. *North and South: a history of the annual cricket classic in Argentina.*

Cashman R, Weaver A. 1991. *Wicket women. Cricket and women in Australia.* New South Wales University Press, Kensington NSW.

Docker E. 1976. *History of Indian cricket.* Macmillan Company of India Ltd., Delhi.

Guha R. 2002. *A corner of a foreign field. The Indian history of a British sport.* Picador, London.

Hall P. 1999. *150 years of cricket in Hong Kong.* The Book Guild, Lewes, Sussex.

Harte C. 1993. *A history of Australian cricket.* André Deutsch, London.

Heyho- Flint R and Rheinberg N. *1976. Fair play. The story of women's cricket.* London, Angus & Robertson.

Hone WP. 1956. *Cricket in Ireland.* The Kerryman Ltd., Tralee.

James A. 1993. *Ratu Kadavu's Fijian cricket XI in Australia 1907/08.* Published privately.

James A. 1998. *The tour of Oldfield's Australian cricketers to Singapore and Malaya in 1927.* Published privately.

James CLR. 1963. *Beyond a boundary.* Hutchinson, London.

Labouchère PGG, Provis TAJ, Hargreaves PS. 1969. *The story of continental cricket.* Hutchinson, London.

Lester JA. 1951. *A century of Philadelphia cricket.* University of Pennsylvania Press, Philadelphia.

Majumdar B. 2004. *Twenty-two yards to freedom. A social history of Indian cricket.* Viking Penguin Books India, New Delhi.

Manley M. 1988. *A history of West Indies cricket.* André Deutsch, London.

Marder JI. 1968. *The International Series. The story of the United States v Canada at cricket.* Kaye and Ward, London.

Melville T. 1998. *The tented field. A history of cricket in America.* Bowling Green State University Popular Press, Bowling Green OH.

Odendaal A. 2003. *The story of an African game.* David Philip, Claremont, South Africa.

Orders D. 1990. *Cricket in Portugal.* APN Sociedade Impressora Lda., Trajoucc – Parede.

Pollard J. 1992. *The complete illustrated history of Australian cricket.* Pelham, Ringwood, Victoria.

Robinson S. 1989. *A history of the Hong Kong Cricket Club 1851-1989.* Centurion, London.

Ryan G. 2004. *The making of New Zealand cricket 1832-1914.* Frank Cass, London.

Sandiford KAP. 1994. *Cricket and the Victorians.* Scolar Press, Aldershot.

Sharp I. 1985. *The Singapore Cricket Club 1852-1985.* Singapore Cricket Club, Singapore.

Siggins G. 2005. *Green days. Cricket in Ireland 1792-2005.* Nonsuch, Stroud.

Snow PA. 1949. *Cricket in the Fiji Islands.* Whitcombe and Tombs Ltd, Christchurch, New Zealand.

Stoddart B, Sandiford KAP. 1998. *The imperial game: cricket, culture and society.* Manchester University Press, Manchester.

Swanton EW, Melford M. 1966. *The world of cricket.* Michael Joseph, London.

Swanton EW, Plumptre G, Woodcock J. 1986. *Barclays world of cricket. The game from A to Z.* Collins, London.

Swanton EW, Woodcock J. 1980. *Barclays world of cricket. The game from A to Z.* Collins, London.

Tennant I. 1985. *Corfu and cricket.* Anglo-Corfiot Cricket Association.

Wilkins B. 1999. *The bowler's art. Understanding spin, swing and swerve.* A & C Black, London.

Winch J. 1983. *Cricket's rich heritage. A history of Rhodesian and Zimbabwean cricket 1890-1982.* Books of Zimbabwe, Bulawayo.

Wynne-Thomas P. 1989. *The complete history of cricket tours at home and abroad.* Hamlyn, London.

Wynne-Thomas P. 1997. *The history of cricket from The Weald to The World.* The Stationery Office, London.